1/12

SPANNING
THE
CENTURY

SPANNING THE CENTURY

The Life of W. Averell Harriman, 1891–1986

Rudy Abramson

WILLIAM MORROW AND COMPANY, INC.
NEW YORK

Library of Congress Cataloging-in-Publication Data

Abramson, Rudy.
    Spanning the century : the life of W. Averell Harriman, 1891–1986 /
Rudy Abramson.
        p.   cm.
    Includes bibliographical references and index.
    ISBN 0-688-04352-6
    1. Harriman, W. Averell (William Averell), 1891–1986.
    2. Statesmen—United States—Biography.   I. Title.
    E748.H35A64   1992
    973.9′092—dc20
    [B]   91-42483
                                                                  CIP

Printed in the United States of America

First Edition

1   2   3   4   5   6   7   8   9   10

BOOK DESIGN BY LYNN DONOFRIO DESIGNS

Dedicated to the memory of my father

Emmett R. Abramson
1907–1978

AUTHOR'S NOTE

In one of his regularly updated plans for the disposition of his estate, Averell Harriman provided for his personal papers to be left to the playwright Robert Sherwood, whose intimate account of the alliance between Franklin D. Roosevelt and Harry Hopkins became one of the monumental works of World War II history and biography. Harriman and Sherwood had been friends since the 1930s, when the writer had been part of the literary crowd that Harriman entertained at Thanksgiving Day house parties. During the war, they had served Roosevelt together, Sherwood a presidential speech writer and director of overseas operations for the Office of War Information, while Harriman was FDR's emissary to Churchill and Stalin. Afterward, Averell had hoped that Sherwood would write the Harriman story with the kind of deft touch brought to the saga of Roosevelt and Hopkins.

But Sherwood died in 1955 and Harriman's career continued off and on for another quarter century, during which time he declined numerous overtures from writers seeking his cooperation in a biography. Over the years, he made several fitful starts at putting down his personal recollections, and during the late sixties he employed historian Mark Chadwin, who conducted extensive interviews with personal and professional friends. During one of the periods when he was more or less retired, he and Elie Abel, then dean of the Columbia University Graduate School of Journalism, wrote his account of his World War II career, *Special Envoy to Churchill and Stalin*. For several reasons, including his

7

advancing age, his plan to follow that with subsequent volumes covering the Truman years and the Kennedy-Johnson period never materialized.

Nor did he succeed in his desire to publish an account of his four years as governor of New York, rejecting two completed manuscripts. One by Daniel Patrick Moynihan, a young aide at Albany and later a United States senator, was deemed too negative; the other, a scholarly study by Professor Frank Munger of Syracuse University, he concluded, had missed the drama and vitality. The present book was undertaken after Harriman was in his nineties, and with the initial expectation that he would continue to decline to cooperate in a biography. But when I approached him, he granted me access to his papers, agreed to interviews, and offered to express approval if friends contacted him concerning my overtures. He was too old, he said, to tell his own story or to oversee an authorized biography.

The Harriman papers proved to be far more extensive than I had imagined. There were, first of all, nearly fifty filing cabinets, plus assorted boxes, suitcases, and other containers in a storage room—referred to as The Dungeon—beneath his house. Correspondence and records left by his mother were still in the office of the manager at the family's Arden estate in Orange County, New York. Documents, clippings, and memorabilia tracing the family back to its arrival in America nearly two centuries ago were at the Harriman estate office at Brown Brothers Harriman and Company, on Wall Street, collected over the years by Josephine Merget, an employee who made the family's history her hobby. The gubernatorial papers—including the two-volume Munger manuscript—fill nearly one thousand linear feet in Syracuse University's George Arents Research Library. Other material spanning half a century of Harriman family history is in the archives of the Union Pacific Corporation in Omaha, Nebraska.

In a dingy Brooklyn warehouse, among canceled checks and the flotsam from decades of overflowing files, I found the long-forgotten records of Harriman's business career in the 1920s. The storage room in what was once a bank also yielded an inventory of material that had been destroyed, evidently for lack of space. Sadly, the list included the personal papers of Kitty Lanier Lawrance Harriman, Averell's first wife, and Mary Harriman Rumsey, the sister who pioneered the American consumer movement and helped lead her brother into public service.

Both the business files found in Brooklyn and the materials from The Dungeon are now deposited in the manuscript collections of the Library of Congress—minus hundreds, if not thousands, of pages of secret and top secret documents and cables removed because they had never been declassified. They range from an account of a long Harriman conversation with Nikita Khrushchev to cables from the 1968 Paris peace talks with the North Vietnamese.

As much as Harriman yearned for and sought recognition for his work as a diplomat and political leader, there remained to the end of his days a wall around his personal life.

When I arrived for one of our talks, he began by again expressing his desire to be helpful, but he then added, "I do not intend to discuss my three wives. I have been married to three wonderful women, and I will not discuss them or get into comparisons." Once, when I mentioned to him that I had just finished reading his brother Roland's memoir, *I Reminisce*, he hesitated for a moment and then said a little disdainfully, "Oh yes, I saw that. It has a great many personal things in it."

After two or three unsuccessful attempts to draw him out about his relationship with his father, the hard-bitten, much-maligned railroad baron E. H. Harriman, I turned to his wife, Pamela, for help, confident that over the years he had revealed to her the formative experiences of his early life. He had not. "This might be difficult for you to understand," she told me, "but he has never really talked to me about his parents and his childhood."

Evidently having some curiosity herself, she suggested that she join the next conversation to see if she could help break new ground. On a sunny Sunday afternoon shortly thereafter, the three of us sat on a patio at Willow Oaks, the Harrimans' country place outside Middleburg, Virginia, and I once again brought up the subject of his father. The clipped answers were the same, and she began trying to follow up. On her first attempt, she was greeted with a gentle dismissal with a wave of his hand. After her second try, he paused for a moment and said, "Darling, please." She made one more attempt. "Darling, I'm being interviewed," he said firmly, "and I will answer the questions as I wish."

Elie Abel, I learned, had encountered the same difficulty even in writing Harriman's own account of his World War II experiences. Most of the book's passages about E. H. Harriman and the private life of the family survived only with the collaborator's pleading and insistence.

It was not, I concluded, that there was anything that Harriman wanted to hide or any old animosity toward his father, but a combination of a failing memory and a constitutional inability to talk about intimate matters that required him to reveal his innermost feelings. Except when it concerned great world leaders, he found it distasteful to explore personalities and motivations. His blunt style did not lend itself to delicate analysis and repartee. "Words were his enemy," said Monteagle Stearns, a foreign service officer who worked for him toward the end of his career. Almost to the end of his days, he was as much interested in looking ahead as he was in looking back, except when he considered his personal experience instructive, as he often did. He was relentless in his determination to remain engaged with the world. When he could no longer read the newspapers, he insisted upon the news being read to him, and more than one reader who skipped paragraphs in haste to reach the end of a story was called up short with a gruff observation, "That makes no sense whatever."

ACKNOWLEDGMENTS

Throughout the course of researching and writing this book, I have benefited from touching and immensely valuable advice, support, assistance, and inspiration for which I can never adequately express my gratitude. It has come from my family, from professional colleagues, from members of the Harriman family, and from scores of people whose careers put them in the company of Averell Harriman during his long journey across the twentieth century. I shall always be indebted to all of them. I particularly wish to thank those without whom this project would have died long ago—first of all, Governor Harriman himself, who granted me access to his papers, struggled with a fading memory to recapture his experiences, and asked of me nothing but honesty. For their candor, indulgence, and encouragement, I am equally indebted to the people who undoubtedly knew and understood him better than anyone else: his wife, Pamela, and his daughters, Kathleen Mortimer and Mary Fisk.

I owe most to my wife, Joyce, and my daughters, Kristin and Karin, from whom I have borrowed important months and years. They have been steadfast, inspirational, totally selfless, and monumentally patient and understanding.

I especially wish to thank Mrs. Barry Bingham, Sr., and the Mary and Barry Bingham Foundation. Their generosity made possible a period of intense concentration on this project and a year as the Mary and Barry Bingham Adjunct Professor at Berea College in Berea, Kentucky.

My life was profoundly enriched by the experience, by the friendship of President John Stephenson, and by the faculty, the staff, and the student body of an institution for which I have deep admiration and respect.

I must also express appreciation to my friend Albert P. Smith of Lexington, Kentucky, who has long shared Berea's commitment to the people of southern Appalachia; to my agent, Elise Goodman, who deserves the credit for conceiving the project; and to my editor, Harvey Ginsberg, whose magnificent professional skill is matched by Jobian patience.

For their support from the beginning, my gratitude goes, as well, to William F. Thomas, the former editor of the *Los Angeles Times*, and to Washington bureau chief Jack Nelson.

Lastly, I must say thank you and offer a heartfelt tribute to Donald M. Irwin, a dear friend and *Times* colleague, who spent many hours in the last months and weeks of his life reading the manuscript of this book, gently but relentlessly exposing its flaws, and urging me on with his wonderful, inexhaustible enthusiasm. It is my hope that the craftsmanship, integrity, and courage that marked his life are reflected in these pages.

CONTENTS

INTRODUCTION

In June 1983, Averell Harriman went to Moscow on what he knew was his last trip to the Soviet Union. He was then ninety-one years old, nearly deaf, and going blind. It had been eighty-four years since he had first set foot in Siberia, a wide-eyed, illegal visitor to a primitive fishing village. It had been fifty-seven years since he first visited the Kremlin to call on Leon Trotsky, forty years since Franklin Roosevelt had made him the United States ambassador to the USSR, and nearly twenty since he had negotiated a treaty with the Soviets banning tests of nuclear weapons in the atmosphere. Following his retirement in 1969, he had gone back five times.

He had known all of the top Soviet leaders since Trotsky and Josef Stalin, and, therefore, with the Kremlin again in transition, he felt compelled to make one more journey to Moscow—to size up Yuri Andropov, the aging former chief of the KGB who had emerged as the transitional leader upon the death of Leonid Brezhnev. It was a dangerous time in relations between the nuclear superpowers. Arms control negotiations were at a standstill, and the Reagan administration was carrying out a stupendous modernization of the American military arsenal amidst a drumbeat of warnings about a "window of vulnerability" when the Soviet Union could theoretically carry out a successful first strike against American intercontinental ballistic missiles and bombers armed with nuclear weapons.

15

The meeting was obviously not a watershed moment in diplomacy, but neither was it a Soviet gesture to humor an old man. As they had since he arrived as one of the capitalists Lenin needed to save his socialist economy, Kremlin officials accorded Harriman a special respect, as did leaders of most of the other important nations of the world. He had not only represented the United States over the years; he had epitomized it. "It didn't make any difference what job he had or where he went," said Richard Helms, a former director of the Central Intelligence Agency and onetime ambassador to Iran. "He was a big wheel because he carried the capitalist system around under his hat." The relationship with the Soviet Union had survived in spite of his being one of the first and most outspoken of the Cold Warriors, for he had continued to advocate civil relations with the Soviet Union. In that, he had been consistent from the time when he was denounced by the American left as a threat to peace until he was attacked by the right for being naive in his view of the Communist threat. For nearly sixty years, he had stuck to a conviction that a workable relationship between the United States and the Soviet Union was vital to both. Heir to one of the United States' vaunted railroad fortunes and prime exhibit of freewheeling Yankee capitalism, he had derived much of his influence from his Soviet ties. At crucial times when his career required a jump start or his ego needed reinforcement, he found it in the Soviet Union. "All his life, Averell needed reinforcement of his self-esteem," said his longtime friend John Kenneth Galbraith, "and his relationship with the Soviet Union was part of that." He had spent more time in the Kremlin than any other American envoy. Even though George F. Kennan, who served under Harriman in the American embassy in Moscow during World War II, became the country's most renowned Sovietologist, the USSR was still Harriman's turf.

His sentimental last visit to the Kremlin was treated as a moment of import by the Soviets. Andropov, who was regarded as a shadowy, unknown, and perplexing figure in the United States, used the occasion to air his concerns over the strategic arms modernization going on in America, the general chill that had settled upon the Washington-Moscow atmosphere, and the danger of a war starting through some miscalculation.

Back home, Harriman reported to Secretary of State George Shultz, the Senate Foreign Relations Committee, and Vice-President George Bush. And then, in a remarkable display of determination, he went on a network television interview program and concentrated fiercely enough to pick up the questions in spite of deadened auditory nerves and to give his assessment of yet one more Kremlin chief.

It was this kind of physical and psychological resilience that more than anything else made him an important twentieth-century diplomat. He was approaching fifty before he took up his first presidential assignment, but he was still traveling the world on missions for the White House a generation after his contemporaries had quit; and when the President and the secretary of state no longer summoned him, he set out on his own, as he did when he called on Andropov.

He never had the commanding presence of Dean Acheson or the analytical brilliance of George Kennan. He didn't have the warmth of his boyhood friend Robert A. Lovett, the grace and smoothness of David Bruce, the humor of Charles Bohlen, or the lawyerly skills of John J. McCloy. He was short-tempered, parsimonious, ambitious, and superstitious. Lord Beaverbrook, the Canadian-born publishing magnate and member of Churchill's War Cabinet with whom Harriman collaborated and occasionally feuded during World War II, once said he knew no one else who had gone so far with so little. With reason, Beaverbrook harbored some jealousy of Harriman, but there were others, especially those who crossed him, who shared a view of him as a dilettante. Among his close friends there were some who thought him intellectually dull.

But none challenged his effectiveness when he had presidential marching orders. Vernon Walters, who rose to the rank of three-star general and to his own ambassadorial career after several stints as Harriman's interpreter, compared Harriman's one-on-one negotiating skills to the legendary persuasive powers of Lyndon Johnson. He received similar marks from Isaiah Berlin, the esteemed English political scientist, who wrote Harriman's widow a few days after his death at ninety-four: "He was an irreplaceable asset to the U.S. government—and to the entire West—because of an uncanny sense of what, as a negotiator, could work, and what could not. In the most essential aspects of international relations, he seemed to me virtually infallible. He sized up people, situations, the nature of contending forces, as art experts determine the authorship, date, and earliest significance of a work of art."

His life, spanning the years between the presidencies of Benjamin Harrison and Ronald Reagan, covered the century in which his country emerged as a world power and exercised a military and economic supremacy that disappeared forever before he was gone. When he was born in Manhattan, the life expectancy for the American male was fifty years. The radio was still in the future; the telephone was in its infancy; and trolley cars were drawn by horses. The last cables of his diplomatic career were transmitted by satellite, and he returned from the last of his more than one hundred round-trips across the Atlantic aboard the Concorde supersonic airliner.

There was a symmetry about his life, a progression that brought him to personal crossroads in phase with the country's own. He was beginning school at the outset of the Spanish-American War, which made the United States a consequential world power. Among his vivid memories was the day he stayed home from school to see the parade for

Admiral George Dewey, the hero of Manila Bay, who was escorted down Fifth Avenue through nearly hysterical crowds. He had toured much of Europe before he was in prep school, and when the treaty of Portsmouth ended the Russo-Japanese War in 1905, he was visiting Tokyo with his parents and saw riots touched off by Japanese opposition to the settlement terms.

Consequently, he had grown up thinking of the United States as a part of a global community, and the oceans as avenues of commerce rather than barriers providing isolation from foreign enemies. His business career took him from the waning days of unfettered capitalism through the years of rampant Wall Street speculation, the Crash and the Depression.

He was a New Dealer during the recovery from the 1929 crash, a dollar-a-year man in preparation for war. He was a Marshall Planner, a Cold Warrior, and in the Vietnam War, finally, a dissenter. When he died in 1986, he had served every Democratic president of the century except Woodrow Wilson, and with notable exceptions, such as Adolf Hitler, Mao Tse-tung, and Ho Chi Minh, he had engaged most of the figures who shaped the course of the world for five decades.

Had he been as articulate as he was determined, and had he been blessed with humor to match his energy, he might have been president. But perhaps because of burdens laid upon him in an upbringing that was as demanding as it was privileged, his goals were always tantalizingly just beyond his reach.

SPANNING
THE
CENTURY

Chapter I

ROOTS
Progeny of a Rich Englishman

Averell Harriman's great-great-grandfather William was financially secure long before he transplanted his family from London to New Haven, Connecticut, in 1795. A man with firm political ideas, robust ambition, and excessive self-esteem, he made few friends and took no discernible interest in community affairs. After coming to America, he was driven around in a flashy four-in-hand attended by outriders, and was enviously and contemptuously referred to as "the rich Englishman."

Beyond that, not much is known about him or his life in Nottingham, where he grew up, or in London, where he accumulated his wealth as a stationer, or in America, where bad luck and the vicissitudes of the shipping business kept him from ever turning his substantial holdings into a real fortune.

Averell and the generations that followed were never much interested in the circumstances of William's immigration or his travails in the shipping business. For them, the saga of the Harriman family began with E.H.

E.H.—Edward Henry Harriman—was old William's great-grandson, Averell's father, the man who created a huge fortune and a troublesome reputation, leaving Averell a name indelibly imprinted in American lore. He was the last and, arguably, the mightiest of all the railroad barons, ruler of the far-flung Union Pacific and Southern Pacific systems, a power behind the Illinois Central, and a moving force in boardrooms of other railroads from coast to coast.

But for Theodore Roosevelt, who made him the object of a political blood feud and a subject of public ridicule, and cancer, which killed him at sixty-one, he might have realized his dream of creating a railroad and steamship empire spanning the globe.

As it was, he died commanding the Union Pacific and the Southern Pacific systems capitalized at $1.5 billion, employing more men than the standing army of the United States, and surpassing state legislatures in influence upon the American West. At his peak, he controlled 75,000 miles of railroad track, possessed $400 million in stocks and bonds, held another $150 million in cash, and enjoyed access to inexhaustible fortunes.

What was remarkable about him was that, having started with nothing, he accumulated most of the fortune and influence in less than a decade. How did he do it? "With this," he would say, tapping on his head with a pencil.[1]

E.H. was a force of nature, a prodigy who arrived on Wall Street a scrawny, nearsighted fourteen-year-old with the cunning of a wolf and enough energy to light the stock exchange. When it counted, he could and did—while still a young man—outmaneuver and outwit even J. Pierpont Morgan, the corpulent captain of American high finance, administering the only defeats that the imperious Morgan could bring himself to acknowledge.

As a railroader, Harriman had no equal, unless it was his Morgan-financed northern rival, James J. Hill, who built the only railroad to the Pacific coast without benefit of government land-grants and who was as ambitious as Harriman to extend his domain all the way to the Orient.

Nearly everything about E.H. was controversial. He was secretive, ruthless, manipulative, relentless. He was also too proud to explain himself, too stubborn to change, and consequently became one of the most vilified men of his time when his friendship with fellow New Yorker Teddy Roosevelt disintegrated.

Averell was just a boy when his father reached the pinnacle of his extraordinary career. While he idolized E.H. and feared his disapproval, he approached manhood hearing his father denounced for watering railroad stocks, corrupting politics, destroying the man who had launched his career, and building an oppressive railroad monopoly. Decades after E.H. was lowered into a solid-rock tomb on the family's country estate, the son remained in the overpowering shadow. Even when Averell himself was a middle-aged, internationally known businessman, he was seldom introduced, written about, or publicly acknowledged without being identified as the son of the famed railroad king. To the end of Averell's life, which lasted nearly a century, E.H.'s legacy was always with him.

* * *

Appropriately, William Harriman brought the family from England in the same year the first primitive rail was laid in the United States—a wooden strip on the side of Beacon Hill in Boston.

The story passed down in the family was that he had been a fervent sympathizer with the colonists' revolution and that his coming to America had been for the love of democracy and not commercial opportunity, for which he nevertheless had an appreciative eye. Whatever the case, his family assuredly did not belong to the ordinary "huddled masses yearning to breathe free."[2]

William Harriman was, on the contrary, a well-born, well-married minister's son. He was thirty-five years old and solidly entrenched in London's commercial establishment when he decided to strike out for a fortune in America. The belongings his family stored in the hold of the ship *Portland* when it departed Bristol were not the meager possessions of emigrants setting out to make a new start. Rather than essentials for survival, the Harrimans' trunks contained valuable china and silver accumulated over generations, parchments attesting to William's standing as a gentleman, and heirlooms passed down from ancestors who belonged to Austrian nobility.

The move was effected over several years. William's business was profitably sold to a young associate, who, in time, became the Lord Mayor of London, and careful plans were laid for a shipping business beginning with service between the booming port of New Haven and the West Indies.

It was a high-risk venture, even for an experienced merchant, but it had the potential of making a fortune. For more than a century, the West Indies had depended upon American vessels to deliver vital foodstuffs. They had suffered along with the American colonies while trade was cut off by the Revolutionary War, but thereafter commerce flourished, bringing prosperity to American port cities such as New Haven. By the time the Harrimans sailed for the United States, however, the French Revolution had made the West Indian trade more adventurous than profitable.

Although 100,000 French and British troops in the West Indies drove food demands and prices to new heights, American vessels bound for the ports risked being seized, condemned, and sold if intercepted by ships from one country with cargo for the other. Hundreds of Yankee merchant vessels had been captured and lay in port at Martinique, Guadeloupe, Antigua, and Barbados facing condemnation by French and British courts. Still, the prospect of fat profits outweighed both the financial uncertainty and the hazards of the skirmishing at sea.

Accompanied by three of his four young sons, two daughters, his pregnant wife, and his sister-in-law, Harriman sailed on April 4, 1795, arriving in New York two months later. For five years his shipping enterprise survived, but New Haven was hardly London and its port did not match the opportunities of New York's. So in 1800, the Rich Englishman moved his enterprise and his family to New York, the vibrant center of American commerce.

He opened an office on Front Street, near the East River docks, and took up residence in a big house on Broome Street, where he had the city's best merchant families for neighbors. New York provided opportunities and challenges unimagined in New Haven, but the shipping business was no less uncertain. Good times, which saw coffee houses near the wharf jammed with traders and docks swamped with cargo, were always followed by spare weeks and idle months. In time, more captured American seamen were involuntarily held in the British Navy than were serving in the American fleet.

As his own trading vessels were captured by French and British warships and his cargoes were hijacked by pirates prowling off the American coast, Harriman saw the assets he had brought to America wiped out.

The Jefferson administration responded to the harassment at sea with a policy of coercion against the British and French. Congress imposed an embargo on all foreign trade, prohibiting the sailing of any American vessel from the United States to a foreign port. For Harriman and every other shipper, the solution was obviously worse than the problem. Instead of forcing Napoleon and the British to respect American neutrality, the embargo crippled the industry. Beside New York's idled docks, six hundred trading vessels were tied up for more than a year, and unemployed seamen stood in long lines outside soup kitchens.

Times improved once Jefferson lifted the embargo, but then came the War of 1812 and a British blockade of the eastern seaboard. Once again, Harriman's idle trading ships rotted at their piers.

On top of William's business reverses, the Harrimans were trailed by personal tragedy. Three of the five children born to them after they reached the United States died in infancy or early childhood. Even more crushing were the deaths of their three eldest sons after they had reached manhood. Young William, who had entered the British Navy before the family left London, died in a midocean engagement with a French warship. Alphonso, who was two years younger, accidentally drowned not long afterward. Their third son, Edward, disappeared at sea in the spring of 1815. Then twenty-eight, he sailed as master of cargo aboard a Harriman vessel bound for the West Indies. Several weeks later, in May or June, he and his crew departed St. Thomas in the Virgin Islands on their way to Curaçao, just off the coast of Venezuela. They planned to spend only a few days there, then head northwest for a port call in

Jamaica before returning to New York. But neither Edward nor his ship was ever heard from again.

The family scoured the islands across the Caribbean, seaports in the West Indies, and docks along the Atlantic coast. For two years, they ran advertisements in newspapers, questioned sailors, and followed rumors. They never found a trace.

Many years later, the family story goes, an old sailor on his deathbed confessed that he had once been in a band of pirates that operated in the area, and that he had been with them when they captured the Harriman ship just off the coast of South America. The handsome young cargo master, he said, had been forced to walk the plank.

Of William Harriman's seven boys, only one, Orlando, survived. The fourth son had grown up planning to become a military officer and follow in the adventurous footsteps of his older brothers, but finding himself the only survivor, he abandoned his dream of following the trade routes or joining the Navy. It was not a difficult decision, for he was already twenty-five years old and had a growing family of his own when his last brother vanished.

Before he was out of his teens, Orlando had married Anne Ingland, the daughter of a well-to-do family that had come to New York from Nova Scotia several years before the Harrimans landed. The Inglands lived comfortably on the corner adjacent to Government House, the mansion that had been built as the residence for President Washington before the seat of the federal government had been moved to Philadelphia. Little knowledge of the Inglands was passed along except that Anne was "a petted only daughter, who knew only the luxurious side of life, whose wishes were all anticipated, who had never even been called upon to decide any arrangements of her wardrobe."[3] The Orlando Harrimans were, one of their daughters recorded, "a beautiful example of conjugal affection."[4] And that was to put it mildly. Orlando emulated his father by producing an enormous family—eleven children altogether, eight of them sons.

Though the family's dream of a shipping empire had slipped away, Orlando was a prosperous commission merchant. And while he had been forced to forget the glamour of the sea, life in New York was an adventure in its own way. Congestion made the city dangerously prone to fires in winter and increasingly vulnerable to epidemics in summer. More than once the family packed up and moved north to the countryside to escape diseases threatening their Greenwich Village suburb, but Anne nevertheless contracted and survived yellow fever during one of the periodic outbreaks.

For weeks bankers and businessmen like Orlando conducted their affairs at home rather than risk going downtown. One day during the terrible siege of yellow fever in 1823, he found it necessary to go to his office. On the way there he found Wall Street so deserted that grass had begun pushing through the cobblestones.[5]

In spite of it all, the Harriman business under Orlando did better than it ever had under his father's management. Profitable domestic markets were developing in the south and the west; industry was expanding on the Atlantic seaboard; merchants were finding new customers abroad.

By the mid-1830s, New York had grown to a population of 250,000, and its suburbs were spreading inexorably northward. Broadway below Fourteenth Street was still the heart of the city, but surveyors had already laid out cross streets as far north as Forty-first Street, and the population had nearly doubled with the passing of a single decade.

In December of 1835, the tinderbox city of wooden buildings was swept by the most devastating fire in its history. Breaking out on the subzero night of December 16, flames engulfed a five-story dry-goods store, destroyed the marble Merchants' Exchange that had been considered fireproof, then threatened to spread north into the residential neighborhoods.

The Harrimans were awakened by church bells as the alarm spread to Greenwich Village and the wind-whipped blaze leaped into a night sky already illuminated by a stunning display of the northern lights. Tragically, it was one of the coldest nights in memory, the East River having frozen so hard that it was possible to walk between Manhattan and Brooklyn. Firemen who rushed to battle the inferno were rendered helpless because both the hoses and the wells that provided their water were frozen solid.

Merchant ships, trapped by ice at their East River docks, were set ablaze, and block after block of the business district south of Wall Street was consumed. Unable to slow the flames' spread, firemen did the only thing they could under the circumstances—try to remove the most valuable merchandise from doomed warehouses.

Even the Brooklyn waterfront was in jeopardy. High winds carried sparks and burning cinders across the river, setting fire to the sails of a schooner in port and igniting the roofs of several warehouses. With the threat to Brooklyn keeping its firemen at home, more and more volunteers arrived from New Jersey to join the fight in Manhattan. But after two days, the inferno continued. More firefighters and equipment came from as far away as Philadelphia, and militiamen marched in to maintain order and prevent looting as the flames spread to more than seven hundred buildings. As a last resort, desperate authorities turned to Fort Jay on Governors Island and to the Navy magazine at Red Hook, New Jersey, for help. Wagons loaded with barrels of gunpowder were brought in aboard barges which battered through the ice, and the troops blew up enough houses to create a firebreak and bring the conflagration under control.

When it was over, the toll was put at $26 million, and the Harrimans were among the hundreds who saw their businesses wiped out. On Front Street, the building occupied by their shipping offices was among the eighty that had gone up in flames. However, Orlando was more fortunate than many of his merchant friends and competitors, who wound up bankrupt, for he had enough cash to rebuild, though the recovery took years.

At the time of the fire, Orlando Harriman, Jr., was two months out of Columbia College, where he had distinguished himself by winning the gold medal for standing first in his class. But Orlando junior took no interest in restoring the business. William Harriman's eldest grandson was preparing himself instead to join the Episcopal clergy, a career more befitting the eldest son of a southern planter than of a Yankee trader. The ministry was not an unprecedented calling for a Harriman, however. Young Orlando's great-grandfather back in London had been an ordained clergyman in the Established Moravian Church. There had been a strong church tradition in his mother's family as well.

He did follow directly in the footsteps of his father and grandfather in one respect, however. He married well. As soon as he became a deacon of the Episcopal Church, he wed Cornelia Neilson, the daughter of a prominent physician in New Brunswick, New Jersey. She was anything but glamorous, but her parents claimed kinship with several of New York's leading families, including the Stuyvesants and the Bleekers, and she counted among her antecedents Colonel John Neilson, who had served on the staff of General George Washington and represented New Jersey as a delegate to the Constitutional Convention.

As a couple, Cornelia and Orlando junior did not cut the romantic figure of the socially prominent Orlando senior and Anne Ingland, who had enjoyed a wide reputation for their style and grace on the dance floor. Orlando junior was a stocky, thick-chested, bulldoggish man whose early and growing baldness exaggerated his strong jaw and heavy brows. Cornelia was a frail woman with thin lips and a mouth that turned downward at the corners. With her hair parted in the middle and pulled tightly away from her face, she had an expression that was perpetually severe, unhappy, and disapproving.

For much of her life as the minister's wife she was as unhappy as she appeared. Where she and her husband were concerned, the Lord's work provided neither material rewards nor social recognition. It was not that Orlando lacked energy or ambition. He simply did not have an engaging personality in or out of the pulpit, and he could never find church positions commensurate with his intellectual gifts. A brief tour teaching prisoners at Sing Sing prison was followed by a year as assistant rector at Christ Church in Tarrytown. Thereafter, he moved to Hempstead, Long Island, as rector at St. George's.

Four years later, following recurring disagreements over salary, he found an opening as assistant rector of St. Paul's at Castleton, Long Island, but there were times when he had no post at all. Through all the moving about, Orlando, in both the Harriman tradition and the popular nineteenth-century custom, saw to it that his wife was regularly pregnant.

Eight years after his ordination, while they were still living in their white, two-story parsonage at Hempstead, Cornelia delivered their fourth child. Born on a cold February 20, 1848, days after settlement of the war with Mexico had made the United States a transcontinental republic. The son was named Edward Henry, in honor of his unfortunate great uncle whom pirates had forced to walk the plank thirty-two years earlier.

It was a name whose usage would never be entirely settled. Orlando and Cornelia and the family called him Henry, which he never liked. His friends later called him Edward, Ed, or even Ned. To his wife, he was also Henry, but to the newspapers, he would always be E.H. The initials had an authoritative resonance more appropriate for Wall Street and railroad boardrooms, and it fit nicely into headlines.

His birth made his parents' hand-to-mouth existence only more difficult. Months after he had found a pulpit on Staten Island, Orlando began following the tales of gold in California. He had no intention of going into the goldfields, but he saw in the flood of migration to California a chance for a new start in the church. Thus, in the spring of 1850, he jumped at an offer to become a rector in Sacramento, and in May he set out for California, leaving Cornelia and the four children—Henry was fifteen months old—behind.

His odyssey was nothing like his grandparents' orderly and carefully planned migration more than half a century earlier. Since he was departing from the East Coast, traveling alone, and in a hurry, he elected to sail rather than join an overland wagon train. That left him the choice of a fifteen-thousand mile voyage around Cape Horn, or a trip aboard a steamer to Panama, where he would disembark and make his way through sixty miles of jungle to the Pacific port of Panama City, then board another ship for the rest of his journey to San Francisco. It was a formidable undertaking, but the trip around the Horn offered the daunting prospect of five months at sea, bone-chilling cold, and violent storms. Cutting across the isthmus would reduce the time and distance by half, and although Orlando Harriman was seeking a parsonage and not the goldfields, he was no less anxious than prospectors to get to California without delay.

The journey was not nearly so simple as the steamship company had promised. Tormented by fleas and mosquitoes, unprepared for the mud and tropical heat, he made his way across the isthmus via foot, flat-bottomed boat, and mule back. He arrived at the Pacific desperately ill. For days, he lay in a camp with a raging fever, and when he emerged from his delirium, he was still too weak to go on. He languished for a month without medical attention, unsure whether he would survive.

When he sailed, the Pacific Mail and Steamship Company's side-wheeler to San Francisco presented new nightmares. Sick men were jammed into quarters where they could only grow worse with cholera, yellow fever, Chagres fever, or a host of tropical maladies loosely called "isthmus disease." For seven of them, Harriman conducted funeral services at sea.

When he reached California, he found that his ordeal had been for nothing. Having received no word of him, the congregation had given up hope of his arrival and had hired another minister, leaving Orlando stranded thousands of miles from home with neither the strength nor the money to undertake the return trip. He was left to preach on street corners, in mining camps, and in the public buildings he could borrow in San Francisco, Sacramento, and Stockton.

He organized two new congregations which survived and eventually became parishes, but California in 1850 was hardly a place for a bookish, displaced minister in search of stability for a family. As soon as he had the money for another steamboat ticket, the chastened Orlando set out for home, making his second trip across Panama, this time without falling victim to a fever. Eleven months after sailing with high hopes of transplanting his family to new prosperity, he was back in New York, facing circumstances that were more pressing than ever.

This time he took up residence in Jersey City, and for the next several years kept the family together by doing pastoral odd jobs, helping out at larger parishes in Manhattan, filling in for absent ministers around Jersey City.

Eventually, a small turn for the better did come. Vestrymen in search of a new minister to tend the flock of St. John's parish in West Hoboken sent him a formal invitation "to become rector of said Church and to take charge of the Parish at a yearly salary of $200," and promised "more if the church can afford it."[6]

Grateful, Orlando accepted the offer the same evening it reached him, although it meant he had to walk back and forth between Jersey City and West Hoboken to attend to his duties.

Rather than poverty, the family's life was one of chronic financial embarrassment. Feeling they were temporarily displaced from their own social class, the Harrimans kept at a distance from their immigrant neighbors, uncomfortable because their circumstances forced their children into public schools and close social contact with poor, ill-bred boys with no apparent future. Cornelia's only defense was to drill into her offspring a sense of ambition, even duty to rise above their dreary surroundings.[7]

One of the ministry's few advantages was that it enabled the Harrimans, in 1860, to send their boys to Trinity School in Manhattan, where the children of ministers were accepted at a fraction of the tuition charged other boys.

Especially in the eyes of their mother, the change of schools was a crucial event in the life of Henry and his older brother, Oliver, for it presented them a chance to break out of their parsonage existence and have better friends than the boys in the streets of Jersey City. But to take advantage of the opportunity, they had to arise before dawn and walk two miles to a ferry slip. Then, after crossing the Hudson, they had another mile-long hike to school.

Although Henry was small for his age, he was quick to defend himself in the streets and he was often the leader of boys who congregated in their neighborhood. Just turned thirteen and barely more than five feet tall when the Civil War broke out, he organized, drilled, and led boys who shouldered sticks and marched ahead of Union soldiers heading south toward Washington in the spring and summer of 1861.

Jersey City was then a town of 29,000, and when Lincoln issued his call for troops, 5,000 of its able-bodied men responded, many of them marching away in the lighthearted belief that they would put down the Southern insurrection and come home without having seriously disrupted their lives. Stirred by the town's patriotism, Henry made serious plans to go on to West Point from Trinity and launch a career as a military officer.

But at the very time he was losing himself in his soldierly dreams, he was also coming to understand that his family lived in perpetual financial crisis. Thus when he was fourteen, he announced he was dropping out of school to go to work.

The early end of the boy's formal education was one more humiliation for Orlando Harriman, because Henry had shown great scholastic promise, standing first in his class at Trinity, although putting forth little effort. He was far better known for his mischief-making than for study. In his family-approved E. H. Harriman biography published in 1922, the journalist-historian George Kennan (uncle to George F. Kennan, the Sovietologist) suggested that the boy decided to quit out of boredom with the school, quoting him as telling his father, "I have become convinced there is something else in life for me besides school and books. I am going to work."[8]

Whatever the motivation, Orlando could muster no forceful argument against it, given the family's financial circumstances. The vestrymen at St. John's had never come up with the raise they had talked about, and in fact, the church was falling further and further behind in payment of his $200-a-year salary.

As soon as he left Trinity, Henry found a $5-a-week office boy's job at a brokerage firm. Even that was more than his father was earning from St. John's, and for the first year that the boy worked, he turned all his earnings over to the family. In the end, as the church fell nearly $400 in arrears, Orlando was forced to seek a financial settlement with the employers he had served longer than any others in his entire career. It was clear that neither possessions nor financial security would ever come of his labors in the ministry.

But then, after more than twenty years of dependence upon near-empty collection plates, Cornelia finally received a family inheritance, enabling her and her husband to live in some comfort—and dignity. They moved into an old homestead in the better section of Jersey City. Orlando was no longer in desperate search for work, and his son, freed from having to support his parents, was able to start salting away his money for his own purposes.

Henry arrived at his job on Wall Street knowing nothing of stocks and bonds, and even less about men rich enough and bold enough to gamble fortunes on a tip, but he was too eager and quick-witted to be wasted sweeping floors and emptying spittoons in the D. C. Hays brokerage office. Promoted to pad pusher, he joined the rowdy army of boys who kept the market running by darting from office to office, stopping only long enough to consult their "pad" and call out the latest quotations. Among the scores of them who hurried about Wall Street during the Civil War years when trading was heavy and speculators enjoyed long runs of satisfying days, Harriman stood out. He was fast on his feet, and once a quotation was recorded on his pad, he remembered it. He pleased ever-impatient brokers because he loudly reeled off listings without ever pausing to consult his pad, and he made no mistakes.

Wall Street was his natural habitat. Its pace suited his metabolism. Its competitive atmosphere riveted his attention and fired his imagination as he saw gigantic decisions made in seconds and fortunes deployed with a nod. Surrounded by men who casually invested sums that took his breath away, and dazzled by speculators trading and constructing paper empires, he soon forgot about West Point.

Before he was out of his teens, he became D. C. Hays's chief clerk and office ramrod. It was a position that paid more and enabled him to qualify for a broker's license. Among his contemporaries, he developed a reputation for being as ruthless as he was precocious. He was a loner who blithely ignored Wall Street traditions and good manners whenever it meant a few dollars to him, especially irritating fellow brokers by brazenly pocketing commissions he earned by taking their customers' orders while they were at lunch.

For eight years, he saved nearly everything he made. Then, in 1870, he borrowed $3,000 from his Uncle Oliver Harriman, who had done well in real estate, and bought a seat on the stock exchange. His broker's license, exchange seat, and personal office opened more doors, but he was scarcely any closer to the wheeling and dealing that fascinated him.

He was still forced to bide his time, saving his commissions as carefully has he had squirreled away his D. C. Hays salary and each $2 commission he had picked up during his first days as a broker. But while his habits antagonized his peers on the Street, he endeared himself to older traders, who found him the kind of man who could be trusted with money.

One well-heeled and overweight client considered his advice so valuable that he agreed to pay Harriman's higher rent for a ground-floor office rather than labor up two narrow flights of stairs to the austere cubbyhole. Besides gaining a reputation as an astute judge of individual issues, he came to be recognized as a sharp analyst of market trends, and when he steered customers away from ruinous losses during an 1873 gold panic, important new clients flocked to him.

The chance to make his first big money came when "Deacon" White, one of the truly fearless speculators on the Street, attempted to corner the stock in a group of small railroads that specialized in hauling anthracite. As White's purchases of the stock mounted, the price moved steadily upward, and Harriman noted that it far exceeded its inherent worth.

When it soared beyond reason, Harriman correctly concluded that somebody was trying to corner the market, and he launched his own raid. As the listing passed $100 per share, he gambled that the effort to corner it would fall short, and that the price would plummet as dramatically as it had gone up. He began selling short, making sales on the assumption that he would be able to acquire shares cheaply to cover his obligations. When the collapse came, within days, he was able to buy shares for $6 to cover sales he had made for as much as $110. As a result, he pocketed a $150,000 profit while White lost a fortune.[9]

It was a heady moment, a glimmering invitation to riches for the taking. He shortly spied a chance for another short-sell windfall when the Delaware and Hudson Railway Company stock began a similarly suspicious upward march. Once again, Harriman sold short and waited for the inflated stock to collapse.

But this time, he had unknowingly gambled against John Jacob Astor, who succeeded in buying control of the railroad. Instead of going down, the stock went up and stayed up and Harriman was forced to cover his short sales at substantially higher prices, losing everything he had picked up at White's expense.

Sobered by these flings at high-risk speculation, he retreated to the less exhilarating strategy of investing and building his reserves from commissions earned from blue-chip clients—including Colonel Astor, who had not confided his intentions toward the Delaware and Hudson.

But it was no longer a matter of saving $2 commissions, for he now counted Vanderbilts and Belmonts, not to mention market manipulators such as Jay Gould and other less-than-respectable marauders, among his clients. All of them had come to admire his nerve and trust his judgment in spite of his youth. C. J. Osborne, one of the boldest speculators in New York, called him "the best broker on Wall Street," and August Belmont gave him authority to withdraw up to $1 million from the Belmont account anytime Harriman saw a promising use for it.[10] He was neither bull nor bear, appearing equally confident whether the market was booming or collapsing. During times of panic, when the new ticker produced a litany of ruin, he actually seemed to enjoy the tension and fear around him. Somehow he knew how to prosper in good times or bad. Sensing tremors before they reached the surface, he led retreats ahead of falling prices. And with the return of good times, he was regularly ahead of the pack in resuming investments.

He cultivated new contacts as carefully as he managed portfolios. He joined the Union Club, the proud "mother" of New York clubs, drilled with the 7th Regiment—the "Society Regiment"—of the New York National Guard, and made friends with young men born to the financial aristocracy.

Before he was out of his twenties, he was financially more secure than any Harriman since his great-grandfather, William, had arrived in America. He had made enough money that wealth was no longer an objective but merely a tool to create power. He had also met the two people who would help him become something more than just a successful Wall Street broker.

Sometime in 1877 or '78, at the home of George Clark, one of the Wall Street social friends he often visited, he was introduced to Mrs. Clark's cousin, Mary Averell, a tall, proper, rather somber daughter of an upstate banker. She was serious-minded, sophisticated, and, like Harriman, somewhat beyond the age when one was expected to be married.

To the Clarks' satisfaction, Harriman and Mary Averell were immediately taken with each other. Shortly, they were in serious courtship, E.H. devoting to Mary all the time he had previously reserved for bachelor dinners, boxing lessons, hunting trips, and his Wall Street baseball team.

About the same time he was courting Mary, he struck up an equally fortuitous friendship with Stuyvesant Fish, who would eventually help him get his start in big-time railroading. It was, to put it mildly, an unlikely alliance. Fish's family had been pillars of New York commerce and society for two hundred years. Stuyvesant's father, Hamilton Fish, had been governor of New York, a United States senator, and more recently President Ulysses S. Grant's secretary of state. Grandfather Nicholas Fish had served under General Washington from the Battle of Long Island to Yorktown, and later the President had rewarded him with appointment as the country's first Supervisor of Revenue.

"Stuyv" Fish had the good looks and a natural social grace to accompany his impeccably aristocratic credentials. A big, easy-going man-about-town, affectionately called the White Elephant because of his size and his blond hair, he was a thorough contrast to E.H.

Though Harriman had a budding reputation as a Wall Street phenomenon, he was physically as unimposing as his parsonage upbringing was unimpressive. It was his pal, White Elephant Fish, not he, who seemed destined for mighty things.

While Harriman was clerking for D. C. Hays and growing up street-smart, Fish had proceeded through Columbia University. And while Harriman was saving his $2 broker's commissions, Fish was getting started as a young executive at the Illinois Central Railroad. After a smooth internship, he was named secretary to William Henry Osborne, one of the company's chief financiers, who had been the Fish family's neighbor at their summer place in the country. By the time he met Harriman, Fish sat on the Illinois Central board and had his foot firmly on the executive ladder at the company embodying railroad tradition.

When it was chartered, the IC was reputed to be the longest railroad in the world. It was the first road in the country to receive a federal land-grant, and after it was completed, it was considered an engineering accomplishment rivaling the Erie Canal and the National Road. Its tracks had been the magnet that had brought families to settle and work some of the richest farmland in the country.

Abraham Lincoln had, as a young lawyer, represented it in down-state Illinois courtrooms, and it was in the railroad's offices that Lincoln had first met George B. McClellan, the line's chief engineer, who would later command the Army of the Potomac.

During the Civil War, the tracks and rolling stock of the Illinois Central had been strategic assets fought over and put to the service of both the North and South. In peacetime, it was no less valuable.

Extended from the ports on the Great Lakes all the way to the Gulf of Mexico, it intersected hundreds of feeder lines reaching into the rich flatlands of the midcontinent to deliver grain and cotton to both northern and southern ports.

The original line in Illinois was built with old New York money, and it was still considered a society railroad, if only because some of its stock remained in the portfolios of eastern aristocrats, such as the Fishes and many of the clients of E. H. Harriman and Company. Its ownership had actually passed into the hands of wealthy foreign investors, but as Osborne approached the end of his own career, he foresaw a bright future for his neighbor and protégé, Stuyvesant Fish.

Fully recovered from the Panic of 1873, the country was moving to the rhythm of the Iron Horse; Fish's friend, E.H., having carefully saved his money for such a day, began to invest heavily in the stock of the Illinois Central.

Harriman also concluded his successful courtship of Mary Williamson Averell by marrying her in 1879—an investment, it turned out, that was as smart as his purchase of Illinois Central stock. Mary's father, William J. Averell, had himself been a Wall Street broker for eleven years, but he had moved back home to the serene environs of Ogdensburg, on the bank of the St. Lawrence River, where he was a pillar of the community and president of the Ogdensburg and Lake Champlain Railroad.

At the Harrimans' rectory in Jersey City, news of the engagement had been joyfully received, especially by the bridegroom's mother. Henry's engagement to a well-bred girl from an old and prosperous New York family was further testament to Cornelia Harriman's inspirational influence on all of her children. Considering their financial handicap, they had done astonishingly well. Henry's brothers, John Neilson and Orlando, were both successful businessmen. His sister Lilly had married Charles D. Simons of Brown Brothers bank, and his sister Annie had wed J. Fleming Van Rensselaer.

Now, even before meeting the bride-to-be, Cornelia rushed a reassuring letter to her. "In making him happy, you may safely trust him," counseled the motherly letter from New Jersey. "Ever dutiful and affectionate as a son and kind and generous as a brother, he will be true and reliable in his more tender relations to you, whom we are hoping in the near future to claim as one of our own."[11]

The cream of Ogdensburg society filled every pew in St. John's Church for the high-noon wedding on September 10. An ailing and frail Orlando came out of retirement to help the Reverend J. D. Morrison, rector of St. John's, read the vows. After a luncheon reception at the Averell mansion, all of the guests trooped down to the railroad station, where a locomotive, emblazoned with a huge red, white, and blue banner identifying it as the *E. H. Harriman*, took the newlyweds' honeymoon car away with a screaming whistle and a cloud of steam.

They moved into a house Harriman had bought on East Forty-fourth Street, and E.H. went back to his brokerage business at E. H. Harriman and Company, but his marriage had made it possible for him to be something more than a stock trader. His father-in-law arranged for him to join the board of directors of the Ogdensburg and Lake

Champlain, and soon he was spending much of his time steeping himself in the railroad business.

His first chance to get his own hand on the throttle of a railroad company came when he and S. J. Macy of the New York merchant family and several other friends bought control of a thirty-four-mile-long upstate line connecting the Pennsylvania Railroad depot at Oswego, New York, with docks on Lake Ontario. The Lake Ontario and Southern, as the little spur line was called, had already gone bankrupt once and appeared to be headed on a second trip to insolvency. Under the circumstances, its chairman, a Wall Street broker named William Alexander Smith, was more than pleased to have it taken off his hands.

Certainly, it was not a property that commended itself to investors. The roadbed and tracks were dilapidated, its freight cars in disrepair, and its aging locomotives long overdue for major maintenance.

With Macy as president and Harriman as vice-president, the new owners undertook a general face-lifting. At the same time they fixed up their rolling stock, they established a new grain elevator company as a subsidiary to help generate business. But nothing they did in more than a year of serious effort significantly improved the road's financial performance or its prospects. With Macy and most of the other partners discouraged and ready to get out, Harriman named a price for which he would either buy their interest or sell his, and all hastened to take his money.

In full command, E.H. was free to do what he had in mind from the beginning—to forget turning a profit and throw everything into making the road attractive to one of the big companies that had always taken it for granted. The value of the Lake Ontario and Southern was not in its rickety rails and worn equipment, but its location. Renaming it the Sodus Bay and Southern, Harriman set out to sell it. Although the spur connected the Pennsy's tracks to the docks on the lake, company officials had never shown a moment's interest in owning it, and to get their attention, E.H. deftly put them in competition with the New York Central.

To the latter, he touted his small line as an opportunity to block the Pennsylvania from getting strategically valuable access to the Great Lakes. He then tweaked the interest of Pennsylvania executives with a batch of statistics showing them that there was money to be made by hauling coal to Sodus Bay for shipment to the Canadian market via Lake Ontario.

Just as he hoped, New York Central men promptly took an option to buy, and their interest brought the Pennsylvania to the bait. When the New York Central's ninety-day option expired, they sought to renew it, but E.H. had disappeared. Although he was unavailable to the New

York Central executives, he arranged to be located by representatives of the Pennsylvania, who were now anxious to buy. The old feeder line brought him a handsome profit, but more importantly, the sale brought him a satisfaction surpassing anything he had ever experienced buying and selling certificates on Wall Street.

And even as he pulled off the deal with the Pennsylvania, he was angling for an important role in the Illinois Central, where his friend Stuyvesant Fish had helped him establish personal connections with company management. His big chance to be something more than Fish's friend came in the summer of 1881 when President Garfield was mortally wounded by an assassin, sending the stock market into a dive. Illinois Central shares dropped with the rest. At the time, the road was trying to raise cash for modernization. Harriman bought heavily into its bonds, and recommended that his wealthiest brokerage clients do likewise. He also counseled against selling off the stock of what he told them was the best railroad in the country.[12]

By 1883, the road's health was again robust. European immigrants were arriving at a record pace. Westward expansion was booming, and with it, the Illinois Central and other American railroads were gathering enormous profits. That summer, Harriman's friend Fish became vice-president of the IC, and E.H. himself was elected to the board of directors.

Within a stunningly short time after taking his seat at the directors' table, Harriman dominated the company. Working through Fish, he succeeded in getting his Uncle Oliver named to the board as well, and he quietly made arrangements to control the proxies of many of the foreigners who had huge holdings in the company. Then, with the wistful assessment that he had wasted fifteen years of his life, he closed his brokerage business, quit Wall Street, and became a railroad man.[13]

To the consternation of the old guard, he and Fish took the conservative IC into a bold expansion, going after more routes and building new track to close weak links they found in the system. They modernized rolling stock, rebuilt bridges, renovated aging stations, took over small lines such as the Mississippi and Tennessee and the Wabash, St. Louis and Pacific.

Their freewheeling management frightened men who had long found psychic and financial comfort in William Henry Osborne's practice of putting the road's earnings into banks instead of boxcars. "I don't like that man Harriman," grumbled Sam Sloan, a veteran railroader and intimate friend of Osborne's, who had watched Stuyvesant Fish grow up. "He and 'Stuyv' Fish are going to get Osborne in trouble with the Illinois Central if he don't look out."[14]

They did not bring down the financial ruin that Sloan and his generation feared, but Harriman's aggressive style put him on track for a head-on collision with J. P. Morgan over an obscure Iowa railroad called the Dubuque and Sioux City.

For twenty years, the Illinois Central had leased the latter's tracks across the state, providing 38 percent of the small company's gross earnings. It was a good deal for Dubuque and Sioux City stockholders, and Illinois Central officials expected to continue it as a matter of course, but it was not the sort of arrangement that appealed to Harriman. It put the Illinois Central in the position of maintaining tracks and roadbeds and footing the bill for improvements and extension of lines it didn't own. Furthermore, competition had increased, and the Dubuque and Sioux City had started to lose money. Harriman could see that the losses were going to mount rapidly unless the system was expanded to reach more grain elevators and stockyards across the state.

The first time the lease came up for renewal after Harriman became a member of the Illinois Central board, he urged that the company simply buy the Iowa line instead of signing another long-term lease. There was no objection, and he immediately started buying Dubuque and Sioux City stock, accumulating, in short order, about fifteen thousand shares. That was nowhere near enough for control, but it was enough to alert stockholders that something was afoot. Seeing a chance to drive the price far higher, they began pooling their holdings, and Harriman suddenly found that no more shares were to be had at a reasonable price.

Anticipating a showdown at the annual stockholders meeting in Dubuque, the holdouts put their pooled shares in the hands of Drexel, Morgan and Company, and began rounding up proxies for an all-out battle for control of the company.

When the meeting was called to order in February 1897, it appeared that Harriman and the Illinois Central had been stopped. The Morgan forces held enough stock and proxies either to dictate a sale price or to set the terms for a new long-term lease. What they had not anticipated, however, was that Harriman had arranged for a huge turnout of small shareholders for the meeting. Holding a majority of the voters in the room, they elected new directors who favored the sale to Illinois Central. When the question of the purchase was put to them, the new directors declared that all of Morgan's proxies were invalid, because he had signed the certificates in his possession as owner rather than trustee. The great lion of Wall Street had been ambushed in Dubuque.

Humiliated by an upstart he didn't even know, Morgan carried his fight to court, and there it sat for several months. When the time was right, Harriman finally made a compromise offer of $80 per share. There was nothing left for Morgan to do but accept, and the Dubuque and Sioux City became part of the Illinois Central system.

Thereafter, "the little man," as Morgan called Harriman, was a detested rival with whom a score had to be settled.[15]

As chairman of the IC's powerful finance committee and Vice-President Fish's confidant, Harriman in effect ruled the Illinois Central.

He had begun his railroad career at a fortunate moment, for the eighties brought a surge of unbridled expansion. During the single decade, railroads added more track than had even existed in 1870. More than six thousand miles of new track were laid every year, and money poured into railroad investment faster than it could rationally be used.

Speculators put down new rails parallel to existing tracks with no purpose but to force the established company to buy them out in self-defense. Every year saw dozens of new railroad securities traded on the stock exchange. Rate wars broke out, making it sometimes possible for travelers to go from New York to San Francisco for as little as $21.50.

Not surprisingly, such a time was littered with victims, some innocent, some greedy. In the midst of the boom, 108 railroads and eleven thousand miles of track were in bankruptcy. But the blue-chip Illinois Central remained the favorite of conservative old New York money.[16]

With Fish and Harriman ignoring the hitherto sacred tenet that the railroad run cheapest was run best, the eighties brought to the IC system 1,500 miles of new track, 274 new locomotives, 234 new passenger cars, and an additional 8,401 freight cars. Annual profits soared from $8.9 million to $20 million.[17]

About the time of the showdown with Morgan in Iowa, Harriman closed his Forty-fourth Street house and moved his wife and children to Chicago. He had gone there expecting to stay only weeks, but he had become so immersed in the day-to-day excitement of running the railroad that he wound up staying for three years, becoming vice-president in 1886 when Fish moved up to the presidency of the company.

There were by 1887 three children—Mary, who was six, Cornelia, who was three, and in between, a blond-haired son named Henry Neilson, just past four and old enough to be aware of his father's absences. He was called Harry, and he matched the Illinois Central railroad in E.H.'s affections. He was the son E.H. had to have to take up his work someday and continue the Harriman line.

The family had been in Chicago only a few months when the city was hit by an outbreak of diphtheria. Harry was stricken and died in February 1888, three months before his fifth birthday. Harriman blamed himself. Although moving his wife and children to Chicago had seemed an expression of his devotion, the ultimate truth was that he had uprooted them for the sake of his career and the Illinois Central Railroad. The loss made Chicago forever a bitter memory.[18]

As long as he lived, Harriman would mention Harry in letters to his wife. Years after the child's death, he stopped at Niagara Falls, where he and Mary had once taken Harry as a toddler, and alone he retraced their old steps with the little boy. In a letter to Mary, he said he wondered whether Harry's spirit was still "hanging about." At other times, when his wife questioned his driving himself toward exhaustion, he would reply that he had obligations because of "Harry's sacrifice."[19]

At the controls of the Illinois Central, Harriman headed off determined competition from Collis Huntington's Southern Pacific in the South and acquired seemingly insignificant spurs wherever he saw opportunity for a profitable new Illinois Central branch to take root. With Fish's acquiescence, he picked up the failed Wabash, St. Louis and Pacific, and launched construction of the Chicago, Madison and Northern, linking the IC's rails in Iowa directly to Chicago.[20]

Proof of his management ability and the wisdom of the expansion strategy was in the railroad's ledgers. The Illinois Central's credit standing was the best in the industry, enabling it to raise money at half what it cost many other railroads during the eighties.

Usually railroad bonds cost 7 or 8 percent interest, but guided by Harriman the IC got rates as low as 4 percent, and at least once Fish marketed bonds at 3½ percent. The secret, financier Otto Kahn observed years later, was that "somehow or other, it never had bonds for sale except when bonds were in great demand; it never borrowed money except when money was cheap and abundant."[21]

Illinois Central planners looked toward the 1890s expecting Harriman and Fish to continue building track and buying new trains at their same intense pace. A planning committee appointed by E.H. made a long study of expansion and modernization needs, and recommended full throttle.

When the report reached him in late January of 1890, Harriman was feeling sickly and taking a few days' rest in New York. His telegraphed reaction to its recommendations stunned the Chicago headquarters. Without warning, the ramrod of ten years' expansion decided to abandon the strategy he had promoted from the day he joined the board. The boldest practitioner of the spend-money-to-make-money philosophy suddenly reverted to the old gospel of William Henry Osborne, urging that all spare cash be put into the bank rather than plowed into the expansion and modernization.

Any policy of large-scale spending, he said, "would be unwise. . . . Our organization is not prepared for it, we haven't sufficient information, and it might lead to extravagance. Our whole force should be devoted to making and saving money. We can make the necessary improvements this year, during the dull season, with the equipment we already have."[22] It was a crucial moment in Harriman's career and in the fortunes of the venerable Illinois Central.

Either ignored or indiscernible to other railroad executives were signs that the boom of the eighties was coming to an end.

A little more than two years later, financial panic spread from Europe to the United States, laying siege to banks and investment houses, leaving farmers and merchants destitute.

Railroads, with their enormous needs for cash, followed financial institutions into depression and bankruptcy, the Union Pacific, the Northern Pacific and the Atchison going down in 1893, along with the Erie, the Reading, the Southern, the Baltimore and Ohio, one household name after another.

By the middle of the nineties, 156 railroads and 39,000 miles of track, capitalized at $2.5 billion, fully a quarter of the American railroad industry, had gone into receivership. Conspicuously missing from the ruin was the Illinois Central, saved because Harriman had taken it onto a siding. With disaster all around, its huge stores of cash allowed it to strengthen its hold on the rich delta of the Mississippi Valley while the country was in the throes of a devastating depression.

It never missed a quarterly dividend payment during the four years that the country was mired in the economic swamp. In fact, at the depth of the crisis it floated a $2.5 million bond issue at an interest rate of 3 percent.

Soon after turning the road away from expansion to build its cash reserves for just such a day, Harriman resigned the vice-presidency and moved back home to New York.

He remained a powerful influence because he was still a director and chairman of the finance committee, but it was time to strike out for bigger things.

Chapter II

RAILS
Rise of the Little Giant

In his prime, E. H. Harriman was a sawed-off, dyspeptic little man standing less than five and a half feet tall, habitually dressed in baggy clothes, and sheltered by a soft felt hat that swallowed his head and made him look even smaller than he was. With his floppy walrus mustache, he was a prototype for political cartoonists in need of a capitalist to portray as either despotic or foolish.

He contrasted so completely with other financial wizards with their tall silks, frock coats, and impeccable beards that later descriptions of him grew outlandishly exaggerated, one assigning him a prison pallor, a frightful cough, foul breath, and a nose that dripped. Foul breath and drippy nose or not, his undistinguished appearance and his go-it-alone habits were but small details adorning his reputation as a fearless competitor with carnivorous instincts.

Within big-money circles Harriman was regarded with both awe and suspicion. Anybody who could publicly skin J. P. Morgan was a formidable figure. Not surprisingly, his reputation also included strong hints that he was a man not to be trusted.

Morgan, who fumed for years over the way Harriman outfoxed him in Dubuque, warned banker friends that the "little man" bore watching in anything he did. James Stillman, president of the powerful National City Bank, who would in time become one of Harriman's closest allies, acknowledged he had received discreet warnings from others to "look out for Ed Harriman," that the onetime pad pusher was "not a safe man to do business with."[1] The suspicion was not confined to Wall Street.

In 1885, about the same time he quit his brokerage business and became a full-time railroad man, Harriman began building what would become a 20,000-acre country estate in the Ramapo Mountains northwest of New York City, buying the first 9,500 acres at a distress sale held by friends who had fallen on hard times. The property, a dozen miles west of the Hudson, was owned by the Parrott family, which had given its name to the famed gun used by the Union Army in the Civil War and whom Harriman had known over years of hunting trips to Orange County.

With four iron mines and a furnace, the estate supported the Parrotts luxuriously until the rich Mesabi Range of Minnesota destroyed the market for ore mined from the modest deposits in New York. Without their income from the mines, the Parrotts had to sell off everything except their immediate homestead, and Harriman had purchased their property at auction. Believing that he had callously taken advantage of their misfortune and prevented them from getting a better price, members of the family never spoke to him again, though he steadfastly insisted that he had entered the bidding because the land was about to fall into the hands of lumbermen who had no interest but to strip the majestic slopes of their valuable hardwood.

In any case, E.H. bought the property for $52,500, the first in a series of acquisitions that would create a domain thirty square miles in extent, with cold, deep lakes and with peaks offering expansive vistas of the Ramapos. It was named Arden for Mrs. Parrott's family, and before Harriman was through with it, the estate was the envy of all the city rich who kept country places in the Hudson Valley.

But the real bargain that Harriman sought was not in the wooded New York highlands, and he did not find his prize until the financial panic of 1893 had taken its toll on American railroads. Amidst the devastation of the battered industry lay the wreckage of the famed Union Pacific, an icon of the country's explosive western expansion. Four years after it fell into bankruptcy, it presented the big opportunity E.H. had awaited.

Running westward from the bank of the Missouri River at Omaha, through Cheyenne and Laramie to Ogden, it had always been more colorful than profitable, its name an inspiration to the stout-hearted immigrants who rode it to the frontier, its history one of scandal, debt, poor management, and unfulfilled promise.

Acquiring branch lines that doubled the mileage of its original tracks, the company had during the eighties stretched its resources to the limit without improving its profits, and when the crisis of '93 hit, it was one of lines that took an early plunge into insolvency. While it was in receivership, its feeder lines and subsidiaries with profit potential had been sold off one by one, and the main line deteriorated into appalling disrepair.

Harriman had patiently bided his time after the crash, adding to his private landholdings, involving himself in civic affairs in Orange County, and engaging in a fight with Morgan over the reorganization of the bankrupt Erie Railroad. He did not have the personal fortune to take charge of a major line, but he knew of other ways to capture control.

While making something of the Union Pacific would require monumental commitment, the possibilities down the road were breathtaking.

Congress had created the Union Pacific and Central Pacific railroad companies in 1862, the year E.H. went to work on Wall Street, giving them the land, the money, and the mandate to forge a great railroad linking California to the rail system and the populous states of the East.

With public money and lands heaped upon the developers by Washington, the patriotic undertaking got under way after the Civil War. Dollar-a-day Chinese coolies pushed the Central Pacific eastward across the Sierra Nevadas from California, and General Grenville Dodge drove the Union Pacific westward with an army of ten thousand destitute Irishmen, grizzled Civil War veterans, adventurers, wanderers, and fugitives. The construction gangs fought Indians, dynamited their way through granite mountain passes, and worked through winters when snow reached the tops of telegraph poles, securing themselves in the folklore of the West. Near the end, with the whole country swept up in the dream of uniting East and West with a ribbon of steel, they put down as much as five miles of track a day.

Four years after construction started, trains from New York and California met at Promontory Point in Utah, and on May 10, 1869, a ceremonial golden spike at last linked East and West. Celebrations erupted from coast to coast as the news chattered along telegraph wires.

In retrospect, the price paid for the triumph was staggering. The unity of East and West had been bought with the labor of the semislave coolies imported for the Central Pacific, the destruction of the Plains Indians, and stupendous graft and corruption. Washington had, during the railroad heyday of the last half of the nineteenth century, turned over to developers land grants with an area greater than that of New England, including some of the continent's most fertile farmland. In no case was the generosity greater than it was to the men who built the Union Pacific and Central Pacific railroads. Besides the twelve million acres of land grants along the Union Pacific right-of-way, public cash subsidies amounted to as much as $48,000 a mile. The Crédit Mobilier construction company, whose stock was handed out to members of Congress by Congressman Oakes Ames of Massachusetts, pocketed profits of $44 million.

And when the line was finished, the concept of the transcontinental road was basically flawed, as far as Union Pacific was concerned. Access to the West Coast was controlled by the Central Pacific link from Ogden westward. To gain control of a route to the coast, therefore, the Union Pacific struck out northwest, buying the Oregon Railroad and Navigation Company and building the Oregon Short Line into Portland.

The connecting line to the sea wound tortuously across the mountains of Wyoming, and crossed mile upon mile of empty plains that produced no revenue. The company was saddled with incompetent management, its trains preyed upon by bandits on horseback, its treasury looted by frock-coated opportunists from back East.

Gunmen who took wallets and vanished into the hole-in-the-wall country of Wyoming were mere mischief compared to Jay Gould, who figuratively put a gun to Union Pacific's head and forced it to buy his unprofitable Kansas Pacific and Denver Pacific systems that ran parallel to the Union Pacific tracks. Threatening full-scale competition, Gould bullied the Union Pacific into exchanging 200,000 shares of stock in exchange for his roads, then dumped the shares for a $10 million in profit.

When the Union Pacific declared bankruptcy in the most spectacular of the collapses in 1893, it surprised no one. Its earnings were declining, the system desperately needed repairs, and it was facing the deadline for repayment of a $53 million government loan. For a year and a half thereafter, a highly pedigreed committee led by J. P. Morgan, and including General Dodge, the hero of Union Pacific's construction, worked vainly to resuscitate it, but there were too many people to be satisfied—including congressmen sensitive about the railroad's past and its outstanding debt. Investors who bought and sold railroad securities had no interest in an abused and chronically ill company whose prospects for profits seemed dim at best. In the spring of 1895, the great Morgan, who had higher callings than to labor over a case so clearly hopeless, quit.

A few months later, George Gould, head of the Missouri Pacific, talked Jacob Schiff of Kuhn, Loeb and Company into picking up where Morgan left off. And for nearly a year, Schiff made difficult but steady progress, gathering support in Washington and gradually reviving the interest of the New York financial community. But then his supporters in Congress began to waver on arrangements for handling the railroad's debt, and investors inexplicably resurrected old questions. Before long, Schiff concluded that somebody had gone into competition against him.

Schiff had no reason to suspect Harriman. They had known each other since E.H. joined the board of the Illinois Central, and they had worked together in opposing Morgan's effort to reorganize the Erie. While Schiff admired E.H.'s accomplishment in saving the Illinois Central from the crash, it did not occur to him that Harriman had the audacity to try single-handedly to take control of the Union Pacific.

As soon as Schiff described the situation to Morgan, however, the latter identified Harriman's clear fingerprints, and Schiff confronted E.H. face-to-face. Typically, Harriman went on the offensive, acknowledging that he had for months been secretly putting obstacles before the committee, and calmly announcing that he intended to reorganize the Union Pacific himself. He would finance his rejuvenation of the system, he explained matter-of-factly, by raising $100 million from the sale of Illinois Central bonds.

Because the IC had hoarded its cash before the collapse, it could now raise money at 3 percent interest, a rate that not even the influential house of Kuhn, Loeb could match. In spite of its access to European capital, Harriman contended, Kuhn, Loeb could not raise money for less than 4½ percent.

It was not an empty boast. Illinois Central's performance in the bond markets was strong enough that Harriman had a real chance to make his grandiose scheme work. Years later, Harriman's biographer suggested that he actually had a more limited ambition than he confessed to Schiff. Instead of taking over the Union Pacific outright, his aim might have been merely to prevent the Union Pacific from falling into the hands of the New York Central and the Chicago and Northwestern. It was also possible that he and Stuyvesant Fish were, at most, out to make the Union Pacific a part of the Illinois Central system and that his objective changed once he succeeded in gaining a dominant position in Union Pacific.[2]

From the beginning of Schiff's effort to take charge of the bankrupt road, there had been gossip in the financial community that the Vanderbilts were behind it, perhaps planning to turn the New York Central into a transcontinental road.

If Harriman's object was nothing more than protection of the Illinois Central, it was one of the few times in his life that he underestimated his own power of persuasion, for Schiff was willing to bargain, and E.H. was willing to listen. The Harriman price for cooperation was simple. He wanted the chairmanship of Union Pacific's new executive committee. Only if he was made the company's top executive would he drop his own effort. Schiff tried to dismiss the demand as unreasonable, if not an outright bluff. In any case, he could not meet Harriman's condition, because he had already arranged for Winslow Pierce, the lawyer for the Missouri Pacific, to be chairman.

Harriman not only stuck to his guns, but made the secret fight public, causing Schiff to realize for the first time that his rival was willing to wreck everybody's chances rather than back down. Inviting Harriman to yet another meeting, he all but capitulated. While he could not back out on his commitment to Pierce, he did promise to make Harriman an executive committee member and suggested the chairmanship could follow. "If you prove to be the strongest man in that committee," Schiff told him, "you'll probably get the chairmanship in the end."[3]

With this huge concession, Harriman became Schiff's collaborator, putting up $900,000 for membership in the Kuhn, Loeb syndicate.

It took almost a year of rugged negotiation, but Schiff succeeded in bringing the government and wealthy investors into an agreement for the syndicate to buy the road and reorganize it, assuming its debts of $81 million, including a government claim of more than $58 million. As promised, Harriman was immediately elected to the new executive committee.

The restoration offered a challenge dwarfing anything E.H. had ever tackled. By experience, he was a financier who spoke and listened to the spirit world of Wall Street, successfully advising railroaders when to sell bonds, when to hoard cash, when to buy new boxcars, and when to make do with the old ones. To reclaim a railroad wrecked by years of mismanagement and buried under monumental debt was quite another matter. The IC had been a well-run company already on the way to vigorous expansion the day Harriman arrived. In that case, it hadn't mattered whether he knew anything about the weight of rails, the traction of locomotives, or the grade of inclines. Now he was suspect because he had not fueled boilers or blistered his hands tightening track bolts.

As soon as the reorganization plan was in place, the new directors headed west for their initial look at the wreck they had claimed. From the first day, Harriman was conspicuous for knowing the company and the territory vastly better than anybody else in the party. After a week of tramping through idle trainyards, deteriorating passenger stations, and rotting boxcars, most of the others returned to New York despondent at what they had seen. Depression-ridden towns across Union Pacific territory were as discouraging as the railroad itself. Even Schiff now doubted that the line could ever be made profitable.

Only Harriman was undaunted. Wherever the directors encountered railroad workers and local officials, he bombarded them with questions that mystified most of the other directors, and showered them with a torrent of observations on urgently needed repairs and changes. By the time the trip was over, word was already going around Union Pacific stops that the little man, Harriman, was the one to watch among all of the new moneybags from New York.

"That's Ned Harriman; used to be with the Illinois Central at Chicago," general manager Edward Dickson was overheard telling another company official at one stop along the way. "He's a comer. They all defer to him, and he knows nearly as much about the property as I do already—except the financial end, and of this he knows all and I know very little."[4]

But Harriman was only beginning to delve into the road's condition. In the early summer of 1898, he took his teenaged daughters, Mary and Cornelia, and left on a five-thousand-mile journey to inspect the line mile by mile.

The shops in Omaha rigged a special observation car to be pushed ahead of a slow-moving locomotive so Harriman could see every bridge and crosstie across Nebraska, Wyoming, and Utah. From the main road they detoured onto every spur, including the feeder lines that had been sold during the frantic efforts to avoid bankruptcy—lines which Harriman intended to recover. From time to time, he would order a halt and climb down. Stuffing his hands in his pockets he would walk the roadbed alone.

Seeing the ends of track bolts extending beyond tightened nuts, he told Omaha to order shorter bolts. Water towers needed larger pipes, he advised, so locomotives could save time at watering stops. Too much money was being spent fixing old boxcars. If they needed more than ten dollars' worth of repairs, he wanted them scrapped.

Traveling only in daylight, the party chugged westward, pausing in North Platte, Julesburg, Cheyenne, and Laramie, then turning northwest on the Oregon Short Line all the way to Portland, with Harriman filling dozens of notebooks with a scrawl indecipherable to anyone but himself.

From Portland, Harriman and his daughters headed back south to San Francisco, picked up the Central Pacific tracks to Ogden, and finally returned to Omaha after detouring once more to inspect the feeder lines running north into Montana. "He saw every poor tie, blistered rail, and loose bolt in my division," said a division superintendent who had been ordered aboard the Harriman's car for a talk between stops.[5]

Since he had been along when members of the board took their first look at the road the previous year, Harriman well knew what to expect when he and the girls left New York. But his detailed inspection through the summer dramatically emphasized the magnitude of the job before him. The roadbed cried out for extensive repairs, and much of the rolling stock was technically obsolete, with freight cars in disrepair and locomotives too small.

The track—"a welded streak of rust," as it was called in later exaggerated accounts—was in a precarious state for stretches of hundreds of miles. The rails were too light, the tracks unballasted, bolts loose, crossties rotted. Streams and gulches were spanned by bridges still consisting of only wood. But as he rolled along, Harriman had more to worry about than restoring decent maintenance. A greater problem was the way the route had been laid out. Although the road's construction had been an enormous engineering achievement for its time, General Dodge and his work gangs had been under enormous pressure to stay on schedules laid down in Washington. They had, for the most part, taken the route of least resistance, negotiating through highland passes most easily accessible to mules and men with picks and shovels. As the tracks crossed Wyoming, there were grades of nearly one hundred feet per mile; some climbs were so steep as to require two engines under full throttle. Tracks wound around curve after sharp curve, to elevations of more than eight thousand feet.

Long before he finished his tour back in Omaha, Harriman concluded that much of the Union Pacific would have to be rebuilt from the roadbed up if it was to become profitable. It would require new locomotives and heavy new freight cars. That meant miles of new roadbed with heavier track, plus steel bridges and solid embankments in place of the old wooden trestles. To cut the cost of hauling wheat and cattle from the plains and the heavy freight from factories, he planned to run long trains and run them fast; that meant shaving the tops from peaks, straightening curves, and blasting new tunnels through solid rock.

While he was still in the Far West, he wired the board in New York a request for $25 million, about half what it had cost to build the main line from the Missouri to its Promontory Point connection with the Central Pacific in the first place—half the $51 million it had actually cost before the promoters tacked on their $44 million profit.[6]

Not even Harriman's confidence and his personal order for another five thousand shares of Union Pacific stock was enough to get the directors to fork over such a sum when they had just taken on an $81 million debt. But when he returned with all the details of his plans to remake the road, they changed their minds, putting up the money and endorsing nearly every recommendation that he unwound from his stack of notebooks.

Moreover, the board members had by then seen and heard enough to make Harriman chairman of the executive committee and chief executive officer, deposing Winslow Pierce. E.H. was suddenly the monarch of the Union Pacific, backed by men whose fortunes would make him America's railroad king: John D. Rockefeller's younger brother, William; Rockefeller–Standard Oil banker James Stillman; Standard Oil mastermind Henry H. Rogers; and Schiff. Later came Henry Clay Frick, captain of his own huge coke and steel empire.

For a time, outsiders, and perhaps the powers at Standard Oil headquarters themselves, had seen Harriman as a mere agent of the oil millionaires, a convenient instrument for deploying their surplus cash.

But once the Union Pacific rebuilding was complete, and Harriman was in search of still bigger stakes, he emerged the leader rather than the tool of America's most potent financial alliance.

As an engineering feat, the modernization of the decrepit railroad rivaled the construction itself. Millions of tons of rock were put into new roadbeds as mile after mile of heavy track supported by nearly a million new crossties stretched along the Omaha-to-Ogden trunk line. Where it was impossible to straighten curves out or to cut grades down to Harriman's forty-three-foot-per-mile grade limitation, the roadway was abandoned outright and the tracks relocated. In one memorable stretch of four miles, the straight new track cut across General Dodge's winding roadbed no less than seven times. Just west of Cheyenne, 800,000 yards of gravel and rock, enough under normal conditions to ballast a railroad track for three hundred miles, was required to build one new crossing of Dale Creek. Thousands of carloads of broken granite from cuts and tunnels in the mountains were hauled down for track ballast, reinforced embankments, and footings for steel bridges that replaced wooden spans. Tops and sides were ripped off hundreds of derelict boxcars, converting them to flatcars for construction trains. New track-laying machines pushed forward, tossing new crossties off on one side of the roadbed and rails on the other. Specially designed ballast cars dumped huge loads of gravel in minutes and moved on.[7]

Old-time Union Pacific hands were incredulous at the avalanche of money thrown behind the rebuilding, money that sent caravans of steam shovels, graders, and snowplows and scores of young civil engineers to carry out Harriman's orders.

Like the original construction crews that had worked through deep winter snow three decades before, Harriman's work gangs labored through the long winter of 1900 in the Wyoming high country, blasting, drilling, hauling, driving hundreds of loaders and graders and tractors. In the Laramie Mountain foothills, they moved five million yards of rock and dirt to level a stretch of eighteen miles. At the peak of the climb over the Rockies, they cut through nearly 1,800 feet of solid rock to open a new tunnel 250 feet below the summit. Between the hills west of Cheyenne and the Wasatch Range east of Ogden, they removed some seven thousand degrees of curvature, the equivalent of nearly twenty complete circles. On only a few brief stretches did they fail to meet Harriman's stringent specification on grades.

As the work parties laid down the new road, Harriman was recapturing the subsidiary lines that Union Pacific had lost during its slide into bankruptcy and the five years it remained insolvent. Some 2,500 miles of track belonging to the Oregon Short Line and the Oregon Railroad and Navigation Company once again became part of the modernized Union Pacific system.

In just three years, Harriman doubled the capacity of the UP freight trains, buying more-powerful locomotives and five thousand new boxcars capable of hauling forty to fifty tons each. But the face-lifting was not the objective itself, and when railroad president Horace Burt expressed satisfaction at the arrival of boxcars, Harriman snapped, "Yes, Mr. Burt, they are fine cars, but there's nothing in them."[8] The cargo was not long in coming, however.

As Harriman had foreseen, the depression was ending as the Union Pacific renewal was finished. As if nature had conspired with him, generous rains ended a long Grain-Belt drought, producing three bumper wheat crops three years in succession—and the Union Pacific was ready.

More than a financial triumph, the reconstructed Union Pacific was also Harriman's personal toy. He delighted in racing over it to set new speed records, taking his children on inspection trips, and talking to customers who rode his passenger trains and shipped their wheat and pigs to market on his freight cars.

When his sumptuous private car traveled the territory, its chef provided a smorgasbord of quail, prairie chicken, elk, and antelope. Near the track in Wyoming, a mountain stream was impounded so strings of speckled trout could quickly be fetched for the chairman's car or for dignitaries he wished to impress as they crossed his territory.

He ordered carloads of soil hauled into the mountains and unloaded around barren stationhouses so trees and flowers could grow, and he formed armed posses and mounted them on long-winded horses to rid his railroad of robbers.

From the moment he assumed control and sent crews to work on the tracks, he was a fanatic about discipline and safety. On one of his inspection trips, his speeding train hit a stretch of rough track without warning and very nearly went off the rails. A construction gang replacing crossties had failed to send a flagman down the track to warn approaching trains. When Harriman found what had happened, he ordered the entire crew fired on the spot, despite protests from Burt that he was being cruel.[9] From such episodes, word spread that an unusual transformation was taking place, and Harriman's reputation soared. One of his promoters was John "Bet-a-Million" Gates, the flamboyant barbed-wire salesman turned market speculator who had been seen to put down a million-dollar bet on a baccarat game. After the rebuilding was completed Gates declared that "I have traveled over nearly every railroad in the United States, and have just been over the Union Pacific by daylight. It's the best I have ever found, east or west, and in my judgment it is the most magnificent railroad property in the world."[10]

Rejuvenated, paying dividends, and in favor on Wall Street, the new Union Pacific made Harriman a part of the financial establishment. The railroad's credit opened doors to any venture he chose to undertake, and its stock, bought during the dog days when he picked it up for $10 to $25 a share, made him an immense personal fortune.[11]

During his years as Union Pacific chairman, Harriman would eventually pump $175 million into modernizing and improving it, but by the time the initial $25 million rebuilding was complete, the railroad had been turned into a mighty financial engine as well as a transportation system ranking with the best in the country.

With the line under his uncontested domination, Harriman made his next move without even pausing to savor his triumph. While still guiding the rebuilding, he established a syndicate to take over and reorganize the troubled Chicago and Alton, a railroad with enormous potential and a special attraction to Harriman because of his Illinois Central interests. He also answered a call from owners of the struggling Kansas City Southern to help overhaul its 778-mile system running from Kansas City to Port Arthur, Texas. And for good measure, he took a place on the board of the Baltimore and Ohio, using his Wall Street connections to raise $32 million it badly needed for modernization.

His big opportunity came, however, when Collis P. Huntington, the last survivor of the mighty Big Four who had pushed the Central Pacific eastward to meet the Union Pacific, died, giving him the chance to get his hands on the biggest railroad company in the world.

With Leland Stanford, Charles Crocker, and Mark Hopkins all dead, Huntington held 37 percent of the huge Southern Pacific Company, which included both the Southern Pacific and Central Pacific railroads. Together, they operated over nine thousand miles of track, from Portland to Los Angeles, into central Mexico, and eastward to New Orleans. The holding company also owned steamship lines, and, in a manner of speaking, the California legislature. Equally important to Harriman, the Central Pacific held the priceless link between San Francisco and the Union Pacific's terminus at Ogden.

Like his three partners, and like Harriman, Huntington was a self-made man. He had struck out on his own as a fourteen-year-old farmhand in Connecticut, and had moved on to become a clock peddler and hardware dealer. His search for riches had taken him west at about the same time that the Reverend Orlando Harriman made his ill-fated trip to California, and he, too, had been delayed in Panama. Unlike the Reverend Orlando Harriman, however, the crafty Huntington took advantage of his misfortune, selling off his $1,200 consignment of time-pieces to his fellow travelers for $4,000, creating the nest egg he needed to strike out in California.

In Sacramento, he set up business in a tent, selling a variety of supplies to gold miners. That had made him a small fortune before he met Mark Hopkins and began dreaming of building a railroad across the mountains.

While Huntington did not hold a majority in either the Southern Pacific or Central Pacific railroads, he exercised control without fear of losing them, for they were protected from marauders by being part of a giant holding company. But when the old man died in August 1900, Harriman pounced. Backed by Union Pacific directors who approved the sale of $100 million worth of bonds, he opened negotiations for enough stock to gain full control of the Southern Pacific Company and thereby get both of the railroads. Although recently in bankruptcy itself, and holding only $4 million in cash reserves, the Union Pacific's recovery had been so spectacular that its bonds opened wide the doors to capital.

By early 1901 Harriman had laid out $42 million, and rounded up 38 percent of the Southern Pacific stock, assuring him that no one else could take over. The directors' authorization of $100 million in bonds meant that another $58 million could be used for other purposes. Again, he had not spent a cent of his own money.[12]

Increasing Union Pacific's holdings in the Southern Pacific Company to 49 percent, Harriman in effect merged the Union Pacific, Central Pacific, and Southern Pacific systems into one gigantic railroad. Then to secure his control, he severed ties with banks that backed Huntington, froze out members of the old Southern Pacific management, and installed himself as president and chairman of the Southern Pacific Company's executive committee. From his cluttered rolltop desk on the fourth floor of 126 Broadway, he dominated the territory from the Missouri River to the Pacific Ocean. His trunk lines ran from Omaha to San Francisco, and from Portland down through Sacramento, San Francisco, and Los Angeles, then eastward through Phoenix, El Paso, San Antonio, and Houston to New Orleans.

Branch lines extended into nearly every western state and deep into Mexico. The only exception to his western domination was the northern tier of the western states crossed by James J. Hill's Northern Pacific and Great Northern roads.

Besides the three railroads and the Southern Pacific's steamship lines operating out of Galveston, New Orleans, New York, and Havana, Harriman now commanded the steamers of the venerable Pacific Mail and Steamship Company, carrying freight and passengers between the United States and major ports throughout the Orient. The Union Pacific subsidiary also continued its steamship runs between San Francisco and Panama, the same route Harriman's father traveled on his ill-fated journey during the Gold Rush.

It was now possible, General Dodge observed, for E.H. to travel from New York to New Orleans by steamship, board a train to San Francisco, cross the Pacific to China, return by a second route, and then take any one of three railroads to Kansas City or Omaha "without leaving the deck or platform of a carrier which he controls and without duplicating any part of his journey."[13]

Once in command of the Huntington lines, Harriman again adopted his familiar strategy of modernizing aging property. He began revamping the old Central Pacific main line to Ogden, rebuilding its approaches to San Francisco, and laying heavier rails along Southern's "Sunset Route" across the Southwest.

The task hardly compared to the rebuilding of the Union Pacific, for the depression had not brought the same destruction to the Huntington lines that it had visited upon railroads in the East. And shortly before he died, Huntington had already prepared for the general economic recovery by ordering his experts to work on a plan to put the thirty-year-old Central Pacific line back into first-class shape.

Harriman summoned authors of the plan to bring their work to New York, and after only one three-hour meeting in his library, he approved every major recommendation they outlined. The initial investment totaled $18 million, much of it for leveling grades and straightening curves to enable heavily loaded trains to run on more-demanding schedules.

But besides his general face-lifting on the Central Pacific, Harriman decided to attack one traffic bottleneck presenting a challenge that dwarfed his construction of Union Pacific mountain tunnels and the replacement of wooden bridges. Just west of Ogden, the Illinois Central tracks curved northward along the shore of the Great Salt Lake. To get around the inland sea, heavily laden freights had to navigate tight curves and pull several steep grades along the loop that added forty-four miles to the Ogden–San Francisco run. When the Central Pacific coolies had laid down the track, it had not occurred to engineers that there might be a way to shorten the expensive journey. Huntington's chief engineer had later recommended a span straight across the lake, but the project was still on the drawing boards when Huntington died.

In January 1902, Harriman, who had often traveled the route around the lake, ordered Southern Pacific superintendent Julius Kruttschnitt to go to work on a twenty-seven-mile-long section running straight across the lake, eleven miles of it supported by trestles above the water.

Hauling rock from opposite sides of the lake, Kruttschnitt's trains dumped thousands of carloads into the water month after month. Though the depth was no more than thirty-two feet, the soft lake bottom absorbed tens of thousands of tons of rocks hauled out of the mountains, and for months pilings sank and trestles toppled as soon as they were put in place. At times the undertaking appeared to be madness, but Harriman rejected suggestions that it be abandoned. Every setback was followed by orders from his office to haul more rock, and an army of

three thousand men worked seven days a week driving pilings and setting
new trestles whenever the foundation seemed stabilized. When the span
was finished after two alternately depressing and triumphant years, the
Lucin Cutoff had cost $10 million, but it eliminated 1,515 feet of grade
and nearly four thousand degrees of curvature, making it possible for
trains to strike straight across the lake and eastbound locomotives roll
into the highlands under full throttle. Freights began taking the cutoff
in the spring of 1904 and passenger trains a few months later, and
thereafter the venture saved the Central Pacific $1 million every year.[14]

Even in control of the Central Pacific and Southern Pacific, Harriman was not altogether satisfied with his hold on the West. He still
worried that his system was potentially vulnerable. Ever since he had
gotten the reconstruction of the Union Pacific under way, he had kept
a wary eye on the Chicago, Burlington and Quincy. Eastward from
Denver, the Burlington's route paralleled the Union Pacific, and in his
dark moments, Harriman could imagine it laying a track from Denver
west, destroying the monopoly the Union Pacific and Central Pacific
enjoyed on traffic into San Francisco from the nation's breadbasket. His
interest did not arise altogether from the threat of competition in the
West, however. The Burlington was a solidly profitable railroad, and
more than that, its tracks ran right into Chicago, the headquarters of the
Illinois Central. For that reason, he had tried unsuccessfully to buy into
the Burlington even before Huntington's death threw open the gates to
the Southern Pacific Company.

As the strategist responsible for the success of the modern Illinois
Central, Harriman fully appreciated the importance of Chicago as the
rail capital of the country. Control of the Burlington would not only
open the Union Pacific's way into Chicago, but would neatly connect it
with the Illinois Central.

What he now had in mind was to use his routes to the West Coast
to tie in with his steamship lines and tap into markets across the Pacific.
Access to Chicago was crucial.

If he was to exploit opportunities in the Orient to the fullest, he
needed lines into the rail hub of Middle America connecting him to the
Mississippi Valley and the ports on the Great Lakes. But when he and
Jacob Schiff had gone to Burlington officials in 1899 with a private offer
of either cash or Union Pacific stock for the Burlington, they had been
turned down out of hand.

Afterward, they tried buying up the stock on the exchange, hoping
they could acquire enough influence to at least prevent the company
from falling into enemy hands. Working with Schiff, James Stillman,
and George Gould, in a pool, Harriman bought eighty thousand shares,
but he concluded it was impractical, if not impossible, to ever get control

through the open market. Too much of the stock was in the hands of small owners. More importantly, Harriman was engaged in the momentous acquisition of the Southern Pacific; he was working on the reconstruction of the Kansas City Southern and arranging financing for the Chicago and Alton.

While he was thus preoccupied, James J. Hill, with the backing of J. P. Morgan, was busily buying thousands of Burlington shares. The boss of the Northern Pacific and Great Northern wanted the Burlington for the same reason that Harriman did. His Northern Pacific ended at St. Paul and the Great Northern at Duluth. Not only was he without his own line into Chicago, he did not have a close alliance there, as Harriman had with the Illinois Central.

The Minnesotan was not one to be taken lightly. Although he was not a financier, he was fully Harriman's equal as a railroad man. Like E.H., Hill had started with nothing, having come to St. Paul from a remote farm in Ontario and getting his start as a shipping clerk and coal dealer. A powerful man with bird legs and a steel-wool beard, he'd had one of his eyes shot out by an Indian's arrow, and was so obviously a frontiersman that it was easy to underestimate his shrewdness and sophistication.

He was also like Harriman in his drive to dominate and to instinctively bull ahead even when wise men urged caution. He so admired Napoleon that he had given himself the middle name Jerome in honor of Bonaparte's brother. In the days when he still had no money, he made wealthy friends, particularly among politicians who he learned could be enlisted and used in return for only modest favors and contributions.

Just as Harriman had captured the imagination of the financial community by rescuing the Union Pacific, Hill had made a name for himself by taking the bankrupt St. Paul and Pacific Railroad and developing it into the Great Northern system.

When he undertook to extend it all the way to Seattle without benefit of federal money or land grants, experts labeled the project "Hill's Folly." But Hill did lay his tracks across North Dakota, Montana, Idaho, and all the way to Seattle without land grants or subsidies. He was the first railroader who ever did that, and he finished the job during the panic of '93, when the Union Pacific and the biggest names on rails found ignominious company in bankruptcy.

When Morgan arrived to reorganize the bankrupted Northern Pacific, Hill was ready to step in as his partner. And the Morgan colossus now stood behind him as he reached for control of a line into Chicago and the rails on E. H. Harriman's Union Pacific flank.

A showdown between Harriman and Hill had been brewing even before they collided over the Burlington. Although they had long been on friendly terms, Harriman had put them at swords' points by engineering a stock swap that recaptured Oregon subsidiaries that the Union Pacific system had lost during its bankruptcy.

The problem was that both Harriman's and Hill's giant continental systems depended heavily upon access to the same strategically located tributary rails. Harriman's control of the Oregon Railroad and Navigation Company made the Union Pacific a competitor in Hill's northwest territory. Hill needed Harriman's lines in order to reach Portland, and Harriman could get to Seattle only on Hill's Northern Pacific. Of all the parties involved, only Jacob Schiff was positioned to act as a peacemaker.

Harriman's banker, adviser, and business confidant, Schiff was also a longtime friend of Hill's. He had helped finance the Great Northern in the days before Hill had fallen in with Morgan. He had been a Great Northern director, and remained on good enough terms to bring Hill and E.H. together.

In March, just as he was winding up his run on the Southern Pacific stock, Harriman learned that Hill was having secret negotiations with Burlington officials and was near an agreement to gain a majority of the company's stock. Schiff arranged a meeting; but when the three of them sat down together at the Fifth Avenue mansion of First National Bank president George Baker, there was not much to be said.

At first miffed because Hill hadn't told the truth when he had first been asked about his activities in the Burlington market, Schiff was now irate because he and Harriman had been badly outmaneuvered. E.H. conceded as much. In the short confrontation in Baker's study, he bluntly demanded to be taken into Hill's Burlington deal. He wanted a one-third interest for the Union Pacific, but under the circumstances, he and Schiff could only appeal for fairness. Hill was uninterested. "Very well," Harriman snapped, "it is a hostile act, and you must take the consequences."[15]

Days later, the Northern Pacific and Great Northern formally agreed to buy 97 percent of Burlington's common stock for $215 million, or $200 a share. And with that, both Hill and Morgan mistakenly concluded that the battle was all over.

Triumphant, Hill headed west, escorting some important guests to Seattle, while Morgan sailed for Europe to shop for art and loll in the baths of Aix-les-Bains, where emperors and others of his class had taken their leisure for centuries.

With their attention diverted, Harriman retaliated, taking a defiant course that would stand Wall Street on its head. If Hill denied him a cut of the Burlington, he would simply acquire control of the Northern Pacific itself and get the Burlington in the process. In early April, he and Schiff began buying Northern Pacific stock, backed by the $60 million remaining from Union Pacific bond issue authorized before the Southern Pacific acquisition. They could gain control, they calculated, if they could acquire somewhere between $80 million and $100 million of the stock held by the public.[16]

At first, the plot smoothly proceeded without notice. On the way west, Hill stopped off at his great gray mansion in St. Paul, and while he was there, he noticed there was heavy trading in Northern Pacific stock. It did not concern him. After the Burlington coup, that was only to be expected.

But returning to St. Paul several days later, after breaking the St. Paul–Seattle speed record both going and coming, he found Northern Pacific quotation continued its upward march. As he proceeded back to New York, he was unaware that even his and Morgan's allies were being seduced by the Northern Pacific's popularity and taking profits on their stock. Northern Pacific's own directors unloaded thirteen thousand shares of their private holdings, and the Morgan bank casually sold ten thousand, all of them winding up in hands of Harriman and Schiff.[17]

Belatedly realizing what was happening, Hill confronted Schiff, who acknowledged that Harriman and Kuhn, Loeb and Company were amassing Northern Pacific stock. Since Hill had denied them a fair share of the Burlington, he went on, "we're going to see if we can't get a share by purchasing a controlling interest in the Northern Pacific."[18]

It was Friday, May 3, and by Harriman's tally, he and Schiff had already accumulated $42 million worth of Northern Pacific preferred stock, and $37 million worth of its common shares. That assured him, he believed, a majority of the total outstanding stock, although he was forty thousand shares short of a majority in the common.

Schiff thought they had won, but Harriman realized that the struggle was not finished. The forty-thousand-share shortfall in the common was potentially fatal because the Northern Pacific charter gave directors the option of retiring the company's preferred stock as they wished. If directors controlled by Hill and Morgan retired all the preferred, leaving only the common shares to be voted, they would remain in control.

On Saturday morning, a sleepy Schiff arose after talking with Hill into the wee hours and went to synagogue. Harriman was not feeling well, and stayed at home rather than going downtown to his office. But the stock exchange was open on Saturday morning in those days, and he telephoned Kuhn, Loeb and left orders for another forty thousand shares of Northern Pacific common to be bought before closing. The instructions were relayed to Schiff while he was still at synagogue, but the banker directed his office not to place the order, because he considered it unnecessary and wasteful. Not until a struggle broke out in the exchange on Monday morning did Harriman learn that the order had never been executed.[19]

It was a monumental mistake. When the market reopened on Monday, the Morgan legions on Wall Street were on full alert, sent forth by orders from Aix-les-Bains to buy 150,000 Northern Pacific shares. James R. Keene, a market manipulator who had gained renown as a hired gun for Jay Gould and lesser-known speculators, led the charge to head Harriman off.

By the end of Tuesday, both sides thought they had won, but the struggle had slipped out of control. Northern Pacific closed at 149¾, far above any rational assessment of its value. As a result hordes of speculators began selling short, confident of a quick windfall when the price descended to a reasonable level.

Instead, it continued to soar. Between them, the Hill-Morgan and Harriman–Kuhn, Loeb forces had cornered the market. No substantial number of shares was available anywhere. After opening at 112 on Monday and climbing to 149¾, it passed 200, then 300. By Thursday, it exceeded 1,000. Speculators who had sold short had lost fortunes and were unable to find stock to cover their commitments at any price. A panic surpassing anything in living memory swept the trading floor.

Blue-chip stocks plummeted as they were dumped by Northern Pacific losers raising money to cover themselves. U.S. Steel sank from 46 to 24, the market value of all its common stock losing $100 million and its preferred $133 million in the course of the day.[20] With the record for trading volume shattered hours before the bell, the ticker fell more than ten minutes behind, and traders who put in panic orders to sell "at the market" later discovered that they had lost another $10 to $15 a share during the delay in execution of their orders.

Brokerage houses found themselves insolvent, and interest rates on call loans skyrocketed to 60 percent. Instinctively seeking mutual security, bankers pooled $19 million to rescue preferred customers, $15 million of it raised by Gallatin National's Frederick D. Tappen in fifteen minutes on the telephone.[21]

Among the young brokers in the melee was Bernard Baruch, who had been taken aside by James Keene's son-in-law on the first day of the battle and told that a Harriman-Hill struggle for Northern Pacific control was behind the surge of the railroad's stock. Baruch enjoyed the scene, for he had stayed clear of Northern Pacific and was in the process of making the biggest killing of his career by picking up blue-chip stocks that desperate shorts threw overboard to raise money to cover their losses.[22]

Wall Street had been primed for just such a calamity. Speculation, encouraged by victory in the Spanish-American War and the election of William McKinley to the presidency, was rampant, with Americans naively operating on the reckless assumption that stock trading would quickly make them rich. Young men could find no higher calling than to make money, and for the first time women, in huge numbers, joined in buying and selling stocks. "Bucket shops," little back-room and back-alley exchanges, did a thriving business in an underground market. At the height of the Northern Pacific panic, police raided one shop in lower Manhatten and found five hundred people gambling on stocks. Like the New York Stock Exchange, the bucket shop was dominated by the Northern Pacific corner.

The city was awash in tales of huge sums made and lost. One story had former president Grover Cleveland pocketing half a million on a tip from Morgan. There were rumors that Harriman booster Bet-a-Million Gates had taken a loss of $50 a share on sixty thousand shares. Both the Harriman and Hill forces had stopped buying before the crescendo, uncertain over control of the Northern Pacific and the outcome of the panic they had created. E.H., who ordinarily worked at home until late morning, was downtown early on the climactic Thursday, closeted with Schiff, William Rockefeller, and George Gould. The struggle for the Northern Pacific was for the moment overshadowed in the market wreckage. The first objective was to restore sanity before they were themselves ruined by the chaos they had started. Conferences moved on to Schiff's conference room at Kuhn, Loeb. In the afternoon at Morgan's office, Schiff sat down with Hill, his banker friend George Baker, and Morgan's lieutenants to complete a truce.

What he proposed and the Morgan-Hill camp accepted was a plan to jointly bail out stricken brokers by providing them with Northern Pacific stock at $150 to cover their short sales. Once the market crisis was over, the two sides were to come to a summit conference to resolve the deadlock over the Burlington.[23]

The arrangement ended the panic, with only a fraction of the damage that had seemed certain a few hours earlier. By the time the agreement was concluded, the market was closed, but even before trading stopped the situation had eased when a Schiff man fought his way through the bedlam and announced from a desktop on the exchange floor that Kuhn, Loeb would not enforce delivery of Northern Pacific stock it had purchased the previous day.

On Friday Northern Pacific was down to $325 at market closing, and on Saturday morning it lost another $175. As the uproar subsided, the word on the street was that Hill had won. Characteristically, Harriman remained mum; when he was asked about the panic later, he baldly asserted there had been no contest at all between Hill and himself. Though he failed to wrest control of the Northern Pacific away from Morgan and Hill, his enormous holding in the railroad left them at an impasse.

Neither fully understood its legal implications. Harriman controlled the majority of Northern Pacific's preferred stock, as well as a majority of the preferred and common combined. But Morgan and Hill still held their narrow majority of the common, and with it the right to retire the preferred shares.

Harriman's heavy holdings raised the possibility, however, that he might be able to elect new directors favorable to him, block retirement of the preferred shares, and take over the Northern Pacific after all. However, neither side had the stomach to go into the trenches again.

For a month, secret conferences searched for a way to take account of the nearly $80 million worth of Northern Pacific stock held by Harriman and the Union Pacific. On May 31, after a meeting at the Metropolitan Club, the two railroaders and their bankers reached a settlement. Harriman and William Rockefeller were put on the Northern Pacific board, with E.H. also becoming a member of the executive committee.

The pact gave him much less than he wanted when he started out to seize the Northern Pacific, but it provided the Union Pacific unquestionable security from the Hill juggernaut on the north. It furthermore prevented the Burlington from extending its rails to the West Coast and going into direct competition with the Union Pacific, and it granted the Union Pacific the right to use Northern Pacific tracks between Portland and Seattle.

Yet while the impasse was being successfully untangled, Hill worried over the chilling possibility of another raid like Harriman's. His solution was to create a holding company bringing the Northern Pacific, Great Northern, and the Burlington together in a single organization big enough and wealthy enough to resist any outside effort to take control. He called it the Northern Securities Company.

Thus, in the fall of 1901, Harriman found himself a skunk at a garden party, part of the new $400 million railroad trust created as a result of his raid. Because of his huge investment in Northern Pacific stock, he and Union Pacific laid claim to a proportionate share of the new company—some $80 million in Northern Securities stock—and became a partner of the man who now detested him with the intensity of a blast furnace, J. Pierpont Morgan.

Hill, naturally, was named president when the trust was set up, but three of its fifteen directors represented the Union Pacific.

Within weeks, it was under attack. Lawyers for the state of Minnesota and Theodore Roosevelt's Department of Justice simultaneously prepared legal challenges on grounds that Northern Securities was an illegal merger of Northern Pacific and Great Northern.

Litigation dragged on for more than two years, and so did the Harriman-Hill rivalry. At times, it was as petty as the Northern Pacific struggle had been bold. Hill's people bristled at Harriman's attempt to move Northern Securities' offices into the same building with his own headquarters, as well as at an apparent Harriman maneuver to steer a contract for new railroad cars to a company in which he held a large interest. Their troubles in the Pacific Northwest still festered.

Both legal challenges to Northern Securities wound up before the U.S. Supreme Court. Minnesota's lawsuit, asserting that the trust was an illegal merger, was dismissed for lack of jurisdiction. But on March 14, 1904, the high court, divided 5-4, ruled that the trust was a violation of the Sherman Anti-Trust Act.

The decision precipitated still another year of wrangling and another test before the Supreme Court. This time, the dispute arose with Harriman's challenge to Hill's method of disassembling Northern Securities. Hill proposed to return Harriman's holdings in the form of Northern Securities stock, but E.H. demanded that he receive Northern Pacific shares instead, for he had surrendered them to Northern Securities when the trust was set up. Taking a pro rata share of Northern Securities stock, he argued, would beat him out of more than $20 million because Northern Securities' assets included the less valuable Great Northern stock as well as Northern Pacific.[24]

In the end, Harriman lost. The Supreme Court in effect agreed with Hill's argument that one might as well go to a bank and demand a return of the same bills one had deposited.

But he had not lost his luck. There was a surge in the market just as the Northern Securities stock was delivered to him, and in the ensuing months, he unloaded it for a $58 million profit.[25] With other spare Union Pacific cash, he had $130 million to put to use. He invested it in nine other railroad companies where he deemed it useful to establish a stronger presence, extending his influence from coast to coast.

Harriman's battle with Hill was, his friend Otto Kahn of Kuhn, Loeb later contended, one of the most serious mistakes of his career.[26] By going after huge holdings in railroads far from Union Pacific territory, he seemed out to monopolize the railroads of the country, a man driven by nothing more than wanton greed.

Chapter III

AVERELL
Son of the Railroad Man

When E. H. Harriman gave up the vice-presidency of the Illinois Central and went home to New York in 1890, he moved his wife and three daughters into a four-story brownstone on East Fifty-first Street behind St. Patrick's Cathedral. The center of the city's fashionable residential neighborhoods was still to the south, but to stay away from commercial development and congestion, well-to-do families steadily moved farther north.

On upper Fifth Avenue, the mansions on Millionaires' Row attracted growing crowds of gawkers. Madison Avenue, a block to the east, was second in prestige only to Fifth Avenue, and the Harrimans' new home was only one door from the corner of Madison and Fifty-first. Although it was beyond the smell and clatter of the crowded cobblestone streets to the south, the family fled New York every summer. In June, as soon as Mary and Cornelia were out of school, the household was transferred to the Harriman's summer cottage at the Arden estate, and there Mary and the children remained until mid-September while E.H. commuted.

It was a tranquil interlude in his life, as he waited for the United States to rise out of the economic doldrums. He often took three-day weekends in the country, but otherwise he boarded the 8:12 Erie at Turner's Corner each morning. At Jersey City, he crossed the Hudson on the ferry, as he had when he was a schoolboy, and walked from the slip near Cortlandt Street to his office on Broadway, arriving two hours after he had left home. When the stock exchange closed in the afternoon, he headed for the country again, getting back in time to go for a late afternoon ride or to fish for bass in Echo Lake before nightfall.

In the late winter or early spring of 1891, not long after their third daughter, Carol, had passed her first birthday, Mary Harriman learned that she was again pregnant. By then, she was nearly forty, and her husband was forty-three, but she was happy to have another chance to deliver a son. Boys were, after all, a Harriman tradition. E. H. was one of four sons, his father was one of eight, and his grandfather one of seven. Since Harry's death, he had needed another son all the more.

Through that summer, E.H. maintained what was for him a casual pace. He exercised his trotters, added property to his estate, expanded his kennels, and taught Mary and Cornelia to ride. In mid-September, the family moved back to Fifty-first Street.

On a balmy Sunday afternoon two months later, E.H. sent for Dr. W. G. Lyle, who came up Madison Avenue at a trot, driving past carriages loaded with sight-seeing families. The Harrimans' family physician arrived just in time to attend the birth of Mary's fifth child. The healthy baby, born without complication, was to the parents' delight a boy. His name had already been selected: in honor of his grandfather in Ogdensburg, the new son was named William Averell Harriman.

His first memories were of the house on Fifty-first Street, the twin towers of St. Patrick's, horsecars taking passengers up and down Madison Avenue, the candle-lit country house at Arden, and train rides with the family.

Before he was of school age, they moved a bit farther uptown, to a bigger house on the northeast corner of Fifth Avenue and Fifty-fifth Street, in the neighborhood of America's most conspicuous millionaires. Just up the avenue were the mansion of Collis P. Huntington, the ruler of the Southern Pacific, and the French Renaissance palace built by Cornelius Vanderbilt. Two blocks south was E.H.'s friend William K. Vanderbilt, whose residence rivaled Cornelius's château. The immediate neighborhood also included the homes of William C. Whitney, Jay Gould, Mrs. O. H. P. Belmont, John Jacob Astor IV, and the latter's estranged cousin, William Waldorf Astor, who by then had resettled in London.

The Harrimans did little to attract attention to themselves. They were not invited to the glittering balls and dinners where Mrs. Stuyvesant Fish, the wife of E.H.'s Illinois Central colleague and sponsor, reigned as Caroline Astor's successor as arbiter and grand dame of New York society. For that, the Harriman fortune was not yet of adequate size or sufficient age.

Neither were they "society" by temperament. Mary Harriman found personal publicity-seeking vulgar. E.H. thought costume balls silly, and formal dinners purposeless and wasteful. On the evenings of the Vanderbilt, Fish, and Astor parties, the Harrimans could be found in their parlor playing Parcheesi or backgammon.

Averell was too young to remember much about the time when E.H. was taking it easy, keeping regular office hours and building up the country estate. By the time he was ready for school, his father was fighting for control of the Union Pacific. He was not yet ten when his father took command of the Southern Pacific system and precipitated the Northern Pacific panic on Wall Street. By the time Averell reached his teens, E.H. was one of the most controversial figures in America, lampooned by cartoonists, investigated by Congress, and ridiculed by the President.

After he was a small boy, he seldom had his father's undivided attention, and so he grew up with kaleidoscopic and confusing images of the powerful, impatient, driven man he was supposed to emulate and someday succeed. Life with E.H. was a long, never-ending lesson in discipline, striving, and self-improvement.

He showered his children with toys, then commanded them to untie the strings rather than cut them, and fold and save the wrapping paper before the new toys could be used. Always there was, from the man accused of ruthlessness and financial piracy, sermonizing on the responsibilities of wealth. There were frequent lectures on honesty, and stern admonitions that men with shifty eyes and limp handshakes were not to be trusted. And there was pressure—constant pressure—to ride properly, to speak properly, to study, to achieve, to do better.

Averell's childhood memories of his father—and his judgments of him in later life—were fraught with contradictions. One of his earliest recollections was going out with him on a cold Christmas Eve at Arden to deliver a gift to a servant's child accidentally left off the list when the family handed out presents at its holiday party for people on the estate. Just as vividly, he remembered E.H. ordering one of his own children's dog killed for its irritating barking. In her own way, Mary Harriman was as demanding as her husband, enforcing rules as rigid as his.

The circumstances inevitably made Averell a somber child. He grew up with a stammer, which became steadily worse under his father's pressure to stop it. Life was a test, an obligation to please Pappa, to measure up to towering expectations of the man admirers called "the Little Giant," and sensationalist newspapers portrayed as an ogre.

Within days of Averell's birth, E.H. put him on the waiting list for Groton, a new prep school in Massachusetts where the Reverend Endicott Peabody had adopted all the time-honored English methods for perfecting young, upper-class gentlemen. Under Peabody's stern guidance, boys scarcely out of their mothers' laps began their academic preparation for Harvard or Yale and their moral and physical tempering for the leadership of the nation's vital institutions.

To prepare the clay for the master potter, Averell's parents sent him early on to a day school which followed English educational tradition as slavishly as did Rector Peabody. He joined the Knickerbocker Greys, boys from New York's best families who learned close-order drill and gentlemanly deportment at the Seventh Regiment Armory, and, much against his wishes, went to Miss Dodson's dancing classes. At his pre-preparatory boys' school on Forty-sixth Street, English headmaster A. Wallpole Craigie instructed his young charges in Latin, English, history, and math, hewing to every detail of British tradition except caning.

Rather than using the cane, Mr. Craigie required his boys to settle differences with their fists. Desks were moved aside, a ring formed, and the combatants ordered to go after each other with bare knuckles. Averell concluded that caning would have been preferable, for the only time he was sent into the ring, it was against a boy with a well-earned reputation as the school bully. He was thrashed, and his ego was painfully bruised because E.H. was a boxing enthusiast who had once taken lessons from a professional fighter, and still traveled with exercise equipment in his railroad car.

School opened at Craigie's two or three weeks before the Harrimans returned to the city each fall, and so Averell moved in with the Craigies until E.H. and Mary arrived at Fifty-fifth Street with the rest of the family. The first year he was brought into the city early for the opening of school, he sobbed so sorrowfully that his father allowed him to skip the first day and spend it playing around the chairman's rolltop desk and listening to cryptic conversations about the Union Pacific.

Each morning, wearing knickerbockers and a starched white shirt with a broad Eton collar, he walked alone to school. He went home for lunch, the trip requiring him either to run or skate to make it back in time, but it was a small price to pay for avoiding Mrs. Craigie's food. After classes in the afternoon, the boys took the Madison Avenue trolley or walked to Central Park to play football, usually returning to the Craigies' to study for an hour before going home.

On occasion, he went up to the Harlem raceway and watched E.H. and William K. Vanderbilt race their sulkies wheel-to-wheel around the track. During the winter, E.H. would sometimes load some of the boys into a sleigh for a jog around Central Park.

Academically, Averell's career at Craigie was hardly illustrious. He was, the headmaster reported at the end of his last year there, "prone to extreme carelessness" and to lack of attention. For the term, he stood dead last among the boys in his form in algebra and composition and near the bottom in English grammar.[1] As a consequence of such performance, he was subjected to tutoring through the summer. No matter where the family went or what it did, Averell's tutor was along.

His first realization that his father was wealthy and that his own life was something far from ordinary came to Averell when he was seven: thanks to E.H.'s doctor, the family embarked upon a grand vacation in the wilderness of Alaska.

After two years of driving himself without respite in his refinancing and rebuilding of the Union Pacific, the new powerhouse of the American railroad industry was ordered by his physician to take a rest. E .H. promised to comply, but characteristically, he turned his summer of relaxation into a spectacular project with its own objectives.

Having long wanted to go hunting for a Kodiak bear, he immediately began plans to make his vacation a hunting expedition and to take Mary and the children along. The trouble was that steamers which carried tourists to the Far North did not make port in the hinterlands where he wanted to hunt. The solution was to hire his own ship. That way, the family could live aboard while he hunted his bear, and they could sail and anchor wherever they wished. By the time the children were told what he had planned for their summer, his vacation and hunting trip had evolved into an ambitious scientific expedition.

Because long stretches of the Alaskan coastline were uncharted, its wildlife unstudied, its glaciers and fjords unexplored, he decided to invite scientists along for an unprecedented study of the wilderness. Unannounced, he walked into the Washington office of C. Hart Merriam, head of the U.S. Biological Survey, and began laying before the puzzled government scientist a full-blown plan to take a research vessel staffed by experts from a dozen scientific disciplines along the coastal wilderness to systematically collect, photograph, and catalog flora and fauna. Knowing less about railroads and Wall Street than Harriman knew of botany, Merriam took the railroad baron for some harmless eccentric until he had listened at some length to E.H.'s carefully laid plan. Once he confirmed Harriman's identity, he was breathless at the thought of an enormous expedition with landmark scientific work conducted free of charge. Before his visitor left, Merriam agreed to recruit a team of nationally known scientists to be Harriman's guests for the summer. Even then he had no idea that he was about to join an undertaking that would dominate the rest of his professional career. His team, assembled within two months of Harriman's visit, included John Muir, the conservationist already renowned for his solitary roaming in Alaska, and naturalist John Burroughs. E.H., meanwhile, chartered an iron-hulled steamship called the *George W. Elder*, ordered it converted into a luxury liner, and hired a crew of sixty-five to sail it and look after the needs of his guests.

Aside from two dozen of Merriam's scientific colleagues, the entourage included in-laws, cousins, friends of the Harriman daughters, Mary, Cornelia, and Carol, plus E.H.'s doctor. There were also three artists, two photographers, two stenographers, two taxidermists, and a chaplain.

Counting the servants, camp hands, hunters, and packers, the vacation party numbered 126 by the time the eastern contingent boarded Harriman's special train, *Utopia*, and pulled out of Grand Central Station on its way to Seattle.

It was Averell's first chance to see the wild West. The train stopped in Idaho, where everyone in the party mounted horses or piled into stagecoaches for a twenty-five-mile detour to the spectacular Shoshone Falls on the Snake River. Later, when the *Utopia* reached the Washington border, E.H. ordered another stop for a brief journey down the Snake on a side-wheel steamer.

News of the expedition preceded it, and a huge crowd awaited the party at the Seattle docks, standing in a chilly spring rain to watch the latter-day ark being loaded. Belowdecks went milch cows, pigs, and crates of live chickens, and into the galley, boxes of oranges and grapefruit shipped up from California. A library of scientific books and journals was transferred from the train, along with microscopes, cameras, guns, fishing gear, butterfly nets, and skinning knives to outfit the research spaces that were set aside for members of the scientific party to study and preserve their specimens.

Once the loading was completed, Mary Harriman arrived with the younger children: Averell, his sister Carol, who was nine, and brother Roland, then three and a half, all turned out in nautical garb. They boarded, the gangplank was retracted, a loud cheer went up, and under clearing skies, the ship eased out of the harbor with flags flying and the "Star Spangled Banner" playing on Harriman's gramophone.

In the two months that followed, the expedition called at Eskimo villages and mining camps, explored glaciers and fur seal rookeries, and visited malodorous salmon canneries. Pressing within thirty miles of the Arctic Circle, the party hunted, fished, and camped in a pristine wilderness, collecting thousands of plants and animals for the American Museum of Natural History in New York.

For Averell, the high moments were not the discoveries that sent excitement through the scientific staff, nor his father's successful bear hunt, but the meetings with Siberian Eskimos, drunken whalers, and down-and-out gold prospectors along the way.

He awoke early, tagged along with shore parties, watched birds and animals killed for museums, and hung around the research spaces. More than eighty years later, the last survivor of the expedition, Averell still remembered the terrifying cracking of icebergs breaking and the thunder of thousands of tons of ice sliding into the sea as they came apart. He recalled the wild-West atmosphere of Skagway, a train ride to the headwaters of the Yukon, and most of all being terrified and torn by fear and revulsion when the party stopped at an abandoned Indian village at Cape Fox, and hunters and deckhands were ordered by his father to cut down its nineteen magnificent totem poles and load them aboard. Watching as the ornately carved poles were brought down, he was afraid that the Indians would come back as suddenly as they had left years before, catch the intruders stealing their sacred religious emblems, and slaughter all of them.[2]

E.H. at last succeeded in killing his prized Kodiak, though his conquest was anything but a classic confrontation of man and beast. The bear that came into his sights was a female with a cub at her side, and she was herded into a narrow gorge where he waited, surrounded by the expedition's professional hunters ready to fire if he missed. But one shot from his high-powered rifle brought her down, and he left to someone else the honor of shooting the cub. With his successful hunt behind him, Harriman devoted himself to amusing his family and supporting the scientists he had invited along.

While the bear hunt had been in fact an execution, Harriman's companions had other occasions to observe physical courage that bordered on recklessness. Once he ordered the crew to take the steamer into a fjord where charts indicated the waters were not navigable. Peter Doran, the *George W. Elder*'s captain, backed up by an expert on Alaskan coastal navigation, insisted on stopping, and when Harriman ordered them to continue through a narrow inlet past a huge glacier, "rocks or no rocks," they renounced responsibility for the vessel.

John Muir believed they might find yet another glacier or hidden fjord ahead, and so for thirteen miles they edged ahead through a narrow and shallow canyon. One of the *Elder*'s propellers hit a submerged rock, but Harriman's luck held. The ship was not disabled, and the channel opened up into another spectacular bay, with brilliant glaciers that white men had never seen before. Averell and the rest of the children stood on deck to get a view of their discovery as the scientific party cheered E.H.'s determination. Future maps would label the secluded niche in the wilderness as Harriman Fjord.

The idea of stopping on Russian soil was Mary's, and carrying it through meant not only crossing the rough shallows of the Bering Sea, but contending with icy fog and poor visibility. The round-bottomed hull of the ship made it roll so unpleasantly, even in the calm waters near the coast, that members of the party jokingly renamed the *George W. Elder* the "*George W. Roller*." Between the Alaskan peninsula and the eastern tip of the Asian continent, the old steamer wallowed through seas more turbulent than anything it had encountered before, and half the party was seasick.

One night the *Elder* ran aground when the stricken members were in their cabins and the rest lingered over dinner. There was a shudder, and then a series of sharp jolts shaking the vessel from its keel to the top of its smokestack as it came to rest on the rocks. Averell slept through the collision and the rush of the frightened passengers to the deck, but within minutes he and his brother were taken from their bunks, strapped into life jackets, and led to abandon-ship stations beside the lifeboats. The final order never came. Captain Doran was able to back off the rocks, freeing the vessel without a hole being torn in its hull. To the children, who enjoyed it all, missing the chance to take to the lifeboats was a disappointment. The shaken adults soon realized the near-disaster would not persuade Harriman to turn back, for within minutes he was playing games with his sons as if nothing had even happened.

When they arrived at Plover Bay on the east coast of Siberia the next day, they were greeted by Eskimos who had jumped into boats and rowed out to meet them. Ashore, they were welcomed into foul-smelling summer huts made from animal skins stretched over frames of whalebone and anchored to the ground by heavy stones to keep them from being blown away by the fierce wind.

The *George W. Elder* was obviously not the first ship that had brought white men to Plover Bay, for some of the natives bore the scars of chronic syphilis, their reward for the hospitality they had extended to whaling parties. The Harriman expedition remained long enough only to swap knives, tobacco, sugar and trinkets for harpoons, sealskin boots, and native fishing gear, but many years later, Averell would boast to Josef Stalin that he had first visited his country without benefit of a passport. As a seven-year-old boy, he was glad to end that first visit, however, for he had found the sight and the smell of its natives more menacing than the frigid wind—and jarringly at odds with his schoolboy image of Eskimos.

The *Elder* returned to Seattle July 30. E.H. was by then weary of vacationing, bored with Alaska's spectacular scenery, and anxious to get back to the renovation of the Union Pacific, his responsibilities at the Chicago and Alton, and his growing interest in the Kansas City Southern. For most members of the scientific contingent, months and years of effort lay ahead before they would wind up their role in what was much later deemed "perhaps the last grand expedition of the nineteenth century." The nine-thousand-mile odyssey produced thirteen volumes of scientific and technical reports that were not finished even when E.H. died.[3]

Averell really saw his father's railroad domain for the first time in the spring of the next year, 1900, after the Pullman Company delivered E.H.'s new private railroad car, the *Arden*. For six weeks, he and Roland traveled the Illinois Central and Union Pacific rails with their parents, tagging along with E.H. in railroad stations, warehouses, and docks as they moved south through Memphis to New Orleans and Galveston. From Texas, their route took them back to Louisiana, then north through Arkansas, cutting briefly into Indian Territory, and on to Missouri and Kansas. As the *Arden* swayed gently through pine forests, cotton plantations, and the flat green plains of spring wheat, E.H. spent hours with Averell going over assignments from Mr. Craigie, reading history lessons, talking about the railroads.

After an overnight stop in Kansas City, the party picked up the Atchison, Topeka and Santa Fe Railroad, crossing the Arkansas River into Colorado at dusk. To Averell's disappointment, a stop at the Grand Canyon was canceled because his mother decided it was too hot and dusty to venture out of the car, and they missed seeing much of the Pueblo and Navaho reservations because they passed during the night. In California, they visited Pasadena, sailed on San Diego Bay, and rode horseback into the mountains overlooking the sea at Santa Barbara.

On their way back to the East, they tarried so E.H. could inspect the progress of the Union Pacific reconstruction. In the Wasatch Mountains, where new lines were being built to cut down steep grades and eliminate miles of tortuous curves, they stopped, unloaded horses from a cattle car, and rode twenty-five miles to view the work at a new tunnel and eat lunch with a construction gang. They raced across Nebraska under bright moonlight in mid-April, traveling hour after hour at a steady speed of seventy miles per hour on the rebuilt Union Pacific tracks.

After reaching Omaha and crossing the Missouri to Council Bluffs, Iowa, they took the Burlington route south to Kansas City, and eastward across Missouri, pausing overnight on the banks of the Mississippi, where they dined with Mr. and Mrs. Jacob Schiff, who had hooked their car to the train in San Francisco.

Back in Chicago, where the weather was now springlike, the Harrimans left the car for an evening at the theater, and met Mr. and Mrs. James J. Hill, who joined the party for the last leg back to New York, neither family suspecting that Hill and E.H. would be engaged in a monumental railroad war within months.

For Averell, the long trip was a more powerful revelation of his father than the Alaskan expedition had been. Wherever they went, E.H. was in control. Whether he was talking with his Union Pacific employees or influential men who boarded his railroad car, he dealt with them as firmly as he did with his children at Arden. Politicians deferred to him, bankers and railroaders listened to him, and businessmen courted him.

Rich men such as E. H. Harriman sent their sons to Groton as much for what it made them as for what it taught them. It was a place where character was honed, where sacred studies—Episcopalian-style—and competitive athletics designed to foster Christian manliness were as important as composition and mathematics. In an atmosphere of uncompromising regimentation, Dr. Peabody's charges absorbed reverence for the social order, confirmed their place in it, and came face-to-face with their special responsibilities. Groton was where the Protestant establishment renewed itself—the school of Roosevelts, Whitneys, Vanderbilts, an academy for America's first families.

Boys lived in six-by-nine-foot cubicles in spartan dormitories, arose for cold showers at 5:45 A.M., attended daily chapel, and dressed in woolen knickerbockers and starched white shirts. When they arrived in the fall, underclassmen turned in whatever money they brought with them and were thereafter given twenty-five cents a week for spending. From this, they were required to put a nickel into the collection plate at Sunday chapel. A rigid hierarchy separated the boys in the lower "forms" from upperclassmen. The older boys stood atop the structure serving as examples, enjoying small but coveted privileges, and assigning black marks against the younger for any of a long list of behavioral infractions. Their disciplinary rituals stopped just short of hazing. Included among them was an unauthorized punishment called "pumping," in which badly errant lower-formers were held under an open faucet until they feared they would drown.

What E. H. Harriman wanted from Groton and its revered and autocratic headmaster was, briefly, to make his son something better than himself. If all parents could make their children better than themselves, he wrote his wife from one of his business trips, "how fast this world would improve."[4] Averell could discern little difference between his father's and Rector Peabody's notions of a boy's obligations. As if he needed reminding that E.H. had set a lofty standard for him, Groton masters were quick to offer his father as his example. And everything the school preached about responsibility was echoed at home.

From his $2,000 yearly allowance, he was required to pay the $850 tuition of another boy at school. He was also ordered to keep a diary, write a postcard home each evening, and provide his parents a weekly report of his grades.

Academically, Mr. Craigie had given him a leg up at Groton, but after the first months his class ranking started to drop. He was failing in his great obligation to please Pappa. The gravity of his shortcomings was brought home to him with the impact of a Groton cold shower when he received a letter that his father was coming for a visit. More than a visit, it was a conference. Reporting to E.H.'s railroad car, the student was confronted with damning evidence that his marks were declining and was warned that he was going to be "just like Uncle Willie," unless he mended his ways. It was the most chilling thing his father could have said, since E.H. regarded his brother Willie as a ne'er-do-well and an embarrassment.[5]

A return visit was unnecessary, but the pressure from home never ended. When his grades improved, he received fatherly congratulations—always accompanied by suggestions that there was still room for improvement. His mother's style was gentler, but her own pressure was just as constant and equally focused on his obligation to be something and somebody.

She visited regularly, always concerned whether he was going to the gym for daily exercises to make him stronger, unfailingly reminding him to do his utmost so he would please Pappa. And the older sisters chimed in to emphasize his responsibilities. Mary and Cornelia signed off their letters with reminders that even his father's health was influenced by his performance at Groton. "It does please Pappa so for you do well," Cornelia admonished him, "and it worries him a lot when you don't."[6]

E.H. himself was, of course, full of specific recommendations. "I should think you would have little trouble in deciding which lesson to work hardest at," E.H. wrote during the difficult early going. "Why not begin with history? Conquer it & see how it feels to have done something." But then, he quickly added, "You need, however, to work English studies and Latin with more vim."[7]

He did not find Averell's response satisfactory, and he followed up. "Your letter is welcome. It is nicely written, well expressed & properly spelled, but all about football. Did you receive my letter about taking up the lesson most difficult to you and working at it until you have mastered it? Please write me at once whether you received the letter & which lesson you select. Now then, my boy, football & all the other recreations are interesting & useful in their place, but should be subservient to real & influential work. Besides, they are enjoyed much more when so done. Talk it over with Mr. Peabody. I will write him if you wish me to. Let me know. Mr. Peabody & the other masters as well as myself are responsible for getting your mind properly started and directed in its development."[8]

Always there was the suggestion that he could do better, and during times when his marks took a turn for the worse, the Sunday-night letters from home were filled with exasperation. E.H. sent back one report card with the comments, "What do you say? Why is it? I'm afraid they won't want you back next year, to say nothing of taking much trouble with Roland. Write me frankly. Dr. Peabody told me when you were getting your best marks this winter that you were not doing your work as they all thought you capable of. Don't you care? What shall I do about it?"[9]

He went regularly to a tutor after breakfast and for other sessions devoted to spelling drills. He worked, as he was told, at exercises that were supposed to help him gain weight, and he struggled to control his stammering, speaking each morning before one of the masters, who would loudly clap his hands the moment he started to falter.

On every front he could usually find the basis for an optimistic report to his parents and his sisters. "I think I am doing better in my stammering because last night when I spoke to the Rector, I did not stammer once," he reported after beginning his daily sessions. "I am also going to try to spell well this year. You said that it would be nice to over come some differculty [*sic*] each year and so I am going to try that this year."[10]

In the summer of 1905, as he wound up his first year at Groton, the mail from home finally brought something more than the usual exhortations to do better. The family was going to the Orient for the summer.

E.H. saw a chance for a huge step toward his goal of putting together a transportation system that would circle the world. With the two-year war between Russia and Japan about to end, there might be an opportunity to get control of the South Manchuria Railway. Even before the Japanese and Russian governments had accepted President Roosevelt's invitation to a peace conference at Portsmouth, New Hampshire, Lloyd C. Griscom, Washington's minister in Japan, had invited Harriman to Tokyo to assess the opportunities for American capitalism. E.H. grabbed the chance. "It is important," he replied, "to save the commercial interests of the United States from being entirely wiped from the Pacific Ocean in the future. The way to find out what is best to be done is to start something."[11]

Harriman was an obvious choice to take the lead in stimulating American investment in postwar Japan. Since he already controlled steamship lines connecting Japan and the west coast of the United States, the situation was made to order for him. Japan stood to get possession of the South Manchuria Railway as its most important gain from the war, but much of the line was in ruin. Withdrawing Russian troops had taken away nearly all of the rolling stock, destroying the tracks and bridges to protect their retreat. While control of the road was a potential windfall, strategically and economically, the Japanese government was facing financial crisis and was in no position to rebuild it quickly.

After securing control of the line in Manchuria, Harriman planned to buy the Chinese Eastern Railway, connecting it to ports on the Yellow Sea. The line belonged to the Russians, and he thought they would be willing to sell it, since they had lost Port Arthur to the Japanese. That would give him a connection from the sea to the Trans-Siberian Railroad terminus in northern Manchuria. If he could acquire access to the tracks of the Trans-Siberian from Czar Nicholas, his steamships crossing the Pacific could connect with a rail line running from southern Manchuria to the Baltic Sea.[12]

With that, the only link required for a round-the-world system would be a transatlantic shipping operation. "It'll be the most marvelous transportation system in the world," he told Griscom. "We'll girdle the earth."[13] The system he envisioned would put the United States in a commanding position in the Oriental trade, and open the least-developed parts of Asia and Europe to American capital.

Then fourteen, Averell but dimly comprehended what his father proposed. At Craigie and at Groton, as well as at home, his education had been strongly European flavored, and the prospect of going to Tokyo, Seoul, and Peiping was even more exciting than going to the wilds of Alaska.

The Tokyo-bound party was tiny compared to that of the Alaskan expedition, but in addition to his wife and all five children, E.H. took along Dr. W. G. Lyle, his personal physician, R. P. Schwerin, the vice-president of the Pacific Mail and Steamship Company, and Mr. and Mrs. Robert Goelet, who were frequent dinner guests and traveling companions. Crossing the Pacific on the SS *Siberia*, the party broke the San Francisco-to-Honolulu speed record by several hours. They paused long enough to go sight-seeing in Hawaii, and stopped again at Midway Island, finally arriving in Yokohama at the end of August.

At a formal reception suitable for a traveling head of state, government officials, businessmen, and bankers showered them with invitations to official parties and dinners days in advance. The Japanese were clearly in a mood to do business, but the streets of Tokyo were in ferment. Six days after the American visitors arrived, demonstrations escalated into full-scale riots. With the U.S.-sponsored Portsmouth peace conference coming to an end, it was obvious that Japan would get far less than it had demanded in damages from the Russians.

Averell and his tutor were touring the city when the violence broke out. Hurrying back to join the rest of the family at the American legation, they had to work their way around mobs fighting pitched battles with police. The skirmishes spread from street jousting to organized attacks on government buildings, climaxed by the burning of the official residence of the Home Minister.

The Harriman party was not an object of the protesters, but Japanese officials nevertheless feared for their safety because the unpopular compromises had been fashioned in negotiations arranged by Theodore Roosevelt. As Averell watched from the window of the legation, army troops armed with bayonet-tipped rifles took up defensive positions around it. E.H.'s physician and his private secretary, trying to make their way back to the building, were set upon by mobs, and Dr. Lyle was slightly injured. Schwerin's ricksha was stopped and his runner beaten.

The violence spread to other cities, where demonstrators torched Christian churches and mission schools and burned Roosevelt in effigy. In the face of it, Harriman's meetings and social engagements were called off, and Averell's carefully planned exploration of Tokyo and immersion in Japanese culture were canceled. The political experience was more enduring than his brief sampling of museums, Japanese food, and the accomodations of a Japanese inn. He had arrived in Tokyo thinking of all Japanese as smiling, bowing, unquestioning servants of authority, but the violent demonstrations, the first rebellion he had ever seen, frightened him, especially since they took on a distinct anti-U.S. flavor.

In spite of the disruption, E.H. pushed on with his bid for the South Manchuria Railway, making no attempt to hide his larger objective of a global transportation empire and assuring his Japanese hosts that they should not be concerned about his gaining a monopoly. "From New York to the Pacific Coast, and from there to Japan, about 10,000 miles, the railroad and steamship lines are practically under one control and one management," he told Japanese dinner guests, exaggerating somewhat. "The economies of operation, the comfort to the traveling public, and the advantages to shippers of this concentrated control can be readily appreciated. The benefits to the people of the United States which follow, directly and indirectly, are incalculable. The same policy, if followed in Japan, is bound to produce the same results."[14]

His prospects improved as order was restored and he prepared for negotiations with Prime Minister Katsura Taro. Deliberations on another important front collapsed, however. Gaining concessions from the Reverend Dr. Peabody back at Groton proved vastly more difficult than dealing with the Japanese government.

It was less than a month before Rector Peabody's students were due for the opening of school, and E.H. had requested special dispensation for Averell so the boy could go with the family to Port Arthur, Peking, Pusan and Seoul, an experience certain to be more enriching than the first week at Groton. Peabody refused to look at it that way. As far as he was concerned, nothing in the trip was as important as Averell's reporting to school on the same day as the other boys. If it was impossible for Averell to arrive on schedule, the rector's last message advised Harriman, then it would be impossible for Averell to continue as a Groton student. The boy was furious and heartbroken.

Even though the rector had treated him more fairly than he had expected when he had been called in to explain his behavioral black marks the year before, he had never liked Dr. Peabody. In a despondent moment during his first year, he had blurted out to his father that the rector "would be an awful bully if he weren't such a terrible Christian."[15]

The ultimatum left E.H. no choice. He had to send Averell home. But he was not to be entirely outdone by Peabody's stubbornness. As it happened, Secretary of War William Howard Taft had been in the Philippines for several weeks and at the time was preparing for a seventeen-day voyage to San Francisco by way of Honolulu. But if the ship took the great-circle route from Manila to Tokyo to Seattle, the trip could be cut to ten days. Averell could stay another full week and still make it to Groton on time. With Taft's connivance, Harriman rerouted the ship under the pretense that the secretary of war was urgently needed in Washington.

In Seattle, Averell and his tutor were immediately put aboard a train for the East, arriving at Groton in time for him to move back into his dormitory cubicle and resume his classes on schedule. Nevertheless, Rector Peabody's pupil still missed the family's trip to Korea, Manchuria, and China, and he never forgave Peabody or Groton. It rankled him because Roland, who was only nine, and all of his sisters got to see battlefields where some of the most savage combat of the Russo-Japanese War had taken place. They came home with tales of their steamer maneuvering past mines still floating in the water, and of sailing near the shattered hulks of vanquished ships. They walked battlefields in the hills beyond the port where they saw arms and legs of fallen Russian and Japanese soldiers protruding from ground where they had fallen.[16]

When he returned to Tokyo, Harriman and the prime minister signed an agreement creating a syndicate to buy the South Manchuria Railway. The terms called for the road between Port Arthur and Ch'angch'un to be operated by a Japanese company that would have Harriman and his American associates as half-owners.

The Americans would put up as much as $100 million, and the Japanese would grant the syndicate rights to work the rich coal mines of southern Manchuria. Harriman left Tokyo confident that he had launched a great new phase of his railroad career. They set out for home on October 12, stopping for a rest in Honolulu, where President Roosevelt's daughter, Alice, joined them for the rest of the trip.

While the party was still at sea, however, the agreement began to fall apart. Japan's foreign minister arrived home from the Portsmouth peace conference, and concluded that the deal would be politically disastrous. The demonstrations had clearly shown that it was not the time to allow American capitalists to step in and take half of Japan's most prized conquest from the two years of fighting.

A cable was waiting for E.H. in San Francisco, telling him that further study would be necessary before the Japanese could go forward with the plan. Actually, the message meant that the long journey had been for nothing—except a supply of captured Napoleon brandy that the Japanese had given him. The idea, nevertheless, stayed alive. Harriman explored a possible alliance with a British syndicate, or an arrangement with the Chinese. Nothing worked. His hopes were dashed by the financial panic that hit the United States in 1907, the deaths of the emperor and empress dowager of China in 1908, and then his own fatal illness.

Harriman took his sons on their last adventure with him in the summer of 1907. It was one of the few occasions that the boys were ever with him for an extended time without an entourage along. For several weeks, they camped in Southwestern Oregon, hunting, fishing, and exploring the backwoods. At E.H.'s Pelican Bay Lodge, Averell and Roland slept in a tent in sight of Mount Pitt, to the west, and California's fourteen-thousand-foot Mount Shasta, capped with snow even in midsummer, far to the south. By day they fished in Upper Klamath Lake, and went on shooting trips, accompanied by two professional hunters, who helped Averell to bag a deer and twelve-year-old Roland to shoot a bear. An ailing back prevented E.H. from spending long days in the woods, so he remained at the cabin, where he could use the telegraph line he had installed to keep him in touch with the office in New York.

They arrived with the first automobiles ever seen by the Oregon backwoodsmen, and entire families came outside and gaped when they passed. Because logging roads were much too rugged for the fragile gasoline-powered buggies, they were preceded by axmen who removed stumps and saplings from their path when they motored out to visit the camps of railroad workers and surveying parties. Whenever their caravan came upon small streams, Harriman would hit the water going full tilt, trying to make it across before his machine drowned out. When he succeeded, he was then able to pull the others across. When he didn't make it, the whole party would wade into the water to push him out.

Although Averell was unaware of it, his father's health had begun to decline seriously by the time they went to Oregon, and E.H. evidently was beginning to think he did not have long to live. "The boys must have their experience," he wrote Mary toward the end of the summer, "and I feel that I must attend to some of it during the time remaining for us to be with them."[17]

As an upperclassman at Groton, Averell was less discontented than he had been when he returned under duress from Tokyo. He enjoyed the status that Rector Peabody's hierarchy conferred upon boys in the upper forms. He was also no longer the smallest boy among his contemporaries: in a tremendous teenage burst of growth when he was sixteen, he had gained twenty-five pounds in a single year and shot up to six feet in height.

His new physique made him happier than nearly anything else. He had fretted at being smaller than his friends, and in his letters home had often noted when he had succeeded in gaining weight. Suddenly, he was a head taller than his father. He boxed, played baseball and football, and took an active part on the debating team. He also handled the advertising for the school paper, the *Grotonian*—successfully, because he sold ads to the Harriman railroads.

When he decided to compete for a place on the Groton crew, his father pitched in to make sure he succeeded. In the spring of 1908, he took Averell and Roland aboard his steam-powered yacht, the *Sultana*, and sailed up the Hudson to Poughkeepsie, where they anchored and watched the spring races between the best college crews in the country.

Harriman knew nothing about rowing, but with his boys in tow, he invited himself into the headquarters of every crew in the meet, interviewed the coaches, and took in everything he saw and heard. Of all of them, he was most impressed by Syracuse coach Jim Ten Eyck. He liked the way Ten Eyck handled himself and the way the Syracuse boys responded to him. The coach had a firm handshake and a steady eye— and although Harriman was only vaguely aware of it, he happened to be one of the preeminent rowing experts in the country.

Hired soon thereafter, Ten Eyck lived with Averell and Roland at a camp on Forest Lake through the following summer. He rousted them from their beds at sunrise, and sent them out for a brisk workout before breakfast. Afterward, they had a strenuous session on a rowing barge to build shoulder and leg strength, then practiced in single sculls. The routine was repeated in the afternoons, and between their hours on the lake the coach lectured them on rowing techniques, training, and crew competition. At night, they fell into bed exhausted.

Food was sent down from the house and visitors came on weekends, but for weeks the boys were consumed by rowing and in touch with the outside world only by telephone. When Averell returned to Groton, he was ready to compete with the strongest of Mr. Peabody's oarsmen.

Other times at Arden were less intense. Averell and Roland, along with boys from school or Tuxedo Park, the colony for the rich a few miles to the south, often rowed out to a small island in the middle of the deep, spring-fed lake and camped for days, swimming, fishing, and cooking over an open fire.

On the miles of trails that wound through the hills to the old iron mines, they rode horseback and across the meadows and fields, they hunted birds and small game. Both learned to handle trotters with dexterity, racing at Goshen and Tuxedo, and got their first taste of polo when E.H. bought half a dozen well-schooled ponies. In the fall, they rode to hounds, occasionally taking a holiday in Virginia, where E.H. had bought property and organized the Orange County Hunt. When winter came and they were in the country only for weekends, the boys skated and played hockey on the lakes while the Harriman girls entertained friends at a big yellow guesthouse which their father had built for them.

Even with the separate guesthouse, the homestead had sprawled to three stories and more than two dozen rooms, including a parlor for billiards. It still seemed inadequate, and not long after Averell entered

Groton, E.H. began construction of a mammoth stone castle near the summit of Mount Orama, on a Ramapo crest offering the highest elevation construction site on the estate.

Among Averell's many Groton friends who carried their own burden of protecting a powerful family name was Hall Roosevelt. His parents had died, and his upbringing had been entrusted to his older sister, Eleanor, and her husband, Franklin. Averell was a year ahead of the Roosevelt boy, but they lived in the same dormitory and they had become friends because their families were friends. Eleanor Roosevelt and Averell's sister Mary were involved in charity work together. Averell's mother and Franklin Roosevelt's mother had known each other well for years. Through his last three years at Groton, Averell and Hall sometimes exchanged visits when they were home for holidays. Eleanor and Franklin occasionally took them to the theater, and sometimes the Harrimans invited Hall to weekends at Arden.

The main connection between the Harrimans and the Roosevelts, however, had been the long friendship between E.H. and Eleanor's Uncle Teddy, which had recently ended in a spectacular feud. E.H. had known the President well in New York and several times had visited him in the White House to discuss both politics and railroad matters, sometimes taking the children with him. After accompanying the Harrimans from Honolulu to San Francisco on their way home from Japan, Roosevelt's daughter, Alice, had joined them on E.H.'s train back East. An incident during the trip illustrated the easy relationship between them. Harriman took the occasion to make one of his speed runs across the country, and it quickly drew the attention of the newspapers. The President sent a telegram to a station stop, cautioning E.H. to be careful, and Harriman replied good-naturedly, "You run the country, I'll run the railroads."[18]

In spite of the public relations problems he brought on himself by episodes such as the Northern Pacific panic on Wall Street, Harriman had been politically useful to the President. In 1904, when Roosevelt ran for the presidency in his own right, E.H. raised $250,000 for Republican coffers, including a personal contribution of $50,000. It was one of the times when the interests of the country coincided with the interest of his railroads, Harriman thought, and he rose to extraordinary public service during his friend's years in the White House.

In the wake of the devastating San Francisco earthquake and then during the flooding of California's Imperial Valley by the Colorado River, when Roosevelt urgently needed him, he stepped forward voluntarily. The struggle to save the Imperial Valley lasted more than two years and preserved over a million and a half acres of the most productive agricultural land on earth. It was an undertaking that rivaled construction of the railroad track across Great Salt Lake and the rerouting of the Union Pacific through the Rockies. Harriman was first drawn into the crisis because the Southern Pacific line into the valley was threatened, but he wound up taking responsibility for averting a public disaster.

Far back in geologic time, the Imperial Valley was beneath the ocean. Then, over centuries, silt carried by the Colorado River built a massive levee that made the northern tip of the Gulf of California an inland sea. In time, the water evaporated under the scorching sun, leaving a deep basin.

As the Colorado changed course, it refilled the empty basin with fresh water, deposited deep new layers of silt, and withdrew again, its shifting course finally creating a valley as rich as the delta of the Nile, but uninhabited until the twentieth century.

In 1901, the California Development Company began digging a network of irrigation ditches to bring in water from the Colorado. Settlers moved in and began year-round farming on homesteads that produced an effusion of fruit and vegetables. Within five years, the dried-up sea and lake bed, given its apt name by developers, had twelve thousand people living on it, with 120,000 irrigated acres under cultivation. But the same kind of silt that had created the rich valley soon clogged the main channels that carried water from the river into the irrigation canals.

With farmers desperate for water, the developer made a new cut just south of the U.S.-Mexican border in the summer of 1904, believing there would be plenty of time to close it again before the spring flood season. But the closing was delayed too long, and when workers tried to fill the cut, the fast-rising river swept away their dam of pilings, brush, and sandbags. No sooner was the cut refilled than it was washed out again. The opening that had been 60 feet wide was suddenly 160, and the Colorado was starting to turn the valley back into an inland sea.

Running low on money, officials of the development company appealed to Harriman for help. But after giving them a loan of $200,000, E.H. discovered that it would cost much more than that, perhaps $750,000, to bring the river under control. Instead of calling in the loan, he ordered the Southern Pacific to turn the river back into its bed.

By the time the Harrimans returned home from Japan in the autumn of 1905, a $60,000 dam had been erected in the cut, but in November it, too, was knocked out, and nearly the entire flow of the Colorado poured into the valley through a gap six hundred feet wide. At the center of the ancient Salton Sea, a new lake covered 150 square miles by the end of the year.

Harriman was in New York and Southern Pacific officials were struggling with a situation worsening by the hour when San Francisco was hit by the great earthquake. As soon as he heard the news of the quake and the fires spreading in the aftermath, Harriman ordered a special train and raced for the West Coast. At every stop, he sent cables ahead, mobilizing the Southern Pacific and the Central Pacific to rush disaster relief to the city, where fires raged out of control. Food, blankets, tents, and medical supplies were given priority over every other cargo on the Harriman lines. Trains brought in hundreds of carloads of supplies and transported 225,000 refugees out of the city in the following days. Idle boxcars became temporary housing for thousands of others who had nowhere to go.

After surveying the smoking city, Harriman became a self-appointed coordinator between local officials and Red Cross experts sent in by the President. He lived aboard his private railroad car parked on the Oakland pier, using it as his emergency command and communications center. At night, he walked through boxcars offering encouragement to refugees who found shelter in them. In the midst of the San Francisco tragedy, the Imperial Valley battle against the Colorado River was being lost. The California Development Company had again run out of money, and thousands of acres of crops were being flooded. The Southern Pacific's track was threatened, and the towns of Mexicali and Calexico were in danger of being inundated. The cut was a quarter of a mile wide, jeopardizing the irrigation system of the entire valley.

Under these grim circumstances, Harriman and the Southern Pacific took control of the California Development Company and full responsibility for the emergency effort. They abandoned the attempt to dam the water with sandbags and brush and went to work on a rock barrier. With the use of three hundred "battleship" cars borrowed from the Union Pacific, rock was hauled from quarries up to four hundred miles away. An army of Indian and Mexican laborers worked day and night through September and into October. The new barrier collapsed in October, the fifth to be washed away.

There was encouragement to be found in the setback, however. The steel-web foundation had held firm, and soon the freight cars were dumping more rock again. In three furious weeks, workers dumped three thousand carloads of new rock into the breach, and dredges scooped up forty thousand yards of gravel and dirt to fill the cracks.

This time the dam held. But downstream, a weakened levee ruptured, and the river cascaded into the valley through a new, thousand-foot break. Estimates were that it would cost $350,000 to dam it, and $1.5 million for twenty miles of levees and ditches would be required for a permanent solution.

E.H. appealed to the President, but Roosevelt said he could do nothing, because Congress was in recess. Furthermore, he said, Harriman had taken responsibility for the California Development Company, which had not "the slightest excuse" for any delay in moving to close the new break.[19] Harriman argued that his loans to the company had not made him responsible for all of its obligations, but he notified the President that the Southern Pacific would go back to work, "trusting that the Government, as soon as you can procure the necessary Congressional action, will assist us with the burden."[20]

There wasn't time to construct another steel-cable-and-brush mat as a foundation for the new dam, so Harriman's engineers drove pilings into the rushing stream and put a railroad trestle across the break. Then they began dumping rocks delivered by a thousand railway cars—some of the rocks were boulders so huge they had to be cracked apart by dynamite charges before they could be dumped. In all, more than eleven thousand carloads were hauled in, and by the time the river was permanently put back in its channel, Harriman had spent more than $3 million from the Southern Pacific's treasury. Assistance from the government never came. Roosevelt appealed to Congress without success, and William Howard Taft, Roosevelt's successor, continued an effort to have the railroad reimbursed even after Harriman was dead. A House Claims Committee recommendation for a special appropriation of $773,000 died quietly after opponents denounced it as a raid on the federal treasury.

The relationship between Harriman and Theodore Roosevelt chilled long before it became a subject of newspaper headlines. Unfortunately for E.H., their disagreement erupted into a public feud when Roosevelt's popularity was soaring and his own reputation was being battered.

For months, he was caught up in a messy and much-publicized struggle over the control of the Equitable Life Assurance Society, where he was a director. Along with Jacob Schiff and other financier friends, he aligned himself against reformers trying to shift control from directors to stockholders and block playboy James Hazen Hyde from becoming president. The financiers were promptly accused of using Hyde, Equitable Life's largest stockholder, in an effort to take control of its enormous assets. Unfortunately for Harriman's public image, the Equitable uproar came at about the same time that he had found it necessary to oust his old friend Stuyvesant Fish from the presidency of the Illinois Central for secretly dipping into railroad funds for personal ventures. If all this wasn't enough, a huge Union Pacific dividend increase was made under circumstances which suggested that Harriman had manipulated the public announcement so he could make a personal killing on insider information.

What permanently tarnished his reputation and became a large part of his legacy to Averell, however, was the famous feud with Roosevelt. Their relationship had actually begun to go sour during a 1904 election misunderstanding, but the rupture did not become publicly known until 1907.

E.H.'s version of the celebrated fight was that the President, concerned about a shortage of campaign funds and squabbling between New York Republicans, had enlisted his help in raising campaign money. In return Roosevelt promised to settle a party conflict in New York by making Senator Chauncey Depew, who had fallen out of favor with upstate Republicans, the United States' ambassador to France.

Soon after he had raised the money, Harriman later claimed, Roosevelt reneged on his promise regarding Depew, a faithful supporter of railroad interests. Harriman, as a result, felt deceived and humiliated before New York politicians who had been told of the arrangement.

Then, during the 1906 congressional elections, Republican congressional campaign chairman James Sherman approached E.H. once again to help raise money for the party. Knowing nothing of what had happened two years before, he was surprised at Harriman's categoric refusal to help.

To explain his attitude, E.H. pulled out and read a copy of a year-old letter he had written to his friend Sidney Webster, a New York lawyer and Illinois Central director, recounting what had happened in 1904: how upstate Republicans had not wanted Depew reelected to the Senate, how Roosevelt asked for Harriman's help with fund-raising, and how E.H. had personally contributed $50,000 to the party's campaign. But after the election, the letter continued, Roosevelt "then told me he did not think it was necessary to appoint Depew as ambassador to Paris as agreed."[21]

Sherman returned to Washington and met with the President, evidently telling Roosevelt that Harriman had said he no longer cared about the future of the Republican party, because he could readily buy political influence. To protect himself in case the differences became public, Roosevelt put down his own version of the 1904 incident, addressing a letter to Sherman recording what Sherman had just told him about the meeting with Harriman.

"You inform me," Roosevelt wrote the intermediary,

> that he told you that he did not care in the least; because those people were crooks and he could buy them; that whenever he wanted legislation from a state legislature he could buy it; that he could "buy the Congress," and that, if necessary "he could buy the judiciary." This was doubtless said partly in boastful cynicism and partly in a mere burst of bad temper because of his objection to the Interstate Commerce Law and to my actions as President. But it shows a cynicism and deep-seated corruption which make the man uttering such sentiments, and boasting, no matter how falsely, of his power to perform such crimes as least as undesirable a citizen as Debs, or Moyer, or Haywood.

The wealthy corruptionist, and the demagogue who excites, in the press or on the stump, in office or out of office, class against class, and appeals to the basest passions of the human soul, are fundamentally alike and are equally enemies of the Republic.[22]

Two months after the meeting with Sherman, Harriman tried to make peace. He sent Union Pacific lawyer Maxwell Evarts, who had sat in on his meeting with Sherman, to give Roosevelt the Harriman version of the meeting. Harriman, Evarts told the President, had declined Sherman's request for a contribution simply because he thought "there was no advantage in making general subscriptions for party purposes, that if there was any desire to spend money it had better be spent in some other way, and that so far as he was concerned he never even got any thanks for campaign contributions." Morever, he told the President, that Harriman "said nothing about him [and] that there was nothing in the whole conversation that could not have been repeated to him or anyone else."[23]

Roosevelt apparently accepted Evarts's version of the meeting, for he asked the Harriman intermediary to meet with Sherman and have the Republican fund-raiser write a statement that there had been a misunderstanding.

But any chance of making peace slipped away. A disgruntled stenographer who had been fired by Harriman sold a copy of the letter E.H. had written to Sidney Webster that told of Roosevelt's broken promise on the Chauncey Depew deal. On April 2, 1907, the letter was published by the New York *World*. With that, Roosevelt released the letter he had earlier addressed to Sherman, its phrases "undesirable citizen," "wealthy corruptionist," and "enemy of the Republic" exploding into headlines.

The fight was particularly disastrous for E.H.'s reputation because it came to light as the Interstate Commerce Commission (ICC) was investigating railroad mergers—zeroing in on the Harriman lines, the Union Pacific's acquisition of the Southern Pacific, the much-debated Union Pacific dividend announcement, E.H.'s effort to take control of the Northern Pacific, and profits he made in the refinancing of the Chicago and Alton Railroad several years earlier.

As a witness in the massively publicized hearings, E.H. was disagreeable and combative. He challenged the commission's authority, questioned its motives, and refused to say how much he had profited when he and members of his syndicate took over the Chicago and Alton, selling themselves discounted bonds and voting themselves a 30 percent stock dividend. He was guilty, the commission finally concluded, of "indefensible financing" in that case, and of eliminating competition in transcontinental business and traffic to and from the Orient by snapping up the Southern Pacific. The surly appearance before the commission was the only effort he ever made to defend himself. Although Roosevelt's attack and the ICC investigation had the odor of political opportunism, Harriman had brought them on himself because he had become the quintessential "railroad baron."

A year after the ICC hearings and the breakup with Roosevelt, the government went to court to force Harriman's Union Pacific to divest itself of its interest in the Southern Pacific, charging the Harriman combination violated the Sherman Anti-Trust Act.

At the same time he was reined in by Roosevelt and the ICC, Harriman was also overtaken by ill health. In his letters to Averell, he increasingly complained of his aches and pains, especially after having surgery for appendicitis. His back hurt him, and he blamed it on having slept on the glaciers several nights during the expedition to Alaska. He had symptoms of rheumatism, pains in his stomach, and pains in his chest.

Still, he drove ahead with his new Arden mansion, building a funicular up to the construction site on a thirteen-hundred-foot peak, opening new roads to make it accessible to automobiles and horse-drawn carriages, and overseeing an army of six hundred construction workers at the homesite carved out of the mountaintop.

In 1908, the Erie Railroad, of which he was a director, faced bankruptcy, unable to pay off $5.5 million in notes coming due. Other members of the board, mindful of Harriman's recent experience and the Roosevelt administration's assault upon the trusts, were jittery. Even when Harriman offered to provide half of the $5.5 million to meet the Erie obligations, other members of the board refused to put their private assets on the line.

In the end, Harriman went to his banks for the full amount, seeing it as necessary not only to save the company but to shore up confidence of the business establishment just beginning to recover from the economic panic of 1907. He was in too much pain to leave his bed and arrange the loans before the deadline. So, he telephoned bankers from home and sent his top lieutenant, Robert S. Lovett, a former Texas judge and railroad lawyer, to help secure loans to prevent the road from going into receivership. As soon as he felt well enough, he went on a series of trips over thousands of miles of his railroads, taking most of the winter and spring of 1909. He went to Georgia to inspect the Georgia Central, an obscure line which gave him claim to a coast-to-coast railroad empire. He had acquired it the previous year because it connected with the Illinois Central at Birmingham, putting the Harriman mark on connecting lines running from Savannah to San Francisco.

He also went west to attend to business in Texas and California, before heading south into Mexico to see a new extension of the Southern Pacific running to Mazatlán. Although losing weight and becoming more stooped, he put on a brave front, and he was cheered to find that his public reputation improved in proportion to his distance from New York. Wherever he stopped, local officials rolled out the red carpet and the press mobbed him, wondering whether Harriman money might be headed for Chattanooga or Savannah. "I've been doing absolutely nothing but taking a much needed rest," he told reporters in Savannah during his southern swing. "I was poisoned by something that I had eaten, and I had to get it out of my system. The rest and climate have been grateful to me, and I shall go back home feeling much better for the visit."[24]

Privately, however, Harriman was gravely concerned about his health. His letters home were uncharacteristically reflective about his career and the damage the fight with Roosevelt had done to his name. He still thought about Harry, his son who had died in Chicago twenty years earlier. Parked on a siding in his railroad car in mid-February, he wrote to his wife, who had urged him to take it easy during his western journey. In his nearly illegible scrawl and careless syntax, he told her, "It was Harry's sacrifice which seemed to give the strongest inspiration for good clean work & the accomplishment of something of lasting advantage that has kept me at it so hard during the last twenty years. It was then that I thought to have the best & quiet life. How little we counted the result of that Chicago trip in 1888. Now, when again we thought of some chance during the last two and a half years, came the attack which made it necessary to protect our good name & leave the boys something to be proud to work for—first the memory of Harry & now the protection of our reputation for Averell and Roland."[25]

At Groton, Averell was much aware that his father had become an object of intense political ridicule, led by the President of the United States. During the ICC investigations, Mr. Peabody's boys adopted the railroads as the subject for their spring debates, and Averell eagerly took the side of the railroads against the Roosevelt administration. He wrote to his father for copies of old speeches and solicited his prediction on the outcome of the antitrust case seeking divestiture of Union Pacific interest in Southern Pacific.

E.H. was delighted. Averell was showing signs of growing up by taking an interest in serious matters. He was approaching graduation from prep school and headed for Yale to prepare for his business career, and in the coming summer he was going to take his first job with Union Pacific, working with a surveying party in the West. Although E.H. had been unwilling to defend himself publicly, he eagerly armed his son for the debate. He sent him personal letters he had written to President Taft, asked the general counsel at both Union Pacific and Illinois Central to provide the young scholar with memoranda, and offered his own analyses of the ICC investigations.

Once during the preparation, he dictated a long letter while lying in bed too ill to sit up and write. The commission's trouble, he said, was not its authority or the law that created it, but members ambitious for power, who took positions on issues before the matters ever reached the panel. "Most of its acts have been unobjectionable, but their methods have been wrong—In fact so it has been with the outgoing administration all through—so you see such a committee is not competent to judge and have control of the affairs of a railroad."[26]

Averell took that to mean there was not much wrong with federal railroad regulation, and E.H., who was by then traveling in the West, hurriedly wrote back to set him straight. The law, he said, ought to allow railroads to expand. "The present act is wrong & its application vicious— It gives too much power to a few men which might be used for blackmail either for money or political consideration & end in control of the government itself." And evidently referring to his erstwhile friend Theodore Roosevelt, he concluded, "It has already been used to satisfy personal vanity & jealousy."[27]

In spite of all the preparation and high-level assistance on the railroad case, Averell succeeded no better than his father had before the ICC, but he assured E.H. that not all had been for naught. "I am sorry to say that we lost," he reported. "The subject was 'Resolved that the government has been justified in its actions against the railroads.' You see that makes it a very sweeping subject.

"I spoke for nine minutes—all the time that was allowed me, and did not stutter at all. I think I have finally got control of it. . . ."[28]

The high moment of his career as one of Rector Peabody's charges came not long before graduation, and it was not in the classroom. On a chilly spring afternoon of 1909, as members of the Groton crew worked out in the two-man shells on the river, Averell helped save the life of his classmate Charlie Fry. Running the launch that was keeping coach Richard Danielson abreast of the young oarsmen, Charlie slipped and fell, and both of his arms were caught between the rotating shaft and the housing connecting the engine and propeller. Danielson struggled vainly to extricate him as the launch drifted unattended.

When the coach began shouting for help, Averell plunged into the frigid river and swam to the launch while the other boys rowed to the shore to find help. Luckily, a medical student who had a first-aid kit in his boat was canoeing nearby and came to the rescue. With the help of Averell and the coach, he succeeded in working the boy's mangled arms free and stopped the bleeding.

The next day, the still-shaken coach wrote a letter to E. H. Harriman praising his son's courage. "In all that time," he said, "Averell helped with a calmness and a courage that was perfectly wonderful. He was gentle and tender, acting with perfect self control . . . and it seemed to me of a very high courage."[29]

By the time E.H. returned to New York in April, his condition had declined so precipitously that his doctors urged him to go to Europe for treatment. He sailed with young Mary just days after Averell's graduation from Groton. Following brief stops at Paris and Vienna, they settled into Badgastein, a health resort not far from Salzburg. For weeks E.H. drank and bathed in mineral waters long reputed to have had remarkable curative powers. Unlike earlier summers, when they had toured the continent by automobile, father and daughter stayed at the spa through June and July with Harriman closely following his regimen of baths and electrical massages, being carried from the baths back to his room wrapped in steaming blankets. "While the attending physicians do not think that his health will be entirely restored, they expect great improvement in his condition," a dispatch from Austria reported in the New York *Herald* in late June. The improvement never came. On the contrary, Harriman continued to weaken, and on the advice of his European specialists, he sailed for home again on the *Kaiser Wilhelm II*.

Arriving back in New York on August 25, he was sallow and hollow-eyed. His hat rested on his ears, and his suit swallowed him, making him appear smaller than ever. Members of the Union Pacific entourage and the five dozen newspaper reporters and photographers who greeted him were shocked when he was unable even to walk across the pier without sitting heavily down to rest on a baggage truck. Still, when he made it to his railroad car, waiting at Jersey City to transport him to Arden, he invited the reporters aboard and lay on a sofa answering their questions while his wife fanned him. On the mountaintop at Arden, he seemed to improve.

Hours after his father reached home, Averell returned to New York from the West. He had spent the summer carrying a chain and driving stakes for a surveying party on the Oregon Short Line in the Bitter Root Mountains of northern Idaho, taking off only long enough to visit the Pacific exposition in Seattle. The physical labor of outdoor life leaving him tanned and hardened had been his father's idea. E.H. had seen it as the beginning of a long and systematic railroad education that would someday prepare him for taking over the Union Pacific.

When he had last seen his father in the spring, Averell still had not realized how gravely ill he was, and even when he got to Arden shortly after the family's arrival, it did not occur to him that his father might be near death.

Construction workers and decorators had worked night and day through the summer on the new mansion but it was far from finished when E.H. returned. The family moved into a second-floor section, settling E.H. into his huge bedroom suite, complete with a fireplace in its bathroom, looking out over the swimming pool and into the Ramapo Valley.

The afternoon after he got home, Averell went to his father's room for their first talk in months. It was mostly about the son's work in Idaho, and more than once E.H. apologized for being away throughout the spring and summer. Even after the talk Averell did not have any serious concern that his father's life was in danger.

For several days thereafter, E.H. was well enough for Roland to roll him about in a wheelchair, equipped with pneumatic tires to give him a cushioned ride across the stone porches and formal gardens.

At the foot of the incline railway, a crowd of reporters stood around, trying to buttonhole anyone they could catch going to or coming from the house. But one visitor who managed to get to arrive and depart undetected was E.H.'s bitter old rival, J. Pierpont Morgan. Responding to what he later called a "pathetic message" from E.H., Morgan arrived to find Harriman "muffled like a mummy" on a sun porch of the great house. They spent an hour deep in private conversation and parted with a handshake. "We made our peace," Morgan later said of the meeting. That was all that was ever revealed about their last conversation.[30]

Despite his weakness, Harriman continued working on business matters, dictating letters to his secretary, talking with Jacob Schiff, who arrived from New York, and catching up on the status of construction work on the house. On Sunday, August 5, he took a sudden turn for the worse. By Tuesday he appeared near death, and two days later he died with Mary and all the children, including Averell, who had rushed home from Long Island, at his bedside.

The bright gas light that burned on top of the hill was turned off, the incline railway stopped, and the two hundred workers on the estate sent home as soon as his passing was announced. On Wall Street, the flag of the Stock Exchange was lowered to half-staff.

Harriman was sixty-one, and his elder son, with one summer's experience on a Union Pacific work gang, was still two months from his eighteenth birthday.

Chapter IV

YALE
Bones, the Boathouse, and a Bride

Not yet eighteen, Averell had less than $400 in the bank and no coherent plan for his future when his father died, leaving an estate worth nearly $70 million and placing upon his elder son a vaguely perceived role as head of the Harriman family. The only time that the presumptive future leader of the empire had ever been remotely on his own was that same summer, the interlude between Groton and Yale when he had spent several weeks on the surveying gang in the Bitter Root Mountains of Idaho.

He arose at dawn and worked until dusk, swinging an ax and lugging a surveyor's chain through gullies, over rocks, and up slopes. He ate beans and bacon out of tin cans, washed his clothes in mountain creeks, and made $40 a month. "The work has been very hard," he wrote his father in Austria. "We get up every morning at 5:45, and usually get back to camp at about 7 or 7:30. We don't even always get Sundays off, but last Sunday we happened to, and I had a grand washing day. I haven't quite recovered from it yet—I still feel pretty clean. We were very lazy that day, too. We slept 'til 6:45."[1]

As much as he had been lectured about responsibility, Averell had actually been given little of it. His father's secretary had looked after his bank account. Stablemen had cared for his ponies. Tutors had helped with his lessons. His older sisters had interceded with his parents, and his parents had protected him from temptation and the unexpected. It had always been accepted that one day he would take the reins of the

Union Pacific. He would sit on the boards where E.H. sat. He would give the Harriman name a respectability that eluded the father. But with E.H.'s untimely death, the first son's preparation was far from complete and left in the hands of his mother.

Mary Harriman had played no discernible role in her husband's career. She had professed to know nothing about business matters, insisting that her duty was to support her husband and provide him a home and family where he could take refuge from the railroad and financial wars. Except to intimate friends, she referred to E.H. as Mr. Harriman, and to outsiders she was so overshadowed by him that she appeared to be devoid of interest in worldly affairs, a Victorian by nature, choice, and habit.

E.H.'s will left her everything he owned. Soon to become famous for its brevity, it made no mention of his children. In less than a hundred words, the fortune was bequeathed to his wife without condition:

> I, Edward H. Harriman of Arden, in the State of New York, do make, publish and declare this as and for my last will and testament, that is to say: I give devise and bequeath all my property, real and personal, of every kind and nature, to my wife, Mary Harriman, to be hers absolutely and forever and do hereby nominate and appoint the said Mary W. Harriman to be executrix of this will. In witness whereof, I have set my hand and seal this eighth day of June, in the year 1903.[2]

The only surprise was that the personal fortune was not much larger.

Suddenly, she had sole responsibility for the whole amount and for seeing Averell and Roland through the business education they had scarcely begun. Her second daughter, Cornelia, was already married when E.H. died, and within months, Mary married sculptor Charles Cary Rumsey and moved away to Long Island. Averell was at Yale and Roland at Groton, leaving Carol the last of the family to keep her company.

Under the circumstances, Averell grew up quickly. He took on responsibilities that had belonged to his oldest sister, such as keeping an eye on the dairy and Arden's stables, and occasionally standing in for his mother when the family required a public representative. After five years with Rector Peabody, he settled comfortably into Yale, though he had become a subject of constant fascination for New York newspapers, which recorded his university acceptance, arrival on campus, and procession through every college ritual that provided an occasion to assess his mettle. He led the freshman class into battle against the sophomores in the annual Cane Rush, a brawl of uncertain origin in which the underclassmen battled for possession of the college fence.

By custom, sophomores wearing hats and armed with bamboo poles took places on the fence each year on George Washington's birthday and defended it against howling, attacking freshmen. It was a form of warfare only slightly more controlled and structured than it had been in earlier times when the battle raged across the campus for much of the day. This year, the struggle was coming in for criticism as being childish and unbecoming of Yale, if not downright dangerous, and faculty observers were on hand to consider whether it ought to be abolished.

Still, nearly two hundred freshmen and sophomores joined the fray. For Averell, it provided an opportunity to establish himself as a regular fellow by playing a conspicuous role in something mildly frowned upon by the administration. It was unusually warm for late February. A springlike rain had washed the snow away, and the combatants met in ankle-deep mud. Averell and his friend Holladay Philbin led waves of freshmen against the sophomores defending the stone fence, knocking them from their perches, breaking their bamboo poles, and trampling their top hats. When it was over, forty members of the class of 1913 reached their objective, making the contest a rout, since the rules required only twenty-five of them to battle their way to a perch. The victory was not without a price. Averell and Philbin, later a star varsity athlete, were made special targets by the sophomores, who pummeled them to the ground and rolled them in the chilly quagmire until they were barely recognizable.

Averell came up with a skinned nose, and while faculty observers looked on askance, the New York *World* reported that he had demonstrated grit—"It was the only hazing he has had since he came to Yale and he took it without a whimper."[3]

Two days later, recovered from the Cane Rush, he was involved in what could have easily been a tragic mishap on the first day of rowing practice. Training began in spite of a gusty wind, and his boat was swept out into the icy Long Island Sound by rough water. The air temperature was below freezing, and he and the seven others were soaked to the skin. Although two of the oars were broken, they managed to swing back upriver and make it to the boathouse with ice forming on their sweaters and "nearly in a condition of collapse." The son of the railroad king had come through it "in fine form," reported the New York *World*.[4]

His passage from the custody of Dr. Peabody to the university campus was made easier because his Groton class had supplied the rector's first substantial contingent to New Haven. It included Vanderbilt Webb, the grandson of William K. Vanderbilt and the unquestioned leader of Averell's form at Groton; George Dixon, Jr., Averell's New York pal who had spent the summer working with him on the surveying party in Idaho; and Charles H. Marshall, a classmate all the way back to the Craigie School in Manhattan.

Averell had been an instigator of the movement toward Yale, considering enrollment at New Haven and membership in Skull and Bones a democratic rebellion against the elitist tradition of Grotonians going on to Harvard and membership in the Porcellian Club. As much as a place to attain intellectual maturity, the campus at New Haven was the setting for wealthy young men to cement the social and business contacts of a lifetime. Fraternities, eating and drinking clubs, and all manner of societies created for purposes great and obscure shaped a subculture of Yale Men as structured and elitist as Harvard's, and, if anything, more dedicated to propagating itself. To be a Yale Man was to be loyal, to aspire, to strive, to conform, to always represent the Blue. Besides society reporters from New York newspapers, the campus was regularly visited by the city's smartest tailors, taking measurements and orders, and representatives of shipping lines, arranging winter cruises to the West Indies and elsewhere.

Averell came to the community well prepared. He was a little aloof, never seeking to ingratiate himself, never allowing it to show when he was impressed or surprised; he was loyal to the Yale Blue, a joiner, a team man, "a good sort" who never in his four years on the campus told anyone that he didn't like being called "Bill." He joined the University Club, the Wigwam Wranglers debating society, and Psi Upsilon fraternity, managed the varsity hockey team, and took an active hand in the growing Groton Club and City Government Club. While still an underclassman, he established himself as one of the most accomplished bridge players on campus.

Every time there was a suitable occasion, his mother pushed him forward as the titular head of the Harriman family. The family endowed a chair in forestry to begin its Yale association, and while he was still a freshman, he went home for his first important public ceremony as an heir to fortune, presenting the state of New York a deed to ten thousand acres of land from the Arden estate and a gift of $1 million to go with it.

E.H. had proposed the gift to Governor Charles Evans Hughes before starting out on his last trip to Europe, suggesting that other property owners also contribute to a vast wild parkland between the Ramapo Mountains and the west bank of the Hudson. The Morgans, the Vanderbilts, and the Rockefellers shortly joined, creating the Palisades Interstate Park, stretching through the Hudson Valley and into New Jersey. As usual, E.H. had been able to advance the Harriman interests with his public beneficence. By giving the state urgently needed parkland, he was able to prevent more desirable parts of the Arden estate from being condemned for park use, and to kill plans by politicians in Albany to build a state prison on nearby Bear Mountain.

Ceremonies making the ten-thousand-acre chunk of the Arden estate the northern end of the expansive interstate park were held on a wind-swept plateau beneath the peak of Bear Mountain and within view of the spectacular Storm King, looking down upon the sparkling blue Hudson. Averell escorted his mother, still wearing her mourning black, and spoke stiffly and formally, but without stammering, as he made the presentation to the Palisades Park Commission. "In accordance with a long cherished plan of my father, to give to the State of New York, for the use of the people, a portion of the Arden estate, and acting on behalf of my mother," he said, "I now present to the Commissioners of the Palisades Park the land comprising the gift. I also hand you my mother's contribution to the expense of further development of the Harriman Park. It is her hope and mine that all through the years to come, the health and happiness of future generations will be advanced by these gifts."[5]

With that, a detachment of West Point cadets fired an eighteen-gun salute, the colors were raised, and down on the river the steamer *Hendrick Hudson* let out prolonged whistles as its passengers stood on deck cheering and waving their hats and handkerchiefs. To the audience, there was nothing memorable about the little speech, but it was the first time Averell had ever felt the warmth of public applause. He enjoyed it, and although he did not know it, it was the beginning of his career as a public man.

The dedication in October 1910 was made more meaningful to him and to the family because it followed a tense interlude between the Harrimans and their neighbors in the village of Turner. Determined to memorialize her husband, Mary Harriman had offered to provide $25,000 for a new railroad station on condition that the village change its name to Harriman. But when the Harriman sign was nailed to the station, villagers called a mass meeting and loudly complained of highhanded tactics by their rich neighbors on the mountain. The disgruntlement had subsided by fall, however, and the gift of the $1 million and the ten thousand acres helped put it to rest.

Aside from E.H.'s death, nothing did more to propel Averell out of adolescence and into manhood than the marriage of his sister Mary to Charles Rumsey, a hard-drinking, polo-playing sculptor, who had first been summoned to Arden to create pieces for E.H.'s new mansion and its gardens.

Because Mary was ten years older than Averell, and because she had their father's genetic disposition to take charge of everything around her, Mary had always assumed the prerogatives of the first-born son in the family hierarchy. Before her father died, she had taken on the responsibility for overseeing the estate, with its dozens of employees, its dairy herd of four hundred cows, its stables, kennels, greenhouses, and private power plant for generating electricity. With such a sibling, Averell had little to be responsible for.

While Mary had been E.H.'s favorite child, she had more than any of the others been a source of concern to him. Headstrong from childhood, she was a "modern woman" long before the term came into vogue. She defied her father by going to Barnard College although he considered higher education both unnecessary and unseemly for a young woman of her means. From then on, she set her own style and, within limits, wrote her own agenda. She drove her horse-drawn carriage to school, accompanied by a secretary who sat beside her typing or taking dictation. Before reaching the campus, she hitched her horses and walked the last blocks to avoid the appearance of privilege. As her friend Nathalie Henderson later told the story, it was while they were at Barnard that Mary got the idea of creating the Junior League.

Dissatisfied because she saw no socially redeeming purpose in her debutantes' parties, she spent months before her own presentation to society mulling over some way to organize the girls of her own class behind some useful project to mark their introduction. Work done by churches was "too sectarian" for her, and hospital service "too limited in scope." She struck on the notion of a permanent organization to go into settlement houses and among families in chronic need of help, the idea coming to her as she drove her snappy sulky down Riverside Drive.[6]

When "Pad" Rumsey appeared at Arden, he endeared himself to the family with his agreeable personality and his skill as a sculptor, but even more with his horsemanship. He was a superb rider in the hunt or on the polo field, and a skilled driver in a sulky. Rumsey had never been presented to E.H. for approval as a son-in-law, however, and when the eldest daughter received a formal marriage proposal, Averell was called upon for advice. He and his mother had reservations about Rumsey's drinking habits and thought "little Mary" ambivalent about matrimony. Though Averell's experience with such matters was nonexistent, he was a good judge of his headstrong sister, and knowing she would not be influenced by any advice, he urged his mother to make no effort at intercession. On May 26, 1910, Mary was married in St. John's Chapel on the estate.

Home from Yale at the end of his freshman year, Averell escorted his sister to the altar and served as the family's host at a brunch for the Harriman and the Rumsey families and the friends who came up from the city. Afterward, he and his mother and the guests made their way down the mountain on the incline railway, leaving the newlyweds to honeymoon in the huge stone mansion.

In the weeks after the wedding, Averell had his first opportunity since his father's death to have long talks with his mother about his own future. He was surprised to learn that she was about to begin passing his part of the family fortune along to him at once, and to give him family and business responsibilities that he expected to come to him only after he was out of college.

His class standing at Yale improved over his undistinguished performance at Groton and, spared the lectures of his father, his sister, and Rector Peabody, he overcame his shyness and some of his stammering. His mother provided him with a Stutz Bearcat and, as promised, transferred to him thousands of shares of Union Pacific and Illinois Central stock as well as bonds and real estate. She also arranged for him to serve on the Palisades Park Commission and work with the Boys' Club, which E.H. had founded in 1876 to provide gathering places and organized activities for boys in danger of aimless and troubled lives in the streets. About the same time, he was elected a director of the Harriman National Bank, which was controlled by his mother, and of August Belmont's Cape Cod Construction Company, which was cutting a shipping canal across the cape.

When senior elections rolled around at Yale, he was among the top ten finishers in selection of the "most to be admired," "most thorough gentleman," "most likely to succeed," and "handsomest." His popularity came to him mainly through his relentless effort to recapture the prestige of Yale rowing at a moment when the school's athletic program was at its lowest ebb in memory.

He had gone to New Haven with dreams of winning a place on the varsity crew and helping reverse the Blue's sagging fortunes against Harvard. The tradition-encrusted rivalry was then the most important event in Yale athletics, and after a long run of victories for the Blue, it had turned sharply in Harvard's favor. During his first term, when one hundred members of his class reported for rowing practice, he was a serious contender, but while he was home for the spring holidays, he had a physical examination and his doctor detected a heart murmur. It had first been noticed while he was at Groton, during his period of rapid growth. Although he was more than six feet tall now, he still weighed only 160 pounds, and the recurrence worried his mother and concerned his doctor enough that he recommend that varsity-level competition be forgotten.

While he followed the sobering advice, his larger commitment to a Yale rowing comeback was only intensified. He still spent hours around the boathouse, rowed in intramural competition, and engaged in long campus debates about whether varsity athletic teams should be coached by professionals or amateurs from the ranks of Yale alumni. His mother encouraged his continuing interest, becoming both a fan and financial supporter of Yale rowing in its quest to recapture elusive glory.

In June of 1911, when Averell was rowing in a sophomore-class boat in a preliminary to the varsity race against Harvard, she arrived aboard the *Sultana* with Carol, Roland, and several guests, and found a berth among dozens of yachts near the finish line. She watched impassively as his boat was badly beaten, but the sophomore-class loss was nothing compared to another varsity disaster. For the sixth year in a row, the Crimson oarsmen flashed across the finish line ahead, this time by a full minute, making it Yale's worst defeat in twenty-eight years. Every potential remedy had abjectly failed. A new boathouse had been constructed; football players had been recruited to put more muscle behind the oars; the training regimen had been changed; the schedule had been revised. But the varsity not only continued losing to Harvard, it lost in 1911 to an inexperienced Princeton eight that was just learning to row.

The crew's unrelieved humiliation was accompanied by a malaise in other sports that troubled Yale men wherever sweaters were worn with the varsity *Y*. In Averell's sophomore year, only the football team produced a winning season in a major sport, and that appeased hardly anyone, because Walter Camp's heroes of the gridiron still fell to Harvard, despite the annual reminder that the game would be the most important event of their lives. The track squad lost to Princeton for the first time; the baseball team lost to Harvard and Princeton in succession, and the varsity crew fell to every serious rowing school in the East except Columbia.

With alumni and undergraduates favoring amateur coaching by Yale graduates and student assistants, crew coach John Kennedy, a professional sculler, was dismissed. No longer a candidate for the varsity, Averell volunteered to coach the freshmen crew, and at the boathouse, where he began to campaign for the presidency of the Yale Navy, he argued for a return to the Oxford stroke that had produced a renaissance in Yale rowing more than forty years earlier.

He made the case persuasively, not only at the crews' quarters but in the office of Dean Frederick Scheetz Jones, who was acutely sensitive to alumni unhappiness over the sad state of Yale rowing. Mary Harriman, having heard about the crisis from the day of Averell's arrival at New Haven, was prepared to invest in a solution, and when Averell proposed a personal mission to England to study English rowing, she agreed to finance it.

Another Yale student, named Robert Cook, had made a similar journey in 1873 and had brought back enough tips from Oxford and Cambridge to revolutionize rowing in America. Now, as Averell argued for reintroduction of English-style rowing at Yale, Robert Cook himself, by then a newspaper manager in Philadelphia, was getting ready for another visit to England in order to return to work with the varsity coaching staff. Under the extraordinary circumstances, the dean agreed to excuse Averell from classes for six weeks in the hope that he might bring some of the English magic back.

Armed with letters of introduction to Oxford rowing coach Harcourt Gold and to William Waldorf Astor, he sailed for England in January 1912. His mother was pleased at his taking the lead, and she wished him well with an indulgent note expressing the hope that "this little mission will prepare you for other & bigger ones. I know your father's spirit is with you always & that he would be pleased with this opportunity, which both interesting and delightful, brings responsibility and will be a test of your good sense & ability."[7]

When he arrived in London, his first stop was at Baring Brothers, his father's London banking house, for a visit with George Rowe, the chairman of Oxford's graduate rowing committee, who was one of the partners. Rowe was anxious to help not only Yale but the son of E. H. Harriman. At the university, however, Averell encountered indifference and outright rudeness from his own contemporaries at crew headquarters. He arrived at the boathouse in a cold rain, and the young men he had crossed the Atlantic to study and emulate did not so much as invite him inside the door. The coach was away, and to members of the vaunted Oxford crew, the Harriman name meant nothing. Nor were they impressed that a sophomore from Yale had crossed the Atlantic just to watch them train.

"If you want to see us row," the imperious varsity captain told him at the entrance, "go down to the tow path. We'll be coming out in another half hour." With that he closed the door.[8]

In the following days, Averell watched from the path as the young Englishmen worked out each afternoon, taking notes on the way their oars caught the water and their long strokes swept them back until their bodies were nearly parallel with the river's surface at the end. Each night, he carefully recorded what he was able to glean from hanging about the boathouse, copiously describing the dimensions of boats, the measurements of oars, the placement of seats, and the theory of the Oxford stroke.

After the coach's return, he was finally invited into the crew dining room, but was left to eat alone, out of earshot of the varsity's honored table. He was close enough, however, to observe and record every particular of their training diet and routine, down to their luncheon menu of cold beef and potatoes, along with stewed prunes and figs.

In spite of the uniform indifference of the oarsmen, he made headway. Rowe came out from London and invited him to go along to a supper honoring the crew of Oxford's Magdalen College for its preeminence in intramural rowing. After the festivities, Averell returned to his hotel amazed at the social familiarity between students, coaches and faculty members, particularly their "curious habit" of downing huge quantities of champagne together, a rite unlike anything imagined at Yale. Only by providence, he thought, had all escaped without being injured by the fireworks that had been shot indiscriminately into the crowd during the celebration.

Continuing to trail the varsity, he was eventually invited to take his meals with the crew; and when they moved to Henley to continue preparation for their coming meet with Cambridge, he went along with them. As they took to the river, he joined alumni and racing devotees who rented horses and rode the paths along the Thames, staying within full view of the boats. Later he was taken on the river by Harcourt Gold, who was largely responsible for Oxford's perennial success. That gave him a rare chance both to soak up technical wisdom from the veteran coach and to make a closer assessment of the individual crew members.

By then he had become familiar enough with the men in the Oxford boat to see room for improvement—technically and personally. "The stroke is considered a marvel but [he] looks very rough," he wrote of Oxford's most crucial oarsman. "He had a hard & marked catch but washes out at the finish, but they leave him alone as he is a hardened sinner."[9]

Though he became more or less accepted as a part of the Oxford entourage during the workouts at Henley and Putney, Averell spent much of his time with towering historical figures of the sport—Bob Cook himself and Rudie Lehmann, a legendary English oarsman, who had transplanted the secrets of Oxford and Cambridge rowing to Harvard after Cook's success at Yale. During several days with Lehmann's family, he carefully took down every fragment of the coach's advice and spent afternoons with him watching Cambridge train. The experience confirmed Averell's belief in Oxford supremacy. "They will never be as good as Oxford," he concluded, "but are much better than I expected. Stroke and Seven are long in the water but the rest of the crew is all out before them. Six is particularly short. They get onto the catch fairly well, but their finish is ragged, not nearly as much swing as Oxford."[10] The Cambridge crew, he concluded, was poorly led and overtrained—mistakes he resolved to see avoided at Yale.

Toward the end of his mission, he caught up with Cook during an Oxford workout one morning and arranged for an interview with the legend who had coached Yale for nearly twenty-five years. Like any Yale oarsman, Averell was awed by Cook's past, but their meeting was a disappointment. During their long talk at a restaurant at Picadilly Circus, Averell found the old coach wholly preoccupied with the immediate Oxford crew rather than the fundamentals of the English rowing technique. Consequently, the long-awaited conference yielded nearly nothing for him to take home to his freshmen, and no reason to think Cook would change the varsity's fortunes as he had forty years earlier.

Averell was also annoyed with himself because he had mistimed his expedition. His six-week leave from classes expired five days before the much anticipated Oxford-Cambridge meet. He was powerfully tempted to stay an additional week so he could see the outcome of the preparations he had watched. The delay would also give him the opportunity to return to New York on the maiden voyage of the new British supership, the *Titanic*.

But a commitment was a commitment, and knowing that any chance to return the following year would be ruined by a late return to the campus, he sailed for home on schedule aboard the *Olympic*. He was back at Yale on April 14 when the stunning news came that the *Titanic* had struck an iceberg and sunk in the North Atlantic, with 1,513 passengers and crew members perishing.[11]

His first big test as Yale's neophyte freshman coach came two months later in the forty-sixth annual regatta at New London, Connecticut. Bob Cook had arrived at New Haven soon after Averell's return from England and had begun working with the new varsity coach, James O. Rodgers, who had graduated in the class of 1898. But as the meet approached, Averell could see that they had little chance of breaking Harvard's streak.

Two days before the race, he wrote friends in England confessing that he feared the worst. "The freshmen eight are up against a very strong &, by their trials, one of the fastest freshman crews that Harvard has turned out, & I don't think that my men will have the strength to beat them. Out of the four crews that race, it now looks as if the freshman four is the only one that can win. It is a very discouraging outlook & and I don't know whether the coaching system can stand the shock."[12]

The frank assessment of the young expert was not shared by Yale supporters, who assumed that Yale's deliverance was at hand with the return of Cook and the Oxford stroke. On the night before the race, students and alumni poured into New London by the thousands, jamming the streets with automobiles and surging along the sidewalks in a sea of Harvard hatbands, Yale streamers, and dyed brooms and feathers. On the day of the meet, hundreds of powerboats found places lining the course, and near the finish line yachts belonging to patrons and influential alumni were moored. Among them, as usual, was Mary Harriman and her party aboard the *Sultana*. Anchored nearby, their owners and guests attended by platoons of servants, were August Belmont's *Scout* and the U.S. government yacht, *Dolphin*, with Secretary of the Navy George von L. Meyer aboard. Harry Payne Whitney's *Dixie II* put on its own show, passing by the crowd at thirty knots with Yale banners flying.

By the time the schedule reached the main events—the four-mile varsity race with eight-oared shells and the two-mile competition in four-man boats—Averell's freshmen had already lost to the Crimson in the two-mile contest between crews of eight. But as it turned out, it was his oarsmen who offered hope to the faithful flying the blue and white. With nineteen-year-old Dean Acheson rowing number seven, the freshman eight challenged the Harvard boat all the way to the finish line before losing by two and a half seconds in the closest contest of the day.

The Crimson freshmen opened a lead after three quarters of a mile, but Harriman's crew, employing the longer, stronger pull imported from Oxford, refused to fade. A quarter of a mile from the finish line, the freshmen from New Haven stepped up their beat in an effort to surge into the lead, but Harvard had correctly anticipated Averell's strategy and held off the stretch rush.

In the late afternoon, the Yale varsity did its best, but Harvard won easily in both its eight-man and four-man shells. The outcome did not shake Averell's confidence in the English system, although the Yale crews came to the end of the race exhausted, oars skimming the top of the water instead of catching effectively and driving the boats forward.

The showing of the freshman crew convinced many of the graduates that Averell was on the right track, and they dramatically demonstrated their confidence by naming him to replace Rodgers as coach of the varsity. It was the first time anybody had been given the job without ever rowing a varsity race, but he had acquired support in important places. In the esteemed estimation of Bob Cook, he was "easily the most promising crew coach in America [and] one of the most competent students of rowing in this country." It was his personal hope, Cook said, that young Harriman would devote his life to the sport.[13]

But the next spring at New Haven brought continued varsity losses; experienced oarsmen encountered more difficulty than did the freshmen in adopting the imported stroke. Still, Averell was invited to stay on as coach after graduation, and he agreed.

Yet after another defeat at the hands of Princeton, letters to the *Alumni Weekly* again ran in favor of hiring an experienced professional coach. Harriman, said Walter Badger, a member of the class of '82, was "a good coach although with limited experience." The trouble, the alumnus added, was that Averell's business interests kept him away from New Haven, leaving the crew in the hands of Dean Acheson, who had never pulled a varsity oar.[14]

Averell did not wait for an invitation to discuss the problem with alumni rowing chairman Frederick Allen in New York. "Yale hasn't got time to wait until I learn to be a coach," he said, and ended what Bob Cook had thought such a promising career. Allen offered no protest. "That," he replied to Averell's assessment, "is exactly what I was going to tell you."[15] But in the end, Harriman felt vindicated. The rowing committee accepted his recommendation to bring in Oxford coach Guy Nickalls as his successor, and by 1915 the Yale eight left Harvard seven lengths behind at New London and won every other race it entered.[16]

At the same time the question of professional-versus-amateur crew coaching was being argued, Yale's venerable senior societies, a bedrock of undergraduate social order and alumni loyalty, were under growing student criticism and public ridicule. Fanned by a new novel, *Stover at Yale*, written by Owen Johnson, Yale 1900, the controversy saw the societies belittled for fostering offensive elitism that was out of place at a modern educational institution. But Averell was no more inclined to support the overthrow of the social order than he was to ignore the decline of Yale rowing. The societies bonded men like himself to Yale and to each other across the generations. As much as he had wanted to row under the Blue banner, he wanted even more to be tapped for membership and inducted into one of the imposing secret fortresses.

He returned from his first trip to Oxford just as the three societies prepared for the annual Tap Day ritual. Vying for men from proper families who had distinguished themselves in ways deemed exemplary, each selected fifteen members from the forthcoming senior class to perpetuate the secret brotherhood.

The taps of 1912 were anticipated with uncommon interest not only because of Owen Johnson's best-seller but because the class of 1913 included a bumper crop of offspring of publicly prominent Americans, Averell being conspicuous among them.

Opinion among the undergraduate cognoscenti was divided over whether he would go to Skull and Bones or to Scroll and Key. The latter made claim to scholarly superiority, but Bones was the first of the societies, the list of its members an awe-inspiring roll of men at the top of America's political, financial, and social institutions. Over the generations, its pledge of secrecy had stood more firmly than marriage vows and professional oaths. Except for the fifteen active members and alumni, Yale men could only guess at what was inside the prisonlike oaken doors of the great ivy-covered mausoleum.

Wolf's Head, the third society, was out of the question for the son of E. H. Harriman, even though the family had no Yale tradition of its own to uphold. Unlike most of his friends, who represented second or third generations and hoped to follow fathers and grandfathers into Bones or Key, Averell could point only to his uncle, William H. Averell, and an Averell cousin as Yale men before him, and he had hardly known them, if at all.

On May 16, as juniors did on Tap Day year after year, members of Averell's class with aspirations for society membership gathered beneath a gnarled oak in front of Battell Chapel to wait for a man from each of the societies to emerge from the fortresses. A spring downpour soaked them to the skin and left them standing in mud. They waited without hats and with their coats draped about their shoulders, seemingly oblivious to the rain as their judgment approached.

Dozens of underclassmen scrambled up into the tree and took places on the lower limbs where they could have an unrestricted view of the proceedings, during which representatives of the societies would walk into the crowd to find the juniors found worthy, whacking them on the back and ordering, "Go to your room."

Every window was filled in Durfee Hall, and faculty members crowded onto the porch of the chapel. Girlfriends, graduates, newspaper reporters, even parents—including athletic director Walter Camp, who was anxious to see whether Walter junior would follow his famous father into Bones—huddled under umbrellas on the fringe of the crowd.

At the moment the clock on the front of the chapel struck five, a man from each of the societies, wearing a derby, a blue serge suit, and his gold society pin in his lapel, approached waiting candidates. The grave emissary from Bones walked straight to Harriman, spun him about and whacked him on the back with the command, "Averell Harriman, go to your room." From the tree, a shout went up, "Harriman goes Bones," and Averell hurried away through the parting crowd to his dormitory.

The supreme honor of the tapping ritual was not being chosen first, however. By long-standing tradition, the moment of highest drama went to the juniors chosen last, and in the class of 1913, the last tap for Bones went to George Cortelyou, Jr., whose father had been an important figure in New York Republican politics before going on to the White House as Teddy Roosevelt's private secretary. Key's last tap honor went to Vanderbilt Webb, chairman of the *Yale Daily News*, who had continued to shine at New Haven as he had at Groton.

There were more poignant moments, however, as others arrived at the crossroads which many considered the most important of their college careers. At times, Owen Johnson's acerbic criticisms of the societies seemed unnecessarily kind. Crises of mutual embarrassment saw several juniors hoping for Bones or Scroll and Key decline a tap by a man from Wolf's Head, quietly saying no or merely shaking their head as the society's representative turned on his heel. Up in the tree, underclassmen injected themselves into wrenching decisions, shouting, "Take it! Take it!" as juniors tapped by one society weighed the odds of later selection by another. Richard W. Robbins, the business manager of the *Daily News*, turned down a Key invitation, hoping for a Bones tap that never came.

Other sure shots were left standing uninvited and humiliated after all the forty-five new members had been taken. Among those rejected

were Averell's roommate George Dixon; Douglas Bomeisler, a rowing
star and contender for the captaincy of the football team; and Joseph
Walker, the son of the speaker of the Massachusetts House of Representatives. Walker's exclusion was astonishing, for he had only recently
defeated Averell for the presidency of the Yale Navy, Harriman's contributions to Yale rowing notwithstanding.

Although being tapped was a momentous occasion, Averell was careful to let his mother know that it was taken in perspective. "I have gotten
a number of letters of congratulations from Bones graduates," he wrote
her in a tone concealing his satisfaction. "It must be a marvelous institution for these men to take it as seriously and to make as much of it as
they do."[17]

After living anonymously in E.H.'s shadow through all of their married life, the widow Mary Harriman emerged as a powerful figure on
her own. The world's richest woman—as newspapers called her—managed the fortune with remarkable confidence. Soon after E.H.'s death,
she sold off property on Fifth Avenue, where her husband had planned
to build a new city mansion, and moved to 1 East Sixty-ninth Street,
pushing ahead, meanwhile, with completion of the new Arden house.

Dividing her time between Manhattan and the estate in the country,
she looked after E.H.'s pet projects, such as the Boys' Club, the Goshen
racetrack, and Island Park Ranch in Idaho. Determined to see his reputation salvaged from the wreckage of his fight with Roosevelt, she began
assembling material for a massive biography of him.

Deluged by six thousand requests for contributions within weeks of
E.H.'s death, she opened an office on Fifth Avenue and hired a "man of
affairs" and two accountants to help her systematically manage family
philanthropy, handling gifts as efficiently as E.H. had operated the
Union Pacific. Rather than turn to a foundation, as had the Rockefellers
and the Carnegies, she kept direct control of her contributions, following
E.H.'s practice of giving only to endeavors in which he took a genuine
interest. The approach caused talk that she was a miser, although she
expanded the family's charitable interests far beyond what they had been
while E.H. lived. It was years before she consented to put money into a
philanthropic trust, and when she did, it was placed not under the control
of professionals but under the direction of Averell and Roland.

She made her interest in education a crusade, supported medical
laboratories, endowed eugenics research projects, took a lively interest
in banking and finance, and put together a company to help artisans
who had worked on the mansion now called Arden House. To the delight
of her daughter Mary, she founded the Association for the Improvement
of the Condition of the Poor, and in time, she began even making public
speeches.

Although she was politically as well as personally conservative, there were times when she undertook surprising crusades against entrenched traditions. She fervently promoted professional and scholarly training to prepare young people for public service. Regretting that public service was a higher calling in Europe than it was in the United States, she went to the presidents of Harvard, Yale and Columbia with a proposal to educate young people formally for public administration. In the face of the widely held conviction that scholarship and politics were antithetical, she tapped the Rockefeller and Carnegie fortunes, as well as that of E.H.'s old ally Jacob Schiff, for help to support a public service training school. It became the National Institute of Public Administration, forerunner of the Syracuse University School of Citizenship and Public Affairs and of formal public administration courses in universities across the country.

Besides pressing ahead with the gift of the land for the Harriman State Park, she forgave a $113,000 mortgage on the Boys' Club building for which E.H. had laid the cornerstone in 1901. She donated an athletic field to Trinity School, where her husband had attended classes before dropping his education to become a Wall Street office boy, and she built a new gymnasium for St. George's Parish at Hempstead, his birthplace.

After endowing the chair in the Yale School of Forestry, she established a fund for research on North American wildlife and put C. Hart Merrian, who had organized the scientific party for their 1899 trip to Alaska, in charge of it. At the Southern Pacific Hospital in San Francisco, she created a trust fund for research on the illnesses and injuries of the railroad's employees; and at Roosevelt Hospital in New York, she provided the funds for basic cancer studies at the Harriman Research Laboratory.

She launched far-reaching exploration of public health problems by establishing a Committee on Public Health, endowing hospitals, and supporting the New York Academy of Medicine. In much of this, she consulted Averell, who became her chief adviser on family matters, while Judge Robert S. Lovett looked after Harriman interests in the railroads.

While Averell regularly came home on business, taking a boat from New Haven, Mary Harriman often traveled to Yale in her private railroad car, staying long enough to entertain her son and his roommates, attend chapel, and call on members of the faculty and administration.

Although she was a stern, imposing woman, who seemingly found little joy in life, her relationship with her children was as warm as E.H.'s had been demanding. Besides encouraging and financing Averell's undertakings, such as his study of English rowing, she indulged Roland in carefree adventures that E.H. would have declared out of the question. One summer, after her younger son had followed Averell to Yale, she turned the *Sultana* over to him for his entire vacation. With several of his buddies, he sailed to Jacksonville, Havana, and Jamaica, passed through the Panama Canal and continued to Acapulco and San Francisco.

While E.H.'s most enduring ambition was for his sons to take over the Union Pacific, circumstances made it impossible for Averell and Roland to emulate him—the court-ordered divestiture of Southern Pacific, the coming of the automobile, the stirring of federal regulation, and the adoption of the income tax had conspired to end the golden age of the railroad barons.

Averell's formal railroad education began in the early summer of 1913, soon after he left the Yale campus. Under the guidance of Judge Lovett, who had succeeded his father as chairman of the executive committee and chief executive officer of the Union Pacific, he went west to begin his ordained climb to the top. Spending most of the next two years in the West, he lived in the home of A. L. Mohler, the Union Pacific boss in Omaha, receiving an intensive course in practical railroading. A favorite of E.H.'s, Mohler had taken his first railroad job when he was sixteen and had made his way up through the ranks from clerk, freight agent, and auditor on half a dozen railroads, finally breaking into management at Union Pacific.

While he was living in Omaha, Averell went through much the same progression that Mohler himself had followed on his more labored ascent of the ladder years before. The internship took him into every operating department. He learned locomotive operations, traffic control, maintenance, and purchasing. He spent several weeks traveling the territory, some of it with gangs working on the tracks.

Through it all, railroad employees from greasy mechanics to stooped auditors who had labored a lifetime over Union Pacific books assumed a familiarity that would have been unthinkable in New York. He was, to most of them, "Bill." His Groton accent, his polished eastern manners, and his imperious reserve made him conspicuous, but E.H.'s upbringing had hardened him.

Behind his back, workers laughed when he went to creeks and washed twenty-five-cent socks worn so threadbare and full of holes that they would have been thrown away by a track hand. He was not robust, but he had a commanding presence and he acquired a physical toughness that surprised railroad men and impressed friends like Judge Lovett's son, Bob, who had known him most of his life. Lovett would always remember riding with him through snow-covered pines during an early mountain spring. Everybody else in the party wore rain gear to protect them from the falling snow, but Averell rode in an open-necked crew sweater, seemingly unaware of the snow falling on him, soaking his sweater and running down his back and chest.[18]

Several months after Averell's arrival in Omaha, Judge Lovett put him in charge of a project to ferret out waste in the Union Pacific from bottom to top, and he spent nearly a year traveling around the system, often alone. He showed up in foundries, car shops, and rolling mills, called on freight agents, and covered long stretches of the road with repair crews. "We've been spending most of our time on the road, starting usually between 7 and 8 A.M., and ending up after dark in the evening," he wrote his mother in the fall of 1914. "Nothing could be better than all day in an open track car. We have been over most of the Colorado division, and in a few days will go on to the Kansas division."[19]

Though he threw himself into his work with an enthusiasm that pleased Lovett, he was bored by the pace of life in Omaha. He was always anxious to get back to New York for a board meeting and a chance to play polo or drive in a harness race. On occasion, he joined the family for outings at the ranch in Idaho, where he and Roland rode, went trout fishing, and shot sage grouse.

His chance to move up came with the death of the railroad's vice-president for purchasing. Judge Lovett had been impressed with his investigation of waste, and he brought him home to New York to become a junior vice-president at the age of twenty-four. The job put him in close contact with every significant aspect of railroad management and operation.

Two years of "knocking around the system" and his investigation for Lovett convinced Averell that the company was wasting huge amounts of money simply because it had never established uniform standards for its contracts and relied far too much on ad hoc purchasing. What especially perturbed him was "collusive bidding" that amounted to price-fixing by suppliers at huge expense to the railroad. For all of Judge Lovett's reputation as a railroad executive, the junior vice-president concluded that his mentor trusted suppliers far too much.

Without consulting the judge, he challenged manufacturers' bids on a huge contract for new locomotives. Suspecting collusion between American Locomotive and Baldwin Locomotive, he threatened to cancel Union Pacific's policy of giving some business to both companies and place the entire order for both freight and passenger engines with the lower bidder. Baldwin had submitted the winning bid for the freight locomotives and American had bid lowest on the engines for passenger trains, their proposals smelling of price-rigging.

Harriman called in a vice-president of Baldwin and announced that both freight and passenger engines would be purchased from one contractor at a lower price than either Baldwin or American had offered. The executive protested, but when Harriman picked up the telephone to call Baldwin president Samuel Vauclain, he backed down and accepted Averell's price. Shut out, American Locomotive loudly objected and appealed directly to Lovett, but the chairman backed his young vice-president.[20]

When he was at Arden, Averell went frequently to the Goshen racetrack where E.H. had made trotting a thriving sport. Mary Harriman had given the track a new $50,000 grandstand soon after her husband's death to go with the band stand she had already provided. The Goshen Driving Club reciprocated by making Averell its president several weeks before he graduated from Yale. Given his early training under E.H.'s expert guidance, he was a skilled driver, more often than not in top contention and sometimes winning matinee races. He also raced at Tuxedo, and occasionally at other tracks on the trotting circuit.

On a hot July afternoon in 1914, he narrowly escaped serious injury when his horse panicked and ran away during a race in Cleveland, hastening his withdrawal from harness racing. As he turned into the home stretch fighting to hold a narrow lead behind a fast trotter aptly named Excito, a part of his harness broke, frightening the horse into a headlong gallop. The animal thundered past the finish line, swiped the fence, and crashed through two barriers before falling into a ditch with Averell still in the driver's seat and clinging to the reins. Surprisingly, neither horse nor driver was injured, but Averell had to withdraw from the competition, leaving it to his teammate Pierre Lorillard to win the main event for the Goshen drivers.

Horses were not his only distraction from the Union Pacific. Home from Omaha, he fell in love with a friend and riding companion of his sister Carol. Kitty Lanier Lawrance was a dark, willowy, pretty brunette of twenty-two who had been orphaned in early childhood and reared by Charles Lanier, her widower grandfather. She had spent her school years at his house on East Thirty-seventh Street in Manhattan and her summers at "Allen Winden," his estate at Lenox, Massachusetts.

Before Averell came into her life, she had been courted by more than one young man who wanted to marry her, including a dashing engineer-adventurer named Lincoln Ellsworth, who would later become famous as a polar explorer. But since he disappeared for months at a time, so, eventually, did her romantic interest. She and Harriman, on the other hand, seemed ideally suited. She was a crack shot with a hunting rifle or a shotgun, a graceful rider, and a sharp-eyed judge of horseflesh, whether thoroughbreds, hunters, or polo ponies. More than that, she was good at bridge and she had become a favorite of Averell's mother during Kitty's visits to Arden to ride with Carol.

The Harriman and Lawrance families had been acquainted for years. Kitty's grandfather was a member of several railroad boards and had been deeply involved in the work of the American Museum of

Natural History, activities that had brought him into contact with E. H. Harriman. He was also an intimate of E.H.'s old nemesis, J. P. Morgan. Both Averell's mother and Kitty's grandfather welcomed the match, so when Averell went to Charles Lanier to formally ask to marry his only granddaughter, Lanier was eagerly anticipating his call. His only response was to inquire whether Averell was "free of venereal disease?"[21]

Oddly for a man who would later acquire a reputation as a womanizer and playboy, there had been no serious romantic interest in Harriman's life until he met Kitty at twenty-four. Girlfriends had usually been Carol's acquaintances who came to prom weekends at Yale, visited Arden, or joined sailing parties on the *Sultana*. They found him attractive, shy, and excessively courteous. They liked his sad, brown eyes—"sheep dog eyes," one called them—along with his impeccable manners and hint of English aristocracy. He also had a slight but elegant stoop that enhanced his aristocratic bearing and made him seem older than he was. Because of his reserve, casual acquaintances found him cold, and he made friends slowly, whether they were women or men.

The marriage to Kitty would probably have never happened if not for an accident in the spring of 1915. On a Saturday afternoon in April they took their horses from their stables in Central Park and set out on a leisurely ride along a bridle path near Riverside Drive. As they were passing beneath a railroad trestle, a train roared overhead and Kitty's mount reared and fell backward with her still in the saddle. The full weight of the animal broke her pelvis, and it was questionable whether she would ever walk normally again. Averell blamed himself for having taken the route.

It was weeks before she could walk with the aid of a cane. For a time, she recovered at Arden, and then she was moved to her grandfather's estate in Massachusetts. She was still unable to walk when their engagement was announced in July, creating romanticized stories that they had met when Averell saved her life from a runaway horse.

In September 1915, soon after she was on her feet again, they were married at the Trinity Episcopal Church in Lenox. A special express train brought the Harrimans and their guests up from New York, but the ceremony itself bordered on the austere, reflecting both Kitty's conservatism and Averell's own aversion to having his personal life put on public display. Roland was his best man, and Yale friends Holladay Philbin and Charles Marshall joined Kitty's brother, Charles Lawrance, in greeting guests as they arrived at the church entrance. There were no ushers, and the bride had no attendant, nor did she carry a bouquet or wear gloves as she was escorted to the altar by her grandfather. The ceremony, performed by Dean William M. Grosvenor of the Cathedral of St. John the Divine and William L. Wood, the Trinity rector, lasted but six minutes.

Their wedding present from the bridegroom's mother was the great house at Arden, where E.H. had planned to establish his dynasty. Mary had overseen completion of the broad corridors with statuary, tapestries, and paintings by American artists, but nine years after construction started, it was still unfinished.

When it was begun, the mansion was a technological marvel, lighted by electricity from its own power plant, served by its own railroad, and supplied by greenhouses that provided not only an unlimited supply of potted plants and flowers but nectarines and vegetables in every season. Strategically placed vents could be opened to catch a mountain breeze from any direction, giving the mansion a rudimentary air-conditioning system. In its organ room was the largest privately owned pipe organ in the country, used for Sunday-afternoon concerts. Mary Harriman stuck faithfully to E.H.'s detailed plans for a house that would represent American art and craftsmanship from its limestone and granite walls to furniture carved, assembled, and finished in the estate's own woodworking shops.

With her older son installed as a railroad vice-president and married to a woman of whom she genuinely approved, Mary Harriman considered the succession almost complete. Six years after the mansion was first occupied, work crews returned to finish Averell's east wing, converting it from Charles Rumsey's seldom-used studio to a residential complex, complete with office space plus quarters for Averell and Kitty's servants and staff. Mrs. Harriman continued to live in the second-floor suite, which she and her husband had shared in the west wing for the few days that he lived in the mansion.

In Manhattan, the top floor of the house on the northeast corner of Fifth Avenue and Sixty-ninth Street was set aside as the newlyweds' residence in the city. Mary Harriman's sun room, her favorite place in the house where she had entertained her guests during the six years she had been alone, became the newlyweds' parlor.

Chapter V

SHIPS

Harriman II, Steamship King

As darkness descended on the last day of January 1917, German ambassador Johann von Bernstorff called on Secretary of State Robert Lansing to deliver the chilling message that made war inevitable for America. Two and a half years after the outbreak of fighting in Europe, Germany was resuming unrestricted submarine warfare against all shipping across a broad expanse of the Atlantic off the shores of Britain, France, Belgium, and Holland. A nine-month-old pledge to give passengers a chance to escape before attacking civilian vessels was being withdrawn. Attached to the formal note was a copy in English, sparing both men the discomfort of sitting through a translation. The ordinarily jaunty von Bernstorff watched in grim silence as Lansing put aside the transmittal letter and scanned the English text of the cable from Berlin:

"From Feb. 1, 1917, sea traffic will be stopped with every available weapon and without further notice. . . ." U-boats, already sinking one of every four ships bound for Britain and France from the United States, would henceforth attack without warning and without regard to destination or cargo. Submarines loaded with torpedoes were approaching their stations, if they had not in fact already arrived, along the perimeter of the embargoed zone. Their new orders would become effective in less than eight hours.[1]

The United States had been moving inexorably toward war with Germany ever since a German U-boat had torpedoed the *Lusitania* off the coast of Ireland on May 7, 1915. One hundred and twenty-eight

112

Americans, including 63 infants, had been among the 1,195 passengers who drowned as the queen of the Cunard Line went down.

Believing now that the United States would not enter the war and confident that Americans could not change the outcome even if they did fight, Germany was brazenly setting out to starve the Allies into submission. The menace of the United States had vanished, Minister of the Interior Karl Helfferich told the Finance Committee of the Reichstag that same afternoon in Berlin. "By fall, the Island Kingdom will sprawl like fish in the reeds and beg for peace!"[2]

That evening as President Woodrow Wilson studied the message alone at the White House, the news swept Washington and awakened government officials in London and Paris. In New York, the harbor was sealed to traffic, and policemen were called away from the annual patrolmen's ball to increase the watch over eight German passenger ships interned at their docks in Hoboken since the war's beginning. Three days later, the President went before a cheering joint session of Congress and announced that the United States was severing diplomatic relations with Germany. Before the month was out, he took the step tantamount to declaring war, asking Congress to arm American merchant ships.

Averell Harriman was then twenty-five years old and the father of a month-old daughter, named Mary in honor of his mother. The war in Europe was not among the things uppermost in his mind. He had set out upon his ordained course of assuming the work of his father. In the offices and shops of the Union Pacific, he was now Mr. Harriman. To a few of the elders who had been closest to E.H., he was still Averell, but otherwise the time for easy familiarity with the son of the boss was gone.

He was precisely where his father would have wished him to be, fulfilling the eldest son's family obligations, performing a respectable amount of public service, and learning the railroad business from the lieutenants the Little Giant had trusted most. Though Averell's sympathy was unequivocally on the side of the Allies, he had developed no passionate feelings about the conflict in Europe. Nor had anyone else in the family. Teddy Roosevelt and his friends in the forefront of the preparedness movement, they all thought, had been, as usual, unnecessarily bellicose in urging the United States toward a conflict that might still remain a European affair.

They took no big hand in politics, but they had enjoyed satisfaction in the withering of Roosevelt's political fortunes, especially after his Bull Moose revolt split the Republican party and helped put a Democrat in the White House. Although they remained steadfast Republicans, they found much to admire in Wilson's neutrality and much to support in his commitment to a powerful influence overseas without entanglement in Europe's political upheavals.

About the time the fighting broke out in the summer of 1914, Averell had completed his Union Pacific internship in Omaha and returned to New York. As a new vice-president, he was in charge of $50 million worth of purchases each year, acquiring everything from desk calendars and table linens to crossties, track bolts, and locomotives. But he was still in training and his mentor was comptroller Charles B. Seger, whose sharp pencil and keen eye for waste had made him one of E.H.'s favorites. Bent on proving himself, Averell continued to put the European war out of mind even after the sinking of the *Lusitania* and the explosion of the military-preparedness movement across the country.

While he and Kitty honeymooned in the summer and fall of 1915, hundreds of young and middle-aged executives and financiers, including many of his classmates from Yale, developed rudimentary military skills at a tent camp on the shores of Lake Champlain near Plattsburgh. Paying for their own uniforms and equipment, they spent hours in saber practice, marched in close-order drill, dug trenches, waged mock battles under the guidance of professional soldiers, and bivouacked in six-man tents. Averell briefly considered getting his own uniform and marching shoes, but playing soldier was not his style.

At Yale, Roland had already seen many of his friends leave school for flight training. Judge Lovett's son Bob had dropped out in his sophomore year to help organize a squadron getting ready for a possible war with Mexico, but he would later transfer to the Navy and win the Navy Cross for flying dangerous submarine patrols off the coast of France. After waiting impatiently for graduation in 1917, Roland took a commission in the Army Ordnance Corps and, anxious to get into combat, applied for the artillery; but he was stricken by pneumonia, then diagnosed as having tuberculosis, and wound up in an Army hospital rather than a trench.

Mary Harriman provided the government with money to construct swimming pools at posts where aviation cadets were in training and gave her aging yacht to the Navy. The elegant old steamer was armed with depth charges and sent on futile submarine patrols, the living spaces filled to the brim with coal.

Averell was slow to comprehend the implications of the war for America and for himself. With the country torn by a thousand political crosscurrents and led by an administration passionately committed to neutrality, he believed for months that it could remain on the sidelines of the conflict. If neutrality failed, American men would still be removed from combat by three thousand miles of salt water.

When he finally did broach the subject of military service to his mother, he found her sternly opposed. He had his responsibilities not only to his wife, whose frail health was a concern from the day of their marriage, but to the larger Harriman family. If war did come, he could do something far more important than shoulder a rifle or serve as a junior officer. Still, he obviously could not watch the United States go to war while he continued as vice-president of the railroad. Across the West, there was already a fiercely held notion that wealthy New Yorkers like the Harrimans were enriching themselves every month that the fighting in Europe dragged on—which was more or less true.

In the autumn of 1916, after Congress passed a massive prepared-ness bill authorizing emergency acquisition of a huge merchant shipping fleet, Averell began looking for a shipyard to buy. The United States faced a crisis in sustaining its commercial interests in Europe, even should it remain neutral in the war. And if neutrality failed, as appeared increas-ingly likely, America would, at the least, have to supply the Allies with convoys of food, fuel, ships, guns, and ammunition, if not troops. The transportation requirements would be staggering. "Shipping," he con-cluded, "would prove the neck of the bottle."[3] It was an opportunity for wartime service as worthy as combat was conspicuous—and it was, potentially, profitable.

There was no American merchant marine worthy of the name. U.S. shipyards could in no way compete with British facilities, nor could the country's ship operators challenge modern foreign fleets served by crews working for a fraction of American seamen's pay. Statistics that ranked the United States as the world's number three merchant power, behind Britain and Germany, were deceptive, for much of the American fleet was confined to the Great Lakes. As a matter of fact, American vessels carried no more than 10 percent of the country's foreign trade in the year before the war broke out in Europe.[4]

It was obvious that the United States would face an industrial task unprecedented in its history if it entered the conflict. A lifeline to Europe would require not only creation of a real merchant marine but a vigorous construction program to replace tonnage lost to German submarines' war of attrition. Already, shipyards were pushed to the limit, with three fourths of their shipways occupied by vessels under construction for an expanded Navy.

Two days before the German ambassador delivered the message recanting his country's pledge to spare neutral merchant ships from torpedo attack, Harriman, with his mother's financial backing, bought a shipyard.

In Chester, Pennsylvania, just down the Delaware River from Phila-delphia, the fifty-six-year-old Roach yard had in better times been an important shipbuilding center. Ten years before Averell was born, three thousand men had worked there, annually turning out ten merchant vessels. C. P. M. Jack, a retired Navy captain, had been operating it for two years when the twenty-six-year-old Harriman acquired its deteriorat-ing shops and seven shipways where minesweepers were being con-structed for the Navy.

Resigning his Union Pacific vice-presidency, Harriman hired Jack as a consulting engineer and began modernizing the plant. What he had in mind was much more than continuing Navy contracts. Anticipating a crash program to build a merchant fleet, he also hired a man regarded by many as the foremost naval architect in the United States.[5]

Richard H. M. Robinson, a forty-two-year-old former Navy officer, had just completed the overhaul of the Lake Torpedo Boat Company in Bridgeport, Connecticut, taking a shipyard that was in financial and mechanical disarray and turning it into one of the finest in the country. His management ability was more than matched by his engineering skills. After graduation from the Naval Academy, he had gone on to graduate study of ship design at the University of Glasgow. Later he served for eight years as assistant to the chief constructor of the Navy and had overseen the building of the battleship *Connecticut*. He subsequently became the Navy's chief designer but retired out of financial necessity.

In addition to two decades of ship design and construction experience, Robinson had impressive political connections. His elder brother, Henry, a California lawyer and banker, had close ties to the Wilson administration and had turned down an invitation to join the Cabinet as secretary of the interior.

Knowing nothing of the shipbuilding business, Harriman made Robinson his chief adviser, executive officer, and confidant, and thus brought about one of the most enduring business associations he would ever have. They started their collaboration with an assault upon the most insurmountable obstacle to an American merchant fleet capable of changing the course of the war: the shortage of shipyards. Less than six months after hiring Robinson, Harriman took a train to Washington with documents and engineering drawings that would become known as "Design No. 371," a plan for mass-producing merchant ships.[6]

The details of the plan's creation were never recorded. But it was revolutionary, and like many revolutionary developments, it had diverse origins. Harriman deserved much of the credit, for as soon as he had bought the Roach yard, he hired the most accomplished ship designer he could find and put him to work on the problem. Robinson himself gave the credit to Captain Jack, the former owner who was still in Harriman's employ, and Max Willemstyn, the yard's engineering manager.[7] In any case, it was young Harriman's shipworks at Chester which produced the first complete plans for a "prefabricated" ocean freighter.

It was a clever scheme to speed shipbuilding by using components produced at far-flung welding shops, bridge companies, and truck plants, and delivering them to assembly yards where they would rapidly be riveted together. Engines, boilers, bulkheads, decks, and superstructures would be identical, making mass production possible and reducing the time a vessel occupied a shipway.

The idea was centuries old. The Roach yard had adopted it on a limited scale as far back as the turn of the century, and it was still used in a limited way when Harriman arrived, but its widespread application in the buildup of the American merchant fleet was one of the important engineering innovations of World War I.[8]

Two months after Germany's declaration of unrestricted submarine warfare, Americans were outraged to learn that Germany had urged Mexico to attack the United States if the Wilson administration joined the Allies in the European conflict. Followed by the quick sinking of three U.S. merchant vessels by U-boats, the revelation made it impossible for Wilson to resist the outright declaration of war any longer. Accompanied to Capitol Hill by a clattering squadron of cavalry, he went before a joint session of Congress on April 2 and asked lawmakers to declare the United States at war with the Central Powers. The Senate adopted the resolution two days later with only six dissenting votes, and at 3:15 A.M. the next day, the House followed suit. The President signed it that afternoon.

Two weeks later, when the U.S. Shipping Board authorized the Emergency Fleet Corporation to undertake a staggering $3.6 billion merchant shipbuilding program, engineering drawings for Harriman's "prefabricated" steel ship were ready, as were designs from scores of other shipbuilders, large and small, proposing steel, wood, and even concrete hulls.

Major General George Washington Goethals, the Army engineer who had been Teddy Roosevelt's ramrod of the Panama Canal construction, was summoned from retirement to take over the effort. He opened shop in four small offices three blocks east of the White House, where shipbuilders in search of contracts created pandemonium. Many of them were without qualification, and some falsely claimed to be already at work under agreements made with the Shipping Board.

Harriman was among dozens of contract hunters who had never built a ship; but unlike many of them, he had made massive preparations, including not only design work but signed agreements with subcontractors and suppliers, including United States Steel and American Bridge Company. The proposal promptly got Goethals's support, but the debate over which design could be built cheapest and fastest went on through the summer. Meanwhile, shipping losses to German submarines mounted to more than a million tons per month.

Goethals was for steel, but his boss, Shipping Board chairman William Denman, wanted to build a thousand wooden vessels because wood was cheaper and supplies were unlimited. The steel industry, on the other hand, was already hard-pressed to meet war demands. Goethals was unshakable in his conviction that steel vessels were superior, even if more expensive. They would be less vulnerable to torpedo attack, could be built larger, and when the war was over they would have a useful lifetime exceeding that of the most optimistic claims for wooden ships. Instead of a risky commitment to wooden hulls, he proposed to speed production of steel vessels by working construction gangs double shifts and swiftly opening new yards.

Harriman's plan was precisely what Goethals wanted to see. The design was simple, and it could be mass-produced. The trouble was that the standardized structures required for mass production gave the Harriman freighter the shape of a shoe box rather than a cruise liner. It had a flat bottom, flat sides, and a flat top, with sharp angles everywhere and a stubby bow and stern. It evoked anything but grace, speed or maneuverability, and some old sailors seriously questioned whether such an inelegant tub could be seaworthy.

The battle between the proponents of steel and wood took a heavy toll. In the end, the President had to fire both Goethals and Denman and take full control. Meanwhile, all of the 431 steel ships under construction in American yards were taken over by the government along with 97 German ships and 87 Dutch vessels interned at the beginning of the war. Edward N. Hurley became the new shipping czar and resolved the ship construction dispute by agreeing with both sides. The United States, he declared, would build 1,700 new steel ships and 1,000 wooden ships.

The most urgent initiative was the construction of three government yards to build prefabricated steel freighters along the lines of Harriman's proposal. Selected to build one of the three yards, Averell found himself with a challenge that would have tested E.H. himself.

As the first small contingents of doughboys arrived in Europe, his Merchants' Shipbuilding Company began work at a 270-acre site at Bristol, Pennsylvania, twenty-five miles up the Delaware from Philadelphia. The operation required construction of shops and facilities to build a dozen freighters at a time, as well as a new town for twelve thousand workers. Averell brought in an old steamer, the *Cape May*, and docked it at the shore to provide living quarters for the first construction gangs. Carpenters, steelworkers, and laborers by the hundreds were soon swarming over the site from dawn until dusk, putting down shipways and raising houses, barracks, stores, a hospital, a movie theater, a post office, and a five-hundred-room Spanish mission—style hotel. Wedged between the bank of the Delaware and the tracks of the Pennsylvania Railroad, the buildings were as austere and unstylish as Averell's cargo ship itself.

Harriman bought himself a comfortable bungalow overlooking the river and acquired a motor launch, christened *Wah Wah*, to shuttle back and forth between the new shipyard community of "Harriman, Pa.," and his property downstream at Chester.

At the Roach yard, welders and riveters rushed to complete Navy minesweepers in order to clear facilities for work on forty freighters ordered by the Emergency Fleet Corporation. Before the first prefabricated hull was in place, Averell had signed a contract for twenty more, the government agreeing to pay him a fee of $64,000 per ship, with bonuses up to $15,000 each for early delivery.

The search for patriotic, noncombat wartime employment was not Harriman's sole motivation for going into shipbuilding. Though he had liked his position at the Union Pacific, he faced the prospect of waiting years for retirements and death to lift him up the company ladder. The railroad would never again expand as it had in E.H.'s day, meaning there would be fewer opportunities to move up, even if his name was Harriman. The company was becoming bureaucratic; the industry was beset by increasing competition from trucks and automobiles. Although Judge Lovett was not far from E. H. Harriman in age, he belonged to an earlier generation and had neither the authority nor disposition to dominate the Union Pacific personally the way E.H. had.

Even if he had been certain that he would someday claim his father's seat as Union Pacific chairman, Averell knew he could never escape E.H's enormous shadow. The most important thing he had learned during his months as an intern and junior vice-president was that he would always be "the boy." To make a mark of his own, he had to find his place outside the railroad industry. Shipbuilding came about almost by accident, his interest first aroused by a Yale classmate who had gone into the coconut business in the Philippines.

When the fighting broke out in Europe, the business ran into trouble because the steamships that transported coconuts to the United States were pressed into transatlantic service. Harriman casually suggested that his friend "buy a couple of ships" and offered to help him arrange the financing.[9] The problem, they soon found, was that vessels were not to be had. On Wall Street, Averell quickly got confirmation of what he might have already known—it was a perfect moment to invest in shipbuilding. Britain had captured or driven German merchant vessels from the high seas, and most of London's own commercial fleet had been diverted to military service. The consequent shortage of merchant tonnage and the German submarine campaign drove construction prices, shipping rates and profits to record heights.

Between 1914 and 1917, petroleum freight rates between New York and Liverpool shot from $4 to $50 per ton. Cotton freights from New Orleans to Liverpool increased from 45 cents per hundred pounds to

$6.25. Prices for ships doubled and doubled again.[10] Boom times came to the American shipbuilding industry long before the United States entered the war. The long-range prospect, Harriman concluded, was for the United States to emerge from the war as a new maritime power rivaling Great Britain and Germany. Consequently, he had bought the Roach yard expecting to remain involved in shipbuilding and shipping long after the war was over.

His first winter in Pennsylvania was brutal, bringing the bitterest cold and the deepest snows in years. Shipyards along the Delaware were icebound for weeks. Loaded railroad cars were stranded in Philadelphia, and for days at a time work came to a halt on both Harriman's shipyard and the new town at Bristol. Progress was slow even in good weather because he encountered labor problems he had never imagined—workers lacking even basic hammer and saw skills and others merely seeking haven from the draft.

Still, in a little more than four months, the new ship town was nearly finished and keels had been laid for the first two freighters. It was, the Emergency Fleet Corporation's resident engineer said, "a remarkable achievement." Once work started on the first hulls, hundreds of rivet guns and hammers banging on steel plates created an unrelenting din that went on for eighteen hours a day. Workers were often left with their hearing permanently impaired. Others were blinded or scarred by shards of hot steel or flying rivets. Four of Harriman's men drowned during a ship launching when scaffolding gave way, dumping dozens of workers into the river only a few feet offshore.

In a brawling, hard-drinking atmosphere tinged with ethnic and racial tension but sustained with patriotic fervor, Harriman's yards sent their freighters down the shipways more or less meeting the schedules laid down by the Emergency Fleet Corporation. But the national effort to create a bridge of ships to Europe was never fully under control. The company waged a continuing, uphill battle against drinking on the job and spent heavily on recreational activities to provide diversion for the thousands of single men working in the yards. There were weekly boxing matches and a company baseball team that became so successful that Harriman was accused of hiring major-league players.

The town of Bristol was not altogether happy about the boomtown prosperity. Burnet Landreth, a wealthy seed merchant who had been its most prominent businessman before Harriman's arrival, carped about the "fabulous profiteering by Harriman and his gang" and the behavior of construction workers building the new town. "This crowd," he wrote in his diary, "was composed of the worst element in the country. They ruined many cars belonging to the railroad, they behaved in a very ruffianlike manner at the railroad station, they thought they owned the whole town. They committed many assaults and many murders. The crush of bad men can only be compared to what might be done by a crowd from the Alaskan silver mines."[11]

Of more concern to Harriman than problems with the locals were official complaints from the Shipping Board and the Emergency Fleet Corporation. Inspectors, finding men sleeping on the job, charged management with laxity, and government auditors complained that company records were in such disarray that they were useless.

Harriman and Robinson blamed most of their problems on government foot-dragging and Shipping Board engineers' demands for picayunish changes that threw assembly work behind schedule. In an angry letter to Chairman Hurley, they complained that they couldn't operate full shifts because the steel plates were not arriving on schedule.[12] The truth was that the explosive buildup was more than the industry could handle. A call by the President for 250,000 shipyard workers had brought 300,000 men within a month. In the year after Averell bought the Roach yard, the population of Chester shot from 38,000 to 125,000.

When the historic flu epidemic struck in 1918, Chester was one of the first towns in the East forced to close its public facilities and meeting places. In shipbuilding communities all along the river, hospitals and clinics were so overtaxed that stricken residents had to be taken by boats to an emergency care station set up in the immigrant quarantine station at Sandy Hook, New Jersey. As many as half a million civilians died across the country, and rumors spread that the outbreak was the work of German agents. After the armistice, the Navy attributed more than five thousand deaths to the epidemic and the Army nearly forty-seven thousand.

Still, the chaos at Chester and Bristol paled in comparison to the havoc at the Hog Island yard operated by the American International Corporation, just south of Philadelphia. There, thirty thousand new workers reported in a year; and once in full operation, the yard saw a new keel laid every five and half days for one of the seven-thousand-ton cargo ships that came to be known in seaports of the world as "Hoggies." While Harriman's shipbuilders lived in stucco bunkhouses and family dwellings, immigrant workers at Hog Island lived in shacks and fed their hogs on Philadelphia garbage. There were labor troubles, charges of graft, and rumors that the yard was infected with pro-Germanism.

Like other shipbuilders who won contracts from the Emergency Fleet Corporation, Harriman saw his yards reach their capacity just as the armistice was signed in November 1918. Several of the Chester minesweepers were rushed into action by the Navy, but the war was nearing its end by the time Bristol launched its first freighter, and before a single ship from any of the new government yards was put into service, the fighting was over. Still, in three years, the United States' moribund shipbuilding industry had vaulted into world leadership, sending more tonnage down the ways in 1918 than any country in the world had ever launched in a single year.

Even at the peak of the war work, residents of Harriman, Pennsylvania, seldom saw the "young man from Yale," as they called Averell a little disdainfully. He left the shipbuilding to Dick Robinson and to William T. Smith, the manager of the Bristol yard, spending most of his time in New York and appearing in the Delaware Valley only for ceremonial launchings, Liberty Bond drives, and special occasions such as a Philadelphia parade of seventy thousand Delaware Valley shipyard workers protesting congressional criticism of the building program.

His absence was to some extent due to his wife's health. Two months after the birth of their first child in January 1917, Kitty Harriman became pregnant again, and in December, their second daughter, Kathleen Lanier Harriman, was born. Kitty was slow to bounce back. She had been seriously weakened by her pregnancies, the first coming not long after her riding accident. In the months after Kathleen's birth, she spent much of her time outside the city—at the "railroad ranch" in Idaho, at her grandfather's summer place in Massachusetts, or at Overhills, North Carolina, where Averell hunted and played polo.

Initially, her doctors thought she would recover within a few months. In August 1918, she was able to make her first and last visit to Harriman, Pennsylvania, to christen her husband's first freighter. She toured the community and the shipyard, and stood for more than an hour at the launching ceremony. She dutifully smashed the bottle of champagne and christened the 418-foot *Watonwan*, but when the blocks were knocked away, the freighter refused to slide into the water. Days after Kitty was back in New York, workers urged the first Harriman ship into the water without fanfare.

In September came confirmation of earlier suspicions that she was suffering from tuberculosis. "Dr. Brown had an x-ray taken last week and Kitty has just written me that there was still a blur in both lungs," Averell wrote his mother, who was visiting the Crocker family in San Francisco. "It is a pretty hard blow as Dr. Miller gave her such hope last spring of things clearing up by the fall. It will probably mean that New York will not be possible this winter. Things are still so indefinite that we are not saying anything about it yet until we can make definite plans. Kitty is very plucky and uncomplaining but it is quite a blow to her. She has been forced to be out of things and feeling badly so consistently for so many years now that it is discouraging."[13]

Soon after the armistice, the government canceled its contract for the last twenty Harriman freighters. Anticipating that, Averell had already planned to use the enormous merchant fleet the government had on its hands with the end of the war as a shortcut into the general steamship business in which he would lease and operate surplus government-owned tonnage. It was hardly a novel idea; the U.S. Shipping Board was deluged by proposals from bankers, shippers, and entrepreneurs with the same thing in mind. Unlike most of the others, however, Averell was thinking on a grand scale. His larger strategy was to expand quickly into ownership of his own merchant vessels, tying financing, construction, and operation together in the manner of the European maritime empires, and to strike out into international trade.

New York, he was certain, was about to become the world's financial center, with U.S. merchant ships carrying exports in volumes never dreamed. He wholeheartedly embraced the Wilson administration's view that long-term prosperity required the United States to move aggressively into foreign trade.[14] He was, he said, "profoundly convinced that the necessity for developing American shipping is upon us."[15] It was his chance to do as E.H. had done in 1897 when E.H. sensed the first faint pulse of economic recovery and went after control of the bankrupt Union Pacific. With his mother again backing him, he went shopping for ships.

"I didn't mean at all to ask you to furnish the funds for our enterprise," he wrote to her in February 1919, "but I did want you to know what I was doing so that, if for some reason or other—a world panic— my loans were called, I could feel you would stand back of me & that you approved of it before I started & not disapproved of it afterwards. I can finance the deal all right with a legitimate use of the securities you gave me to back a loan & had intended to do so, but since you have suggested it, I would much prefer to get the funds from you & and pay you more interest than you can get from other investments & guarantee the loan so that if it is not successful, you or the estate will not lose.

"I have enough securities other than the ones you have given me, which I can sell and pay off the loss. In other words I want to stand on my own feet, face the risk personally & and take the profits."[16]

He acquired his first important shipping interest in April, obtaining for about $7 million a one-fifth interest in the American-Hawaiian Steamship Company, one of the more solid merchant shipping operations under the American flag. Founded in 1889, the company had prospered in the sugar trade, carrying cargoes to and from the east coast of the United States in the days before the Panama Canal. When the United States entered the war, the company was operating sixteen steamships in the eight-thousand- to thirteen-thousand-ton class, and thirteen of them had been requisitioned by the government to serve as transports for the Army.

To his ten thousand shares purchased from the Mexican government, Averell added several smaller purchases over the following months while enticing his friends to acquire shares of their own. At the first board meeting after his initial acquisition, he was named vice-president of the company. Just a year later he became president, when George S. Dearborn, one of the commanding figures of the American shipping industry, died. By then, he had also gained control of his first three steamships based on the East Coast by buying out W. H. Randall and Company, a Boston shipping business, and its operating subsidiary, the Shawmut Steamship Company.

Again backed by his mother, along with the Guaranty Trust Company, and with Percy Rockefeller and several other friends taking an interest, he then organized W. A. Harriman and Company as the financing arm of his new empire. It acquired Monks, Godwin and Shaw, a firm with a well-established maritime insurance underwriting business, and moved into its own building on lower Broadway's Shippers' Row. Before the first month was out, W. A. Harriman and Company closed a $6.5 million deal to purchase the Coastwise Transportation Company in Boston and its fleet of ten new colliers.[17]

Seeking a share of the international trade that had belonged to Germany before the war, Averell quietly departed for Berlin in April 1920, hoping for an arrangement with Hamburg-American Line, which had been the world's premier shipping company before the war. The company was still a vast repository of expertise, but its docks were vacant, its warehouses in Europe and America empty, its mighty fleet dispersed by the victorious governments. Some former Hamburg-American vessels now sailed the oceans under new names and flags, while others rusted in ports where they had been docked after the armistice. Among several deteriorating at anchor in New York was the 54,000-ton *Vaterland*, reputed to be the world's largest ship. Impounded by the United States at the outbreak of the war, it had later been renamed the *Leviathan* and used to transport 558,000 American troops across the Atlantic.

Since the war, Hamburg-American had been casting longing eyes toward both England and America in hopes of arranging a marriage that would enable it to use foreign ships to resume service on its routes. The U.S. Shipping Board had similar ideas, seeing the Germans' route structure and port facilities as a shortcut to American maritime supremacy. Board officials enlisted Will G. Sickel, a German-American who had represented Hamburg-American in New York before the war, to sound out his old employers on reopening their trade routes under an arrangement with American interests in control. Sickel returned from Berlin with a draft contract and word that the Germans were ready to come to Washington to formalize an agreement. But Shipping Board officials had backed away from an alliance, deciding that a cooperative venture properly belonged in the hands of private enterprise.

Although he was quick to go after German routes, Harriman had powerful competition from the American Ship and Commerce Corporation, organized at the same time he was putting together his own maritime conglomerate. Headed by General Goethals, the first boss of the Emergency Fleet Corporation, and Teddy Roosevelt's youngest son, Kermit, the company controlled Philadelphia's venerable Cramp shipyard and the Kerr Navigation Company, which had a fleet of ten steamships. Goethals and Roosevelt had reached the Germans first, hoping to secure a pact to operate their routes and gain the needed vessels from the Shipping Board. But the board refused to guarantee them the ships they needed and the negotiations collapsed. Conveniently for Averell, the impasse occurred just as he was preparing to sail for Europe.

He remained abroad for several weeks, spending most of the time in Germany, where he and Wilhelm Cumo, Hamburg-American's director general, assembled the framework of an agreement for Harriman to provide the ships with which to reestablish passenger service between New York and Hamburg. Under the arrangement, he and Hamburg-American would have a fifty-fifty role in furnishing additional tonnage, when and if it became necessary. Each would provide half of the vessels for the freight service between Germany and the United States and between Germany and other countries. Hamburg-American would offer technical expertise, port facilities, and its prewar route structure and act as agent for the American line in European ports, while the Harriman organization would represent the Germans in the United States.

Averell returned to New York elated, anxious to present his triumph to the Shipping Board.

The last of the emergency wartime agencies remaining in existence, the Shipping Board had become one of the most controversial of Washington's bureaucracies. Already experienced in dealing with it, Harriman understood the perils ahead of him. Concerned that the board might resume its own negotiations with the Germans, he went to Admiral William S. Benson, its chairman, as soon as he returned from Europe. After explaining his agreement, he followed up the meeting with a letter reiterating his case:

> It has occurred to us in addition to the information we left with you on May 5th, it is advisable to give you a complete picture of the shipping activities of our group:
>
> 1. We build ships.
> 2. We finance ships.
> 3. We own ships.
> 4. We operate ships.
> 5. We insure ships.
>
> It is our feeling that our activities, covering as they do many phases in the marine field, present a rather unique picture so

far as America is concerned, although, of course, there are
similar combinations in England. In conclusion, perhaps it is not
out of place to point out to you that our complete organization
probably has a broader and more real ship knowledge than
perhaps any other in this country.[18]

In spite of the pitch, Benson was not impressed with the arrangement. "At first sight," he wrote Harriman after reviewing the document,
"the impression made is anything but satisfactory."[19] His skepticism had
justification, because Harriman was not prepared to carry out the obligations he proposed to assume. Most of his steamships were committed to
Pacific and coastal routes. He did not yet have an organization capable
of operating the old Hamburg-American schedules. Moreover, American Ship and Commerce was still in the competition.

Briefed on the continuing efforts of Goethals and Roosevelt, Harriman struck on a scheme worthy of E.H. in his prime. He went to Philip M.
Chandler and Company, the financier underwriting American Ship and
Commerce, with a bold scheme to take over American Ship and Commerce just as his father had tried to take control of the Northern Pacific
Railroad from James J. Hill. Chandler, having exhausted his patience
with the ineffective efforts of Goethals and Roosevelt, listened to Harriman's scenario fascinated. Seeing the possibility of both profits and a
U.S. foothold in trade competition with Britain, he agreed to join Averell
in taking control.

With Chandler as his intermediary, Harriman then offered American Ship and Commerce his agreement with Hamburg-American in
exchange for being taken into the company. Their foot in the door, W.
A. Harriman and Company and Philip Chandler and Company bought
100,000 shares of stock at $25 a share, with options on another 100,000
at the same price. It was enough to give the two of them control, and
they promptly elected Harriman president, deposing General Goethals
in a coup engineered with astonishing ease. With that, Averell took over
the ten freighters owned by Kerr Navigation Company, including those
already operating between New York and Hamburg. Impressed, Benson
and the Shipping Board were ready to give the Harriman arrangement
with Cumo their blessing.

The announcement that he controlled American Ship and Commerce and was entering an operating arrangement with the Hamburg-
American Line catapulted the Harriman name into the headlines—not
since E.H. panicked Wall Street during the Northern Pacific affair had
the name been so prominently on display. For the first time, Averell had
a public identity of his own. He was no longer just the son of E. H.
Harriman. He was now "Harriman, the Steamship King."

Coming as it did during a high tide of postwar chauvinism, the alliance with the German company stirred a political uproar. It was held up by critics as a blueprint for the restoration of Germany as a maritime giant at the United States' expense. Hamburg-American's very name fired the emotions of Americans who had not forgotten how the company's ships had served as bases for spies and saboteurs during the long months when they were interned in U.S. ports.

Although Harriman was not publicly attacked for it, the fact that he had not served in uniform during the war was not forgotten. Some of his old Yale friends thought his behavior shameful—first avoiding service in uniform, then rushing into a lucrative business collaboration with the Germans. His former roommates, Charley Marshall and George Dixon, stopped speaking to him for years. Most members of Yale '13 had fought in the war, and eight of them had been killed. "Averell was regarded as something much less than the beau ideal during those days," said his friend Bob Lovett, who had been one of the first American flyers sent to France by the naval air service.[20]

Cutting their ties with American Ship and Commerce as soon as Harriman took control, Goethals and Roosevelt attacked the Harriman–Hamburg-American deal as egregiously tilted in favor of the Germans. They were joined by the general counsel of the Shipping Board, who urged Benson to withhold approval on grounds that it would lead to "the promotion of German rather than American commerce." Editorial writers demanded a congressional investigation.

"That another German plot to injure the United States has been discovered must now be apparent to everyone who peruses the daily press," declared *The Nation*, a respected voice of moderation. "The contract between the Hamburg-American Line and the Harriman shipping interests has been so beclouded by charges and counter charges, by criminations and recriminations, by revelations as to the conduct of Hamburg-American officials during the war, that any reader is entitled to feel that the Germans have been caught once more at their old tricks. True, Admiral Benson is most emphatically in favor of the contract, and somehow one does not regard a Harriman as the kind of person who readily has the wool pulled over his eyes, but even this will not avail. Plainly, America has been gulled once more."[21]

The most serious opposition came from Alfred E. Clegg, a onetime Shipping Board employee who had headed an American Ship and Commerce subsidiary. During the war, Clegg and his partner, H. Farquharson Kerr, had bought eight Austrian steamers which had been taken over by the U.S. government. The story was that their firm, Kerr Navigation Company, had reaped windfall profits by charging as much as $160 per ton to deliver cargo through German and Austrian submarine patrols to ports in the Mediterranean. With the armistice, they were positioned to begin quick service to South America and Japan as well as to Europe and

Scandinavia. One of their freighters was the first commercial vessel to dock at Hamburg when the United States again licensed trade with Germany.[22] When American Ship and Commerce was formed in 1919, Kerr Navigation Company became its operating subsidiary; and in the company's discussions with Hamburg-American, Clegg was its principal negotiator.

American Ship and Commerce held an option to acquire Kerr and Clegg's vessels, and as soon as Harriman took over the presidency of the parent company, he announced plans to exercise it. He needed the ships to fulfill his commitment to the Germans, but he also wanted to get rid of Kerr and Clegg. That both were British subjects made him vulnerable to allegations that his organization was further tainted by foreign influences.

Under their arrangements with American Ship and Commerce, Kerr and Clegg were to receive cash payment for their vessels upon exercise of the option. A Harriman emissary met the pair in the lobby of the Chase National Bank on lower Broadway one Saturday morning in late August and escorted them to a safe deposit where they were given their $4.9 million in stacks of crisp $10,000 bills. But before they could get out the door with their money, they were intercepted by U.S. Treasury agents, who impounded the cash on grounds that they were about to take it out of the country without paying excess profits taxes. It was never established that Harriman had anything to do with tipping the government to the transaction, but the circumstances suggested that he had personally let officials know about the payment, perhaps suggesting that Clegg and Kerr were about to leave the country without meeting their tax obligation.

Under a law passed just months before in an effort to shore up the U.S. merchant marine, they were exempt from excess profits tax on the sale of their ships as long as they intended to reinvest the money in the U.S. maritime industry. This, they stoutly insisted, had been their plan.

Angry at having their fleet captured and their money impounded, leaving their shipping ambitions in tatters, they retaliated. When the steamer *Kerlew*, one of the vessels Averell had bought, arrived from Hamburg and docked at a Harriman pier in Brooklyn a week later, burly longshoremen sent by Clegg and Kerr boarded the ship and took control. It was six A.M., and by the time Harriman reached his office, a tug had moved his ship to a Fifty-seventh Street dock belonging to Kerr and Clegg, and its cargo was being unloaded by the former owners. Before he could decide how to respond, he was served with a restraining order signed by Justice Richard H. Mitchell of the New York Supreme Court, explicitly barring Harriman from retaking possession. Chagrined at being hijacked and then legally outflanked, Harriman and Richard Robinson, the new vice-president of Kerr Navigation, went into federal court in the afternoon and got an order that put U.S. marshals aboard the *Kerlew* and stopped further cargo from being unloaded.

The maneuver was only momentarily successful, for back in the state supreme court, Justice Mitchell took heated exception to having his mandate so cavalierly brushed aside by a federal judge. He held Harriman, Robinson, and Ira Campbell, their lawyer, in criminal contempt of court, announcing that all three would immediately be sent to jail unless they undid their mischief.

With that, Averell meekly withdrew his federal court action, removed the marshals from the *Kerlew*, and returned the ship's papers to Clegg and Kerr. The New York court then issued an injunction preventing him from taking possession of the eight steamships until October 22, ninety days after the agreement was signed. The decision allowed two of the vessels to make another round trip to Hamburg for Kerr and Clegg before the transfer became effective.

It was not until the dispute broke out over possession of the *Kerlew* that the newspapers learned of the secret cash payment and the impoundment of the $4.9 million. Embarrassed by the whole affair, Harriman stayed out of sight, but Clegg and Roosevelt were more than willing to accommodate reporters, suggesting that the worst of the tale was yet to be told. The seizure of Kerr and Clegg's cash, Roosevelt contended, was nothing but a Harriman-orchestrated plot "to stifle all shipping competition."[23]

But the chief objection that they and other critics raised to Averell's deal with Hamburg-American was that it permitted the Germans to provide half of the new ships to be added to the jointly operated routes. Since American ships would make up the entire fleet at the beginning, they contended that American-flag vessels would have to be withdrawn once Germany started building ships again. In this light, Harriman's twenty-year contract was held up as nothing more than a clever German maneuver to use American ships to preserve German routes until they could be reclaimed with German vessels—in short, a blueprint for the return of the German merchant marine to world dominance.

The controversy went on through the summer. Admiral Benson and the Shipping Board stood firmly with Harriman in defense of the agreement, the formerly skeptical chairman having decided that it was a heaven-sent opportunity for the American merchant marine. His endorsement and heavy lobbying by the Shipping Board were not enough to calm the uproar, and Harriman concluded the only way to stop the hounding by the press and avoid a prolonged investigation by Congress was to make the entire agreement public.

On October 6, 1920, New York's major newspapers printed the full text. When it appeared, Kermit Roosevelt declared that the document only confirmed his contention that it miserably failed to protect American interests. Clegg claimed that Harriman still withheld separate agreements containing the most serious concessions to the Germans. But the tactic worked. The public accepted Benson's conclusion that Harriman was "a full blooded American citizen," said *The New York Times*, and Harriman was to be commended for "the risks he is taking in his attempts to develop American shipping."[24]

That chapter closed, Harriman controlled one of the largest merchant fleets in the world. His routes, including the joint service with Hamburg-American, extended from New York, around Cape Horn, and into the Pacific. His ships sailed as far north as Hamburg, as far south as Capetown, and across the Far East beyond Manila, Hong Kong, and Yokohama, to Vladivostok.[25] To simplify his management and control over the companies he had bought, created, or reorganized, he brought them all together under the banner of United American Lines, with Harris Livermore as president.

The wheeling and dealing that put him in command of the largest merchant fleet under the American flag would have warmed his father's heart. E.H. had been fifty years old when he became chairman of the Union Pacific's executive committee and started his historic rebuilding of the bankrupt road, but his son, now hailed as "Harriman II" and "the Steamship King," was not yet thirty.

The shipping experience had taught Averell at least one lesson which eluded his father to the end—that it was sometimes necessary to fight bad publicity. His exposure to the spotlight during the Hamburg-American uproar was excruciating, and after it was over he sat down, as his father never did, and discussed his business and his ambitions with journalists.

Forbes Magazine published a breathless interview in which B. C. Forbes himself boasted that he was revealing "the first pen picture of this new captain of industry." The interviewer was reverent, and Averell was stiff, defensive, and unctuous, his reflections an amalgamation of E. H. Harriman and Endicott Peabody discourses on the obligations of wealth and the nobility of labor.

It was indefensible, he said, for a rich man not to use his money to benefit his country:

> Idle capital or capital misapplied is as destructive economically as the conduct of the loafing workman or the bomb thrower.
>
> It is the duty of everyone, rich or poor, to work. The rich man must not apply his money or his effort for purely selfish purposes. His duty is to consider how he can do the most to develop his nation's resources along sound lines and thus pro-

vide useful remunerative employment to as many breadwinners as possible.

The man who uses the dollar as a yardstick to measure the success, or non-success, of his activities, and who doesn't take very much broader—national—considerations into account is not the highest type of citizen, nor does he get the fullest satisfaction out of life. I am striving to do the thing which I believe is the best and the most important thing I can do for the interests of America. I love work—I cannot see how anyone could prefer to be idle.

When I took up this work I am now in, I fully expected to encounter all sorts of difficulties and knotty problems. Therefore, I am not in the least bit discouraged over the criticisms that are being leveled at me. I am willing to have my work tested by time and by results. I am trying to build not for today only, but for ten, twenty, and more years ahead.

His contract with Hamburg-American was just an example of his building for the future, "merely a step towards the great ultimate object" of making the United States the mercantile power of the world. "Even shipping itself is but a means to an end."[26]

He talked to the *Marine Review* in the same vein. For the first time, he even invited comparison to E.H. "Father always had a desire to build up merchant shipping," he said, "but during his day the opportunity was not right."[27]

Nor, as it turned out, was the opportunity right for Averell. Tactically, he had been brilliant in his negotiations with the Germans and in gaining control of American Ship and Commerce, but strategically, he had been fatally shortsighted. The eighteen-month economic boom that followed the war and heavy American investment in foreign trade had temporarily concealed a stupendous global surplus of merchant ships, most of it in the hands of the United States.[28]

In his Delaware shipyards, there had been enough commercial business at first to take up some of the slack left by cancellation of the emergency fleet vessels. At Chester, there was work on new freighters for the Shawmut Steamship Company and on diesel-powered motor ships for the American-Hawaiian line. Other contracts were lined up to build ten-thousand-ton oil tankers for the Atlantic, Gulf and West Indies Steamship Company, Union Oil Company, and Tidewater Oil Company.

But by 1920, when he was completing his Hamburg-American coup, the high tide of the economic boom had passed. When the government work was finished, employment at his yards dropped to less than half of the wartime peak, and shipways stood idle. The Bristol and Chester shipbuilding operations were merged, workers' housing at Chester was sold off, and lawyers were negotiating to wind up his government contracts.

Shortages of railroad cars disrupted delivery of materials, causing such a pileup of ship components in suppliers' storage yards that expensive parts were lost or buried wholesale. Interest rates soared; ship orders slacked off; foreign competition increased; and British shipbuilders dumped surplus tonnage on the market at prices grossly undercutting American yards. Averell was hit by strikes: first the carpenters and painters, and then the metal tradesmen. Shipping companies lost interest in prefab freighters, turning to specialty vessels, but even there orders were hard to find. Just as Averell was about to lay the keel for the first of six tankers for Atlantic Gulf and West Indies Steamship Company, the whole order was canceled.

He sold his house at Bristol, turned his personal launch, *Wah Wah*, over to the company, and negotiated an agreement for the government to assume ownership of the town he had built. His final claim submitted to the government came to $10 million, but after a year of discussions he settled for $560,000 and the deed to the Victory Hotel. At Robinson's recommendation, he took his Chester organization out of shipbuilding and into general engineering services. New forecasts saw even darker times ahead for shipbuilders.[29]

Besides running global cargo lines, Harriman entered his alliance with Hamburg-American expecting to capture a healthy share of the booming North Atlantic steerage trade. Through 1919 and 1920, the flow of European immigrants mounted steadily, exceeding fifty thousand a month, causing some ships bound for the overwhelmed Ellis Island to be diverted to Boston.[30]

He launched his passenger service on Christmas Day, 1920, sending his steamer *Mount Clay* out of New York to Hamburg. The vessel had belonged to the Germans under the name of *Prinz Eitel Friedrich* before being detained, but it had been taken over by the United States and renamed the *DeKalb*.

While owned by the Shipping Board, it had been ravaged by fire, and Harriman, picking it up for $800,000, had refurbished it. Introducing the Harriman–Hamburg-American third-class passenger service, the vessel, renamed once again, provided new comfort and dignity for immigrants traveling to America. Followed into the transatlantic service by the *Mount Carroll* and the *Mount Clinton*, the ships provided sitting rooms, smoking rooms, cabins accommodating two to six passengers, washstands, mattresses, and clean linens—amenities never dreamed of by earlier immigrants, who crossed the Atlantic like cattle, crowded into open steerage.[31]

The service began with soaring expectations, Averell believing that still more ships would be needed soon after the first three were in service. Even before the first sailing, he was urging the State Department to station an official in Hamburg to issue American visas so chaos would not be caused by thousands of emigrants seeking to board his ships. Because the United States was still technically at war with Germany, the request got nowhere. Nevertheless, he predicted the third-class traffic would be "heavy, and we believe continuous."[32]

Congress soon changed that with the "percentum act." The new law put national quotas on immigration. It had been pocket vetoed by Woodrow Wilson, but in May 1921 it was sent to President Harding. With his signature, it restricted the yearly number of immigrants from any country to three percent of the number of persons born in that country who were in the United States in 1910.

That limited the influx from southern and eastern Europe, where Harriman got most of his steerage traffic. He did not object to the new law on grounds of discrimination, as did its most vocal critics, but because it would cut third-class passenger traffic "to less than half of the capacity of shipping in the Atlantic trade." It would, he said, mean "ruin to new American passenger lines."[33]

But in spite of the restriction, his third-class passenger trade was profitable. His three cabin ships usually arrived fully loaded. As the vessels came into New York Harbor, Harriman clerks carrying suitcases of cash boarded an Immigration Service cutter at daybreak to meet them. They scrambled up rope ladders to hand out requisite packets of $25 to each immigrant before they were herded through an Ellis Island medical receiving station where LCDs and DCDs—those with "loathesome contagious diseases" or "dangerous contagious diseases"—were detained. The former, usually with active venereal disease, were shipped back to Europe, the latter segregated for treatment.[34]

While Harriman could blame Congress for limiting his prospects in the third-class passenger trade, his larger problem was that he had not appreciated the signs of economic retreat around him as he put millions into his shipping operations during 1919 and 1920. The United States was sliding into a depression along with the rest of the world, and just as he completed his Hamburg-American arrangement, the bottom fell out of the shipping business.

The huge surplus of ships having become obvious, Congress tried to speed the government's turnover of the emergency fleet to private hands, but the Shipping Board was stuck with hundreds of idle vessels. By March of 1921, 35 percent of the government-owned ships were docked, and the figure was mounting to an eventual 70 percent.[35]

Having used the Shipping Board to help him build his fleet, Harriman became one of its bitterest critics. Cargo ships on his major routes sailed half empty, and he had to go to the board for cash advances to maintain some of the vessels he operated for it. He continued to demand withdrawal of government ships from the seas, taking aim on such competition anywhere he could find an important public forum. The content of his message was often as bombastic as his delivery was stultifying. Before the convention of the National Merchant Marine Association in Washington, he acidly complained that his business had been disrupted because government ships were "operated by persons who are totally disinterested in whether the ships are run at a profit or at a loss."[36]

He was especially irritated by competition from Shipping Board vessels on the routes of his American-Hawaiian line. Under these circumstances, he complained in a speech to the National Republican Club in New York, it was impossible to make money, because the shipowners' conference was tied to rates that could not be cut to match competition from government-owned vessels. "The Shipping Board has made an agreement with us on rates and is maintaining those rates. So we are going to tell the government that we will get out of the conference unless it takes its ships out of the trade."[37]

The threat of a rate-cutting war against government-owned freighters infuriated Admiral Benson, who replied with an accusation that Harriman had been naively taken in by the "insidious influences" of the International Mercantile Marine Company, which operated ships under both the British and the American flags.

"I have stood fearlessly and strongly behind you in the Hamburg-American combination, and have been severely criticized by the public press for my stand in connection with you and your company in this matter," he told Harriman in a stinging letter, "so I feel I am warranted in telling you very frankly that your attitude toward the officials of the I. M. M. in your address here, and your attack upon the Shipping Board and its methods . . . indicates very strongly to my mind that you have been won over by the representatives of the International Mercantile Marine Company and other shipping interests in New York that are known to be inimical to the proper development of an American merchant marine."[38]

Harriman's problems with the Shipping Board were minor compared to those suffered by his chief competitor, the U. S. Mail Steamship Company. The latter had formed an alliance with North German Lloyd along the lines of Averell's arrangement with Hamburg-American. With thirteen government-owned ships to operate the North German Lloyd schedules, the U. S. Mail combine fell into serious trouble, the Shipping Board complaining that it had "failed to meet the conditions and obligations" of its contract and "failed to show anything like sufficient energy and efficiency."[39]

As tightened immigration and the depression on both sides of the ocean cut into passenger traffic, U. S. Mail dropped $400,000 behind in its lease payments to the board, and drifted into financial crisis. Officials suspected it of fleecing immigrants by diverting funds advanced for their lodging and transportation after reaching America. Finally the new Shipping Board, headed by Albert D. Lasker after Harding's inauguration, moved to regain control of the government ships leased to the company. In the late afternoon of July 22, 1921, Shipping Board officials, accompanied by U.S. marshals, boarded the liners *George Washington, America, Susquehanna, President Grant,* and *Agamemnon* at their docks in New York, and took them from U. S. Mail's control. Four more ships were reclaimed the following day, and the board announced that all would be turned over to Harriman's United American Lines.

U. S. Mail fought back in court, claiming collusion between the Board and Harriman, but the seizures were promptly upheld, and U. S. Mail Steamship slid into bankruptcy. Instead of turning the ships over to Harriman's exclusive control, however, the board asked him to join the Roosevelt Steamship Company and the Moore and McCormack Company as temporary unpaid joint managers, operating the vessels as a "patriotic duty."[40]

The board could not have created a more prickly relationship. Roosevelt and his friends H. F. Kerr and Alfred Clegg, now in the steamship business in London, saw a chance to dominate the Atlantic passenger trade. They immediately suspected Harriman of using his inside position to get control of the huge liners. "He is making very definite efforts, both in England and in Germany, to swing everybody over to the opinion that . . . they will be in full possession, and rightly so, in the course of a few months," Clegg warned Roosevelt. "In Germany, we found several of the Hamburg-American Line people . . . already talking authoritatively on the subject of the money which was to be spent by the board on the ships in order to put them into proper running order, and in other ways talking as if the business was entirely under their own management."

Clegg urged Roosevelt to "adopt the policy of checkmating him and of covering his designs where possible, and save ourselves for the real tussle when the time comes that the board relinquishes the ships. I think you should take the attitude of suspecting selfish designs in every proposal Harriman puts forward, and while you will only be able to object on thoroughly sensible grounds, I should so object on every such occasion if I were you."[41]

But Harriman lost interest. The Shipping Board was ambivalent about the future of the ships, and Prohibition was proving disastrous for passenger service under the American flag. Instead of using the custodianship to secure permanent control, Harriman wanted out altogether. He was looking instead toward first-class passenger ships that he could sail under a foreign flag, avoiding the ban on liquor. "We have understood," he told the Shipping Board, "that the arrangement was merely a temporary one, and we trust that you will not consider it advisable or necessary to extend it for a period of more than sixty days. We now feel that in any case we should withdraw at the end of that time."[42] He wound up remaining as one of the managing operators for six months, but then quit.

In early 1922, he bought two nearly new twenty-thousand-ton Dutch-built passenger liners for $2 million each. The *Brabantia* and the *Limburgia* had been ordered by Hamburg-American before the war, but they had been sold to the Royal Holland Line, which operated them between Rotterdam and South America. The acquisitions gave Averell the two largest privately owned passenger ships under the American flag. He renamed them the *Reliance* and the *Resolute*, and announced plans to put them into the transatlantic service along with his third-class steamers. Outfitted with swimming pools and luxurious staterooms, and capable of providing three classes of passenger service, they compared favorably with the most luxurious vessels of the Cunard Line.

It was a proud moment, Harriman declared, not only for himself but for the United States. "We have felt," he told Admiral Benson, "that this transfer to American registry of these splendid passenger ships was an important addition to the American merchant service, as well as an auxiliary to our Navy particularly because our marine is lacking in ships of this type. Although the enterprise is basically commercial, I do not believe I am wrong in feeling that it is of distinct national importance."[43]

He celebrated the *Resolute*'s arrival in New York with a lavish dinner party aboard ship, hosted by his wife. For the occasion, a special train fetched members of Congress, members of the President's Cabinet, and immigration and Shipping Board officials from Washington. Hired cars awaited them at Pennsylvania Station and whisked them away to the pier. Boarding the ship, they found they had been assigned their own staterooms where they could rest and refresh themselves before joining their hosts on deck.

As Averell feared, the courts refused to relax Prohibition aboard American-flag ships, a development which many shipping executives predicted would eventually make the Stars and Stripes an oddity in the world passenger trade. With satisfaction, Kermit Roosevelt predicted that Harriman's first-class passenger service was headed for deep trouble "unless some very skillful juggling can be worked out with Hamburg-American."[44]

But Harriman had bought the *Reliance* and the *Resolute* with the Shipping Board's agreement that he could transfer them to Panamanian registry if he did not get a favorable decision on serving liquor. With Prohibition entrenched, he switched flags. Then, surveying the overpowering competition presented by the British lines, he deployed both the *Resolute* and the *Reliance* on long charter cruises.

The impact of Prohibition on the passenger business was just another of the host of problems that Harriman failed to anticipate. He hadn't foreseen the more restrictive immigration policy, nor had he expected a requirement that American-flag vessels use American shipyards when they required repairs.

By the mid-twenties, the U.S. economy had made a robust recovery, and so had the German merchant marine, led by North German Lloyd and Hamburg-American. But just as Harriman's critics had predicted, his joint service with Hamburg-American was dominated by his German partners. At a time when rampant inflation made Germany's currency nearly worthless, the dollars it earned in its operating arrangement with Harriman made it possible for Hamburg-American to pay off its debts and bounce back as strong as ever.

Averell's difficulties were never confined to the passenger trade. In order to cut costs, some freighters were sold off and others moved to foreign flags. The steamers that once belonged to Kerr and Clegg went to Polish registry and moved from the Atlantic trade into the trade on the Black Sea. He completed his withdrawal from his wartime shipbuilding facilities, selling the old Roach yard to Henry Ford as a site for an automobile plant, and he took W. A. Harriman and Company into investments that had nothing to do with the maritime industry.

His mother, who had encouraged his venture into shipbuilding and backed him at important moments in the acquisition of his fleet, now thought the steamship business a dead end, although she came to his building on Shippers' Row two or three times a year to emphasize her support. Before her arrival, doormen would roll a red carpet from the lobby out to the sidewalk, put huge potted palms outside the door and stand by. She would arrive in a black limousine, attended by a footman in immaculate livery, and walk through the lobby where tickets for the Harriman steamships were sold. Her mysterious visits seldom lasted more than a few minutes, and then she would depart, leaving shipping clerks whispering that she had no doubt recharged the treasury of United American Lines.[45]

Elsewhere she let others in on her opinion. She confided to Luther Gulick, a young protégé who spearheaded her efforts to improve the preparation of young men for public service, that she was concerned that her son "had pushed himself too far." Averell was, she said, "trying to match in shipping what his father had achieved as a railroad man, and the effort so far only brought him losses amounting to several million dollars."[46] She rarely spoke of such matters beyond the family, and the fact that she acknowledged Averell's problems to Gulick reflected the depth of her concern.

In the spring of 1925, Averell sold two of his third-class passenger ships, the *Mount Carroll* and the *Mount Clinton*, for $280,000 each, and there were increasing signs that the alliance with Hamburg-American had run its course. The approaching demise became obvious when the German line, preparing for another expansion, borrowed $10 million from American banks without even bothering to approach W. A. Harriman and Company. A few weeks later, Averell and Wilhelm Cumo met secretly in London, and Hamburg-American formally asked to buy him out.

Under the arrangement, Hamburg-American got not only the *Reliance* and the *Resolute*, but also the *Cleveland*, the only other Harriman ship offering first-class passenger service. For the three vessels and the stock of United American Lines, Harriman received $5.5 million in cash, bonds, and securities, plus 10 million reichsmarks' worth of Hamburg-American stock.

The circumstances were ideal for an acrimonious parting, but Harriman was satisfied to get out. "Have closed with friends who guarantee approval by their company," he cabled his office in New York. "Have sold three ships and United American Lines, Inc., and three shipping subsidiaries. As pier lease being negotiated by United American Lines, it is of greatest importance that lease be signed before announcement or leak."[47]

"The H. A. L. board of directors was rather upset at the size of the purchase price," he wrote his mother on the train between Hamburg and Paris. "It is an excellent deal from our viewpoint and liberal from theirs. I am satisfied with it. It is considerably better than I expected."[48]

When the announcement was made in July, it generated little attention, for the fear of the Germans had dissipated. Ironically, on the same day of the announcement marking the passing of Harriman as an important maritime figure, the Shipping Board in Washington adopted a resolution ordering that the big government-owned passenger ships of the United States Lines be put up for sale.

Chapter VI

MINES
Manganese, Moscow, and Trotsky

After he entered the shipping business, Harriman went to Europe twice a year and usually stayed for weeks at a time. His Hamburg-American connection and a close association with the Warburg financial empire in Germany made him one of America's best-known business figures abroad.

New York had become the new financial capital of the world, but Berlin was the hot attraction for aggressive American investors; Averell's tie with the Warburgs was a natural one, for the families had known each other for a generation. The American branch of the Warburg family was by both marriage and money connected to the Kuhn, Loeb and Company establishment which had backed E. H. and the Union Pacific, and it was through these European connections, far more attuned than Wall Street to the financial repercussions of the Bolshevik revolution, that Averell came to do business in the Soviet Union.

Though he would later claim that his chief interest in the USSR was to understand the Soviet political phenomenon, the evidence argues that his overwhelming objective was to make money. Certainly, he was, like capitalists everywhere, concerned about the Marxist virus; but he was never swept up in Red paranoia, nor distracted from the possibility of business opportunities on a scale that challenged the imagination.

As Western governments debated strategies for meeting the Bolshevik problem, German businessmen aggressively moved to reestablish their Russian trade at the same time they pressed their comeback in

139

Atlantic shipping. But while they were determined to exploit every market, many investors questioned whether the Bolshevik government would survive long enough to make good on its long-term commitments. Though it was necessary to accept Soviet securities, the more cautious Westerners promptly discounted them and sold them to speculators willing to gamble that the government would be there to redeem them at maturity. Harriman, along with the Warburg interests, began buying the discounted securities.

As its economy floundered, the Soviet government warily and unsuccessfully encouraged Western investment, finally confessing that it desperately needed capitalists to keep it afloat. In exchange for hard cash and modern technology, Lenin opened the doors for big Western money to exploit the country's stupendous natural resources, cloaking the ideological compromise of his New Economic Policy by characterizing Russian resources as "bait" that would "win over the capitalist to cooperate and help reconstruct a socialist economic system."[1]

When the opportunity was offered in 1920, Harriman was in no position to weigh it seriously. He was just emerging from the maelstrom caused by his deal with the Hamburg-American line. The American economy was going into a stall, and his shipping business was threatened by the competition from government-owned vessels.

But two years later, he tested the waters by going into a small steamship service working the German-Russian trade between Hamburg and ports on the Black Sea. The Russians owned half of it and the Harriman–Hamburg-American combine owned the other half. It operated without the public or, apparently, even any substantial number of his business friends in America knowing anything of Harriman's dealings with a government the United States regarded as an international pariah. In 1924, when the Amtorg Trading Corporation was set up to handle the Soviet government's import-export business in the United States, the Harriman–Hamburg-American partnership became its forwarding agent and shipping broker. Deutsch-Russiche Transport Gesellschaft, or Derutra chartered steamers that carried cargoes shipped between the United States and the Soviet Union.

By the time the new direct channel for the increasing U.S.-Soviet trade was announced, Averell was secretly on the trail of a windfall in the USSR. His new interest was manganese, a mineral without which it was impossible to make steel. On the rugged plateaus of the Caucasus Mountains, one hundred miles from the Georgian port of Poti on the Black Sea, lay the largest known deposits of manganese in the world— as much as seventy million tons of ore. Before the war, fully half of the world's production had come from this one concentration, its output in 1913 reaching a million tons.

But after the Soviets' bloody annexation of the Republic of Georgia and confiscation of property from private owners, production had fallen to less than a third of that prewar peak. Nevertheless, in the mid-twenties, the American steel industry was importing 100,000 tons—$10 million worth—of Georgian manganese each year. The idea of a mining and marketing project in Georgia was brought to Harriman's office early in 1924 while Averell was on a long trip to Germany. Mark Rascovich, a Russian-born consulting engineer, walked in unannounced, claiming to have connections with Georgia mine owners who needed an international firm to market millions of dollars' worth of ore. He was promptly shown the door.

W. A. Harriman and Company was not interested in mining, he was told, certainly not in Soviet Georgia. But to get rid of the persistent Rascovich, the office accepted a prospectus he had written, and sometime later it was read by John Speed Elliott, one of Harriman's vice-presidents.

The possibilities were as appealing as they were unlikely. For an investment of $250,000, Rascovich claimed, there were potential profits running into the millions. His prospectus was just plausible enough that it could not be dismissed out of hand, and when it was put before Harriman himself, Elliott was ordered to sail for France, where Rascovich promised that Harriman's lieutenant would find a Georgian named Nikoladze, who was chairman of the mine owners' organization. Nikoladze would be accompanied by lawyers prepared to sign a marketing contract on the spot.

It was not to be so simple. Before it was over, Elliott's trip turned into an odyssey that continued from Paris to Constantinople, across the Black Sea to the manganese deposits ninety miles from the Georgian capital of Tiflis, and finally to Moscow.

For starters, Nikoladze was not in Paris when Elliott got there. The purported leader of the mining organization had gone back to Georgia, leaving word that he could not return to Europe but that he could come to Constantinople. With good reason, the missed connection increased Elliott's skepticism. Even if Rascovich was truthful and Nikoladze was genuine, doing business in Georgia would be an enormous gamble. Harriman's man, nevertheless, went on to Turkey. In Constantinople, he was denied a visa to enter Georgia, and the mine owners' representative was then refused permission to leave the USSR. For six weeks, Elliott and Rascovich, who had accompanied him from New York, collected gossip, toured mosques and bazaars and waited.

Meanwhile, a personal investigation by Harriman himself produced a picture altogether at odds with the assurances that had taken Elliott to Turkey. From Amtorg representatives in New York, he learned that the Soviet government was planning to award a manganese mining concession in Georgia, granting exclusive rights to mine the deposits. Rumors were that the contract would go to the Germans because they had been heavily involved in the area before the war when the manganese market had been dominated by the Krupp interests.

With Elliott continuing to pester Soviet representatives in Turkey for a visa, Averell sailed for Berlin hoping to talk with Soviet diplomats and trade officials before a deal was closed. While he was crossing the Atlantic, Elliott finally got into Georgia.

Suspected of being an economic spy, since he had turned up without Moscow's having sent word of him, Harriman's lieutenant was kept waiting in Tiflis for a full week before he was permitted to go on to the manganese fields. When he finally got to the mines at Chiaturi, he found that, contrary to everything he had been told, there was no organization of mine owners. There was no mining organization; there was no one in Georgia with authority to do business. The whole story Rascovich had brought Harriman, evidently in good faith, was a pipe dream.[2]

Certainly there were in fact massive manganese deposits, but the mines that had been in the hands of private owners in the days of the Georgian Republic were in shambles and under control of the Soviet government.

Their equipment was primitive, worn out, and broken down; the former owners were bitter at both Moscow, for confiscation of their property, and the foreigners for coming with ideas of mining it. Ore was dug out of the plateaus with picks and shovels, and barefoot Georgians and Armenians, clothed in rags, loaded it into donkey carts and hauled it down to railroad cars. At night, the workers slept on the ground in the same stables with the animals. Making the operation even more inefficient, Elliott learned, was the fact that the railroad changed from a narrow-gauge to a standard-gauge track halfway between the mines and the seaport, meaning that the ore had to be laboriously transferred from one ramshackle train to another.

In Berlin, Harriman was not so discouraged. In spite of the glum reports from Elliott, he concluded that with modern mining technology the plateaus outside Chiaturi might dominate the world market for manganese ore. But while control of the thick seams lay with the Soviet Concessions Committee in Moscow and not with some Georgian association, it was clear to both Harriman and Elliott that both the former owners of the property and the titular government of the Georgian Republic had to be satisfied before the mines could be successfully operated. Before the revolution, large tracts had been held by foreigners, mostly Germans, and now these absentee owners, like those who remained in the area, resented the prospect of the American financier moving in to take huge profits under Soviet auspices. Averell sought to mollify them with pledges of royalty payments and offers to take European investors into the new mining company he planned to organize.

Elliott, meanwhile, got the signatures of Georgian officials on a draft agreement and set out for Moscow, arriving in early September. The proposal gave Harriman exclusive rights to work the Chiaturi mines for twenty years, paying the Soviet government a royalty on every ton, and providing a share of his profits to the former owners.

In spite of intense efforts to keep it all secret, word of a Harriman move on the Caucasus swept European financial circles; and when Elliott reached Moscow in September, he found serious competition, not only from the Germans but from British, French, and Dutch companies as well. Incredibly, the U.S. government did not learn of Harriman's wheeling and dealing until late October, when British prime minister Ramsay MacDonald referred to it in a speech in the House of Commons.

The negotiations dragged through the fall and winter and into the spring of 1925. Averell organized his mining company and brought in friends as investors, but he still made no contact with either the State Department or Commerce Department. If he had, he might well have withdrawn. Certainly, he would have driven a harder bargain, for the files at the State Department's Division of Eastern European Affairs were replete with evidence that he was headed for serious trouble.

"Until Russia is recognized by the United States and a proper trading agreement is concluded between the two countries, every kind of American investment is less than safe," warned the American embassy in London. "The Russians realize this, but they are doing their best to provoke indignation and troubles in commercial and diplomatic circles. Harriman would be well advised first of all not to take such a big concession, and second, in any enterprise he undertakes, he should do it with international groups."[3]

The skepticism was not limited to the government. Enough of his partners in W. A. Harriman and Company were opposed that he agreed to underwrite the deal with $4 million of his own cash, leaving the company out of it.

Their doubts were sobering, however. And while he was no less determined to press ahead, he was also anxious to protect himself. Very nearly causing the negotiations to collapse, he demanded that the Soviets add language explicitly stating his right to withdraw from the concession if it proved unprofitable.

In return, the Russians extracted from him a pledge to modernize the mines and to rebuild the railroad running to the seaport at Poti. He considered that unnecessary for the operation of the concession and balked for several months before relenting in June of 1925, in effect giving the Soviets $4 million for the right to walk out on a losing proposition.

The contract required him to pay the Soviet government a royalty of three dollars per ton for all the ore he exported during the first three and a half years, increasing it to four dollars thereafter. After producing

300,000 tons in his first year, he was to increase output to 500,000 tons by his fifth year and maintain that pace for the next fifteen years.

For exclusive export rights, he guaranteed $1.5 million a year in royalties to the Soviet government, a sum that was of little concern to him, for he confidently estimated production sufficient to give the Soviets $62 million over the term of the contract, while his own profits would amount to $120 million.

In the view of the Kremlin, the political ramifications were as important as Harriman's cash, the American capitalist's large presence in the USSR being a potentially significant step toward diplomatic recognition by the United States government.

When Harriman's Georgian Manganese Company took control of the mines in the summer of 1925, the early signs were that he had engineered a coup. By August, he had orders for 100,000 tons of ore to be delivered by the end of the year. Bethlehem Steel Company, his number one customer, ordered 30,000 tons per month beginning in October and told Harriman it expected the demand to continue at that level at least through the following year. Production started at 33,000 tons per month and went up to 45,000 tons in October. The only problem, it appeared, was to get the ore to port and find enough freighters to deliver it.[4] Closing the books on 1925, the company showed a profit of $315,000 for the first six months, and much more was expected over the long haul.

His zealous pursuit of the concession led him into mistakes that would prove disastrous, however. He had plunged into the venture on a huge scale without ever seeing his property, taking his advice from Elliott, who knew nearly nothing about mining, and from Rascovich, who had misled him at the start. They were mistakes that E. H. would never have made.

Backed by heavy investments from Germany and England and subscriptions by a long list of friends and associates from railroading, shipping, and banking, including James P. Warburg and Chicago merchant Marshall Field, he made separate agreements with the former owners of the mines, promising to pay them a two dollars per ton royalty on the first 600,000 tons.

It was not long before the trouble started. The cost of the promised railroad improvements had been grossly underestimated. Nearly thirty bridges needed rebuilding, new tunnels had to be cut, narrow-gauge rails replaced, and rolling stock modernized. Realistically, it would cost $12 million to $15 million.

Relations between Harriman's men and the former mine owners soured almost overnight. Georgians resented the company because it had made its deal with Moscow; trade unions despised the capitalists, and Harriman employees aggravated the situation by behaving in the manner of colonial governors. There were physical confrontations; the state bank cut off credit to former owners in the area; and mining costs escalated.

Once the downhill course began, it was irreversible; the operation was "full of most unfortunate surprises," as one report to Harriman put it. "In general money is being spent too loosely and is often wasted. . . . The staff is huge, employees are appointed without sufficient attention being paid to their efficiency or their moral and social standing. Most of the girls are from such a milieu and of such a reputation that no decent man will dare appear with them in the streets. Relations with most of the private owners are very strained. The Georgians especially are dissatisfied; they all seem to think that the concession has been particularly hostile and unfriendly toward people of their nationality."[5]

Communists harassed non-Communists in the mines; labor unions conspired to hold down productivity; workers interfered with hiring and had foremen and supervisors arrested for working men overtime without permission. Thievery was rampant, but authorities refused the company permission to arm security guards and would not prosecute workers accused by management.

Worse, there was a softening in world manganese prices. Brazil and the Gold Coast of Africa, the principal competitors for the market, stepped up production, increasing supplies and bringing prices down. There were rumors of production increases in India, and reports of newly discovered deposits in South Africa. The situation was further aggravated by a prolonged British coal strike which shut down steel mills. Prices skidded downward from the nearly $100 a ton which ore had been bringing at Pittsburgh at the time the concession was signed.

The Soviet government was as much responsible for the glut as was production elsewhere. Just as the Harriman organization was getting started at Chiaturi, the Soviets, using German interests to handle the marketing, began exporting manganese from the Nikopol mines in the Ukraine, sending ore to the world market from resources previously reserved for domestic use.

Harriman was in no position to tolerate falling prices, because he had tied himself to a fixed royalty. No matter what manganese fetched on the world market, he was obligated to pay the Soviet government the three dollars per ton—going up to four dollars after three years.

Typically, though, he was too busy to fret with such details. There were more deals to be made, and he pursued them at a frenetic pace. In Germany, he arranged a $7.5 million loan for the Good Hope Steel Company, $10 million for waterworks and streetcar lines in Cologne, and millions more for utilities in Breslau. With Lee Higginson and Company, in New York, he marketed German securities to raise capital for the segment of the transatlantic cable running from Emden to the Azores. At the same time, he was gaining control of new mining operations in Poland, buying a stable of thoroughbreds in New York, and taking an increasingly keen interest in competitive polo.

In spite of the warning signs from the Caucasus, he looked seriously at other Soviet concessions. He considered a timber project, but backed away because his organization had no shred of expertise in forestry or sawmills, and began organizing a pipeline and refinery project for transporting and processing crude from the Baku oil fields near the Caspian Sea. He also went so far as to take a lively interest in opening a bank in Moscow.

For weeks at a time, he was constantly on the move, living out of his suitcase. "I have been traveling around Europe in circles," he wrote his mother from a train. "I think I wrote you from Berlin. I then went to Hamburg, the Hague, London, then Paris, Cannes (via Italy and Switzerland), London again, Paris, Berlin, and now I am enroute to Hamburg. I stay there 24 hours, then night train to the Hague for one day, then the night boat to London."[6]

In the spring of 1926, while he was in Germany negotiating to sell his first-class steamships to Hamburg-American Lines, he was approached by German and Russian trade officials and representatives of the Deutsche Bank with an idea for a German export organization that would finance Soviet purchases of German turbines and farm machinery. Since American loans to the Soviet government were not allowed, they devised a scheme for him to sell securities of a German export company in the United States and for the Germans to use the proceeds to provide credit to the Soviets, enabling them to import industrial and agricultural equipment. For starters, Averell proposed to market $25 million to $35 million worth of the corporation's notes in the United States to help back 300 million reichsmarks' worth of credits to the Soviets. Half of the credits were to be secured by the banks and manufacturers in the export corporation and the other half by the German government itself.

Rumors of the plan were picked up by American diplomats in Berlin and relayed on to the State Department before Harriman's lawyers broached it to officials in Washington. By the time he went to discuss it with American ambassador Jacob Gould Schurman in Berlin, the U.S. government had already decided that such an arrangement would be tantamount to making direct loans to the Soviet Union. In the first place, such loans were not available to countries that had not settled their war indebtedness to the United States—and the Soviet Union was among them. In the second, Washington was not interested in seeing Americans finance trade between any two foreign powers. And thirdly, it was opposed to American money being funneled to support imports by the Soviets. While Washington had approved short-term credits in the export of American commodities, such as cotton, to Russia, Harriman was proposing to deal on a scale that would strengthen the Communist government politically and enable Germany to capitalize on the Soviet trade at the expense of the United States.

While the Treasury and Commerce Department bureaucracies expressed no strong opposition, the State Department was adamant. There, it was even suspected that the proposed loan was a further Harriman payoff to the Soviets for his manganese concession. "It should be observed that W. A. Harriman & Co. recently obtained an extensive manganese concession from the Soviets," Robert Francis Kelley, chief of the State Department's Division of Eastern European Affairs, observed cryptically, "and it is probable that the proposed loan is the outcome of this business relation with the Soviet regime." In State's hard-nosed view, the only way the United States could influence Soviet political behavior was to keep up relentless economic pressure. And that pressure, Kelley warned, "would be considerably relaxed if the Soviet government succeeded in obtaining foreign loans or long-term credits, thereby permitting it to proceed with its economic and political experimentation. . . ."[7] In the face of the opposition, Averell persisted for weeks, believing that he could eventually convince Washington of the plan's logic.

He made his pitch to Schurman in May. While he was in complete sympathy with the policy of withholding diplomatic recognition from the Soviet Union, he told the ambassador, hamstringing trade and business dealings was another matter. Washington and the Coolidge administration had to choose between two clear economic-policy options. The United States could take the hard line, ban commercial and trade dealings with the Soviet government altogether, and try to isolate it economically as well as politically, or it could relax its restrictions and permit not only trade but the financing of trade as well.

The former course he deemed totally unrealistic, since the Allies had already normalized relations with Moscow. In defense of his own proposal, he argued that it would do nothing to enhance Russian imports from Germany at the expense of the United States. In the long run, Soviet purchases of German farm and industrial equipment would serve to stimulate its basic economy and, in time, enhance the Soviet demand for consumer goods such as cotton which the Soviets could buy from the United States.

Schurman listened patiently, and faithfully relayed it all to the State Department; but after three months went by, there was no sign that he had made any dent in the government's position. Realizing that the administration was probably waiting for the idea simply to fade away, Averell finally went to Washington to deal with officials at the State and Commerce departments face-to-face. At Commerce, Secretary Herbert Hoover went on the offensive as soon as he walked in the door. The scheme, the secretary announced, was altogether out of the question.

The President's Cabinet had considered and already rejected it because the Soviet government had made no move to honor its war debt to the United States. The plan's economic merits did not even enter into consideration.[8]

While he was forced to give up on that, he was no less enthusiastic over his other possibilities in the USSR, including the Moscow bank, which he was exploring in cooperation with Guaranty Trust. Even as he was in Washington to see Hoover, one of his collaborators, Guaranty's William Hamilton, was on his way home from Moscow, where he had discussed plans for the bank with Foreign Minister Maksim Litvinov. The banker had found Soviet officials "very anxious to see such a bank established" and ready to "do everything in their power to make its creation feasible and attractive." Very soon, he told Harriman, it would be possible to conclude more "interesting financial and industrial operations."[9]

Hamilton had also taken the opportunity to remind the Soviets of the importance of the troubled Harriman manganese concession. Harriman was, after all, not some opportunist out for a quick buck. If his concession succeeded, the Soviets would have established a useful institutional relationship with the capitalist community. According to Hamilton, the Russians' reaction had been that they would endeavor to work with "substantial, reputable American interests, rather than with the shoestring speculators who heretofore have been America's chief representatives in business with Russia."[10]

In the three years before Harriman's negotiators arrived in the Caucasus, the Soviet Concessions Committee received more than 1,500 applications from Western Capitalists. The winners, Germans, Swedes, Americans, who made leather, cut timber, and mined asbestos, found it increasingly frustrating and unprofitable to do business with the regime. Although Harriman was still publicly insisting that his mining concession was going well, the truth was to the contrary. While the Soviets still regarded the manganese concession as the showpiece of Lenin's New Economic Policy, Averell was headed down a rough road already traveled by lesser capitalists who had gone into the USSR.

Weeks after his mining operations got under way, he learned that the Soviet government had withheld the richest deposits in his concession area—fifteen million tons at a site called Perevissi Hill—planning to develop it once the Americans were gone. To make matters worse, he failed to secure a contract with United States Steel Corporation, the single gigantic customer whose business could have ensured his success, the company finally opting to use manganese from its own mines in Brazil. All of the circumstances surrounding the deal had converged to put him fundamentally at odds with the Soviets. For his enterprise to survive, he needed to hold production down in order to keep price up.

But since the government's income was determined solely by tonnage, its object was to get maximum production.

Harriman's response was to go slow on both capital improvements and production increases. A year after his contract was signed, his exports were hovering just above the minimum required for him to retain the concession, and it was becoming common knowledge that the much-publicized venture was faltering. The Soviets were complaining that he had paid too little for the concession and that his real aim was merely to use the Soviets' vast manganese resources to capture control of the American steel industry.

Dispatching Richard Robinson to the Caucasus for an inspection in the fall of 1926, Harriman called on Herbert Hoover for the second time in a few months, but this conversation with the secretary was no more satisfactory than the first. Since he had not bothered to consult the secretary or anyone else in the administration, and in fact had worked on the manganese deal in great secrecy, the administration had no sympathy for his predicament. In its difficulties with Moscow, Georgian Manganese could expect no help or advice from the U.S. Department of Commerce.

On November 3, Averell and Kitty sailed for Germany on the first leg of a journey to the Soviet Union to deal with the deteriorating situation. In Berlin, he complained to German government officials that their embassy in Moscow had continued working against him, even after he had gotten the concession in Georgia. He now suspected that the German and Soviet interests were in an outright conspiracy against him, marketing manganese from the Ukraine at a loss to force him to keep his own price down and push production up. German business interests were going along with it because other American businessmen would be discouraged from going into competition with them for Soviet business if Harriman encountered insurmountable problems.[11]

The Germans' attitude had stiffened after the State Department blocked the effort to finance exports to Russia with American capital. Still determined to market industrial products abroad, the Berlin government now viewed any movement toward accommodation between Washington and Moscow as threatening.

Having been unfortunately cavalier in taking on the concession, Harriman looked at the negotiations ahead of him in Moscow as a critical moment in his life. As the train approached the Russian border, he scrawled a note to his mother telling her he feared his negotiations would be "slow and difficult." But he added, "It is pioneer work & of real use"[12]

His party, now including Dick Robinson, who joined them after his own inspection trip to Chiaturi, and William Hamilton of Guaranty Trust along with his wife, Constance, reached Moscow on December 9, after a roundabout trip through Austria and Poland and a visit to Leningrad. Robinson had told them what to expect, but they were, nevertheless, taken aback by conditions in the Soviet capital. Harriman was especially struck by the pervasive atmosphere of oppression and the persistent evidence of destruction.

Nine years after the revolution, the Soviet capital reflected not a classless society but a stark coexistence of extremes—oppression and poverty face-to-face with sophistication and privilege. Some czarist remnants stubbornly survived beneath scars of the revolution, and others were protected and nourished. Foreigners moved about the city in aging luxury cars which the new regime had taken from the old; they were segregated in a few "tourist" hotels, such as the Bolsha Moscovskaya where Harriman made his headquarters, eating his meals in dining rooms still using linens, silver, and porcelain china from royal palaces. Away from the small enclaves of privilege, waifs in rags wandered frozen, cobblestone streets, surviving by begging and stealing.

Though he was the best-known capitalist doing business in the Soviet Union, and presumably helping perfect the socialist state, Harriman found the Soviet bureaucracy a mighty challenge. He was told that Josef Stalin, the ascendant figure in the Communist party and the government, would be unavailable. For the most part, the negotiations were carried on with Adolf A. Joffe, deputy director of the state Concessions Committee headed by Leon Trotsky. One of the sophisticates among the Bolsheviks, Joffe had been an original member of the War Revolutionary Committee, and after the revolution had been sent to Germany to reestablish diplomatic and commercial relations. While he was the Soviet official best equipped to address the problems of Georgian Manganese, Harriman chose not to deal extensively with a bureaucrat, sending his man Robinson to handle the details and remaining personally out of view, as though waiting to be presented with a treaty. The tactic bestowed an aura of importance and an anticipation of his personal arrival at the negotiating table.

During two weeks of discussions between Robinson and Russian bureaucrats in an old palace that had once belonged to a Russian tea merchant, Harriman called on Western diplomats and dined with Armand Hammer at the mansion where the Soviets had ensconced their favorite concessionaire. Hammer was the one foreigner who was prospering mightily in the USSR, taking advantage of his father's personal friendship with Lenin. His first concession had been an asbestos mining operation similar to Averell's manganese enterprise, and it had been a bust. After bailing out of it, Hammer had pursued several other ventures, including the export of furs and artworks, and a highly profitable pencil manufacturing business at four plants in Moscow.

The German embassy, aware of Harriman's blunt talks in Berlin just days earlier, hosted a dinner party, hoping to smooth ruffled feathers, but Averell regarded the occasion as a heavy-handed attempt to cover up the obvious German efforts to undercut his concession. He was especially infuriated when, in the presence of Foreign Minister Litvinov, the German ambassador told him that the problems of the Chiaturi mining concession were the result of his inexperience. The difficulty, the envoy said, could have been avoided if Harriman had only consulted the Germans and taken the benefit of their valuable advice.[13]

In spite of the stiffness of his negotiations and the certainty that he was kept under surveillance, Harriman found the Russian capital more open to him than he had expected. Soviet officials were accessible, and the government made little effort to prevent him from contacting dissidents and intellectuals.

Before he left, he made a satisfying little foray into diplomacy. Just before his arrival in Moscow, the Soviets had buried the ashes of Leonid Krassin, their ambassador to Great Britain and the government representative who had been the best known and most highly regarded in the West. Now Krassin's widow, who had grown up in England and made no secret of her fierce anti-Bolshevist views, wanted to return to London with her two daughters, but was being denied permission by authorities. Unable to get a personal audience with Litvinov, she asked Harriman to intercede, and he warned the foreign minister that the case would soon attract wide attention throughout the West. In the United States, the unfavorable impression created would seriously damage the Soviets' chances of gaining diplomatic recognition. Krassin's family was shortly permitted to depart.

Harriman's main object in the manganese talks was to get relief from the onerous fixed royalty and agreement on less extensive improvements to the railroad. He also wanted an understanding on the competition from the Nikopol mines. Under the circumstances, he warned, the Soviets could no longer dominate the world manganese market. If the Soviets responded to increased foreign competition by dropping prices, they would only set off a new price war. Since manganese use was entirely dependent upon world steel production, a cut in its price would not increase consumption.

While Harriman had pushed his production from 436,000 tons up to 772,000, an increase of 24 percent in his first year, the South Russian Ore Trust, operating the Nikopol mines with the financial backing of the German firm of Rawack und Grünfeld, had raised its output from 380,000 tons to 815,000, a 115 percent increase.[14]

At first, the Soviets argued that Harriman's management, not the soft world manganese market, was responsible for his trouble. He had done nearly nothing, they charged, to carry out his agreement to modernize the mines in the Caucasus. There was truth in the assertion that he had been slow to replace the picks, shovels and donkeys with steam shovels and aerial trams, but for that he blamed the Soviets themselves. After Moscow's agreement to permit the first 600,000 tons of ore to be mined by former owners and operators, the Soviet state bank had demanded full payment of all their outstanding loans. Harriman had to provide them money to settle these and to pay off their obligations to their workers. Then he had to advance them more money to continue their operations.

Altogether, the bailout of the former owners had cost him $1.4 million of the $4 million he had agreed to invest. The project direly needed more capital, but "much as it is to be regretted," he told Joffe, his mining equipment and stocks of manganese ore in the Soviet Union were not considered acceptable security for loans from Western banks. Under these circumstances, and facing the possibility of a price war, he could justify no further investment. It was, in effect, an ultimatum.

Unable to see Stalin, he took his case to Trotsky. Lenin's great organizer and commissar of war had suffered the first of his ultimately fatal reverses in Bolshevik politics. Just before the signing of the manganese deal with Harriman, he had become chairman of the Concessions Committee, taking a job he considered a risky and distasteful assignment. He confided as much to Litvinov, complaining that "it shouldn't be difficult to spread the rumor that Trotsky has sold himself to International Capital. . . . Young people who see me so often on the Tverskaya sitting in a car with foreign businessmen could easily fall for such slanders. . . . It's already being said that I'm on Averell Harriman's payroll."[15]

Harriman's encounter with the man whose power was second only to Lenin's in the revolution was tense and formal. Armed with English and Russian texts of the agreement and copies of the written exchanges between Averell and Joffe, they sat across a huge conference table, attended by an interpreter and sustained by Russian tea. For four hours, they worked through the document line-by-line. There was no sign of the fire that had made Trotsky one of the most captivating of the Bolshevik leaders. Rather than risk using his limited English, Trotsky spoke through George Andrechin, a Bulgarian who had learned his English while growing up in the United States.

Harriman was uncomfortable, and he was sure that Trotsky was, too, probably knowing that their conversation was being monitored, and fearing that the changes being requested in the manganese concession would only add to his troubles. There was no debate, and nothing but a smattering of social conversation, although Harriman made a stab at ingratiating himself. "If your government continues in the same pace to develop industry, and your rich resources," he said, "I will venture a prediction: the 20th century will no doubt go down in history as the American Century, but it is not impossible that the 21st century may become known as the Russian Century." "Oh, no," Trotsky replied, "all I am willing to grant you is the first half of the 20th century."[16]

In detail, Harriman again laid out the whole case that he and Robinson had already presented to Joffe, and then set forth his demands for continuing his operation. Given his requirements for capital improvements, payments to the former owners, and royalties to the Soviet government, he was in no position to reduce prices to steel companies. But if relieved of some of the obligations to modernize the transportation and loading system in Georgia, he could afford to lower his prices and meet his export obligations. He wanted to limit his modernization costs to $2 million and to base his royalty payments on the market price.

Trotsky gave no inkling of his reaction to any of the proposals. When the meeting was over, he bowed stiffly and left the room by one exit while Harriman was escorted out another.

On Christmas Eve, the Harrimans and the Hamiltons boarded a private railroad car, opulent even by the standards of his father's contemporaries. In the relic of czarist times, they departed for the Caucasus, leaving Robinson behind to continue the negotiations. The journey was tedious. Mile after mile, the train jostled over rickety track and deteriorating roadbed at a speed of no more than twenty-five miles per hour, lest it jump off the rails. Across the countryside, evidence of the economic crisis, the aftermath of war and famine, was more gripping than in the streets of Moscow.

South of Astrakhan, their route took them along the shore of the Caspian Sea through the Baku oil fields. Though his troubles in Georgia had tempered his enthusiasm for an oil pipeline and refinery project, Averell still took the time for an overnight stay in Baku and a tour of the fields.

Working conditions there were no better than in the manganese mines, many of the men living in stables built for animals in the days before the fields were mechanized. At the hotel where they spent the night, Harriman was struck by the incongruity of a dinner table where butter was not to be found yet dishes overflowed with caviar.

Turning west toward Tiflis the next day, the Americans crossed the Caucasus and descended through foothill villages of flat-roofed, mud-colored cabins, ruins of whitewashed stone houses, and churches plundered during the Georgian Republic's last stand against Bolshevism. Crossing spectacular table lands, they traveled an hour at a stretch without seeing a human being, reminding Harriman of his boyhood trips across the western United States on the Union Pacific.

They arrived in Georgia's capital on December 28. Harriman spent a day meeting with disgruntled officials of the former republic and bureaucrats from Moscow. Neither the locals nor Soviet functionaries exhibited any sympathy for the company's predicament or for his explanation that he had been misled about the work necessary to modernize the mines. They insisted that even while Elliott was drawing up the preliminary contract before going to Moscow, Elliott had been warned that the project would cost far more than the $4 million he had estimated.

The hosts were more impressed by Harriman's stamina than by his arguments. After hours of briefings, he was still ready to sample a dozen Georgian wines from a store of six thousand bottles in the State Wine Library that had once been the private stock of Grand Duke Nicholas. Then, to their surprise, he appeared fresh, sober, and on schedule for an evening at the opera. At midnight, after a second grueling day in the capital, the party boarded their train and resumed their journey to Chiaturi, arriving at the Scharopan intersection at dawn. There, they paused just long enough for breakfast in their car before transferring to a less commodious service train on the narrow-gauge railroad to take them on to the mines.

When Harriman finally saw his mines on New Year's eve, a cold rain was cutting gullies down the ore-blackened slopes, turning the mining camps into dark, filthy mudholes and making it foolhardy to venture outside without high-topped rubber boots and heavy raincoats. Soon after the party arrived, the hammering rain sent mudslides and rockslides from the steep slopes onto the railroad tracks, knocking out telegraph lines and cutting communication with the outside world.

The mood of the union officials and former mine owners who awaited them was as disagreeable as the Georgia winter. Competition and the slack market had forced Harriman's managers to lay off 4,500 men and limit operations to two sites. Union representatives complained about the layoffs, grumbled about workers' pay scales, and demanded that the company move faster to improve the miners' living conditions. After hours of listening to the union representatives and displaced owners, Averell slogged through the rain and mud to see Chiaturi's mayor. He was told that his honor had gone to Tiflis, but the Americans suspected that he had merely made himself unavailable, for the underling who received them was rude and uncommunicative. "He evidently wanted to show us how he despised capitalists," Harriman's interpreter noted in his diary. "He was absolutely lacking in the most ordinary courtesy. I felt thoroughly ashamed. So we left him and went to the State Bank where Mr. H. inquired into the working of the Bank."[17]

Harriman found the sloppiness and lack of interest in the railroad he was modernizing disgusting, though he had hardly expected the Union Pacific. Trains were delayed while men with shovels added or removed a few tens or hundreds of pounds of ore to make each car weigh precisely thirteen tons. Managers of the operations could find little time to be concerned with such tactics because they were constantly occupied in dealing with the Soviet bureaucracy.

Much later, Averell would maintain that his inspection convinced him that it was impossible to do business in the Soviet Union and that he decided then and there to withdraw from the concession. But if that was the case, he gave no such indication at the time. To the contrary, his assessment at the end of his visit was full of optimism, and he departed the Soviet Union apparently thinking he had reversed the hopeless situation.

Before leaving Chiaturi, he wrote a long letter to Robinson back in Moscow, detailing the progress that was being made at their two active mines. Aerial tramways would be operating within two months, bringing ore from the slopes down to the expanded washing plants. New housing for workmen had been completed. Machine shops were going up, and the components had arrived for steam shovels to be assembled at the washing plants to load ore onto railcars. Pneumatic drills had begun to replace picks and shovels, and mine foremen predicted that it would soon be possible to load and ship 250 carloads of washed ore every day.

With the relatively inexpensive improvements, he still looked toward mining the area indefinitely. Having already learned a great deal from his experience, he ordered Robinson to conclude firm agreements on duties he would be charged on goods and materials shipped in from the United States. "There are some things that we will have to import for some years," he said, "and I think it is of great importance that we should not put our necks in the noose and accept the obligation to pay undefined duties."[18]

He was also concerned that valuable deposits would be left beneath the villages in the area, and he told Robinson to begin arrangements for mining beneath them and making settlement with residents for any damage done in the process. Not only did he intend to persevere with the manganese concession, he was still interested in the Baku oil field project. More productive wells were coming in, thanks to Western drilling technology, and he assured Robinson he was satisfied that the financing of a pipeline "will be a safe venture."[19]

On the last leg of the trip to the Black Sea, he intended to stop and inspect the seven bridges that he still planned to repair under his scaled-down railroad modernization. But when they got back to Scharopan and the end of the narrow-gauge rails, there was no train to meet them. Local Soviet functionaries would not take the responsibility for dispatching a train for him, and nothing happened until he surmised the cause of the delay and agreed to forgo the inspection stops. When a train finally did arrive, another two hours passed while its crew awaited permission to move.

Harriman sat swearing and watching the rain splatter in the muddy railyard while Kitty and Averell's interpreter played bridge with the Hamiltons. By the time the train was permitted to roll, it was late afternoon, and the brief winter twilight was fading. Weary and irritated at the final display of pettiness, the party crossed Georgia in the dead of night. There was no reason even to slow down at the bridges. The wind raged as the train chugged toward the Black Sea, and when Harriman arose at Poti the next morning, he found work at the loading dock at a standstill, the elevator having been toppled to the ground by the gale.

It was another month before they got back to New York. After crossing the Black Sea on a Danish freighter, they spent several days in Constantinople, then Averell and Kitty sailed for a vacation in Italy and on the French Riviera. As usual, Harriman's vacation was also business. In Milan, he discussed plans for a hydroelectric project with Italian bankers and businessmen and explored the future market for manganese at Italian steel mills. When he warned his hosts that the Italian government's deflation program would present mounting problems in marketing its securities abroad, he was given an appointment to see the dictator, Benito Mussolini. While he tried to speak seriously to the bald, hulking Mussolini about the volatile manganese market and the serious effect of a higher lira on Italy's world trade deficit, the comic-opera Fascist used the meeting as an opportunity to practice his English. He received Harriman in the style of a medieval ruler, sitting at the back of a cavernous office in Palazzo Chigi, once the Austrian embassy. The formal trappings created a splendid atmosphere for an audience but hardly for a conversation.

Mussolini's barely serviceable English could not communicate whether he understood the intricacies of the manganese market, but when Harriman brought up the increased value of the lira, his eyes bulged and he declared he was restoring Italian pride that had been missing since the time of the Roman Empire. "I must restore the pride of the Italian nation," he kept saying. "The value of the lira must be protected."[20]

Several days later in Cannes, Harriman arranged a meeting with Winston Churchill, Britain's vacationing chancellor of the exchequer, in part because it was a convenient opportunity to add another important political figure to his growing list of acquaintances, but more than that because he wanted to hear Churchill's views on the future of relations between London and Moscow. As he expected, Churchill told him nothing that lent confidence in the future of the New Economic Policy or his own concession. Churchill's view, simply put, was that it was pointless trying to do business with the Bolsheviks, his own country's recognition of the Soviets notwithstanding. The chancellor was clearly less interested in helping Harriman bring the future into focus than he was in analyzing his own failed effort to rally support for intervention in Russia eight years earlier. Had Britain and America been decisive, he grumped, the Communist government would have fallen before it became established.[21]

When Averell and Kitty finally reached New York aboard the White Star Line's *Olympic*, reporters following the developments with the manganese concession were waiting for him. Expecting them, he had written a press release to keep them at bay: "Matters under discussion would be adjusted," and meanwhile mining operations were "being conducted satisfactorily."[22]

In seeking to get the agreement rewritten, Harriman had driven a much harder bargain than he had in the beginning, and Concessions Committee finally consented to nearly everything he had demanded, including an agreement to accept $1 million in annual royalties instead of $2 million and to adopt his proposal for royalty payments tied to market price.

It was obvious, however, that the entire concessions program was in decline. The German press carried new allegations that foreigners were being mistreated by Soviet authorities, and Joffe acknowledged that some of the big concessionaires, Harriman among them, were having serious difficulties. A huge German timber concession was struggling because of high interest rates and a slump in the lumber market. Even the fabulously successful Krupp interests made a serious mistake, trying to produce grain on Russian land suitable only for livestock ranges.

The controversy over the manganese mines and Harriman's unsuccessful attempt to finance Russian trade through the Germans obscured more profitable European investments—including a huge mining operation in Silesia, undertaken in collaboration with the Anaconda Company, the world's biggest copper miner. Scarcely noticed in the United States, the Harriman-Anaconda interests secured a foothold in some of Europe's richest deposits of zinc and coal with lesser interests in stone quarries, silver mines, timber tracts, and brickyards.

Only months after the agreement was signed on the Georgian manganese concession, Harriman arranged a $10 million loan to the mining interests of Germany's Georg von Giesche estate, which had lost control of much of their most valuable property when Silesia was divided between Germany and Poland following the World War.

The financing was arranged through a new Harriman-Anaconda holding company called the Silesian-American Corporation. With $15 million raised from a stock offering eagerly snapped up by investors, it acquired control of Giesche Spolka Akcyjna, with the von Giesche interests as minority partners. The powerful combination dominated Polish zinc and coal mining and held options to acquire rich Giesche zinc mines just across the border in Germany.

Over a period of five years, Harriman envisioned huge increases in production through modernization and increased efficiency, agreeing to invest an additional $10 million in improvements during that period.

But not surprisingly, the deal ignited a political furor in Germany, with the press and politicians bitterly objecting to what they considered Harriman's "greedy tactics" and "slavery of German industry."[23] He found it, he said, "rather amusing." Although the Prussian government interceded and the option on acquisition of the German zinc mines expired, Silesian-American still held the rights to buy and process in its Polish smelters all of the zinc mined on the Giesche properties.

As the first big American capitalist to venture into postwar Poland, Harriman received a welcome dramatically unlike his reception in the Caucasus. The same summer the Soviets began cutting corners on the Georgian manganese concession, the Diet in Warsaw passed a law exempting foreigners—Harriman—from property taxes on zinc-smelting operations and providing for the duty-free export of zinc products for a period of twenty-five to thirty years. It was hardly surprising that he was followed into Poland by Standard Oil, General Motors, and International Match Corporation, among other American investors.

With the American stock market booming in the summer of 1928, Harriman moved to acquire three steel mills, employing about thirty thousand workers in northern Poland, along with several more mines. The $50 million deal provoked new alarm in Germany. The Harriman interests were already in control of a quarter of the world's zinc supply, and German nationalists saw imminent danger of his undercutting European steel cartel prices with cheap Polish iron and steel.[24]

In the face of the German opposition, it took eight months for the acquisition to go through. When it was completed in the spring of 1929, he had financial control of the biggest industrial complex in Poland, and he had laid the foundation for further expansion with nearly unimaginable potential. Even while the acquisition of the steel mills was pending, he had, at the suggestion of the Polish government, gone to work on a plan to generate and distribute electricity.

With vast coal resources plus zinc smelters and steel foundries consuming enormous quantities of electric power, Harriman could hardly avoid building generating plants. Once that step was taken, the possibility of constructing an electrical transmission system across Poland would be irresistible. In the summer of 1929, he began negotiations, providing the government with detailed plans for a sixty-year concession to generate electricity and distribute it to a third of Poland's population. His territory would include the northern industrial district, Warsaw, and seventy-five other towns and communities. At the outset, he proposed to buy an eighty-thousand-kilowatt steam plant at Chorzów and more than double its capacity. Then he would undertake construction of both hydroelectric and coal-fired generating stations. He proposed spending $15 million in the first five years, $10 million in the second five, and $1.5 million each year thereafter. After electrification of larger towns across northern Poland, the system would be extended to villages down to three thousand inhabitants.

The government was willing for him to press ahead, and he invested $400,000 in further plans for the system and for a new Polish company that would be organized to manage the concession. But opposition stirred quickly as the proposal was put before provincial governors. The Polish press took up the opposition, and party political leaders on both the left and right joined in. Harriman was characterized alternately as a tool of the Germans and as a dictatorial capitalist reaching for control of the country.

From outside Poland, there was a drumfire of press and political criticism, as well as competition from French interests, but Harriman expected to survive it because he had first undertaken his study of electrification at the request of the Polish government, and because he had the cooperation and support of the American embassy.

But after nearly a year, the plan was suddenly rejected. A message from the government said only that the Harriman terms were "unfavorable for the State from an economic point of view."[25] Privately, Irving Rossi, the European representative of W. A. Harriman and Company, was euphemistically told the obvious, that the concession had been scuttled "for reasons of state."[26] The Harriman interests had, in other words, gotten too big, too visible, and he had become a political problem within the country and without. Representatives of the American embassy went to the Foreign Ministry in search of a fuller explanation, but were "left to share the prevailing ignorance."[27]

Averell's lawyers, the brothers Allen and John Foster Dulles, were inclined to let the matter cool off and then try to restart the negotiations, but Harriman's interest faded. It took three years for him finally to settle on $100,000 worth of Polish bonds for the $400,000 he had invested in developing the electrification plans the government suggested.

Gradually, he withdrew from his investment in the country entirely as Poland backed away from the policies that had opened the door wide to him. Silesian-American's Polish mining subsidiary fell behind in its payments on the $13 million in loans for its modernization. New currency restrictions reneged on the favorable treatment of zinc exports. Harriman's men in Poland concluded the government was trying to force Americans out, but the American staff continued to run the mining operations until the Nazi occupation in 1939.

*   *   *

Although Harriman's negotiations in Moscow in 1926 and 1927 were successful, they did not make the manganese mines profitable. With Stalin solidifying his dictatorship of both the Soviet Communist party and the government, Lenin's idea that Western capital could be used as a tool of the revolution waned, as did Harriman's optimism.

Vernon Taylor, a Pennsylvania oil expert Harriman had sent on a follow-up visit to the oil fields of the Caucasus, left Baku thinking the pipeline project foolish. First stopping in Moscow, Taylor had been favorably impressed by his talks with Foreign Minister Litvinov and other officials, but after an inspection tour in the Caucasus, he concluded their assurances were worthless. His conclusion was "not only that Russia was not at present a suitable field for investment but that the propagandist activities of the Soviet regime constituted a menace to all capitalist countries."[28]

The fatal blow to the manganese concession, in the view of State Department analysts, came when the Soviets prevented Harriman from protecting himself against the anemic ruble. Under his contract, he was required to buy the Soviet currency from the state bank for two years, vastly adding to the cost of his operations when the Soviet currency could be bought elsewhere at a fraction of the official rate. Georgian Manganese turned to Turkey.

Under their trade agreement with the Soviets, the Turks sold their goods in Russia and accepted payment in rubles. This left them with the problem of getting rid of the Soviet currency. When Harriman offered to buy it in large amounts to meet his payroll and expenses in the Caucasus, the Turks jumped at the opportunity. The transactions saved him $750,000 before the Soviets objected.

The dispute compounded a host of other problems. During the winter after Harriman's visit, rain, snow, and cold made it nearly impossible for miners to work, and the uncertainty of ship schedules at Poti disrupted loading and transportation operations. Boats would fail to arrive on schedule and then dock in twos, threes, or fours.[29] Relations with the unions and former mine owners continued to deteriorate. When an old washing plant mysteriously went up in flames, Harriman's men could only conclude that arson was the cause.

Although the Soviets cut production at Nikopol as promised, they still undersold Harriman, as did new foreign producers. Manganese from Georgia had become the most expensive on the market.

J. C. Hays, an engineer dismissed as mining operations were cut back, told American officials upon reaching Helsinki: "The workmen do as much or as little work as they see fit and you cannot say anything to them if they loaf on the job as all do. The workmen feel that they are the government; they simply do you a favor by being connected with

your business, that it is not for the employer to say how much or how
little work a man is to do. There is no incentive at all for a workman to
do first class work. High class work does not necessarily bring increased
compensation. Practically, a premium is placed on mediocrity. The result
is that there is no efficiency, that there is no attempt on the part of any
of the workmen to acquire skill in their particular work. Everything is
reduced to a dead level bordering on stagnation."[30]

On top of all this, manganese prices continued to drop. Even with
the benefit of the sliding royalty scale, Harriman was losing $2 on every
ton he sold. Scarcely more than a year after his own Moscow negotiations,
he finally realized that it was impossible to do business in the Soviet
Union. He served notice on the Soviet government, demanding arbitration and cancellation of the contract.

Both he and the Russians, mutually embarrassed by the failure, were
reluctant to put the matter before an arbitrator who would conduct his
review somewhere outside the Soviet Union. The inevitable bad publicity
would damage hopes of expanding trade with the West and winning the
diplomatic recognition of the United States. In a last try at dissuading
Harriman from his decision to get out, the Soviet labor commissar solemnly promised the engineers at Chiaturi that the labor troubles would
be stopped forthwith, but it was too late.[31]

The concession had been doomed from the beginning. Operating
from afar, Harriman had gone into the enterprise without understanding that the Soviets really did not care whether concessionaires made
money from their operations, and most of his difficulties had resulted
from that. "The initial contract signed by Harriman representatives
would have made old E. H. Harriman turn in his grave because it was
so utterly inept," Walter Duranty wrote in *The New York Times*.[32]

Ultimately, the Soviets agreed to negotiate a settlement. The task
fell to Robinson and George Piatakov, chief of Moscow's Paris trade
delegation, who had represented the Soviets when the initial agreement
had been concluded three years earlier. Not surprisingly, the talks
dragged on for weeks, with both sides trying to escape with their pride
intact.

For Harriman and Robinson, settlement was complicated by their
minority partners. Germans who had broken ranks with their government and joined Harriman only to come up empty felt that he had
not taken advantage of their expertise. Now they wanted a separate
settlement in which Harriman would buy them out.

But after suffering three years of their petulance, Harriman had no
such intention. The Germans, he told Robinson, were "as much responsible as anyone for failure of the enterprise. . . ." In fact, he said, it was
"because of their familiarity with the business that I was much influenced
to go ahead with the original concession." And once the trouble started,

they had been "destructive, critical, and when pinned down have never made a concrete suggestion."[33]

Later, in a more charitable vein, he suggested that he and the Germans might together coerce the Soviets into buying back the bonds that would be given in settlement of the concession. "After Robinson has closed his deal," he cabled Disconto Bank chairman George Solmssen in Berlin, "would you care to attempt to force government to purchase at discount notes we would then hold? Threat to make public market for notes at low price which would injure their credit might be used to force purchase of at least part."[34]

Solmssen wasn't interested, but he still had enough regard for Harriman as a financial operator that he asked to be taken into the Silesian mining enterprise. "Perhaps," the chairman cabled in fractured English, "this business or some other profitable transaction in which we may take part enables you to give us the opportunity to make good the considerable loss encountered at Tchiaturi. We would regard an offer of this kind as a reciprocation of the many good services which we believe to have rendered in Germany to your good firm."[35] If Harriman replied, the answer was evidently no, for Disconto was not among the participants in the Silesian mines.

The outline of a settlement with the Soviets began to emerge soon after the talks began. The Harriman group would be reimbursed for its capital investment in the mines, the railroad, and the seaport, and Harriman would grant the Russians an additional loan so they could take over operation of the mines themselves. The negotiations then settled into bickering over the true amount of the American's investment, the size of the loan, and the terms for repayment.

In the end, the Soviets agreed to a figure of $3,450,000 for Harriman's capital investment. For his part, he agreed to accept payment in the form of fifteen-year bonds bearing an interest rate of 7 percent, and to provide the Soviets with a five-year loan of $1 million to keep the mines going. Both he and the Russian government claimed satisfaction from the experience. The loan became a trophy for officials in Moscow, held up in Europe as testament to their credibility with one of America's foremost capitalists. It was to Moscow "the final breach in the American policy of restriction on trade with the U.S.S.R."[36]

With Harriman's departure, the Georgian mines came under control of Rawaek und Grünfeld, the German operators of the Nikopol field. The richest deposits of all, the Perevissi Hill area, which had been withheld from Harriman's concession, became the major source of their exports. The Soviets had cleverly gotten Harriman to mechanize low-grade deposits and install loading facilities so they could subsequently open up the highest-grade deposits themselves. In a cruel blow to Averell's ego, the Germans soon signed a five-year contract to sell as much as

150,000 tons of ore per year to the United States Steel Corporation, the crucial customer he had never obtained.

When the Soviet press announced that the concession was being turned over to a Soviet trust, there was no hint that Harriman had quit Georgia in disgust. It was, instead, made to appear that the Harriman deal had come out entirely in the Soviets' favor, which was almost true. The capitalists had served their purpose and now the Soviet government was prepared to step in, bring the management directly under the control of Soviet experts, increase the mines' output, and create thousands of new jobs for workers.

"The collapse of the Harriman concession is not a collapse of the concession policy of the Chief Concession Committee," *Economic Life* editorialized in Moscow. "It is the collapse of a generally wrong business policy of the concessionaire; it is a collapse which was the result of a change on the world's market."[37]

Harriman chose to regard the end of the affair as testament to his own perspicacity and skill in liquidating a potential disaster. He had negotiated his way out of a dead end, escaping without losing money, while concessionaires who lingered suffered heavy losses. Some of his associates, doubting that the Russians would ever redeem the bonds, sold theirs at hefty discounts, but Harriman did not join in a public effort to embarrass the Soviets as he had suggested to his German associates. Among the purchasers of the discounted Soviet bonds was Armand Hammer, who, nearing the end of his long stay in the Soviet Union, had established a small banking operation in Paris.

Though under ordinary circumstances it would never have approved the $1 million Harriman loan to the Soviets, the State Department decided not to challenge the settlement, figuratively dropping the last of its barriers to commercial relations with the USSR.

There were difficulties back in Georgia, however. As the Bolsheviks took control of the mines, cutting pay and selling off clothes and boots that had been imported for the miners, the Russians and Georgians who had worked closely with officials of the company were arrested, and some were sent off to Siberia. Concerned over his million-dollar loan and still not certain that the Soviets would redeem the $3,450,000 worth of their bonds that he owned, Harriman held his tongue—and his bonds. In private, however, he had concluded that Americans doing business in the Soviet Union were falling prey to "the grandest aggregation of corruption, incompetence, and utter brutality that the world has seen for centuries."[38]

The final settlement of the account came on schedule fifteen years later, the last payment of $137,000 being deposited to his account in the Chase National Bank in New York.

Chapter VII

PLAYBOY
A Moment at Meadow Brook

As the Harrimans celebrated Christmas, 1927, at Arden, railroad cars parked on a siding at the estate were loaded with polo ponies, heavy trunks of saddles, bridles, mallets, and farrier's gear, a La Salle automobile, and the personal effects of grooms, trainers, and their families. Averell was headed for the California sunshine and the fields of combat at clubs in Carmel, Santa Barbara, and Pasadena.

In spite of the increasingly precarious state of his Soviet manganese concession and grumbling among his associates that he was not paying sufficient attention to business, he had decided to give much of the coming year to the game that had become his obsession. Although he was anything but a gifted athlete, he had developed into a remarkably good polo player, and he was getting much better. Riding at full tilt, he could smack powerful drives downfield, receive passes without breaking stride, and turn with the confidence of an Indian brave to defend against an opponent's charge.

He now rode with the country's best players, the elite of an elitist sport—men who reigned over an ancient Persian game that found its way to America via India and England. Adopted by Anglophiles, it had been vastly improved and transformed into a spectator sport by the eastern rich, blossoming in the twenties when its pace, style, and abandon expressed the vibrant atmosphere of a robust America. Polo symbolized the good life. It *was* the good life. In the winter, Harriman and his friends played in California, in the spring in North and South Carolina,

164

in the summer at the Meadow Brook and Piping Rock clubs on Long Island, and in the fall at his own fields at Arden. At the offices of W. A. Harriman and Company, the joke was that he would have long since been a world-class player had he not allowed business to interfere.

The trip being prepared as Averell went through the ritual of delivering gifts to the estate employees on Christmas Eve was not an ordinary vacation. During the coming fall, the best polo team the United States could assemble was scheduled to play Argentina for what amounted to the world championship, and Harriman intended to be on it. He had been playing the game since he was a teenager and his sister Cornelia had begged a reluctant E.H. to buy Arden's first polo ponies. Although Averell rode well, it was not until his sister Mary married Charles Cary Rumsey that he took up polo in earnest. His sculptor—brother-in-law had grown up playing in Buffalo, where one of the first polo clubs in America had been established. He was good at every known skill of horsemanship, polo included, and harbored ambitions to play in international competition himself. When Rumsey brought serious polo to the flat fields at the bottom of Mount Orama, Averell was caught up in it as he had been in no other sport except rowing.

It was more satisfying than riding to hounds or driving a sulky, because it called for strategic wisdom and tactical instinct in addition to physical skills. He had never really loved harness racing, a sport that required him to crouch down close behind a horse's hindquarters, catching the dirt and dust of the track as he hunched forward in a sulky, with his long arms and legs stretched out uncomfortably before him. After driving, he was inevitably seized by fits of sneezing and troubled by watery eyes, symptoms of what he considered a classic case of "horse asthma." His interest in trotting waned sharply after the horse ran away with him in the race in Cleveland. The episode had embarrassed him in a sport that had brought acclaim to his brother. Roland had begun breaking trotting records at the Goshen Driving Club while he was still in his teens, and his wife, Gladys, was herself a championship racer. The two of them were trotting patrons and promoters as well as competitive drivers, and Averell had no taste for vying with them on their turf. He was, after all, the first son.

Polo had drama and suspense. It had beauty and grace. The men who played it and the people who followed it had a style and verve and glamour missing from the hunt and the trotting track. It required superior riding skill, coordination, reflexes, and patience. To play it well, one had to have both upper and lower body strength, good peripheral vision, and an instinct for the ball. Although he was an excellent horseman, Averell was willowy and thin, lacking the thick shoulders and torso to muscle opponents off the ball, or hit the long drives that launched scoring assaults. Seasoned players who watched him at Arden and during the early days at the Meadow Brook Club at Old Westbury, Long Island, saw no likelihood that he would ever be anything more than an ordinary weekend player.[1]

But he had well learned his early lessons from Pad Rumsey. His brother-in-law had not only helped him hone his mallet skills and understand the finer points of tactics and strategy, but he had also showed him the special kind of horsemanship required by the game. On the polo field at Arden, Rumsey had introduced a rough-and-tumble game in which riders tried to unseat each other from galloping ponies by grabbing a kerchief worn around the neck. The only object was to be the last survivor in the saddle, but the competition demanded the same kind of agility and balance required on the polo field, and from it Harriman acquired robust confidence. He did not hesitate to ride headlong into scrimmages with mallet flailing, challenging opponents for a free ball shoulder-to-shoulder at breakneck speed. He was unintimidated by larger horses or stronger riders. Struck by an errant mallet, he drove ahead. Unseated, he scrambled back into the saddle.

He began playing organized polo at Meadow Brook in 1915, but he was not awarded a rating by the U.S. Polo Association until 1921, when he was assigned a handicap of one, the lowest rung of a rating scale that made a ten-goal handicap a level achieved by only a tiny fraction of the world's best players. In 1923, he moved up to a four, and from 1924 to 1927, he stood at five, meaning that he was much more than an ordinary club player but at least a couple of notches below international caliber.

Because it was impossible for him to get home to Arden to play in the afternoon, he took a cottage near the Rumseys' at East Williston, Long Island. Then he could slip out of the office in the afternoon in time for a full game before dusk. Later, when he acquired a bungalow on Long Island Sound at Sands Point, he often commuted to the foot of Wall Street in a speedy motor launch, avoiding the entanglement of automobile traffic crossing the East River.

About the same time he began playing at Meadow Brook, he started to import world-class polo ponies from England and Argentina, crossbreeding them with Thoroughbreds, following the trend toward bigger and faster mounts that had already changed the American game to one of speed and wide-open offense. He hired an English army captain to come to Arden to school his ponies and develop his own trainers, and long before his handicap was anything to attract attention, his ponies were the envy of Long Island.

His real ascension began when he met Tommy Hitchcock, a World War I air hero who was well on the way to recognition as the greatest polo player in the world. Before he was out of his teens, Hitchcock had shot down two German planes, and in turn had been shot down and imprisoned for five months before escaping and making his way to Switzerland. He had first played polo when he was so small that he had to be lifted onto the back of his pony. By the time he was twenty-one, he was already a member of the United States' international team, revealing the same daring he had demonstrated as a *pilote de chasse* in Lafayette Escadrille.

He was the sport's Babe Ruth, bringing to it an electricity and excitement produced by no one else. Idolized by fans who had never seen a match until they pushed their way into grandstands just to watch him ride, he had the perfect polo physique: muscular shoulders, a long waist, and short, powerful legs that allowed him to do battle standing erect in his stirrups. Wielding his mallet with fluid, sweeping strokes, he could drive the ball awe-inspiring distances. He instinctively organized and led, his uncanny anticipation always putting him wherever control of the ball was contested. He rallied offensive charges and snuffed out enemy assaults without raising his voice, lifting his teammates to play beyond their own abilities. Harriman idolized him.

After practice in the afternoon and club matches on weekends, Averell kept him behind to talk tactics, and it was not uncommon for him to persuade the star to practice with him in the early morning and to visit Arden after the Long Island season was over. There Averell's teams played autumn weekend matches against cadets and faculty members from nearby West Point, and continued to have pickup games until they were driven to shelter by cold wind and muddy ground.

In the city, Hitchcock shared a townhouse with George Gordon Moore, a rough-edged lawyer and avid sportsman who had made a fortune in stocks and mining investments and played rather ragged polo with extraordinary zeal on both coasts. Through the winter, Moore's uninhibited parties at the house on East Fifty-second Street drew a crowd of polo players, unattached women, theater people, and journalists who followed the game, and Harriman was one of the regulars in what Moore considered his little "corporation."[2] When time came for play in California, Moore's estate in the mountains overlooking the Pacific became the headquarters for his New York friends. "What they now call the roaring twenties was ours," Moore wrote Harriman many years later, after he had lost both his fortune and his health. "It is my private conceit that in those years our little coterie had the greatest robust fun . . . ."[3]

It was Harry Payne Whitney who made Long Island—Meadow Brook and Old Westbury—the mecca of polo in the United States. The first American to reach the exalted status of a ten handicap, he had assembled and led the American team that went to England and swept the International Cup in 1909. England recaptured it in 1914, and it remained overseas through the war, but a new American team established supremacy in 1921. With the British team decisively subdued and no challenge for the cup due for three years, Argentina emerged as the chief threat to the dominance of the gentlemen on Long Island.

The gauchos won the U.S. Open championship in 1922, and would have completed their conquest unblemished but for a stunning upset by Harriman's Orange County team. Made up of Pad Rumsey, Raymond Belmont, Malcolm Stevenson, and himself, Averell's team was given little chance. Stevenson was the only one of the four who had ever ridden in international competition, and the others had only recently begun playing as a team. But the squad shocked the Argentine national team, 13–10, igniting in Averell a burning ambition to play on the United States' international squad. Almost overnight the victory over the Argentines also made Orange County a highly regarded competitor on the U.S. tournament circuit. Just days afterward, however, the team was shattered. On the way home from practice Rumsey was thrown from the rear seat of an open car and killed. The team was finished for the season, and Averell was without the friend who had most encouraged his polo ambitions.

By 1924, when he at last got his opportunity to contest for a place on the U.S. international team, Averell was twenty-eight, well beyond the age when world-class polo players ordinarily break into competition; but with the British coming to Meadow Brook to play for the Westchester Cup, he got into test matches and established himself in the front ranks of emerging new players. Unfortunately for him, all of the Big Four who had beaten England three years earlier, regarded by many as the greatest polo team in history, were still playing near their peak, even if their formidable physical skills were diminished. Therefore, it surprised no one when the United States' Defense Committee announced the same lineup that had taken the field at Hurlingham in 1921—Devereux Milburn, the captain, playing at back; J. Watson Webb at number one, Tommy Hitchcock at number two, and Malcolm Stevenson at number three. Aside from Hitchcock, who was still only twenty-four, all were older than Harriman. Milburn was forty-three, Webb was thirty-nine, and Stevenson was thirty-seven. So, there was still time.

In their battle for the cup that fall, the American four overpowered the British in two straight games and popularized polo as a spectator sport, not only for the well-to-do who kept summer places on Long Island but for more ordinary New Yorkers being swept along in the uninhibited twenties.

The game epitomized the good times that existed for monied Americans. The rich, comforted by the unintrusive presence of Calvin Coolidge in the White House, reveled in their wealth, and the middle class pampered themselves with cars and radios and toasters. Adventurers celebrated triumphs of speed of the automobile and the airplane, and ordinary people briefly escaped their ordinary lives in the dim, carpeted, crushed-velvet–luxury of marble movie palaces. Million-dollar purses came to boxing. The home run came to baseball, and bobbed hair, shortened skirts, and cigarettes came to liberated American women.

The 1924 English team was followed to the United States by the rakishly handsome Prince Edward of Wales and his own string of eight polo ponies. The presence of a future King captivated the eastern seaboard, bringing thousands of young women out to Long Island hoping for a glimpse of him. As he docked on a private launch that fetched him from the ocean liner *Berengaria* at the quarantine station, gawking, flag-waving crowds spread along the shoreline from Oyster Bay to Glen Cove.

After a quick trip to Washington for lunch with the President, he settled in at the James R. Burden estate at Syosset for nearly a month to play polo, ride to hounds, take in the races and party until dawn. Harriman and Kitty dined with the heir to the throne at the Piping Rock Club, and Averell played polo with him on fields sealed off from crowds and the clamoring newspapermen. The year after the prince's sojourn on the island, Harriman and his Orange County team again surprised the experts by winning the United States Open, defeating a heavily favored Meadow Brook team that included both Hitchcock and Devereux Milburn. Hitchcock was in his prime, and Milburn, although approaching the end of his career, was still one of the world's most formidable players. Against such a team, Harriman's Orange County four was supposed to have little chance, and the championship finale was as surprising for its intensity as it was for the 11–9 Orange County victory. Mallets were shattered and helmets were lost, and on one occasion, Hitchcock was very nearly knocked off his pony in a ferocious scrimmage that moved from sideline to sideline.

Though it played beautifully, Harriman's team was also the beneficiary of unusual luck—it scored one cheap goal while Hitchcock was on the sideline replacing a broken mallet, and it received a gift of another when Hitchcock accidentally knocked the ball into his own goal. Averell scored three goals, riding shoulder-to-shoulder with Hitchcock and Milburn.

The battle established Averell as one of the top players in the country, bringing him attention rivaling that he had received from the steamship business. He was in the public mind a rich man's son, still not quite grown up, though he was approaching thirty. If he succeeded in business, he was reminded that he had been given E.H.'s millions. If he succeeded in polo or his other diversions such as horse racing and dog breeding, he was a playboy. And he did succeed, not only as a player but as a racing-stable owner and a breeder of champion Labrador retrievers. He got into horse racing almost as a family obligation, since his sisters owned Thoroughbreds and his wife adored racing. In 1922, he started his own string of racehorses with George Herbert Walker, his partner in W. A. Harriman and Company whose grandson, George Herbert Walker Bush, would become President of the United States. Two years after they organized Log Cabin Stables around a few colts bought from Harry Payne Whitney, August Belmont's death gave them a chance to get into racing on a larger scale.

Through close family friendships, Averell had long been familiar with the stable and the Belmont bloodlines. His older sister Cornelia had come within $500 of buying Man o' War, the most famous Belmont colt of all, bidding $4,500 for him at the 1918 yearling sale at Saratoga. But her husband, Robert Gerry, refused to go any higher, on grounds that no colt could be worth such an astronomical amount.

In January 1925, soon after Belmont died, Averell and Walker bought all of his horses in training. For $225,000, they got seventeen untried colts, a four-year-old stallion named Ladkin, considered one of the better racehorses in the country, and two established three-year-olds.[4] The real gem, however, was a colt called Chance Play, a son of Man o' War who went on to become the country's top racehorse as a four-year-old, winning the Saratoga Cup and the Jockey Club Gold Cup and making Harriman a big name in racing. Indeed the horse was good enough to cause the breakup of Averell's Log Cabin Stables partnership with Walker.

The latter got his racing satisfaction at the betting window, and, therefore, he wanted to keep their best horse on the racing circuit. Harriman favored a few prestige races and careful preparation for a long and successful career at stud. Because of continuous differences over when, where, and how often to race Chance Play, they dissolved their partnership, with Averell keeping the horse and organizing his new Arden Farms Stables around him. By the time the big chestnut stallion was retired at the end of the 1928 racing season, he had won sixteen of thirty-nine races and purses totaling $137,946.[5] Averell was on hand for most of the victories, from Saratoga to Belmont Park to Havre de Grace in Maryland, but when he ended his career in the winner's circle at Belmont, the owner was absent, enjoying the pinnacle of his own career in polo.

At the same time he was wheeling and dealing in shipping and international finance and making his name as a sportsman, Harriman was also carrying on a long-running liaison with a dark-eyed actress—cabaret singer named Teddy Gerard. He had to be discreet about it in New York, but in Europe he had been rather careless, and the word quickly circulated around Long Island and lower Broadway that she was often with him during his business trips overseas. Gerard had got her start as a teenaged dancer-singer-actress in Argentina before making her 1909 New York debut as a member of the chorus of *Havana*. Six years later, she launched her film career in *Billy's Spanish Love Spasm* (sic), and then moved on to Europe. In London during the war, she was a nightclub singer popular enough to start a fad of Teddy Gerard hats and gowns and to make a fan of Winston Churchill, who knew the lyrics of a number of her songs.

In the early twenties, she moved back to New York, where she played the Amsterdam Roof Garden, appeared in Florenz Ziegfeld's *Midnight Frolic*, and earned several small Broadway roles, all while she tried to establish a film career working for Inspiration Pictures. Her later films—*Cave Girl* and *The Seventh Day*—were scarcely more successful than *Billy's Spanish Love Spasm*, although she was the heroine of *Cave Girl*, playing opposite Boris Karloff.

During her stays in New York, the sultry Gerard lived in a stylish apartment Averell provided for her in Greenwich Village, amusing herself painting portraits and making herself far less conspicuous than she did when they were in Europe. In 1924 and 1925, Averell and Kitty spent months apart. In the midst of one separation when Averell and Kitty were both in Europe but following separate intineraries, Gerard quit the cast of *The Rat* on Broadway and sailed for England on the *Leviathan*. The press quoted unnamed informants to the effect that she was headed for Europe to marry Harriman.[6]

When the ocean liner reached Southhampton, the *New York Daily News* reported, she was to be met by Harriman. "That the young Harriman and Miss Gerard are engaged is insisted on as a fact by those claiming familiarity with their plans," continued the *News*. "That they are to wed soon after Miss Gerard reaches England is the understanding along Broadway.

"Miss Gerard's departure was hasty. It followed her receipt of a cable message early Friday. Although she sailed on the Leviathan, her name did not figure on the passenger list. Considering her normal chattiness, she was singularly uncommunicative."[7]

Divorce had become inevitable, but not because of Teddy Gerard, although she was becoming an embarrassment. Averell and Kitty had not known each other well when they were wed, and probably would never have married but for the riding accident in the midst of their courtship for which he felt responsible.

After the first two or three years, it had hardly been a marriage at all. When Kitty was barely recovered from the accident, there were the two babies in less than a year, and then tuberculosis. Because of her health, she was often confined or away from the city in more healthy environments: the ranch in Idaho, Arden, Lenox, or Overhills, the North Carolina retreat where Averell and several friends built cottages. In the Long Island polo crowd, she was seldom seen, and some of Averell's friends had no idea that he was married.

In September 1924, Kitty, her daughters, and their tutor, took an apartment in Paris and a house in England. Sometimes accompanied by the children and at other times alone, she spent the fall and winter taking trips about Europe, including a Mediterranean cruise and a sojourn in the Alps, where she renewed her friendship with adventurer and polar explorer Lincoln Ellsworth.[8]

She regularly got letters from Averell, but they were usually about polo, how he and his various ponies had performed, and about the prominent mares being taken to Arden to be bred to his prized sire, Prince Friarstown. She was still in Europe when he arrived to round up more investors for the manganese mines in January 1925. Before leaving New York, he had wired her that he would be at the Carlton in London for a few days before going on to Germany, and was "awfully keen to be together as much as possible."[9]

In the spring, they reunited for a trip to Spain and to the south of France, where he spent several days playing polo, but they were once again going their separate ways when the Teddy Gerard stories got into print in New York.

As Gerard sailed, Roland Harriman, who ordinarily kept his distance from his brother's personal life, sent a stern letter recommending that Averell and Kitty return from Europe together. "Things have quieted down considerably about your troubles, but everyone is keenly interested still & watching for the next move. I won't go into details, but I think it is essential that you & Kitty *return together*, no matter how inconvenient it may be. Otherwise, I am afraid no amount of denial will avail. Altho' I didn't see it, I understand there was an article in the Daily News when T. sailed announcing her departure in order to marry you. I am afraid, therefore, that unless you come together, the reputable papers will not hold off. I am not trying to frighten or argue with you, but would like you to take my word for it." He went on to talk about Mary Harriman's frail health, intimating that Averell and Kitty could ease her of some of her worries.[10]

But for Mary Harriman's adamant disapproval of divorce, the marriage might have already ended. The matriarch's view of acceptable moral behavior had not been altered by the jazzy twenties. She joined Episcopalian churchwomen, including Mrs. James Roosevelt, the mother of the future President, Mrs. J. P. Morgan, and others in proposing an organization to discourage any "excess of nudity" and "improper ways of dancing."[11] When dresses became shorter, she insisted that conference rooms have tables so that the legs of women present would not be subject to view.[12] To her, divorce was categorically unacceptable, and besides that, she had developed a special relationship with her daughter-in-law, who, during Averell's travels, had often stayed at Arden.

Neither Averell nor Kitty wanted to risk a divorce that would hasten the old lady's decline, so their unavoidable breakup was delayed by mutual consent. As Roland recommended, they came home from Europe together in the spring of 1925 and continued to live together in their house on Washington Square. To Mary Harriman's delight, Kitty even joined Averell when he made his trip to the Soviet Union to try to salvage the manganese mining enterprise the following year.

Teddy Gerard's departure for England and his return with Kitty did not end the "troubles" that worried Roland and the family, however. When movie producer Charles Duell wound up on trial for perjury after a bitter contract dispute with screen star Lillian Gish, testimony revealed that Averell owned $400,000 worth of preferred stock in Inspiration Pictures, Gish's studio. The company had encountered a financial crisis during the filming of the Gish picture *Romola,* and he had made it additional loans of $600,000. Actually, it had been an arrangement between Yale men—Averell, his 1913 classmate Walter Camp, Jr., who worked for W. A. Harriman and Company, and Duell. Although there were hints in court that Harriman had a romantic interest in Gish, the real reason for his using Camp to conceal his interest in Inspiration Pictures was not Gish but Teddy Gerard.

Harriman's chances of breaking into international polo were fading when his seventeen ponies were loaded for the trip to California at the end of 1927. Even though his team had upset Argentina in 1922 and had won the U.S. Open in 1925, he had not even been among the players invited by the Defense Committee to take part in a month of trial play to pick the U.S. team for the 1927 showdown with the British, his handicap of six notwithstanding.

The coming year, 1928, when the United States would again play Argentina for the championship of the Americas, would be his best and probably last opportunity to make the international team. Only Hitchcock would remain from the squad that had dominated international competition through the decade. The United States would be searching for a new Big Four.

The journey to California for the first weeks of 1928 was the beginning of an eight-month campaign to ratchet his game up to a level that would put him on the United States' team in the September match with Argentina. Home base in the West was George Gordon Moore's 22,000-acre ranch near Santa Barbara, where Moore put up Averell, Hitchcock, and the other Long Island players in their own guest cottages near his fifty-seven-room hacienda. They had the use of his polo field, his ponies, golf course, and private game preserve. To ward off boredom, Moore always arranged at least one wild boar hunt in which, on horseback, they went after their prey with spears.

During two months in California, Harriman played polo every day.

When there was no game, he and J. A. Crawford, his groom, who had ridden the train delivering his mounts and equipment to the coast, schooled his ponies. After Hitchcock arrived in February, the two of them teamed up with Moore and Aiden Roark, playing in matches from Carmel to Santa Barbara to Pasadena, winning the Pacific Coast Tournament at the Midwick Country Club in Los Angeles with relative ease. The fiercest competition came in the semifinals, when they faced the Midwick club's own team that included Cheever Cowdin and Robert Strawbridge, who were also members of Harriman's Orange County four. Averell was the high goal man, scoring four times as Moore's San Carlos Cardinals won 10–8.

Two days later, playing before a crowd of nine thousand, they romped past a team led by the Marquis de Portagos, a Spaniard with international aspirations, who had two members of the English international team riding with him. As always, the game was dominated by Hitchcock, but Harriman was rapidly improving. Playing at the number three position, where he had to fight for possession of the ball and pass it down field to Moore at forward, he still managed to score twice in the 12–6 victory for the Pacific championship. After that, Hitchcock headed back for New York, but Averell stayed on for another month, organizing another team and continuing match play.

Hollywood in the twenties was in love with polo, and because Harriman was a rising star in the eastern firmament, he was envied by weekend club players without handicap and courted by fixtures of the movie colony. Young Bob Lovett's wife, Adele, visited Pasadena that winter, and when Averell took her along to a party given by the famous movie producer King Vidor, she was astonished that the man who had seemed to her hopelessly stodgy and dull in New York was at home among the glamorous figures of the film industry.

Harriman was back at Moore's ranch at the end of February when Roland cabled that the Russians were refusing to send a representative to meet with Richard Robinson on the deteriorating situation with the manganese concession. The only thing left to do was to demand arbitration and bring the whole thing to an end. But not even the collapse of the mightily promoted deal with Moscow was enough to interrupt polo. He stayed in California until winter ended in the East, and then headed back on schedule, remaining just long enough to see his mother and the children. Then, with Kitty, Hitchcock, and Peggy Laughlin, Hitchcock's fiancée, he took the train south to Aiken, South Carolina to resume serious training.

Aiken was a hunting and shooting paradise with carefully manicured racetracks and ten polo fields, one of which Averell leased from the Whitneys. The prospect of riding in the warm Carolina sun had a special appeal because Cornelius Vanderbilt "Sonny" Whitney was there with his wife, Marie, and the Harrimans were to be their guests. Sonny was in his mid-twenties and usually acted considerably younger, but he was a Yale man, a former member of the varsity crew, and a polo player of promise. Averell had known him since he was a boy, and for several years they had played against each other and occasionally traded ponies.

But more than polo or the Carolina sunshine it was Marie Whitney who made the Aiken trip compelling: Harriman had fallen in love with Sonny's wife. Unlike his frolic with Teddy Gerard, his interest in Marie Whitney had not drawn attention, because she and her husband were in the polo crowd that partied together during the Long Island season.

Mrs. Whitney was still a month short of her twenty-fifth birthday, a stunning brunette with violet-blue eyes, an eye-catching figure, and a merry irreverence for money, the Long Island social order, her husband, even polo itself. She laughed, swore, chewed gum, and danced the Charleston. She also golfed, played tennis, rode horseback, and shot birds. Nonetheless, she had about her an unusual maturity for a woman her age, and Averell found her irresistible.

Marie and her sister, Frances, had spent their childhood summers at Glen Cove, Long Island. The daughters of Sheridan Norton, a moderately well-off lawyer, and Beulah Einstein, a quintessential Jewish mother, they were only eleven months apart, and they were decorous attractions at polo matches across the island and parties on the North Shore.

Sonny Whitney had met Frances Norton at a Piping Rock polo match while he was still a student at Yale, and had invited her to one of his parties aboard the Whitney yacht, *Whileaway*. Out of both habit and prudence, "Frankie" Norton took her sister along. The decision ended Sonny's blooming interest in her, for the moment he saw Marie, he shuffled place cards, banished Frances to the opposite end of the table with his cousin, Douglas Burden, and gave Marie the rush. To the consternation of his mother, Gertrude Vanderbilt Whitney, they were engaged within months.[13]

Although they had stayed together for six years, the marriage was a disaster almost from the beginning. While they were still engaged, Sonny was hit with a massively publicized $1 million breach-of-promise lawsuit by Evan Burrows Fontaine, a dancer who had performed at one of his parties and claimed that in a subsequent relationship he had fathered her child and promised repeatedly to marry her.

It was a tabloid dream: illicit love, a show girl, high society, the scion of a great fortune put on display in daily headlines. Sonny was not an ordinary rich man's son. He was a great-grandson of old Commodore Vanderbilt himself, and the son of the man reputed to possess a fortune second only to the Rockefellers'.

Fontaine's claims were exposed as fraudulent when the sleuths retained by the Whitneys discovered that she had been married to a sailor at the time Sonny supposedly proposed to her. The upshot of the case was that both Fontaine and her mother were charged with perjury and she was briefly sent to jail for falsely swearing that her marriage had been annulled at the time of her fling with Sonny. Because of the notoriety of the case, however, Sonny and Marie went to Paris to be married, but even there, guards had to be hired to prevent reporters and photographers from infiltrating the church. Their honeymoon in Europe and the Middle East lasted several months, and when they returned, they moved west. Sonny was put on a retainer from his father and given a position in which he was supposed to learn about the family's mining interests, an assignment which conveniently kept him beyond the reach of the New York press. The subsequent course of the union was as uncertain as its beginning, however. Once the Fontaine affair faded, Sonny fully recovered his roving eye and justified all of his parents' doubts about his maturity.

He was the one who first broached the subject of divorce, and when Marie's father tried to bring about a reconciliation, he ignored the overture. So Harriman was hardly in the position of a wife stealer, although he received the accusation. Averell, like the rest of the young Whitneys' friends, became aware of their troubles during evenings when Sonny drank too much and became publicly insulting. At one of Tommy Hitchcock's parties, Marie fled the house in tears, but in the boisterous atmosphere the incident went unnoticed by all except Averell and Charles Lindbergh, who followed her outside and consoled her. It was the first time Averell and Marie had ever talked seriously, and it was the beginning of a romance.[14]

By the time of the Harrimans' trip to Aiken in the spring of 1928, anybody who knew Marie and Sonny was aware that their marriage was a wreck. When they were together, they were surrounded by friends to ease the tension of each other's company.

Not long before Aiken, Sonny had organized a bonefishing trip and had invited half a dozen friends, including playwright Philip Barry and his wife, Ellen. They sailed from Palm Beach at midnight aboard his yacht, *Adventure*. Expecting rough water, they fortified themselves with champagne, hoping to sleep as they crossed the choppy Gulf Stream on the way to Bimini. But they had barely fallen asleep—Marie sharing a cabin with Ellen Barry—when they hit a raging storm, and for the rest of the night, all clung desperately to their bunks. When daylight came, no one aboard, including the pilot hired to find the bonefish waters, had any idea where they were. Marie blamed Sonny for stupidly sailing with a crew that had never made the Bimini trip before.

At midmorning, deliverance came when they spotted a rum boat pitching and rolling in the waves but maintaining a steady heading. They followed it, winding up in Nassau, where they docked beside a yacht even more imposing than Whitney's *Adventure*, and shortly afterwards they met its owner—Al Capone, the country's most successful bootlegger.

For Sonny, it was a chance to salvage something worthwhile from the whole misadventure, for he and the gangster had a mutual interest in horse racing. That evening, Capone and his bodyguard joined the Whitneys' table at the casino, but it was quickly obvious that his interest was in Marie and not in discussing Miami horse racing with her husband. Marie found his attention hilarious; her husband was livid.[15]

At Aiken, Averell and Mrs. Whitney, who was a notoriously late riser, were up at dawn for long horseback rides across the fields and through the pine forests while all the others slept. The only other person out at that hour of the morning was Peggy Laughlin, Tommy Hitchcock's fiancée, and she was usually invited along. It did not occur to her that she was being used as insurance against rumors until others began taking her aside to cross-examine her about Averell and Marie. "I was as dumb as anything," she later recalled. "I didn't even know they knew each other."[16]

With three months of steady practice and match competition behind him in California and at Aiken, Harriman went home for the opening of the Long Island polo season playing better than he ever had in his life and ready to make his all-out bid for a place on the United States' international team. He was hard and lean, and his ponies were in midseason condition. He stabled them at Meadow Brook, moved to Sands Point early, and continued practicing every day.

On a Saturday in June, he was in the clubhouse when an Army airplane being tested over Old Westbury snapped a wing during a maneuver and plunged to the ground. Two lieutenants aboard the Curtiss Falcon parachuted to safety, but their crippled plane crashed through the roof of his stable, killing Gay Boy, a big Thoroughbred gelding, and March, an eight-year-old chestnut mare. Both had been trained hard through the winter and spring in preparation for the test matches, so the loss could hardly be calculated. Harriman had paid $3,000 for Gay Boy as a green three-year-old. The pony had since been ridden by Malcolm Stevenson in competition against Britain, and at the age of nine he was in his prime, fast, intelligent, strong enough to play three chukkers at top speed.

When he recovered from the immediate damage to his polo career, Averell was furious at the government not only for killing his ponies but for then demeaning them. Washington dismissed his claim for $15,000 as excessive, but Harriman hounded the government for eight years, as much to force acknowledgment of his ponies' worth as to collect damages.

As far as Congress's Claims Committee was concerned, there was not much difference between a world-class polo pony and a truck horse, and it was willing to give Harriman no more than $1,000. Congressman Robert Bacon of Long Island finally introduced a special act in the House providing for payment of $7,500, and brought it to the floor when it seemed least likely to attract attention. But adoption required unanimous consent, and there was a chorus of objections. Providing financial relief for a Harriman was not good politics, especially in midst of a depression, and most especially when the relief was sought for the loss of polo ponies, the epitome of a rich man's plaything. Before the matter came to a conclusion, Averell was prominently identified with the Roosevelt administration, and he unhappily settled for a paltry $1,000 when the prices for ponies of Gay Boy's class were routinely exceeding $20,000.

At the time of the accident, only a few weeks remained before the Argentine match, and Averell faced an uphill struggle against Captain C. A. Wilkinson of the U.S. Army for the forward's position vacated by the retirement of J. Watson Webb, the high scorer on the United States' greatest championship teams. The rivalry stoked sizzling competition in test matches throughout the spring and summer. Although he had elevated his game to a level he had never before approached, the experts still thought he would lose the number one position to the young army officer, who had an edge in both the accuracy and the distance of his shots.

About the time the Argentine team arrived in New York to begin preparation for the series, however, Wilkinson suddenly faded. He began to ride and pass poorly, missing scoring chances because he was caught badly out of position. His mallet lost its thunder, his steady aim faltered, and his timing deserted him.

In the judgment of the polo columnists and experts around the practice fields, Wilkinson had simply played himself into the ground. He got up early every morning and schooled his ponies for several hours and then played in afternoon games. As the competition with Harriman came to its conclusion, he was exhausted.

Harriman's strategy had been perfect. He paced himself, leaving his ponies' schooling to his trainers, and devoting all of his own energy to game competition and practice with Hitchcock. Even after his loss of Gay Boy and March, his ponies were as good as any in the country, and because of that as much as anything, he gradually emerged as the choice over Wilkinson. But just when his place on the team at last seemed secure, a new challenger appeared.

Stephen "Laddie" Sanford, who had often played with Averell on Orange County and Sands Point teams, returned from England, where he had spent months practicing and training. Almost as much as Harriman, Sanford's success as a polo player had been achieved by having superior ponies. His family owned a profitable carpet-manufacturing business, and, like Averell, he went after the best ponies money could

buy in the United States, England, or Argentina. When he returned to
Long Island in the summer of 1928, he was so much improved that he
had to be seriously considered for number one. Fortunately for Harriman, his arrival came too late for all of the test matches, so when the
Defense Committee settled on the American team, Averell was on it.

It had been the longest competition in memory. America's new Big
Four had Harriman at Webb's forward position, and Cheever Cowdin,
one of his regular Orange County teammates, at the back position where
Devereux Milburn had reigned as America's greatest player until he was
overtaken by age and Tommy Hitchcock. Harriman and Cowdin would
join the great Hitchcock, now captain of the American squad, and Malcolm Stevenson, who once again postponed retirement.

"The uniform sentiment of all concerned," the Defense Committee
announced, "is that Harriman and Cowdin fill out the strongest team
possible for the series. The team has been selected purely on the strength
of individual playing in the practice season and it is felt that the men
named have proved themselves in action."[17]

The decision put Harriman in a delicate predicament, for besides
being a participant in the unprecedented competition, he was himself a
member of the Defense Committee. He therefore reclused himself from
discussions concerning the new number one, but his selection was still
controversial because the competition had been so nearly even.

The announcement should have ended the matter, but there was a
long delay in getting the match under way. No sooner had the Argentine
team arrived than its ponies were hit by an outbreak of flu, forcing
postponement. At first Hitchcock thought it was an opportunity. Uneasy
about a new team with two men who had never played in international
competition, he scheduled another round of intense practice.

For the first test of the United States' newly anointed Big Four, he
arranged a match against a team composed of Sanford, Earle Hopping,
the retired Webb, and Winston Guest, a strapping young Yale graduate
who had recently carried the highest polo handicap of any collegiate
player in the country. Instead of solidifying the new international team,
however, the practice, played in a light rain, called into question the
wisdom of Averell's selection. Sanford played circles around him all
afternoon. At the same time, Guest made the selection of Cowdin look
like a serious mistake as well. Relieved of all pressure, the "scrubs" rode
like demons, humiliating Hitchcock's varsity 10–8. Suddenly, the selection of Harriman and Cowdin was subject to change, and Averell had
himself to blame. He had left his best ponies in the stable when he rode
out for the practice match, while Sanford played his finest mounts.

Hitchcock and the Defense Committee were embarrassed, but the
team captain still favored his friend Harriman over Sanford, even
though, deep down, he had private doubts about Averell's tenacity. Al-

though they had played together for years, Hitchcock wondered whether Averell had the steel and steady nerves for international competition.

Sanford was so clearly the superior forward in the practice game that the Defense Committee had no choice but to bench Harriman in his favor, and to replace Cowdin with Guest. It fell to Hitchcock to deliver the news, and it was, he told Averell, the toughest chore he had as American captain.

Finding disarray in his lineup and fending off second-guessing that spread from the committee into the newspapers and to the stables of polo clubs from Old Westbury to Illinois, Texas, and California, Hitchcock called for yet another practice match to give the latest team one chance to play together before facing the hard riders from Argentina. More than ever, it appeared the United States' team was setting itself up to lose.

Everybody had practiced and played test matches until they now risked riding themselves into the same exhaustion that had befallen the unfortunate Wilkinson. The team from Argentina, meanwhile, took advantage of the delay and controversy, working out easily on borrowed ponies while their own mounts recovered. Harriman weathered the controversy around him, his confidence intact. With the second practice game coming up, he told Hitchcock, "I think you will find me back on the team."[18]

He arrived at the Piping Rock Club determined to recover his place. Sanford, he knew, was "soft" in close combat, inclined to give ground when he was challenged for a free ball. So before the game, Harriman went to Manuel Andrada, a muscular, thick-chested member of the Argentine team who had been recruited for the practice, and urged him to "keep Sanford off the field."[19]

This time Harriman brought out his best ponies and scored three goals while Andrada harassed Sanford mercilessly. The practice team took the lead over the newest international squad and led for most of the game, before finally losing 10–8. Just as planned, Sanford was muscled off the ball and thoroughly roughed up by Andrada. Not until many years later did Harriman confess his underhanded tactic against his friend. Polo was called a gentleman's game, Will Rogers would later observe, for the same reason tall men were called "shorty."

At Hitchcock's request, the Defense Committee reversed itself once again and put Harriman back on the Big Four. The captain said he had simply not felt comfortable with Sanford out front to receive his passes downfield, while he knew Harriman's every move. They had practiced together for so long that each could anticipate the other the moment they surged downfield.

On a Saturday afternoon, the American team finally rode out to meet the Argentine four. Harriman's first game in international competition placed him in a struggle against one of the game's premier players. Defending Argentina's goal was Canadian-born Lewis Lacey, the world's only active ten-goal player aside from Hitchcock, Stevenson, and Milburn.

Averell broke the ice, scoring against him in the opening moments of the first chukker. Coming out of a midfield skirmish in control of the ball, he raced clear on a three-stroke scoring drive. Hitchcock hammered a free shot into the center of the goal after a foul was called against Argentina moments later, and the United States had a quick 2–0 lead. But thereafter it appeared that the experts' prediction of victory for the South American team had been right. Argentina scored five goals in a row, threatening to turn the game into a rout.

Hitchcock rallied his team late in the first half, and struggled back to within one point. When play resumed after a halftime intermission, he and Harriman scored two more quick goals to give the United States a brief 6–5 lead.

One of international polo's most memorable games was unfolding. The play was furious. Malcolm Stevenson, the United States' number three, had his helmet knocked off in one melee, and moments later play had to be stopped briefly when Lacey was hit in the throat by an errant mallet. Argentina opened the sixth period of the game with a thunderous assault on the U.S. goal. Its first shot went wide, a second was turned back by Hitchcock, but a third was driven high between the goalposts by Jack Nelson, Argentina's number two, tying the score at 6–6.

The match was still tied when the eighth chukker, the final seven-and-a-half-minute period, began. A light, chilly rain was falling, but no one had left the packed bleachers where the crowd was on its feet. Halfway through the period, after a U.S. shot was blocked, Argentina rode into position for a game-winning shot. But Stevenson got his mallet down, blocked it, and drove the ball back toward Argentina's goal.

Riding Miss Mark, a powerful mare he had already used for two periods, Harriman wheeled in a flash and broke ahead of Lacey and John Miles, Argentina's number three. His first shot carried him beyond the defender's reach, and a second brought him in front of the Argentine goal, forty yards out. With Miles and Lacey trying vainly to overtake him, Harriman whipped his mallet down on the white willow ball for a third shot. He connected solidly and the ball carried into the left side of the South Americans' net. The crowd went wild.

Grantland Rice described what he called "one of the greatest plays ever seen on a polo field":

> Out of a tangled scrimmage of ponies and riders, the white
> ball [had] bounded along the green turf, a good seventy yards
> away from the Argentine goal at a hard angle. It was a hole in

one, two home runs, [and] a 90-yard run in football in a pinch.
Lacey and others attempted to ride Harriman off as he came
to the ball. But he came to it like a flash . . . waving the bat of
Babe Ruth or the driver of Bobby Jones. It was all or nothing
with Harriman here. There was no one around to whom he
could feed the ball. He could see the two goal posts seventy
yards away; he came tearing up and he let fly with everything
he had. The long drive carried a slight slice and it was this slice
that turned the trick as the ball struck twenty or thirty yards
short, and then bounded over the line with the winning score."[20]

In the dying seconds, a desperate Argentine shot struck the United
States' goalpost, but caromed away from the net, and the game ended
before the ball could be put back into play.

Harriman was an authentic hero, his name in headlines above
Tommy Hitchcock's, the U.S. victory even taking the top sports-page
play away from the 1928 World Series, which was about to open with
the New York Yankees facing the St. Louis Cardinals. It was, declared
New York Times polo writer Robert F. Kelley, "the most exciting and the
best game of international polo that International Field has seen since
they stopped keeping scores in fractions. . . ."[21]

Averell's unforgettable day didn't end with his heroics at Meadow
Brook. A few miles away at Belmont Park, Chance Play, the pride of
Arden Farms Stables, came home ahead by a length to win the Aqueduct
Handicap. Three days later, Argentina staged a comeback, winning
10–7, administering the United States' first loss in international competition since 1914, and forcing the match into a decisive third game. Harriman and Hitchcock scored three goals each, but from the opening
seconds Argentina held the momentum, turning back one North American drive after another, recklessly riding Hitchcock's team off the ball
and driving toward the American goal with a fury they had never mus-
tered in the first game.

The only real suspense came early in the game when it appeared
that Lacey had been seriously injured. His pony fell on top of him,
pinning him to the ground, but he got to his feet, mounted another
steed, and played on as though nothing had happened. He turned back
Averell's shots and passed deftly to his forward, Arturo Kenny, who sent
five shots into the North American goal.

With the match thus tied at one victory each, more than forty thousand spectators, said to have been the largest crowd ever to witness a
polo contest in the United States, turned out for the showdown, overflowing the bleachers and standing shoulder-to-shoulder in the end
zones. They began arriving at noon—special trains from Manhattan
filled with young men from the financial district; motorcars loaded with

families; the entire crowd from the just-ended Piping Rock Horse Show. Charles Lindbergh slipped into the crowd almost unnoticed. Colonel Robert McCormick, the Chicago publisher, arrived with an entourage that included Archduke Leopold of Austria. There was a party from the Metropolitan Opera, including Mrs. Dorothy Benjamin Caruso. The fashion show and social gathering had reached a crescendo to match the drama on the field.

In a clubhouse box among the players' families, Kitty Harriman cheered Averell on—as did Marie Whitney, who was seated nearby with Sonny. For drama, Harriman could hope for nothing to match his winning goal in the first game, but he played just as well as he had on the first day.

The real difference was that Hitchcock emerged for the first time as the dominant force in the game after moving himself from number two to the number three position and calling upon twenty-year-old Earle Hopping to replace Malcolm Stevenson. Benching the man who was one of only four ten goal players in the world was a huge gamble for the young captain; but knowing it would be a high-scoring game, Hitchcock sacrificed Stevenson's tactical savvy and experience under pressure for the longer drives from the mallet of young Hopping, and it worked. Hopping and Hitchcock hammered long passes downfield. Averell picked them up, and converted six of them into goals, while Hitchcock himself scored four. When it was over, the United States had won 13–7 and had taken the championship of the Americas.

It was the end of Harriman's brief, shining career in international competition. The glorious autumn of 1928 was also the end of his marriage with Kitty. Within days of his polo triumph, Harriman called his daughters up to his bedroom in the house at Washington Square and told them brokenly and rather incoherently that he and their mother were parting. The breakup was for reasons the girls would not understand until they were older, he said, but, painful as it was, it was best for all of them. The only reasonable thing was for the girls to remain with their mother.

Movers shortly took their things away, and the four-story brick house where Mary and Kathleen had spent all of their lives was subleased to a new tenant. Harriman moved uptown to the Knickerbocker Club, and Kitty and the girls took an apartment on Park Avenue at Seventieth Street.

In the spring, she established residence in Paris, where a simple charge of desertion was sufficient grounds for divorce. It was also the place where wealthy Americans could part ways without all of the attention that they would have attracted at home. Averell got an address of his own on the Champs-Élysées, and on May 24, he was formally served with a sheriff's summons requiring him to return to her or face divorce.

He declared that he firmly intended never to go back, and the divorce laws of France in their due course produced the decree.

Marie Whitney, meanwhile, took a somewhat less fashionable route of shedding Sonny. Where he was concerned, not even the refuge of a foreign court could divert attention. In July, she and her sister moved to the Nevada shore of Lake Tahoe to establish residence in preparation for a Reno divorce, which was granted two months later.

The following February 21, she and Harriman were married in a private family ceremony in All Souls Church in Manhattan, and at midnight sailed for Europe aboard the liner *Bremen*, escaping New York before the word spread. They remained abroad for several weeks, spending much of their honeymoon roaming Parisian art galleries to collect paintings that would shortly appear in Marie's own gallery in New York.

The bride, who had briefly studied art history, had exquisite taste and a special fondness for Postimpressionist works, and probably at her suggestion Averell purchased for $72,000 a stunning van Gogh still life called *White Roses*. He planned to own it jointly with his mother, but back home, Mary Harriman made her half a wedding gift. Although she had realized that Averell and Kitty's marriage was hopeless, she was crushed by the divorce because she had grown to love Kitty as one of her own.

After his marriage to Marie, Averell's interest in polo waned, and he began to withdraw from horse racing. The U.S. Polo Association awarded him a handicap of eight after the Argentine match, making him one of the five top-ranked players in the country since Milburn was dropped to six, and Stevenson to eight. Only Hitchcock was a ten. Young Winston Guest was the only nine, and Hopping, along with Harriman and Stevenson, carried an eight. Averell continued playing for fun, maintaining a handicap of four as late as 1940. But instead of Meadow Brook, he made his headquarters at Sands Point, which accepted Jewish members, including his friend Robert Lehman, and permitted play on Sunday.

His divorce also concluded the illustrious career of Arden Farms Stables' star, Chance Play. Under their parting arrangement, Kitty bought the stable's most successful horse and several colts for $180,000 and sent him to stud at her own breeding farm in Massachusetts. He was later sold to Averell's sister Cornelia, and he wound up his days at Kentucky's famed Calumet Farm, where he died twenty years later, having sired twenty-three stakes winners.

A little more than a year after their divorce, Kitty married New York surgeon Eugene Pool, who had attended several members of the Harriman family, including Averell's daughters, his mother, and Kitty herself. In 1936, at only forty-three, she died of cancer. She and Averell had remained friends, and he had, oddly, seemed more attentive to her than he had while they were married. His daughter Mary urged him to come to her funeral, and he would have gone but for a concern that her husband would not approve. For the rest of his life he spoke of Kitty so rarely that many of the people who knew him for decades were unaware that there had been such a marriage. Although it had lasted for fourteen years, they had been apart for most of the time because of her frail health. It was one of his failures that troubled him.

Chapter VIII

BANKER

Mergers, Partners, Wings, and a Crash

Harriman was an exception, but to most of the American financial establishment, aviation was in the 1920s still more of a curiosity than an industry. While the war had created a generation of adventurers and dreamers with a visceral love of flying, Wall Street was slow to realize that there was money to be made from airplanes. At the time, it took a visionary to see clearly how the flimsy flying machine could ever challenge trains and motor vehicles, much less ocean liners, for passengers and cargo. A visionary Harriman was not, but he had powerful faith that new technology always brought with it investment opportunity. So while he was not swept up in the romance of flying, he regarded aviation as a prudent field in which to put money.

It was the middle of the decade before ordinary investors realized that a vast new industry was already at hand. Then, when Congress adopted the Kelly Act, transferring airmail service from the Post Office Department to private operators in 1925, entrepreneurs began to create new "airlines" overnight, some of them with nothing but a single monoplane and one stout-hearted pilot, who was often president or chairman of the board. To carry the mail, the government paid them $3 a pound. Then with Charles Lindbergh's conquest of the Atlantic two years later, ordinary market speculators fell in love with aviation stocks, and suddenly, more money was available than the fledgling industry could rationally use.

Early in 1929, Averell's Yale classmate Robert Lehman came to him with a proposal to invest in everything from airplane manufacturing to schools for aspiring pilots. The idea was to create a publicly owned aviation conglomerate and use its stock to acquire small struggling enterprises, weaving them into an efficient enterprise that would thrive on both the expansion and consolidation of the industry. It took no persuasion to bring Harriman aboard.

He had made his first investment in aviation even before the war, backing Kitty's brother, Charles Lawrance, who was working on an air-cooled aluminum engine in the hopes of making it possible to build planes bigger and faster and capable of carrying several passengers hundreds of miles. At the time, expert opinion was still on the side of water-cooled motors, and Harriman considered his brother-in-law's prospects so farfetched that he limited his commitment to $10,000; he had gone to several friends, including Vincent Astor, Dorothy Whitney Straight, and Percy Rockefeller, however, and they had put up similar amounts, enabling Lawrance to continue work that made him a historical figure in aviation.

Lawrance's big break came when the French government agreed to buy his engine for its military planes, although the onset of the war kept the deal from going through. Shortly afterward, he sold 450 of the engines to the U.S. Navy for its training planes, however, and won a contract to continue his work on air-cooled engine technology.

In 1920, when the Army launched a competition for a 350-horsepower radial air-cooled motor, the Wright Company, the predominant engine manufacturer in the United States, hired Lawrance to design its entry. His engine was the winner, but Wright then refused to share the patent rights, leaving the inventor with little return from the ideas he had been developing for years. So when the Navy also decided to adopt the air-cooled engine, he prepared to enter competition for the contract. With that, Wright relented, paid him $500,000 for his company and his patents, and took him back into the company as the brains of its engine-design team. A year later, Lawrance was president of the Wright Company, and three years afterward, his Wright Whirlwind engine powered Lindbergh and the *Spirit of St. Louis* from New York to Paris.

Having passed up his chance to finance his brother-in-law's work on a serious scale, Harriman had invested in a company manufacturing bombers and amphibious planes for the Army in the mid-twenties. Soon thereafter, he became one of the original investors in a forerunner of Pan American Airways, organized by former Wall Street bond salesman Juan Trippe the month after Lindbergh's solo crossing of the Atlantic. Well connected at the polo clubs on Long Island and married into the Diamond Match fortune, Trippe had bought surplus Navy seaplanes in the early 1920s and started an air taxi service. His planes were old and unreliable and the service failed under an accumulation of mechanical problems and a shortage of spare parts, but with an eye on the lucrative airmail route between Key West and Havana, Trippe went to Harriman and other wealthy friends, raising the capital to buy more planes and launch the Aviation Corporation of America. Sonny Whitney became chairman of a board of directors, and Robert Lehman, William Rockefeller, William H. Vanderbilt, and Sonny's cousin John Hay "Jock" Whitney joined Harriman among the company's principal investors. A year later, Trippe negotiated a merger with two competitors, creating the Aviation Corporation of the Americas. Its subsidiary, Pan American Airways, was to become one of the world's dominant airlines.

Pan Am's three-engine Fokkers were profitably shuttling mail bags and capacity loads of six passengers between Key West and Havana when Lehman and Harriman created the new conglomerate that would span the continent, taking in manufacturers, mail routes, airlines, and landing fields at an astonishing pace and at remarkably little cost. By then, the field was crowded. Railroad men, steamship owners, and automobile manufacturers—General Motors and Ford among them—had also seen the opportunities and joined the surge into the business. Small operations were rapidly being absorbed by competitors with superior assets, who promptly consolidated them into bigger companies, monopolized territories, created new markets, and turned profits by centralizing management. Aviation no longer belonged to the flyers and mechanics who had attended its birth—they had been displaced by bankers as aviation fell into a pattern that was evident throughout American industry. More than one thousand corporate mergers had swallowed six thousand companies during the twenties; it was said that two thousand corporate directors were positioned to dominate the economic life of the United States. Harriman was undoubtedly one of them, sitting on the board of fifty-four corporations by 1932.

His alliance with Lehman was a natural one, for in addition to their Yale friendship and mutual involvement with Pan Am, they had been social friends on Long Island, and polo teammates from Sands Point to Pasadena. Lehman was not in Averell's class on the polo field, but he was easily an equal when it came to identifying investment opportunities. In temperament, he was as daring and innovative as Harriman—and ultimately more successful as a Wall Street operative. During the years while Harriman had been in shipbuilding, shipping, and mining, Lehman, then a new partner in his family's investment-banking firm, had gotten into aviation, radio, retailing, and the theater.

The Aviation Corporation of America, or AVCO as their conglomerate was called, was actually an idea of Sherman Fairchild, another of Trippe's original backers and an inventor who had created a profitable and important new role for the airplane with his development of the aerial camera. After receiving his first camera patent in 1918, Fairchild had started designing planes to provide a stable platform for his photographic system, and shortly became one of the country's foremost aviation manufacturers.

His stubby-winged monoplane, called the FC-1, not only served the needs of his camera but by happy coincidence proved to be an ideal machine for airmail operators. It was rugged and economical, and it had an enclosed cockpit, greatly improving mail pilots' chances of survival in a business that had already seen more than two hundred crashes and the loss of fifty lives by the time the first FC-1 took off in 1926.

Fairchild's vision of a giant conglomerate and his approach to Lehman and Harriman arose, however, from a serious threat to his survival as an airplane manufacturer.

Early in 1929, the Post Office Department awarded the Cincinnati–Chicago airmail contract to the Embry-Riddle Company, a Cincinnati flying school and charter operation which lacked the cash to buy the planes it needed for the service. The company had been Fairchild's most important customer for the FC-1, but faced with the requirement for more planes than it had ever considered owning, it went in search of help. Curtiss Aircraft Company offered assistance—provided, of course, that Embry-Riddle used Curtiss planes instead of Fairchilds.

Facing a crisis, Fairchild persuaded his directors to create a subsidiary that would heavily invest in Embry-Riddle and prevent it from falling into the clutches of Curtiss. The new company would also buy other small operations that stood to become profitable enterprises through mail contracts. With that, Fairchild went to Lehman in search of financing, describing his concept as a "General Motors of the air."

On March 3, 1929, shortly after talking with Fairchild, Lehman and Harriman chartered AVCO, with Averell as chairman of the board and Lehman as head of the executive committee. The two of them quickly raised $35 million from an offering of two million shares of common stock, selling it for $20 a share. Several special friends, including Tommy Hitchcock, their polo mentor, and Mrs. Beulah Einstein Norton, Averell's Long Island neighbor who was soon to become his new mother-in-law, were given a chance to invest ahead of the rush; and Averell and Lehman each took 25,000 shares at $17.50.

Before a month was out, Fairchild's companies were brought under the new corporate tent with a swap of $5 million worth of AVCO stock for all of the stock of Fairchild Aviation Corporation, Fairchild Airplane Manufacturing Corporation, Fairchild Aerial Surveys, Fairchild Aerial Camera Company, and Fairchild Flying Corporation.

Almost overnight, the conglomerate went into airline operations, acquiring Colonial Airways and Universal Aviation Corporation, both sizable holding companies created by acquisition of small mail carriers that had grown large enough to get into the passenger business. Within six months, they controlled nine companies operating scheduled passenger services. Of all of them, Colonial was most promising because it came into their hands on the eve of its inauguration of a New York–Boston passenger service which had the potential to become a gold mine. With gleaming, fourteen-passenger Ford trimotors, it transported capacity loads of passengers between Logan Field in Boston and suburban Queens in scarcely more than an hour. Linked with the Embry-Riddle system, it also gave AVCO a network of routes reaching as far west as Kansas City.

Universal Air Lines, the operating subsidiary of Universal Aviation Corporation, had been created by investment bankers in the Midwest. Starting business as Continental Airlines, it took over two smaller competitors at the height of the economic boom and adopted its grand new name only months before it was in turn absorbed by Harriman and Lehman. By the time of its merger with AVCO, Universal was preparing to forge a transcontinental air-rail service by linking its air routes with rail lines. The Union Pacific had no role in the scheme, but Harriman was nevertheless taken with the plan. Not only did it present the possibility of bringing new passengers to trains, but it also hinted of the day when airplanes and trains would be bona fide competitors for passenger business. The opportunity was at hand for transportation companies to have their stake in both railroads and airlines, just as E.H. had tried to fashion a worldwide transportation system from ownership of trains and steamships.

As AVCO and Universal laid plans to inaugurate this rail-plane service, Averell proposed that Union Pacific work out a similar arrangement with United Airlines, which had routes roughly paralleling the Union Pacific tracks across the West. The railroad was interested, but United did not yet have planes capable of providing the air link.

Three months after the Universal merger, Harriman launched transcontinental service under the banner of the Aviation Corporation, in cooperation with the New York Central and the Atchison, Topeka and Santa Fe railroads. The offer to transport passengers from New York to Los Angeles in a mere two and a half days made headlines; and for the few who tried it, it was a grand and exhausting adventure. But more vividly than anything else, the service demonstrated how close aviation still was to the days when it belonged to men in scarves and goggles. Weather forecasts were dubious, navigation equipment rudimentary, and emergency landing fields poorly lighted. The hazards were vividly emphasized by regular accounts of mail planes quitting on the wing or flying unexpectedly into foul weather. Universal's strategy for dramatically reducing cross-country travel time was to fly its passengers by day and have them continue their journey through the night in the relative comfort of railroad sleeping cars.

On June 14, Harriman, New York mayor Jimmy Walker, and a host of dignitaries saw the first California-bound expedition off from Grand Central Station. Presiding over the festivities, Averell proclaimed the new service "a great step in the linking of the commercial and social lives of the two great seaboards of our country."[1] With a band playing and a crowd of several hundred cheering them on their way, the thirty-six travelers departed in the late afternoon aboard the New York Central's *Southwestern Limited*. Through the night, they chugged north. At dawn, having traveled through Albany, then westward past Buffalo and along Lake Erie, they arrived in Cleveland, where they were shuttled from the station out to the airport, put aboard three twelve-passenger Fokkers and flown on to Chicago for breakfast. They reached Kansas City in time for lunch, and Garden City, Kansas, for an early dinner. There, twenty-four hours after leaving New York, they wired a progress report to Harriman and boarded the Atchison, Topeka and Santa Fe's *California Limited* for the rest of the trip. Sixty-two hours and fifteen minutes after leaving New York, they stepped from the train in Los Angeles. Mrs. Mabel Walker Willebrandt, a former U.S. assistant attorney general, presented Mayor George E. Cryer a thermos of Atlantic Ocean water and a three-day-old copy of *The New York Times*. The party was exhausted.

Less than a year after its stock was offered, the Aviation Corporation of America was in possession of a passenger system extending from Montreal to El Paso and back to Atlanta. Its 6,500 miles of routes were served by 220 planes flying 20,000 miles every day. Its subsidiaries connected fifty-four of the country's largest cities and held twenty-nine domestic and ten foreign mail contracts. Besides its passenger businesses and manufacturing companies, it owned airfields and flying schools, and held rights to designs for flying boats and aircraft engines. Subsidiary companies numbered eighty, and Harriman presided over a huge board of seventy directors, some of whom he barely knew.

But long before there was any inkling of the disaster ahead for the national economy, there were signs of danger for the company. As he had in his earlier ventures into new territory, Averell displayed more affinity for making deals than attending to details of corporate management. And while Lehman, as chairman of the executive committee, was responsible for AVCO's operations, he was, like Harriman, stretched thin by other far-flung investment concerns. The rapid expansion had seen companies swept up helter-skelter with slight regard to their corporate role and with little attention to their value. Minority holdings were bought out in subsidiaries which the corporation already controlled, and companies run by men too proud to be conglomerate team-players were allowed to operate as independently as ever. With no coordination of connecting flights, routes and schedules were duplicated wholesale, causing huge losses.

Weeks before the market disaster, David K. E. Bruce, a member of the board who was also a partner in W. A. Harriman and Company, raised a warning flag. He was alarmed by the loose management, he told Averell, and the inflated prices being paid for properties. Management, he thought, had taken a particularly foolish risk in putting day-to-day control in the hands of forty-four-year-old Graham Grosvenor, whose experience included nearly nothing relevant to his new responsibilities. Bruce recommended the exact course E. H. Harriman had taken in 1893 in saving the Illinois Central from the economic crash. AVCO still had on hand $23 million in cash, and Bruce urged Averell to desist from further acquisitions and save it. It was time, he said, to tighten management and take firm control of the disjointed collection of subsidiaries.

Neither Harriman nor Lehman paid attention. They had been able to make nearly all of their acquisitions with stock swaps. The heavy reserves of cash made it possible for them to ignore losses by their passenger operations because they could offset them with proceeds from high-interest, short-term loans to brokerage houses doing a booming business in the bull market. Averell was rarely seen at AVCO headquarters on Forty-second Street, and he was never available for inspection of new properties or flights on company planes. Some executives and board members, including Fairchild, were convinced that he had no personal interest in the business.

Actually, the problem was that the chairman had more pressing concerns. Besides running W. A. Harriman and Company and Harriman Brothers and Company—the latter a bank he had founded in partnership with Roland—he was taking on new responsibilities in the railroad business. Specifically, he had, at the request of Judge Lovett, spent several weeks evaluating the troubles at the Illinois Central. He was also at the time of AVCO's most rapid expansion in the midst of divorcing Kitty, a process which required him to establish temporary residence in Paris. Moreover, AVCO had early in its existence turned into something Harriman had failed to anticipate when he and Lehman arranged the stock issue. Instead of a vehicle for investment in aviation securities, it was soon a massive operating corporation.

Just as serious as the lack of attention by Averell and Lehman was the lack of aviation experience on the part of the people they had put in management. Executive ranks were filled by men with investment-banking backgrounds, and for advice Averell turned to old friends such as Charles B. Seger, chairman of Union Pacific's finance committee, and Richard Robinson, his adviser and lieutenant going back to the shipyards in Pennsylvania.

Although the chairman knew plenty about shipping and railroading, he had neither gained a deep understanding of aviation nor grasped the bewildering pace at which it was changing. Unlike railroading and

Averell and brother Roland, circa 1903. Even as small boys, their privileged lives were dominated by the demands of a father preparing them to follow in his footsteps. To the end, Roland, the younger by five years, lived in the shadow of his more aggressive and ambitious brother.

The Harriman Brothers at Arden. From childhood ponies they graduated to trotters, polo ponies, hunters, and Thoroughbreds. Adopting one of his father's favorite sports, Roland became one of the country's foremost harness racers, but Averell got the headlines as a world-class polo player and Thoroughbred owner.

Groton School's Varsity Crew, spring 1909. Averell (*fifth from left*) arrived at Groton as one of the smallest boys in his class. A stringent exercise program ordered by his parents, a burst of growth, and a summer of training by a professional coach on one of the lakes of the family estate made him one of Groton's top oarsmen. An irregular heartbeat prevented him from earning his varsity letter at Yale.

E.H. and Mary. In the spring of 1909 the Harrimans sailed for Europe, where E.H. sought treatment for an increasingly serious abdominal condition. When they returned in August, his condition had seriously deteriorated, and on September 9 he died of cancer at his Arden estate.

Launching—a Ship and a Career. Harriman's wife, Kitty, already in fragile health, came to her husband's shipyard at Bristol, Pennsylvania, to christen his first World War I freighter at its launching. The shipbuilding venture led to several years as a maritime operator and financier, but Harriman would always regret that he had not gone into the armed services during World War I. His marriage to Kitty ended in divorce after fourteen years.

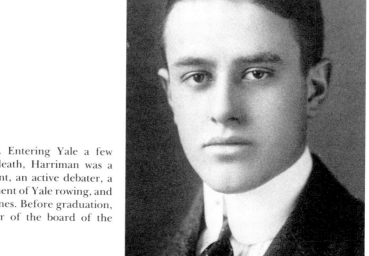

Freshman at New Haven. Entering Yale a few weeks after his father's death, Harriman was a better than average student, an active debater, a crusader for the improvement of Yale rowing, and a member of Skull and Bones. Before graduation, he was already a member of the board of the Union Pacific.

Harriman II, Steamship King. After building freighters for the government in World War I, Harriman became, in the 1920s, a powerful figure in maritime affairs, evoking comparisons to his father. At left is Richard H. M. Robinson, a naval architect, who was an important adviser and associate in Averell's shipbuilding, shipping, aviation, and mining ventures. The ship's captain with them is unidentified.

On the Homestretch at Belmont. With business partner George Herbert Walker, grandfather of the future president, George Herbert Walker Bush, Harriman entered Thoroughbred racing with horses purchased from the estate of August Belmont, Jr. Although the banking and finance partnership with Walker continued, their racing association was short-lived because they disagreed over the relative priorities of racing and running a Thoroughbred breeding farm. Harriman then formed his own stable and won stakes races with his stallion Chance Play, a son of Man o' War.

An Eight and Three Tens. At the peak of his polo career, Harriman led the United States to victory over Argentina in the 1928 America's Cup matches, tantamount to the world championship, and was awarded a handicap of eight (ten being the maximum achievable) by the U.S. Polo Association. On the left here, he prepares to ride with three who had achieved the exalted rank of ten: Americans Watson Webb and Malcolm Stevenson, and Argentine star Lewis Lacey. Never regarded as a natural athlete, Harriman became a world-class player by riding the best-trained ponies and practicing for months with his friend Tommy Hitchcock, still considered by many the premier player in the history of the game.

The Former Mrs. Whitney. Seven months after his divorce from Kitty, Harriman married Marie Norton Whitney, recently divorced from Cornelius Vanderbilt "Sonny" Whitney. Beautiful, witty, and an astute art collector, Marie was soon afflicted with serious eyesight problems. She stayed behind in New York as Harriman took up his diplomatic career.

In E.H.'s Shoes. At the depth of the Great Depression Harriman assumed the chairmanship of the Union Pacific Railroad as it faced the most serious problems it had confronted since his father had rescued it from bankruptcy three decades earlier. Before a map of the system in the company's New York boardroom, Harriman is flanked by the men who anchored its management and guided modernization of its passenger operations: *from left,* President Carl Gray; Harriman; F. W. "Woody" Charske, the controller; and William M. Jeffers, who would later succeed Gray.

shipping, aviation as yet had no recognized hierarchy, no center of gravity; insofar as it was led at all, it was guided by people and forces not well known to the financial establishment.

AVCO president Grosvenor was an inventor, whose personal expertise concerned elevators rather than airplanes. He had been vice-president of Fairchild Aviation only briefly before its merger with AVCO and his selection as president. Since he knew neither Harriman nor Lehman very well, he lacked the confidence to bring the company's accumulating problems to them forcefully. Besides the two principal figures and the huge corporate board, Grosvenor had to deal with separate boards of directors of most of the dozens of subsidiary companies, plus aviators and minor executives going their own way.

Fairchild pleaded with Harriman and Lehman to split the corporation into three grand divisions and hire a recognized expert at the top of each, but his advice, like Bruce's warning, was ignored. When the market crashed, AVCO stock had already descended several points from its springtime high. On Monday, October 24, the day the catastrophe began, it skidded from 20 to 9⅝. The next day, Black Tuesday, the worst day in the history of the exchange, saw it fall to 6¼. For most of the next three years, through the duration of Harriman's active association with the company, it hovered between 2 and 4. The collapse wiped out the demand for call loans, which had kept the company's cash reserves flush, and for the first time, Harriman and Lehman were forced to confront the serious operating losses, which were growing dramatically worse.

In the first full year after the crash, the company lost $4.7 million, and the year after that, despite efforts to cut costs and sharpen management, it lost another $4.2 million. Belatedly, they tried to bring order to their competing fiefdoms by reorganizing along the lines Fairchild had recommended. They consolidated all of the subsidiaries flying passengers, mail, and cargo into a company called American Airways. The new creation, the forerunner of American Airlines, eliminated some of the bureaucratic morass; but government regulations prevented them from shifting mail contracts from one company to another, so the corporate shells of all the subsidiaries had to be preserved.[2]

The crash and the losses did not prevent Harriman and Lehman from striking out toward more ambitious goals, specifically development of a four-engine flying boat for transatlantic passenger service. Proposed by Fairchild, the project immediately appealed to Averell because it offered a possible use for the idle Cramp Ship Yard in Philadelphia, which he owned. He envisioned flying boats being assembled on the old shipways and launched on the Delaware River, but Virginius Clark, the new plane's designer, and Roland Palmedo, who was Robert Lehman's aviation expert, inspected the Cramp yard and fled. Both were horrified at the thought of trying to convert the derelict shops and rusting shipways into a modern aircraft plant. It was, said Palmedo, "a dreadful, lugubrious place."[3] It was not the lack of a construction site that killed the flying boat, however. The chief problem was that neither the Navy nor Juan Trippe at Pan Am was interested in buying the plane. The Navy had no hangars large enough for it; Pan Am was skeptical. Though the company had ordered a Sikorsky flying boat, Trippe thought it was more likely that passenger service to Europe would make intermediate stops at airfields in Greenland or Iceland.

Finally acknowledging that they had a management crisis, Harriman and Lehman turned to outside experts for help, giving Sanderson and Porter, an engineering consulting firm with impressive experience in the aviation industry, dictatorial authority for corporate management. The consultant's first step was to replace Grosvenor as president and install Frederick G. Coburn, one of its own partners, with a mandate to impose order. Coburn liked the superplane idea, and after the flying boat was abandoned, he was eager to try another approach to a new-generation passenger plane. Under his guidance, the company undertook to design a dramatically more efficient land-based plane. Analyses of the passenger market and the state of engine technology suggested two types of planes with potential: a four-engine design with a capacity of thirty passengers and an aircraft with a capacity of ten, powered by a huge single engine.

Two- and three-engine designs were dismissed out of hand. Engines were still prone to go out of control, requiring them to be shut down, and a dead engine with a windmilling propeller created such a powerful drag that one or two remaining motors would have difficulty keeping a plane airborne, much less meet a government safety requirement to maintain level flight at ten thousand feet after an engine failure. Under those circumstances, neither a two-engine nor a three-engine plane made sense. At the Super Plane Corporation, designers preferred a four-engine plane, but management decided instead to build a prototype of a new single-engine transport, to be designed and assembled at the Farmington, Long Island, plant of the Fairchild Airplane Manufacturing Corporation. By then Fairchild himself had pulled out of AVCO in frustration after making a deal with Harriman and Lehman to regain Fairchild Aerial Camera Company and Fairchild Aerial Surveys.

The superplane might have succeeded, but as the prototype was being completed, development of the controllable-pitch propeller produced a giant leap forward in engine efficiency. New engines were less apt to stall or run away; and if they did, propellers could be "feathered" so they did not produce a fatal drag on the aircraft. As a result, twin-engine planes burst to the forefront of commercial aviation, more efficient than airlines had ever dreamed.[4] AVCO's superplane came to nothing.

*   *   *

The Harriman fortune, though battered by the diminished value of railroad stocks, withstood the crash because it was too massive and too securely rooted in the productive machinery of the country to be pulled down by the collapse of inflated stock prices. In earlier times, E.H. had become wealthy by anticipating the market's booms and busts, and the wealth he left behind made it unnecessary for his sons to risk their future on the rise and fall of the market.

Rather than trading, they profited on a grander scale by creating new corporations, issuing stocks, and marketing the bonds of foreign governments and corporations. Averell had made his share of tactical retreats—notably from the shipping business and from his manganese concession in the Soviet Union—but his routine investments, in steel, in banks, in bonds, even in a Broadway production with James Warburg, steadily paid off. The twenties had been good times for him in every way. Union Pacific stock, having hit a high of 129½ in 1920, reached 297⅝ in 1929; company profits marched to record highs, and dividends held at 8 percent.

Harriman and other American bankers who traveled Europe after the war provided much of the financing that enabled the Germans to keep up their war reparations payments to European neighbors they had attacked, so the others could, in turn, repay their debts to the United States.[5] His risky shipping and manganese-mining ventures aside, he was generally cautious, investing in German enterprises that did much of their business overseas, thereby insulating themselves from the rampant inflation at home. His stake in the German cable system to the Azores was safe because the government had secured the loans with its postal receipts. His loans to German steel interests were equally secure, because the companies he financed did fully 40 percent of their business abroad.[6]

With his personal connections with European customers, and with ties to banks in London and Berlin, Averell handled the search for business abroad, leaving Roland to see after their affairs at home. It was an arrangement that entirely suited the younger brother, who did not share Averell's fondness for travel, his love of Europe, his interest in international politics, his hobby of collecting art, or his eye for beautiful women. Roland was happy to go to the bank at nine, home to Gladys at five, and up to Goshen to drive his trotters on the weekend.

Averell was restless, relentless in chasing deals—mines and steel in Germany, an oil concession in Iran, an airmail contract in China, an electrical power plant in Poland, gold prospecting in South America. The possibilities never ended.

His instinct was always to charge ahead, to continuously expand. On St. Patrick's Day of 1927, just days after his return from the Soviet Union, he jumped more heavily into foreign investment and trade underwriting with the new partnership bank with Roland. Each put in $1,130,000 in cash. They took four other partners, and set up business with four employees in a single room at 39 Broadway. Knight Woolley, one of Roland's Yale classmates, who borrowed $400,000 from the brothers for his share, was put in charge. Averell's only instructions were, "Here's $4 million—go ahead and run the bank."[7]

From the day the bank opened, business boomed. Twice in its first two years, it had to move to larger quarters, the four-man staff expanding to seventy. The secret was its adroit use of a device called the banker's acceptance, which substituted the institution's credit for that of its customers. Woolley, who had published a book on the subject in 1924, was the expert, and with him in charge, Harriman Brothers and Company swept up the accounts of importers and exporters by the hundreds.

Still, Averell was uneasy about the stampede of speculation on Wall Street. Americans of modest means were buying stocks on margin, then using them as collateral for loans to buy more. Seduced by tales of fortunes created from nothing, they were gambling dangerously under the delusion that they were investing, some taking advice from psychics, horoscopes, and newspaper columns, expecting fat profits within days, if, indeed, not hours.

In early March of 1928, trading broke the one-day record set nearly three decades earlier, during the panic created by E.H.'s grab for the Northern Pacific Railroad. By autumn, there were days when several million shares—a huge volume for the time—changed hands on the New York Stock Exchange, and the Dow-Jones average had climbed 200 points from where it had been when Harriman Brothers and Company opened its doors. To Harriman's relief, the Federal Reserve tried to rein in the rampant speculation by telling its member banks in early 1929 to stop providing funds to brokers who made loans for credit purchases of securities. President Hoover expressed personal concern, but nothing slowed the rampage. Though he supported the Federal Reserve's effort to discourage speculation, Harriman saw no cause for personal retrenchment.

Among the partners, there was feeling that W. A. Harriman and Company could have been doing much better had the chairman given less attention to amusement and more to business during his long trips abroad. Internal memoranda revealed consternation among both European customers and the partners in New York. "We are extremely well known in Germany," said one. "The Giesche [steel] deal gave us a big reputation, as did our shipping efforts, and the several bond deals have established our general standing. In addition to that, Mr. W. A. Harriman personally has quite a reputation for courage, conservatism, and wealth." But under the circumstances, it concluded, "there is no reason why we should not get more business in Germany than anybody else. The connections which will get us this business—or at least will give us an opening to bid on everything that comes along—have yet to be established. . . ."[8]

Roland had occasionally needled Averell about his style. On one of his own infrequent trips to Europe, he was so disturbed by what he heard from customers that he wrote to Averell about it rather than waiting to discuss it at home. "You will remember," the younger partner recalled, "I said W. A. Harriman & Co. was stepping out to do a lot of business and trying to build up an organization to cope with development without having the proper means of introducing a smooth working organization which would function properly during the construction period. I realize, of course, that the only way to break in an organization is to give it work to do, but the work must be done in a reasonable, businesslike way. . . . To put it in a nutshell . . . you are continually interested in getting new business and . . . handicapped by not having the proper means in the way of organization to carry out any unusual or new focus of business outside the regular routine."[9]

In spite of his brother's concern about lax management and his own worries over the real health of the market, Averell continued to do nothing to tighten up his organization. And although they were attuned to money markets and economic conditions on both sides of the Atlantic, neither of the Harrimans foresaw the market crash. When it came, though, it moved Averell to take seriously the advice he had been ignoring for months.

In the spring of 1930, with the magnitude of the economic crisis becoming obvious, he ordered spending cut throughout W. A. Harriman and Company. But six months later, the picture was still grim. There had been no improvement in the business climate, and in search of further ways to economize, Harriman ordered a formal review led by G. H. Walker's son-in-law, Prescott Bush. A partner in both W. A. Harriman and Company and Harriman Brothers and Company, the father of a future President of the United States, Bush issued a stern report that called for drastic and immediate additional measures. It was costing $100,000 a month to operate the New York offices, and another $100,000 for offices in Europe. Bush urged him to close shop in both Warsaw and Paris, and to put operations in Berlin on a budget of no more than $18,000 a year. Such a retreat was personally offensive, but Averell reluctantly agreed to it.

The Harrimans' chief competitor, Brown Brothers and Company, faced even heavier pressures. Like nearly everyone else, the Brown bank, a pillar of financial conservatism which had weathered the vicissitudes of Wall Street since 1825, had failed to anticipate the market collapse. The crash caught the firm with millions of dollars' worth of foreign securities on its shelves waiting to be marketed. Afterward, most of them could be sold only at enormous discounts, and some, such as $15 million in bonds issued by the government of Argentina, now facing bankruptcy, could hardly be sold at any price. The Browns' plight was aggravated by the retirements and the deaths of several partners and the removal of their assets from the partnership. In Thatcher Brown's delicate phrasing, he and his partners were "doing too large a business for our capital."[10]

Under these circumstances, he approached Averell with a proposal to merge the Brown and Harriman banking and investment interests into a banking partnership. The deal was completed within weeks.

Like the Harrimans, the first generations of Browns in America had been merchants. About the same time William Harriman was setting up his shipping business in New Haven at the end of the eighteenth century, Alexander Brown arrived in Baltimore from Belfast. Of the two, Brown prospered more easily. He imported Irish linens and exported cotton and tobacco. After the family's interests expanded to Philadelphia and New York, Alexander's son, George, founded the Brown banking dynasty.

It was at George Brown's house in Baltimore that the United States' first railroad company—the Baltimore and Ohio—was organized, with Brown as its treasurer. At the time of the 1827 meeting, there were only two railroads in the world, but Brown and two dozen Maryland businessmen made a bold decision to build a road from Baltimore over the Allegheny Mountains, all the way to the Ohio River.[11]

The family's enduring interest and influence was in banking, however. Attuned to the increasing mobility of businessmen, it created the traveler's letter of credit, forerunner of the ubiquitous credit card. Among the artifacts in the firm's offices were the letters of credit Woodrow Wilson had drawn from Brown Brothers when he set out for the Versailles conference, and the one carried by Charles Lindbergh as he flew from New York to Paris.

The first bond between the old Brown banking house and the Harrimans was established a generation before the merger, when Charles D. Simons, manager of Brown Brothers' foreign exchange department, wed E. H. Harriman's sister, Lilly. More recently, the two families had amiably competed for business across Europe, Harriman and his partners encountering the Browns in hotels, and clubs, and trains. Although Averell was the first son in the Harriman house, Roland became the more visible figure in the new partnership, for six of the twelve partners in the new company had been at Yale with the younger Harriman brother. Knight Woolley and Prescott Bush, Harriman partners before the merger, had been Roland's classmates, as had Robert A. Lovett, the son of E. H.

Harriman's counsel and his successor at the throttle of the Union Pacific. Ellery James, like Lovett, a young partner at Brown Brothers, had been Roland's friend since they were small boys.

In fact, Ellery and Roland had talked as far back as the mid-twenties about a combination of Harriman and Brown interests. The drift of the casual conversation had been that the cordial competitors could someday find it mutually profitable to put their interests "under a single roof."[12] In the troubled spring of 1930, the matter came up again as James, Bush, and Woolley played cards in a New Haven Railroad parlor car on their way to their Yale class reunion. It was only weeks after Bush's committee had finished its study of the problems confronting W. A. Harriman and Company.

Back in New York, James broached the subject to Thatcher Brown, and the senior Brown Brothers partner took the idea to Averell, who embraced it at once. In November, he and Roland sat down with Thatcher Brown and Charles Denston Dickey, one of the Brown partners, to begin formal negotiations. In less than two weeks, the evening talks at Dickey's Park Avenue apartment produced an agreement. Under the arrangement, Averell and Roland each put $1.33 million in cash into the partnership, in addition to the assets of W. A. Harriman and Company and Harriman Brothers and Company, bringing their contribution to more than $8 million.[13] The merger was a source of anxiety at Kuhn, Loeb, the Union Pacific's bank ever since Jacob Schiff had collaborated in E. H. Harriman's takeover. When Averell and Roland created their own partnership bank in 1927, the brothers had called for and gotten a share of the railroad's banking business. But as partners in Brown Brothers Harriman, they would make no move to push aside Kuhn, Loeb, which continued as the railroad's primary bank.

There was but one sticking point. With enormous family pride at stake on both sides, the final issue to be settled was what to call the new bank. Brown wanted to keep the revered name Brown Brothers and Company, but Averell balked. Since he and Roland were bringing a huge amount of urgently needed capital, he deemed it out of the question for the Harriman name to be omitted from the nameplate. Under the circumstances, he told Brown, a logical name would be Harriman and Brown Brothers, but that was unacceptable to Thatcher. As much as both needed the deal, the touchy question had the potential of causing it to fall apart. Realizing that, Averell and Brown agreed to put the decision into the hands of a committee whose members were long-standing friends of both the Harriman and Brown families. But the committee split and the decision finally fell to its chairman, Frederick Allen, a senior partner in Lee Higginson and Company, who years before had counseled Averell to give up coaching the crew at Yale. The name, Allen decided, should be Brown Brothers Harriman and Company. The announcement of the merger was made on December 12 after reporters were summoned to a press conference in the library of Brown's home on Park Avenue. The next day it was very nearly the only positive financial news to be found. In the morning papers, the story was flanked by gloom—bank stocks were again under assault, and police were in the financial district to keep crowds of angry depositors at bay outside the locked doors of the Bank of the United States, across the street from the new Brown Brothers tower.

In this dreary atmosphere, New York's newspapers took the merger as a bright spot, emphasizing the importance of the Harriman family wealth in shoring up the four-generation-old Brown bank. The *Wall Street Journal* suggested that the announcement had in fact been hastened to bring some relief from the pounding of financial bad news.[14]

On a raw day at the end of December 1930, with soup kitchens a fixture of American cities and able-bodied men hawking apples on Manhattan street corners, four bank clerks rolled heavily laden handcarts out of 39 Broadway and along the sidewalk to Wall Street, turning down the gentle slope of Wall Street past the New York Stock Exchange, to the new thirty-six-story tower of Brown Brothers and Company. There was no police escort. A few steps behind them, providing security, an officer of the Harriman Brothers bank kept pace, unnoticed. Bundled against the biting wind, he thrust his hands deep into his overcoat pockets, his right hand clutching a loaded revolver.

Stacked neatly into the carts and carefully protected from the elements were the accumulated assets and obligations of Averell and Roland's investment careers—stocks and bonds from Germany, Austria, Poland, and Hungary; investments in mines, steel mills, oil wells, railroads, ships, and airplanes; credits to exporters and importers on both sides of the Atlantic and the Pacific.

The unheralded passage of the carts consummated the Harriman-Brown union. Fourteen months after the crash of the market, the brothers were partners in a blue chip banking house that had prospered in international finance over 112 years of good times and bad. With their assets transferred to Wall Street, Averell and Roland took their places at rolltop desks in Brown Brothers' quiet, gentlemanly partners' room, where all sat together in the fashion of an old European counting house, waited upon by English clerks, conducting business uninterrupted by telephones and secretaries, and unimpeded by closed doors.

The country was sliding deeper into the trough, notwithstanding rallies on the stock exchange and the continued prosperity of the very wealthy, whose lives had been undisturbed by paper losses. Prices continued to fall, unemployment to climb. Across the country, banks were still failing. On the Illinois Central Railroad, track hands made $1 a day.

Market touts, who had stubbornly insisted, and even believed, that the Crash was a momentary convulsion that would pass as soon as investors regained their nerve, had fallen silent. President Hoover himself had taken to calling the situation a "depression" because he found the word more benign than "panic" or "crash."

Besides a share in expanded business, the merger presented a chance for the Harrimans to benefit from the Browns' prestige and tradition. As visible as Averell was in Europe, the Harriman name was in banking circles no match for Brown Brothers' reputation. "They had enjoyed a long and honorable career," Roland observed, "and we had enjoyed a short and honorable career."[15] Putting the interests together provided the prospect of bringing badly needed discipline to the Harriman organization, which had distinguished itself far more with its imagination and aggressive pursuit of opportunity than with its management.

The new partnership inspired confidence because of Brown Brothers' long tradition of responsibility and Harriman's reputation for boldness and enormous wealth. Moreover, it was not a corporation in which officers merely managed the money of stockholders. It was a partnership whose members' own resources were at risk and who stood personally liable for commitments of the institution. Such an arrangement was possible, Roland Harriman said, only because it was "a joining of forces by people who thought alike and liked each other."[16]

As a business arrangement, Averell was happy with the alliance, but in spite of the stability of Brown Brothers and the collegiality brought to the partnership by Roland and the "Horsemen" of Yale '17, he was not comfortable in the paneled partners' room. His freewheeling style was out of place in the meticulous execution of commercial banking transactions. He was adrift. The younger partners, who had encouraged the marriage from the beginning, were friends of his brother. They, and all the rest, looked not to Averell, who was then thirty-nine, but to fifty-four-year-old Thatcher Brown as their de facto leader. Although the Harrimans accounted for the largest portion of the partnership, the elder Brown was referred to as the "The Captain," and his special status was confirmed by an honored seat beside the big window overlooking the site of the fabled buttonwood tree where two dozen brokers had first swapped stocks on Wall Street in 1732.

Averell blamed the AVCO fiasco on Coburn, whom he had disliked from the beginning because of a dictatorial disposition and a self-righteousness assumed with his license as a troubleshooter. "I just can't understand how Coburn led us on as he did in the expenditure of money in the development which is impossible for us to recover," he complained to David Bruce after the ill-fated superplane project. "I do not see any solution to it, except turning the key in the door and hoping someday we can sell the plant. The advice you and I were giving him for so long was unheeded. It makes me sick, but that's that."[17]

But Coburn's mistakes as president were minor compared to the one Harriman himself was about to make. Against strong advice, he persuaded Lehman in the spring of 1932 to join a stock swap bringing Errett Lobban Cord, a onetime automobile salesman, into AVCO as the conglomerate's largest stockholder.

Cord had begun his business career by dressing up and selling used cars while he was still in high school. He had created one of the first car washes in the country before becoming a salesman of Moon automobiles in Chicago. Eventually in control of Auburn Automobile Company, he marketed the prestigious high-powered Duesenberg and manufactured a front-wheel-drive car named for himself. He also built motors for Auburns, Cords, and Duesenbergs and branched out to Lycoming aircraft engines as well.

By the middle of 1930, Cord was building Stinson passenger planes; and the following year, he founded Century Air Lines and Century Pacific Airlines, each equipped with a dozen of his Stinson trimotors.

Linking the principal cities of the Midwest, Century competed directly with American Airways, providing frequent service between Bloomington, Chicago, Cleveland, Detroit, Springfield, St. Louis, and Toledo. In California, Century Pacific operated between the state's larger cities and on eastward routes from Los Angeles to Yuma, Phoenix, and Tucson.

The secret of Cord's success was that he went further than any of his competitors to control operating costs. Paying his pilots less than other carriers, he earned the enmity of both industry management and organized labor. He was distrusted by the Post Office Department and, therefore, had to survive without government airmail contracts. After his pilots went on strike and the Post Office Department rejected his desperate effort to negotiate a cut-rate mail contract, he went to Harriman with an offer to swap his airlines for AVCO stock. Although the corporation was losing money, Cord viewed its depressed shares as a huge bargain because of its still hefty cash reserves.

From Harriman's perspective, the deal was attractive because it offered American Airways an opportunity to dominate routes across the Midwest and to get rid of Century Pacific's nettlesome competition on the Phoenix–Tucson leg of American's transcontinental route. There was also the possibility that Stinson planes could reduce operating costs. He had already been advised that American Airways' $300,000-a-year losses on the New York–Boston run could be cut in half by replacing Ford trimotors with the lighter Stinsons.

The downside of the equation was that Cord might make a run on AVCO itself. With E.H.'s example and his own successful takeover of American Ship and Commerce before him, Harriman certainly knew the tactic; but still he dismissed warnings about the Chicago wheeler-dealer, and on April 2, 1932, he announced the merger. AVCO would acquire control of Cord's airlines and twenty-seven planes valued at $622,000 in exchange for 138,000 shares of Aviation Corporation stock. Cord would also get a spot on the board of directors.

With the merger, Century's service competing with American Airways in the Midwest was canceled, as were its flights between Los Angeles, El Paso, and Tucson, leaving nothing of Cord's western operations but the schedules between Los Angeles, Sacramento, and San Francisco. On routes where Cord and American Airways had battled head-to-head, American now enjoyed a monopoly.

While the negotiations with Cord were still under way, Sanderson and Porter announced that it had finished its overhaul of the corporation's management. To Harriman's delight, that ended Coburn's tenure as president, and the board promptly elected in his place Lamotte Cohu, a stockbroker and president of an AVCO subsidiary called Air Investors.

At the same time, Lehman and Harriman swallowed their pride and asked Fairchild, still a major stockholder although he had quit management, to take a hand in the day-to-day running of the company. Fairchild's view of the corporate leadership had not changed during his absence. The executive committee, he noted in a letter to Averell, still had only three members with significant aviation experience. Only seven of the thirty-five directors could claim any competence in the field whatever. "It seems to me if we are unfortunate enough to make anymore of the expensive blunders we have in the past," he said, "stockholders might justly place the responsibility for them largely in the makeup of the board and the committee."[18]

But unlike many of the directors who knew Cord's reputation, Fairchild was enthusiastic about Harriman's deal, thinking Cord would bring to policy discussions urgently needed practical insight. He was, like Averell, mistaken. Instead of adding stability and aviation savvy, Cord plunged the boardroom into furious controversy. He quarreled with Cohu over the use of Stinson airplanes, which the new president considered underpowered and inadequate for the American Airways routes, and belittled Cohu's management of pilot discipline, aircraft maintenance, and daily operations. The disputes escalated into an outright challenge of the president's authority, and shortly split the board into factions, leading to friction between Harriman and Lehman, between Harriman and Cord, and between Harriman and directors angry at him for bringing Cord onto the scene in the first place. Fairchild concluded that Averell would always be hopelessly ineffective because, he said, the chairman lived in fear that "something would happen that would besmirch the Harriman name."[19]

Critics of the Cord deal soon proved to be correct. The new director struck for control of the corporation. With the stock trading for less than $3, he bought thousands of additional shares to go with the 138,000 he had received in exchange for his airline properties, bringing his holdings to more than a fourth of the outstanding common stock, dwarfing Harriman's and Lehman's own holdings. Too late, Averell recognized his folly. "My friends told me I'd be a damn fool to take you into the company," he angrily told Cord in front of the assembled directors, "and they were right. I'm a damn fool."[20]

Luckily, though, Harriman had a way out. He had been elected chairman of the board of the Union Pacific, so three weeks before Cord's takeover attempt became public, he simply quit as AVCO chairman to pursue his destiny at the railroad. His Union Pacific election had taken place upon the death of Judge Lovett four months earlier, and he had spent two of the intervening months in Europe. But with the Cord affair about to blow up, Cohu contended that the chairman had just headed for the bushes "scared to death" of being publicly outmaneuvered by a hustler like Cord.[21] In any case, he was no longer chairman of AVCO when Lehman mounted the defenses against Cord's takeover.

At the suggestion of board member Eddie Rickenbacker, directors loyal to Lehman and Harriman moved to acquire North American Aviation, Inc., a huge holding company whose subsidiaries included Eastern Air Transport, Inc., Sperry Gyroscope, and substantial pieces of both Douglas Aircraft Company and the new Curtiss-Wright Corporation.

The merger via a gigantic stock swap promised uncontested domination of the nation's passenger traffic. In control of Eastern Air Transport, AVCO would add the profitable New York–Atlanta route plus a new southern run to the West Coast and a link to the Pan American system and its connections to Florida and on to Havana.

Cord saw it for what it was—a ploy by the bankers to keep control in the hands of the old Harriman-Lehman board. Since the merger would bring a big expansion of board membership, Cord's influence would be dramatically diluted. Indeed, the additional two million shares of stock to be issued in exchange for the North American holdings stood to reduce his percentage of the shares outstanding from 25 percent to 15 percent.

He retaliated with a campaign to round up enough proxies to gain control of the board before the merger could be approved. While his lawyers went to court and obtained an order temporarily blocking the deal, he put together his own slate of candidates and demanded a special meeting of shareholders. That done, he launched an offensive of paid newspaper ads, charging that Harriman and Lehman had squandered $38 million through waste and stock speculation.

"The control of your company," he said in one message, "has been in the hands of a small group of New York bankers whose combined holdings, according to records of recent date, aggregate less than 7 percent of outstanding stock. Shortly after organization of your company these same men furnished the New York Stock Exchange with a consolidated balance sheet showing assets of approximately $54,000,000. Today the latest available balance sheet shows assets of approximately $16,000,000."[22]

Returning from Europe, Averell kept his distance from the spectacle, adopting his father's practice of saying nothing in response to the accusations. Publicly, the fight was waged by Cohu and Cord Corporation executive vice-president L. B. Manning, who was as combative as Cord himself. Ridiculing AVCO management for its three years of losses, Manning boasted that he and Cord had made $10 million in profits and paid out another $3 million in dividends in the same period of time. Cord fully intended, Manning said, to bring a new era to American aviation: "We're going to meet the railroads at their own rates. We're going to fly freight just as cheap as the railroads can haul it."[23]

When it appeared that the fight would be thrown into the laps of 28,000 stockholders, an agreement amounting to a huge triumph for Cord was worked out. The Lehman-Harriman interests would reduce the board to fifteen members, with five of them to be named by Cord, five by the existing management and five more to be mutually approved by the opposing factions; at the same time, the North American Aviation merger was dropped. The New York establishment had been routed by the car salesman from Chicago.

With the election of the new board, Cord's influence was doubled. Besides Cord himself, it included Manning; Lyndol R. Young, Cord's personal attorney; R. S. Pruitt, general counsel of the Cord Corporation; M. C. Meigs, a Cord ally who was chairman of the Illinois Aeronautical Commission; Frank Vanderlip, former president of National City Bank, who had backed the takeover; and Carle C. Conway, a longtime associate of Vanderlip's. Averell and Lehman remained as representatives of the original board.

Inevitably, the first meeting of the new directors accepted Cohu's resignation and replaced him with Richard Hoyt, a St. Louis broker, early aviation investor, former chairman of Curtiss-Wright and former chairman of Pan American Airways. A diplomat with cordial relations with both factions, Hoyt took on the chore of making Cord's takeover complete. Whipped, Harriman discreetly helped him remove Cord's final opposition from the board.

On March 1, 1933, Hoyt wrote Harriman:

Dear Averell:

I saw Mr. Cord last night and told him that if he would do absolutely nothing to 'spill the beans' that I was confident the whole matter could be worked out as he wishes. I told him we could make no commitment but that you were going to proceed in an orderly manner, having received a favorable reception from the Lehmans; first get Bobby lined up and then make arrangements with the others; and that he would hear from us a little later on.

He is going to California and says he will have nothing to say about the matter whatever until we are prepared to make an announcement and that as far as any statement goes I can write it and he will sign anything that I say and say nothing else.

I outlined to him in general that it was our idea that such a statement would be along the following lines: Cord et al had substantially increased their holdings up to more than x shares; that Cord had expressed a desire in view of the critical times, etc., to have actual control of the corporation and management. In view of his large ownership the other directors felt it proper to accede to his wishes, and he made the following arrangements, etc. . . . .

Sincerely Yours,
Dick[24]

Two weeks later, Harriman, Lehman and their remaining allies on the AVCO board resigned. In a terse farewell to a company now ruled by Cord, Averell simply wrote "I hereby tender my resignation as a director of the Aviation Corporation and all of its subsidiaries, such resignation to take effect at once."[25]

It was not the end of his interest in aviation. Soon after he became chairman of the Union Pacific, board member Frederick Warburg began pushing for the railroad to buy control of United Airlines. Finally, in 1934, after Congress required the separation of aircraft manufacturing from the transport business, Harriman ordered a study of the airline industry. In the end, the price of a buyout of United was too high, but the idea of a Union Pacific–United relationship persisted until 1940, with Warburg suggesting that the railroad buy into the airline and establish a cooperative marketing and ticketing arrangement. Harriman opposed it as impractical.[26] His cautious view of a Union Pacific–United merger was perhaps influenced by his unhappy experience at AVCO. In any case, for the rest of his life, he rarely spoke of the latter. He made no mention of it in the brief account of his business career in his book *Special Envoy to Churchill and Stalin*, and whenever he was asked about it, he passed it off as something of no importance, an undertaking of Robert Lehman's.

It was, nonetheless, his last foray into an enterprise in which he might have measured up to his father as a capitalist. And in this attempt, he had, as before, fallen short.

Behind the optimistic facade of the new partnership with Brown Brothers, the Depression weighed heavily. For two years, neither Averell nor his brother accepted any earnings from the bank, and, in fact, came to the rescue of a few of the other partners who were in personal financial difficulty.

The new bank had gotten off to a rocky start because the merger was shortly followed by Europe's own economic crisis. Fortunately, Brown Brothers Harriman saw the trouble coming, and dispatched Knight Woolley and Ellery James to Europe to terminate and reduce lines of credit which had before the merger been extended to customers across the Atlantic by both the Brown and Harriman organizations. It was a close call, for Woolley and James were still on their way home from Switzerland when the crisis broke.

At midcrossing, Woolley spotted the chilling news in the ships bulletin that Kreditanstalt, one of Vienna's major banks, had reported losses for the preceding year equaling its entire capital reserves, and faced the possibility of closing its doors. The news swept through the European banking community, sending German banks to exercise all the credits they had with banks in the United States.

Although Brown Brothers Harriman had been able to shed substantial German credits, it still suffered heavy losses when the Hoover administration responded to Germany's plight by suspending war debt and reparations payments. The Stillhalte Agreement, as it was called, cost the firm $1.58 million in Germany, $247,000 in Austria, and $681,000 in Hungary, but the partners considered themselves lucky.[27] Had they not moved when they did, the losses might have been millions more.

Mary Harriman was by then feeble, but she was much aware of the bank's troubles. Although she had over the years distributed much of the fortune to the children, she came to their rescue with additional cash when they encountered heavy seas. In the spring of 1932, when the bank was feeling the full impact of the European payments suspension, she called George A. Ellis, her personal lawyer, to her house on Fifth Avenue and told him she wished "to turn over $1,000,000 to Averell and Roland's firm."

"She knew the two sons were worried about the financial situation," Ellis later recalled, "that they had suffered enormous losses; she did not want them to become discouraged, but on the contrary felt that they were entitled to great credit for carrying on the name in the business world instead of leading a life of ease as they could have done without the worry and strain of business and the financial risks involved therein.

"I explained to her that the firm was a partnership and that while her sons had a majority interest, it was hardly practical for her to make a gift of that amount to the firm with outside partners, and I suggested that the same purpose could be accomplished by a gift to her two sons."[28]

That afternoon, Averell and Roland each received a $500,000 check. Both checks were immediately turned over to the bank, and, perhaps, saved it. Outside the partners' room, the episode was never discussed, but the Browns privately expressed their gratitude to Averell, evidently unaware that the emergency infusion of cash had come directly from his mother.

"I heard only yesterday afternoon what you and Roland are again going to put the firm in a practically invulnerable position," James Brown wrote Averell.

> It is difficult for me to find words to express my appreciation and my admiration for the courage you are showing under such uncertain conditions. The contributions you have made since Dec. 31 last at such great sacrifice to your personal fortunes is something that no partner of the firm can ever forget. Your treatment of the red figure partners is generous to a degree unparalleled and would have been done only by men with vision and big hearts. Such actions deserve high reward and I have faith that the position you are creating for the old firm will result in a great future. What I can do to help is little but you must both count on me to do anything possible to lighten your burden and build for your future.
>
> Faithfully Yours,
> James Brown[29]

By the mid-thirties, the crisis for the bank had passed. With all of the partners out of the red, 40 percent of its earnings were plowed back into the firm's capital and 60 percent went to the active partners. Though the bank never rivaled the brothers' railroad holdings, it contributed steadily to their personal fortunes for half a century.

Ironically, the partnership was the beginning of the end of Averell's career as a capitalist and his professional teaming with his brother.

Chapter IX

TRAINMAN
Little Zip, Challenger, and Ketchum, Idaho

When Harriman became chairman of the Union Pacific Railroad, it was a billion-dollar corporation facing the hardest times it had seen since his father salvaged it from bankruptcy. It was sapped by the Depression and challenged by trucks, buses, automobiles, and airplanes. Its chief consolation was that the condition of just about every other railroad in the land was worse.

More than a hundred railroads were failing to muster enough money to pay their taxes and interest on big debts they had assumed during expansion and modernization projects in the aggressive twenties. A third of the country's railroad companies were in receivership, and industry giants such as the Baltimore and Ohio, the New York Central, the Southern Pacific and the Burlington had to have government assistance to remain solvent.

The B&O went to Washington for a $55 million government loan in the spring of 1932, and it was followed by Vanderbilt's proud New York Central, which lost $11 million in one six-month period and required $43 million from the public treasury to survive. The latter's stock fell from a 1929 peak of $256.50 to $8.75, the B&O's from $145 to $3. The Union Pacific's crisis, a possible suspension of dividends, was nothing in comparison to all that, but it was unprecedented in the Harriman era.

Before the market crash, the whole industry was already ailing, though few people in it and fewer outside of it recognized the symptoms.

209

During the twenties, railroad executives had put 15,000 new locomotives and 850,000 new freight cars on the tracks.[1] Yet in the months just before the Wall Street debacle, tracks and locomotives were being used at no more than half their capacity, and terminals had empty docks and deserted warehouses although railroad stocks soared from one peak to another.[2]

In love with the automobile, attracted to the bus, and charmed by the airplane, passengers abandoned trains. Day coaches rattled along with more and more empty seats, and Pullman cars deteriorated into seedy relics from better times. Freight customers once captive to railroad companies took their business to barges, pipelines, and trucks breaking into the long-haul business. The fickle government, so generous during the age of railroad building, now favored aviation with subsidies and motor carriers with compassionate regulation.

More vulnerable than it knew, the railroad industry collapsed like a rotten trestle when the Depression hit. Traffic fell another 50 percent. Freight cars still owned by banks rusted in train yards. Nearly three quarters of a million railroad employees were put out of jobs, and tens of thousands more worked only sporadically. Desks at the Interstate Commerce Commission in Washington collected railroads' applications to trim schedules and to abandon more and more of their unprofitable routes. Between 1929 and 1933, one hundred stations were closed, dozens of diners taken out of service, coaches parked, and shop hands, ticket agents, and train crews laid off.

After going off the Union Pacific payroll before World War I, Averell had remained a director, but in the late twenties he had increasingly taken a hand in the company, correctly expecting that, in time, he would be called to succeed Judge Lovett as chairman.

At Lovett's instigation, he was elected chairman of the executive committee of the troubled Illinois Central in 1930. It was sort of a trial by fire, a post where he could gain valuable experience while keeping an eye on the family's heavy investments and the Union Pacific's $50 million equity. He took a slow trip through the same IC territory he had traveled with E.H. as a boy, this time to size up the troubles of a company reeling under the threat of financial collapse.

The "mainline of middle America" was losing $3.5 million a year, and the bottom had fallen out of its stock. From a high of $136.75 in the raging bull market, it had plummeted to $4.75 a share.[3] Freight business was being lost to the Federal Barge Line operating on the Mississippi River and to the competing Missouri Pacific. Its passenger traffic was drying up. The good news was that highways in the Mississippi Valley were still inadequate, and construction was at a standstill. It was a perfect time, Harriman thought, for Illinois Central to go on the offensive and gain the upper hand before its competition revived.

He came home from his trip and persuaded the old Harriman and Union Pacific allies at Kuhn, Loeb to take $20 million worth of IC notes so the road could meet its obligations for another year while he pressed for drastic spending cuts. But in spite of the reductions, the road stayed in the red. Dividends were suspended, and cash reserves dwindled until the company was on the brink of bankruptcy.[4] It survived because Harriman got it into line for a loan from the new Reconstruction Finance Corporation, created by Congress in early 1932 to provide emergency assistance in critical sectors of the economy.

At the same time Averell was fighting the wolf from the door at Illinois Central, Judge Lovett had him take another long journey to assess the Union Pacific's own retrenchment. For a month, he traveled alone in his private car, stopping across the West to meet shippers, bankers, and station agents, to speak to chambers of commerce, and entertain mayors and governors. Although thousands of employees had been laid off, schedules trimmed, track retired, and projects deferred, the Union Pacific was in no way threatened like the Illinois Central, and he returned recommending that it, too, take the offensive rather than simply wait out the Depression. Considering the shape that the rest of the country's railroads were in, the situation at the Union Pacific was "remarkably satisfactory."[5]

With the ailing Judge Lovett approaching his seventy-second birthday and looking longingly toward retirement, the trip was as much as anything an occasion for Averell to prepare himself for the chairmanship, and he was already anticipating decisions that would be left to him. He intended to ease Carl Gray, the sixty-four-year-old railroad president, out of the day-to-day operations and put control in the hands of William Jeffers, a backslapping, hand-pumping Irishman who had been with the railroad since he was fourteen, rising from station janitor to company vice-president.

Gray, who had directed the operation of all the United States' railroads under government control during World War I, had been president of the Union Pacific since 1920. In government offices and corporate boardrooms, he was one of the country's best-liked and most respected railroad executives, and among Union Pacific employees he was revered. At the same time, train crews, telegraphers, station agents, and small-town customers regarded Jeffers as the epitome of the railroader. Among subordinates, he was as much feared as admired, but there also was a feeling of camaraderie because he was one of them.

"Jeff" had dropped out of school in the ninth grade, and at sixteen, he was a UP telegraph operator. A year later, he was an assistant foreman of a track-laying crew, and before he was out of his teens, he was a train dispatcher. At thirty-two, he was vice-president of the Utah division. He had not taken a vacation in forty years, and except for reading western histories and detective stories, he had no hobby other than the railroad. Quick-tempered, blustery, and demanding, he claimed to know ten thousand employees by name, and he expected all of them to drive themselves as hard as he did. It was a point of pride with him that he had come up through the ranks, and while his ambition could not be concealed, he went out of his way to associate himself with the gandy dancers, telegraphers, and brakemen he regarded as the real railroaders.

Jeffers, Harriman wrote in his notes as he headed home from his inspection, was an "energetic, feet-on-the-ground clear thinker," who would "develop to the top of the railroad world." Even more important was his commitment to the company. "UP is his life," Harriman scribbled as he thought his plans through. "With Gray, Gray first, UP second. With Jeffers, UP first, UP second." His plan for Gray was to "divorce him from details at Omaha still more and have him devote more time in New York, Washington, & Chicago to promote general interests of railroad problems with the investors' community, politicians, and railroad executives."[6]

Six months after the trip, Lovett died unexpectedly after checking into a Long Island hospital for abdominal surgery, and Averell was elected chairman. Carl Gray remained president until October 1937, but Jeffers, in the new position of executive vice-president, was increasingly the man running the railroad.

Averell and Jeffers took control of a system that remained in good health because Lovett and Gray had been quick to make cuts across the board to protect cash reserves when the market collapsed. But more than that, Lovett had for two decades used E. H.'s strategy of keeping tracks and equipment up to date and holding down expenses by financing new projects at times when money could be borrowed at the most favorable rates. Because it was kept in tip-top shape, the system could weather hard times by making huge spending cuts without plunging into immediate deterioration.

Still the pinch of the Depression could not be avoided. And while it was tempting to blame every problem on the national malaise, it was also clear to Harriman that the railroad industry suffered serious problems not attributable to the Depression. During the twenties, Union Pacific's passenger revenues had declined by half, and in the three years following the Crash, they had declined by half again—which meant it was carrying only a fourth as many passengers as it had ten years earlier.

Lovett had in his last years come to believe that the best days of American railroads were gone. In a gloomy moment, he had advised Roland Harriman to take up another career. The imagination that had created the American railroad empires had been stifled by overregulation from Washington, and passenger service had been allowed to disintegrate while management concentrated on making easy money hauling freight.

Day coaches were worn, noisy, dirty, and attended by crews with studied surliness. The same was true of dining cars and sleepers on the long runs where luxury had once been the hallmark. Managers slicing budgets to save money during the Depression made unprofitable passenger trains their targets. In cases where the government denied applications to terminate service, conditions grew still worse.

Harriman took it personally because he had more or less grown up on trains; and even during the years when his attention was on shipping and mining, he peppered Union Pacific officials with suggestions for improving passenger trains. Just before the Crash, he had recommended that Union Pacific install telephones on all of its long-distance trains and arrange to show motion pictures, but he had gotten a gentlemanly rebuff from Carl Gray. If they did that, the president said, it would just provoke the competition into a response that would have to be answered in turn, and the upshot would be more escalation of expenses.[7] In the winter of 1932–33, Harriman took another trip to the West Coast, accompanied by Gray, Jeffers, and other officials, finding the passenger business so bleak that he wondered aloud whether it should be abandoned altogether.

That was out of the question, he knew—for one thing, nothing so drastic would ever be approved by the government. Besides, he had already made a deep commitment to modernize passenger service, convinced that he could in the process save the credibility of the railroad. "There was a greater stake in the passenger business than just the saving of a loss," he later said. "That stake was public opinion. . . . We set ourselves the job of regaining public confidence. Instead of being conservatives we now became radicals. . . . We had been afraid of innovations, afraid to disturb the picture. . . ."[8]

The characterization of the approach as radical was hardly an exaggeration. In the midst of the Depression, Union Pacific management invested $50 million on passenger trains that had accounted for less than 10 percent of its income in 1932. With trains running half empty and passenger cars standing idle, they ordered revolutionary new high-speed trains, betting that passengers would reappear if they found comfortable and economical service once again. The time for change was ripe. For years, the Union Pacific had kept an eye on the development of diesel-powered locomotives as a possible replacement for the venerable steam engines that had for half a century symbolized America's industrial might. Through his shipping interests, Averell had kept up with developments in diesel marine engines in the 1920s, and when engineers representing manufacturers in Germany called on him at his shipping office, he had sent them along to see officials at the railroad. Returning from a trip to Europe for Brown Brothers and Company, Bob Lovett brought drawings of diesel locomotives he had seen being built in Germany. Averell took them to Carl Gray and persuaded him to send a locomotive expert to investigate. The conclusion was that the German engine was still too small for American freights. Undaunted, Harriman kept raising the subject, and within weeks Union Pacific men were back in Europe to visit diesel motor shops in Switzerland and England, as well as Germany.

When Averell succeeded Judge Lovett, new aluminum and steel alloys being used in airplanes presented an opportunity for designing a radically new diesel-powered passenger train. So, in 1932, the Union Pacific went to work on a plan for a streamlined train, powered by a new engine that could take it down the track at more than one hundred miles an hour and travel nonstop for hours at a stretch.

On May 24, 1933, a few months after he had mused over the possibility of abandoning the passenger business, Harriman announced that the company had ordered this "entirely new type of passenger train." The Union Pacific, he said, had concluded that "a radically different type of passenger equipment" was necessary to save rail travel.[9] His plan was to present the new train to the country in highly publicized demonstrations and then put it into scheduled service.

It was a move of stirring audacity, considering economic circumstances and the outlook for the passenger business. There was no guarantee that the streamliners could ever be profitable, even if they did capture the imagination of the public. Harriman took the risk because he was certain that passenger trains would otherwise continue to deteriorate, dragging the entire railroad industry down with them. Officials of other companies had come to similar conclusions.

Although he was hopeful that the prospect of speed and glamour would attract interest, Harriman was wholly unprepared for the public excitement that greeted his "train of tomorrow" when it dramatically rolled out of the Pullman shops in Chicago nine months after the board approved the purchase. Awaited by hundreds of gawking spectators, hordes of photographers, and network radio correspondents with live microphones, it glided into the open and stopped on a track beside a huge steel sleeping car drawn by a steam locomotive. There was a buzz of admiration and a spontaneous eruption of applause at the sight of its compact, low-slung contours, its canary yellow and chocolate brown colors, and gleaming chrome grillwork covering the nose. The guttural rumbling of the distillate-burning experimental engine as much as its strikingly modern appearance suddenly made the huge, boxy steam train on the adjacent track a relic.

Altogether, the train's three cars weighed only eighty-eight tons, about as much as a single Pullman sleeper. Only eleven feet high, their undercarriage cleared the roadbed by less than a foot. They were air-conditioned, equipped with indirect lighting, and outfitted with adjustable seats. In the tanks beneath the floor of the engine was enough fuel to travel 1,200 miles nonstop.

Tests of a scale model in a University of Michigan wind tunnel had shown that it could cruise at a steady ninety miles per hour, fully loaded. It had, in fact, already cruised at eighty-six miles per hour in a secret run and had not gone faster only because Averell wanted it to be in the Union Pacific's possession when it began to shatter the speed records of steam trains.

Streamlining was not an innovation of Harriman or the Union Pacific. A spinoff from aviation, it was about to sweep both the railroad and automobile industries. Other solvent railroads, led by the Burlington, rushed to acquire their own streamlined cars and diesel engines. Automobile manufacturers were turning to plans for vehicles with rounded fenders, sloping roofs and hoods replacing the familiar square bodies that had found their ultimate expression in Henry Ford's Model A.

As he accepted America's first streamliner in the cold Chicago railyard, Harriman announced that he had already ordered three more of them, complete with sleeping cars and equipped with more-powerful diesel engines. Union Pacific's goal was a passenger service that would cut twenty to twenty-four hours off the trip between Chicago and Los Angeles.

Before the test train was finished, he had already laid plans to publicize it massively by racing from Chicago to Washington faster than anyone had ever gone before, rolling triumphantly into Union Station. There President Roosevelt would board it for a personal inspection and a ride to Baltimore and back.

But the grandiose plan to make a big splash hardly fit the style of the old-timers around the Union Pacific boardroom; it even frightened young men like Bob Lovett, who was now a member of the board and the executive committee. Although Lovett was inclined to defer to Averell on both banking and railroad matters, he thought the speed run foolhardy.

The train represented untested and potentially risky technology, and he was adamantly opposed to taking a chance of wrecking it in a publicity stunt. The Texas and Pacific Railroad had been working on a fast train with a new type of wheel and it had jumped the track and been all but demolished in a test run. Being an old family friend, Lovett could challenge Harriman's judgment as could no other board member. With the speed-run announcement about to be made, he called Averell in Washington and tried again to talk him out of it, then emphasized his concerns in a sobering letter:

We have a brand new untried train. It will not get much of a workout after the christening in Chicago. Now assume a lot of advance publicity is put out about its arrival in Washington and that, when there, it will be inspected by the President and other notables, and then assume that, after all this hullabaloo it jumps a switch point and gets cracked up, or some bad engineering bug develops in it and makes the affair a fiasco. It seems to me that it would retard the whole program of speed trains so much as to make it awfully unwise to run such an unnecessary risk. The safer and more reasonable procedure would be to get it safely into Washington, shine it up and polish it within an inch of its life, and then make the announcement.[10]

Lovett renewed his concern a week later, telling Harriman he was still "scared to death," and Averell relented.[11]

Passing up the speed demonstration that he saw bringing the railroad a million dollars' worth of free advertising, he had the train travel to Washington three days after the ceremony in Chicago with its throttles under firm restraint. Even without a dramatic arrival at the end of a record-breaking speed run, the excitement surpassed anything the Union Pacific had imagined. Accompanied by his daughter, Anna, several members of the Cabinet, and a gaggle of White House aides, President Roosevelt boarded the train at the station and spent nearly half an hour being shown through it by Averell and Carl Gray. Afterward, he sat in his limousine and watched as it was backed down the track and moved up again to give him a better view, but he passed up the offer of a ride to Baltimore, evidently thinking himself sufficiently exploited by the massively reported show at the station.

Several members of the party did board the train with members of Congress and journalists for a seventy-five-mile-per-hour demonstration, which produced giddy accounts. "There is a sense of security and peace and comfort as you rush through the air at 75 miles an hour that is lacking even in the newest of the old fashioned trains powered by huge iron monsters," reported the *Washington Star*. "There is no noise or dust, and hardly any vibration. This new gas-engined bullet cleaves its way through the air at break neck speed. . . . Harriman and the Union Pacific will go down in history among the pioneers in railroad development in the United States."[12]

With nationwide fascination fired by the presidential inspection, *Little Zip*—as railroad officials had taken to calling their toy—drew huge crowds everywhere it was put on display. Thousands more waited along its route to see it pass and hear the piercing air horn that humbled the familiar wail of the steam whistle. Before it was ever allowed up to its cruising speed, *Business Week* magazine delivered the Harriman message more clearly than he and the company had been able to put it. The Union Pacific, it said, had put the railroads into competition with the airlines, leaving behind "the crash bang school of railroading."[13]

In Washington, Harriman received steady reports from his men aboard the train as it began its introductory tour. "Marvelous outpouring of people all along Pennsylvania from Baltimore to Pittsburgh, not only in cities but all the small towns and along countryside," Carl Gray wired him four days after it left Washington. "Almost solid concourse from Johnstown to Pittsburgh. Ran slowly and everybody had opportunity to see train. Pennsylvania officers exhibited greatest interest and were responsible for advance publicity. Had preview [for] invited guests last night, something like 250 and today crowd is comparable with that at Washington. Count at Washington over 33,000, Baltimore over 25,000. It is no exaggeration to say that 500,000 people saw the train enroute yesterday."[14] At times, the crowds were so dense and close to the tracks that Gray feared for the people's safety. The story was the same day after day as it made its way to the Chicago World's Fair and on to Boulder Dam and the West Coast. Its performance was as satisfying as the public reception. On a run between Omaha and Columbus, Nebraska, it hit ninety-three miles per hour as easily and quietly as it ran at seventy.

When the more powerful version, complete with sleeping cars and a new nine-hundred-horsepower diesel engine, was delivered in the fall of 1934, Lovett could no longer restrain Averell from dramatically showing off what the new speed trains were meant to do. Having passed up his high-speed dash from Chicago to Washington, he decided to set a new transcontinental speed record instead. More than that, he would shatter the coast-to-coast mark that E.H. set in 1906. The old man's personal train had raced across the country in seventy-one hours and twenty-one minutes as he returned to New York after directing the evacuation of San Francisco earthquake victims. Now Averell planned to erase the twenty-seven-year-old mark and show the feasibility of cutting a full day from the trip between the Pacific coast and Chicago. He also wanted to emphasize Union Pacific's preeminence in the new age.

Although he had taken delivery of the first streamlined train, other railroads were driving equally hard to recapture the fading passenger traffic with streamliners. The Burlington's new diesel-powered *Zephyr* had hit a top speed of 112.5 miles per hour during a run between Denver and Chicago, and the company had, in fact, used a diesel engine before the Union Pacific.

All the publicity had ignited a new fascination with trains and speed, producing pressures for the railroads to even run their old steam trains faster. Union Pacific, Southern Pacific, and the Santa Fe all cut two to two and a half hours from their schedules between Los Angeles and Chicago.[15]

On the way west for the assault on the cross-country record, the Union Pacific speed train easily set a record for the trip between Omaha and Los Angeles, covering the 1,880 miles in thirty-three hours and forty-two minutes, nearly thirteen hours less than the scheduled service.

Harriman's departure for New York from Union Station in Los Angeles on the night of October 22, 1934, generated the excitement of a first-night film opening. A crowd of five thousand milled around the stucco station, trampling shrubs and flowers as popping flashbulbs reflected off the shiny new aluminum cars. Extra police were sent in to hold people back as Averell and Union Pacific officials greeted business leaders and political dignitaries invited to see them off.

At ten P.M., the new diesel, more powerful by a third than the engine in the first streamliner, eased out of the station, five cars behind the engine gliding away, as *News Week* reported the following week, "as silently as a snake."[16]

Somewhere in the darkness of the desert, the party zipped past the eastbound *Los Angeles Limited*, which had departed two hours earlier. By the time Harriman and the fifty-odd guests awoke in the sleeping cars— the *E. H. Harriman*, the *Abraham Lincoln*, and the *Oregon Trail*—the next morning, they were in Utah.

Ahead of them, guards stood at every switch, and section hands patrolled mountain passes for fallen rock. Sixteen hours out of Los Angeles, they stopped in Salt Lake City to pick up officials of General Motors and the Winton Engine Corporation before streaking across the Great Salt Lake and into the mountains. Through the night, they flashed past junctions and way stations in a blur, the wail of their air horn piercing the silence and receding rapidly into the distance as station managers consulted their railroad watches and wired ahead the message, "On Schedule, On Schedule."

They were seven minutes late leaving Cheyenne, but on a long straightaway between Dix and Potter, Nebraska, the two-hundred-ton streak of yellow and brown hurtled eastward at a new record speed of 120 miles per hour. At the controls, chief engineer Harry Robinson monitored the speed gauge while his foot held the locomotive's "dead man's pedal"—a safety device designed to bring the train to a controlled stop if the engineer fell asleep or dropped dead—against the floor.

Crossing the Nebraska plains between Cheyenne and Omaha, they established another record by averaging eighty-four miles an hour over a stretch of more than five hundred miles. They reached Chicago's La Salle Street Station at three o'clock Wednesday afternoon, thirty-nine hours after leaving Los Angeles, nearly five hours faster than any train in history. A forty-hour scheduled service was clearly feasible, for they had dawdled at Salt Lake City, Omaha, and Cheyenne while an NBC broadcasting team aboard filed network reports on their progress.

The rest of the trip was leisurely because they had to stay behind the New York Central's *Twentieth Century Limited* on its regular eighteen-hour run from Chicago into New York. Still, when they arrived at Grand Central Station, fifty-six hours and fifty-five minutes after departing Los Angeles, the streamliner had beaten E. H. Harriman's trip home from the West Coast by fourteen hours and thirty-two minutes. It had also made the transcontinental journey in five hours and twenty minutes less than the combined air-rail service that Averell himself had initiated five years earlier for the Aviation Corporation. The trip had convinced him that streamliners could cut the cross-country time down to forty-eight hours, and there was already talk of a hundred-mile-an-hour train between Chicago and New York.

Grinning and waving his battered hat, Harriman led the passengers from the train onto a platform swathed in red, white and blue bunting, covered by a red carpet, and jammed with hundreds of well-wishers. He embraced Marie and then city officials who shouted congratulations above a thunderous rendition of "California Here I Come" by a New York Central redcap porters' band. "We have made all the cities of the East closer to the coast by one day," he said into a cluster of microphones. "I think I may say that rail travel has already been revolutionized. Eventually this type of train is sure to replace the old sort. It is too much faster, too much cheaper to run, not to win in the end."[17]

In the commotion, much of what he said was drowned out. Adding to the confusion, Robinson, the exhausted engineer who had been at the controls of the train through most of the journey, fainted. He was taken away in a wheelchair after being sufficiently revived to give a brief account of how he and two other crewmen had guided the bullet cross-country.

The next day, 58,700 people trooped through the train before it was closed to the public. After that, it was moved on to be briefly put on display at Philadelphia, Bridgeport, New Haven, Boston, Cleveland, and St. Louis before it was sent back to Omaha to be outfitted for routine service as the *City of Portland*.

While the streamliners were the headline-getters, there was more to Harriman's design for rehabilitating the passenger service. No matter how glamorous the streamliners were, the majority of Union Pacific's passengers would never set foot on them. Real modernization required elimination of the anxiety and discomfort being inflicted upon ordinary day-coach passengers. For them, Harriman's objective was as revolutionary as the speed trains themselves—he wanted a service, he said, "to make each of our coach passengers feel he was our most valued patron."[18]

With Jeffers personally ramrodding the project, $600,000—three times the cost of *Little Zip*—was spent modernizing what Averell had already started calling an "old type train," combining low fares and first-class accommodations into a model passenger service. The ideas came from the passengers themselves, gleaned by Avis Lobdell, who was hired to travel the system and gather their complaints. There were enough gripes and suggestions to quickly fill notebooks—passengers were fed up with dirty cars, rude attendants, tasteless food, uncertain schedules, and petty premium charges for extra service. Pullman customers were equally disgruntled. As far as they were concerned, Will Rogers had been on the money with his observation that the only Pullman service improvement in a generation had been a washbasin slot for used razor blades.

The refurbished test train that would determine whether good service would bring passengers back was aptly christened the *Challenger*. Its cars were outfitted with plush carpets, tapestries, and upholstered bucket seats. Taking charge of the interior decoration, Marie banned the drab colors that had served since E.H.'s day and introduced bright tablecloths, blankets and cushions. All the cars were air-conditioned and equipped with commodious lounges and dressing rooms. Taking an idea from the airlines, Harriman ordered the cars staffed by stewardesses, all trained as nurses, who pampered passengers with sweets, fluffy pillows, and constant attention. Brakemen and conductors were ordered to desist from their old habit of going through the train yelling out station stops during sleeping hours, and to awaken gently each passenger scheduled to leave the train at stops during the night. Dining cars were routed through to the end of the line to avoid the crashing and banging caused by their being detached while passengers tried to sleep.

Berths were extended several inches, affording tall passengers the luxury of stretching their legs, and new brakes were installed to cut down running noise and eliminate screeching stops. Two coaches reserved for women and children were an instant hit: they gave women who traveled without male escort a sense of security and allowed them to be more informal and relaxed, and provided for children who traveled alone to be looked after by Union Pacific stewardesses. Week after week, these coaches accounted for 60 percent of the *Challenger* passengers. To top it off, the dining car served breakfast for a quarter, lunch for thirty cents, and dinner for thirty-five cents. And the *Challenger* offered a round-trip between Chicago and Los Angeles for $57.35—$3 less than the same journey by bus.

Soon it became the Union Pacific's most profitable train, even making money on the cut-rate food service. Passengers who had previously taken lunch boxes began crowding into the diner in record numbers— on one day in the winter of 1935, more than seven hundred meals were served as the *Challenger* rumbled toward Chicago. Leaving Los Angeles only minutes after departure of the ten-car *Los Angeles Limited*, it often rolled out of the station filled to capacity while the *Limited*'s passengers numbered a few dozen.

Although he was taking an increasing interest in politics, Harriman was obsessively attracted to details of both the *Challenger* service and the new streamliners. Recovery of the passenger service became a consuming personal mission. The man who had kept an eye on his Soviet mining enterprise between polo matches and who had casually chaired the Aviation Corporation fussed over the *Challenger* like a professional housekeeper, installing electrical outlets and telephones and equipping streamliners with windows that polarized light and eliminated glare.

In spite of the hard times, the improvements began to pay off even before the *Challenger* trains were in full service. In 1935, passenger service saw a 21.4 percent revenue increase, followed by another 34.7 percent jump the year after that. Even at the height of its modernization program, the company continued its dividends to stockholders, paying $6 per share in 1935, a generally dismal year for nearly everybody.

The improvement of the railroad, its new passenger cars, and its bright colors had an impact on the customers as well as on the railroad and its employees who ran the trains. "We have noted instances," Harriman said, "where passengers boarded the train in unpressed or untidy clothes but retired to change their clothes after noting the looks of the train."[19]

Fast trains, fresh flowers, and fluffy pillows made passengers happy, but Averell had learned at E.H.'s knee that a railroad prospered only when its territory prospered. Union Pacific country produced cattle and grain and bought lumber and farm equipment, but it needed destinations for passengers, and in the summer of 1935 Harriman toyed with an idea for generating new traffic.

During his travels over Europe in the twenties, he had often lost time because men he needed to see were off in the Alps skiing. Although he had invested heavily in polo ponies, racehorses, and bird dogs, he had never really thought about sports as a serious investment opportunity until after the 1932 Winter Olympics at Lake Placid, when European-style skiing began to catch on in the United States. The Boston and Maine and the Boston and Albany railroads had started to make money running "snow trains" to New England on winter weekends. The Union Pacific, going back to E.H.'s time, had recognized tourism as a potential source of revenue, and much earlier, it had, with considerable success, developed tourist traffic by running a spur line to Yellowstone National Park and by joining in development of the north rim of the Grand Canyon. Until Averell came up with the idea of Alpine skiing, however, no one in the company had ever regarded snow as a potential asset. Every winter, it cost the railroad millions. Now Averell imagined trainloads of passengers journeying to the Rockies from both coasts.

At first, he had thought about organizing a club made up of his friends and building a lodge somewhere out West near the Union Pacific line. He and CBS president William Paley kicked the idea around at Arden, and he later mentioned it to Herbert Swope, Dorothy Schiff and few other possible investors and members, but there was no great enthusiasm. The obvious alternative was to make it a railroad project. That idea, in Harriman's mind, meshed so neatly with the improvement of passenger trains that it became a part of his overall modernization strategy.

One of the European skiers he knew was Felix Schaffgotsch, a young Austrian count who was something of a dandy, and an excellent skier. Harriman had once rented a cottage from the Schaffgotsch family while in Austria hunting chamois, and he had later arranged for Felix to have a stint in a trainee's job at Brown Brothers Harriman. Since the western mountains resembled the Alps, Harriman recruited him to find the place for a railroad resort investment.

Carl Gray and Bill Jeffers, who had seen more schedules wrecked and budgets destroyed by blizzards than by rockslides, train robbers, and crop failures put together, thought it was crazy. The only skiing done in Union Pacific territory was by small boys and by ranchers, who had to strap heavy runners to their feet to search for cattle lost in winter storms. As far as the UP president and executive vice-president were concerned, the best advice they could offer the chairman was to forget his resort and stick to railroading.

It was already too late for that. Averell's research showed ski sales skyrocketing on both the East Coast and the West Coast; country inns and tourist homes in New England were turning away customers on weekends and filling most of their rooms even during midwinter week-days.

Schaffgotsch arrived in New York in late November. Sent immediately to Union Pacific headquarters in Omaha, he launched his expedition under instructions to report only to Harriman. The boss wanted a place close to Union Pacific tracks, obviously, but it also had to be far enough from a city to prevent it from being overrun by weekend skiers arriving in their automobiles. Through December and January, the Austrian toured the Rocky Mountain West—from Denver to Mount Ranier, Mount Hood, and Mount Shasta, to Lake Arrowhead and Mount Baldy. He skied, hiked, rode horseback, and traveled by sled and airplane. Every promising spot proved to have some fatal flaw. Either the snow conditions were unacceptable or the location was unsuitable. He rode a straw-filled sled over the Grand Tetons to Jackson, Wyoming, and was favorably impressed, but he could get no assurance from state officials that they would keep the pass leading to the area open in winter. Aspen, Colorado, was attractive, but there were too many trees, and it was so high that Schaffgotsch feared that guests unaccustomed to the altitude, would have difficulty sleeping.

While Schaffgotsch searched and took detailed notes, Averell enrolled in skiing lessons at Saks department store in New York and got ready to join him when he found a site to recommend. Two days before Christmas, the count reached Los Angeles and checked into the Beverly Wilshire Hotel for the holidays, having vetoed every mountain he had seen. "I have done practically all the developed ski resorts from Mount Baker (Seattle) to Mount Baldy (Calif)," he wrote Harriman. "All these places are purely weekend resorts, and no competition of any sort. Besides, most of them are about four to seven hours drive from the towns, which makes it too near for a longer stay and again too far for every weekend. The hotels and inns are all built as summer resorts and now only adapted for winter sports, which is jumping and tobogganing."[20]

After the holidays, he moved on to Utah, then eastern Idaho, and back to Colorado. He was at the Brown Hotel in Denver and about to give up when he got a wire urging him to come back to Idaho for one more look. William J. Hynes, a Union Pacific freight agent at Boise and former member of the Idaho legislature who had been his guide in the state, had forgotten to take him to Ketchum, a backwater sheep town in a Sawtooth Mountain valley in the south central part of the state.

During the 1880s, mining around Ketchum had boosted the town's population to two thousand, and the Union Pacific's Oregon Short Line had laid a track linking it to Shoshone. But the silver ore had long since been exhausted and the Depression had taken its toll on the sheep farmers who stayed after the miners were gone. The summer population was only 270, and during the winter months half of them left for Shoshone or Twin Falls rather than stay in the Wood River valley, cut off from the world except for the thrice-weekly train.

As Schaffgotsch and Hynes headed north from Shoshone behind a county snow plow, Harriman's scout thought he was once again wasting his time. The valley was far too wide to provide the kind of shelter a resort required. But it dramatically narrowed as they approached Ketchum, making it more likely that they would find slopes protected from the gales bringing winter snow. As they got into town, Schaffgotsch was struck by the stench of sulfur. But once he went out to a little valley to the east, he forgot the foul smell coming from hot springs bubbling to the surface in Ketchum. A mile from the main street, he found what he had been looking for all across the West. There, the road led into a small, open valley, surrounded on three sides by mountains free of trees, and open to the south. It was the ideal site for a ski lodge, protected from the icy north winds, and near gentle, open slopes perfect for beginning skiers. On the other side of town, towering above Ketchum's on the west, was the taller, truly impressive Baldy Mountain, with stands of evergreens reminiscent of those of the Swiss Alps and wide natural openings perfect for ski runs. On the mountains and in the valley, the snow was light, squeaky-dry powder. The locals claimed that the storms that delivered it usually came at night and quickly moved on, leaving still, sparkling, sunny days. A review of weather records would bear them out.

There was already skiing in Ketchum, but it was unlike anything Schaffgotsch had ever seen. Out of necessity, the hearty winter residents traveled about on twelve-foot-long homemade slats, moving and braking themselves with poles the size of pitchfork handles, their heavy boots held to their skis with "housings" made of canvas. Except for small boys, who slid down the hillsides, no one regarded skiing as amusement.

On the day after his arrival, Schaffgotsch enlisted a youngster to accompany him and spent three days skiing the slopes and exploring the valley. When he got back to Shoshone, he wired Harriman that he had at last found the place—with "more delightful features than any other place I have seen in the U.S., Switzerland, or Austria for a winter sports center."[21] Within days, Averell and Marie, accompanied by his daughter Mary, plus William Paley and his wife, Dorothy, boarded Averell's private car, the *Overland*, at the end of a New York Central train and headed west. They stopped in Omaha for updated reports from Schaffgotsch, picking up the Union Pacific for the rest of the journey. In Shoshone, they were diverted to a siding, and a waiting locomotive took them north through the ascending foothills, passing Picabo, Bellevue, and Hailey as the snow along the track grew deeper and the Sawtooth Range loomed higher.

When they arrived, on Washington's birthday, Schaffgotsch was waiting for them with an enclosed wagon, warmed by a woodstove. He was surrounded by most of the town's population, which had turned out to see him deliver on his promise that the famous Averell Harriman would appear in Ketchum.

The Union Pacific chairman was sold on the count's Idaho discovery the moment he climbed out of the wagon for his first look at the valley east of town. "There were all the mountains with gold in the background and the hills covered with snow," he recalled. "I fell in love with the place then and there."[22]

The party stayed for several days, living in the railroad car, exploring the valley in the wagon, laboriously climbing up mountainsides to ski down in pristine snow. For the first time, the ranchers and merchants started to believe the incredible story that the Union Pacific Railroad might build a hotel east of town. If he was serious about it, old-timers advised Harriman, they knew where there was a warm spot in the valley. It was a place at the east end where the cattle always huddled on the coldest days. Harriman took their advice, and the sunny corner of a broad meadow became the site for his lodge.

As soon as he had seen Ketchum and the mountains around it, he was anxious to get back to New York to sell the story to his skeptical Union Pacific officers and get planning started in time for an opening for the following ski season. Without even waiting for their formal endorsement, he sent in land agents to start negotiations for property. He also hired Steve Hannagan, the public relations man who would make the valley outside Ketchum world famous.

Hannagan had previously done some work for the Union Pacific, and he had earned a reputation as a promotional genius by mesmerizing snowbound New Yorkers with images of sun, golden sand, and tropical luxury at Miami Beach, turning it into a thriving winter playground. He was a brainstormer, promoter, and nonstop talker who poured out so many ideas that some were inevitably winners. He had all the machinery and contacts that Harriman needed to sell the novel idea of a winter vacation in Idaho.

A city boy, Hannagan had never been on skis and took no interest in any known form of outdoor recreation. His natural environment was the Stork Club in New York or one of its imitations in Miami Beach, not an Idaho sheep town with one restaurant, a single grocery store, and a motel with a hot spring that stunk. But he accepted Harriman's case and in March he arrived in the wild West. Expectedly, he was attracted neither to Ketchum nor the magnificent mountains around it. Wearing a light tweed suit and low-cut city shoes that filled with snow the moment he stepped off the train, he looked for the mountains bathed in golden light that Averell had rhapsodized about; but half-blinded, he could see nothing but one "Godforsaken field of snow."[23] Nevertheless, personal feelings could not be allowed to hobble a professional pitchman, and he doggedly proceeded into the wilderness.

As he later told the tale, the sales spiel for Harriman's valley came to him as dramatically as the story he fabricated about Harriman getting the inspiration for an Alpine resort in America while waiting out a snowstorm at St.-Moritz. As he inspected the valley in the late Idaho winter, Hannagan claimed, the sun had come out and he had begun to sweat, even though the snow didn't melt. Then and there, the name Sun Valley had come to him, and thereafter ideas for Harriman's resort flowed as clearly as a mountain stream.

Averell's plan had been to build a one-hundred-room hotel—to be called the Ketchum Inn or something like that—financed in part with a stock issue, with the balance covered by a loan from the railroad's cash reserves. Hannagan would publicize it, and if it caught on, it could be expanded. But Hannagan returned to New York with much bigger ideas, beginning with a million-dollar luxury hotel where glamorous and famous guests would themselves become a part of the attraction. Instead of promoting the luxury and self-indulgence, however, they would evoke images of robust health and vigorous exercise in the sun and snow.

Around the lodge and slopes there would be heated outdoor mineral pools, skating rinks, dogsleds, a bowling alley, a movie theater, and Union Pacific club-car comfort would bring guests from both coasts. The key was to do it all with "class and snap."

"If it is not done on this scale it should not be done at all," said his first detailed report to Harriman. "It would be my hope to make every newspaper and magazine reader, every theatre goer, every radio listener conscious that there is a great winter sports resort in America—a resort more colorful, modern, more exclusive than any other in all the world. . . . This needs to be done with unusual pictures showing the unusual climate of Idaho which suggests sun bathing in three-cornered, uncovered ice houses, skiing in shirts skinned to the waist, bathing in natural hot water pools in the open." Done right, he promised, Sun Valley would get national attention.[24]

Harriman bought it all. Hannagan's gusher of suggestions became his blueprint. Union Pacific executives, having said all they prudently could to temper the chairman's excitement, loyally fell into step, with Harriman and Hannagan setting a fast pace. Paying a little more than $10 an acre, railroad agents acquired four thousand acres of grazing land from Ernest Brass, a rancher who had seen his cattle business ruined by poison larkspur weeds and his sheep herding devastated by the Depression. Architects produced blueprints for a 250-room hotel, and as the snow melted, surveyors arrived to stake out the building site.

To Hannagan's recommendations, Harriman added touches of his own. He began with a ski club for his New York social and financial friends, including Tommy Hitchcock, Nelson Rockefeller, and William Paley, and a ski school run by the Austrian downhill champion Hans Hauser. Union Pacific's engineering department at Omaha was ordered to work on a new system for lifting skiers to the top of the runs, and it responded in a fashion that he boasted was typical. The solution was a modified version of the hoist used to load stalks of bananas aboard fruit boats, suspending chairs instead of bananas along a moving cable transporting skiers as gently as ripe fruit.

Out of the Idaho backcountry, hundreds of unemployed men carrying their bedrolls, some accompanied by their families, flocked into Ketchum on foot, on horseback, and atop logging trucks, looking for jobs on the project. From the south, laid-off Union Pacific employees joined them. Since many were penniless, the payroll office handed out

$5 ticketbooks used by railroad employees to exchange for meals until their first payday.

Harriman ordered additional rail sidings put down and sent in boxcars outfitted with bunks, showers, office equipment, and commissary stocks, creating a huge construction camp near the Ketchum depot. Workers who brought families with them lived in relative privacy in "family cars." All walked out to work at Sun Valley at dawn each morning and back to their railcars at sunset.

By summer, Ketchum was taking on the atmosphere of a gold-rush town. Besides the normal rowdiness that went with having men with money in their pockets, there was enough friction between the locals and the New Yorkers who came to supervise that Harriman sent in railroad detectives to maintain order. Their responsibilities included escorting Marie and the Harriman daughters whenever they were in town.

Instead of building the lodge with logs and having the potential for fire, Harriman and his architects struck on the idea of hollowing the logs and filling them with concrete, preserving the rustic look and providing safety at the same time. It was an expensive and laborious process, but the hotel was already taking shape by the time the Harrimans returned for a long summer visit. Marie's retinue included her old school chum Marjorie Duchin, the wife of society band leader Eddy Duchin, who had joined her in redecorating the passenger cars of the Union Pacific. Together, they took on the interior decoration of the lodge, ordering custom-built furniture, touching off the rooms with cherry red carpets and pastel drapes, bedspreads, and washcloths to contrast with the winter vistas of white. Even white sheets and pillowcases were forbidden.

Ketchum watched the race toward a December grand opening with amusement and bewilderment. As the hotel went up, an army of workers on the flank of the mountains behind it erected towers and strung steel cable between them. Not since wagon trains rumbled into town with ore from the silver mines had Ketchum seen such prosperity.

Harriman and Hannagan spared no effort. Together, they provided Schaffgotsch with a notebook filled with addresses and private telephone numbers, sending the count off to Hollywood with special invitations for people they especially wanted at Sun Valley's opening—actors, actresses, producers, directors—the Gary Coopers, the Samuel Goldwyns, and the Darryl Zanucks among them. Walt Kuhn, the painter whose work graced the new Union Pacific streamliners, arrived to advise on the interior of the lodge, and Marie's sister, Frances Lord, was retained to spread the word back on Long Island. Dartmouth ski coach Charles Proctor spent much of the summer in Idaho overseeing the location of the lifts and the first ski runs, so pleasing Harriman that a mountain was immediately named in his honor.

Creating press releases and planting newspaper articles was easy, but Hannagan had one problem that defied even Harriman's bankroll. He needed a picture that would do for Sun Valley what photographs of bathing beauties in the surf had done for Miami Beach, but the resort as yet consisted of a construction site surrounded by mountains with rocks and patches of sage grass. Harriman's PR man was up to the challenge. In a Manhattan photographer's studio, he arranged the picture that made the resort famous. It showed a perspiring, deeply tanned young man, stripped to the waist, with sweat glistening on his handsome brow and muscular chest. He was on skis, leaning on a pole supposedly anchored in an Idaho mountainside. Of the millions who saw it, few suspected that his ski poles anchored him in gauze or that the perspiration was created not by attacking a Sun Valley slope but by a jar of petroleum jelly.[25]

With autumn, Austrian ski instructors, German waiters, and French chefs arrived from the East. Local women hired on as chambermaids; Lane's General Merchandise made room for ski poles and sunglasses among its stocks of pitchforks and sheep-dip; and families prepared to stay on through the winter as Ketchum braced for the arrival of movie stars and money from both coasts of the United States.

December arrived with everything in place the way Harriman and Hannagan had planned it. The ski lift was perfected, the hotel was finished, Hannagan's well-advertised sun was shining—but there was not a trace of snow. When a couple of inches did fall, a warm rain immediately followed and washed it away. Not in living memory had the valley seen a December so balmy. Guests who arrived expecting to be among the first on the slopes of the new Alpine resort had nothing to do but ride horseback, play backgammon, or drift into Ketchum to shoot craps at the new casino.

Mercifully, Harriman was detained in New York by a debutante party for his daughter, Mary, and unaware that his first guests had already renamed Sun Valley the "Ketchum Con." But as the hotel filled up for the grand-opening party, he sent orders that no one was to be charged for lodging as long as there was no snow. Hannagan took bolder steps of his own, sending invitations that brought unattached studio starlets from Hollywood.

The grand opening took place with the slopes bare and tension rising among the guests looking out upon dusty ski runs. At the gala dinner dance, one of the Hollywood guests punched a Chicago banker in the nose before hundreds of people, including several members of the press. The banker had approached a table where movie actresses Joan Bennett and Claudette Colbert were seated with their husbands and producer David Selznick. Something he said offended the film-maker, who knocked him flat on his back on the dance floor, bloodying his face sufficiently that he had to be removed from the room. Harriman was horrified, but Hannagan was delighted with all of it, for it made Sun Valley news across the country.

Two days after Christmas, snow finally began to fall. By New Year's eve, it was two feet deep, but that still didn't cover the tall sage grass, which no one had remembered to cut and which gave the mountains the look of a man who needed a shave.

By then the Harrimans had arrived from the East, and trains from Los Angeles had brought more of Hollywood's biggest names—Errol Flynn and Madeleine Carroll among them. Colbert, Robert Young, and Melvyn Douglas had already been in Idaho most of December with Selznick and a film crew shooting sequences for a new movie, which, to Hannagan's chagrin, was called *I Met Him in Paris*.

Despite the shaky start, though, the massive publicity campaign succeeded wondrously. Sun Valley was an American St.-Moritz. Skiers from both coasts found it exciting to cross the country in Union Pacific luxury and ski in the remote western mountains, and Hollywood adopted it all with more enthusiasm than even Harriman and Hannagan had dreamed. Film stars loved it for its informality. When they learned from Hannagan that being photographed allowed them to write their Sun Valley trips off as a business expense on their tax returns, they even more gladly allowed themselves to be used as the centerpieces of Sun Valley—and Union Pacific—promotion.

For the opening of the second season, the new, less expensive Challenger Inn adjacent to the lodge was finished, as was Averell's own six-bedroom cottage. The family, along with dozens of their friends, arrived in Ketchum aboard a spanking-new *City of Los Angeles*, being touted as the world's longest streamliner.

Unlike the year before, the snow arrived on schedule, and guests were greeted at the railroad station by dogsleds and sleighs drawn by horses and reindeer. The first occupants of the Challenger Inn arrived just as the workmen were packing their tools and leaving the site, checking into the new hotel whose facade had been inspired by the set for *I Met Him in Paris*.

The reindeer were among the few failures among all the schemes Hannagan and Harriman dreamed up to create atmosphere. Taken off their moss diet when they were moved from Alaska to Idaho, they nearly starved before they accepted Idaho alfalfa. Fearing their imminent death, Union Pacific rushed in a carload of moss to save them, but while the shipment was en route, the animals made their reluctant switch to hay and then refused to return to their native diet. They were nervous and ill-tempered, and when they were hitched up for sleigh rides, their Eskimo handler could exert no control over them. To keep them from running away or attacking the passengers, he had to hold their antlers until his sleigh was loaded, then release them and leap into the driver's seat. Averell did not find it amusing when the animals who delivered Santa Claus for the lighting of the Christmas tree in front of the lodge turned on St. Nick and chased him away in full flight.

For Averell, the ski resort was the most satisfying venture of his business career. Union Pacific did not make big profits on Sun Valley traffic, but the notion of rail travel was romanticized and the company's image was polished. He stayed at his cottage for nearly two months during Sun Valley's second winter, working at becoming a competent skier before heading back to New York. To some extent the sport replaced polo in his life. "No one has really lived," he decided, "until he has skied."[26]

With the opening of Baldy Mountain, world-class skiers descended upon Sun Valley, along with eastern society and the California movie crowd, and Averell established the Harriman Cup to promote the sport. Although eastern resorts had started earlier, Sun Valley was the most important influence in popularizing downhill skiing in the United States. Baldy was in the view of many experts the best ski mountain in the world, and on it young American skiers began to compete with Europeans for the first time.

Dick Durrance beat the Austrians down Baldy, winning the downhill, the slalom, and the combined, taking the Harriman Cup for the first two years. A pigtailed girl named Gretchen Konig, later world-famed as Gretchen Fraser, trained on the slopes to sharpen her skills for the Olympics, where she became the first American woman skier to earn a gold medal.

For five years, Harriman fussed over Sun Valley as he had none of his other business enterprises. Whenever there was repainting, samples had to be kept to prove to him that the original colors were unchanged. He dictated the precise location of the furniture in the lodge's famous Duchin Room, ordering it moved if he arrived and found chairs and tables had drifted from their original places. When he was away, general manager Pat Rogers wired him daily reports on snowfall, skiing conditions, sales of lift passes, and news of notable guests arriving for the first time, including women establishing Idaho residence in preparation for dissolving unsuccessful marriages.

Without being unseemly, the resort catered to what Rogers called the divorce "carriage trade" from both coasts. Hannagan's public relations operation, phenomenally successful at pushing photographs of Sun Valley visitors who wished to be publicized, was equally adept at protecting guests who didn't. Expert divorce counsel was available just down the road at Hailey, where Ernest "Phez" Taylor, a New York lawyer, put out his shingle after he and his wife, Dorice, arrived aboard the *City of Los Angeles* for Christmas, 1937.

Three years after the grand opening, Ernest Hemingway was lured to Idaho from Montana. He drove up to the lodge one afternoon in September 1939 with his companion Martha Gellhorn and stayed for two months, sampling the hunting and fishing along Silver Creek and enjoying one of the lodge's prime corner suites—number 206—facing Dollar Mountain. He returned to shoot duck and pheasant again in the fall of 1940 and 1941, hunting on a few occasions with Harriman, accompanied by Averell's prize-winning Labrador retrievers sent out from Arden for the use of special guests.

During his second long stay in the lodge, Hemingway spent hours on the patio outside suite 206 going over galley proofs of *For Whom the Bell Tolls*. The arrangement between the writer and the resort was beneficial to both. Sun Valley was happy to provide accommodations in the off-season in exchange for the bonanza in publicity that the famous author and sportsman generated by hunting in the valley. When Averell arrived in 1939 and found Hemingway had moved into the less expensive Challenger Inn with the beginning of ski season, he promptly ordered him back to his suite in the "Glamor House," as Hemingway called the lodge.

Harriman's last visit to Sun Valley before the war was in late 1940. The resort was about to begin its sixth season when the Japanese attacked Pearl Harbor, and it stayed open the following winter. But in 1942 it was turned over to the Navy and converted into a recuperative hospital, the lodge housing officers and the Challenger Inn accommodating enlisted men. The flatland in the valley was turned back into grazing land for sheep, the saddle horses were sold, and the sled dogs that had greeted snow trains were sent back to Alaska. During the war years, some of the Hollywood regulars—Clark Gable and Gary Cooper among them—used their leaves from the military to come back and ski on the empty slopes, staying with friends in Ketchum.

Harriman's much-publicized Austrian ski instructors had become objects of venomous suspicion in Ketchum and Hailey even before the United States entered the war. Two days after Pearl Harbor, Sun Valley's top ski instructors—Austrians Hans Hauser, Friedl Pfeifer, and Sepp Froelich—were arrested by the FBI as enemy aliens, and Hauser and Froelich were shipped off to an internment camp in North Dakota. Averell, who was by then in England expediting the flow of American arms and supplies across the Atlantic, wrote letters supporting them, and Froelich and Pfeifer were released. Both joined the Army. Before the war was over, Froelich won a Silver Star for gallantry in the Pacific, and Pfeifer lost two ribs to a shrapnel wound while fighting with the 10th Mountain Division in northern Italy. Hauser, who had a brother in the German Army, remained in confinement until the war ended.

The only avowed Nazi in Sun Valley had left in 1939 when the war began in Europe—Harriman's friend Felix Schaffgotsch, it developed, was an admirer of Hitler and a disciple of national socialism. He had confided his sentiments to Averell's daughter Kathleen, and he had once told the actor David Niven that he had planned to bring Nazi friends from Austria to work as Sun Valley ski instructors.[27] Otherwise, he kept his politics to himself; but after Hitler invaded Czechoslovakia in 1939, he went home and entered the German Army. Harriman never heard from him again, and it was not until after the war that he learned that the count had died on the Russian front.

The resort was returned to the railroad after the war, and once again the ski trains rolled into Ketchum from Los Angeles. Harriman returned regularly—if not frequently—until he was nearly ninety and Sun Valley was in the hands of its third owner. He never fully forgave the Union Pacific for selling it.

In its heyday, Sun Valley brought the Union Pacific treasury $250,000 a year in additional passenger revenues, adding to the recovery already under way when the late snow finally arrived for its first winter. By the end of 1936, streamliners filled to capacity were running regular schedules between Chicago and Los Angeles, Chicago and San Francisco, Chicago and Denver, and Chicago and Portland. More trains were on order.

The *Challenger* service, launched on the Los Angeles–Chicago run, had been so successful that new cars were being rushed out to extend it to San Francisco and Portland. With less fanfare, Harriman turned to modernizing the freight trains with renovated boxcars and more-powerful steam locomotives to handle longer freights at speeds comparable to passenger trains.

As he fidgeted over the barren Sun Valley slopes that first December, the railroad had come into a windfall that had as much impact as his management on Union Pacific's improved financial health. In the Los Angeles suburb of Wilmington, General Petroleum Corporation—later Mobil Oil—brought in an oil well that produced nearly 1,400 barrels of high-quality crude per day. The gusher was within yards of a 1,100-acre Union Pacific industrial site.

The find was in an area where wells dug with spades and drilled by augers had mysteriously yielded oil years earlier. But even when Ranger Petroleum Company drilled a well producing seventy-five barrels a day in 1932, Harriman and the Union Pacific management had paid it little attention. They were satisfied that industrial development of the property that E.H. had acquired with the Los Angeles and Kansas City Railroad would pay off handsomely with new freight business. The railroad had already sold Ford Motor Company a seventy-acre parcel near Long Beach Harbor, where the company had built the country's biggest auto assembly plant.

Oil became a serious consideration only in the summer of 1936, when General Petroleum conducted a thorough geological study of the neighborhood, finding a production zone at 2,430 feet, then another at 3,000, and still another between 5,300 and 5,500. Six months later, the drilling boom exploded, and Union Pacific officials feared the company was in danger of losing its oil through wells drilled all around the railroad property, draining the pool beneath it.

While he was in Idaho, Harriman renewed efforts to get an agreement with Edsel Ford to pace the drilling from their properties so both would get the maximum long-term production and keep oil prices from collapsing. With the General Petroleum strike, it was too late for that. Since the richest deposits lay at a depth of only 3,500 feet, a well could be completed in a month.

Ford's property, in the middle of the Union Pacific tract, was leased to General Petroleum, and the oil company was positioned to drain huge amounts of oil from the railroad land legally by merely drilling adjacent to the property line. After meetings between Ford and Union Pacific officials and his own contacts with Edsel Ford, Harriman thought he had an agreement to restrain drilling. But by early 1937, it was clear that Ford Motor Company, too, wanted to pump out its oil as quickly as it could so it could expand its auto plant. Uppermost in Harriman's mind as the oil problem came to a head was the challenge of learning to ski satisfactorily. Sun Valley's first holiday crunch was over, and he remained in Idaho until March, spending much of each day on Dollar Mountain. He arranged conferences between Union Pacific and Mexican Seaboard Oil Company in case it became necessary for the railroad to start drilling to protect itself, but he left most of the negotiations with Ford Motor Company and General Petroleum to Jeffers and Gray, who got nowhere.

Jeffers arrived in California and found the situation more threatening than he had imagined. The first well on Ford land, he wired Harriman, was already "draining our property to a greater extent than previously thought."[28] Two more wells had also begun production near the property line, and four more were being drilled.

The potential of the Wilmington field was staggering. Wells were being started at the rate of a dozen a week. Besides the wells on Ford land, Union Pacific was threatened by others on private leases along its northern boundary. After receiving Jeffers's on-the-spot assessment, Harriman gave the railroad's executive committee his approval of a $538,000 emergency program to drill seven offset wells along the property line and begin preparations for six more.

For decades the railroad had leased its promising drilling lands across the West to oil developers who paid royalties, but Averell was putting the Union Pacific directly in the oil business. In March, William Reinhardt, a well-regarded oilman, was hired away from a drillers' association to become a Union Pacific vice-president in charge of oil development, and by spring the company had three wells in production and twenty-one more in various stages of drilling and preparation.

The first came in on April 1, producing three thousand barrels a day. By midsummer, daily production had soared to forty thousand barrels. A year after General Petroleum brought in the first important well, the last pretense of self-restraint on the part of the drillers had vanished—389 wells had been drilled without a single dry hole.

By the end of 1937, Union Pacific itself had seventy-two producing wells and another eighteen under way, and it had begun to lease small detached parcels of land that could not practically be made a part of its own drilling program. The year following, another forty-eight wells were brought in, and the railroad netted more than $4.7 million from the California field, and that was only the beginning.[29]

The industrial land that E.H. had bought casually was in the center of a gigantic field that would produce more than 1.1 billion barrels of oil over the following thirty years, during which time it would remain the most productive field in North America. By the 1940s, the ground began to settle dangerously, so great was the extraction from the deposits. Eventually, Ford Motor Company had no choice but to close the huge Long Beach automobile assembly plant.[30] No such ill luck attended Averell with his strike, however: following his aggressive move to the diesel-powered streamliners and his successful promotion of Sun Valley, Harriman's oil made him one of the more successful railroad men in the country—in times that were as tough as any his father had known.

Twenty years after he had left his job as a junior vice-president to strike out for himself in the shipbuilding business, he had made his mark on the Union Pacific. Impressive though it was, his success in restoring passenger service was ephemeral. The heyday of the passenger train was gone, in spite of the streamliners and the *Challengers*. Under the circumstances, he and the rest of the Union Pacific management might have even made a historic mistake in their decision to save it. They had, said railroad historian Maury Klein, "put too many eggs in the wrong basket. . . . If the financial resources and competitive energy devoted to passenger service between the wars had been funneled instead into a concerted effort to improve freight operations, the postwar history of the railroads might have turned out very differently. Freight made most of the money, after all, and it desperately needed new thinking, new technology, and new techniques. But in the 1930's, the threat to passenger traffic looked far more grave. Few people believed another world war was coming, and fewer still grasped what effect it would have on the national transportation system."[31]

With the modernization program behind him and Sun Valley established as the country's foremost ski resort, Harriman's characteristic restlessness was increasingly evident.

Since the spring of 1933, he had spent more and more of his time in Washington. In the first days of the Roosevelt presidency, he had been on the fringe of the New Deal and ambivalent about the Roosevelt administration, but he had found the electricity in Washington and the trappings of political power irresistibly seductive.

Chapter X

NEW DEAL
FDR, General Johnson, and the Blue Eagle

Although he would in retrospect claim membership in the New Deal as a badge of honor and mark his conversion to the Democratic party in 1932 as one of the defining moments of his life, the launching of Harriman's public career was not the dramatic triumph of conscience that became immortalized in political folklore. He had never taken an active interest in Republican politics, though he had gained a private meeting with Warren G. Harding in 1921 and supported him because he was persuaded that Harding would press to make the United States the world's leading maritime power. He voted for FDR in 1932, as he had for Al Smith in 1928, largely as a protest against Herbert Hoover, high tariffs, and Prohibition. Then, too, there had been the Depression, which had touched even the Harriman family and still had not hit bottom.

Not only had Averell and Roland needed the $1 million in cash from their mother to see Brown Brothers Harriman through, but Averell had twice gone to her to get financial help for his sisters. Mary Rumsey, who had never demonstrated the Harriman touch where money was concerned, had suffered heavy losses in a newspaper syndicate and needed $500,000 to put her affairs in order. Carol, who had married R. Penn Smith, a banker and polo player, was widowed at the age of thirty, and had to have $100,000 to straighten out loans and investments that went bad after the Crash. In both of the daughter's cases, the money was provided with the understanding that Averell and Roland would thereafter approve their investments. Of all of E.H.'s children, only

Cornelia, who had married Robert Livingston Gerry and into a fortune comparable to the Harrimans', got through without one of her mother's "little gifts," aside from the $100,000 bestowed on each grandchild at its birth.

Mary and Carol's problems were among the minor things that made 1932 the unhappiest year of the Depression for Averell. He faced stupendous problems as the new chairman of the Union Pacific at the same time he came to the unhappy end of his involvement with AVCO. Then, just as the showdown came with E. L. Cord, his mother died.

In the last days of October, she closed the Arden mansion as she had every autumn since E.H.'s death and moved into the city for the winter. At eighty-one, she had been in seriously declining health for more than two years, and a few days after her return to her house on Fifth Avenue, she collapsed and was rushed to New York Hospital. She died before dawn on November 7, surrounded by her five children. Her body was taken back to Arden to spend the night before being buried beside her husband. The next day, Tuesday, was election day, and Averell went down to the village of Harriman and voted for Franklin Roosevelt and all of the other Democrats on the ballot, including Herbert H. Lehman to succeed Roosevelt as governor of New York.

He did not think about it at the time, but he had left the rails his father had laid for him.

Harriman's twenty-five-year acquaintance with the President was nothing more than that. They were not, as was later so widely presumed, close personal friends in the Hudson Valley aristocracy. When Averell had spent weekends as the guest of Groton classmate Hall Roosevelt in the home of Franklin and Eleanor, he had been in his early teens, and though less than ten years separated his age from FDR's, the circumstances of those early encounters made it seem as if they belonged to different generations. FDR was already a young family man, helping his wife with the upbringing of her young brother. Later, Roosevelt would seem to have no clear recollection of those early meetings. And Eleanor, perhaps because she had first known him as a "child" and the little brother of her friend Mary Harriman, never came to regard him as a gifted public servant.[1]

Over the years, Averell had considered Franklin a consummate example of the Hudson Valley gentry, a man whose abilities and accomplishments had always been exaggerated because he was who he was: the regent of a family prominent for so long that its name was no longer associated with any sort of grubby commercialism. Averell's legacy was, by contrast, new money, and E.H.'s reputation was as one of the foremost buccaneers in the days of unfettered capitalism.

Harriman had never called on Roosevelt when FDR was an assistant secretary of the Navy in World War I, nor when he was governor of New

York, but over the years they had crossed paths when both were involved in fund-raising for the Greater New York Council of Boy Scouts. Neither had taken the initiative to develop a friendship. After the Democratic National Convention in 1932, Averell was invited to Hyde Park to discuss the plight of the railroad business, and before he went back across the Hudson to Arden, the Democratic nominee had offered to make him finance chairman of the Democratic National Committee, an honor he declined because he was still ambivalent about politics, pressed by his railroad and AVCO responsibilities, and uninterested in campaign financing.[2]

Roosevelt, he thought, lacked any deep comprehension of economic matters. Certainly he had much to learn about the country's embattled railroad system, for he had offered a personal view that its principal problem was that it was overbuilt; there was more capacity than the country needed. But the candidate had vigor, intensity, and an open mind, all of which Averell had found lacking through twelve years of Republican administration in Washington. The obvious willingness to try bold and unconventional policies to ease the economic and psychological lethargy was enough to make him much preferable to Hoover, for whom Harriman had developed a personal as well as a political aversion.

The four months between the election and Roosevelt's inauguration were the darkest of the Depression. Seventeen million people were out of work. Family farms were being foreclosed; railroads were going bankrupt, banks failing at a frightening rate. Although faring better than most railroads, the Union Pacific was still laying off employees and trimming service. In mid-February 1933, less than three weeks before Roosevelt's inauguration, the governor of Michigan responded to a crisis at several banks around Detroit by ordering all banks in the state closed for eight days, triggering panic across the country. In the following week, $700 million in cash was withdrawn by frightened depositors asking for their money faster than currency could be distributed to vaults by the Federal Reserve. Hoover appealed to Roosevelt to help restore confidence, and the President-elect went to the White House for a conference; but he would have no part of a lash-up with a leadership discredited and in shambles.

On the Saturday of Roosevelt's inauguration as the thirty-second President of the United States, Harriman left Marie sleeping and went down to Wall Street, spending a grim, lonely morning waiting for the radio broadcast of the ceremony in Washington. On his way down Broadway, he passed banks with doors locked and guards standing outside. Just before dawn, Governor Lehman had ordered them closed. Not since Averell's great-grandfather had gone there in the midst of a cholera epidemic and found grass growing through the cobblestones had the financial district seen more gloomy times.

The "spread of hysteria," Lehman said in his 4:20 A.M. announcement, had "placed upon the New York banks a burden so great that it has finally rendered drastic action imperative here."[3] The order had come too late to make the morning papers, and stunned customers arrived to find the doors sealed behind the posted official notices. Guards stood by explaining over and over that they would be open again on Tuesday.

After going by the Union Pacific offices, he went on to see James Warburg, a new member of the railroad's board of directors and one of his few banker friends who had supported Roosevelt. They spent an hour talking about the banking crisis; then, just before noon, Harriman walked to his office at Brown Brothers Harriman, and, like millions of Americans across the country, turned on his radio to listen to Roosevelt's inauguration, anxious to learn what the new President proposed to do about the economic ruin and the banking crisis.

Even though conservatives and reactionaries on Wall Street held Roosevelt to be a radical and a dangerous enemy of free enterprise, he had steered such a determined middle course in his campaign against Hoover that Walter Lippmann had observed that he hardly seemed a dangerous enemy of anything. He had been so far ahead of Hoover in the campaign that it had been unnecessary for him to antagonize the political right or pin himself down with specifics about his intentions. He even managed to attack the Hoover administration from the right, chastising it for centralizing power in Washington and failing to balance the budget.

But as he stood before the microphones for his first presidential attempt to summon America from despair, Roosevelt laid the blame for the nation's misery at the feet of the "rulers of the exchange of mankind's goods." The cadence and resonance fired his message with authority and hope, but his stirring declaration that "the only thing we have to fear is fear itself" was drowned out on Wall Street by his attack on "unscrupulous money changers" who stood "indicted in the court of public opinion."

"The money changers have fled from their high seats in the temple of our civilization. We may now restore that temple to the ancient truths. The measure of the restoration lies in the extent to which we apply social values more noble than mere monetary profit."[4]

When it was over, Harriman was furious. He switched off his radio, took the elevator down to the lobby, and walked out into the empty street, where the only sound was the snapping red and white flag above the portal of Brown Brothers Harriman and Company. The President's confidence and the applause washing across the plaza of the Capitol and spilling out of the radio had been lost in the withering attack on the bankers. Roosevelt, he thought, had been unfair, superficial, and unnecessarily demagogic. He was not only crushed by Roosevelt's broadside against the financial community, but angry at himself for letting it be known that he had voted the straight Democratic ticket and inviting ridicule from most of his friends and banking partners.

A month after Roosevelt was sworn in, Harriman concluded a long tour of the Union Pacific and went to Washington for his first call on officials of the new administration. The worst of the banking crisis was past. Spring was about to burst forth, and the city was swarming with politicians looking for jobs and bankers trying to convince the government that they were in condition to reopen after the national banking holiday that the administration had ordered for the purpose of choking off the panic Roosevelt had inherited. Lights blazed through the night as the President's "brain trusters" drafted reform and recovery bills that were being obediently approved by lawmakers called into special session. The pace and energy of the capital surpassed even the first days of World War I, when Harriman had arrived with his plans for his prefabricated ship.

Harriman was not looking for a job in the administration. To the contrary, he took the train down from New York because he was concerned about bills being drafted to reform Wall Street—the securities industry, the stock market, and banks—and to deal with the financial crisis of the country's railroads. In principle, he was not opposed to reform, but he was fearful of policy decisions being left in the hands of liberals who had neither experience nor discernible sympathy for business interests. Reform was at the top of every agenda; and what troubled Harriman, even as a moderate businessman and Roosevelt supporter, was that it was so often in conflict with recovery. Unless there was recovery, much of the reform would be worthless.

Where the railroads were concerned, he had already taken the opportunity to urge the new administration to lift the onerous hand of the Interstate Commerce Commission, which had restrained railroad mergers ever since Teddy Roosevelt had gone after E.H.'s empire. After the meeting with the Democratic nominee at Hyde Park the previous summer, Harriman had received a visit from Raymond Moley and A. A. Berle, two of the candidate's policy planners, to discuss his specific recommendations. His chief advice had been for the government to allow profitable mergers that could help save beleaguered companies from bankruptcy and to stop federal subsidies that he saw bestowing competitive advantages on the barge and trucking industries.

What was most on his mind in early April, however, was securities reform and what he could do to tone down the legislation before it was shouted into law by a House and Senate already swept off their feet by administration initiatives. Wall Street, well remembering Roosevelt's inaugural attack on the money changers, was alarmed not only that reformers bent on protecting small investors would require securities dealers to provide the government details on every issue offered for sale but that the thousands already listed would have to be registered with the government as well.

The problem for Averell and all the rest of the businessmen, politicians, and emissaries who filled the hotels, swamped switchboards, and haunted government offices was that Roosevelt was sending trains through the switches too fast for passengers to know where they were headed. To outsiders trying to fathom what the White House was doing, the style seemed helter-skelter and reckless.

After two days in town, Harriman was unnerved by what he found. James Warburg, who had been enlisted to help the administration prepare for the upcoming World Economic Conference in London, met him for dinner and found him with "his hair pretty well standing on end over some of the radical suggestions he [had] heard on railroads, banking reform, and security legislation." The administration, Harriman complained to his friend, had altogether too many chefs stirring the broth; reformers were starting with the answers and then figuring out the problems, putting down the wrong figures, adding them up, and getting the right answers.[5]

The handling of securities and stock exchange reform was typical. Immediately after the election, Moley, the organizer of Roosevelt's "Brains Trust," had received the approval of the President-elect to begin preparing legislation protecting customers in both the stock exchange and the securities market. He recruited Sam Untermyer, who had led a sensational congressional investigation of "money trusts" twenty years earlier, and the seventy-five-year-old reformer had returned to Washington with his crusader's zeal undiminished. Since stock and securities dealers were engaged in interstate commerce and used the U.S. mail for transactions, Untermyer drafted a bill empowering the Post Office Department to regulate both the stock exchange and the securities industry.

Neither Moley nor the President thought it made sense to make the department charged with delivering the mail the watchdog of Wall Street, so they put Untermyer to work on a different approach, and Roosevelt evidently forgot about it. In any case, the President called in Attorney General Homer Cummings and Commerce Secretary Daniel Roper after the inauguration and gave them the same task he had placed before Untermyer. The two Cabinet officers, in turn, employed former Federal Trade Commission chairman Huston Thompson; and unbeknownst to Moley or Untermyer, Thompson drafted a bill putting government regulatory authority in the hands of the Federal Trade Commission. It required that every offering listed with the FTC be accompanied by a list of explicit details.

When the competing efforts were discovered, two acrimonious White House meetings tried to merge the drafts, but got nowhere because Untermyer ridiculed Thompson's work and refused to compromise. The upshot of it was that Untermyer was assigned to work on legislation regulating the operation of the stock exchange. Thompson deleted the stock exchange provisions from his draft, and the rest was sent to Congress as the administration's securities reform act.

Averell found the proposal "theoretical, impractical, and unworkable." It was laden with irritants, such as a requirement that full information be made available thirty days in advance of any security offering, and that a formal prospectus be read to prospective purchasers in every sales interview concerning a security offering. Its effect, he insisted, was to put the government in the position of passing judgment on the soundness of securities in the market.[6]

He took all of his objections to Moley, who conceded that the bill was an "impossible confection" which needed to be entirely rewritten. The view was shared by Congressman Sam Rayburn, who had responsibility for it in the House, and warned that the whole thing had to be thrown out. The matter might have been put aside for another year at that point but for the possibility that Roosevelt would take the United States off the international gold standard and unleash an orgy of financial speculation.[7] Determined, therefore, to salvage some measure of securities reform, the administration turned to Harvard law professor Felix Frankfurter for help.

The professor arrived from Cambridge with two of his brightest protégés—James M. Landis, a youthful faculty colleague who would later become chairman of the Securities and Exchange Commission, and Benjamin Cohen, an expert on British securities law, which would be used as a model for their reform proposals. Added to the team in Washington was Thomas Corcoran, a former Frankfurter student, who had joined the New Deal at the outset as counsel to the Reconstruction Finance Corporation.

Although Harriman's purpose in Washington was to make it impossible for the securities reformers to ignore Wall Street's views, he avoided being cast as an obstructionist. Moley regarded him as "a man of fine, discriminating intelligence, and a distinctly liberal stripe" and told the new drafting team to consider him the designated representative of what Rayburn called the "enlightened men with experience" in the securities business.[8] Frankfurter's team was to look to him when it needed a realistic assessment from the industry. Thinking he had become a full-scale participant in the process, Harriman sent for two New York securities lawyers to join him, expecting that the three of them would be asked regularly to analyze the work of the drafting team as it proceeded. Soon, however, he found himself and his experts excluded, Moley preoccupied with other presidential assignments, and Frankfurter back at Harvard. Not only was Harriman unconsulted, he could find out nothing about what Frankfurter's charges were doing, and the fragments he did pick up only added to his anxiety. It looked as if a bill was coming that would make it nearly impossible to market new securities. Harriman hounded Moley and Warburg on the telephone and haunted their offices until Moley started to complain of being fed up with "all the yawping from interested parties in New York."[9]

When the Frankfurter bill, largely the handiwork of Landis, was finished, Rayburn finally arranged a conference between the drafters and Harriman's lawyers, then sent the measure through his committee to a vote on the floor of the House without even bothering with further hearings. After a few changes by the Senate, the Securities Reform Act was signed by the President on May 27.

It required underwriters and dealers to make full advance disclosure about their offerings, put a damper on ventures such as the Lehman-Harriman financing of the Aviation Corporation, and prohibited institutions from both accepting deposits and issuing securities—that put Brown Brothers Harriman and Company out of the securities business. But it was, in good measure because of Harriman's diligence, only a modest reform, though Wall Street took small comfort from his achievement. Resentment of Roosevelt and the New Deal, muted in the first weeks of the administration, spread new and more bitter roots in the financial and business communities.[10] The securities reform begun in 1933 would be completed the following year with creation of the Securities and Exchange Commission.

To Wall Street acquaintances and some of his old friends, Harriman's hobnobbing with the New Dealers marked him as vainglorious, unreliable, and unfaithful to his kind. There were times when he walked the street in the financial district and saw people he knew cross to the other side to avoid shaking his hand.[11] His association with the new administration in Washington, said Brown Brothers Harriman partner Prescott Bush, "didn't help us a damn bit. People would ask, 'What the hell is your partner doing down there with this bunch of Communists and Socialists?' "[12]

While he was bird-dogging the securities bill, Harriman's curiosity about Washington and the Roosevelt administration became an infatuation, especially with recovery ideas still overshadowed by the drive for reform on every front. Disorganized though it was, the New Deal had purpose. It attracted men who, like Harriman, found joy in the exercise of power. Several weeks of trailing the securities bill had made clear to him what most of his friends on Wall Street feared and suspected—the real power in America had shifted from New York's financial district to Washington. Sensing that, the Union Pacific chairman had begun scratching at the door of the administration, Warburg recommended Harriman to Roosevelt as the United States' ambassador to Germany. The President invited him to the White House for tea and a conversation that seemed designed to size up his diplomatic talents, but Roosevelt either forgot the recommendation or Harriman flunked the audition, for nothing was ever heard of it.

During one of the days while he vainly waited to find what Frankfurter's men were concocting for the securities industry, Harriman had taken Warburg's advice and looked up Hugh Johnson, a recent recruit in the army of bill drafters at work across Washington. Johnson had arrived in Washington about the same time Harriman came down to work on the securities bill, and Moley enlisted him to help draft industrial recovery legislation.

After leaving the Army as a brigadier general, Johnson had worked for a while for financier Bernard Baruch before going off to be an executive of the Moline Plow Company in Illinois. He returned to Baruch's employ in 1927, living on Long Island and serving as Baruch's man Friday on Wall Street; but he had not been especially successful, and, therefore, had not had occasion to cross paths with Averell. As Baruch's agent, he had worked diligently against Roosevelt's nomination before the Democratic convention, but he had rallied to provide valuable service as a speech and memo writer in the campaign against Hoover.

Harriman found him in a hideaway office in Moley's suite at the State Department. Red-faced with slicked-down black hair and steel gray eyes, Johnson was as gruff and unpretentious as a cavalry sergeant. His specific charge from Moley was to outline a massive program that would stimulate recovery through the establishment of business and industry codes setting maximum hours, minimum wages, and rules of competition. From an economy thus organized, fair prices, better wages, and increased employment would supposedly flow. There would be protection against overproduction as well as security of consumer buying power. To take up the slack and get men out of the soup lines and hobo camps, hundreds of thousands would be put to work on public projects in fields such as conservation and construction.

Rather than tinkering, reforming, and placing additional obstacles in the path of business and capital, Johnson saw himself putting the trains on the tracks. He shared Averell's concerns about securities reform and tried to help him follow what was happening. Harriman liked him immediately because, unlike many of the reformers, he put recovery first. Rather than of a perfected democracy, his vision was one of invigorated markets, of Americans returning to work, and of the country shaking itself from its lethargy. He was a doer, a blunt, take-charge leader in the mold of William Jeffers at the Union Pacific. They spent an hour together on Averell's first visit and then met for dinner a couple of days later. Harriman went back to New York fired by Johnson's pep talks, and with new interests far beyond securities reform.

While the White House offered him no position in the administration, there was one avowed New Dealer, as yet without portfolio, who was anxious to recruit him: Mary Harriman Rumsey. Averell's sister had none of Averell's ambivalence about politicians in general and about Franklin Roosevelt in particular. She harbored no question about the rightness of the New Deal's course, nor doubt of its ultimate success. She was decidedly a reformer; but she held no grudge against the recoverers, and she encouraged her brother to join them.

Averell and Mary had received more than their share of E.H.'s genes and the template they provided for the old man's incessant urge to strive and achieve. They had grown especially close in the years after Pad Rumsey's death. Mary's French château at Sands Point and her penthouse in Manhattan became gathering places for a richly varied collection of social, political, and intellectual friends, from fox hunters and polo players to economists and poets and Junior Leaguers and journalists. Her guests included Scott Fitzgerald and William Butler Yeats, the latter brought from Ireland to read for friends. At Sands Point, Averell had a cottage next door and was more or less a regular at his sister's salon, where she showed him off to newcomers and he took in perspectives on politics and economics that he never heard spoken on Wall Street or around the clubhouse at Meadow Brook. Mary's three children, who were required to make an appointment when they wished to discuss something with their always preoccupied mother, looked upon him as a substitute father, seeing him more than his own daughters saw him during his estrangement from Kitty and after his and Kitty's divorce. His namesake, Mary Averell Harriman Rumsey, and her younger brother, Bronson Rumsey, delighted in being taken on rides in his cabin cruiser or the small seaplane he sometimes used to commute to Wall Street. He taught Charles Rumsey, Jr., to play polo well enough for him to make the team at Harvard.

As his sister looked to him for financial advice, he was increasingly influenced by her politics, and when she publicly announced that she was voting for Al Smith in 1928, he was prepared to go quietly along with her.

With Roosevelt's election, Mary moved her headquarters to Virginia, where she had for several years spent considerable time on a farm at The Plains, an hours' drive west of Washington. There she kept horses and raised enough corn and wheat to feed a sizable herd of beef cattle with some grain left to send to market. When the Depression came, she organized an Emergency Exchange Association, which bartered skilled labor for merchandise; and inspired by the Irish poet-economist George Russell, she founded the Eastern Livestock Cooperative Marketing Association to try out a plan for farmers' cooperatives throughout the country.

With Labor Secretary Frances Perkins, a friend and ally going back to settlement-house work in 1918, she rented a three-story, octagon-shaped house in Georgetown. Washington's "very air was supercharged with a new vital force," she said, and she added to the voltage. Transferring her New York salon to the House on O Street, she presided over a new social and intellectual crossroads where writers, artists, social icons, and foreign dignitaries who had regularly visited her château on Long Island met New Dealers from Cabinet rank down to secretaries in agencies whose initials still mystified the out-of-towners. Eleanor Roosevelt came to tea. Will Rogers came to dinner. On a given evening, the gathering might include polo player Tommy Hitchcock, New York *World* editor Herbert Swope, Bernard Baruch, General Douglas MacArthur, United Mine Workers chieftain John L. Lewis, and New Deal brain trusters such as Moley and Rexford Tugwell.

When he was in Washington, Averell was a regular, as was his new friend Hugh Johnson, who sometimes brought his wife but often dropped by alone looking for support from his confidante and adviser, Madame Perkins, especially after his tempestuous personality began to create problems for him all over Washington. For the general and a host of others, the Rumsey-Perkins house was a place where gossip was assimilated, new ideas were tried out, and political careers were assayed.

Unlike Averell, who made no attempt to presume familiarity with the Roosevelts, his sister was on an intimate basis with the White House. To Mary, the President of the United States was still "Franklin."

"Dear Franklin," she wrote him after he took the United States off the gold standard. "All these weeks I've resisted the impulse to write you, but after your splendid decision today about the gold standard, I just can't help writing. . . . It is difficult to choose between the magnitude of creative events you have brought about in so short a time. But out of all, your May 7th address on the Partnership of Government and industry was so perfect—it touched such a high peak of courage and wisdom— it was such a fine work of art that I wanted to cheer and cry at the same moment—the way one feels before a glorious picture or a great piece of sculpture. It will live as an eternal message—complete in itself—perfect for all time."[13]

As close as she was to the Roosevelts and all the insiders of the New Deal, Mary held no official position in the spring of 1933. Thus she began talking with Moley about buying the *Washington Post* and appointing him her editor. Since she no longer made serious business decisions without consulting her brother, Averell was brought into the conversations soon after he arrived to work on the securities bill. It was well known around town that the ailing *Post* was about to be put up for sale. It was down to as little as a dozen pages a day and losing money at the rate of $25,000 a month. When it was unable to pay its newsprint bills at the end of March, it fell into bankruptcy, and Mary saw an opportunity to make it a new voice for liberal principles in the capital. Beyond that, she wanted to branch out and publish a liberally oriented national public-affairs magazine.

Moley was willing to quit his job in the administration and join her. He was still the powerhouse of Roosevelt's Brains Trust, but he was financially pressed and went back to New York to teach at Columbia University once a week so he could remain on the institution's payroll at the same time he drew his government salary as an assistant secretary of state.

At first, Averell was not excited about the plan, because he had seen too many of Mary's brainstorms produce schemes for socially meaningful business ventures that had no hope of being self-sustaining. Years earlier, he had tried unsuccessfully to negotiate an agreement for her to buy the *Des Moines Capital*, but his offer of $800,000 had been turned down. Afterward, she and Hearst columnist Arthur Brisbane agreed to buy a newspaper in Perth Amboy, New Jersey, but the deal fell through because Hearst enforced a provision in Brisbane's contract preventing him from investing in other publishing interests. Unfortunately, she had persisted. She had then purchased a syndicate which provided papers with feature articles, cartoons, and political columns, and it soon began losing money at an alarming rate, making it necessary for her to go to her mother for help.

It was not a first-time trip into financial difficulty for Mary, and this time her mother put stern conditions on her bailout. Besides getting Averell's consent to future investments, she was to sell her Sands Point house and her late husband's studio to raise additional cash. The latter requirements were never met, but thereafter she faithfully consulted Averell on business affairs. By the time he was brought into her plan to buy the *Washington Post*, however, the idea was already in full bloom. Rather than try to dissuade her when she was already under a full head of steam, he agreed to join her, but he resolved to spread their risk around.

Vincent Astor, who had nearly limitless assets and a pocketbook open to anything supportive of Roosevelt and the New Deal, agreed to take a 50 percent interest in the venture. They would pay up to $500,000 for the ailing *Post*, with Astor kicking in $250,000, and Mary and Averell contributing $125,000 each.

When the paper went on the auction block on June 1, 1933, a crowd of several hundred, including lawyers, socialites, political figures, and newspapermen worried about their fate, gathered at the steps of the *Post* building to watch the bidding. From her office above the street, Evalyn

Walsh McLean, wearing the Hope diamond around her neck, watched, hoping that her own attorney could buy the paper back and give her a chance to rescue it from the ruin brought by her former husband.

Averell, Mary, and Astor stayed away, as did other serious bidders, but V. V. McNitt, a newspaperman associated with Mary's ill-fated syndicate, who represented them, never had a chance. The bidding opened at $250,000, and McNitt immediately made their offer of $500,000, but after that the price shot upward in jumps of $25,000. Within minutes, former Federal Reserve Board chairman Eugene Myer bought it for $825,000.

The bid to buy the *Post* having failed, Harriman was back in New York looking after the modernization of the Union Pacific passenger service and investigating the possibility of a magazine venture with Mary and Astor when Congress adopted the centerpiece of the New Deal program—the National Industrial Recovery Act that Hugh Johnson had been sweating over in April. Providing for coordination of the economy through a host of industrial codes, it established the National Recovery Administration as a huge new federal bureaucracy to restore economic vigor. Its exquisitely delicate mission was to get people back to work and the wheels of production turning, if not humming, while protecting workers' buying power from runaway price increases. General Johnson and the NRA would give Averell his uncertain start in public service.

Like the writing of the reform bills, the creation of the recovery program was anything but orderly. Roosevelt contrived to have rival construction gangs at work on its framework without mutual agreement on what they were building or to what purpose. But out of the disorder came a strategy and a bureaucracy reflecting the ideas of nearly everybody. The National Recovery Administration, like just about everything created in Washington that spring, sent shivers through the money changers Roosevelt had figuratively chased from the temple on Inauguration Day. To them, it smacked of collectivization.

It was controversial in Washington, too.

No one had worked harder on it than Hugh Johnson, and he logically became its director. Besides the code-making NRA, the recovery act had established the Public Works Administration to run pump-priming projects putting people to work on the federal payroll. Johnson also envisioned it as a lever to encourage private industry to adopt codes. But at the moment he was sworn in as director of the NRA, Roosevelt took from him the $3.3 billion public-works portion of the program and put it under the auspices of the Department of the Interior. It was a slap in the face for Johnson's fragile ego, and he very nearly balked at taking his oath of office. But flattered and consoled by Frances Perkins and

Mary Rumsey, he undertook the mountainous task of producing business and industrial codes which the New Dealers hoped would delicately balance the interests of capital, labor, and consumers while fostering a return to economic growth.

Johnson encountered the precise difficulties skeptics had predicted. Code negotiations dragged, and companies maneuvered to protect themselves with quick price increases before higher wages could go into effect. After six weeks only one industry—cotton textiles—was covered by a code.

Supremely confident of his own persuasive power, however, Johnson went to Roosevelt with a proposal for a single nationwide code mandating wages of $12 to $15 for a thirty-five- to forty-hour work week. It would remain in effect while codes were written by individual industries. With consumers, small businessmen, and shop owners endorsing it, Johnson could see a tidal wave of popular sentiment sweeping reluctant industries into acceptance.

Roosevelt gave the go-ahead, and Johnson launched public-relations and propaganda campaigns unmatched in peacetime. NRA's emblem was a blue eagle—actually a Navaho thunderbird—with talons clutching lightning bolts and cog wheels. Above the motto "WE DO OUR PART," it began appearing in barbershops, grocery stores, and on the windows of row houses in Queens and farmhouses in Iowa. By the hundreds of thousands, businesses promised to abide by the code and consumers pledged to patronize those displaying the blue eagle.

In July, Johnson enlisted Averell to lead the crusade in New York, charging him to make the nation's largest city and the President's home state beacons for the country. Establishing his headquarters in the Roosevelt Hotel, Harriman took less than a week to put together rudimentary organizations in half the counties in the state. By recruiting Republicans to serve with Democrats as county cochairmen, he gave the effort a patina of bipartisanship. He enlisted the editorial support of newspapers, recruited four-minute men to speak from courthouse steps and theater stages, and took to the airwaves himself to give a statewide radio pep talk on patriotism. Herbert Swope composed a tailored code for the state and the city, laying upon New Yorkers a special responsibility to follow the leadership of their native son in the White House.

New York responded, as did much of the rest of the country. The highlight of its crusade—and of the short-lived National Recovery Administration—came on September 13, 1933, with the President's NRA Day parade up Fifth Avenue. State and city employees were released on holiday, the stock exchange and banks were closed, and more than a quarter of a million workers and employers marched along the avenue for ten hours. One and a half million spectators jammed the sides of the route as chanting and waving units representing labor groups and employer associations marched past a reviewing stand at the New York Public Library.

The New York City police band, playing "The Yanks Are Coming," led the units of the National Guard in dress uniform past the reviewing stand. Dozens of military planes swept overhead, and confetti showered onto marching union locals and on floats bearing Miss NRA and Miss Liberty in bathing suits. No one was left out. Stockbrokers, teachers, cops, barbers, cabbies, and waiters lined up for the march, causing the spectacle to last hours longer than planned. At Sing Sing prison, inmates were excused from their labor assignments for the day so guards could carry their Blue Eagle up the avenue.

The procession began in the early afternoon and went on until past midnight. Predicting that the outpouring of support would have grass roots repercussions across the land, Harriman stood on the reviewing platform with Governor Lehman, General Johnson, Mayor John P. O'Brien, and the inevitable clutch of Tammany political factotums. With nightfall, several members of the reviewing party surrendered to fatigue and slipped away. But when the last unit, a platoon of weary cigar makers, marched past the library after midnight, Harriman was still at his post, sipping black coffee from a cardboard cup and exchanging final tributes.

Through that spring and summer it had seemed that the country was beginning a surge toward recovery. Production jumped, employment increased, and General Johnson became, with the exception of FDR himself, the most publicized man in America. He flew around the country rallying, pleading, badgering Americans to get behind the codes. In Washington, visitors stood in line outside his office on the fourth floor of the Commerce Department, and he often stayed at his desk through the night.

It was not a time for discordant notes, but Harriman discreetly sounded one to the general and the President in his report summing up the New York campaign. It pointed to a flaw that would in a short time become obvious. "Too good a job of selling NRA has been done throughout the country as a whole," he warned—the agency was mistakenly regarded as the whole national recovery program in itself.[14]

The plan for a national magazine received unexpected impetus not long after the *Post* auction when the controversial Moley took a spectacular and generally unmourned fall from grace in the administration, making him available to become editor.

In the midst of the chaotic World Economic Conference in London, the professor arrived as Roosevelt's special representative, assuming authority and the spotlight and throwing the conference into confusion over Roosevelt's monetary policy. His conduct outraged Secretary of

State Cordell Hull, who chaired the American delegation. When Roosevelt backed away from the conference's efforts to stabilize world currencies, the session was effectively wrecked, and Moley was humiliated.

Moley's temper, tactlessness, and lack of respect for turf had made him the most resented figure in Washington and suddenly expendable.[15] When the London debacle led to a resignation threat from the angry Hull, it became necessary for Roosevelt to publicly cut his lieutenant loose. Easing him out of the State Department, where Hull would no longer tolerate him, the President detailed his brain truster to the Department of Justice to briefly study the administration of criminal justice, giving him an opportunity for an "honorable exit."[16]

The first issue of the Astor-Rumsey-Harriman magazine, *Today,* appeared in October with Franklin Roosevelt as its first subscriber. Calling itself "an independent journal of public affairs," it featured an attack on chiselers who undermined the NRA and an article by General Johnson on a favorite Harriman theme—that the NRA was only part of the Roosevelt administration's recovery strategy. Even the founders thought the inaugural issue awful. "It proclaimed the amateur, even to our parental eye," Moley admitted. "We realized suddenly how very green we were, how much we still had to learn about the publishing business."[17]

Printed on the kind of limp, gray pulp used by fiction magazines, the first issues were larded with reprinted cartoons to fill up space and featured a signed editorial by Moley. Both Averell and Mary's names were on the masthead, as was that of Astor, who wrote a weekly commentary. Nearly all the space was taken up with initiatives of the New Deal.

It soon showed improvement. Some of the capital's best-known newspaper correspondents began to write for it, as did big-name authors such as Sherwood Anderson and Theodore Dreiser. Photographs were substituted for the cartoons; the subject matter took on more variety; and the publishers made a leap to a new aesthetic plateau by replacing the gray pulp with a paper that was almost glossy. But after a first-issue circulation of 100,000, it quickly settled back to 50,000 and stayed there for months. Arthur Brisbane, who had contributed an article to the first issue, predicted failure and advised Averell "not to go any deeper financially into the little weekly venture than you would do purely as an amusement. I think that the weekly has done well and that it has been very well managed. But as I said to Vincent Astor at the beginning, even before the first number appeared, I think I know that it is absolutely impossible for a weekly of that kind to pay expenses. I do not think that the Angel Gabriel could do it, if he were in the place of Professor Moley and McNitt. I hope that your sister is not putting very much money into it. It is not possible for it to do otherwise than lose heavily, I am afraid."[18]

Averell was distressed about *Today* even before he got Brisbane's assessment, but his unhappiness was caused by the editorial columns rather than by the meager advertising linage. The news coverage was weak and, Harriman thought, too strongly colored by the prejudices and opinions that Moley developed as an early insider and one of the New Deal's creators. He wished he had never gotten into the venture in the first place, and wouldn't have, he told James Warburg, but for his obligation to look after his sister's interests.

Bob Lovett, who was a Republican but devoid of anti-Roosevelt fanaticism and not given to personal invective, wrote Averell long letters filled with blistering criticism of Moley. The magazine, Averell's old friend complained, was "no longer a 'personal journal of public affairs,' but rather Moley's personal journal of his PRIVATE AFFAIRS—of petty hates, of little crushes on people, and of news tinged with his ideas."

Lovett thought the magazine was so completely a Moley soapbox and instrument of personal vindication that it lost sight of its purpose. "Moley's pet hates," he told Harriman, "may increase circulation but I think pornographic stories will accomplish the result more quickly and do the cause of liberalism less harm in the long run. The magazine is becoming increasingly cheap and increasingly colored by Moley's own views. It is becoming a magazine of bias and indicates that it is written by a person whose sense of humor has been replaced by a sense of self importance."[19]

Harriman was in no position to demand Moley's dismissal, even if he had been willing to go that far. The editor still had Astor's unqualified support, and Astor controlled the magazine. He nevertheless got his unhappiness across in several blunt conversations with Moley, who then issued a four-page mea culpa, emphasizing to the staff that he had left the government, that *Today* was neither a house organ, a primer, nor an appendage of the New Deal, nor a "peep hole into the secrets of the administration."[20]

After several months, *Today*'s circulation climbed back to 75,000 and continued to increase. It reached 100,000 again, and with a format emphasizing news rather than analysis, it gradually wore down its rival, *News Week*, as the chief competition of Henry Luce's *Time* magazine. In 1937, at the age of four, *Today* acquired *News Week*, creating *Newsweek*. Malcolm Muir was brought in from McGraw-Hill as its editor, and Moley was made a columnist with the title of contributing editor.

Four months after concluding the New York Blue Eagle campaign, Harriman took his first real government job. In January of 1934, he hired on with General Johnson to administer the NRA codes for the nation's heavy industry. Theoretically, the recovery agency was now ready to fulfill its mandate. Ninety percent of the country's industry was "codified"—covered by thousands of pacts resembling "something between a charter of a medieval guild and the agreement of a modern cartel."[21] Millions had signed the blanket codes, put the Blue Eagle emblem in their windows, and marched in support of the NRA. But Harriman had been correct in his warning that the effort was more public relations than substance. It had fallen far short of General Johnson's heady prediction that it would send six million people back to work.

The exhilaration had faded. Businessmen, who had been swept along in the 1933 momentum of the New Deal and the tentative recovery, now regained their bearings and their intuitive distrust of Washington and the Roosevelt administration. Prices were advancing; and among the working class, the "we do our part" patriotism of the summer past was tainted with a sourness over "NRA prices and Hoover wages."[22]

As the most publicized vehicle of recovery and the ostensible beacon of economic democracy, the NRA and its system of codes were obvious targets for everybody's discontent. Industry executives wanted to use the codes to ensure profits. Labor leaders looked to them to help them unionize workers; consumers expected them to preserve buying power.

Harriman was on the opposite side from Mary Rumsey and his other Washington mentor, Secretary Perkins. While Rumsey headed the Consumer Advisory Board and Perkins chaired the Labor Advisory Board, Averell was, until joining the NRA staff, a member of the Industrial Advisory Board, chaired by Pierre S. Du Pont and made up of leading figures from manufacturing and big business. He arrived in Washington to begin his new job and a round of code hearings, appeals meetings and revision debates in the aftermath of an angry flap between his sister and Hugh Johnson. Mary and her consumer allies had concluded that the NRA codes were allowing the buying power of ordinary Americans to be seriously eroded. After the big New York parade, they badgered Johnson until he agreed that Rumsey could hold public hearings on price policies. The trouble was that the Christmas shopping season was fast approaching. Businessmen, concerned that Mary was about to publicly skewer them for overpricing, stormed the NRA. Uncharacteristically on the defensive, Johnson promised to hold the consumer board off until after the holidays. When word of that promise spread, Mary and a consumer delegation marched into Johnson's office, and there ensued a shouting match in which Johnson—"Old Ironpants"—was answered "roar for roar."[23] The general stuck to his commitment to delay the hearings until January, but he invited Leon Henderson, an economist who led the consumers' shouting, to become the administrator's assistant for consumer problems.

Rather than a bona fide New Dealer, Averell was regarded by members of Mary Rumsey's staff and her consumer allies as one more big businessman working from the inside to undermine the agency's real purpose. When he joined an unsuccessful move to abolish codes covering dozens of trades such as shoe repairmen, barbers, and beauticians, they considered all their suspicions confirmed.[24]

There was never a hint that Mary's consumer fervor was moderated by her brother's presence in the NRA hierarchy. To the contrary, reports got back to the consumer panel that Averell had expressed alarm that his sister "was becoming a captive of a bunch of subversive left wingers on the staff of the board."[25]

Johnson had not liked the idea of a Consumer Advisory Board at the beginning of the NRA, but it had been urged upon him by Perkins, and Mary Rumsey had been his only choice to head it. No job could have suited her better. While she lacked bureaucratic experience and made mistakes, she became a powerful influence in the recovery program. She brought together economists, sociologists, and other academics, built strong political ties with the liberals and reformers within the administration; and created a consumer network across the country. Whenever consumers mentioned the idea of a Cabinet-level Department of Consumer Affairs, her name usually led the speculation for secretary.

Rumsey was perpetually in motion. Whether on the train between New York and Washington or in her car being chauffeured about either city, she was accompanied by a secretary frantically taking dictation. A telephone was beside her at her dining table, and it was not unusual for her to make business calls in the middle of the night. As soon as she awoke in the morning, she went through several newspapers and magazines before leaving her bed, marking and clipping and collecting notes. When she was about the capital on business, she often had a sandwich for lunch in her car. Members of her staff, frequently called to the phone soon after dawn, would be fired and rehired in the course of a day, and wind up the evening with a glass of sherry and a new batch of instructions at O Street.

When excited, as she usually was, she was inclined to begin and end conversations in the middle of thoughts, her words tumbling out in a torrent that challenged old friends and caused strangers to wonder about her mental and emotional stability. Dexter Keezer, the consumer board's executive director, concluded that "she thought faster than she could talk, although she was a rather high-speed talker.

"The result was that to keep the talking and the thinking fairly evenly balanced, she frequently left out words. The result was that her talking sometimes seemed a rather unintelligible jumble. There was a system in her word-skipping, however, [which] if understood, could be made to line up her thinking and her talking evenly, and restore order to the word jumble and give the phenomenally fast-moving mind an equally well-organized voice." Once he discovered the logic of her scatter-shot speech pattern, Keezer found conversations with her "often brilliant, and almost always enjoyable."[26]

Family members were more direct with her than were her friends in trying to slow her down. When her enthusiasm made her unintelligible, Averell's solution was to raise his voice above hers and, sometimes stammering himself, command, "For Ch-Christ's sa-sake Ma-Mary, slow it down."[27] Although he had been for several years a major figure on Wall Street, he was in his early days in Washington totally in his sister's shadow, their early roles in the family hierarchy resumed. She was far closer to the Roosevelts, and she was spiritually in tune with the reformers who shaped the character of the New Deal. Once more she counseled her brother almost as intensely as she had when she presented him with a watch and a hastily scrawled letter urging him on his way to Groton:

Dear Averell,

Here is something to remind you that the world is always moving. Don't let it get ahead of you! Also that time flies. Never let it catch up with you. Time is the one thing that you can never recover. This also is to make you never have to say "in a minute." Make the other fellow say it to you. Remember, too, that Time brings Truth and "Truth is the stronger thing. Let one's life be true." And it is not the truth that a man possesses or thinks he possesses, but the spirit & the desire a man has to gain and to live the truth that makes a man strong. Averell, always "beware with thy might and grow straight in the strength of the spirit" . . . you must know your self (& judge yourself). But then to be yourself, you must forget yourself. Remember the Ancient Mariner. He liveth best who loveth best, all things both great and small.

So now that I have spouted quite enough stuff at you, I'll tell you to go ahead because it is so good to live hard & love hard & learn hard & school is such fun. But in spite of it, we are going to miss you hard, too.

Lovingly,
Mary[28]

His arrival as the administrator of the agency's heavy industry division put him in the position of serving a chain of command and attending to inconsequential details for the first time since he had been a junior vice-president at the Union Pacific. But he took the job seriously, if at times impatiently, putting in eighteen-hour days at the NRA headquarters. Before the winter was over, he was made one of Johnson's four special assistants.

The job lasted less than a month. Under pressure to do more about code enforcement, Johnson responded with a broad reorganization of the agency, and Averell emerged the senior assistant administrator and, effectively, Johnson's chief of staff. The assignment made him responsible for a much-debated reform of code administration as well as oversight of compliance and enforcement. He was potentially the most powerful figure in the NRA, for he arrived in the administrator's inner circle as Hugh Johnson lost his grip.

The general was driving himself beyond his limits, and Harriman tried to get him to ease up by spreading responsibilities around the top of the agency. But Johnson was on an emotional trapeze, thirty pounds overweight, drinking too much, and swinging from emotional heights one day into inconsolable depths the next. He went on work binges when he stayed at his desk all night, threatened subordinates, berated visitors, and quarreled with newspaper reporters. When he was discouraged or exhausted, he was prone to disappear without warning, leaving his office in the hands of Frances Robinson, his red-haired secretary and gatekeeper, who did her best to protect him. During such times, Averell kept his mouth shut and avoided his sister's house where he would be put in an embarrassing position when others gossiped that the NRA chief was somewhere consoling himself with a bottle of bourbon. But no amount of precaution could hide the fact that the tantrums, disappearances, and riffs with other administration liberals were increasing in frequency.

From a growing array of critics, there was agitation for Johnson's replacement, and rumors spread that Harriman was being groomed for the job. Instead, in April 1934, Averell announced his resignation; he was not discouraged with the agency or his own role, but he was wholly frustrated with Johnson. Although he had agreed to stay only two months in the first place, he remained until June before quitting his first tour with the government and going back to New York to resume his responsibilities with the railroad and the worrisome magazine.

Johnson's personal problems did not abate, and in October Roosevelt finally extracted his resignation. Responsibility for the NRA was turned over to a new National Industrial Recovery Board, and Harriman, four months after he had quit, was asked to come back as its chief administrative officer.

Once again, he told the Union Pacific board that he was needed in Washington for two months; after making his record-breaking coast-to-coast run in the new streamliner, he moved to the capital for the second time in the year.

Nowhere was his return more welcomed than at the Rumsey-Perkins residence in Georgetown. Perkins had long since concluded that Johnson had to be removed, and she had helped the President ease him out. Mary saw the general's departure and her brother's return as good news for the consumer. Even if Averell still looked at the world through the lenses of big business, he did not share Johnson's skepticism of the consumer board. She saw little of him, however, for he worked eighteen-hour days. On Friday night or Saturday morning, he either took the train home for the weekend in New York or went out of town to do gospel work for the NRA, while Mary drove down to her farm at The Plains.

With fox-hunting season, she regularly went to the country to ride across the fields where the Harrimans had hunted since the turn of the century, when E.H. brought the whole family down from New York. On Friday, November 16, she worked at her office until near midnight, and then drove to the farm. She was up again with the brisk dawn of Saturday, and near Upperville, Virginia, she and her friends in the Piedmont Hunt climbed into their saddles. It was her fifty-third birthday, and a big weekend in the Virginia hunt country, for it also happened to be opening day of the fall steeplechase season at Middleburg.

Just after noon, when the hunt was almost over, her horse stumbled after clearing a stone fence and fell forward. She was riding sidesaddle, and was thus held to her mount by a clamp, so she had no chance to fall clear. Her right leg and several ribs were broken when the horse landed on her. Dr. Archibald Randolph, Piedmont's master of hounds, was riding just ahead of her, but he did not hear her fall and rode on. The following riders found her lying on the ground minutes later.

At Emergency Hospital in Washington, she was given a blood transfusion and rushed into surgery to repair the compound fracture of her thigh. Her injuries were painful but seemingly not life-threatening. Averell had left Washington on Friday to make several NRA speeches before business groups, and by the time he got back, she was apparently beginning her recovery.

After a few days, she felt well enough to summon members of her staff to bedside conferences and to spend more time talking with her children than she had since any of them could remember. Her son Charles had married Mary Maloney just a month earlier; and while they visited the hospital room, the patient instructed them on buying furnishings and decorating their home. Each morning, Ruth Pedersen, her social secretary, appeared to take dictation, read to her, and receive instructions for the day. Averell, still settling into his new job as administrative officer at the NRA, stopped by daily en route to the office and saw her again at the end of the day. The O Street regulars visited in the evenings.

She was going ahead with plans for a speaking tour she was arranging for her Irish friend George Russell; and when she was not receiving visitors, she sat up in bed and dashed off notes in longhand, assuring friends that she was on the mend and exhorting her charges to keep up the pace at the Consumer Advisory Board:

Dear Friends,

    I am sorry that I am not able to be at the staff meeting with you all. It has been a great inspiration to me to realize how magnificently everyone on the staff of the Consumers' Board is standing by and carrying on your work. I do expect it to go forward with all the judgment and skill of which you are capable and I know that it will do so. It has been a great help to me in my illness to know that the idea was so familiarly established in your minds and in the minds of the other officers of the government. Best of luck to you! I shall keep in touch with your work regularly.

Sincerely Yours,
Mary Rumsey[29]

    But the recovery faltered. Damage to her kidneys proved to be more serious than her broken bones; and in mid-December, after she had been in the hospital for a month, she developed bronchial pneumonia. Her condition was again critical, but her doctors reported that she was "fighting gamely" and there was still "every hope" that she would recover. On December 19, however, she went into a precipitous decline after being given another blood transfusion. In the early evening, doctors told the family there was little hope. With Averell, her three children, and Frances Perkins at her bedside, she died at 10:50 P.M.

    Eleanor Roosevelt, nearly all of the Cabinet, and most of the principal figures of the New Deal attended her funeral service in Washington before Averell took her home on a train for burial beside her parents and her brother Harry.

    The hospital attributed her death to pneumonia; but Averell, seeing how her condition had dramatically turned for the worse after her transfusion, demanded an autopsy and a review of her case. Two months later it was concluded that she had been the victim of a transfusion reaction, though evidently not a case of mismatched blood types. Instead, doctors told him, she "belonged to that excessively [*sic*] rare group who are sensitized in some way by an initial transfusion." Beyond that, her death was unexplainable, "a tragic, mystifying affair."[30] The premature deaths of Mary and her husband did not end the tragedy of her family. Her daughter, little Mary, who had been Averell's favorite of the three, suffered a serious "schizoid breakdown," the beginning of problems that haunted her for years, including suicidal periods when she wished to die on the hunting field where her mother had been injured. And then, in April 1939, Bronson, the younger of the two sons, was killed in an airplane crash. He had flown to Mexico with Hall Roosevelt's son, Daniel, and on the way home, their private plane crashed into a Mexican mountainside.

Harriman spoke little of his sister's death, then or in the later years when efforts were made to examine his transformation from Republican orthodoxy to Democratic liberalism. Undoubtedly, the tragedy of Mary hastened him on the road he had already started.

He dug into his job as administrative officer of the NRA with his usual intensity, but the glitter of the recovery's showpiece was gone. Small firms felt they were oppressed by monopoly and overburdened by costs resulting from codes. Big business, never comfortable with the alliance, fretted over code enforcement and concessions to labor.[31] Labor and consumer criticism mounted; the agency's compliance machinery faltered; and challenges proliferated. Perhaps influenced by the persistent fight that had been waged by Mary and her consumer forces, Averell himself parted ways with businessmen pushing for codes with price-fixing provisions. The de facto price-fixing, in the form of codes banning sales below production cost, had been opposed all along by labor and consumer groups fearing they would be the ones to suffer from price and production controls.

At the same time, Harriman went to work on his mandate to open the NRA to public scrutiny, allowing reporters to attend hearings and holding daily press briefings which he deemed models of government candor, even if journalists did not.

In the spring of 1935, Roosevelt considered making him chairman of the National Industrial Recovery Board overseeing the agency. When Reynolds Tobacco Company chairman Clay Williams resigned after holding the job ineffectively for sixty days, Harriman and deputy administrator Arthur D. Whiteside, the chairman of Dun and Bradstreet, emerged as the candidates to replace him. When the choice between the two sparked a factional struggle behind the scenes, Roosevelt decided against naming either of them "for fear of creating a discordant board."[32] Instead, he left Averell as administrator and put Donald Richberg, who had already been given so many special assignments he was being called the Assistant President, in charge of policy matters.

By then, however, the NRA's days were numbered. Harriman prepared legislation to extend it for two years beyond its June expiration date, and the bill was making its way through Congress when the Supreme Court ruled the NRA unconstitutional. In a lawsuit arising from the New York code for the live poultry industry—"the sick chicken case" as it would be remembered—the court unanimously held that Congress had, in approving NRA writing, unconstitutionally delegated legislative authority to the recovery agency.

It was hardly a satisfactory way to end the first chapter of his government career, but without Mary the NRA, the administration, and Washington had lost some of their vitality. On the morning the court's decision was reported in newspapers, Roland Harriman was in Washington and went by Averell's apartment for breakfast, expecting him to be demoralized. Surprisingly, he found his brother in good spirits. He "really didn't give a damn" that it was over.[33]

It was the end of his work for the New Deal. There were rumors from time to time of a Cabinet job, but the only thing he was offered was a chance to be Federal Housing administrator, which he declined, going back to New York to throw himself into modernizing the Union Pacific passenger service and acquiring more efficient locomotives to fight off the threat of competition from trucks, buses, and airplanes.

He was appointed to the Business Advisory Council, however, and that kept him in the forefront of Roosevelt's most visible and "tame millionaires." The post continued his contact with the administration and with the President; and having learned from his sister, he now took advantage of opportunities to ingratiate himself at the White House. Whenever there was an occasion, he sent FDR a laudatory note and occasionally a pheasant shot at Arden along with bottle of vintage wine from the cellar.

During assignments for the New Deal, and later when he served Roosevelt during World War II, Harriman received the acquiescence of his banking partners and the Union Pacific board of directors, announcing his intention to return as soon as he completed his assignment for the administration. But the trip to Washington to monitor securities-reform legislation in the spring of 1933 had in effect brought his financial career to an end, leaving Roland in charge of the family interest in the bank and in the railroad industry.

In earlier years, it had seemed ordained that he and Roland would work in tandem, their personalities perfectly suited to a long-term collaboration in the style of the Warburg and Lehman families. After his discharge from the Army, the younger brother had spent more than a year in Santa Barbara overcoming tuberculosis, then returned to join Averell in the shipbuilding business and on the Union Pacific board of directors. At both W. A. Harriman and Company and Brown Brothers Harriman and Company, Roland was an ideal partner, willing to do the plodding detail work and leave to Averell the wheeling, dealing, and world travel. They had played their roles from the time they were boys. Averell had been brought up with the burdens and perquisites of the eldest son and Roland granted the indulgences of the baby in a large family.

Long after their merger with the Browns and Averell's commitment to more or less permanent government service, the brothers' fortunes remained closely linked. While their sisters had gone their own ways with their inheritances, Averell and Roland's investments in railroads, airlines, utilities, steel, rubber, gas and oil, and foreign and domestic securities were managed by their jointly owned Merchant-Sterling Corporation and Orama Securities Corporation, with Roland close at hand after Averell was gone.

While compatible, they were in many ways opposites. Ambitious, aggressive, stimulated by pressure and comfortable with controversy, Averell was attuned to being a Harriman, committed to keeping the name in lights. Roland, affectionately known as Bunny, since he had kept rabbits as a small boy, was conciliatory, unassuming, and patient— perhaps because it had taken him years to overcome completely his latent TB infection. He was also more generous, and over the years fund-raisers such as Yale University president Kingman Brewster, Jr., would find that the most effective way to get support from Averell was first to go to Roland who would, tongue in cheek, make a contribution contingent upon a matching amount from Averell.

No one compared the brothers more succinctly than Bob Lovett, their partner at Brown Brothers Harriman and fellow board member at Union Pacific. The difference between them, said Lovett, finding an apt metaphor in Averell's polo prowess and Roland's equal devotion to harness racing, was that Averell ran and Roland trotted.[34]

Personally, the brothers had gone their own ways after Roland's marriage in 1917 to Gladys Fries, the daughter of a New York chemist. Conservative in her background and tastes, she did not care for Averell's life-style, had little in common with Kitty, and even less with the free-spirited Marie. In time, one might have concluded that the brothers contrived differences.

Roland remained a true-blue Republican—as did Cornelia and Carol—serving as a Hoover delegate in the electoral college in 1928 when Averell bolted to vote for Al Smith. Once Averell began breeding championship Labrador retrievers, Roland's kennel at Arden became home to equally distinguished cocker spaniels. While Averell vacationed in Europe, Roland and Gladys sought seclusion on the ten-thousand-acre Idaho ranch, fly-fishing in the Snake River, shooting grouse, bear hunting on horseback, and riding in cattle roundups.

In spite of their divergent interests, the Harriman clan had remained intact because the matriarch still presided over its headquarters at Arden, where she lived from spring until late autumn. In the summer, Averell's family occupied his "wing" of the mansion, while Roland lived in the renovated "homestead" used by the family until Arden House was built. During summers, Mary's grandchildren, eventually numbering thirteen, roamed the estate on their horses much as her children had, but the habit of settling in for the entire summer went out of style, and she was at times alone, except for her servants and staff. Still, the family gathered on September 10 each year for the observance of Harriman Day, the anniversary of E.H. and Mary's marriage. She kept alive the other traditions that went back longer than Averell or Roland could remember—an afternoon ride in her horse-drawn carriage, the Sunday afternoon concert in her music room, the Sunday breakfast delayed until the servants returned from church, the Christmas party for employees of the estate. With her death, however, the reunions ended and children drifted their own ways.

For Averell, the great empty mansion became a problem. He had few occasions to use it, and he could hardly close it. Marie thought it gloomy and depressing, its dimensions overwhelming. The idea of turning it into a retreat for their friends occurred to them, and not long after his mother's funeral Averell wrote to the Lovetts, the Hitchcocks, the Paleys, the Swopes, and several other couples, suggesting that they use it as a club. There would be no dues, but he proposed to charge each person $5 for a weekend—"to cover near-beer, beefsteak, and onions." For his part, he offered breakfast on trays, a buffet lunch, afternoon tea, and dinner. Servants, including a chauffeur, would be provided. Ponies would be available, as would the croquet lawn, the pool, and the other amenities.

Most probably, the prospective members shared Marie's opinion of E.H.'s castle, for the invitation and subsequent club newsletters stirred no interest, and the mansion stood foreboding and vacant except for the staff that looked after it. But from the lame club notion came Marie's inspired idea of a party big enough to fill the place. The long Thanksgiving weekend provided an occasion, and through the thirties the autumn holiday brought rocking laughter to the dim corridors. For the first time the house was lit from the wine cellar to the cupola that E.H. had ordered so he could look down at Tuxedo Park a dozen miles away.

As much as his public alliance with the Democratic party or his sojourns in the vineyards of the New Deal, the Thanksgivings at Arden revealed the new Harriman. Not to be found among the guests were the bankers, railroaders, and Republicans with whom he had always kept company. With Alexander Woollcott, the critic and public scold, deputized to approve the guest list, Arden's doors were opened to a menagerie of writers, artists, croquet players, journalists, and New Dealers. Regulars included the playwright Robert Sherwood and his wife, Madeline, Heywood and Connie Broun, George and Beatrice Kaufman, Bill and Dorothy Paley, the Tommy Hitchcocks, the Ralph Pulitzers, the Herbert Swopes, Charles MacArthur and his wife Helen Hayes, Harpo Marx, Steve Hannagan, and later, Harry Hopkins.

Altogether, the guests numbered several dozen, filling all of the thirty-odd bedrooms. They began arriving on Wednesday afternoon, and the last did not depart until Monday, some friends learning only when they were back in the city that they had been at the same party.

The music hall at the front of the house in which E.H. had planned to receive guests at formal receptions was converted into a badminton court where exuberant drives sent the shuttlecock into the recesses of Mary Harriman's giant pipe organ. At a bowling alley installed by Averell in the basement, Heywood Broun could be found sliding about in sock feet, competing against Britain's Lady Diana Cooper, bowling in evening dress.

The host made provision for riding, hunting, duck shooting, or fishing in his stocked lakes, and occasionally he led guests, dressed in city clothes hardly appropriate for the wilderness, on deer-stalking forays into the woods. For the most part, though, his friends contented themselves with parlor games that continued through most of the night, encouraged by flowing champagne. A particularly zany game called murder sent guests roaming through the house in search of clues to an imaginary killing, each providing an alibi for himself. When one investigation pointed to Broun, the founder of the American Newspaper Guild explained that, at the moment of the murder, he had, in fact, been in Harriman's kitchen organizing a strike by the help. Another search, to the great amusement of all, revealed that Marie Harriman had no idea of the whereabouts of her kitchen.

The Arden kitchen was, in fact, a matter of some curiosity, for the food at the parties acquired a reputation for genuine mediocrity or worse. Guests claimed that duck was put before them half-cooked and reeking of fish, and that even the fresh vegetables from the estate's greenhouse were somehow rendered inedible. Random House publisher Donald Klopfer discovered the Red Apple Diner in the village of Harriman and began to slip away in an automobile always filled with friends in search of a hot dog or greasy hamburger. Dorothy Paley arrived with her own provisions—huge boxes of Sherry's chocolates, which she hid in her room. Others included food hampers among their luggage.

The heating and hot water systems so rarely put to use often failed the test of the yearly gathering. The regulars took pains to cultivate friendships with Marie Harriman's maid, Victoria, who could see to it that certain baths were drawn before the hot water ran out. After their first exposure to the chill of Arden's November nights, some prudently brought along hot-water bottles to take to bed with them.

Many who made Woollcott's Arden invitation list were also Harriman's summer friends on Long Island, where he played world-class croquet after giving up polo. On lawns at Sands Point, Manhasset, and Great Neck, he reigned at the top of a pastime that Herbert Swope said "gives release to all the evil in you" and "makes you want to cheat and kill."[35] Their game was not the ordinary backyard diversion of the elderly; rather, as Swope suggested, it was a vicious test of nerve, psychological fiber, and spiritual endurance, played with finely balanced mallets from Abercrombie and Fitch. Imported cast-iron wickets provided only a fraction of an inch of clearance for balls. Mastery of the game, claimed those who played it well, required muscular strength, the heart of a lion, and the mercy of a cobra.

Swope's course at Great Neck was laid out so that an opponent's ball might be driven into a roadside gutter that would carry it downhill, around a curve, and out of sight of the estate. Bromo-Seltzer heiress Margaret Emerson's court, reputed to be the most challenging in the East, required balls to be played through the entangled surface root system of an ancient tree. The traps there destroyed men and women of less than heroic patience. Averell's own lawn at Sands Point provided opportunities to smack the enemy into the waters of Long Island Sound.

Twice Harriman won the Brooks championship trophy awarded each year for what Long Island regarded as the world championship of English croquet, defeating the likes of Swope, Woollcott, Moss Hart, and Richard Rodgers. His second championship, in 1938, came in a classic match with Herbert Swope's son, Ottie, played on a course swept by the torrential rains of an approaching hurricane and illuminated by the headlights of a dozen automobiles. Play was suspended by mutual agreement when the balls began to float out of position, the rule books failing to yield guidance for the circumstances. One of Averell's admitted regrets for going into public service during the war was that it took him out of the championship competition and gave Ottie Swope his chance to win the Brooks trophy for three successive years and retire it.

The near-obsession with the game stayed with him for the rest of his life, making him a member of the Croquet Hall of Fame and leading to erroneous claims that he always had his custom mallet in his luggage as he traveled the world. He played the game with the intensity of a chess master, but without a clock to move him, he was known to take upwards of an hour contemplating a shot, giving opponents time to go off for lunch or a drink. He was at times bewilderingly impatient with less-than-worthy adversaries, and some wondered whether he even enjoyed the game at all, for he played as though he were waging some great inner struggle for elusive perfection.

The Arden Thanksgivings, like the croquet championships, came to an end because of the war. In 1939, though, the guests made their way up to Arden House as usual, and for four or five days, the war in Europe was almost put out of mind. Presiding over dinner in the formal dining room, Broun had newcomers make speeches on what they were thankful for, and Robert Sherwood was coaxed into entertaining with a soft-shoe routine singing, "When the Red, Red Robin Comes Bob, Bob, Bobbing

Along." Balmy weather coaxed most of the guests out to go walking or horseback riding before they started drifting away to the city on Sunday. It was the last of the big parties, but before Christmas many of those who had been present would see each other again at Heywood Broun's funeral.

Chapter XI

LONDON
Anchoring the Lifeline

In April of 1940, shooting stomach pains put Harriman in the hospital in New York and his doctors quickly determined that he had an ulcer. He was taken off cigarettes, cocktails, and nearly all nourishment except a glass of creamy, tepid milk every two hours, and told to rest. For a week, he did nothing except read a new book or two, write a few letters, and try to cultivate an interest in classical music.

The attack, he concluded, had been brought on by anxiety over the war in Europe. With Poland overrun and Allied shipping suffering mounting losses to German U-boats, he hadn't been able to shake off the feeling that the country had learned nothing from World War I. Seven months after Hitler's invasion of Poland, Americans seemed content to watch the Nazis conquer Europe and force the surrender of Britain. If such a disaster was allowed to happen, he was sure the bell would eventually toll for the South American continent, and in time the United States would be at Germany's mercy—it would have no choice but to accept "what Germany dictates in the way of what we can sell and buy and at what price."[1]

He was angry at the Republican isolationists pursuing the presidential nomination—all in full cry against a commitment to stopping Hitler. And he was frustrated at the Roosevelt administration's waffling. With the election six months away, the President looked like the only Democrat who could win, but setting a controversial precedent with his bid for a third term, he was handling the war issue so gingerly that neutrality was being widely embraced as realistic policy.

As a matter of principle, Harriman was opposed to a third presidential term, and into the spring he confidently predicted that Roosevelt would decide against breaking tradition with a race for another term.

If FDR dropped out, it was easy to see a Republican isolationist, maybe even Senator Arthur Vandenberg of Michigan, the most determined of them all, winning the presidency. As a hedge against that, he would later contribute $25,000 to Wendell Willkie's campaign for the GOP nomination, because he found ex-Democrat Willkie the only one in the pack with an appreciation of the Hitler threat. He took care to keep the contribution secret, but he confided to John J. McCloy, a Republican who shared his concern over a retreat to isolationism, that he would be glad to join the government under a Willkie administration.[2]

While he was in the hospital, the Nazis swept into Norway and Denmark. In May, while he was still feeling too poorly to go to the office, they invaded Holland, Belgium, and Luxembourg. By the time he was again at full speed, France had fallen, Italy had entered the war, and Winston Churchill had succeeded Neville Chamberlain as Britain's prime minister.

At the end of the month, Roosevelt at last moved toward industrial mobilization. After asking for breathtaking production increases, including fifty thousand airplanes a year, he sent for seven prominent businessmen to lead the rearmament. Harriman, who had just finished a two-year hitch as chairman of the Business Advisory Council, was disappointed not to be among them. The job he wanted—mobilizing the railroads and the rest of the transportation industry—went instead to Ralph Budd, chairman of the Chicago, Burlington and Quincy. Harriman was left to his Union Pacific board meetings, but he did not intend to be ignored by the mobilizers.

On the same day the chiefs of the new National Defense Advisory Commission went to the White House to get their marching orders from the President, he gave a rousing speech to businessmen in Omaha, calling for urgent support to governments at war with Hitler "in the hope that they can win the war on the other side of the ocean instead of finding ourselves with the job to do in this hemisphere." The time had come, he said, to "sell them everything they need. And if they can't pay for it, let's send it to them anyway."[3] The rallying cry was intended for an audience far from Omaha, but it moved Union Pacific president Bill Jeffers to fatuously suggest that Harriman himself was Democratic presidential timber if Roosevelt took himself out of the race.

Averell airmailed a copy of his text to Washington with a note assuring Edward Stettinius, the new commissioner for industrial materials, that support for war mobilization was sweeping the great plains of the Union Pacific territory. The hint for a job could not be missed, and as soon as Harriman got back to New York, he was invited to spend two or three days a week in Washington, coordinating the transportation of raw materials. He arrived on the train the next morning, bringing his private secretary with him.

Although he would remain chairman of the Union Pacific for another three years, Harriman would never return to a major role in running the railroad. In the army of dollar-a-year men pitching in to help prepare for war, he went to Washington every Monday morning. Instead of staying two or three days as Stettinius had suggested, he remained on the job all week. Operating in uncharted territory outside the jurisdiction of any department, the National Defense Advisory Commission was chaotic—dozens of consultants, advisers, and coordinators shared desks and competed for telephones, ashtrays, and straight-backed chairs in offices appropriated from the Federal Reserve Board.

Before he finished his first week, Averell unilaterally expanded his own assignment and began advising the commission on railroad matters that technically belonged to Budd. The industry, he knew, was in no condition to support explosive economic expansion and military mobilization, because it had never recovered from the Depression. Although executives would not admit it, Harriman insisted that 100,000 new freight cars were direly needed just to replace derelicts carried on the books as operational rolling stock. He couldn't persuade Budd of that, however. As far as he could tell, the man in charge of transportation mobilization was "satisfied that the railroads need do nothing to prepare themselves."[4] By autumn, Harriman was proven right. There were not even enough cars to move the fall grain crop to market, and he went public with what he had been telling commissioners in private.[5]

He not only moved in on Budd's railroad territory but began a free-lance investigation of rubber and magnesium shortages. When the administration ditched the hopelessly inefficient commission and created the new Office of Production Management, he was an obvious candidate to take charge of the industrial materials division. In the eyes of some, however, his reputation rested on polo, Sun Valley, record-breaking streamliner trips, and parties at Arden. When he called on OPM director William S. Knudsen to discuss the job, the first question from the former General Motors president was whether he was "ready to stop butterflying around" and get down to work.[6] He remained in charge of the industrial materials division at OPM just long enough for a spat with the irascible Harold Ickes, secretary of the interior, over the use of electricity from the government-owned Bonneville Dam on the Columbia River.

There was already a shortage of electricity in the country, and the aluminum industry would need much more to support the crash air-plane-manufacturing program. Harriman proposed to make the Bonneville power available to the Aluminum Company of America, but Ickes insisted that it go to Reynolds Aluminum Company in order to preserve competition in the industry. Although Harriman and Under-secretary of War Robert Patterson argued that ALCOA, which had al-ready increased its aluminum production by 50 percent, was better positioned to boost its output further, Ickes was unimpressed. The dis-pute was not resolved until long after Harriman was gone from OPM, and in the end Ickes prevailed; but Harriman and others thought the secretary had needlessly delayed the production of hundreds of urgently needed planes.[7]

The confrontation was typical of the quibbling that went on in the early months of the mobilization, and Harriman was anxious to get out of the OPM bureaucracy and into a job where he could have a real impact. To achieve this end, he looked not to Roosevelt but to Harry Hopkins, the sickly former social worker who had rapidly taken firm personal control of America's mobilization and production machinery. Except for the President, he was now the most powerful figure in Wash-ington, and he had over the years become not only a staunch Washington ally, but a warm personal friend.

Hopkins had moved into the upstairs residence of the White House on the day Hitler struck the Low Countries. Nominally, he was Roose-velt's secretary of commerce, but he had been ailing as long as he had held the job and he had hardly been in his splendid office on the top floor of the department's huge new building. He had gone to the White House for dinner with the Roosevelts that evening and afterward he was feeling so poorly that he was invited to stay the night. He would remain for three years, living in Abraham Lincoln's study and sharing the se-crets, burdens, and powers of the presidency. He saw Roosevelt before the President left his bed in the morning, spent much of the day at his side, dined with him five nights a week, and usually joined him on the presidential yacht on Sunday. In the President's inner circle, in the Democratic party, and in the country at large, Hopkins's unrivaled in-fluence and access to the President caused him to be regarded with mistrust, fear, and envy. "He was generally regarded as a sinister figure," Robert Sherwood wrote at the outset of his much-admired study of the Roosevelt-Hopkins relationship, "a backstairs intriguer, an Iowan combination of Machiavelli, Svengali, and Rasputin."[8] More than any-body else, Hopkins was responsible for Averell's emergence as an insider in wartime diplomacy. They had known each other since the early days of the New Deal when Averell was in and out of Washington, working on the recovery program and getting his first taste of politics. Hopkins was then the new $8,000-a-year chief of the Federal Emergency Relief Administration and a close friend of Mary Rumsey and Frances Perkins.

Neither could remember for certain, but Averell and Hopkins met either on a train between Washington and New York or at Herbert Swope's house at Great Neck, Long Island, where Hopkins became a regular visitor, along with Harriman, Sherwood, Bernard Baruch, and other Roosevelt friends and New Dealers who played croquet and attended Swope's all-night parties.

The friendship blossomed, although they had little in common but their commitment to the Roosevelt administration. Averell embodied the privileged class which Hopkins had long held accountable for the condition of the poor. While Harriman had proceeded through Groton and Yale and into shipping, aviation, and international finance, Hopkins had grown up in Iowa, working on farms and putting himself through Grinnell College. Harry's father, David Hopkins, was a onetime harness maker who operated a small newspaper and magazine store during those years. His mother was a devout Methodist and leader of the church's Home Missionary Society in Iowa.

Hopkins saw New York for the first time when she took him east during a summer vacation from high school. After graduation from Grinnell, where he was a successful campus politician and athlete, he returned to the big city to find a job as a social worker. Subsequently, he did a stretch of settlement-house work, served in World War I, represented the Red Cross in the South, and spent several years with the New York Tuberculosis and Health Association. After Roosevelt was elected governor, he joined New York's Temporary Emergency Relief Administration. In 1932, he was appointed the agency's chairman. The following year, toward the end of the furious first one hundred days of his presidency, Roosevelt sent for Hopkins to take charge of the Federal Emergency Relief Administration and the distribution of about $150 million a month to four million families on relief.

Devoted as he was to the poor, Hopkins also had a powerful attraction to the good life, and it was his fascination with eastern luxury and sophistication, not welfare work, that brought him from Iowa to New York City. He loved nightclubbing, although his delicate stomach kept him a respectful distance from alcohol. He was also an avid horse-racing fan who cared little for the paddocks and farms so admired by his wealthy friends like Averell, but who got elemental satisfaction from cashing in a winning ticket at the $2 window.

Since his exposure to the tenements and settlement houses, he had been an unwavering adherent of federal support of public welfare and workfare in preference to the handout. From the early emergency relief program, he moved to the Works Progress Administration, where he dispatched $10 billion for the construction of roads, bridges, and public toilets, for the painting of murals, and for the composition of short stories. All the while he cultivated his friendship with Harriman, Swope, Bernard Baruch, John Hay Whitney and other rich friends with progressive ideas, Manhattan town houses, Long Island croquet lawns and South Carolina shooting boxes.

Even after he had become part of the President's inner circle, he still cherished weekends with his Long Island cronies; and the Roosevelts joshed him for preferring the fast track on Long Island and the theatrical and literary crowd at Harriman's Arden parties to their own weekend hospitality at Hyde Park.[9] Ickes, who was Hopkins's implacable critic, gossiped that the President's friend was in the financial keep of Harriman, Baruch, and Chicago millionaire John Hertz.

Until he began his mobilization work, Harriman had not had extensive professional contact with Hopkins, but he liked him. There was in this dyspeptic, chronically ailing servant of the President an admirable toughness and a willingness to cast aside his liberal theology anytime it got in the way of objectives.

They shared a contempt for the inefficiency of Washington's bureaucracy. Both were fidgety, impatient, compulsive workers. Hopkins divided all people into two groups, the "talkers" and the "doers," and he proudly placed himself among the latter. The same was true of Harriman, who had little time for reflection and less interest in philosophical repartee. He seldom read a book for the joy of it and, like Hopkins, wrote letters devoid of intimacy or texture. Whether they were intended to convey sensitive personal communications or accompany government documents, they had the same tone.

Neither found it easy to reveal intimate feelings. Robert Meiklejohn, who was Averell's personal secretary for more than a decade, left his service feeling that he hardly knew him, although he had traveled the globe with him, taking his dictation, making his appointments, running his errands, handling his trivia, organizing his daily life. "He was not inconsiderate," Meiklejohn would recall. "He was just no good at human relations—naturally aloof. God only knows how many thousand hours I spent alone in his company, but I do not know one interesting anecdote about his personal life."[10] It was, then, a measure of Harriman's special regard for Hopkins that he would uncharacteristically say many years later, "I loved Harry. That is the only way to express it. He was a dear friend."[11]

The alliance really began when Roosevelt got a passing notion of making Hopkins his successor in the White House rather than seeking a third term. This was the origin of Hopkins's unlikely selection to be secretary of commerce. In his case, appointment to the Cabinet was not a promotion. He would have less influence than he already exercised.

But for political purposes, he would be endowed with credibility and dignity that he could never have as a behind-the-scenes operator.

Roosevelt knew how controversial the nomination would be, and he prepared the capital accordingly. He sent White House aide Thomas Corcoran to see what Harriman could do to sell the idea to the business community. Averell was by then chairman of the Business Advisory Council. The panel had never been very effective and its members had been ridiculed by fellow millionaires, but it was still the administration's most serviceable conduit to big business.

Not even members of the council were enthusiastic about Hopkins as secretary. Although his interests had moved beyond social welfare, he was to more conservative businessmen a dangerous leftist if not an out-right socialist. He had flaunted his suspect ideas by publicly taunting capitalists for sitting in "pompous enclaves" during the Depression while "giving the needy unemployed a ham sandwich and letting it go at that."[12]

Whether Harriman liked the nomination or not, Corcoran observed, the smart thing to do was get behind it because "Harry Hopkins has the keys to the White House, not only the front door, but the back, too." The fact was that Harriman did like the idea. He not only admired Hopkins personally, he knew that the White House insider was far more moderate than his public image. His arrival at the Commerce Department would be an opportunity for business.[13]

That isn't to say they always agreed. Two years earlier, when Hopkins was still the reformer incarnate, there had been a testy disagreement over welfare. Harriman and the Business Advisory Council did a study of the Federal Emergency Relief Administration and came to the orthodox businessman's conclusion that control over welfare programs ought to be transferred to the states. Managed at the grass roots level, relief would be more apt to reach the people who needed it, making better use of government resources. When Harriman took the report and its conclusions to the President, Roosevelt sent him to see Hopkins, who exploded when he heard what Harriman and the council were about to propose. To him, the notion of removing Washington interference was a naive invitation to local corruption. "I thought he would leap across the table and choke me to death," Harriman recalled of Hopkins's outraged reaction.[14] The report passed into oblivion, quietly.

After the visit from Corcoran, Harriman went to work to get the council behind the nomination of Hopkins to head the Commerce Department. The panel had a meeting scheduled in St. Louis, and he arranged for everybody to go out together on a train. That gave him hours to lobby his guests as they traveled west. Members did not need to be reminded that the council had accomplished nearly nothing during Daniel Roper's years as commerce secretary, simply because Roper had minimal clout with the White House. With Hopkins, it would be different, Harriman assured them. Having Harry's attention and support would be almost as good as dealing with the President himself.[15] When the meeting adjourned, Harriman had in his pocket a formal endorsement of Hopkins.

The choice was greeted, naturally, by an avalanche of editorial criticism, much of it stirred up by Hopkins's famous remark, which he denied making, that the policy of the Roosevelt administration was "tax and tax, and spend and spend, and elect and elect."

Averell asked to testify when the Senate Commerce Committee took up the nomination, and he cut short his winter vacation at Sun Valley to get back to Washington for his appearance. By the time he was called, however, Hopkins himself had silenced most of the antagonists who had hoped to hold him up as a radical. About all Averell could do was deliver the Business Advisory Council's endorsement and offer his personal confidence that the new secretary would "move in directions that are sound and in the interest of the stimulation of business."[16]

Roosevelt's whimsical notion of Hopkins as a candidate for the White House quickly faded; but as long as there was any chance of a Hopkins-for-President campaign ever being launched, Harriman was prepared to be at its forefront. A month after the Senate confirmed him as secretary, Hopkins went home to Iowa on a dual mission of reestablishing his country-boy bona fides and courting the business community. Averell went along with him, his presence about as subtle as Hopkins's sudden decision to buy an Iowa farm. His role, as Sherwood described it, was to be a "sort of chaperone or guarantor of economic stability," and he played the part with surprising aplomb.[17] He was chosen to introduce Hopkins for a speech to the Des Moines Economic Club, and he showed up for the black-tie affair dressed in a brown business suit. He had been unable to get a tuxedo, he told the home folks and a national radio audience, because Hopkins had rented the last one in town.

The trip home amounted to Hopkins's only campaign trip. With it ended one the country's most unlikely presidential boomlets.

Long before Hopkins completed his metamorphosis from relief administrator to Roosevelt's chief wartime operative and confidant, Harriman had become an outspoken advocate of American assistance to the Allies. His decision to avoid military service in World War I was a lingering and painful embarrassment to him, and he awaited America's entry in the new European conflict intending to square his personal account for the mistake. To him, it was out of the question for the United States to separate itself from Europe economically, politically, or militarily: "Anyone who says we are not affected by that conflict and its results is not facing reality," he said in the first days of 1940. "America has a destiny at this particular moment in the world's history."[18]

His travels through Union Pacific territory, always isolationist country, persuaded him that public opinion in support of the Allies was building faster than politicians realized, and he regularly sent Hopkins both observations and recommendations which he knew would find their way to FDR.

"I can assure you that public opinion regarding the international situation is moving much faster than I believe Washington thinks it is," he told Hopkins.

> There is a desire, so far inarticulate, for leadership outlining what we can and should do for the Allies under a broad program, with specific steps to be taken immediately. There is a sense of frustration, both personally and for the nation. People want to know what we are going to do as a nation and what they can do as individuals to help. . . . Specifically, and with all due modesty, I believe the time has come for the following:
>
> 1. It should be made clear to everybody that it is our national policy to help the Allies in every way short of war—with the cooperation of as many Republican congressional leaders as possible.
> 2. People should be made to understand that to carry out the above, together with our armament program, will require the cooperation and sacrifice of all our people. The time has come to call for sacrifice rather than stress temporary benefits such as increased employment, better business, etc. . . .
> 3. Leadership should be given to help individuals and private organizations find useful things they can do. . . . A demand for the repeal of hampering acts such as the Johnson Act and Neutrality Act and the enactment of affirmative legislation will follow naturally and quickly.
> 4. The people have confidence in industrialists and not politicians to do a production job. The organization of industry to supply our military forces and the allies is such a job. It should be turned over to industrialists with the advice and joint responsibility of labor leaders and the public should be given to understand that they have been given a free hand.
>
> We have got to cut the unit cost of preparedness or we are licked before we start. General Marshall tells us that it costs twenty-one times as much in this country to put a man in the field and keep him there as in a European country.[19]

Two days after Harriman thus unburdened himself to Hopkins, Italy declared war on France and Britain. That same evening, as German troops advanced on Paris, Roosevelt spoke to commencement ceremonies in the gymnasium at the University of Virginia. There were cheers, whistles, Rebel yells, and a thunderous stomping of feet as he departed from his text and declared: "On this 10th day of June 1940, the hand that held the dagger has struck it into the back of its neighbor. . . .

"In our unity, in our American unity, we will pursue two obvious and simultaneous courses: we will extend to the opponents of force the material resources of this nation and, at the same time, we will harness and speed up the use of those resources in order that we ourselves in the Americas may have the equipment and training equal to the task of any emergency and every defense."[20]

The speech laid the foundation for the Lend-Lease program that would send more than $42 billion worth of arms, food, and chemical, industrial, and medical supplies to the Allies over a period of four years, although it would be another nine months before Congress codified the policy of assistance to "opponents of force" by passing the Lend-Lease Act. Three days after the President's remarks, Harriman joined the mobilization effort.

Washington in 1940 had an air of urgency reminiscent of the early days of World War I and the first weeks of 1933. Harriman was in the same predicament he had been in after Roosevelt's election in 1933—on the fringe, trying to find a place in the action. And he was not alone. The hotels and offices around town were again filled with people anxious to pitch in, many of them Wall Streeters who had despised the New Deal.

Drafted by Oscar Cox, a Maine lawyer who had been in Washington since 1938, the Lend-Lease program sent to Capitol Hill after Roosevelt's Charlottesville speech was a way to get around a British dollar shortage so severe that it had become nearly impossible for Britain to purchase American arms. The act authorized the U.S. government to buy hardware rolling out of American plants and lease or lend it to any country the President deemed vital to the defense of the United States. Roosevelt gave the outlines in one of his famous fireside chats, characterizing the United States as the "Arsenal of Democracy," and at a press conference in which he used the memorable analogy of lending a neighbor a fire hose.

As the program took shape, Harriman took his first vacation in a year. He went to Sun Valley for Christmas, and stayed into the new year, skiing the challenging runs down Baldy Mountain during the day and joining guests around the fireplace in the Duchin Room of the lodge during the evening.

Still, he was anxious. He called back to Washington every day, and when he phoned on January 5, the White House had just announced that Hopkins was going to London to meet with Churchill. It was an opportunity Harriman could not let pass, a chance to see the war first-hand and get himself in on the ground floor of Lend-Lease.

Within minutes, he got Hopkins on the phone and pleaded shame-lessly to go along. He could end his vacation that moment, he said, and get back in time to join him. He knew Churchill, he knew Britain, he knew London. He was available to do anything. He would carry Hop-kins's bags. Nothing worked. Roosevelt had been reluctant to approve the mission in the first place, and now that he had, Hopkins wanted to leave immediately and alone. He did drop a hint—and Harriman did not miss it. The President, Hopkins said, "might have something" after the trip.[21] Harriman returned to his prosaic chores at the Office of Production Management and waited.

Hopkins at first planned to be in England for only a few days, but he remained for six weeks. He was with Churchill from morning to far into the night, sharing meals, walking through the destruction created by nightly German air raids, inspecting military bases, and calculating and recalculating Churchill's emergency needs. In the first two weeks, they spent twelve evenings together, talking alone for hours at 10 Down-ing Street, at Chequers, and at Ditchley, the estate north of Oxford where Churchill retreated on the weekends during full moons, when Chequers was vulnerable to German bombers. Hopkins's skepticism about Britain's leader was replaced by unbounded admiration. "Churchill is the gov't in every sense of the word—he controls the grand strategy and often the details—labor trusts him—the army, navy, air force are behind him to a man," Hopkins told Roosevelt in a letter scrawled on Claridge Hotel stationery and sent to him outside of diplo-matic channels. "The politicians and the upper crust pretend to like him. I cannot emphasize too strongly that he is the one and only person over here with whom you need to have a full meeting of minds. . . . This island needs our help now, Mr. President, with everything we can give them."[22]

While his foremost purpose was to ascertain Britain's defense needs, Hopkins's further mission was to help the prime minister understand Roosevelt's political problems. In a long Sunday-night conversation at Chequers in January, he divided American public opinion into four segments. On the war issue, he told Churchill, there were Nazi and Communist sympathizers who favored a negotiated settlement and Ger-man victory; a larger group, typified by former ambassador Joseph P. Kennedy, who favored no-risk support of Britain; a majority which fa-vored all assistance, even if it led to war; and another minority that was for immediate declaration of war.[23] Harriman was one of the more vocal members of what Hopkins considered the majority.

When Hopkins's flying boat landed in New York in mid-February,

Averell was standing at the dock waiting for him. So was former New Hampshire governor John G. Winant, just named to replace Kennedy, who had wrecked his tour as ambassador by leaving the city when the Nazis launched the blitz against London and talking loosely of Britain's defeat. Having returned by way of Lisbon, the west coast of Africa, and Brazil, Hopkins was exhausted, but at his hotel, he invited Harriman and Winant in to hear the whole story of his mission.

He was optimistic because of Churchill's great character and the political support behind his government, but Britain's needs dwarfed anything the American government had imagined and the British public was convinced that Lend-Lease aid would promptly be followed by the arrival of U.S. combat troops.

Hopkins reported to the President on February 17, and the next day Roosevelt summoned Harriman. In a rambling, offhand conversation, he talked as though it had been long understood that Averell would go to London as the administration's special liaison with the British government. The President had no specific instructions. He knew that Averell was unimpressed with the Office of Production Management, so it was understood that he would not report to it. He was also to be entirely independent of the State Department. In other words, he was to be an extension of Hopkins and the White House.

The experience was unsettling. Besides the President's vagueness, Harriman thought Roosevelt was "far more humble, less cocksure" than usual and showing obvious strain. When he called reporters into his office and made the announcement, he was as cloudy as he had been in the private talk. Harriman, FDR said, would be leaving "as soon as the defense program under the Lend-Spend, Lend-Lease—whatever you call it—bill is perfected.

"I suppose you will ask about his title," the President went on, "so I thought I would invent one; I talked over with him what his title would be, and we decided it was a pretty good idea to call him an 'Expediter.' There's a new one for you. I believe it is not in the diplomatic list or any other list. So, he will go over there as 'Defense Expediter.' " The press, suspecting that Roosevelt was once again establishing a wartime operation outside the established bureaucracy, wondered whether Harriman would report directly to the President or through the conventional channel, Ambassador Winant. "I don't know," Roosevelt replied, "and I don't give a damn, you know."[24]

Two weeks later, Harriman returned for lunch and another conversation that was scarcely more satisfactory than the first. Roosevelt was recovering from a cold and, Harriman thought, "obviously tired and mentally stale." More than the war, he was interested in talking about the deficiencies of the British diet, its need for more vitamins, more protein, and more calcium. While he talked, Roosevelt polished off a spinach soufflé and followed it with a stack of pancakes drenched in butter and syrup.[25]

In spite of his presidential mandate to expedite the flow of equipment to British forces, military leaders looked at Harriman and his mission with consternation because they faced a crisis in the Pacific as well as in the Atlantic. American forces needed everything that Britain was calling for. "We are so short," Harriman noted, "that everything given up by the Army or Navy comes out of our own blood; there is practically nothing surplus and will not be for months."[26] Under these circumstances, senior officials were skeptical of requests coming from London and concerned over the prospect of doing business through Hopkins, who had yet to convince them that he had any understanding of strategy, tactics, or weapons. Indeed, as Averell made his round of the chiefs' offices, Hopkins was without an official government job. He had resigned as secretary of commerce and he was still waiting for Congress to pass the Lend-Lease Act so he could officially become the program's administrator.

Accompanied only by Robert Meiklejohn, Harriman boarded a flying boat on the first leg of his journey to England on March 10, 1941. After four decades and dozens of Atlantic crossings, he was making his initial trip by air. It was the first of sixteen sea and air crossings he would make in the next two and a half years, and it took him with jolting suddenness into a war that still seemed far away to much of America. On the approach to Bermuda, shades were ordered drawn over the windows in the cabin, and passengers, including a delegation of Republican congressmen bound for England on an inspection trip, were warned they could be heavily fined for looking out during the descent and landing. Arriving at Darrell's Island in Bermuda for an overnight stop, they docked beside seaplanes with bulging gun turrets and encountered Scottish Highland troops who had been evacuated from Britain's near-disaster at Dunkirk.

Harriman used the stopover to put down notes about his last frenetic days in Washington. Even before his arrival in England, he was sure that the United States would have to do more than provide Lend-Lease war supplies. For starters, it would have to consider protecting convoys of British ships. "All in all I left feeling that the President had not faced what I considered to be the realities of the situation," he wrote, "namely, that there was a good chance Germany, without our help, could so cripple British shipping as to affect her ability to hold out. The President obviously hoped that he would not have to face an unpleasant decision. He seemed unwilling to lead public opinion or to force the issue but hoped, without the background of reasoning, that our material aid would let the British do the job. I am fearful that if things go against England our more specific aid will come so late that it will be costly. Hopkins is the one man in official position who appears to be ready to force a decision."[27]

In the afternoon, they took off for the Azores, flying through the night, and arriving to refuel at dawn. Before another dusk, they reached Lisbon, landing on the Tagus River where, for an hour, a fourteen-knot current carried them past their anchorage every time they attempted to dock, causing landing crews to break three grappling hooks in the process. Once on the ground, he and Meiklejohn were forced to find space aboard a flight on the Dutch airline, KLM, because the Neutrality Act still kept Pan Am from flying into England.

Getting a seat took three days, in part because Anthony Drexel Biddle, the new ambassador to European governments in exile in London, pulled rank and took the first available space. Being only a minister, Averell had to wait his turn, fuming because Biddle had been rushed to London for work of little import while his own critical mission was stuck. He finally got to England on Friday afternoon. The trip had taken nearly a week, during which the President had finally signed the Lend-Lease Act, with an initial appropriation of $7 billion. Churchill was anxious to get to work.

Roosevelt had been pleased with himself for coming up with the "expediter" title, no matter how bureaucratic it sounded. An expediter could have been a clerk-typist keeping track of schedules and manifests or a sergeant directing the flow of cable traffic. In Harriman's case, there were few jobs more crucial to the White House in 1941. He was responsible for all war matters between the White House and 10 Downing Street at a moment when Britain's very survival was questionable. Given the extraordinary circumstances, he was in effect serving both governments; he was the eyes and ears of Roosevelt and Hopkins, and he was also Churchill's principal instrument for conveying his needs to Washington. His most difficult task at the beginning was to communicate the urgency of Britain's needs to the American military establishment. Being asked to give up hardware they critically needed themselves, senior officers felt entitled to share British military secrets, including sensitive details about Britain's own production and reserves. The Navy would provide flying boats for antisubmarine patrols, but it insisted on evidence that Britain had sufficient crews and facilities to put them into immediate service.

Churchill's naval aide was waiting when Harriman landed at Bristol, and within minutes they were aboard a military plane on their way to Chequers. The cold Elizabethan house an hour's drive northwest of London was the Prime Minister's official country residence and Churchill's favorite retreat. There he could escape the constant pressures and distractions that trailed him at 10 Downing Street and surround himself with inner-circle advisers who had become part of his family.

Harriman had his first serious conversation with Churchill after dinner and came directly to his requirement for access to the sensitive information demanded by the American military. Unless he had the whole story of what Britain had and what it needed, he told the Prime Minister, he could be of little use. Churchill required no convincing. Harriman would get anything he needed. "Nothing will be kept from you."[28]

The word had already gone out. From his first day at work, Harriman was a regular at the late-afternoon meetings of the War Cabinet's subcommittee addressing the struggle against German U-boats in the Atlantic. He was given office space at the Admiralty and the North American Supply Committee as well as access to secret cables and documents on production and supplies. Instead of a monitor or a watchdog over the American pipeline, he found himself "treated as a partner in a vast enterprise."[29]

London was anxious to bring the partnership onto an equal footing, while Washington continued to maintain its fig leaf of neutrality. Harriman was ready to help, going beyond the support of British Lend-Lease requests to promote initiatives that could only edge the United States toward belligerency. Working with the Admiralty, he arranged for battle-damaged British ships to be repaired in American yards, thereby reducing their time out of action. It was a clearer departure from neutrality than Lend-Lease itself. At the same time, he pressed for direct shipment of arms and equipment from the United States to British forces in the Middle East. As it was, the matériel was being exposed to the German submarines twice—on the way from the United States to Britain, and again when shipped from Britain to the Middle East. The fearsome losses of shipping had forced Churchill to send even his coastal defense forces to the Mediterranean and far into the Atlantic to escort convoys and engage the German surface fleet. In the face of possible invasion, Britain was left with only one of her fourteen battleships in home waters. Happily, direct shipment became possible when British forces drove the Italians out of Eritrea, Ethiopia, and Somaliland. With the area secured, Roosevelt declared the Red Sea and the Gulf of Aden to be no longer combat zones, permitting American merchant ships to operate in the area.

Averell's general exuberance for Britain's cause raised hackles in the ranks of the administration in Washington. He agitated for the shipment of surplus foods and lobbied for a huge increase in the canning of salmon so more could be sent to British troops in the Middle East and to victims of the blitz even though it was already in short supply in America.

Such requests were delicate. When Lord Woolton, the British food minister, issued a call for Americans to cut down their consumption of milk, cream, sugar, cheese, and meats to increase supplies available to Britain, Harriman got a testy cable from Hopkins that Americans would take their rationing advice from the Department of Agriculture. "The burden of this message," he said, "is to tell his Lordship in a nice way to pipe down."[30]

During his first weeks in England, Harriman was adopted by Churchill just as Hopkins had been the previous winter; and like Hopkins, he quickly developed a personal devotion matching his political admiration for Britain's leader. Four nights after his arrival, he was at dinner with Churchill and Biddle at 10 Downing Street when he heard the wail of air raid sirens for the first time. Instead of being ushered to the bomb shelter, however, the Americans were handed helmets and led to the roof of the Air Ministry, where they listened to the pounding of antiaircraft guns and watched their shells explode over the city as German planes unloaded their cargoes of incendiary bombs.

Whenever Churchill went out to Bristol, Cardiff, Swansea, or Dover to encourage the King's defiant subjects digging out of the rubble from German air raids that spring, Harriman was his frequent companion, along with Winant.

On their trips to towns still smoking from fires set by Luftwaffe bombs, Churchill introduced the Americans over and over. "He seems to get confidence in having us around," Averell reported to Roosevelt, "feeling perhaps that we represent you and the aid that America is to give."[31] On a Good Friday visit to southwest England, where German bombers had been striking night after night, they arrived just as an air raid hit. From Churchill's darkened train, parked on a siding outside Bristol, they watched bombs exploding from the docks to the center of the city. When it was light on Saturday morning, they joined residents searching the smoking rubble for dead and injured.

In spite of the devastation, Bristol University went ahead with its commencement exercises. Graduates and faculty members left work in the wreckage of the city and put on academic gowns over their soot- and mud-caked clothes to watch the Prime Minister award degrees—one of them an honorary doctorate to Harvard president James Conant, who was in England to expand collaboration between British and American scientists on projects including their top secret collaboration on the atomic bomb. As their train left the station that afternoon, Harriman saw a crack in Churchill's gruff exterior for the first time. When townspeople stood outside his railway car to see him off, he had to shield his face momentarily with a newspaper to hide the tears welling in his eyes.

Arriving back at Chequers that night, Churchill found joyful news. The U.S. Navy, advised a personal cable from the President, was extending its patrol zone all the way to the twenty-sixth meridian, with a dogleg that would include Iceland. American warships would therefore begin providing British convoys with warnings of German U-boats. It was a potentially telling development in the battle against the blockade, for it would allow the Royal Navy to concentrate its ships nearer its home shores. At lunch the next day, John Colville, the Prime Minister's private secretary, asked Harriman whether the decision might not even put the United States at war with Germany. His only reply was, "That's what I hope."[32]

In mid-May, Averell's younger daughter, Kathleen, then twenty-three and a neophyte journalist, got a British visa with the help of Harry Hopkins and arrived in London to find her father still living out of his suitcases in temporary quarters at the Dorchester, and recovering from another bout with his ulcer. She had at first planned to go back to New York after a short visit; but swept into the excitement of the war and seeing her father an important player in history, she took a job as a reporter for Hearst's International News Service and assumed the roles of hostess, social secretary, and companion to her father.

Although he was in the middle of the war working with Churchill, Harriman felt seriously out of touch with his own country and worried that he was not effectively conveying Britain's peril to Americans. Public-opinion polls showed that the number of Americans willing to risk war by aiding Britain was declining.

The cable traffic that cascaded across his desk told him so little of the atmosphere in Washington that his whole view of the war was increasingly skewed to the British perspective. Hopkins seldom wrote, and when he did, his letters were stale because it took more than a month for them to arrive.

Averell complained to the President that there was "almost a stone wall" between London and Washington. "My source of information is entirely from British ministries," he wrote Roosevelt after he had been in England for a month. "My usefulness will be in direct proportion to the extent to which I am kept informed of the developments in fact and thought at Washington."[33] When he suggested going home to catch up, Hopkins waved him off. "If I were you, I would not come home for the present," he replied. "I realize you don't always get what you want but we are after it hard every minute of the day. I think it is particularly important right now until some important decisions are made here that you be in London."[34]

What Harriman wanted was for American naval and air power to join Britain's fight. Lend-Lease alone, he feared, might even be doing more harm than good. "Limiting our participation to sending supplies to Britain can never win the war, and in fact may lose," he wrote Bill Jeffers back in Omaha. "Every week we delay active participation in the

use of our navy and air force, at least, multiplies the eventual difficulties.
I believe that our naval and air help to the British can win the Battle of
the Atlantic against the German submarine raids and air attack. As it is
now, shipping losses are already sapping the vitality of Britain to the
danger point."[35]

In some ways, the Prime Minister himself made Harriman's job
more difficult. Although he was willing to share some of Britain's deepest
military secrets with the U.S. government, he stubbornly refused to reveal publicly the extent of shipping losses, fearing the morale and the
propaganda value the information would have to the enemy. Harriman
argued, to no avail, that full disclosure would, to the contrary, rally
flagging support in the United States.

In Washington's view, Britain's strength was also being drained by
Churchill's commitment to strategic interests in North Africa and the
Middle East. That war, too, had gone sour since the defeat of the Italians.
Field Marshal Rommel's Afrika Korps had driven General Archibald
Wavell's forces, plagued by inferior tanks, a thousand miles across the
desert, recapturing all of Libya. Greece had fallen with fifty thousand
men of the overpowered British expeditionary force evacuated under
darkness. The strategic Mediterranean island of Crete had capitulated
after a battle that raged for ten days. A year after Dunkirk, the heroic
evacuation removed 16,500 troops from Crete to safety in Egypt. "It has
been as if living in a nightmare," Harriman wrote Hopkins, "with some
calamity hanging constantly over one's head. I have not expected any
war news that would make us happy. . . ."[36]

In moments of doubt, Churchill worried that the Germans would
make good on their grand design, with Rommel pushing all the way to
the Suez Canal. The possibility of just that disaster had been the reason
that Britain had risked even an invasion of its home islands in order to
defend its strategic interest in North Africa and the Middle East. The
power that controlled the Middle East controlled access to oil and the
route to India. Now, in spite of the determination to defend the region,
Churchill faced the real prospect of losing everything.

His pride, his judgment, his perception of the war were deeply tied
up in the commitment. He doggedly stuck with it, convinced that the
war in the Middle East had been badly managed. In his moments of
gloom, he fantasized about what he would do if only he were in direct
command himself. He would, he once told Colville, "gladly lay down his
present office—yes, and even renounce cigars and alcohol" if he could
have field command in the Middle East.[37]

In the wake of the Crete disaster, he asked Harriman to go to
the region for a firsthand assessment. Although it was to be chiefly an
evaluation of what the United States could do to help change the ill
fortune, Churchill wanted more. His letter of introduction reflected the

depth of the trust he had gained in the American envoy in just two months. "Mr. Harriman enjoys my complete confidence and is in the most intimate relations with the President and Mr. Harry Hopkins. No one can do more for you. . . . I commend Mr. Harriman to your most attentive consideration," it told British commanders. "He will report both to his own government and to me as Minister of Defence."[38] To emphasize further Harriman's role as his personal representative, the Prime Minister ordered his son, Randolph, an army commando captain based in Cairo, detailed as Averell's military aide.

At first, the mission was thought of as a job requiring a week or two; but before it was over, it lasted thirty-seven days and covered sixteen thousand miles, taking Harriman to visits with British troops and civil servants from the west coast of Africa to the Red Sea, and from Cairo to Baghdad. He inspected ports, ship-repair docks, and secret aircraft-assembly hangars on the Atlantic. Then from Lagos, Nigeria, he followed the cross-continent ferry route taken by new planes on their way to British forces in Egypt, covering five hundred miles a day and stopping off at remote landing strips to inspect facilities and interview pilots.

The situation in the field was as bad as he had expected. There were shortages of tanks, ships, fuel, and transport vehicles. At the assembly plant in the Gold Coast, planes sat in the blistering sun because there were not enough ferry pilots.

With Meiklejohn following along taking copious notes, Averell cataloged the depths of harbors, the lengths of backcountry landing strips, the equipment in repair shops, and the intolerable losses of fighter planes through accidents. He slept in sweltering tents and on rooftops, rode out dust storms, endured mosquito bites, and baked in the sweltering sun for ten days before reaching British headquarters at Cairo. In the following days, sometimes accompanied by Randolph Churchill, he made more trips into the field to talk with pilots, tank crews, and unit commanders in underground dugouts.

His arrival in Cairo came at a delicate moment, for two days later Churchill ordered General Archibald Wavell, Britain's commander in chief, replaced by General Sir Claude Auchinleck, the commander in India. Given the British reverses in the desert and in the Mediterranean, Harriman had arrived prepared to dislike Wavell; and coming into Cairo after more than a week crossing the continent, he thought the comforts enjoyed by the general and his staff were extravagant. That impression was overturned, however, when he saw the loyalty of Wavell's troops and witnessed the general's dignity when Churchill relieved him of command.

From Cairo, Harriman sent the Prime Minister a somber report. There had been no preparation for use of Red Sea ports in case the

Suez Canal was closed; there was no facility to repair American aircraft engines or salvage battle-damaged tanks; tank crewmen were not adequately trained; the aircraft ferry was poorly managed, and there was waste everywhere. Between air, land, and naval forces, coordination was pathetic. Aerial reconnaissance pictures did not get to commanders of armored units; there was little communication between armor and artillery commanders; the Navy got inadequate air cover; and no one received sufficient intelligence data. "There appears a somewhat fatalistic attitude in attempting ventures without proper preparation or appraisal of assets and enemy strength," he reported. "One feels a sense of complacency in Cairo and absence of urgency."[39]

Among British officers, one of the uppermost concerns was the strategy for retreat if Rommel's tanks moved on Cairo and the Suez Canal. If that happened, the options were to withdraw up the Nile or pull back across the canal. Auchinleck, who arrived July 2, two weeks after Harriman made his first call in Cairo, favored the latter. In such a case, the new headquarters could be established in Iraq, where there was already a British base providing a possible jumping-off point for a counterattack.

Harriman was still in Cairo when Hitler invaded the Soviet Union. Western intelligence had seen the momentous change in the war coming, and had warned Stalin. But when German artillery began pumping shells into Soviet territory on June 22, the Russians momentarily took the all-out offensive to be a mere border provocation.

Averell's feeling was one of enormous relief. Hitler had squandered his opportunity to invade England while the United States hesitated. There would now be another year, he guessed, in which to win the battle against the U-boats in the Atlantic. By then, the Lend-Lease pipeline would be in full operation, and Britain would be too strong for the Nazis to consider an invasion.

British military men kept their own optimism in check. Wavell thought the Russians would last no more than six weeks. When the Red Army capitulated, Hitler would have a choice of attacking England herself or striking British forces in the Middle East. The general's nightmare was that the Nazis would move through Spain, close the western end of the Mediterranean at Gibraltar, and then bomb the Suez Canal, shutting off the eastern exit and trapping the British fleet.

Before heading back to London to report to Churchill, Harriman flew to Basra to size up the situation British forces would face if they were forced to withdraw into Iraq. Foremost among the problems would be the daunting prospect of defending Basra's port and the eighty-five-mile-long waterway linking it to the Persian Gulf. But by holding Iraq, Britain would still have access to the gulf and the oil from the huge

Abadan refinery in Iran. Equally important in light of Hitler's attack on the Soviet Union was the fact that Iran provided a route into the USSR from the gulf.

Britain's difficulty in maintaining its footing in the Middle East was never more evident to Harriman than at the end of his journey. Aboard a slow, four-engine Australian Sunderland flying boat, he had to skim the Mediterranean at an altitude of two hundred feet all the way from Alexandria to Malta to avoid being spotted by German fighters. Gunners manned positions in the cockpit, in the tail, and in the nose, their machine guns ready. As a further precaution, his schedule was arranged so Malta was approached under cover of darkness. Safely there, he remained just long enough for a quick inspection of British aviation operations, taking off again at two A.M. to get beyond the range of Italian fighters before sunrise.

At Gibraltar, where soupy weather grounded him for five days, Harriman was given a tour through caves being hollowed out of The Rock so British defenders could dig in if the Germans mounted a serious threat to take it.

Then he went to work on a long list of recommendations, led by advice that Churchill shake up his Middle East organization to stop the destructive intraservice bickering. Another port on the Persian Gulf needed to be considered should mines seal off Basra. He also proposed that the United States take responsibility for ferrying combat planes from their assembly plant on Africa's Gold Coast to the Middle East, and that American technicians, mechanics, and ordnance experts be sent to support RAF squadrons.

Although several of his suggestions were followed, he was again ahead of Washington in his eagerness to support the British. Back home the assessment was that the British could do no better than maintain a standoff in the Middle East. Its navy and its air force were too small to give its army the support it required.

Even as Harriman waited for the weather to clear at Gibraltar, Hopkins was on his way to London to reemphasize the American military's skepticism about the commitment in the Middle East. In the view of the chiefs of staff, the Battle of the Atlantic, the overarching engagement of the war, was being risked and the British Isles exposed to possible invasion by Churchill's bullheaded commitment to an indefensible position so far away. Hopkins's other reason for crossing the Atlantic was to arrange a face-to-face meeting between Roosevelt and Churchill. The two had wanted for months to get together, and the decision was to rendezvous secretly off the coast of Newfoundland, accompanied only by their military chiefs.

By the time Hopkins arrived in London, it was obvious that the war had been changed by Hitler's attack on the Soviet Union. Churchill had immediately promised British support to the Red Army, but in the United States the new war on the eastern front had resuscitated the isolationists. The question of aid to Stalin would obviously be one of the chief matters before Roosevelt and Churchill. After his meetings with the Prime Minister, Hopkins—having just enough time to go to Moscow and get back with an assessment of the eastern front before the upcoming meeting—departed for the Soviet Union.

On July 30, three days after Hopkins sailed from Scotland on his way to see Stalin, Harriman flew home to report to Roosevelt and the chiefs on his inspection trip to the Middle East, knowing what he had to say would provide additional ammunition for the critics of the British course. Upon arrival, he went to General George Marshall's office to pay his respects and make arrangements to deliver his conclusion. It was a Saturday, but he unexpectedly found himself giving full-scale briefing for Marshall and Admiral Harold Stark, the chief of naval operations. Rather than focusing on Averell's recommendations, they were most interested in the disaster on Crete and what they regarded as Britain's inept conduct of the campaign. They disagreed with Churchill's priorities. Marshall's position was that the British had been told what the United States could provide under Lend-Lease—they would have to get by with that, using it as they saw fit. Stark was unimpressed by Harriman's case for the U.S. Navy's taking over ship repairs in the West African port of Freetown. Harriman left the meeting and walked back to the Mayflower Hotel thoroughly discouraged by what seemed complete lack of appreciation of Britain's predicament.

Later, Secretary of War Henry Stimson was similarly skeptical. He was willing to send equipment to the Middle East, but he took no interest in West Africa, where Churchill wanted to see American troops enter the war. Like Marshall, Stimson was determined that the United States would not risk failure in a first commitment of armed force. Both regarded West Africa as too risky—German submarines off the coast might cut supply lines, increasing the possibility of a German land attack from the north.[40]

Though he held his tongue, Harriman was indignant at what seemed to be pervasive Washington shortsightedness. "Britain, and therefore America, is on the defensive," he wrote after his discouraging conversations. "Is the idea that we should wait until England is on the offensive and we can pick a nice plum which is safe because Germany is no longer dangerous? Is the idea that we should let England undertake all the difficult tasks and we take over only the fruit of their efforts? Is the role of our Army . . . such venturesome and dangerous tasks as relieving British troops from their occupation in Iceland?"[41]

*   *   *

Home for the first time since becoming expediter, Averell found that Washington did not regard his role as seriously as he had imagined. He was crushed to learn that he was not invited to the meeting in Newfoundland. When he told Roosevelt that Churchill had expected to see him there, the President gave him a polite brush-off, emphasizing that it was to be a small, no-frills get-together.

Under the pretense that he was taking a little vacation cruise on the presidential yacht, *Potomac*, FDR slipped away for his journey to Placentia Bay, leaving the White House press behind. Not even the chiefs of staff knew anything of the meeting until they were ordered to prepare for departure on an "inspection" trip. On Monday morning, as the President secretly transferred from the yacht to the cruiser *Augusta* off Martha's Vineyard, Harriman was at Sands Point, working out his frustrations with a croquet mallet.

That afternoon, however, there was a message from the White House. He was to get to Boston and meet Undersecretary of State Sumner Welles. Without realizing it, Churchill had made it possible for him to be at the meeting by bringing Sir Alexander Cadogan, the permanent undersecretary of state for foreign affairs. Hearing that Cadogan was coming, Roosevelt added Welles and Harriman to his own party. Averell flew to Boston with his ego on the mend.

The next day, he and Welles landed on Placentia Bay, off Argentia, aboard a four-engine flying boat. By then, the President and the military chiefs had already dispensed with the two issues that most concerned him in London, the supply situation and the protection of Atlantic convoys. But that evening, he and Welles went aboard the *Augusta* for dinner, giving him a chance to talk with the President at length about the Middle East. It was a subject that would be sharply debated by the military officers at the conference, but in the larger drama of the first meeting of the two leaders, it disappeared from priority.

Harriman spent most of the four-day meeting playing the role of a liaison between the two leaders. Although Churchill and Roosevelt had developed an intimate correspondence over the preceding two years, the Prime Minister was still anxious about the impression he would make on the President, and it comforted him to have Averell around to give him a feel for the Americans' perception of the conference. Every day, he found time to pull Harriman aside and quiz him about the kind of impression being made on FDR. After Sunday-morning religious services on the foredeck of Churchill's flagship, HMS *Prince of Wales*, the Prime Minister took a break from meetings and went ashore, inviting Harriman to join him. They rode in a launch to a narrow, rocky beach, and spent an hour walking the coastline, climbing its boulders and talking before a rain squall drove them back to the ship.

The rendezvous off Newfoundland would be remembered for the dramatic staging and its Atlantic Charter renouncing aggression and setting forth principles for a peaceful world, but more importantly at that moment, it produced an agreement for Anglo-American action in the event of Japanese aggression and set in motion the massive program of military aid to the Soviet Union.

The battle on the Russian front had been going on for eight weeks when Roosevelt and Churchill sailed out of the bay for home. Already the Soviets had lasted longer than pessimists had predicted. To buy time, the Russians had paid a heavy price, giving up enormous stretches of territory, but there was no sign of collapse. Hopkins, who had arrived off Newfoundland with Churchill after returning to Britain from his visit to Moscow, predicted that the Red Army would hold on until winter brought Hitler's offensive to a standstill.

He had assured Stalin that the Soviets could count on American help in addition to the support Churchill had already promised, and the Soviet dictator had reeled off needs for antiaircraft guns, machine guns, gasoline, and aluminum. But Stalin had barely scratched the surface of what would be required when fighting resumed in the spring of 1942. Keeping the war going on the eastern front would be a stupendous challenge not only for the Red Army but for American factories. Britain would have to share its Lend-Lease pipeline with Stalin, and together, somehow, the American and British fleets would have to get the stuff into Soviet hands.

Before they weighed anchor, Roosevelt and Churchill cabled Stalin proposing a high-level joint delegation to hammer out agreements on what Russia's new allies would provide. It was a mission that logically would have gone to Hopkins; but he was near exhaustion, and sending him back was out of the question. Although Secretary of the Treasury Henry Morgenthau and Secretary of the Navy Frank Knox both coveted the assignment, Roosevelt, back in Washington, named Harriman instead—undoubtedly on the recommendation of Hopkins.

It was an exquisitely complex assignment. American military officials would be asked to make heavy sacrifices to help a government they detested almost as much as they hated the Nazis. For British officers, the thought of sending war matériel to the Russians was even more painful, like "flaying off pieces of their skin," as Churchill put it.[42] To begin the unpleasant task, the prime minister named Lord Beaverbrook, the prickly newspaper magnate then serving as his supply minister, to head the British delegation.

Although Harriman and Beaverbrook were cochairmen of the mission to Moscow, it was understood that Averell would be the de facto leader, since the United States would be the chief source of the assistance to the Kremlin. Playing second fiddle was not a role that came easily to

Beaverbrook. When the joint delegation met to make final preparations, Beaverbrook moved to take control. The Americans, he insisted, needed only to declare the overall allocations they would make, and then in Moscow he and Stalin would decide on additional contributions to be made by Britain.

Harriman dug in his heels, demanding that committees of British and American experts work out joint lists of weapons, supplies, and ammunition that could be put before Stalin. If Beaverbrook insisted that the negotiations take place between Stalin and himself, he said, it would be pointless for the Americans to go on to Moscow.

Beaverbrook retreated, but word of the dispute immediately got to Churchill, who invited Harriman to dinner to pacify him. When the delegation departed for Moscow, it carried carefully prepared lists of what the two countries together were prepared to offer.

Having foiled Beaverbrook's attempt to cast himself as the principal negotiator, Harriman did make one big concession for the sake of harmony with his lordship. Beaverbrook detested flying, and the thought of a high-altitude B-24 journey through skies haunted by Luftwaffe fighters terrified him. To placate him, Averell agreed to make the trip aboard the heavy cruiser HMS *London*, crossing the Norwegian Sea, going beyond the Arctic Circle and into the Soviet port of Archangel. The journey was hardly without peril.

Their departure from Scotland was surrounded by security precautions unusual even for wartime. Members of the ship's crew were told neither their destination nor the identity of their passengers until they were at sea. Indeed, the names of Field Marshal Gort, Britain's commander at Gibraltar, and Ambassador Winant had been put on cabin doors to make crew members think they were headed for the Middle East. Once the ship was under way, catapult-launched Walrus patrol planes took turns watching out for submarines ahead; heavily armed destroyers covered their flanks; and the captain sailed a zigzag course at top speed. Fortunately, whenever the *London* did pass within range of German bombers based in Norway, its movement was covered by a thick blanket of clouds.

As the ship sliced through the Norwegian Sea, the B-24s spurned by Beaverbrook landed in Moscow with the delegation staff, and the Soviet government announced their arrival as though the entire mission had been aboard.

Five days after leaving Scotland, Harriman and Beaverbrook entered the White Sea and anchored at the mouth of the Dvina River, where Soviet foreign minister V. M. Molotov awaited them aboard a Soviet destroyer. In a frigid rain, they headed upstream to Archangel, transferring at dusk to spend the night on an admiral's yacht tied up at the dock. The next morning, they took off for Moscow in twin-engine military transport planes. What followed was one of the more unnerving experiences of the whole war for Harriman, surpassing any of the bombings he experienced in London. Escorted by fighters, the four transports flew in formation at altitudes ranging from one hundred to eight hundred feet for five hours. Then, on approach to Moscow, they inexplicably came under Soviet antiaircraft fire, shells exploding close enough for all aboard to hear their *crump* and see the puffs of smoke.

Harriman was trying not to notice an airsick Englishman throwing up when he heard the first shells explode. In a split second, even before the passengers realized what the noise was, the Soviet pilots rolled the planes violently to evade the gunners' sights and dove toward the trees, coming so close it seemed they could touch the leaves. Beaverbrook, who had been standing in the aisle, was thrown sprawling.

That night, when Stalin began describing the Soviets' need for Western arms, antiaircraft guns stood near the top of his shopping list. Harriman, hardly known for joking even under the most relaxed of circumstances, dryly remarked without explanation that he might object to furnishing Moscow antiaircraft weapons.

Compared to London, the damage German bombers had inflicted on Moscow was still minor, but the city was nonetheless under siege. Besides the hair-trigger antiaircraft guns around it, there was evidence everywhere that the Russians were prepared for a fierce defense of their capital. The Kremlin had been elaborately camouflaged. Nets concealed its onion-shaped spires, and its walls were covered with canvas backdrops from the Bolshoi theater, making them appear from a distance as rows of small houses. Lenin's tomb was covered with an imitation house, and the body had reportedly been moved. Major avenues and the riverbanks were concealed by phony canvas roofs, and live trees had been planted in pots and scattered about boulevards now traveled by trucks camouflaged with tree branches. Walls about the city were plastered with texts of a speech broadcast by Stalin, explaining what was to be done in the event of an evacuation order. Not a liter of gas, not a kilogram of wheat was to be left behind. Bridges and highways were to be destroyed, houses and forests burned.

The night after their shaken arrival, Harriman and Beaverbrook were driven into the blacked-out Kremlin for their first meeting with Stalin. Averell's initial impression was that the Soviet dictator was much shorter and outwardly more benign than he had expected. The Man of Steel was soft-spoken. He had a limp handshake and he avoided much direct eye contact, characteristics that Harriman instantly noted because E. H. Harriman had so often warned that men with these traits were supremely untrustworthy.

For the better part of three hours, Stalin described the Soviets' most urgent combat needs, with tanks leading the list, closely followed by antitank and antiaircraft guns, and stupendous amounts of barbed wire. Stalin impressed Harriman and Beaverbrook, as he had Hopkins, with his engineer's grasp of technical detail and his accountant's command of statistics. He knew the speed, range, and payload of American planes, the rate of fire of American guns, and the fuel consumption and horsepower of tank engines. He easily recited the quantities of raw materials he had on hand and listed his needs for various kinds of ammunition and vehicles to win what he called the "war of motors." He was accompanied only by Molotov and former foreign minister Maksim Litvinov, who served as their interpreter.

Harriman left the meeting flush with satisfaction. He had prepared himself well, and it had gone perfectly. One more meeting and an aid package could be tied up for Roosevelt and Churchill. But when he and Beaverbrook returned on the following evening, they encountered an altogether different reception. Stalin was restless, boorish, and spiteful, angrily puffing on his pipe, pacing the floor, interrupting them to make telephone calls, and accusing them of being niggardly in their offers. The United States and Britain, he insinuated, wanted to see Soviet forces defeated by the Germans. When Beaverbrook presented a message from Churchill, Stalin tossed it onto a table and, with calculated rudeness, left it unopened.

By the end of the session, they had accomplished nothing. Harriman was mystified and Beaverbrook, who had been equally ecstatic after the first meeting, was rattled. The only conclusion they reached was that they would have to meet a third time. Then, they would put before Stalin their final lists of what the United States and Britain would provide.

Returning to the Kremlin prepared for the worst, they were surprised again. Twenty-four hours after he had denounced their proposals as pitifully and calculatedly inadequate, Stalin listened patiently, nodding his approval over and over as Harriman ticked through the revised lists developed by working groups. He interrupted only to ask for additional scout cars and to enter a new request for eight thousand to ten thousand trucks per month. He had also decided that he needed still more barbed wire. "If possible," he said, he would like to receive ten thousand to fifteen thousand tons the first month, instead of the four thousand he had first requested.

What emerged was a list of seventy specific items, including raw materials such as bauxite, which both the United States and Britain badly needed to maintain aircraft production schedules and which Beaverbrook had to clear personally with Churchill by telephone. Besides trucks, scout cars, and barbed wire, the hit included 1,800 warplanes, 2,250 tanks, 562,000 miles of telephone wire, and prodigious quantities of chemicals, TNT, and cloth.

The first wartime agreements with the Soviet Union were concluded in deceptive harmony.

Averell hurried back to Spaso House, the American ambassador's residence, where he was staying, clicking his heels. He had just accomplished the most important thing of his life, he told his secretary, something that would have an important effect on the course of the war. It was the first time in the four and a half years on his staff that Meiklejohn had known him to unbend in such a fashion. "He looked," the secretary noted, "like the cat that had swallowed the mouse."[43]

For an hour, Averell sat in a hot tub and dictated cables for Hopkins and the President. The meeting had ended in "the most friendly fashion possible," he wrote in his notes. "Stalin made no effort to conceal his enthusiasm. It was my impression that he was completely satisfied that Britain and America meant business. . . . I left feeling that he had been frank with us and if we came through as had been promised, and if personal relations were maintained with Stalin, the suspicion that has existed between the Soviet government and our two governments might well be eradicated. There can be no doubt that Stalin is the only man to deal with in foreign affairs. Dealing with others . . . was almost a waste of time."[44]

All that remained was for the conference to be blessed by a banquet with the obligatory toasts, and for the signing of the protocol. For Harriman that presented a problem. The President had not yet made the Soviet Union eligible for Lend-Lease assistance, so he was without legal authority to sign an agreement promising Stalin anything. Communications delays made it impossible for him to get prompt instructions from the White House. If he refused to sign, it would leave the mission in shambles, so with no plausible way to avoid it, he joined Beaverbrook and Molotov in formalizing the seven-page commitment that would amount to $1 billion over the next nine months. One column listed the arms, ammunition, and supplies the Russians had requested, the second the quantities they asked, and the third the U.S. and British responses. There were no cost figures. It was not until November, a month later, that the President formally declared the defense of the Soviet Union vital to the defense of the United States, making the USSR formally eligible for Lend-Lease assistance.

Aside from establishing supply shipments to the Russians, the mission began regular and frequently troublesome three-way dealings among Roosevelt, Churchill, and their unlikely partner in Moscow.

As a direct result of the Harriman-Beaverbrook talks with Stalin, both Ambassador Laurence Steinhardt of the United States and Ambassador Sir Richard Stafford Cripps of Great Britain, and perhaps Constantine Oumansky, Moscow's ambassador to Washington, were replaced, and Averell assumed an additional role as the most important personal link between the White House and the Kremlin. When Stalin complained about both of the Western envoys, claiming Steinhardt was a "rumor monger and a defeatist" preoccupied with his own safety, Harriman had defended the ambassador and retaliated with his own criticism of Oumansky's work in Washington, but back home he told Roosevelt he believed that Steinhardt's effectiveness in Moscow was finished.[45] The President evidently agreed, for Steinhardt was replaced by FDR's old friend, Admiral William H. Standley, a former chief of naval operations, who had been a member of the Harriman mission. Although Oumansky was already on his way out in Washington, Harriman later attributed the ambassador's prompt reassignment to Mexico to his own Kremlin conversation with Stalin.[46]

The trip back to London was as harrowing as the journey to Moscow. Bucking gale-force winds, the planes were buffeted between the ground and low-lying clouds all the way to Archangel, and nearly everyone aboard them was sick. By the time the mission completed the yacht trip back down the storm-swept river to the bay, the tide had gone out. The party, therefore, had to transfer to a minesweeper to be ferried out to the *London*, which had moved into deeper water. Darkness had fallen by then, and it took three attempts and nearly an hour to come alongside the cruiser in the rain and wind. On the first try, a line between the vessels snapped. On the second, the two ships crashed together so violently that they bent plates in the cruiser's side and holed the minesweeper's hull above the waterline. When a gangway was finally secured between the wet, pitching decks, members of the mission dashed across by twos and threes each time the two vessels rose together to the crest of a wave. Harriman made it across, carrying an armful of sable skins, followed by Meiklejohn with a heavy mailbag filled with caviar. Petrified, Beaverbrook had to be lashed to a stretcher and carried across the slippery gangway. Back on the solid cruiser deck, all were soaked and shivering— and relieved that they would not spend another night in Archangel. All but Harriman dashed for the warmth of their quarters; he alone stood on deck waving to the shore party as the cruiser headed slowly out to sea.

He was exhausted and stricken with a sinus infection. For three days he was confined to bed, attended by Sir Charles Wilson, Churchill's physician, who had come along as the mission's expert on medical supplies. But Sir Charles refused to administer anything but advice, and Harriman finally summoned the ship's doctor and demanded medication. He was accordingly filled with sulfanilamide, and by the time the delegation docked in Scotland on October 9 and boarded a special train waiting to rush its members to London, he was recovering.

Welcomed back as heroes, he and Beaverbrook turned to work on speeches to their nations. Harriman spoke on both the BBC and a CBS network broadcast back to the United States, trying to relieve both British and American suspicions of the Russians and summon confidence in their new ally:

"Stalin himself is interested in one thing and one thing alone—the Russian nation. He kept talking about her present needs, her future hopes, how this nationalist Russia could develop relations with the British empire and the United States, believing that a common base could be found to work together.

"If the Russian soldier, the Russian airman continue to get the needed guns, the tanks, the planes, they will fight on," he reported. "We don't know just where the front line is tonight. We don't know where it will be tomorrow. But I am convinced that, given the tools, Russia will fight on."[47]

After seeing Churchill, Harriman was off for the United States. The morning after his arrival, he drove from Arden to Hyde Park for lunch with the President and Hopkins, giving them a full account of his meetings with Stalin, reiterating his belief that the Russians would hold the Nazis off until winter, though Stalin had just declared a state of siege and ordered foreign diplomats evacuated from Moscow to Kuibyshev, six hundred miles to the east.

The pace Harriman had set since March, especially during the three months when he had crossed the Atlantic three times besides making his trip to the Soviet Union, had left him exhausted. Suffering a lingering reaction to the sulfanilamide he had been given aboard ship, he underwent a physical examination in New York and was ordered to bed. Hopkins, doubting that he should ever return to England, sent Stettinius to discuss the possibility of a replacement. The patient brushed the concern aside. "He is truly appreciative of your thoughtfulness for his health and welfare," Stettinius reported, "but he feels quite certain he will run no risk in returning to London as soon as he is comfortable. He was touched by the thought of a substitute and seemed to feel that if that became necessary Jack McCloy was the best bet. In view of the fact that he has been away from London practically since June, he feels that for him to return there now for a month and then come home for Christmas would be much the best course if it is feasible."[48]

The presidential envoy's most debilitating and persistent symptom was a carbuncle on his behind. When he was otherwise recovered, it was still excruciatingly painful to sit erect, so he equipped himself with an inflatable rubber ring that somewhat reduced his agony and boarded a plane for London carrying it under his arm.

What bothered him more than his carbuncle as he went back to his post was the United States' continuing role on the sidelines of the war. While he was recuperating, a German submarine had sunk the U.S. destroyer *Reuben James*, killing all 115 members of the crew and moving

Congress to modify the Neutrality Act and permit armed American vessels to enter the war zone for the first time. Encouraging as the congressional action was, he told Churchill, the American public retained its aversion to a declaration of war, and there were increasing murmurings that the British were being too slow to go on the offensive against Hitler.

While it had not been altogether Averell's idea to do all of the traveling, there was a feeling in Washington that he had drifted away from the mission that had originally taken him to London. Stettinius expressed concern to Hopkins that Harriman's interests were reaching too far afield. For the record anyway, Hopkins agreed that he should emphasize that "his job is London and not Russia or the Middle East."[49]

The end of November and the beginning of December gave Averell the opportunity to be with Churchill again for extended periods, and they were once again at Chequers on the weekend of December 7, 1941.

After getting his cables off to Washington on Saturday, the 6th, Harriman, along with Kathleen and Randolph Churchill's wife, Pamela, drove to Chequers. Sunday was Kathleen's twenty-fourth birthday, and the Churchills, who had taken a parental interest in her, had arranged a family birthday dinner on Saturday evening. In spite of the occasion, it was not a pleasant weekend. The weather was cloudy and cold. As was often the case, the group was joined on Sunday by Ambassador Winant, General Hastings Ismay, the Prime Minister's chief of staff, Commander C. R. Thompson, Churchill's naval aide, and John Martin, his private secretary. They found the Prime Minister tired and depressed.

The Germans still hammered at Moscow. Japanese aggression in the Pacific was certain. Not feeling well, Clementine Churchill remained upstairs Sunday evening. The Prime Minister sat for long periods in silence, putting his elbows on the table after dinner and sitting with his chin in his hands.

Following an after-dinner ritual, Churchill's valet appeared at nine o'clock, put before him a little flip-top radio that had been a gift from Hopkins, and switched on the BBC news. After the headlines, the announcer moved into the top stories. "The news has just been given that Japanese aircraft have raided Pearl Harbor, the American naval base in Hawaii. The announcement of the attack was made in a brief statement by President Roosevelt. Naval and military targets on the principal island of Oahu have also been attacked. No further details are yet available."[50]

At first there was confusion around Churchill's table about what had been said. Thompson argued with Harriman that the announcer had said "Pearl River," not "Pearl Harbor." As Winant recalled it, Churchill, shaken from his dark mood, thundered, "We shall declare war on Japan," and the ambassador had rejoined, "Good God, you can't declare war on a radio announcement."[51] With Harriman and Winant at his heels, Churchill headed for his office down the hall from the dining room. Before he got there, the Admiralty was on the telephone with confirmation. Winant placed a call to Roosevelt and, after getting the President on the line, handed the phone to the Prime Minister. There was still no full accounting of the damage from the air raid, but it didn't really matter. "We are all in the same boat now," Roosevelt said. He would ask Congress for a declaration of war the following morning. He left the line telling Churchill, "God be with you."[52]

Harriman and Winant were dumbstruck. "They did not wail or lament that their country was at war," Churchill recalled. "They wasted no words in reproach or sorrow. In fact, one might almost have thought that they had been delivered from a long pain."[53] In Harriman's case anyway the Prime Minister's assessment was on the mark. At last the waiting for the inevitable was over, and for that, Harriman was as happy as was Churchill.

Among the early cables that flowed from Chequers was one jointly signed by the two of them. It went to Hopkins at the White House: "Thinking of you much at this historic moment—Winston, Averell."[54]

Chapter XII

PAMELA
A Country Girl from Dorset

The call might come in the early evening or toward midnight, but the invitation was nearly always the same: Would the Ambassador come for a talk? When he needed to unwind, Churchill would routinely ring up Harriman, and Roosevelt's expediter would head through blacked-out streets to 10 Downing Street, or on weekends join the Prime Minister's party at Chequers, where they played bezique, Churchill's favorite card game, until two or three o'clock in the morning. The old parlor game required 192 cards, and with his stubby fingers, he found the task of shuffling them a daunting, time-consuming challenge; but while he contended with slithering cards, he would talk in stream of consciousness about whatever was on his mind. He liked to play the game with Harriman because Averell was a willing sounding board, a source of reliable gossip, or a formidable card-playing adversary, depending upon Churchill's mood. More importantly, he was the epitome of discretion.

For Harriman, the old parlor game became a valuable instrument of diplomacy. Over the course of the war, he and Churchill played hundreds of hours in good times and bad—in the garden at Chequers, at Churchill's hideaway at Chartwell, in heavy seas crossing the Atlantic, on the Prime Minister's train, and aboard thundering American bombers. Although there were times when the Prime Minister's spirits flagged and he played the game to escape his burdens, he was more often talkative. While Harriman dealt the cards, the PM would try out proposals he was thinking of putting to Roosevelt, ruminate over problems with

Beaverbrook, or formulate climactic lines for speeches. Churchill was a genuinely bad player, while Harriman was as good at bezique as he was at bridge and gin rummy. The Prime Minister regularly lost and often squared accounts by writing Harriman a personal check on the spot—a draft for two or three pounds and change drawn on Cox's and King's branch of Lloyds bank.

The games were therapeutic for both. They helped Harriman become an adept reader of Churchill's moods and quirks as well as Roosevelt's and Hopkins's open line to Britain. They also made him a member of the Prime Minister's extended family. For a time, the circle also included John Winant, whose commitment to Britain's cause was as unequivocal as Averell's. Alexander Woollcott, who ordinarily passed out anything except bouquets, considered the Harriman-Winant tandem and concluded that the United States was "more credibly represented" in London than it had been since the eighteenth century, when Benjamin Franklin crossed the Atlantic as a special emissary for the colonies.[1]

Certainly there had been no time when diplomacy was more personal. Besides Harry Hopkins and all the military and political friends now brought together in the war against Hitler, Harriman and Churchill had mutual long-standing social friendships on both sides of the ocean. Duff Cooper, the veteran diplomat who served a tour as the British cabinet minister of information in 1940 and 1941, and his wife had been Harriman's guests at Arden. Churchill had known the financier and elder statesman Bernard Baruch since World War I, and he had long been acquainted with Averell's croquet rival and self-appointed adviser, Herbert Swope.

The Prime Minister was fascinated by Baruch's great fortune—as he undoubtedly was by Harriman's—and the mysterious workings of Wall Street. Over and over, he told Averell the tale of how he had begun investing in the American stock market during a long visit to the United States in 1929 and, having profited handsomely—with the help of tips from Baruch—had waded deeply into speculation just before the collapse. Recently out of office as chancellor of the exchequer, he had gotten a £10,000 advance for a book, but he lost £20,000 in a single day when Wall Street was caught in the terrible maelstrom. He had gone home to England chastened and facing a long, slow recovery from his losses. Still, when he would tell Harriman about the debacle, he would fantasize aloud about "what a wonderful life it would be to be a speculator."[2]

Unlike a good many of the Prime Minister's intimates, especially Beaverbrook and Brendan Bracken, the minister of information, Harriman was also a favorite of Churchill's wife, Clementine. They were backgammon rivals, and rulers of Chequers's croquet lawn where, except for each other, they had no competition worthy of the name. In continuing challenges to Mrs. Churchill, regulars at Chequers had tried bastard forms of the game—versions called robber croquet and golf croquet among them—but achieved no more success than they had under classical English rules. So, when mallets were brought out on the first chilly weekend of the 1941 season, her regular victims watched with unconcealed joy as the American newcomer administered her first defeat in the memory of anyone there.

Clementine's affection for Harriman was cemented when he helped dissuade her daughter Mary from a hasty wartime marriage. The Churchills' youngest was then seventeen, and feeling left out because everyone else, it seemed, had a mission to fulfill in the war. She was being assiduously courted by Eric Duncannon, a son of Lord Bessborough, who had been governor general of Canada during the 1930s. When the young soldier suggested marriage, she was ready to accept, though neither of them had looked beyond the end of the war. Matrimony, it seemed, was the only means they had to take some control of their uncertain lives.

Mrs. Churchill had nothing against Mary's suitor, but was categorically opposed to the talk of marriage because of her daughter's age and the uncertain atmosphere. Considering the matrimonial experience of her two other daughters, her anxiety was well-founded. Her second daughter, Diana, had already been divorced, and the eldest, Sarah, was headed in that direction. Randolph's marriage to Pamela Digby had begun showing signs of stress far too soon. Churchill himself had always been too busy to counsel the older children on their marriage plans, and now he was too preoccupied with the war and the coming and going of visitors to comprehend how far the teenage romance had gone or how much it distressed his wife. He kept promising that when the time came he would be firm and simply explain to Mary that she must wait, but he never found time for a heart-to-heart talk. On the weekend when it seemed that he finally had to deal with it, the Prime Minister and his party went to Ditchley, the country estate of American-born MP Ronald Tree in Oxfordshire, but as circumstances turned out, it was anything but the right atmosphere for a long talk about love and marriage.

On that Saturday night, May 10, London was hit by the worst air raid of the war. Incendiary bombs destroyed the House of Commons, damaged Westminster Abbey, started more than two thousand fires, and killed three thousand people. While reports of the disaster were still coming in, Churchill received word that one of Hitler's principal henchmen, Deputy Führer Rudolf Hess, had parachuted into Scotland and declared himself to be on a mission to make peace with Britain. It was, said Churchill, as if Britain's foreign secretary "had parachuted from a stolen Spitfire into the grounds of Berchtesgaden."[3] The news came as

Churchill, Harriman, and several others were watching a Marx brothers movie.

Mary Churchill, meanwhile, was going ahead with plans to announce her wedding intentions just three days later, in spite of the pleas from her mother. On Sunday, Clementine Churchill turned to their American guest for help with her family crisis, having no inkling of the irony in using Harriman as a counselor.

He had hardly been a traditional father. During his daughters' early years, his far-flung business interests and polo had kept him on the move. When he and Kitty divorced in 1929, Mary was twelve years old and Kathleen was eleven, and the girls had gone to live with their mother. As teenagers, both were off to the Foxcroft School in Virginia, and then to Bennington College in Vermont. Six years after Kitty's marriage to Eugene Pool, a prominent New York surgeon, she died of cancer, and Averell invited the girls to live and travel with him and Marie. But by then they were young adults.

Though he had less experience advising teenaged girls than Mrs. Churchill imagined, he talked with Mary about his own daughters, the uncertainty of the war, and the risk of hasty decisions. His daughter Mary had been married just a year earlier at Arden, but she was twenty-three and had graduated from college; her husband had completed medical school and started his practice. Kathleen, having no intention of marrying soon, was expected in London momentarily. Churchill's daughter had already heard all of the reminders about the seriousness of marriage, the opportunities before her, how her view of the world would soon change. But she was touched that Harriman was also a willing listener who patiently waited for her to talk herself out before he began reminding her of all the things she needed to consider.[4] Accepting from him the same advice she had spurned when it came from her mother, she went to Duncannon and told him she had decided to postpone their announcement.

Shortly thereafter, the secret engagement was dissolved; and in the fall, Mary found a place in the war by joining the Auxiliary Territorial Service and going off to train for service in an antiaircraft battery. Before she left, she wrote to Averell and thanked him for his "sympathy and helpfulness at Ditchley. It was most sweet of you—when you are so busy and have so many important claims on your time—to listen so patiently to a recital of my stupidities and heart aches. You helped me such a lot—and made me take myself less seriously—which was an excellent thing!"[5]

The interest he displayed in Mary was just the beginning of an avid courtship of the Churchill family. Every time he visited New York and Washington, he returned to London with bags bulging with items that had long since disappeared from stores in England—smoked Virginia hams, fresh fruit, handkerchiefs, stockings, cigars.

His being gathered into both the personal and official family of the Prime Minister was hardly surprising, for he was in 1941 the most important American in England: not only was he the President's symbolic representative, but he was a vital cog in the increasingly complex meshing of the military bureaucracies, the embodiment of the Lend-Lease program, and the symbol of the American financial and industrial machine.

He was also congenial company, available for dinners, weekends in the country, and tours of military bases, hospitals, and feeding stations. Harriman's intimacy with the Churchills, in addition to his personal ties to Hopkins and Roosevelt, made him the middleman in the extraordinary friendship between the President and the Prime Minister. When he was in Washington, Roosevelt would show him secret personal letters to Churchill, inviting him to read them before delivery. In London, the Prime Minister used him to critique cables being drafted for dispatch to the President. Harriman was unfailingly deferential, but he soon realized that Churchill was showing him messages because he wanted and expected to be challenged. "If you gave in, he paid no attention to your comments," Harriman later recalled. "But if you stood up to him, he'd pay attention. I would frequently say, 'Mr. Prime Minister, I would like your permission to raise this subject again at a later time.' But very frequently the next morning I would get a message . . . He would say, 'Read this.' It would be a telegram revised in accordance with my suggestion and I would say, 'I think this is all right.' "[6]

The circumstances unavoidably created problems for Winant. Without stopping to consider that he was poaching on embassy turf, the more aggressive Harriman took over a host of matters properly belonging to the ambassador, and Winant's relationship with the Prime Minister consequently faded. During his first weeks on the job, Winant had been what Colville called "almost an appendage of the Prime Minister."[7] The relationship extended to the rest of the family as well. He was, "a dear friend of us all, entering into our joys and sorrows, jokes and rows (in these last always as a peace-maker)," said Mary Churchill. "He was particularly fond of Clementine, and intuitively understood her character and the strains and difficulties in her life."[8]

In contrast to Joseph Kennedy, who left London during the blitz and opposed the Lend-Lease program when he returned to Washington, Winant went out of his way to share personally the tribulations the war imposed on ordinary people. He lived on British rations and took a Grosvenor Square flat next door to the embassy rather than use the ambassador's official residence. On mornings after air raids, he was always in the streets, offering encouragement to people who had lost homes, businesses, and families. His gaunt face, deep-set eyes, and unruly forelock gave him a noticeable and constantly noted resemblance to Abraham Lincoln, and he soon became more widely recognized than Harriman to ordinary people. With the working class and with Churchill's Labourite critics, he had a special cachet, for he had come to his diplomatic post after serving as head of the International Labor Organization. As much as the ambassador's integrity and sympathy for Britain were admired, he had weaknesses that were discreetly noted by the Foreign Office, where he was described as "very earnest and very shy, and, therefore, a poor mixer and not blessed with small talk."[9]

With Harriman's arrival to tend the lifeline, operating independently and in far more substantive contact with the White House and 10 Downing Street, Winant drifted into eclipse. American correspondents, ever sensitive to the ebb and flow of influence, were quick to recognize what was happening. Most of them were young, and all of them were attuned to military issues, so they found it more useful and more enjoyable to pursue Harriman, and he cultivated their friendship. Harrison Salisbury, a United Press correspondent, was somewhat offended at the way many of his colleagues began to brush off the ambassador. Continuing to call on him regularly, Salisbury more than most of the others realized how far Winant had been pushed into the background. "Averell not only took the glamour out of Winant's job," Salisbury said many years later, "he substantively undercut his relationship with Churchill." Like others who called on the ambassador, Salisbury would go to his office and find him sitting in near darkness. Sometimes minutes would pass before he spoke a word.[10]

Harriman, meanwhile, led a thriving operation. As soon as furniture could be borrowed, his eight-man mission had commandeered twenty-seven rooms in the building adjacent to the embassy, and he settled into a huge office that had once been the living room of an opulent flat. With the extra space, he was in a position to invite all manner of visiting government officials to use his quarters, and through them to keep attuned to matters far afield from his mission. He controlled his own payroll and his own communications, operating with little regard to the State Department. Not surprisingly, the embassy official most incensed by the Harriman operation was Brigadier General Raymond E. Lee, the military attaché, who saw himself becoming irrelevant and complained that Harriman was using his position "to interfere in anything and everything."[11] Lee looked forward to Averell's special missions that took him away from London, but he discovered that when Averell was gone, members of the Lend-Lease-mission staff moved in to protect the turf they had taken from the ambassador. Although it was to no avail, the embassy warned British officials that when Harriman was away they could expect Brigadier General Alfred Glancy of the Lend-Lease mission to "meddle in business which is not his concern."[12]

By summer, Winant himself was having serious doubts about his position. The only responsibilities left to him, he complained, were trivial things that could easily have been handled by a middle-level foreign-service officer. When he asked Washington to clarify his authority, he received assurances only in the form of boilerplate job descriptions extracted from government manuals. Rumors recurred that Averell was about to replace him. Aware that Winant felt threatened and undercut, Harriman tried, at first anyway, to shore up his colleague at home. "I want to tell you of the complete confidence and respect that your Ambassador has won from all classes of people in England," he wrote the President in April 1941. "He will become, I believe, before he leaves the most beloved American who has ever been to England. His sympathies are warm, his devotion complete, and his judgment sound. I appreciate the opportunity of working with him."[13]

The sensitivity of the situation was not lost upon the White House. When Hopkins visited London in July 1941 to set the stage for the Roosevelt-Churchill meeting off the coast of Newfoundland, his instructions included a directive from the President to tell Churchill that Harriman's role was to implement Lend-Lease, not make policy.

At the embassy, he picked up more reports of Winant's being embarrassed by Averell's taking charge, and he assured the unhappy General Lee that already he "had given Harriman the most strict and explicit instructions not to touch anything which is any way political. That is the ambassador's business and his alone." He said he had "also told Churchill that we had at the moment in England the best, the finest, and most highly qualified man for ambassador that we have had for 25 years, and a man who is the sincere friend of Great Britain, and therefore that he must deal with Winant direct and fully in all matters which had any political aspect whatever."[14] On the face of it, it appeared that Harriman had received a thorough dressing down, but there is every reason to conclude that he was chastised with a wink, if indeed at all. More than once, in the presence of Kathleen and Randolph Churchill's wife, Pamela, Hopkins was heard to casually warn Averell to "be careful" because Winant "was, after all, the ambassador."[15]

After Hopkins's departure, there was no change. Averell only became more important in the Roosevelt-Churchill relationship, and Hopkins himself would make it clear that he considered Harriman the key figure in London. When Mrs. Roosevelt visited England in 1942, he told her she need not bother with the ambassador, she should deal with Averell. The First Lady, who was especially fond of the ambassador and always dubious about Averell, did quite the opposite.[16]

Winant wondered whether Harriman hadn't quickly grown too big for the Lend-Lease job. By August when he left for Moscow to work out aid arrangements with Stalin, the ambassador wondered aloud whether he would return, and his demeanor suggested that inside he fervently hoped not.[17]

* * *

When Harriman flew to London to take up his mission for Roosevelt, Marie stayed in New York. Not long after their marriage, she had begun having difficulty seeing while driving an automobile, and doctors discovered that she was suffering from glaucoma. By the time Averell went into war-mobilization work in Washington, she had already undergone eye surgery; her condition was a source of continuing concern and required constant attention. Under the circumstances, specialists caring for her deemed it inadvisable for her to leave the city for a prolonged stay. She probably would not have gone to England in any case.

She had her art gallery and a menagerie of children for whom she was responsible, even though there were governesses and various others to look after them. Her own children, Harry and Nancy Whitney, were away in prep school, but living in an Arden cottage where she moved after the mansion was occupied by the Navy were Betty and Nikki Brierley, two English girls who had been evacuated from the blitz and taken in before Averell's departure, and Peter Duchin, who had become to her the son she and Averell never had.

The boy had been in her care since 1938, when he was a year old. His mother, who had been Marie's classmate, best friend, and collaborator in decorating the Sun Valley Lodge, had died a few days after his birth. Suffering a serious lung ailment, he had spent the first year of his life in California; then, when he was strong enough, Marie had him moved to Arden where he spent his boyhood while his father, Eddy, toured the country with his orchestra. To him, Marie was "Ma"; and to her, Peter was as close as her own children.

Averell was alone in London for only two months before Kathleen arrived. Just out of Bennington, she had solicited the help of Steve Hannagan in lining up her London job with Hearst's International News Service, and used the personal intercession of Harry Hopkins to get State Department permission for her trip. But when she left New York on a flying boat following her father's route through Bermuda, the Azores, and Lisbon, she had no intention of remaining abroad for the duration of the war; she had taken the Hearst job mainly to help get the State Department's approval for a visit with her father.

Having heard little from him since his arrival, she found the war devastation worse than anything she had imagined. But she was mesmerized by the atmosphere of tragedy, defiance, patriotism, and romance; and she was as impressed as she was surprised to find Averell a significant figure in the drama that now captivated and alarmed Americans. "He literally knows everyone of note," Kathleen wrote Marie days after her arrival, "everyone who has a constructive part in the workings of the war, and they all love him."[18]

Harriman was still living out of his suitcases. Occupying a ground floor suite at the Dorchester Hotel just off Hyde Park, he was at one of the busiest crossroads in what remained of free Europe. The hotel had become the more-or-less permanent residence of royalty displaced by German tanks, transient generals and admirals, American businessmen, and politicians from across the continent. With the blitz, some well-to-do Londoners left their houses and flats and moved in because the building was located near the Hyde Park battery of ack-ack guns, and had a steel frame, which everyone assumed made it safer than older London buildings.

Kathleen occupied Averell's tiny sitting room, and in her spare hours began a search for more permanent quarters—with the help of Pamela Churchill, the Prime Minister's daughter-in-law, who was also living in the hotel and working in an office at the Supply Ministry. Randolph Churchill's wife, wrote Kathleen to her sister Mary, was "a wonderful girl, my age, but one of the wisest young girls I've ever met—knows everything about everything, political and otherwise."[19] She also wrote Marie all about her new friend, and Marie, appreciating the kindness to her stepdaughter, sent along little presents for Pamela's seven-month-old baby, Winston Churchill II, accompanied by affectionate notes.

It was soon thereafter—before she had been in London a month— that Kathleen discovered that her new pal was also her father's lover. Since she had heard about his long liaison with Teddy Gerard, and since the war had obviously brought on an epidemic of marriage suspensions, she was less surprised than she would have been otherwise, and she kept the little secret to herself. It was nothing to discuss with either her father or her friend, and it was certainly nothing that she planned to report to Marie. Nevertheless, she decided that she would stay in England rather than going home to the comfort and security of New York.

Pamela Digby Churchill was in the spring of 1941 but twenty-one years old, more than a year younger than Kathleen. She had dimples, light red hair, becoming freckles, a splendid figure, and what Evelyn Waugh called "kitten eyes full of innocent fun."[20] She was not a beautiful woman in the classic sense, her female contemporaries would sniff jealously, for she did have freckles and was a bit round-faced. But she was, nevertheless, stunningly attractive. It was not altogether because she was Churchill's daughter-in-law that *Life* magazine had put her on its cover the previous January. She was jolly and uninhibited, but she was also sophisticated beyond her years. She was as comfortable with the diplomats, ranking military officers, exiled royalty, and displaced chiefs of government as she was with people her own age—self-assured without being bold, charming without seeming to work at it. She was an asset to the Harrimans as well as the Churchills, especially socially. "I made another of my lovely social errors last night," Kathleen reported to her sister after several months in London. "Coming into the Dorchester at about ten o'clock, Pam and I met a friend with an obvious foreigner. They were both being very funny and I thought perhaps drunk. I was introduced to the foreigner and as you know, I never listen to names. I said 'How do do' and left it at that. Pam curtseyed and made a helluva fuss. It turned out to be the King of Greece."[21]

Worldly as she was, the young Mrs. Churchill had recently been a country girl. She was born on a 1,500-acre estate in Dorset, the eldest daughter of the eleventh Lord Digby and Lady Digby—"Carnation" and "Pansy," they were affectionately called, out of their attachment to their favorite flowers. The Digby family was not a great one, but a good, solid one—conservative, public-spirited, faithful in service to the crown and to Dorset. Lord and Lady Digby were caricatures of country aristocrats, he the gentleman farmer, gardener, dairyman, and breeder of Guernsey cattle, polo ponies, and hunters; she the activist in Dorset charities, patron of schools and garden clubs. During World War I, he had commanded a battalion of the Cold Stream Guards and was twice wounded in France. With Hitler's invasion of Poland, he returned to uniform—as did Lady Digby—with the rank of general and a war-office assignment as assistant inspector of infantry.

Faithful to tradition, the Digbys envisioned for their eldest daughter a life like her mother's—a comfortable marriage to a dependable man like her father and a house like Minterne. Put on ponies soon after she learned to walk, she was at home in the show ring; and by the time she was a teenager she was not only at home in the show ring but rode to hounds with manly confidence. As a child, she was socially and intellectually precocious, and as an adolescent, headstrong, impetuous, bored with Dorset, and determined to live in the city.

In time, she would evoke memories of her great aunt, Jane Digby, who had scandalized the family when she abandoned her husband, Lord Ellenborough, and her infant son to follow Austria's Prince Felix Schwarzenberg across Europe. She was subsequently the friend, confidante, and, evidently, lover of Bavaria's King Ludwig I before taking German, Greek, and Bedouin husbands in that order. It was said that she was still beautiful when she died in Damascus in 1881 at the age of seventy-four, voluntarily exiled from England for nearly half a century and dividing her last years between her house in the Syrian capital and her husband's tent in the desert.

Carnation and Pansy's eldest daughter was fascinated by the story, but she was never permitted to know the juicy details of Lady Ellenborough's career because Lord Digby had perused Jane's diary and excised most of it except the first and last twenty pages. Long before Lady Jane's carefree affront to Victorian propriety, a distant ancestor, Sir Everard Digby, had burned the name into English history. Tutored by Francis Bacon and knighted by King James I, he was beheaded at the tender age of twenty-eight for his role in the Gunpowder Plot, a conspiracy to blow up the King and all of Parliament in protest against the sovereign's anti-Catholic laws.

When she was fourteen, Pamela finally talked her family into letting her go away to boarding school in Hertfordshire. There, her classmates included Winston Churchill's niece, Clarissa, and girls from London who remembered her as chubby, a little shy, and not quite as clever at games as her friends from the city. But she was on her way; she never really returned to the country again. In the fall of 1937, when she was seventeen, she went to Germany to begin her "finishing off," as it was called. The custom at the time was for upper-class English girls to take a year in Germany, France, or Italy; her choice was Munich, in part because the Digbys had relatives not far away in Austria, which made her parents feel more comfortable. It was also a big moment of self-assertion and independence for her, for she had grown up on her father's frightening stories about the Germans in World War I and on his fuming about the tactics and radicalism of Hitler and his ruffians.

She lived in Munich for half of her year abroad, and then moved on to Paris and the Sorbonne. Although she found the Hitler fanatics and their strutting and glowering frightening, she got in touch with Unity Mitford, a friend of the family and one of the famous English sisters who had become devoted Nazis. While Unity's beautiful sister Diana had secretly married the British Fascist Sir Oswald Mosley, Unity had moved to Germany and become a Hitler groupie. Out of curiosity, Pamela jumped at the opportunity to go along to tea with her hero, the Chancellor. There was nothing memorable about the conversation, other than Hitler's acknowledgment of her presence and a perfunctory welcome to Germany. She found him personally less threatening and less maniacal than the figure she had expected from hearing his ranting on the radio and seeing his pictures at rallies and military parades. Nevertheless, the atmosphere he created was intimidating, and the adoring followers such as Unity Mitford were unfathomable.

She was still a student at the Sorbonne when Hitler annexed Austria and sent German tanks into Czechoslovakia. In April 1939, with Britain introducing conscription, erecting antiaircraft defenses, and vowing to come to Poland's rescue if attacked, she went home to London. That fall, days after Hitler's invasion of Poland and Britain's declaration of war, she met Winston Churchill's son, Randolph, whose work for the London *Daily Mail* had made him one of the country's best-known journalists. He was by then a twenty-eight-year-old Army lieutenant at home on a weekend pass and at loose ends because the mobilization had scattered his cronies almost overnight.

Pamela was nineteen, a little lonely, a little frightened, but determined to hang on in London and get into the war effort on her own terms rather than go back to Dorset or follow her younger sister, Sheila, who had been enlisted in the Army by their mother and was already cooking in an officers' mess. Since she was fluent in French and spoke passable German, she was able to find a job as a translator at the Foreign Office. She was introduced to Randolph by Lady Mary Dunn, a mutual friend who was in the process of moving out of the city for the security of a house in the country. On a Saturday afternoon in September, she went to Lady Dunn's flat, which she was about to rent, and she was there when Randolph telephoned in search of a dinner companion. Unavailable, Lady Dunn put Pamela on the telephone.

According to Randolph's cousin, Anita Leslie, he was chacteristically blunt, and she coquettish. "Mary Dunn said I could invite you out to dinner," said he. "What do you look like?"

"Red-headed and rather fat," she replied, "but Mummy says that puppy fat disappears."[22] They went to dinner, and Randolph fully lived up to Mary Dunn's description of him as "slightly impossible, but good company."[23] He was smitten and she was amused, and both were looking for a balance wheel as they were swept along in the early days of the war with little control of their lives. There was a frenetic courtship over three successive weekends, then an engagement announcement. She had not yet paid the second month's rent on Mary Dunn's flat.

But for the war, Lord and Lady Digby might have counseled caution—in his travels Randolph's reputation for boozing and chasing girls had more than kept pace with his notoriety as a journalist. But back in uniform, both parents were too preoccupied with the war for lengthy consultation about wedding plans, not that they could have exerted any influence on their headstrong daughter anyway. A match with the Churchills was obviously a good one for the first family of Dorset, abundant evidence of Randolph's unreliability notwithstanding. With the benefit of a special license exempting them from the normal thirty-day waiting period, they were married on October 4, a week after Poland was partitioned by Hitler and Stalin and the day after the surrender of the last significant units of the Polish army.

Crowds stood outside St. John's Church in Westminster applauding as the wedding party arrived and as the couple departed beneath an arch of swords formed by the groom's fellow officers. Randolph was resplendent in the uniform of a cavalry lieutenant and his bride exquisite in a long, navy coat, adorned by a fox fur collar dyed to match. But the war was not far away. Guests and even the rector of St. John's, who officiated, carried their gas masks to the ceremony. And, as Churchill, just named First Lord of the Admiralty for the second time in his career, left the church for the reception at Admiralty House, there were cheers along with shouts of "Good Luck, Sir," "God bless you, Sir" from the spectators on the sidewalk.

Romantic as it was at the beginning, the union was a calamity. Some of Randolph's friends thought he had been swept away not so much by Pamela's charms as by a melodramatic notion that he must perpetuate the Churchill line before laying down his life for his country. If he indeed had visions of death, he successfully concealed them. As much as anything, Pamela had been taken with his supreme confidence not only in himself but in Britain's eventual triumph over the Nazis. Others Randolph's age would leave the 400 Club, a dining and dancing club where he and other young, upper-class Londoners were regulars, on their last night before shipping out, dramatically presenting their scotch bottle to Rossi, the maître d', predicting they would never return for it. Not Randolph. He had been an early Nazi hater, predicting at the time of Hitler's election that it would lead to war, and he took it as Britain's destiny to eliminate the Nazi scourge. In his heroic view of himself and Britain, Pamela found "an enormous sense of relief that there was somebody who really believed that there was a future."[24]

For her, the marriage was a declaration of independence: "You were treated as a child until you got married. The status of being married gave you your first freedom."[25] But, impressed with the Churchill name, she had married a man she hardly knew, taken with the exceeding good looks that went with his confidence in the future. After the wedding, she briefly took up the role of an Army officer's wife, first at her husband's station on the Salisbury Plain, and then in Yorkshire. In the spring of 1940, Randolph's 4th Hussars were shipped off to Scotland, and she returned to London, moving into her in-laws' flat on the top floor of Admiralty House.

She was showing her first signs of pregnancy when Hitler invaded Holland, Belgium, Luxembourg, and France, and the King summoned Churchill to Buckingham Palace and asked him to become Prime Minister. Less than a year out of finishing school, she lived at 10 Downing Street.

As the baby's arrival approached, London endured night after night of pounding by two hundred or more German bombers. The windows were blown out at 10 Downing, and the family's bedrooms were moved into the basement. Because hospitals were filled with people maimed and burned by the bombs, leaving no place for routine maternity cases, Pamela went to Chequers with her mother-in-law to await the baby's arrival.

In the country, she was bored, lonely, uncomfortable, and indignant at her obstetrician, who saw her case as his opportunity to escape the nightly bombing. Beginning many days before the baby was due, the doctor arrived at Chequers to check on her each evening, and then decided he should remain overnight in the event that the baby decided to come while London was under attack, making it impossible for him to return promptly.

With the arrival more than a week overdue, she insisted upon going back into the city to see Randolph sworn into the House of Commons. He had made two futile campaigns for a seat several years earlier, seemingly putting an end to his political aspirations. But on October 10, 1940, he came home from his military post in Scotland to be sworn in to fill a seat vacated by a member's death. Under orders from her cautious physician, Pamela and Clementine arrived in the visitors' gallery armed with a large box of laughing gas in case she suddenly went into labor during the ceremony.

Winston Churchill II, the PM's first grandson, was born two days later, the first baby delivered at Chequers in two hundred years. It had momentarily appeared that the event would have to be arranged elsewhere, for on the previous afternoon a German bomb had hit the grounds, raising fears that Luftwaffe pilots had succeeded in targeting the Prime Minister's country residence.

It was a happy occasion for the Churchills. Having seen their daughter Diana end her first marriage after less than a year, and Sarah run off to America and marry an actor seventeen years older than she, they were hoping Pamela would cause their spoiled son to settle down. But baby Winston's arrival was not enough to save a marriage that had begun to go sour within months. Neither wedlock nor impending fatherhood appreciably changed Randolph. When he came home on leave just before the baby's birth, he had created an uproar at 10 Downing by promptly disappearing and staying out all night, storming about a suite at the Savoy, giving speeches to show friends that in Parliament he would be a greater orator than his father. He got home after sunrise, leaving classified military maps in his unlocked car where they were found and turned in by security people, making the Prime Minister so livid he refused to speak to him for hours.

His wife was furious at him as well, and for additional reasons of her own. While he was stationed in Scotland, Randolph's gambling debts had accumulated until she was forced to go to the Prime Minister for financial help. Infuriated, Randolph accused her of trying to turn his family against him, but then made passionate resolutions to change and broke them before going back to his regiment.

A few months later, when he left for the Middle East, she accepted still another pledge that he would stop gambling so they could live on his military salary. On the strength of the unequivocal commitment, she moved out of 10 Downing, took a small house outside London, and even disposed of some of their wedding gifts to raise cash for his debts; but before the boxes were unpacked, Randolph was back at it. Aboard ship on the way to Egypt, he lost eight hundred pounds, and when he got to Cairo, his luck got even worse. She was too stubborn to confess the crisis to her parents; she had already been to the Churchills; so she turned to Lord Beaverbrook for a loan. Then vowing to take care of herself, she put the baby in the care of a nanny, found a job at the Supply Ministry, and moved into the Dorchester.

She met Harriman at the hotel the first week he was in London. Lady Emerald Cunard, one of the city's foremost hostesses and party givers, had moved out of her house on Grosvenor Square for the safety of the hotel early in the blitz. There, she gave a regular Wednesday-night dinner for the residents, and Pamela often went. On this chilly evening in March, Harriman was Lady Cunard's star attraction, fresh from America and believed by many to be the leader of an advance party preceding the United States' entry into the war. Quite naturally, he was seated by the Prime Minister's daughter-in-law, and found her captivating.

In the midst of dinner, the air raid sirens started to wail and the whole party trooped downstairs with their wineglasses and resumed their conversations. The rest of the guests heard less than they had hoped about Lend-Lease, because the expediter was not chatty when it came to war business. Besides, he was more interested in talking with Pamela.

As he waited for the end of the second German air raid since arriving in England, she gave him a useful briefing on Lord Beaverbrook, whom he was about to meet to discuss aircraft production. Beaverbrook had a reputation for being temperamental and difficult as well as for being the adviser with unmatched influence on Churchill, and Pamela was practically a member of his family, too. Beaverbrook was Baby Winston's godfather, and the child was in fact living much of the time at his Cherkley estate in Surrey when he was not at Chequers. But not only did Pamela know Beaverbrook, it seemed that she knew everyone.

It did not occur to Averell that she was barely twenty-one, nor did she think about his being nearly fifty. In the atmosphere of wartime, age, like the past and the future, lost its relevance. She knew nothing of the Union Pacific railroad, Sun Valley, his polo career, his politics, or his family. She did know that as Lend-Lease expediter and Roosevelt's and Hopkins's emissary, he was the most important American in London. What she later remembered most about the dinner and waiting out the air raid together was that Roosevelt's diffident millionaire was devastatingly attractive: "He was the most beautiful man I had ever met. He was marvelous, absolutely marvelous with his raven black hair . . . very athletic, very tan, very healthy."[26]

Well aware of her father's affinity for beautiful women, Kathleen Harriman was neither shocked nor offended when the extent of his friendship with Pamela became obvious to her. Her own relationship with her father had become one of easy friendship. She had long since begun addressing him as Averell or Ave, and he treated her as a friend and intimate colleague. While her relations with Marie had always been cordial, there had never existed the kind of devotion that would have caused her to be concerned about her stepmother's interests. So she did nothing to intrude or even suggest that she suspected anything. She did decide, however, to stay on in London where she could at least watch Averell's flanks. Her presence as much as anything kept the affair from becoming blatantly obvious. Not even Bob Meiklejohn, Harriman's personal secretary, had an inkling that the young Mrs. Churchill was anything more than a pal to Kathleen.

To correspondents, warriors, ambassadors, and officials of governments in exile, Harriman and his daughter became principal attractions of London. In a city short of nearly everything, they were showered with theater tickets, gasoline rationing stamps, attention, and invitations. "Life is unbelievably social," Kathleen wrote her sister. "God only knows why. Every night next week is booked up already and the weekend hasn't started. The only thing people seem scared about is being lonely, so they date up way ahead of time to ensure against an evening alone."[27] At the Dorchester, the Savoy, or Claridges, they were surrounded. At Churchill's dinners at Chequers, Beaverbrook's parties at Cherkley, and diplomatic affairs that would have otherwise been grim and overburdened by the war, they were ornaments that sparkled. When William Walton of *Time* magazine arrived to take up his assignment as a war correspondent, he asked his colleague Mary Welsh—later Mrs. Ernest Hemingway—to introduce him to the most beautiful redhead in London. Pamela shortly appeared to give him a tour of the city. Like most of Harriman's friends, the Churchills did not see anything unusual in Pamela's constant presence in the Harriman circle. But a few who knew the young Churchills' marriage had been foolish and hopeless from the beginning caught the little signs of affection, and there were whispers among them that Averell was creeping down the chilly corridor to another warm bed on Saturday nights at Chequers. One of the first to seriously suspect anything was the Prime Minister's private secretary, John Colville. In mid-April, on a morning after 450 German planes raided London in waves, he went for an early-morning walk to survey the massive damage. Few others had yet emerged; but crossing the Horse Guards Parade, he encountered an unsuspecting Averell and Pamela walking arm-in-arm. The tenderness between Randolph's wife and the tall American envoy, who had been in the country only a month, was unmistakable, and Colville jotted down a note in his diary. At Chequers, Diana Churchill Sandys's perceptive husband, Duncan, intercepted glances, felt vibrations and came to his own conclusion that Roosevelt's special envoy had more than an avuncular interest in Pamela. Like Colville, he kept what he knew to himself.

While Averell was in the Middle East in the summer of 1941, Pamela and Kathleen rented a house in the country where they could relax on weekends and where the nanny could live with baby Winston. There, with remarkable ease, they could escape the war that had battered and blackened London, leaving the homeless to sleep in subways, schoolhouses, and recreation halls, and stand in line for meals at communal feeding centers. From the wharves on the Thames and burned-out working-class neighborhoods to Whitehall and St. Paul's Cathedral, block after block lay in rubble and ashes.

But in the country, their two-century-old cottage was serene, surrounded by wildflowers and fields of grazing sheep and cattle. The only sounds from the war came from an occasional convoy on a road nearby and the planes passing overhead. "This weekend, seven of us sat in the garden and watched the planes coming back from France," Kathleen wrote her sister. "If it hadn't been that three of the boys wore uniforms, it might have been on Long Island on a summer evening with transport planes flying overhead."[28]

The interludes gave Pamela the most time she'd ever had with her young son, but there were not many of them. She had, in addition to her job at the Supply Ministry, a feeding station which she sponsored. She had Randolph's political constituency to look after, and she joined Kathleen as a greeter and guide for the waves of Americans passing through London or settling into war work. The Yanks, Evelyn Waugh told Randolph after a visit to London, were "ubiquitous and boisterous" and had occupied "the place in England which the Germans had in Italy in 1939," but Pamela was showing "exemplary patience" with them.[29]

In the Middle East, Randolph himself had become fast friends with Roosevelt's expediter. After accompanying Averell on several of his inspections, he was an unabashed Harriman fan. "In 10 very full and active days he has definitely become my favourite American," he wrote his father from Alexandria, telling him he found Harriman "the most objective and shrewd of all those who are around you." He added, "I have become very intimate with him and he has admitted me to all the business he has transacted. I am sure you would do well to back his opinions on the situation out here to the limit."[30]

Randolph remained in the dark about Harriman and Pamela for months thereafter. When he arrived in London on a ten-day leave at the beginning of 1942, he was disappointed to find Harriman had gone to Washington. They exchanged telegrams filled with regret that they couldn't be together. "Randolph home for ten days," Pamela cabled. "Has already fallen for Kath. We make a happy trio. Wish you were with us."[31] From Washington, Harriman immediately wired Randolph that he was "bitterly disappointed" over the missed opportunity for a reunion. "Lots of things I wanted to talk out with you."[32] Kathleen was amused by it all, and baffled by her father's message to Randolph. On the face of it, the cable sounded as though Pamela were the subject in mind, but obviously that was not the case.

When Averell and Kathleen had left the Dorchester and moved into the apartment at Grosvenor Square adjacent to the embassy, Pamela had moved with them, later taking her own flat in the building. A year later, she was still the only English resident of the complex and so thoroughly Americanized that her friends claimed she had even acquired a Yank accent. She was, she confessed, "very much a promoter of the Americans," which was an understatement. She was also bored with the Supply Ministry, and she decided to quit the job and become a ferry pilot, seeing the delivery of planes to fighting forces as a more useful contribution than shuffling papers. Her friends were horrified. Clementine Churchill objected because of the baby and because Mary and Sarah Churchill, not to mention Randolph, were in uniform already. Kathleen argued that she drove an automobile only passably, was less than a whiz at mathematics, and therefore not prime pilot material. From Washington, Averell weighed in with discouragement of his own.

It looked as if they were all going to lose, until Brendan Bracken came up with the idea of a high-class service club where doctors, lawyers, businessmen, and other professionals finding themselves in uniform could mingle with their own kind. He even had the place for it—stately old Ashburnham House just behind Westminster Abbey. It had been the library of the Westminster School before the students were evacuated to the country, and remarkably it had come through the blitz unscathed.

With Mrs. Euan Wallace, the wife of Churchill's minister of agriculture, as her cohostess, Pamela opened the doors to an opening-night crowd that overwhelmed the kitchen, the bar, and all the club rooms. Dwight Eisenhower, then the U.S. Army's chief of operations in Washington and a visitor in town, realized that her kitchen was hopelessly undermanned and went back to help out with the cooking.

The huge success of the first night continued. She brought in entertainers and organized lectures on science, politics, and literature, but no matter who was on the program, the hostess was always the main attraction.

In April of 1942, Averell went to Northern Ireland with Hopkins and General Marshall to visit the first American troops sent across the Atlantic in preparation for an invasion of Europe, perhaps before the end of the year. While they were there, they stayed in a country house of a retired army officer, drinking from an old well on the property, and when Averell returned to London, he fell violently ill with paratyphoid.

He was wracked by chills and soaring fever and was at times delirious. Until they decided that professional nurses were required, Pamela and Kathleen took turns caring for him around the clock, feeding him oranges shipped in by Lord Gort, the British commander at Gibraltar, young Winston's baby food, and beef broth prepared by the chef at Claridge's.

It was about this time that Randolph finally learned the extent of the relationship between Averell and his increasingly distant wife, his suspicions confirmed by his brother-in-law Duncan Sandys, among others. As far as Randolph's marriage was concerned, it made no difference. The union was a wreck. Pamela's patience with his excesses had long since expired, and his ego was crushed by her prominence, most brutally when he came and heard himself ridiculed as "Mr. Pamela." During one of Randolph's visits, Evelyn Waugh walked into a family spat, which Lord Digby was unsuccessfully attempting to moderate, and went away certain that Pamela had come to hate her husband so much she could no longer bear to be in a room with him.

When he did realize that his wife had for months been Harriman's girlfriend, Randolph irrationally concluded that he had been deceived not only by his wife and the expediter but by his friends and even his parents. Winston and Clementine, he bitterly complained to John Colville, "had condoned adultery beneath their own roof."[33] There would be some who would later suspect that the Prime Minister chose not to know about the affair because Harriman was too important to him and to Britain. But Colville, for one, was certain that neither Winston nor Clementine Churchill was aware of it until years afterward. "They would have been horrified," he said, "and Lady Churchill would have been indignant."[34]

When Harriman's tour of duty in London ended in the fall of 1943, Pamela remained at Grosvenor Square and fell seriously in love with another American, the celebrated CBS correspondent Edward R. Murrow. But she stayed in close touch with Averell in Moscow, and he made it possible for her to be one of London's premier hostesses as the war's tide turned and the Allies slogged inexorably toward victory. John Colville was among her guests at what he remembered as "marvelously organized dinners." "We were really sort of puritanical in England about rationing," he said, "unlike Paris, where there was a great black market. Everybody took pride in sticking pretty closely to rationing. But if you dined with Pamela, you would have a five- or six-course dinner, eight or ten guests, and foods you didn't ordinarily see. My guess is that all of us around the table were sort of smirking and saying that Averell was taking good care of his girlfriend."[35]

When the war ended, divorce for Pamela and Randolph was only a formality. Before she instituted the proceedings, accusing him of desertion, she went and told her father-in-law, who had been turned out of office. It was painful to Churchill to see them part, but he said he could never wish her unhappiness, and in honesty, he knew that was all Randolph would ever bring her.[36] The decree was granted on December 18, Randolph offering no challenge to her charges. Three weeks later, the former prime minister wrote to Lady Digby to express continuing friendship for the family and his commitment to the happiness of their grandchild, Winston II. "I grieve so much for what has happened which put an end to so many hopes for Randolph and Pamela," he wrote. "The war strode in however through the lives of millions. We must make the best of what is left among the ruins."[37]

Several months after Pearl Harbor, Arden House, like the Sun Valley Lodge and the Challenger Inn, had been turned over to the Navy to become a convalescent hospital. Air raid lookouts were posted in the tower, and the railroad to the summit was ripped up for scrap iron. Marie moved her charges into smaller quarters, took an apartment on East Sixty-sixth Street, closed her gallery, and distributed its paintings between her cottage at Arden, the apartment, and the house at Sands Point. Thereafter, she devoted much of her time to volunteer work for the Ships Service Committee, organizing twice-a-week dances for sailors on shore leave in New York and raising money to buy them washing machines and amenities to put aboard ship.

Until he went off to the Navy himself, she had Eddy Duchin for male companionship, and an occasional boxing match at Madison Square Garden and her inept wartime New York Giants baseball team for diversion.

During the summer, she moved to Long Island, dividing her time between Sands Point and her sister's house at East Hampton, dealing each season with a new avalanche of teenagers' problems. Nancy crashed her car at East Hampton, and wound up in the hospital with a broken collarbone, while her passenger, Betty Brierley, lost a finger. Nikki Brierley, convinced that no one loved her on either side of the ocean, was receiving regular psychological counseling. And until he joined the Seabees, Marie's son, Harry, who was banned from various Long Island estates, celebrated his vacations with antics such as ripping about Arden in an open Model T, firing a shotgun at targets of opportunity and frightening horses, cattle, and tenants on the estate.

Considering Averell's attraction to beautiful women and the wartime circumstances that produced foolish marriages and saw good ones annulled, suspended, and dissolved by the millions, Marie found the news of Averell and Pamela hardly earthshaking. As much as his unfaithfulness annoyed her, she was a little amused that he would risk involvement with a woman as conspicuous as Pamela Churchill. She told him he was a fool. If he wished to continue the affair, she would divorce him, and he could go on his way. His response, Marie told her sister Frances, was a promise to end it. He could hardly have done otherwise. Even in wartime, a divorce would produce ruinous publicity. And since he was nearly thirty years older than Pamela, the idea of marriage did not seriously occur to either of them.

The problem was waiting to be resolved when Franklin Roosevelt took care of it by naming Averell ambassador to Moscow.

Chapter XIII

SECOND FRONT
Encore at the Kremlin

Six days after Pearl Harbor, Harriman traveled to Scotland with Churchill, Lord Beaverbrook, and Britain's top military leaders and boarded the spanking-new battleship *Duke of York* bound for the United States. With America outraged by the sneak attack in the Pacific, the Prime Minister was concerned that Washington might turn its attention to Japan and leave Britain and the Soviet Union to carry on the fight against Hitler alone. Both official communications and the American press in the first days after Pearl Harbor gave him the impression that "the whole fury of the nation would be turned upon Japan," and he worried that "the true proportion of the war" would be lost after the Japanese attack in the Pacific.[1]

Although the Atlantic crossing was perilous, it was urgent in Churchill's view for him and the President to sit down for a top-to-bottom discussion of Allied strategy against the Axis powers and to assess the industrial output required to carry on a full-blown world war. The duration of the struggle, the Prime Minister told Harriman, would be determined by the United States. If it decided to defend every town across the Pacific against the Japanese, the fighting might go on for five long years, but if the government in Washington was courageous and stuck to the President's commitment to defeat Hitler first—"then it can be finished in two years."[2]

The trip from Scotland to Hampton Roads, Virginia, took nearly ten rolling, tossing, miserable days. With waves breaking over the bow of the great ship, the passengers were confined to quarters for much of the voyage, and at times the ship's speed had to be reduced to no more than three knots so it would not outrun its storm-tossed destroyer escorts. Like Churchill, Harriman spent most of the days in his bunk, working on matters to be taken up in Washington and seeing his fellow passengers only in the wardroom for meals and for the movies shown after dinner. Except for the Prime Minister, few members of the party got over their seasickness. But dosing himself with Mothersill's tablets, the medication then in vogue for motion sickness, Churchill overcame his queasiness and regaled his companions with tales of seasickness and lectured them on the evolution of the life preserver and the procedures for ditching in case they were torpedoed or hit by German bombers.

After they docked at Hampton Roads on December 22, Churchill flew on to Washington, arriving in the early evening. Roosevelt was waiting for him at the airport and minutes later escorted him into the White House, the Prime Minister striding jauntily into the mansion, brandishing his special walking cane outfitted with a flashlight which helped him get around in the London blackout. His arrival on his first wartime visit to America was not publicly announced until he was inside the residence. Harriman and the rest of the party came by train hours later.

It had been less than two months since he had been home to report on his mission to Moscow with Beaverbrook, but Pearl Harbor and the declaration of war had turned Washington into a different city. Guards were stationed everywhere. There were air raid wardens on rooftops, blackout drills, and talk of sabotage. When the President left the White House, he rode in an armor-plated limousine; and wherever he went, he was surrounded by a beefed-up contingent of security men with revolvers and submachine guns. German and Japanese diplomats were still in the city, but their embassies were shuttered and surrounded by armed guards.

For the next two weeks, Roosevelt and Churchill were constantly together. The visit planned to last a week ran until the middle of January, when the Prime Minister broke away for a trip to Canada and then a short rest in Florida. At the White House, he was ensconced in a bedroom across the hall from Harry Hopkins, with his map room and command post set up near Roosevelt's own bedroom. The residence was brightly decorated for Christmas, and Churchill had to pick his way among wrapped gifts waiting to be distributed. As a gesture of respect, he pushed Roosevelt's wheelchair when they went about the mansion together, and as their deliberations progressed, he occasionally went into the President's bedroom during the morning to talk with his host, who, like himself, worked the first hours of the day in bed. He joined Roosevelt in the ceremonial lighting of the national Christmas tree on the south lawn of the White House, accompanied him to holiday religious services, and on the day after Christmas addressed a joint session of Congress.

The leaders were regularly joined by Beaverbrook, Hopkins, Secretary of War Henry Stimson, and the military chiefs, whose staffs held their own conference at the new Federal Reserve Building several blocks away on Constitution Avenue. But with much of the business being conducted between only Roosevelt and Hopkins on the U.S. side and Churchill and Beaverbrook for the British, General Marshall, now first among equals of the American chiefs of staff, and other military advisers feared that an exuberant Roosevelt would buy Churchill's agenda all too quickly.

They were soon given good reason to be concerned. With the country focused on the battle for Manila, the President offhandedly agreed on Christmas Eve that American reinforcements headed for the embattled islands in the Pacific could be turned over to the British if they were unable to get through. When the word got around, the American chiefs saw a British design to get the President to write off the Philippines and switch the Allies to a defense of Singapore instead. Marshall and General Henry H. Arnold, chief of the Army Air Corps, protested to Stimson, who went to Hopkins furiously objecting. In the face of Stimson's reaction and the firm opposition of the chiefs, Roosevelt backed down, contending that the conversation had been misrepresented.

But in the long, difficult talks, the conference, code-named Arcadia, produced much, beginning with a reaffirmation that the defeat of Hitler was the first strategic objective. Beyond that, the leaders drafted the framework for a "United Nations" coalition arrayed against the Axis and, upon the insistence of the United States, created a unified command—American, British, Dutch, Australian—for the gigantic new theater extending from the Bay of Bengal to Australia, with Britain's General Wavell named commander in chief. The latter was an idea that Harriman had been vigorously advocating to both Churchill and Roosevelt ever since his mission to the Middle East the previous summer. Churchill also agreed to strengthen British forces in the Pacific while Roosevelt promised to send American bombers to England. With the conference still going on, the first American troops crossed the Atlantic and moved into Northern Ireland to replace British units sent to the Middle East. But of more immediate import, the meeting produced a plan for an Anglo-American offensive in North Africa, adopting the substance of a long memorandum drafted by Churchill as the *Duke of York* bucked the heavy seas toward American shores.

On the night he arrived at the White House, Churchill put the plan before the President, proposing a landing as early as March of 1942 if acquiescence could be obtained from French authorities in Algeria and Morocco. Originally called Gymnast, and later Super Gymnast before coming to belated fruition as Operation Torch, the plan envisioned an attack by two British divisions backed by additional armored units, with about 25,000 Americans going ashore from the Atlantic. With the beachhead established, an American buildup would continue for six months, bringing 150,000 troops. Together, the British and American forces would consolidate control of the south flank of the Mediterranean from Gibraltar to Suez. Meanwhile preparations for a 1943 thrust against occupied Europe could proceed. The concept appealed to the President even before he read the Churchill scenario. After their first White House meeting, joined by Secretary Hull and Undersecretary Welles from the State Department, British ambassador Lord Halifax, plus Hopkins and Beaverbrook, the Prime Minister recalled, "We all found ourselves pretty well on the same spot."[3] With the whole coast of North Africa in allied hands, the direct route from the Atlantic to the Middle East would be secured, and long voyages around the Cape of Good Hope to the Red Sea eliminated.

By the end of Churchill's visit, his outline, filled in by the military chiefs, had evolved into a plan for a Super Gymnast expedition of 90,000 British and 90,000 American troops, backed by impressive air support, to consolidate control of the south flank of the Mediterranean. Despite its obvious appeal, the plan had to be put on hold because shipping wasn't available to support it. U-boats in the Atlantic were still taking a chilling toll—sinking 132 ships in the western Atlantic during the first two months of the year—and Rommel was on the rampage in the desert. The United States faced new requirements of the war in the Pacific, and supply shipments to the Soviet Union were lagging behind the commitments of the protocol Harriman and Beaverbrook had signed in Moscow.

Although he had regularly been taken into Churchill's confidence on both operational matters and great secrets like the atomic bomb, Harriman had not been given the specifics of what the Prime Minister intended to propose at the White House. Consequently, he had arrived in Washington with his own agenda for discussion with administration officials, and it was close to the one composed by Churchill; but in some respects his concerns went beyond those on the mind of the Prime Minister, suggesting initiatives which two years later would be his foremost responsibilities: inducing the Soviet Union to enter the war against Japan, and getting permission for American bombers to use Siberian bases for raids against Japanese territory.[4]

But even more than the shipboard conference off Argentia, the Washington talks relegated Harriman to the sidelines. Beaverbrook and members of Churchill's entourage were far better informed about the progress of the meeting than Harriman, the State Department, or the U.S. military chiefs; for unlike their American counterparts, they were called to the White House for consultation as the work progressed. Averell had time to go to New York for the Christmas and New Year's holidays. At home, as in Washington, the United States' entry into the war had already made an obvious impact. Mary's husband, Shirley Fisk, was preparing to go into uniform; and in the face of Marie's objections, her son, Harry Whitney, was agitating to enlist. To Averell's amusement, a lookout had been posted in the tower atop the Arden mansion, and after he had been at the apartment in the city for a few days, the building's air raid warden had mistaken him for a new resident and asked him to take a regular turn on the roof watching for enemy planes over Manhattan.

While the President and Churchill held forth in the White House, Harriman and Beaverbrook, backed by platoons of economists, went to work revising war production goals secretly laid down only weeks earlier in response to Roosevelt's conviction that a detailed of list of specific targets would be the most effective stimulus to industrial mobilization.

The U.S. Army was now talking of seventy-one divisions in uniform by the end of 1942, with costs estimated as high as $150 billion, and British experts were pressing Washington for still more steps for lifting industrial mobilization "out of the prison of peacetime conceptions of national productive capacity. . . ."[5] Roosevelt accepted their argument for going to an all-out wartime footing, hence Harriman's and Beaverbrook's chore of setting down goals for an American industrial machine that was about to stop producing cars and washing machines and turn fully to tanks and jeeps.

Their new plan, given to the President and Churchill at the end of the second week of conferences, looked beyond 1942 to increases of as much as 70 percent by 1943. By the next year, it said, American industry should produce 45,000 combat aircraft, 45,000 tanks, eight million tons of merchant ships, 720,000 tons of bombs, 20,000 antiaircraft guns, and 500,000 ground and tank machine guns. That was double the previously planned force of airplanes and tanks and triple the earlier goal for antiaircraft guns. The new requirements for machine guns, bombs, and dozens of other vital items demanded even more from American plants. "We had all agreed," Harriman said, "that it had taken the British too many years to get full war production, and Hopkins had the idea, I think with Roosevelt's full approval, that this time could be shortened if we set our sights high at once."[6]

The goals were promptly accepted by the President and embraced by Churchill, who credited Beaverbrook with creating new "ferment" in the mind of the President. Roosevelt arbitrarily increased some of them even more before he announced them in his State of the Union speech. The targets were ridiculed by industrial executives as unjustified, unattainable, and unattuned to real military requirements.[7] Rather than rallying the country, critics argued, impossible objectives would serve only to damage morale when they could not be met. They heaped the blame on Hopkins, still remembered as a big spender from New Deal days, assuming that he had been taken in by Beaverbrook and the British.

Averell had doubts of his own; and as debate raged over the targets, he did not raise his voice to defend them. Indeed, he did not acknowledge even to his lifelong friend Robert Lovett, who had become assistant secretary of war for air, that he had anything to do with them. Not until much later, after American industry had made its historic conversion to war work, did he publicly endorse the President's acceptance of the goals as a crucial step in making the United States the "arsenal of democracy." It was one of the many occasions when it seemed to him that Roosevelt operated on intuition. Without question, he said, the President's action "forced the United States to more complete mobilization, more rapidly than if we had allowed the production people to set their own goals."[8]

After the Churchill party returned to London, Harriman remained in Washington for another two weeks, trying to find more cargo ships. The shortage was delaying supply movements to the Soviet Union, holding up preparations for North Africa, and putting off further deployment of American troops to Northern Ireland. Pacific convoy requirements stood to reduce the shipments to the Soviets even more. Roosevelt, Churchill and their military advisers had spent days juggling operational plans to free up shipping to help the Red Army keep fighting off the Germans in the East, fearing "unfortunate repercussions" if they failed to carry out the commitments made by Harriman and Beaverbrook.[9]

Before heading back to London, he got the President's approval and sent the Kremlin a personal reassurance that the arms, ammunition, and equipment commitments would be kept. "I am satisfied that the material will be made available substantially as promised except as modified in a few items due to our entry in the war," he cabled Stalin. "Every effort is being made to fill the additional requests. Shipping, however, is increasingly difficult on account of increased demands for transport of our troops and air forces to the Far East and other theaters of war. My government is, however, determined to make available all the ships possible and it is my hope that you will be satisfied with the increased number of ships placed in your service during the next month.

"In spite of the disappointing results during the past four months I find all concerned endeavoring to ship what has been promised and to increase the quantities as soon as practicable. I find at the present time in the United States an ever increasing sympathy for and understanding of the people of the Soviet Union. The American people listen hourly with intense interest to the reports of the continued advances of your gallant troops."[10]

While Washington and London were in full accord on the necessity of keeping Stalin's supply line open, there was no such harmony on the overarching issue of a second front in Europe. That had become a touchy subject between London and Moscow before the United States even entered the war, with Stalin nagging at Britain to get Hitler off his back. During Averell's 1941 trip to Moscow to arrange Lend-Lease aid, Stalin had more than once suggested that it was time for British troops to divert some of the fury from Russia. At a Kremlin banquet, he had publicly taunted Beaverbrook and General Ismay, telling them that there should be an immediate offensive, lest the British Army "lose its spirit." Harriman thought it "supremely tactless," considering that Britain was struggling to survive.[11]

American military leaders had never cared for Churchill's heavy commitment in the Middle East. Marshall was concerned that U.S. forces would be deployed piecemeal into small crises where they could accomplish little toward Hitler's defeat. Victories in out-of-the-way skirmishes would neither generate political support for the war at home nor take pressure off the Red Army. If the administration adopted an unproductive course in the war in Europe, pressure from isolationists for the United States to give top priority to the Pacific might become irresistible.

A month after Churchill went home, Major General Dwight Eisenhower, the new chief of the War Plans Division, produced a scenario for a second front in northwestern Europe, with the British Isles as the staging area, and Marshall took it to the President. To Roosevelt, the Army chief's arguments for an early offensive on the shores of northern France were too compelling to be dismissed, and after hearing him out on March 25, he directed him to press ahead with a plan for an invasion of France. Six days later, a document already in preparation by Eisenhower was finished, laying out a large-scale invasion of the continent from staging points in the British Isles. Given the president's endorsement, it was personally taken to Churchill by Marshall and Hopkins.

"What Harry and Geo. Marshall will tell you all about has my heart and mind in it," Roosevelt said in a letter to Churchill. "Your people and mine demand the establishment of a front to draw off pressure on the Russians, and these people are wise enough to see that the Russians are today killing more Germans and destroying more equipment than you and I put together. Even if full success is not attained, the big objective will be."[12] Roundup, as the plan later to become Operation Overlord was first called, envisioned an April 1943 crossing of the English Channel by thirty American and eighteen British divisions, supported by 5,800 aircraft. The American package also provided the option, strongly backed by Marshall, for a smaller attack in the autumn of 1942. After two weeks in Britain, Hopkins and Marshall left London thinking the Churchill government was in full agreement. A European invasion had been accepted by both the military chiefs and the War Cabinet, and blessed in an enthusiastic cable from the Prime Minister to the President. "We wholeheartedly agree with your conception of concentration against the main enemy," he said, "and we cordially accept your plan with one broad qualification." The qualification was that necessary actions continue in other areas, meaning North Africa, while pressing ahead with "your main project."[13]

Harriman did not take part in the talks, but he was kept abreast of them by Hopkins and Marshall. Better than any other American, he knew the depth of Churchill's apprehension about a landing on the beaches of France. His memories of World War I trench warfare were vivid, as were the recent evacuations from Dunkirk, Greece, and Crete. In spite of Churchill's ebullient message to Roosevelt, Averell suspected there had been a profound misunderstanding. While the President's military advisers embraced an early assault on the shores of France, the North African campaign remained the linchpin of the Prime Minister's strategy. Besides securing North Africa and the Middle East, Churchill wanted to move against the Germans in Norway. The idea was simply to drive the Nazis from the northern bases, preventing them from striking convoys bound for the Soviet ports of Archangel and Murmansk. Getting convoys safely through, he was sure, would dramatically reduce Soviet pressure for Britain and the United States to attack the German Army in France. The problem was that the Prime Minister could arouse little support in Washington or among his own military. "Churchill is the greatest military genius in history," an exasperated General Hastings Ismay complained to Harriman one weekend at Chequers. "He can use one division on three fronts at the same time."[14]

Averell's suspicion that there was still no real understanding on the time and place for the second front was confirmed as soon as Hopkins and Marshall departed. The possibility of an unsuccessful assault, and of British troops once again being stranded on the shores of France, was to Churchill unthinkable. To fail, he had repeatedly emphasized, would be worse than doing nothing at all. In the meetings with Hopkins and Marshall, Britain had only agreed to preparation for a 1943 attack across the Channel. Sledgehammer, the plan for an operation before the end of 1942, Churchill thought, was "impossible, disastrous." With the United States as yet providing limited support, the Prime Minister feared that British divisions landed in a smaller offensive against the continent would be destroyed.[15]

What he told Harriman privately was altogether different from what Averell had heard when they were all together at Chequers and what he had been told by Hopkins and Marshall in hours of talks during the ten days they were in London. At the end of the conference, he had accompanied them to Ireland for Marshall's inspection of the first American troops to cross the Atlantic, and during the trip the Army chief made it clear he was still committed to Operation Sledgehammer because it would divert German forces from the Russian front in the autumn of 1942.

Harriman did not take the opportunity to disagree with the general; but where the early invasion was concerned, he was more in tune with Churchill. Marshall, he thought, had seriously overestimated the readiness of the British units available for a cross-Channel operation. None of the twenty-eight divisions in the British Isles was yet fully equipped, and some were at no more than 25 percent of their authorized strength. They were paper divisions.[16] Averell was also sure that the British had purposely been misleading, giving the impression that they agreed to an early second front in Europe because they feared the United States might otherwise turn to a "Pacific first" strategy. Ismay would later admit that the British had been guilty of a lack of candor. The Defence Committee had offered Hopkins and Marshall only one reservation, which was not even relevant, "and our American friends went happily homewards under the mistaken impression that we had committed ourselves to both Roundup and Sledgehammer."[17]

Saying good-bye to Hopkins and Marshall as they sailed from Scotland, Harriman went back to London on April 19 and saw Churchill again the next day. The meeting convinced him that his friends had gone home with the wrong picture. Alarmed about the possible consequences, he began making plans to go to Washington himself. The differences had become too subtle and complex to be resolved by cables. The following morning, however, he fell ill with paratyphoid, his soaring temperature making him delirious. When the worst of it was over, his chance to resolve the misunderstanding had passed and by then he was confronted with new problems that demanded his immediate attention.

Supply convoys headed for Archangel and Murmansk were being riddled by German planes and submarines, now that winter darkness had lifted, and appalling numbers of sailors were dying in the icy sea as their ships went to the bottom. Loaded vessels were backed up in port in Iceland awaiting escort. While he was still in his sickbed, Harriman had sent a member of his mission to Reykjavik to identify critical cargoes for transfer to vessels ready to sail and arrange for some ships to be unloaded in Scotland so they could return to service.

All the while, the Soviets were increasing pressure for an invasion in the west. Visiting London to sign a much-debated Anglo-Soviet friendship treaty, Molotov again raised the subject with Churchill and Foreign Secretary Eden, and they offered him no hope of action before the end of 1942. But Harriman concluded that Moscow's foreign minister had sensed the strategy disagreement between between Britain and the United States.

At the White House on May 30, the misunderstanding was compounded. When Molotov asked Roosevelt point-blank whether there would be a second front in 1942, the President, after looking at General Marshall and receiving his assent, answered in the affirmative. Later, when the State Department drafted a formal joint statement to be issued by the Allies upon the foreign minister's arrival back in Moscow, Molotov objected to the language concerning the second front because he deemed it less clear than the President had been in conversation. Against the advice of Marshall, who thought it unwise to mention 1942 formally, Roosevelt accepted a Molotov revision saying that "full understanding was reached with regard to the urgent tasks of creating a second front in Europe in 1942."[18]

On his homeward journey, Molotov again stopped off in London for a talk with Churchill, the Prime Minister having indicated that he could be more definitive in the wake of Molotov's meeting with Roosevelt. Although he did not dispute the joint statement Roosevelt had approved in Washington, Churchill did not like it, and he handed Molotov an aide-mémoire, stating a strong condition. While preparations were going forward for an offensive operation in August or September, it said, "it is impossible to say in advance whether the situation will be such as to make this operation feasible when the time comes. We can therefore give no promise in the matter, but provided that it appears sound and sensible we shall not hesitate to put our plans into effect."[19]

Harriman caught a ride home with General H. H. Arnold on June 2, traveling with Lord Louis Mountbatten, who was on his way to belatedly advise the American chiefs that Britain had problems with the second front as it had been discussed with Marshall and Hopkins. By the time he arrived, the Soviet foreign minister and the President had completed their meetings, the Russian having headed for home, satisfied.

As soon as Molotov left, the President went to Hyde Park for a few days and Harriman joined him there. From the President's account of the sessions, Harriman was sure that Roosevelt had misled the Soviets exactly as the British had misled the Americans six weeks earlier. He had intentionally sent Molotov home with the wrong impression because he thought the prospect of an early second front would encourage the Russians to continue their fight.[20] Churchill's aide-mémoire notwithstanding, Molotov's conferences in London and Washington cheered Moscow.

The Prime Minister now resolved to settle the confusion before matters got worse, so once again he crossed the Atlantic to confer with his partner at the White House. On June 18, he landed on the Anacostia River at Washington aboard a Boeing flying boat, paying his third call on Roosevelt in less than a year. He spent the night at the British embassy and left early the next morning to join the President at Hyde Park.

This time, he was determined to sell Roosevelt on going ahead with the invasion of North Africa, in spite of Rommel and British reverses wrecking the schedule, and to make himself understood on invading Europe. That afternoon, he handed the President a memorandum that concealed none of Britain's qualms about an early crossing of the English Channel.

"Arrangements are being made for a landing of six or eight divisions on the coast of Northern France early in September," it said. "However, the British government do not favour an operation that was certain to lead to disaster, for this would not help the Russians whatever their plight, would compromise and expose to Nazi vengeance the French population involved, and would gravely delay the main operation in 1943. We hold strongly to the view that there should be no substantial landing in France this year unless we are going to stay. No responsible British military authority has so far been able to make a plan for September, 1942, which had any chance of success unless the Germans become utterly demoralised, of which there is no likelihood. . . ."[21] The only way to get American troops into the war quickly, he argued, was the landing in North Africa. Harriman had warned Roosevelt what to expect.

That afternoon, he and Marie crossed the Hudson to join the President and Churchill for tea. It was oppressively hot for June, and to the Prime Minister's relief, the host had suspended business. In a light-hearted mood in spite of the Prime Minister's directness on the second front, the President had loaded his guest into his convertible equipped with special hand controls and chauffeured him about the estate, all the while entertaining him with a stream of stories that had nothing to do with the war.

Back at the house after the Harrimans arrived, all had fun teasing Hopkins, a widower since 1937, about his blossoming romance with Louise Macy in New York. From the ribbing about a potential wedding, they turned to gossip about Lord Beaverbrook, who, although he had left the government and was back running his newspapers, was still a presence in Churchill's personal and official circles. Beaverbrook always reminded one, Churchill said, of the mother who told her older child to find out what the baby was doing and tell him not to do it.

Although Churchill joined in the banter, Harriman could see that he was preoccupied with the business that had brought him to Hyde Park and "could not seem to free his mind from serious matters for very long at a time." And when he was briefly alone with the President, Averell found that beneath his relaxed air, Roosevelt was disturbed over Churchill's stiff note on the second front. Since the fall of Bataan and Corregidor a month earlier, the war in the Pacific had, in Americans' minds, again overshadowed the conflict in Europe. The loss of the Philippines had not shaken Roosevelt's commitment to the "Europe-first" strategy; but he confessed to Harriman that he was seriously troubled by the difficulty of "finding a place where the soldiers thought they could fight."[22] If Churchill's nightmare was the possibility of an invading force being destroyed on the shores of France, Roosevelt's was to have American forces stand idle while control of war strategy was taken over by advocates of a "Pacific-first" strategy. In that light, Churchill's North African landing was still an appealing alternative to a Channel crossing.

But the chance to resolve the matter finally while Churchill was in the United States was lost the following morning. Back at the White House after an overnight train ride together from Hyde Park, a grim Roosevelt handed Churchill a telegram with the news that Tobruk, Britain's strategic bastion on the northeastern Libyan coast, had fallen to Rommel. More than 25,000 British soldiers had been taken prisoner in a disaster that surpassed the capitulation of Singapore five months earlier. It opened the possibility of German air attacks on Alexandria, an offensive against Cairo, and even German conquest of the Suez Canal. Defeat was one thing, Churchill said, disgrace quite another.[23] From the second front, the conference turned to the new emergency. American bombers in India were ordered to Cairo. P-40s were put aboard ship in Rhode Island, B-25s rushed east from California, and other planes bound for the Soviet Union diverted to Egypt. There was consideration of sending the United States' desert-trained 2nd Armored Division from California; but since ships were unavailable, it was decided to send three hundred more American tanks and ninety 105-millimeter self-propelled guns instead. In the House of Commons, the disaster produced a no-confidence resolution against the Churchill government.

Though the most vital element of the Allied strategy remained unresolved, a romance that had fascinated insiders on both sides of the ocean was successfully concluded during Churchill's visit—Hopkins asked Louise Macy to marry him and she accepted. With the end of the conference, the Prime Minister hosted a dinner at the British embassy, and for the occasion Marie Harriman put in one of her rare Washington appearances. Mrs. Macy joined her on the train from New York. In the Harrimans' suite at the Mayflower, Hopkins popped the question as the four of them were about to leave for the dinner, and Marie walked into the room just as he kissed her.

The following evening, as Churchill said rather grim good-byes, Averell's old friends at the Business Advisory Council gave a dinner in his honor where he spoke briefly, praising Britain's courage against the blitz and the wolfpacks of U-boats. Then, as the others turned to their meal, he slipped out a side door and drove to Baltimore. On a darkened ramp at the harbor, he and Churchill boarded the Prime Minister's flying boat and took off for London by way of Newfoundland.

Three weeks later, they were followed by Hopkins, Marshall, and Admiral Ernest J. King, the new Chief of Naval Operations, under orders from the President to settle the second-front issue at last. This time, they had instructions in writing—to press for a landing in France in the fall. They were to yield in their insistence upon an early invasion "only if you are completely convinced that Sledgehammer is impossible of execution with reasonable chances of serving its intended purpose," Roosevelt told them. "If Sledgehammer is finally and definitely out of the picture, I want you to consider the world situation as it exists at that time, and determine upon another place for U.S. troops to fight in 1942."[24]

The beginning of the climactic conference was anything but promising, the American officers arriving in a combative mood. Harriman met them in Scotland with an invitation to join Churchill at Chequers for the weekend, but instead they went immediately to London and a conference with Eisenhower, now the commander of the European theater. The Prime Minister was furious, and it took a face-to-face visit by his chastened friend Hopkins to restore his good humor.

For two days, Marshall argued for the fall invasion, presenting a detailed plan calling for a Sledgehammer landing on the Cotentin Peninsula, where a beachhead would be held until an all-out invasion in 1943. The British chiefs were unbending, and they were backed by a unanimous War Cabinet, not to mention the Prime Minister. In the face of the uniform intransigence, Marshall asked the President for new instructions, and Roosevelt threw his support to North Africa. The Prime Minister had won. Disastrously, Marshall thought. In his view, going into North Africa precluded an invasion of Europe in 1943. "It looked," he said, "like the Russians were going to be destroyed. . . ."[25]

From the time of his first conversations with Stalin, Harriman had been impressed by the Soviets' determination to hold out; but after Roosevelt's assurances to Molotov, he was afraid there would be serious repercussions from on-again-off-again second-front signals sent from the West, especially when Soviet help was needed to defeat Japan.

On Friday night, a week after Hopkins, Marshall, and King had gone back to Washington, he was invited to Chartwell. Arriving just before dark, he met Soviet ambassador Ivan Maisky leaving the Churchill estate. The Prime Minister was in his little cottage down the hill from the main house, and there they had dinner and played bezique for several hours. Between hands, the Prime Minister reconstructed the second-front decision. He was pleased that it was finally settled, but he, too, was uneasy over the reaction it would provoke in Moscow. He had received a cable from Sir Archibald Clark Kerr, his ambassador to the Soviet Union, recommending that he meet Stalin and personally explain the decision to fight Hitler in North Africa rather than attack in France. Since he had already planned a trip to Egypt, Churchill had got in touch with Stalin to say he would continue on to Moscow to discuss the second front. It was the only way to get past the suspicion and establish some "relationship of trust" with Stalin.[26]

The idea of going along did not occur to Harriman immediately. He left Churchill and returned to London in the small hours of the morning. On Saturday, he went to the cottage in the country with Kathleen and Pamela; and for the rest of the weekend, he brooded over the unpredictable reaction awaiting Churchill on the Prime Minister's first trip to the Kremlin. Given the assurances to Molotov in Washington, he was afraid that "Stalin would not believe a word of what Churchill was telling him. He would think that the British alone had blocked the second front." An American presence might make it clear that the United States was now fully behind the North African plan in spite of everything.[27]

Hopkins was obviously the man who could prevent a damaging misunderstanding, but he was unavailable. As soon as he had returned home from the negotiations in London, he and Louise had been married at the White House and were now honeymooning at a farm in Connecticut. The notion of personally joining Churchill developed on Tuesday when Harriman called on Anthony Eden and went over his concerns. The Prime Minister was by then already in Cairo, but the foreign secretary, who had been in Moscow for several days immediately after Pearl Harbor, thought it a splendid idea for him to catch up. He cabled the recommendation to Churchill and in similar language Harriman wired the proposal to the president.

At one-thirty the next morning, Meiklejohn awakened Averell with a message from the White House, saying No. Considering the sharp differences that had persisted between Washington and London on the second-front matter, Roosevelt was concerned that Harriman would be seen as America's watchdog, sent along because Churchill was not fully trusted. "I hesitate to have you go," the President said, "for I do not want anyone anywhere to have the slightest suspicion that you are acting as an observer. You would, I know, be useful, but I think it is wiser not to run any risks of misconstruction."[28] The President's position was understandable, but Harriman suspected that his reasoning was far more complex than the message indicated. Ever since the United States had come into the war, Roosevelt had wanted to have a one-on-one meeting with Stalin; he had made no secret of his certainty that he could be more effective than Churchill in dealing with the boss of the Kremlin. Months earlier he had directed Averell to talk with Ambassador Maisky about a possible Roosevelt-Stalin tête-à-tête. Now, he guessed that the President's real reason for the veto was that he "didn't want to establish a precedent that would let the British have an observer present if he ever got together with Stalin."[29]

Churchill simply liked the idea of having company. He had first proposed taking Maisky, but Moscow had ordered its ambassador to stay in London—a signal, Maisky thought, meant to convey Kremlin disapproval of the hints it had gotten from Churchill on the second front and the slowdown of the supply convoys.[30]

Seventeen hours after reading the message rejecting the suggestion, Harriman got a second cable from the President, who had received a wire from Churchill enthusiastically endorsing Eden's suggestion. The new message ordered him to catch up with the Prime Minister as soon as possible but offered no guidance or instruction as to what he was to do or say.[31] When he received the go-ahead, Harriman was about to host a stag dinner at his apartment: fortuitously, his guests included Harold Balfour, the undersecretary of state for air. Balfour knew of a B-24 scheduled to take off for Cairo at midnight with with General Charles de Gaulle aboard. He called the Air Ministry and ordered takeoff delayed for Harriman's arrival.

After dinner, Averell packed while talking with Eden, who had been one of his dinner guests, and a barefoot Ambassador Winant, who came in from next door in his bathrobe after hearing the news. At 3:30 A.M., leaving orders that his whereabouts were top secret, he rushed off to the airport. It was 8:30 by the time the plane was finally airborne, and de Gaulle was visibly displeased at being delayed for eight hours, especially since Harriman offered no hint of what his obviously important mission was about.

The twenty-hour trip was as socially awkward as it was physically uncomfortable. On tightly spaced, facing benches in the tubelike bomb bay, Harriman sat directly facing the general, the close quarters forcing the starchy American envoy and the imperious Frenchman to intertwine their long legs and either look each other full in the face or feign sleep. Hour after long hour, they sat in silence, neither condescending to attempt conversation, which would have been hopeless anyway given the debilitating noise and the language barrier.

Although Harriman had sold himself onto the Churchill mission as a symbol of Anglo-American unity, the journey through the Middle East would give him a chance to address a crisis of his own—the supply line to the Soviet Union. Marshall and Stimson had urged Roosevelt to scale down the shipments to the Soviets after the war started in the Pacific, but the President had refused to relent in the effort to get the convoys through, even at a horrendous price in lives and lost shipping. With the possibility of a Soviet collapse still alive, he badgered the Navy to find ships that could be diverted to convoy duty, and pressured Churchill to keep them moving. But the problem was not a shortage of vessels so much as the inability to get convoys through the German blockade in the North Atlantic and the Greenland Sea. With the Soviets desperate for arms, ammunition, and food in the spring of 1942, convoys were especially vulnerable because the Arctic darkness had lifted but the ice had not melted enough to allow the ships to steer far north and beyond range of German aircraft from Norway. Besides seventy bombers and one hundred fighters from the northern bases, the Germans had available packs of submarines and surface ships, including two cruisers and the forty-thousand-ton battleship *Tirpitz*.

In April, heavy ice forced fourteen of twenty-three merchant vessels in one convoy to return to port. During the same month, another convoy saw five of nineteen ships sunk. In all, eighty-four shiploads of tanks, trucks, barbed wire, oil, and ammunition left American ports for Archangel and Murmansk in April, May, and June, but only forty-four got there, the rest being sunk or forced by long delays to be unloaded in Scotland so the ships could return to duty. At the same time, more merchant ships jammed the harbor in Iceland, awaiting escort.

There were other ways to get the supplies to Stalin, but while they were less dangerous, they were hardly satisfactory. Soviet ships could still cross the Pacific to Vladivostok unmolested, since the Japanese did not want to bring the Russians into the war in the Pacific; but when convoys reached the port, their cargo remained thousands of miles from the front. Matériel could also be sent to the Persian Gulf for transshipment through Iran; but with the Mediterranean closed, ships had to go all the way around the Cape of Good Hope, and when they finally reached the Persian Gulf, the ports, docks, and the obsolescent Iranian railroad created a hopeless bottleneck.

Harriman got daily Admiralty briefings, and he passed along to the White House its arguments to reduce the number of convoys, scale down their size, and demand more Soviet help in protecting them. But Roosevelt pressured to keep them moving, brushing aside Churchill's suggestion that Stalin be asked to accept reduced shipments. In May, when the President urged that a huge additional convoy be dispatched to relieve the backup of cargo loaded and waiting, Churchill was exasperated. "With very great respect, what you suggest is beyond our power to fulfill," he told the President, protesting that the Royal Navy was "absolutely extended."[32]

Except for the debate over the second front itself, nothing caused more continuing tension in 1942 than did the convoys. While Molotov was in Washington, the President had raised the possibility of reducing the shipments. If the Soviets could trim their requirement for noncombat items from the 4.1 million tons called for in a new protocol to 2.5 million tons, he said, many additional ships could be thrown into the U.S. buildup in Europe and hasten the day of the second front. Molotov had stiffly responded that "the second front would be stronger if the first front still stood fast."[33]

Finally, in early July, the Arctic supply line was struck by full-blown disaster. A convoy of thirty-four merchant ships, ten more than normal, had set out with a formidable close escort of six destroyers, two antiair-craft ships, two submarines, and eleven smaller vessels. Eleven more submarines, three cruisers, two battleships, several destroyers, and the carrier *Victorious* maintained stand-off positions. Near the northern tip of Norway, the convoy commander mistakenly concluded he was about to come under attack by a major German surface fleet, including the *Tirpitz.*

Fearing the entire convoy was about to be lost, Admiral Dudley Pound, the First Lord of the Admiralty, responded to the commander's report by ordering the cargo ships to scatter. That only made them easy prey for what turned out to be a modest force of Nazi dive-bombers and small surface raiders. Before the fiasco was over, twenty-three of the supply vessels were sunk. Besides the loss of nearly all of their crews, 130,000 tons of the convoy's 200,000 tons of arms, ammunition, and supplies, including five hundred tanks, were sent to the bottom of the Barents Sea. Altogether, in one week, 400,000 tons of Allied shipping were lost. With that, Roosevelt agreed with Churchill that it was time to abandon the Arctic route for the summer.

Ever since his trip to the Middle East and his inspection of the Persian Gulf port at Basra the previous year, Harriman had thought of the route from the Persian Gulf through Iran to the Caspian Sea as a way to vastly increase the flow of supplies to the Soviet Union. In April, he and Hopkins discussed it with War Cabinet members Eden and Oliver Lyttleton, encouraging Britain to improve the Persian Gulf ports and make more use of the route, but they aroused little interest. "That does not seem too encouraging," Hopkins reported to the President. "Eden showed me a paper that had apparently been prepared by the soldiers about supplies to Russia after July 1. The memorandum clearly indicated that some of the military people here aren't too anxious to get supplies to Russia and that we have got to overcome a good deal of resistance."[34] But the United States kept the notion alive. After the President's meetings with Molotov, the United States began arrangements to deliver three thousand trucks per month to the Persian Gulf, to be assembled there and driven in convoys to the Soviet Union. Then, in the wake of the July disaster, the Persian Gulf ports and the rail and truck routes across Iran took on urgent priority. Supported by several detailed studies, Harriman pressed for the United States to take over operation of the Iranian railroad, a step he had recommended in the spring but dropped because the Russians had shown little interest in it.

Arriving in Cairo, he received General Marshall's permission to recruit two officers who knew the railroad route; then he drafted Loy Henderson, a former officer of the American embassy in Moscow who was passing through Egypt on a State Department mission. With Henderson, Major General Russell L. Maxwell, commander of American supply operations in the East, and Brigadier General Sidney Spalding, a Lend-Lease officer from Washington, in tow, he flew on to Teheran, leaving Churchill mildly irritated that he had taken up an agenda of his own.

By the time the PM's party arrived in the Iranian capital two days later, Harriman had concluded that the 3,300 tons a day that Britain expected to ship over the route could easily be doubled. On the afternoon before they took off for Moscow, he put the details before Churchill and General Sir Alan Brooke, chief of the Imperial General Staff.

The Prime Minister's later account was that the decision for the United States to assume operation of the route was made then and there; but as Harriman remembered it, British officers continued to have serious reservations about turning a vital national asset over to another country. In any case, the mere prospect of expanded shipments was one of the few bits of bright news they had to deliver to Stalin.

The flight to Moscow took them north from Teheran, across the Elburz Mountains, along the eastern shore of the Caspian Sea, and almost within sight of the Baku oil fields that Harriman had visited during his travels in the Caucasus in 1927. They skirted Stalingrad, where the German offensive raged, crossed the Volga, and bypassed Kuibyshev, their fighter escort leading them through heavy air defenses and directly over the capital to the airport.

An extraordinary reception awaited. Beside a hot, heavily guarded taxiway, a military band played, a snappy Red Army honor guard paraded, and a long row of Stars and Stripes and Union Jacks ruffled in the breeze beside the hammer-and-sickle banners of the USSR. The brightest luminaries of the Soviet capital's diplomatic community, including the British and American ambassadors, Soviet foreign minister V. M. Molotov, and gaggles of aides, lined up in a huge greeting party. Although the Prime Minister brought bad news, the Soviets had not turned out such a welcome since the beginning of the war.

The twenty Soviet fighters ahead of the three Liberator bombers swept low over the field with an ear-splitting roar. In their wake, the plane bearing Churchill and Harriman landed and taxied into place as the dignitaries surged forward. When the clam-shell doors in the belly of the plane swung open, Churchill's stubby legs stretched uncertainly toward the pavement, but before anyone could step forward to help, he dropped heavily from the bomb bay, quickly followed by Harriman.

Both showed the full effects of a ten-and-a-half-hour flight from Teheran, wrapped in army blankets, deafened, hungry, and chilled to the bone. As he emerged from the plane's shadow, the Prime Minister's thin hair was tousled, his bow tie was askew, and his suit was rumpled, reminding the British ambassador of a fighting bull coming out of the darkness into the bright sunlight of the ring. Harriman was a step behind, suffering a stiff neck and back and moving more creakily than the Prime Minister.

Taken in tow by Molotov, they stood at rigid attention as the goose-stepping Red Army detachment marched before them and the military band played wavering renditions of "God Save the King" and the "Star Spangled Banner." Churchill then stepped before an array of microphones with a defiant reaffirmation of the Allies' commitment to stand together against Hitler.

"Whatever our sufferings, whatever our toils," he said, "we will continue hand in hand, like comrades and brothers until every vestige of the Nazi regime has been beaten into the ground, until the memory only of it remains as an example and a warning for a future time."[35] Harriman didn't try to match the eloquence. He had come to the Soviet Union, he said, to make it clear that President Roosevelt and the United States government fervently shared the commitment to Hitler's destruction.

With that, the visitors were whisked away to prepare for the distasteful moment when they would have to inform Josef Stalin that there would be no Anglo-American second front in 1942. Making that known to Stalin, Churchill had told Roosevelt, was going to be a "rather a raw job."[36]

After months of debate and Churchill's two trips to Washington, the decision to proceed with the delayed invasion of French North Africa rather than Europe was unequivocal. With Stalingrad still under siege and U.S. and British Arctic convoys to Archangel and Murmansk suspended, it was a terrible moment to bring the Kremlin even more bad tidings. Having been there for negotiations twice before, Harriman knew the hours ahead would be far more difficult than the others realized because Stalin had counted so heavily on a second front in Europe pulling forty German divisions away from the Russian offensive. When Churchill had proposed the journey to Moscow, his only explanation had been that he wanted to tell Stalin of "plans we have made with President Roosevelt for offensive action in 1942."[37] But given the aide-mémoire that had been handed to Molotov in London, the Soviets had good reason to expect the worst.

Three hours after they landed, they were ushered into Stalin's office. Harriman thought the dictator had visibly aged in the ten months since they had first met, but he seemed "no less vigorous" than he had in the early days of the German offensive.[38] Conscious of his role as a member of the supporting cast, Harriman said little. Churchill quickly dispensed with the battlefield situation in Egypt and got directly onto the matter of the second front. There could be no invasion of France in 1942, he said, because the United States and Britain did not have enough landing craft to put their forces ashore. Furthermore, weather over the Channel would soon be unreliable, and the planned buildup to a million American troops in Britain for a full-scale 1943 invasion was just beginning. If a landing of 150,000 to 200,000 troops could divert significant German forces from the Russian front, it could be undertaken, he said, but if such an operation failed to lift the siege on the Russian front and succeeded only in delaying an all-out Allied invasion, then it would be a tragic mistake.

Stalin agreed with none of it, challenging point by point every argument Churchill made. At heated moments, he rose from his chair and went to a table where he fished out cigarettes and tore them to bits, using the tobacco to refill his pipe. He insisted the Germans had no first-class divisions in France and questioned American and British courage. Why, he asked Churchill, were they afraid? In the face of the provocation, Churchill managed to hold his temper, chomping on his cigar, fidgeting, and occasionally arising to pace the room, tugging at the seat of his trousers as he waited for his chance to speak. When the visitor got the floor, Stalin listened impassively until the Prime Minister plunged into the case for the North African campaign.

The outline of Operation Torch foresaw British and American forces in control of all the North African coast by autumn. Small diversionary raids would keep Hitler's attention on northern France, and Anglo-American outfits would be positioned to thrust northward into the soft underbelly of Europe. Here, he used his famous crocodile sketch to illustrate his strategy, the snout representing northern France, and the soft, vulnerable underbelly the European shores of the Mediterranean and Adriatic. With that, the Prime Minister suddenly turned the floor over to Harriman to explain the perspective of the United States. There had been no discussion of what he should say, or if, indeed, he should say anything, so he merely assured Stalin that Torch had Roosevelt's unequivocal support. Obviously, he said, Americans were preoccupied with the war in the Pacific, but the President's eyes were "turned upon the European theatre of the war as of primary concern," and he would "support it to the limit of the resources at his disposal."[39]

Stalin nevertheless had doubts about the political soundness of Operation Torch. Since de Gaulle had been told nothing about it, he questioned whether the invasion would be interpreted by the Free French as an American attempt to annex French North Africa. Tactically, he appreciated the plan, however. The idea of striking Rommel's tank corps from the rear and creating friction between the Vichy French and Germans in North Africa appealed to him. But Churchill failed to mention one of the chief enticements that had interested Roosevelt in North Africa from the beginning. As they were about to leave, they paused beside a large globe in Stalin's office, and Harriman could not pass up the opportunity to emphasize the obvious, using the prop to point out the immense strategic benefit of a successful Torch. With the south flank of the Mediterranean secured, Stalin would be closer to his Allies. It would no longer be necessary for them to send convoys thousands of miles around the Cape of Good Hope.

After the first two hours, which Churchill described as "bleak and sombre," the meeting had taken on an unmistakably upbeat tenor, and Churchill and Harriman went home delighted. "The Prime Minister . . . felt it had been the most important conference of his long life," Harriman recalled. As they drove together to the dacha where Churchill was staying, he thanked Harriman generously for his "help in getting over some of the rough spots. No Prime Minister," he said, "has been better supported by a representative of another country."[40] At the dacha, there was vodka, caviar, a long dinner and a full recounting of the whole conversation for American ambassador William Standley, who was miffed at Averell for being left out while Sir Archibald Clark Kerr, Britain's envoy, had been invited to the session. Exhausted, Churchill, for once, started to nod before Harriman.

The rough time was yet to come, though.

On the second evening in Moscow, Harriman and Churchill agreed that the Prime Minister would meet with Stalin alone. Averell had served his purpose, and an evening off would give him an opportunity to invite American correspondents to drinks and dinner. Journalists were always eager to see him, and usually he could get more useful insights from them than from diplomats without giving them much information in return. This time, he wanted to make sure they grasped the importance of the secret conference that the Soviets would announce only after he and Churchill had departed. As they were about to sit down to dinner, a call from one of Churchill's aides advised him that Stalin wished Harriman to join the second meeting at the Kremlin.

What followed was reminiscent of Harriman's experience a year earlier. It was as though the meeting of the previous evening had never happened. Aggressive, rude, and insulting, Stalin accused Britain and the United States of breaking their promise of a second front in 1942 and defaulting on their pledges to provide him with arms to fight the Nazis. He renewed his bitter charge that the British were afraid to engage the German Army and added to it an accusation that the American and British navies had fled the enemy in the disastrous convoy dispersal the previous month. Harriman interjected that both the United States and Britain were "ready for any sacrifice that promised a reasonable prospect of success," but Stalin ignored him.[41]

Inflammatory as it was, the diatribe was delivered in a low monotone, and while it was translated, Stalin avoided looking Churchill or Harriman in the eye. As the Prime Minister sat swelling with indignation, Harriman slipped him a note—"Don't take this too seriously—this is the way he behaved last year."[42]

On a few specifics Churchill briefly interrupted, but not until Stalin talked himself out did he unleash his retaliation. In a withering torrent overwhelming his interpreter, he chastised Stalin for a lack of "comradeship," took exception to the insinuations of cowardice, and lectured the startled host on the folly of an ill-prepared second front.

Riveted, Harriman listened without taking a note and Churchill's interpreter put down his pencil in defeat. Thus one of the great moments of Churchill's wartime leadership went unrecorded. What most impressed Averell was that the devastating response to Stalin's insults came without mention of the Kremlin's notorious nonaggression pact with Hitler.

Stalin's truculence withered. Although the translation had collapsed, he had gotten the full flavor of the message, and he broke into a wide smile. "Your words are of no importance," he told Churchill as the Prime Minister paused to ask his interpreter what he had translated into Russian. "What is important is your spirit."[43] For the rest of the evening, the talk proceeded in a more relaxed atmosphere, and Stalin invited them to return for dinner the following day.

The upbeat conclusion of the meeting was not enough to placate Churchill. He was furious about the bullying and unimpressed by Harriman's contention that Stalin's boorish behavior was a negotiating tactic and his prediction that the rest of the conference would find Stalin conciliatory.

When Ambassador Clark Kerr arrived for lunch the next day, he found Churchill "like a wounded Lion," even threatening not to attend the scheduled Kremlin dinner with Stalin.[44] In large measure, the ambassador blamed Harriman for Churchill's black mood. Averell, he thought, fawned over the Prime Minister much too much, congratulating him excessively when he succeeded, and trying too profusely to cheer and encourage him when he faltered. Churchill, in his view, responded with unnecessary gratitude. "Every now and then he would . . . take Harriman by the hand, making remarks like this," Clark Kerr recorded in his personal notes, " 'I am so glad, Averell, that you came with me. You are a tower of strength.' . . . I think Harriman's presence is bad for him." Roosevelt's envoy, the jealous ambassador complained in his diary, was "no more than a kindly ass . . . a champion bum sucker."[45]

For all of Harriman's efforts to cheer and reassure him, Churchill was still in a cross mood when he set out for the Kremlin dinner on their third night in Moscow. To Clark Kerr's horror and Harriman's amusement, he wore his famous "siren suit," or "rompers" as his friends in London called the one-piece zip-up outfit, fashioned so he could dress quickly during an air raid.

Just as Harriman expected, Stalin was once more as cordial and reasonable as he had been on the evening of their arrival. By Kremlin standards, the dinner was sedate, notably omitting the orgy of vodka toasting that often left both hosts and guests—Stalin always excepted—thoroughly drunk. When Churchill left at 1:30 A.M., Stalin went with him down a long corridor to the exit, almost trotting to keep up, and Harriman took the gesture as truly significant.

The dinner gave Harriman his only opportunity to talk with Stalin out of Churchill's hearing, and he used it to raise Roosevelt's desire to have a face-to-face meeting and to touch on the situation in the Pacific. Although the Europe-first strategy was sacred, Harriman assured Stalin, the United States would keep Japan so occupied that it would have no temptation to invade Siberia.

Trying to be casual, he mentioned that Siberian bases offered the only opportunity to bomb Japan; but Stalin deftly sidestepped the subject: America's big B-24s, he said, could make bombing runs on Japan from Alaska. Nevertheless, he agreeably joined Harriman in a toast to the "great day when Soviet and U.S. planes go together" to bomb Japanese targets.

Difficult as it had been, Harriman was satisfied that his journey with Churchill had fully served its purpose. Stalin had no basis to doubt Anglo-American unity. Harriman was not on hand, however, when Churchill and Stalin had their most useful talk—an eight-hour conversation that began with what was supposed to have been the Prime Minister's brief farewell call. Accompanied only by interpreters, they retired from Stalin's office to his apartment in the Kremlin. There, they had dinner after midnight, talked politics and rehashed the early years of the war. In the course of it, Stalin at last acknowledged that, contrary to his earlier position, the North African landing would provide some relief to the Red Army. It could truthfully be construed as a second front.

The ecstatic Prime Minister got back to his villa at 3:15 A.M., just in time to begin preparations for his departure. Harriman joined him in a chilly rain at the airport before dawn. Not until they were in Teheran that evening was their mission publicly disclosed.

There, Churchill cabled Roosevelt his account of what happened. On the whole, he said, he was "definitely encouraged." The bitter pill had gone down. "Now they know the worst," said the PM, "and having made their protest are entirely friendly; this in spite of the fact that this is their most anxious and antagonizing time. Moreover, M. Stalin is entirely convinced of the great advantages of Torch, and I do trust that it is being driven forward with superhuman energy on both sides of the ocean."[46] With a touch of amusement, Harriman noted that the implacable old foe of Soviet communism was now "all for Uncle Joe. . . ."[47]

With his own commitment to helping the Russians reinforced, Harriman returned to his effort to increase the flow of arms and ammunition through the Persian Gulf. Officials in Moscow had made it clear that they still preferred to take their Lend-Lease deliveries at Murmansk; but after the experience of the last northern convoy, the best hope of increasing the flow of supplies, including the Russians' desperate need for more trucks, was via the Persian Gulf route and the trans-Iranian railroad, or Persian railroad, as it was usually called.

Churchill flew on to Cairo after one night in Teheran, and Harriman stayed behind to inspect the railroad and the ports. He called on the young Shah of Iran, who had been installed in place of his deposed pro-Nazi father and was now cooperating with the British and Russians who occupied his country. Iran wanted American trucks and wheat, and the Shah entered an early plea for further American assistance after the war was over. He disliked the British, he told Harriman, and he feared there would be serious trouble with the Russians.

Averell promised to do what he could to get the Shah's views before the President. Thus began the close, and ultimately explosive, personal ties between Shah Mohammad Reza Pahlavi and the United States. At dawn the next day, August 18, Harriman flew low over the length of the railroad from Teheran to the Persian Gulf. Accompanied by several British and American officers, he visited locomotive repair shops, roundhouses, port facilities, a truck assembly plant, and the Abadan oil refinery. The railroad itself, he discovered, was even more of a wreck than he had expected—"the worst mess I have ever seen."[48]

Completed in 1939, the main line from the gulf through Teheran to the Caspian Sea tortuously covered rugged terrain, including one 165-mile stretch marked by 135 tunnels and bridges. There were grades steep enough to bring steam locomotives to a standstill. The ports were equally outmoded, without either manpower or equipment to unload supply ships and move trains northward with dispatch.

Harriman caught up with Churchill again on August 19 in Cairo, and the next day presented him with the formal proposal for the United States to take over operation of the railroad. If Britain would agree, Harriman promised Churchill, he would lobby the President to increase the road's capacity dramatically and appoint "one of the most competent railroad operating men" to take over. After receiving Harriman's memorandum, characterizing the move as a benefit to British forces in Iran as well as to the Russians, Churchill formally asked the United States to take charge of the road. "Only in this way," said his message to the

President, "can we insure an expanding flow of supplies to Russia while building up the military forces which we must move into northern Persia to meet a possible German advance."[49]

Within the week, Averell was off for Washington in Churchill's Liberator bomber to give the President a detailed report on the meetings in Moscow. At his Shangri La retreat in the Catoctin Mountains of Maryland, Roosevelt listened with amusement as Harriman recounted Churchill's fencing with Stalin and the Prime Minister's anxiety after Stalin's nasty outbursts.

His presidential briefings done, he set out to prepare for the U.S. Army's new role in supplying America's ally facing Hitler on the eastern front. Engineers at Union Pacific were put to work on a new six-wheel diesel locomotive powerful enough to climb the steep grades through mountain passes but light enough to be sustained by the bridges.

At his suggestion 57 powerful new diesel locomotives, less affected by the desert heat and capable of pulling longer strings of cars, were put on the road, along with 1,000 new twenty-ton freight cars and 650 forty-ton freight cars diverted from Europe.

By the following spring, 28,000 American troops were assigned to the Persian Gulf supply convoy, moving matériel from the gulf northward to Soviet-occupied territory in northern Iran. Arrival of the new rolling stock and the equipment to modernize the docks coincided with increased shipments of armaments for Stalin, creating a traffic jam that threw the project six months behind Harriman's schedule. For a time, the effort to open the route to heavier traffic even aggravated the shipping shortage because of lines of vessels anchored in the gulf waiting to unload. In the end, however, the route paid off more handsomely than even Harriman had expected. The railway that could haul no more than 200 tons a day when it was opened in 1939 averaged 3,397 tons once it was fully under the operation of the U.S. Army.

Chapter XIV

MOSCOW
The Patriotic War at Spaso House

Roosevelt and Hopkins considered appointing Harriman ambassador to the Soviet Union after his trip to Moscow in 1941, going as far as to make him an informal offer, but he turned it down. It wasn't an easy decision for him, considering that one of his principal recommendations when he came home to report on his meetings with Stalin was that Laurence Steinhardt be replaced. Averell's experience in the Soviet Union and his intimate knowledge of Lend-Lease made him an obvious prospect for the job, and Hopkins gently pressured him to take it. But for one of the few times in his government career, he begged off. In London he was a principal figure on the war's diplomatic front line. There he could take a hand in moving tanks, trucks, and barbed wire to the Red Army at the same time that he was the President's personal link with the British government. In Moscow, he could see himself a lonely, isolated, glorified messenger. Hopkins understood that, and so the President replaced Steinhardt with retired Admiral William H. Standley, an old friend and former Chief of Naval Operations, who had been a member of the 1941 Harriman-Beaverbrook mission.

The new ambassador's tour was an unhappy one. Standley spent most of his time six hundred miles east of Moscow in Kuibyshev, where foreign diplomats were sequestered when the fall of Moscow appeared imminent. He seldom saw Stalin or Molotov. He had limited patience, and it was severely tested by the Soviets' paranoia and the President's offhand way of doing business. After a year, both he and Washington knew his assignment had been a mistake.

Although the war turned for the better with the Anglo-American victory in North Africa and the beginning of American bombing of Germany, Roosevelt's and Churchill's relations with Stalin remained as distant and difficult as ever. Standley wanted to deal with the Kremlin in a combative, tit-for-tat fashion, but his advice was routinely ignored in Washington, where neither the President nor State Department bureaucrats understood the obstinance the ambassador confronted every day. America's hand and purse were open; and believing he could bring Stalin into an alliance that would survive the war, Roosevelt was ever willing to accommodate.

Harriman himself contributed substantially to Standley's personal dissatisfaction as he did to Winant's in London. He regularly involved himself in U.S.-Soviet affairs, communicating directly with Stalin without consulting Standley and urging the Soviet boss to deal directly with Roosevelt. The ambassador took it as an effort by the Lend-Lease expediter to make himself Roosevelt's link to Stalin as he was the President's channel to Churchill. To Standley's irritation, one of the State Department's first messages after he arrived in the Soviet Union was an admonition not to discuss several of the most sensitive policy issues between the two governments—including the question of the second front. When Molotov went to Washington to discuss the new front and the problems of the supply convoys, Standley knew nothing about it until the foreign minister turned up in London on his way over.

In March 1943, the frustrated Standley hastened the end of his short diplomatic career by publicly accusing the Soviets of concealing the billions of dollars' worth of American and British war aid from their people. The authorities in Moscow, he told surprised American correspondents, "seem to want to cover up the fact that they are receiving outside help. Apparently, they want their people to believe that the Red Army is fighting this war alone."[1] The remarks provoked a tempest, the Soviet Foreign Ministry demanding an explanation from the State Department, and Standley being called in and lectured by Molotov.

Washington was as much as Moscow to blame for the ambassador's outburst. While Standley was left to twiddle his thumbs, a procession of conspicuous and sometimes meddlesome special envoys on assignment from the White House appeared in the Soviet Union. Month after month, Standley grumbled, he "saw Special Representative after Big Dignitary come to Russia, leapfrog over my top-hatted head, and follow out the Rooseveltian policy—do not antagonize the Russians, give them everything they want, for, after all, they are killing Germans, they are fighting our battles for us."[2]

Wendell Willkie particularly infuriated him. The 1940 Republican presidential nominee breezed in for private talks with Stalin, expounded loudly on the failings of the Lend-Lease program, and criticized the United States and Great Britain for moving too slowly to open a second front.

General James H. Burns, the executive director of the Lend-Lease Administration, paid a visit and aggravated already frosty relations between Standley's military and naval attachés and Burns's liaison officer, who reported to Washington through his own channels. Captain Eddie Rickenbacker, the World War I Army Air Corps hero, arrived on a solo mission of uncertain purpose and without the knowledge of anybody in authority in Washington. Patrick Hurley, Hoover's secretary of war reincarnated as an Army major general, appeared in the course of a global mission for his own private talks with Stalin.

Then, Harriman came with Churchill, seeming to the wounded ambassador to be newly self-important and insensitive. The admiral was offended and angry at being left to "sit vacuously and pleasantly at dinner . . . listening to the service chatter of four American Army generals" while Averell went off to meet with Stalin and Churchill.[3] Harriman's contribution to the historic meeting was minimal, Standley sniffed, like "a moth fluttering around the sparks and flame of the interchange."[4]

More serious than the Harriman episode or the succession of other emissaries, however, was his systematic exclusion from anything concerning military assistance. In that arena, the chief irritant was Brigadier General Philip R. Faymonville, Harry Hopkins's personal choice as the Lend-Lease Administration's man in Moscow. Like Standley, Faymonville had been a member of the Harriman-Beaverbrook mission to Moscow in 1941, and on Hopkins's orders, he had been promoted from colonel to brigadier general and left behind to handle day-to-day Lend-Lease matters. Few Americans knew the Soviet Union as well as did Faymonville, who had been the military attaché in Moscow for five years during the thirties. Fluent in Russian, he had visited the remote provinces of Siberia, steeped himself in Russian lore, and developed a passionate sympathy for the Red Army.

He shared little of what he knew with Standley or the military and naval attachés, who resented both his Soviet contacts and his political connections in Washington. In time, Colonel Joseph Michela, Standley's fiercely anti-Communist military attaché, even stopped speaking to him. Standley did not question the young general's loyalty, but Faymonville's attitude caused others in the embassy to gossip that he was a "parlor Pink."

After only six months on the job, Standley asked for and got permission to go home and discuss the problem. At the White House, he complained that Faymonville was "playing Santa Claus" for the Soviets, agreeing to every demand "from a darning needle to a tire factory, which they won't have operating ten years after the war."[5] A session with Hopkins and the President produced vague assurances that Faymonville would be reined in and brought promotions for the military and naval attachés, but in the end nothing was done.

The final insult was the appearance of former ambassador Joseph Davies with a secret presidential message to Stalin proposing a private meeting between the two of them. Davies spent eleven hours closeted at the Kremlin, excluding the ambassador entirely. Even after he had been presented to Stalin by Standley, Davies pointedly declined to present Stalin the sealed letter from the President in the ambassador's presence. With that, Standley wrote the President that he didn't want to spend another winter in Moscow. He was no longer willing, he said, "to attempt to continue service in a position where it can be better rendered by someone else."[6]

By coincidence, Harriman was in Washington as the administration again confronted the task of filling its most important diplomatic post. In May, he and Churchill had crossed the Atlantic on the *Queen Mary*, which was also carrying five thousand German war prisoners to camps in the United States, for the Prime Minister's second meeting of the year with the President. After Churchill departed for a visit to North Africa, he stayed behind, and once again talk turned to Moscow.

As an indication of the importance attached to the assignment, Cordell Hull recommended that Hopkins be sent to Moscow; but to anyone who knew Roosevelt, the idea of letting Hopkins leave was out of the question. No doubt aware of that, Hull made Harriman his second choice. If Hopkins could not go, he said, Averell was the "logical" man for the job.[7] Evidently the President did not attach as much urgency to the assignment as did his advisers, for he toyed with the notion of sending Davies back for another tour.

One of the largest contributors to Roosevelt's political campaigns, the politician-financier Davies had made a fortune representing Standard Oil and had married another when he wed Post Toasties heiress Marjorie Post Close Hutton. He had succeeded William Bullitt in 1937 and had proved to be a disaster, he and his wife making a spectacle of themselves with their excesses. They shipped tons of food and twenty-five deep freezers to Moscow as part of their personal effects; and, once there, Davies amused himself collecting Russian antiques and yachting on the Baltic. He fawned over Stalin and the Soviet government, and Harriman considered him to have been utterly inept. He shuddered when Roosevelt had sent Davies back to Moscow on his special mission, in May 1943, fearing that he might even botch the delivery of a letter.

*   *   *

The President's new offer of the Moscow assignment was masterfully couched to appeal to Harriman's ego. At a private dinner at the White House, Roosevelt talked intimately about the imperative of having a personal relationship with Stalin, emphasizing that Harriman was one of the few diplomats in the world who could honestly claim to know him. No one would have as much chance to thaw Stalin's icy suspicion of the West. The Moscow post was not a mere assignment to impose order in a quarrelsome embassy and expedite the most sensitive communications between the White House and the Kremlin, it was a great calling to national service.

Harriman was trapped by his own rhetoric. He had lobbied for the admiral's appointment in the first place, and he shared Standley's impatience with Soviet pettiness about Lend-Lease. He was glad that the admiral had stood up and complained about it, even if indiscreetly. There was in London, he declared, a growing belief that "we are building up trouble for the future by allowing the Russians to kick us around."[8] It hadn't been two years since he had pointed out the importance of having someone in the post who was a personal friend of the President. Now his own reasoning was turned back upon him by Roosevelt. The prospect of leaving London for Moscow was no more appealing than it had been in 1941. He liked his job in England. He was doing work critical to the war, serving in the supporting cast for the Roosevelt-Churchill conferences, acting as conduit between world leaders and a buffer in their troublesome moments. The Moscow proposal was seductive, but there were before him the unhappy examples of Bullitt, Davies, Steinhardt, and Standley. From his own visits to the Soviet Union, he knew that Western diplomats were "hopelessly restricted . . . fenced in." He could not but fear that in the Soviet Union he would be "at the end of the line, probably losing such value as I had in London."[9]

He also knew about the Faymonville problem, and he understood how totally Standley had been defeated trying to lead a delegation whose troubles had become the talk of the Western diplomatic ghetto in Moscow. Davies's mission had made it obvious that the ambassador was neither kept informed nor given a real chance to use his influence, Britain's Archibald Clark Kerr advised the Foreign Office in London. "In the eyes of the Russians, the whole American embassy has suffered, and the ambassador in particular. It saddens me to watch the attrition of something as good and solid as the Admiral was making of his mission, and the losing of ground that need not be lost, when the holding of it is of the highest importance, and when we seem to be gaining it all the time. What I should like would be to move on to winning the confidence of the Russians abreast and hand in hand with the Americans. Anything else is stupid."[10] As soon as the candid assessment reached London,

Sir Richard Stafford Cripps, London's former ambassador to Moscow, passed it along to Harriman.

After the dinner with the President and several talks with Hopkins, Averell flew back to London in June, having asked Roosevelt for a bit more time to think about the offer. There, he discussed it with Churchill, mulled it over for another two weeks, then suggested a compromise. He would go back to Moscow to try to sell Stalin on a private meeting and to run the embassy for a sort of trial period, during which he would retain the option of returning to London.

"I would know within a couple of months in Moscow whether I could be of value and would ask that, if I have not been able to do a job, I could then return or be fired," he told FDR. "I am so keen about the work you have given me in London, which I feel is of increasing value as the time for the offensive approaches, that I would like to go back to it if I cannot do a real job in Moscow. I am sure I can be of more use to you and the war in London than to remain in Moscow as a glorified communications officer."[11]

The suggestion provoked no interest at the White House, and the matter was still unresolved a month later when Harriman accompanied the Churchills to Quebec, where Roosevelt and the British leader resumed their planning for the invasion of France. One afternoon, while Roosevelt and Churchill napped, Harriman and Hopkins went trout fishing on Grand Lac de l'Paule, forty miles north of the city, getting one of the rare chances that they had enjoyed since Averell moved to London for a casual talk.

Hopkins was in an unusually reflective mood. His marriage, his health problems, and the course of the war had changed his relations with the President; now he and Louise were about to move out of the White House into their own bungalow in Georgetown, and he was beginning to look toward peacetime and a return to private life, his personal and political ambitions behind him. One of his chief concerns would be finding a job in which he could support himself and his family while he wrote about his experiences in the New Deal and the war.

As he mused about his own future, Hopkins subtly lobbied Harriman to take the job in the Soviet Union: obviously, his most important work in London was finished; the Moscow post was far more crucial because Washington now needed Stalin's commitment to enter the struggle against Japan as soon as Hitler was defeated; and the President had to have someone in whom he had confidence to address the overarching matter of postwar relations with the USSR. Having just turned down another Roosevelt suggestion of a private meeting, Stalin was at that moment dragging his feet on the most basic areas of potential cooperation—even denying the United States permission to land damaged planes on Soviet soil after raids on Romanian oil refineries.

Under these circumstances, Harriman could hardly dismiss the assignment. He accepted it at the end of August, but it was another month before his name was submitted to the Senate for confirmation. During the interim, he was at the White House nearly every day for long talks with Roosevelt about the future of France, the role of postwar Germany, and Stalin's territorial ambitions. The President, still optimistic that he could work with Stalin after the war, was open to the idea of providing economic and technical assistance to help the Soviets rebuild; and he was willing to consider internationalizing the trans-Iranian railroad to give the Russians access to a warm-water port on the Persian Gulf.

When Standley arrived in Washington on September 24 to brief the secretary of state for the upcoming foreign ministers' conference in Moscow, he was yet to be advised that he was being replaced. Not until he reached National Airport did he learn that Harriman was taking over. The two of them met by chance when the admiral checked into the Mayflower, and that evening they had dinner in Harriman's suite. Standley poured out all of his frustrations—about Soviet recalcitrance, Faymonville, and the interference by special envoys. The meeting was cordial enough; but Standley did not offer any advice, nor did Harriman ask for it. The ambassador-designate had no qualms about the task before him. Stalin, he told the bemused admiral, "could be handled."[12]

Although he was skeptical of Roosevelt's vision of a postwar order including a cooperative Soviet Union, Harriman believed that unlike his predecessors he could succeed in getting a Kremlin hearing for Roosevelt's message. After all, he had dealt successfully with Stalin before. The Kremlin would understand that he, more than the previous ambassadors, would speak personally for both Roosevelt and Hopkins.

His first problem, however, was to stop the in-house bickering that had humiliated Standley and to straighten out an embassy "seething with cliques and gossip."[13] Unlike Standley, he was in a position to deal with the Faymonville problem.

With General Marshall, he worked out an arrangement in which the Moscow military mission would operate under the ambassador while simultaneously reporting to the Army chief of staff. It was precisely the opposite of the arrangement he had in London, where he conducted Lend-Lease business with the British military completely independent of Winant and the embassy; but now that the shoe was on the other foot, he insisted that the ambassador have responsibility for all of America's business in his country. His first use of his authority over the military mission in Moscow would be to replace Faymonville. Marshall agreed. And since the chief of staff approved, so did Hopkins, who had repeatedly spurned advice to remove Faymonville.

Averell's choice to take over the military office was Major General Albert C. Wedemeyer, a Marshall protégé he regarded as "one of the few men in the Army who had any idea of the difficulties we would have with the Russians after the war."[14] But Wedemeyer's robust skepticism of the Soviet government and the people who ran it had occasionally irritated Hopkins, so the post went instead to Brigadier General John R. Deane, secretary to the Combined Chiefs of Staff.

Harriman had never met Deane; but the general was highly regarded by Marshall, and that was enough. In time, he would operate almost as a full partner in one of the most successful professional relationships of Harriman's career. Deane's orders paralleled Averell's instructions from the President—"to promote the closest possible coordination of the military efforts of the United States and the USSR." Given the rank of major general to allow him access to higher levels of the Soviet military hierarchy, he had explicit authority to go to the Russians whenever he felt it necessary and talk about sensitive plans, operations, and strategy.[15]

While the military mission was being reorganized, Harriman secured his own independence from the State Department hierarchy by arranging with Marshall to have routine access to the military mission's communications system so he could exchange messages with Hopkins and the President, as he had in London, without going through the bureaucracy. The changes were set before his selection was ever announced, and they made him America's most influential envoy. While he had no responsibility for shaping policy, he exerted a powerful influence on it through his connections with Hopkins and Marshall and his insider's position with the British government.

By the time his nomination was sent to the Senate, he was already back in London saying his farewells and conferring with the Prime Minister at Chequers, where he and Kathleen spent their last weekend before departing for Moscow. So intense had been his preparation in Washington that he had not even told his daughter they were moving. Kathleen learned of the appointment only hours before he returned from Washington. She had less than a week to dispose of their flat and find clothes for a Moscow winter.

Their new home in the Soviet Union was a remnant of czarist opulence, now frayed and suffering fresh scars from wartime battering and neglect. It had once been the residence of a wealthy Russian sugar merchant, and the story was that the unfortunate capitalist had died before he had the opportunity to surrender it to the Bolsheviks—murdered by his own drunken son after a quarrel over money.

A fifteen-minute walk from the Kremlin, Spaso House was said to have cost $2 million, and in its heyday it was the finest house anywhere in Moscow. Its two-story great hall was set off by a spectacular crystal chandelier. Columns and stairways gave the illusion of marble, and rooms decorated with satin wall coverings retained some of their elegance in spite of neglect. The war's toll had been heavy—most of the shrubbery had died, and during the summer of '41, a thousand-pound bomb had hit fifty yards from the door, shattering nearly all of the windows. After the embassy was evacuated to Kuibyshev that autumn, the house accommodated a small liaison staff that stayed behind while the chancellery stood boarded up, its offices dark, its water pipes burst, its corridors empty but for the rats. For this diplomatic skeleton crew, Spaso provided offices, a home, and a warehouse for the belongings of other American diplomatic outposts evacuated ahead of the advancing German Army.

Gradually, the house had fallen into egregious disrepair, its heating and plumbing systems barely functioning, its drapes and wall coverings tattered, and frescoes and cornices crumbling. Shattered windows had been covered with plasterboard, with pipes from oil-burning stoves protruding inelegantly from several bedrooms. Dirt covered the back yard, where a bomb shelter had been excavated.

But Moscow was a different city from the one it had been in 1941 when the Germans were almost at the gates. Now the streets were cleaner and more alive, and there were signs of confidence in the people. The capital, Harriman also discovered, was less hospitable to resident diplomats than it was to the President's special emissaries. During his previous visits as America's Lend-Lease negotiator and as Churchill's traveling companion, he had been accorded entrée and courtesies which he now learned were unknown to members of the Moscow-based diplomatic corps. Socially and officially isolated, he spent most of his hours awaiting instructions from Washington or responses from the Kremlin. In the new light, it was obvious that the President's wish to batter down the suspicion dividing America from her Soviet ally was a fantasy.

Shortly after he moved into Spaso, Averell was stricken with a sinus infection. Tending toward hypochondria anyway, he took to his bed, making his second-floor bedroom his office. Even after he recovered, there were many winter days when he never left the house, never received an official visitor, and stayed abed until late morning, reading and writing cables.

In London, he had continued to be a dollar-a-year man doing his patriotic bit to help fight the war; but when he arrived in Moscow, he had gone on the State Department payroll at $17,500 a year. No matter if he answered directly to the President, he was in the grasp of diplomatic bureaucracy. Accordingly, he had to consider matters like conflicts of interest; and before taking the job, he had checked with the bank in New York to make sure that he and the Soviet Union had closed the books on their old manganese concession. It had been years since he had checked on the account, and he found that in July the Soviets had redeemed the last $137,000 of its notes that he held.

"During the day, the phone practically never rings," Meiklejohn noted after they had been in Moscow for a month. "He only placed one call today, to the British embassy, and except for his duty calls, he has virtually no appointments."[16]

Occasionally, there were informal morning visitors, such as Harrison Salisbury, the United Press reporter Harriman had known in London, or some other correspondent. But ordinarily, little happened until 1:30 P.M., when several of "the boys," as he called the top embassy staff, walked over from the chancellery to have lunch and listen to the two o'clock BBC news. Afterward, Meiklejohn would trudge down the stairs and spread the files and cables on the dining room table, and he and Harriman would dispose of the day's business.

For some of the Americans in Moscow, the gray cold and the isolation were more than they could bear. Sam Spewack, a onetime Moscow correspondent brought in to act as press attaché and run the Office of War Information, quickly fell into depression. His room leaked so badly that he had to erect an umbrella over his bed, where he encamped and began to write a novel. He started to drink heavily, and after four months he went home for a visit and did not return.

Minister Counselor Maxwell Hamilton, the senior staff member, was a China specialist increasingly discontented in Moscow and anxious to get out. When he was reassigned to Helsinki, Harriman was equally happy because it provided an opportunity for him to bring in his own Soviet expert. His choice was Charles E. "Chip" Bohlen, a seasoned hand and gifted linguist; but the State Department was willing to send Bohlen to Moscow only temporarily because he was considered vital in his post as assistant chief of the Division of European Affairs. The assignment as the top career officer in Moscow went instead to George F. Kennan, who had gone to Moscow in 1934 as an aide to William Bullitt, the United States' first ambassador to the Soviet Union. By 1943, Kennan was on his way to becoming America's best-known Sovietologist.

In spite of his own confident, assertive front, Harriman was, in his first Moscow winter, lonely and often idle, rankled by the State Department and dissatisfied with his dealings with Soviet officials. He had obviously not expected to have the kind of clout he had enjoyed in London, but given his standing with Hopkins and the President, he had thought that he could establish effective communications with Stalin. For the first time in the war, he started regularly writing letters to Marie telling her what he was doing; and when Spewack and Bohlen left for America, he sent her a gloomy letter confessing his unhappiness and suggesting that she consider a visit.

"The routine will be tough now," he told her,

as I am sending home today the only two men I enjoyed talking with—Sam Spewack & Chip Bohlen. Sam has made life at least amusing and has been a relief and a safety valve when I couldn't stand the State Department any longer. He says he will look you up when he gets to N.Y. Do see him and get all the dope. I am counting on his return in two months at most. Besides being fun, he is doing a really first class job & has accomplished some very important things. His wife, Bella, will probably come back with him. I wish you could come then or perhaps later in the spring. The summer may be better than now. It is hard to take now. One is so shut in both physically and mentally. Everyone is a bit on edge. If it wasn't for the war side of my work, I would be too. As it is, the things I am involved in are so vital that it is a real satisfaction & something is at least being accomplished. . . .[17]

Confined to their routine, members of the Spaso House family wore on each others' nerves. Meiklejohn complained that the boss was taking on airs. "His nibs has acquired, or I have just recently come to notice it, an authoritative, imperious way of announcing his views on even the most inconsequential matters," the secretary wrote in his diary.

He asks endless questions, rarely with any view to gaining information but rather to bring out his own detailed knowledge of the matter in question or to put the other party on the defensive. I suppose these are techniques that are useful in diplomatic conversations or business deals but they certainly make him a person to be avoided so far as recreational conversation is concerned. It really is an experience to witness him giving birth to an important cable. He dictates with extreme slowness and then goes over and over and over every sentence, changing words, phrases and paragraphs time after time 'till nobody but him has the slightest idea of what the end product is."[18]

When Harriman was summoned to the Kremlin on business, it was nearly always late at night, and sometimes past midnight—in which case reports to Washington were drafted before dawn. Rousted from bed to take dictation, Meiklejohn would join him before the fireplace, occasionally dozing as Harriman groped for words and labored over nuances. When important cables were finished, the secretary would go off in the darkness and awaken a code clerk at the chancellery who would get them off to Washington.

On Saturday afternoons, Western diplomats, journalists and a collection of "tame Russians" cleared by the Foreign Ministry came to Spaso House to watch movies. Hollywood films being the capitalist import prized above everything except American cigarettes, film fans were ecstatic when an exploration of the Spaso attic turned up stacks of reels left behind by Standley. The film was so dry and brittle that it snapped every few minutes, nearly always at an inopportune moment, but Kathleen became an expert at splicing, and the reels were shown over and over.

Otherwise opportunities for social contact with the Russians mainly came on special occasions, such as the President's birthday. When FDR turned sixty-two on January 30, 1944, Harriman brought in an orchestra, rolled up the carpet in the formal dining room, and threw a dinner-dance. A huge crowd turned out, and the affair was proclaimed the highlight of the winter season. Although the orchestra knew only marches and played foxtrots with a parade-field *oompah-pah*, there was enough vodka to evoke Glenn Miller.

Between the sanctioned parties, members of the military mission threw bashes awash in viciously spiked punch and raucous enough to send Harriman home early. When summer came, the monotony was relieved by weekends at the embassy's dacha, located in a grove of trees twenty miles outside of Moscow and equipped with a Turkish bath and a greenhouse attended by a Russian farmer who lived there.

Steinhardt had prepared it as a place for the American delegation to retreat if the Germans overran Moscow; when the crisis passed, it was forgotten. Averell paid a visit as his first Russian spring arrived; finding the plumbing, electricity, and a telephone all out of order, he launched an extensive renovation. Chequers it wasn't, even after the repairs, but it was a good place for summer picnics. Beer and softball brought fleeting psychological emancipation, and a vegetable garden provided seasonal relief from the Lend-Lease rations.

Whenever and wherever he moved about Moscow, Harriman was trailed by four NKVD agents who fell in behind him at Spaso's gate. When he went to the ballet or to dinner, they followed him and ejected nearby patrons to claim seats for themselves. The assignment was more challenging for them on the Sunday afternoons when he took to the ski slopes of Lenin Hills. Outfitted in gray flannel trousers, a tweed jacket, and a woolen cap that would have made him the laughingstock of Sun Valley, he took the modest runs at frightening speeds while the agent detailed to pursuit duty seldom stayed upright through the first turn.

Harriman took the surveillance in good humor. His "bodyguards" were insurance against getting lost, and the fact that he rated a four-man detail instead of the two who tailed other ambassadors was testament to his importance. Once, when he went into the country in the early spring, the NKVD car slid into a ditch and buried itself in the mud. To their embarrassment, Averell stopped, backed up, and gave them a ride on his running board.

With good news steadily coming in from the battlefield, the twenty-sixth anniversary of the Bolshevik Revolution—a month after Averell's arrival—was the occasion for Moscow's first celebration since the beginning of the war: a Foreign Ministry party marked by the first appearance of Soviet officials in new diplomatic garb drooping with medals and decorations worthy of Roman centurions. Harriman hadn't a white tie and tails anywhere closer than New York, and a search of friendly embassies produced nothing that would fit. He, therefore, appeared in his basic banker's suit, looking positively proletarian beside embarrassed old Bolsheviks turned out in their splendid uniforms.

What made the occasion truly memorable was that he and Clark Kerr were singled out for the hosts' special "treatment." Surrounded, they were offered toast upon vodka toast, requiring them to drain their glasses in response. The two accepted the honors heroically and foolishly, downing each new drink thrust into their hands to the last drop. Sir Archibald's evening ended when he passed out on his feet and crashed onto a table. By some later accounts, he struck his head on a punch bowl as he fell. Other stories had him going face down into a plate of fish before descending onto the floor. In any case, he was rendered unconscious and, quickly surrounded by his countrymen, had to be helped away.

The hosts themselves did not escape unscathed. Under the effect of the toasts, the combative Andrei Vishinsky, the deputy foreign minister, loudly told the Swedish minister that neutrals were not appreciated in the Soviet Union. Molotov disappeared for an hour or more, returning to action chalky-faced but still on his feet after a call at a sobering station where rumor had it that stomach pumps and caffeine injections were employed.

Thanks to Kathleen, Averell avoided the calamity that befell his British colleague. Seeing that her father had reached his limit, she rounded up a rescue party of officers from the American military mission and steered him toward the exit.

Some days later, the cobwebs having cleared, he dutifully wrote a memorandum describing the affair to the President. But it was, to say the least, inadequate. "The party was getting somewhat hilarious shortly after midnight," he reported. "Clark Kerr showed signs of weakening. Kathleen, who had contributed a great deal to the interest and entertainment of our Russian friends, had the good sense to suggest leaving before it was too late. I proposed a farewell toast to Marshal Stalin and the Red Army he led, and Molotov immediately added your name and that of the Prime Minister to it."[19] The memo was never sent, its author evidently unwilling to give the President less than the truth and unable to confess the graphic details. Meiklejohn's diary recorded that Harriman did not arise until midafternoon on the day following the celebration, having made one "wild foray in search of Bromo Seltzer" before falling back into bed.[20] Thereafter, when he was bound for a Russian party where there was a risk of more special honors, he gulped down hot tea and bread thickly lathered with butter. It was an old Skull and Bones precaution based on the dubious wisdom that the butter would line the stomach and inhibit the rush of alcohol into the bloodstream.

Outside these Kremlin affairs, Harriman met few Russians except members of the crowd authorized to come to Spaso House parties—artists, writers, actors, musicians, many of whom undoubtedly served as intelligence functionaries.

There was rarely a moment when he could be unguarded, so Harriman cherished any opportunity to get out of Moscow and see something of the country. His most enlightening exposure to wartime Russia came by accident and gave him new respect for ordinary Russians. As a prelude to the Big Three conference in Teheran in November 1943, Roosevelt and Churchill had arranged to meet in Cairo, where their military chiefs could plot strategy and the President and the Prime Minister could have their first talk with Chiang Kai-shek. Ordered to join the American party in the Egyptian capital, Harriman, Deane, Meiklejohn, and Bohlen, who was to be the President's interpreter, took off from Moscow on November 19, accompanied by Clark Kerr and Lieutenant General G. LeQ. Martel, chief of the British military mission in Moscow.

About noon, as they flew over tank traps, artillery emplacements, trenches and bomb craters where German troops had weeks before encircled the city of Stalingrad, warning lights in the cockpit showed dangerously low oil pressure in two of their engines. Fearing a bona fide emergency, the crew put the Liberator bomber down at an airfield five miles outside of town.

Armed guards immediately hustled them into a dugout serving as the airport operations center and held them at gunpoint. But authorities arriving from the city minutes later were "beside themselves with delight" when they learned that the man they regarded as the father of Lend-Lease had dropped out of the sky.[21] The unexpected guests were piled into a convoy of captured German automobiles and driven into the ruins of the city. On the way, they had to maneuver around shell holes, wrecked planes and disabled tanks. In Stalingrad itself, scarcely a building was standing; and to negotiate the wreckage and debris, the party had to make its way on foot. Not even in bombed-out London had Harriman seen such destruction. Introduced to curious crowds, he was surprised to find himself a hero to Russians, who shouted his name and crowded around offering him mementos taken from the bodies of dead Germans.

Away from Moscow and the scrutiny of the NKVD, ordinary people's friendship was uninhibited. In a barracks building serving as city hall, the chief of the Stalingrad Defense Council arranged a banquet of sausages, cheese, black bread and cabbage, accompanied by water tumblers of vodka.

Fortified, the visitors were led back into the chilly streets. With guides reciting tales of heroic resistance by women and children, they were escorted around crucial positions where the battle for the city had been decided, and past the cellars, lean-tos, and tar-paper shacks where the survivors were preparing to face winter.

That evening, they sat down to a dinner of the same dishes they had been offered at lunch, the celebration continuing past midnight and soaring to new heights of conviviality. Still not fully recovered from lunch, the visitors manfully drank more toasts—twenty-two of them by Meiklejohn's sober count—and loudly sang old drinking songs in Russian, English, and combinations of the two. Waitresses put down their trays of sausages and danced to whistling, clapping, and cheering. Harriman held forth on Russian heroism and the inevitability of Allied victory, then accepted more war trophies—German sabers, pistols, watches, and medals.

Bohlen, the travelers' most forceful singer as well as their interpreter, slept at the table for a full hour before reviving and resuming his duties. Even General Deane, ordinarily a model of military sobriety, accepted the Russians' invitation to sing. Rising unsteadily to his feet, he soulfully crooned "Show Me the Way to Go Home," his baritone stirring with feeling as he belted out the line, "I'm tired and I want to go to bed."

Not even Deane's singing was enough to arouse his colleague, General Martel, however. At lunch, a toast had caught the British officer with a full tumbler of vodka in hand. He drained his glass, but he never recovered during the afternoon. After the opening toasts were tossed down at dinner, his head fell onto his chest, and he could not be revived. Mercifully, he was finally helped away and laid out on his cot for the night.

At 5 A.M., two hours after the heartiest had fallen into bed, all were rousted to confront breakfast—the same meal for the third time, complete with the cold sausages and vodka. Then, in darkness, they were trundled off to the airfield to resume their journey.

The group's return to Moscow from the eventful Teheran conference days later was an adventure of its own. Low-hanging clouds and icing conditions forced them down to treetop height. After missing their first landing approach, they turned back in search of an alternative runway, narrowly clearing a hilltop as they gained altitude. For an hour, they were lost in thick clouds before breaking out above a railroad track which they followed for 150 miles back to Moscow. "We were so low we could count the trees," Harriman wrote Marie the next day. "I think of my flying experiences, it was by far the toughest."[22] As soon as he got back, Harriman came down with flu again, joining Kathleen, who was stricken with mumps, on the Spaso House sick list. He was just recovering when another of the President's special emissaries arrived.

Army intelligence chief William J. "Wild Bill" Donovan was one of the more imaginative and unlikely of all of Roosevelt's special missions to the Kremlin. Loaded with Christmas presents from home, he had White House authority to arrange collaboration between American and Soviet intelligence, including the establishment of an Office of Strategic Services (OSS) mission in Moscow in exchange for the NKVD having an office in Washington. Considering that the Soviets were refusing to allow Americans the use of Siberian airfields, had witheld the location of Moscow's radio-navigation transmitters from Harriman's pilot, and bugged Spaso House and the embassy, the idea of exchanging spy offices was unorthodox to say the least. But Harriman became one of its enthusiastic supporters. On Christmas Day, he and Donovan went to the Kremlin for a discussion of the project with Molotov, agreeing to the arrangement in principle and clearing the way for details to be worked out directly with the NKVD hierarchy.

Without any of the usual bickering, Donovan soon got an agreement to exchange missions composed of a single officer with a small staff. The two groups were to swap information picked up behind enemy lines and cooperate in dealing with German counterespionage. It was also, Harriman thought, a marvelous opportunity to learn more about the way the Soviets' mysterious intelligence apparatus worked.

But both he and Donovan were jolted back to reality before the latter even got out of Moscow. When Averell asked for his Liberator bomber, *Becky*, to fly the visitor to Teheran, officials refused permission for the plane to leave the Soviet Union. Instead of using the American plane with sufficient range to easily make the trip nonstop, they insisted that Donovan had to fly in a twin-engine Soviet transport, which required at least one refueling stop, and perhaps two. Harriman's stiff protests got nowhere, but he persisted.

For eleven consecutive days, he, Kathleen, and Deane arose at six A.M., and went to the airport with Donovan in the subzero darkness. Each day, they were told the weather made it doubtful that the Red Air Force plane assigned to Donovan could land at Stalingrad or Baku to refuel. And each day, they were told that the American plane could not be used. To make sure that the hardheaded Americans did not defy them, the Russians refused to provide the flight crew with weather details, merely telling them that conditions were unacceptable.

Fuming, Harriman addressed a formal protest to Molotov; on the eleventh day, the authorities finally relented and Donovan flew out on Harriman's bomber. That did not end the test of wills, though. Molotov then refused to let the plane return. Thereafter, he decreed, it would be kept in Cairo and brought to Moscow only when Harriman himself or General Deane had arranged to fly out of the country.

Two months later, the OSS-NKVD arrangement was shelved by the President. It had been decided, Roosevelt cabled Harriman, that the timing was bad.[23] Averell protested that an opportunity was being thrown away and asked to come home to make a case for going ahead, but Washington was no longer interested. Harriman's suspicion that the initiative had been killed by Admiral William Leahy, the White House chief of staff, was confirmed when he got to Washington in May. General Marshall thought the reason was basically personal: the admiral, Marshall said, still harbored anti-Harriman feelings because he blamed Averell for Standley's losing his job in Moscow.[24]

Being one of a few American women in Moscow, Kathleen was as conspicuous as her father, serving as the official hostess at Spaso House, working for the Office of War Information, and making herself a favorite of Western diplomats. She picked up rudimentary Russian, chauffeured herself about Moscow, went to Russian church services, visited hospitals, called on wives of ambassadors. She was a familiar figure at the theater, the symphony, the ballet, and the ski slopes. At the latter, she placed third in the 1943 Moscow slalom championships. At her father's side at Soviet social functions, she was undaunted by the excessive toasting and unintimidated by the formidable challenge of the Russian language. Tall and pretty, and much matured by the two years in London, she had some of the instinctive aloofness that made Averell distant even in the forced intimacy of wartime Moscow, but she was also blessed with an un-Harriman—like sense of humor.

With aplomb, she presided over a residence nearly always filled to the rafters, directed its Russian staff, and found clever ways to conceal Spam and similar Lend-Lease delicacies on the ambassador's table. She shrugged off the affections of amorous Russians and the depressing darkness of Moscow's long winters, overcame bouts with scurvy and mumps, and cheered her father in his moments of frustration. With John Melby, a young foreign service officer who oversaw the operation of Spaso House and became acting director of the Office of War Information in Moscow, she produced the first issues of *America* magazine, a slick publication designed to give Russians some appreciation of what the United States was like. It became possible when Averell worked out an agreement with Molotov, allowing the magazine to be sold for a few kopecks in Moscow while the Soviets offered their own magazine to readers in the United States. *America* quickly became more popular than the embassy newsletter, already much sought after in the Moscow black market.

Since Harriman made no serious attempt to learn Russian, his daughter was also pressed into the role of interpreter at moments when he was caught without a Russian-speaking staff member at his side. And it was in part because of her that he was able to form personal friendships with a few Russians outside official circles. One was with Aleksey Tolstoy, a cousin of the literary giant, whose classic, *War and Peace*, Harriman first read after his arrival as ambassador.

Tolstoy was a hulking, gregarious man who stood out at embassy parties because of his bald dome and long hair hanging from the back and sides of his head. One of the "tame Russians" regularly at the Spaso House affairs, he was a prodigious drinker who wound up happily intoxicated even at the occasional party where sobriety prevailed, taking pride in his capacity for the scotch available at American and British affairs. He and his wife, a small woman half his age, were almost the only Russians who entertained Averell and Kathleen in their home. It was a friendship that required real effort on both sides, for neither Tolstoy nor his wife spoke English any better than Harriman spoke Russian. The wife, therefore, translated her husband's Russian into French, and Kathleen translated the French into English for Averell. Then the process was reversed. After a film or a heavy dinner, when Harriman was sleepy and Tolstoy was mellow, the late-evening conversations were mighty tests of determination.

Kathleen described one of their evenings in a letter home. "As time went on, Averell got sleepier and sleepier, and I found his yawns very catching," she reported. "Mme Tolstoy was having a progressively more difficult time translating her husband's flowery Russian into French; she was getting sleepy too, but Tolstoy was on top of the world, discussing his favorite subject, the Russian soul."[25]

Harriman also used his daughter as an unofficial aide-de-camp whose judgment and instincts he trusted as much as professional expertise. That confidence put her in the middle of one of the war's most sensitive diplomatic predicaments—the Soviets' attempt to absolve themselves of the massacre of Polish Army officers during the occupation of eastern Poland.

In January 1944, a commission operating under the auspices of the Kremlin opened mass graves in Katyn Forest outside the town of Smolensk and displayed the bodies of Poles systematically executed by bullets through the brain. The atrocities had already been revealed by the Germans while the area still lay under their occupation the previous year, claiming that the victims had been captured by the Russians during the Soviet occupation of 1939 and 1940, put to forced labor, then slaughtered before the Red Army withdrew. With the recapture of the area, the Soviets reopened the graves and set up a commission which proclaimed the executions the work of the Nazis, who had taken the region in August 1941.

When Harriman learned that Western correspondents had been invited to see the evidence, he got permission for Kathleen to join them and to take John Melby along as well.

The circumstances were treacherous, and the ambassador's daughter proved herself a careful diplomat. Ghastly as the executions were, Harriman was at the time more concerned with the diplomatic repercussions and working with the Soviets on the future of Poland than he was in solving the mystery.

Discovery of the massacre had already caused serious repercussions: the Polish government in exile was infuriating Stalin by demanding a full investigation by an international body. Harriman did what he could to avoid a rift, but the Poles mistrusted Stalin as much as they mistrusted Hitler, and they refused to back down. Moscow broke relations with them.

The grisly evidence now displayed by the Russians was contradictory. Many of the victims had their hands bound behind them with Russian rope, but the bullets that penetrated their skulls were of German manufacture. Although the Soviet's scenario had the atrocities being carried out in August and September, 1941, most of the victims were dressed for winter in greatcoats and boots.

Kathleen, Melby, and seventeen correspondents were taken to Smolensk on a posh special train from Moscow on January 21, then driven ten miles to the forest, which was actually a grove of unimpressive scrub pines that had been a picnic ground before the war.

There, Soviet experts guided them into tents where long rows of corpses in varying stages of decomposition lay on tables. Inside, in the glare and warmth of the klieg lights, there was a sickening stench. Kathleen, fortunately suffering a severe head cold, took clinical notes as a doctor performed a fast autopsy for her benefit, opening a chest and withdrawing internal organs, and slicing into muscle to show her that the flesh was still red. The Americans inspected bullet holes penetrating the base of the skulls at the rear and exiting through the foreheads, and went through documents and memorabilia missed when the victims' pockets had been ripped open and searched during the investigation by the German commissions. Later, there was a press conference with members of the commission, and then about midnight, the visitors were put back aboard their train for Moscow.

While the Germans had reported finding about four thousand bodies, the Soviets contended that eleven thousand men had actually been shot in the forest. The Germans, the Kremlin maintained, had exhumed all of them and removed documentation dated later than April 1940, then reburied them, and soon thereafter announced their "discovery." Although witnesses seemed to Kathleen "well rehearsed" and the Soviets suspiciously reluctant to be questioned closely, her report to her father said that the men had probably been killed by the Germans. She was much aware of the diplomatic implications, but her opinion was not entirely based on politics or the show the Russians had put on for them. The most convincing evidence, she thought, was the "methodical" manner in which the executions had been carried out.[26]

Journalists who went along could be no more certain than she. "Our verdict," Harrison Salisbury wrote in his journal, "was: a lot of Poles have been killed by revolver shots in the back of the head. They have been dead for some time. We wish we knew who killed them."[27]

As far as Averell was concerned, the commission's presentation supported what he wanted to believe—that the Germans had carried out the atrocities and duped the Polish government in exile. He rushed a report on to the President and Secretary Hull. It was impossible, he said, to judge the scientific evidence of autopsies performed in the presence of witnesses, but from the general evidence and the testimony, Kathleen and Melby believed that in all probability the massacre was the work of the Germans.[28] Eventually the Soviet government would acknowledge the responsibility of the Red Army, but Kathleen's memorandum would remain for years the version of the tragedy most widely accepted by the State Department.

Nine years later, both Harriman and his daughter were called as witnesses in a congressional investigation bent on publicly calling the Soviets to account. Both acknowledged that, after all, the accumulated evidence pointed to the Russians, but Harriman made no apology for Kathleen's earlier conclusion, nor his acceptance of it. It was entirely plausible, he said, that the Germans had "tried to frame the Russians to create friction among the allies," and it was only logical for Kathleen to have concluded just what she did.[29]

She would later acknowledge that, deep down, she had suspected that the Russians had been responsible, but on the basis of what she had seen she could not dispute the Soviet story. After the congressional hearing, the State Department proposed to put an official reprimand in Melby's file for his report from the forest; but Harriman demanded that it desist. He had sent Melby to Katyn Forest, he said; he had agreed with the report at the time; and if blame was to be assessed, it was his own.

Oddly, the job of being the United States ambassador in the Soviet Union became more difficult as the war's momentum shifted to the

Allies. Yet in spite of increasing Kremlin obstinance, Harriman had periods of satisfaction he had never known in business or government, when he felt he was having an important impact on the war. No moment was sweeter than the arrival of the first American bombers in the Soviet Union.

After months of tedious negotiations, Stalin agreed in February 1944 to let American planes use Ukrainian bases for the shuttle bombing of eastern Europe, thereby opening the way for Army Air Corps planes based in Italy to hit targets that had been beyond their reach, landing and reloading in the Soviet Union, then bombing again on the return trip to Italy. The agreement was not only a step toward access to Soviet bases in the Far East for the war against Japan, it was a crack in Stalin's wall against foreign military forces in Soviet territory. No concession was more difficult for the Kremlin to make.

Following a trip home, Harriman returned to Moscow in June 1944 just in time to change clothes and fly to the new shuttle base at Poltava for a party celebrating the triumph of diplomacy and air power in advance. As the diplomatic corps and military officers exchanged vodka toasts in the Ukraine, planes of the U.S. Fifteenth Air Force were loading their bombs in Italy for a strike on rail yards in Hungary before landing in the USSR.

The next morning, Harriman and Kathleen were driving toward the airfield when scores of Flying Fortresses trimmed in their familiar red, white, and blue markings filled the sky in a gigantic V formation. They shook the earth with a low-level pass over the field, sweeping off to the east and lining up in a holding pattern where they peeled off one by one for their landing approach. In the back seat of a Lend-Lease Buick, Soviet major general A. R. Perminov threw his arms around Harriman and tried in vain to kiss him on the cheek as they careened toward the field. Beside the landing strip, Soviet officers stood transfixed as the bombers touched down on the runway with such precision that three planes were on the runway at a time, coasting to their turnoff where they taxied into parked formation. Young women in Red Army uniforms stood by to hand each pilot a bouquet of wildflowers as he stepped from his cockpit. Ambulances and crash trucks mobilized for the arrival were never needed.

Striking with complete surprise, the planes had hit their targets in Hungary with devastating effect. Only one had been lost and it was claimed by an accident, its fuel tank exploding and enveloping it in a midair fireball.

As soon as the lead plane, *Yankee Doodle II*, shut down its engines, Harriman and Kathleen were beside it to welcome their old London friend, Lieutenant General Ira Eaker, whose first act on Russian soil was to present the U.S. Legion of Merit to Perminov. Altogether, 120 bombers and eighty-odd fighter escorts landed at Poltava and two other bases at the end of the first mission and almost immediately began reloading and refueling to hit more targets on their way back. Eaker meanwhile was taken to Moscow to be toasted by Stalin himself.

Spaso House was still tingling with the triumph two days later when German radio, and then a flash cable from Washington, brought the news of the Allied landings at Normandy. For days thereafter, the tired Soviet capital was "awash in boozy good feeling."[30] Americans were all heroes, getting their backs slapped and hands wrung everywhere they went. From one dawn until the next, Russians were ready to drink to the great—and long-awaited—second front.

The invasion coincided with the arrival of the best balmy days of Moscow's late spring, transforming the city. At Spaso House, the sunlight streamed into Harriman's room for the first time since his arrival, the beaverboard over the windows having at last been replaced with glass. More invigorated than he had been in months, the ambassador chopped down a dead tree by the residence, and then armed himself with a heavy hammer and began demolishing a brick wall that had been erected around the mansion to protect its lower windows from bomb damage early in the war.

Official goodwill was as warm as the outpouring in the streets. A Soviet courier arrived with a huge polar bear rug for Harriman and enough Astrakhan skins for Kathleen to make a coat, gifts from Anastas Mikoyan, the commissar for foreign trade. Stalin, who had for so long belittled the difficulty of crossing the English Channel to invade the shores of France, now told Harriman the feat ranked among the great military operations of the ages. "The history of war has never witnessed such a grandiose operation," he declared. "Napoleon himself never attempted it. Hitler envisaged it but he was a fool for never having attempted it."[31]

As the offensive closed in on Hitler, Harriman played host to a deluge of visitors. Eric Johnson, the president of the U.S. Chamber of Commerce, who had unconcealed White House ambitions, paid a long visit that included a late-night call on Stalin and a trip to the front. General Hurley stopped off on his way to Chungking, Roosevelt's crony Ed Flynn appeared to reemphasize the President's concern for religious freedom in the Soviet Union. There were the inevitable congressional delegations—vodka visitors, as the resident Americans called them with good reason.

The week after the invasion of France, Vice-President Henry Wallace, who was in the process of being dumped from Roosevelt's fourth-term campaign, arrived for a stopover on his way to China. Washington saw to it that his itinerary kept him far from Moscow and the American press, so Harriman went all the way to central Asia to meet him. They spent four days trooping around model farms and agricultural experiment stations where Wallace engaged Soviet officials in discussions of plant genetics, wheat yield, and potato diseases. It was a monumental waste of time, but Harriman thought that Wallace might be his own ticket to the Far East and a chance to size up Chiang Kai-shek's war against the Japanese. A cable to Washington, suggesting that he join the Vice-President's entourage, was ignored.

That autumn, while he was away reporting to the President on Churchill's just-ended Moscow conference, Lillian Hellman turned up as a houseguest at Spaso. Full of sympathy for the Soviets and leftist causes, the celebrated playwright had undertaken a cultural mission arranged by the Soviet Foreign Ministry, making the long journey to Moscow via Alaska and Siberia. She had traveled in an unheated Soviet cargo plane that had been forced down by bad weather several times along the way. She had taken refuge for hours in miserable shacks at Siberian airfields, and by the time she reached Moscow, she was coming down with pneumonia. Thinking it dangerous for her to stay alone at the National Hotel, George Kennan cabled Harriman suggesting that she be moved to the ambassador's residence, where she could receive constant medical attention. Averell agreed, hoping her illness would be brief, for Hellman was not only politically controversial but a difficult and demanding woman.

When he and Kathleen got back two weeks later, their guest had made a remarkable recovery; moreover, she had found charming male companionship in John Melby. He was literate, politically sophisticated, and alone. She was in the midst of one of her separations from her longtime lover, Dashiell Hammett, and so romance had blossomed under Harriman's roof.

She stayed on through Christmas 1944 and into the new year, living in Kathleen's sitting room and conducting the business of her cultural mission at an office in the chancellery. She also kept her hotel accommodations where she lived when it suited her and had her own Soviet car and driver on call. Socially, she added new life to the American enclave; and when she left, Melby was not the only one who was sad to see her go. Harriman gave her a farewell party, inviting all the Russians who had entertained her, plus the casts of her plays *Watch on the Rhine* and *The Little Foxes*, which the Soviet theater had produced during her visit.

Years later, at the height of the congressional searches for Communist subversion, Hellman was one of the most badgered and publicized witnesses grilled by the House Un-American Activities Committee; and she pleaded the Fifth Amendment when interrogators went fishing for details about her past political associations. Melby, already a sensitive subject with the State Department because of the Katyn Forest incident, was under investigation at the same time because he was among the young foreign service officers who had served in China in the late forties and whose views did not comply with Cold War orthodoxy.

In 1953, he lost his security clearance and, consequently, his job in the foreign service—in large part because of his affair with the woman who zealots insisted was a fellow traveler, if not a Communist.

Harriman was then out of government and unable to help him. But the matter did not rest. Twenty-seven years later, when Averell was nearly eighty-five, he persuaded the Carter administration to restore Melby's clearance. His old Moscow aide, who had become a college professor in Canada, returned to work briefly as a State Department consultant and qualify for government retirement benefits.

Nearly all of the concerns Harriman put to the President about the Moscow assignment in 1941 were borne out. Most of the time, the circumstances called for nothing more than a messenger and an analyst with infinite patience, and Averell was not a patient man. He had no more interest in the grunt work of diplomacy than he had in sitting in the partners' room at Brown Brothers Harriman. "He wanted to operate on a higher plane," George Kennan said. "He felt that he could learn more that was important in one interview with Stalin than the rest of us could learn in months of pedestrian study of Soviet publications."[32]

His strategic mission was to help create an atmosphere in which Roosevelt and Stalin could make the historic war decisions and plot a course for the future. As Hopkins's health and influence waned, his own role became more crucial.

At the early Roosevelt-Churchill meetings, Harriman had been on the fringes, moving easily between delegations and helping both prepare for their talks, but he was not much needed when the leaders now got together. His appearance at the summits without any apparent responsibility raised hackles at both the State Department and the British Foreign Office.

During the Cairo conference, Sir Alexander Cadogan, the undersecretary of the Foreign Office, bristled at his unsolicited criticism of the British draft communiqué. And in Teheran, Cadogan was deeply annoyed that the American ambassador had lectured him and Foreign Secretary Anthony Eden on "how to conduct international conferences" when "I've forgotten a great deal more than he ever knew."[33]

Even the ordinarily placid Edward Stettinius, while undersecretary of state, complained to the President that the constant attendance of both Harriman and Hopkins at the conferences was deeply resented at the State Department. But with the first Big Three summit, Harriman became a player rather than an appendage. After Stalin had turned down Khartoum, Basra, Nome, and Fairbanks as potential meeting sites, Harriman urged Roosevelt to accept Teheran in spite of the inconvenience in getting to the Iranian capital.

The American and British parties flew to meet the Soviets after four days in Cairo, and there Harriman became the de facto tour director for the loosely organized American delegation. For a momentous occasion anticipated from the beginning of the war, the gathering opened in astonishing disarray.

Louis Dreyfus, the American envoy to Iran, had no idea that the summit was even taking place until he returned from a trip out of the city and found Army tents pitched on the lawn of the legation and soldiers installing White House communications gear. Ousted from his residence and not even permitted to greet Roosevelt at the airfield, he tried to help out by ordering a supply of liquor so the Americans could entertain; but when carpenters constructed a ramp for Roosevelt's wheelchair, the structure obstructed the liquor cabinet so the door couldn't be opened to retrieve its contents.[34]

At midnight, just hours after their arrival, Molotov sent for Harriman and told him German agents were planning to disrupt the conference, and perhaps were even plotting to assassinate one of the leaders. Averell was skeptical and questioned Stalin's foreign minister to what he considered "the limits of civility," without getting any details.[35] Roosevelt was unquestionably vulnerable, since the legation was across the city from the meeting site and the British and Soviet embassies. Although he doubted a plot, Harriman accepted Molotov's invitation to inspect a villa in the secure Soviet compound and the next morning he recommended that the President move into it. The U.S. security detail was in full sympathy. Mike Reilly, its chief, had surveyed the harrowing security problems while the President was still in Cairo, and in meetings with the NKVD, he, too, had been tipped that Nazi agents had parachuted into Iran and were in the city.

Roosevelt settled into his new quarters on his second afternoon, after taking a circuitous route to the compound while his heavily guarded limousine was escorted through Teheran's clogged streets as a decoy. Minutes after his arrival, Stalin appeared. Harriman and Hopkins were there for the historic greeting, but they immediately withdrew, leaving the leaders with their interpreters.

From their private talk, Roosevelt and Stalin went immediately to a plenary meeting on plans for the warfare in France. To the Americans' embarrassment, General Marshall and General Arnold were both absent. No one having briefed them on the schedule, they had gone sight-seeing.

Although the U.S. delegation was small, it was loaded with people whose presence contributed to the disorganization and who had no role in the conference—among them Colonel Elliott Roosevelt, the President's son, Major John Boettiger, his son-in-law, and Ambassador Winant from London, who was preoccupied with arranging a personal meeting with the young Shah of Iran.

Belatedly, Averell created a semblance of order. Each morning he met with Molotov and Clark Kerr for a minute-by-minute journey through the day's schedule. He took charge of arrangements for Roosevelt's dinner for Churchill and Stalin and pressed Meiklejohn, a professional stenographer, into service as keeper of the U.S. delegation's record of the conference's plenary meetings. While Hopkins stayed at Roosevelt's side in all of the conversations, Harriman provided liaison between the President and the other two leaders outside the meeting room.

Churchill required more pampering than usual at Teheran because Roosevelt was blatantly trying to curry favor with Stalin. The anxious Prime Minister sent the President an invitation to lunch before Roosevelt went to have his chat with Stalin at the Soviet villa, but FDR politely turned him down. Warned that "storm signals were flying at the British legation," Harriman scurried to "calm the waters."[36] Meiklejohn was more than a little impressed. "Mr. Harriman," he noted in his diary, "is getting to be a regular fixer."[37] All said and done, the meeting in Teheran was the most crucial—and successful—of the wartime conferences of the Big Three, although the pleased participants, Harriman among them, exaggerated what had been accomplished. Nevertheless, the last big military issue before them had been resolved at the meeting. With the Anglo-American front open in France, they agreed that the Red Army would close from the East, preventing Hitler from concentrating on a defense of France. The coordinated drive would crush the German Army in a giant pincer.

Tangled political questions were set aside for another day.

Accompanied by Kathleen, Meiklejohn, and Eddie Page, the embassy's second secretary, and trailed by his NKVD detail, Harriman boarded a Russian train for Yalta on January 21, 1945. It still was nearly two weeks before the opening of the climactic meeting of the war; but since he was responsible for the President's comfort and the shepherding of a huge American delegation, he had to be there days in advance.

Soviet assurances aside, the Black Sea resort was a potentially disastrous place for the leaders to plot the course of the postwar world—the area had been occupied by the Germans, and the waters offshore were still seeded with mines. Rail lines were wrecked; communications problems were fiendish; and the site was reachable only by a long, winding drive through the mountains. All of this was fully understood, but Stalin was adamant about meeting on his own turf.

This time, he had turned down suggestions of Scotland, Malta, Athens, and Cyprus, all far more accessible than the Crimea. Doctor's orders, he claimed, prevented him from leaving the Soviet Union. For Roosevelt and Churchill, Yalta was an even poorer compromise than Teheran had been. "We could not have found a worse place if we had spent ten years on research," the Prime Minister grumbled before leaving London.[38]

Before Harriman's advance party got to the summit site, Averell was wishing he had gambled on good weather and taken a plane. The war had exacted a heavy toll on Soviet railroads—which were hardly comparable to the Union Pacific even in the best of times. Their train had no dining car, and the party subsisted on hard-boiled eggs, chocolate bars, sardines, bouillon, and bourbon as they rattled southward. They were attended by a female porter, who tidied the beds and went about squirting water through her teeth to soften spots of dirt on the floor. At station stops, elderly women came aboard with brush brooms and swept the cars, and locals hawked black bread and stale potatoes. Several times the Americans were delayed for hours, waiting for oncoming traffic to clear a long section where single tracks had to be alternately used by trains going in opposite directions. Night brought little rest, for their compartments were infested with savage bedbugs. Stations all along the way were jammed with refugees.

Reaching the end of the line at Simferopol in a heavy snowfall, they were advised by the Red Army general in charge to remain overnight, but Harriman insisted that they press on. They covered the winding, fifty-mile trip across the mountains in darkness, creeping along switchbacks until they neared the coast, where the skies were clear, the weather was warmer, and a full moon illuminated the coast and outlined Livadiya Palace, where the President and his party would stay. The marble and limestone retreat built for Czar Nicholas in 1911 overlooked the sea from a height of 150 feet. It was one of the several royal lodgings tucked in between the mountain peaks and the shore, and by far the most impressive, built on a commanding slope with a thick pine forest rising steeply behind it.

Harriman was preceded by a party from the American military mission in Moscow, plus U.S. Navy and Army Air Corps technicians and scores of Russian plumbers, painters, electricians, cleaning women, cooks, and undoubtedly agents of the NKVD. All were swarming over the palace, whose sumptuous furnishings, down to the doorknobs and plumbing fixtures, had been stripped during the German occupation. For the meeting, an army of Moscow hotel workers brought furniture, dishes, silverware, pots, pans, and linens, plus buckets of whitewash to cover the walls, and fumigants for warfare against lice and bedbugs.

A Soviet honor guard had already taken up positions, and Romanian POWs were at work setting out shrubs. Offshore at Sevastopol stood the USS *Catoctin*, a Navy utility ship equipped with a canteen, a hospital, a PX, and a communications center. Around the palace, Navy technicians hurried to install an emergency power station and lay transmission lines to the conference sites. To Kathleen and Eddie Page fell the responsibility of assigning quarters.

The Czar's bedroom suite, the only one with a private bath, was reserved for the President. Private bedrooms nearby were set aside for Stettinius, who had succeeded Hull as secretary of state, Hopkins, Harriman, Bohlen, and James F. Byrnes, director of the Office of War Mobilization. General Marshall and Admiral King were put on the second floor, the latter in a suite that had once been the Czarina's boudoir. The others were less fortunate. Major generals were billeted four to a room, colonels sixteen. Thirty-five officers were assigned to a single bath and forced to shave at water buckets beside their cots.

After two days, Harriman boarded the President's plane, the *Sacred Cow*, which had been ferried from Washington to Sevastopol, and flew off to meet Roosevelt nearly 1,400 miles away at Malta, while Kathleen was left behind to complete preparations at the palace.

Churchill was already there when he arrived, as were the American and British military chiefs, who had been in a day-long debate over General Eisenhower's strategy for crossing the Rhine. Hopkins had also joined the party, arriving from Paris, where he had gone to see de Gaulle. Worn out from his trip, he dragged himself off to bed early, leaving Harriman and Churchill to play bezique for several hours and to hash over what they expected from Stalin.

The following morning, Roosevelt arrived aboard the cruiser USS *Quincy* after ten days at sea. It had been the kind of interlude that ordinarily rejuvenated him physically and spiritually, but this one obviously had not. Harriman was shaken by his "worn, wasted" appearance, alarmingly deteriorated since November. But haggard as he was, Roosevelt was alert and clearly excited about meeting Stalin with the end of the war in sight. He had only one short night to rest before jumping off on the last leg of his journey.

The flight across the Mediterranean, over Greece, the Macedonian peninsula, and the Black Sea to the Crimea was the most hazardous part of the journey because there were still Nazi-controlled airfields along the route. To take advantage of darkness, they took off at three o'clock in the morning, under escort by half a dozen heavily armed P-38s. Churchill followed ten minutes later. Aside from the fighters, they entrusted their security to the darkness, radio silence, and a course carefully charted to take them around the enemy-held island of Crete.

The precautions were now especially serious, for American intelligence had learned that the Germans had discovered the location of the conference. And just the day before, an American plane taking equipment to Yalta had carelessly flown so close to Crete that German antiaircraft guns had attacked and damaged it before it got out of range.

Seven hours after leaving Malta, they arrived at Saki Airfield at Sevastopol. In a huge tent, the Russians had laid out the inevitable refreshments—tables laden with cold cuts, eggs, curd cakes, wine, champagne, and Crimean brandy. Roosevelt skipped all of it, staying just long enough to join Churchill in inspecting the honor guard before leaving on the ninety-mile drive to Yalta.

By the time the party reached the palace, Hopkins was so spent that Admiral Ross McIntire, the President's physician, seriously considered putting him aboard the *Catoctin* so he could have intense medical care. Hopkins would have none of that, but he stayed in his room throughout the conference, convening a few bedside meetings and, with obvious effort, taking the few steps down the hall for each day's plenary meeting. Harriman stepped into his friend's customary role. He was, therefore, at Roosevelt's side through much of the day; and on several evenings, he and Kathleen shared a quiet dinner in the President's suite with Roosevelt and his daughter Anna.

The President immediately went to work where he had left off at Teheran, trying to promote a civil relationship with the Russians after the war, but Stalin was as obstreperous as ever. To Averell's consternation, the President made little effort at coordination with Churchill, allowing five days to pass without a private talk with the Prime Minister.

Although Yalta would be ridiculed as a capitulation by an exhausted President, its political agenda had been thoroughly explored at Teheran and in the intervening fourteen months had dominated Harriman's contacts with the Kremlin. Particularly in the case of the Far East, Yalta confirmed what had already been worked out through Harriman during the fall.

The Pacific had been one of his urgent priorities from the day he arrived in Moscow. He had dogged the Russians for permission to use Soviet airfields in the bombing of Japan's home islands, and since the Teheran conference, he had pressed Stalin to name his conditions for a Soviet declaration of war in the Pacific.

As far back as the Moscow foreign ministers' meeting in October 1943, Stalin had voluntarily assured Hull that the Soviets would help defeat Japan after Hitler was finished. Although he had extended his personal assurances to the President at Teheran, he had been reluctant to lay out his conditions.

While Churchill was in Moscow in October 1944, Stalin had told Averell that the Red Army could mount an offensive against Japanese forces in Manchuria three months after the capitulation of Germany. He had thirty divisions in the Far East, and he would move about thirty more from Europe after Hitler's surrender. In preparation, he wanted the United States to stockpile supplies for two or three months' fighting. He did not think the war would go on much longer.

But aside from the American arms and ammunition, he continued, "political considerations" had to be taken into account. The Russian people had to know what they were fighting for. They fought against the Germans because they had been invaded. They would have to understand why they were fighting against the Japanese.[39]

Two days later, Stalin handed Harriman the long list of supplies he wanted and promised to let him know in two weeks when the United States could begin delivering the four-engine bombers it was providing the Red Air Force. Clearly, the Soviet dictator now wanted to play a larger part than the Americans had in mind. In Washington, strategists envisioned the Soviet role as one of securing the railroads and taking control of Manchuria. But Stalin's plan sketched for Averell was to drive south across the Mongolian desert into China, all the way south to Peking.

With that, Harriman had flown home to give Roosevelt a full account of Churchill's Moscow visit and his own talks with the Premier. The President was pleased with Stalin's new forthrightness and not particularly disturbed that references to "political considerations" indicated that territorial demands were coming. But Stalin's comments about driving all the way to Peking caused him to wonder aloud, "If the Russians go in, will they ever go out?"[40]

With the second Big Three summit delayed by quibbling over the site, the Soviets' political demands in the Far East were finally spelled out to Harriman when he met Stalin at the Kremlin on December 14. In brief, Stalin wanted the Kuril Islands, an archipelago stretching from the northern tip of Japan to the Kamchatka Peninsula, plus the southern half of Sakhalin Island, which the Japanese had got in the 1905 Treaty of Portsmouth. With control of the Kurils and all of Sakhalin, the Soviet Navy would have unimpeded access to the Pacific. He also wanted leases on the Manchurian ports of Dairen and Port Arthur, as well as on the Chinese Eastern and South Manchuria railroads. The rails would link Dairen and Port Arthur with the port at Vladivostok.

Harriman was skeptical of Stalin's assurance that the Soviets would do nothing to interfere with China's sovereignty in Manchuria, but Washington indicated neither disapproval nor acceptance of Stalin's claims, and there the matter still stood when the leaders gathered at Yalta.

It seemed as urgent as ever to bring the Soviets into the Pacific war. During their stopover at Malta, the combined military chiefs had reconfirmed their judgment that it would take eighteen months after Germany's surrender to defeat Japan. Estimates suggested that as many as 200,000 American casualties could be prevented by prompt Soviet entry into the conflict.

At Livadiya Palace, Harriman sat with Roosevelt and Stalin as the Marshal went over his demands again. Despite their profound implications, the President accepted them almost casually, and Harriman raised no question. The agreement had to be protected with extraordinary secrecy because it would take time to move the Soviet divisions across Siberia and into position for the offensive. If it was revealed to the Chinese, both Stalin and Roosevelt feared, the Japanese would promptly learn about it and might even attempt a preemptive attack on the port of Vladivostok to prevent the buildup of stockpiles.

Even Roosevelt's secretary of state was kept in the dark. When Stettinius inquired whether his department should not be involved in the Far East discussions, the President politely told him that it was a military matter. Asia was never mentioned in the plenary meetings, nor in the sessions of the foreign ministers. When the conference ended, the only American copy of the agreement was taken back to the White House and locked in a safe by Admiral Leahy. Not even Chiang Kai-shek learned of the concessions until after the President's death.

While he raised no objection to Stalin's demand for the islands, Roosevelt balked at the proposed lease arrangement for the ports and the rail lines. He preferred to see Dairen operated as a free port controlled by an international commission instead of being leased to the USSR. The Manchurian railroad, he insisted, should be jointly operated by a Soviet-Chinese commission. After one meeting on the subject, drafting was turned over to Harriman and Molotov. As Harriman shuttled the various versions back to Livadiya, the President insisted upon keeping his amendments on both the railroads and the port at Dairen. Besides finally accepting the American position, the Soviets also bowed to Roosevelt's insistence that the ten-paragraph agreement require the approval of Chiang. The President reciprocated by dropping his demand that Port Arthur be put under international control, accepting Stalin's contention that a lease was necessary, since the port would become a Soviet naval base.

Years later, the secret accord would become an exhibit for Yalta critics contending that the President had been fleeced by the Soviet dictator. Bohlen, who interpreted all of the conversations between the President and Stalin, thought that where the Far East was concerned, the United States had indeed been caught napping.[41]

Being the American most involved, Harriman shared the blame, but he did not readily accept it. In his memoire, *Special Envoy to Churchill and Stalin*, published in 1975, he insisted that he himself had been unhappy with parts of the agreement. He did not, he said, like the railroad and ports section, which stated that the Soviet Union's "pre-eminent interests" would be protected at the international port of Dairen. Nor did he like the pledge that the Soviet claims would be "unquestionably fulfilled after Japan has been defeated." He had told the President as much, but the President "was not disposed to fuss over words."[42] Harriman said he had hoped that the military chiefs would complain and give him an excuse to go back to Roosevelt, but they raised no objection.

In demanding the Kurils and southern Sakhalin, Stalin insisted that he merely wanted a return to the situation that existed before the Russo-Japanese War forty years earlier. The well-known truth was that Japan had gotten only the portion of the island below fifty degrees north latitude at the end of the conflict. The Kurils had been acquired from Russia by treaty in 1875. If Roosevelt had forgotten that, the State Department had not, and neither had Harriman. A memorandum describing the issue in detail was prepared before the President left Washington, but apparently he never saw it. When Harriman mentioned the history of the island chain, Roosevelt casually dismissed it. The Kurils seemed to him "a minor matter."[43]

The agreement was not accompanied by a map or list of the islands. Consequently, decades later, Russo-Japanese relations remained soured by Japan's insistence that four of the islands ceded to Stalin at Yalta were, in fact, a part of the Japanese homeland, not the Kuril chain.

Harriman saw Franklin Roosevelt for the last time on the day after the conference ended.

Following a jovial luncheon to celebrate the signing ceremony at Livadiya, the President drove eighty miles down the coast to board the *Catoctin*, still anchored off Sevastopol. At the suggestion of his naval aide, Vice-Admiral Wilson Brown, Roosevelt agreed to spend the night aboard the ship as a gesture of thanks to the crew that had supported America's Yalta contingent around the clock.

Having watched the President at close range for nine days, Harriman had become truly alarmed over his physical condition. Now, following the strenuous conference, Roosevelt faced a trip home that would be as taxing as his journey to Yalta. From the Crimea, he would fly to Egypt, where he would reboard the *Quincy*. Before sailing, he was to meet with King Farouk, Haile Selassie of Ethiopia, Ibn Saud of Saudi Arabia, and Churchill.

Under the circumstances, Harriman thought the President should rest another night at Yalta. He was furious at Brown's insensitivity in suggesting that he go through the rigor of boarding ship and spending the night in cramped quarters. Nevertheless, the party went aboard in the late afternoon and passed what Harriman called a "ghastly night" in stifling heat.

They departed at daybreak, and back at Saki Airfield, Harriman said good-bye. After Roosevelt had been lifted into his plane in a marrow-chilling rain, the giant C-54 lumbered down the runway and climbed slowly into the sky over the Black Sea.

As Roosevelt flew toward Egypt, Harriman and his party, now including Stettinius, Bohlen, the President's political pal Ed Flynn, and a young foreign service officer named Alger Hiss, headed north to Moscow. As they looked out at a country beginning to come back to life after the Nazi occupation, doubts about Yalta had already begun. In an atmosphere of gallows humor, little wagers were being laid on how long the honeymoon would last. Harriman was only slightly less pessimistic than Bohlen, who gave it forty-eight hours.

Back in Moscow, Harriman began to look to the conquest of Germany as a day of personal deliverance. He was anxious to leave the Soviet Union, as were most of the others who had been there through the war. An exodus of sorts was already beginning, with the departure of John Melby, who had been assigned to Chungking. It was a move that Harriman heartily endorsed. With the Soviet Union a new world power, Harriman favored putting diplomats with Russian experience at every important diplomatic post, and Chungking was high on the list. There, Melby could be counted upon to catch Soviet attempts to undercut Chiang Kai-shek. The entire American community and all of the usual tame Russians came to Spaso for Melby's farewell party. The rugs were rolled up again, the Victrola brought out, and the punch bowls filled with the naval attaché's favorite concoction of vodka, white wine, and champagne—called "Iron Curtain Punch" a dozen years before Churchill immortalized the phrase.

The floor was still crowded after midnight when Kathleen called Harriman aside for a telephone call. When he returned he was ashen. The music was abruptly turned off, and tipsy guests were ushered toward the door without any explanation. As soon as they were gone, the residents and a few others from the embassy gathered upstairs where Harriman told them the President was dead, felled by a stroke at Warm Springs just hours earlier.

The end came as relations between the United States and the Soviet Union disintegrated. It had only been two months since Yalta, and Harriman now feared what the end of the war would bring.

Chapter XV

STALIN
Selling the Same Horse Twice

After he emptied his bomb bay on Tokyo in April 1942, Major Edward York aimed his B-25 for China; but running out of gas, he was forced down outside the Soviet Union's Pacific port of Vladivostok. There, astonished Russians took him and his four-man crew from Jimmy Doolittle's raid into custody at gunpoint.

For practical purposes, the American airmen were prisoners of war. While they would later receive mail from home, a visit or two from a U.S. embassy official, and a certain respect from their captors, every indication was that they would be interned for the duration. Moscow was of no mind to risk its neutrality in the Pacific war by setting them free.

Over the months, the guard over them was gradually relaxed, however, and they were given the run of the grim village of Okhansk, where they spent the autumn and winter. Their life was one of such isolation and stupefying boredom that they finally addressed a letter to Stalin, asking to be moved to warmer climes and given something useful to do, if they could not be released to fight the Germans.

Either the letter or persistent entreaties from the embassy and the War Department worked. In the spring of 1943, they were moved more than three thousand miles to Ashkhabad, a village of mud houses ten miles from the Iranian border, and put to work in a shop overhauling training planes. Six weeks later, with the collaboration of a smuggler paid $250, they hid in a Russian cargo truck and slipped across the border into Iran.

By the time Harriman arrived in Moscow in October 1943, sixty other American airmen on missions receiving none of the fanfare accorded Doolittle's raiders had landed, crashed or bailed out into Soviet territory. Like York's crew, they were treated with relative civility; nevertheless, they were confined in a schoolhouse in the central Asian city of Tashkent, prisoners of war for all practical purposes. Although Standley had gotten nowhere arguing for their release, Harriman took up the matter during his first days in Moscow and continued to badger officials until a U.S. Army doctor was permitted to visit them. As a result, one flyer who was recovering from surgery was released and flown to Teheran.

When Harriman pressed Molotov to free the others, he could get no commitment, though it was obvious that the Foreign Minister wished the problem would go away. It was a great mystery, Molotov said in a tongue-in-cheek reference to York's men, but Soviet authorities could no longer find the crew from the Doolittle raid anywhere in the Soviet Union. And while offering no potential solution, he said he thought the crews still being detained in Tashkent should not have to waste another year there. That made it clear, Harriman advised Washington after the conversation, that the Soviets were willing to let the aviators "escape."[1]

Shortly thereafter, Soviet intelligence called on General Deane with a plan for precisely that. Orders would be issued for the internees' transfer from Tashkent to Ashkhabad to help assemble Lend-Lease aircraft arriving in the Soviet Union via the Persian Gulf and the trans-Iranian railroad. Just before they reached their destination, their train would break down. Soviet and American escort officers would go for help, returning with trucks and telling the prisoners the drivers had been bribed to take them into Iran. The sixty made it across the border unscathed, but a later "escape" by another one hundred Americans was delayed when an account of the York crew's adventure got into a newspaper column. Once the concern caused by publicity abated in Moscow, however, the Soviets regularly helped other downed pilots slip through Ashkhabad into Iran and back to squadron ready rooms.

The operation shored up Harriman's early conviction that the Russians were prepared to become reliable allies. In spite of all the headaches that Steinhardt and Standley had encountered in Moscow, Harriman found a streak of encouraging pragmatism in Stalin. Their encounters in 1941 and 1942 suggested that ruler of Soviet Union could be dealt with like a hard-nosed railroad man. He was ruthless and brutal, certainly, but basically dependable. As far as the war was concerned, Stalin's objectives were compatible with America's, Harriman had assured an audience in New York. Moreover, he said the man in the Kremlin believed that close Soviet cooperation with the United States and Great Britain "should and must extend beyond the war, if the world is to be wisely reconstructed." "I quote his program of action . . . from his recent speech: 'Abolition of racial exclusiveness, equality of nations and integrity of their territories, liberation of enslaved nations and restoration of their sovereign rights, the right of every nation to arrange its affairs as it wishes, economic aid to nations that have suffered, and assistance to them in attaining their material welfare, restoration of democratic liberties, the destruction of the Hitler regime.' These are Stalin's words. We can accept this program unhesitatingly. It is our own."[2]

Before his first Moscow winter was over, Soviet officials promised Harriman that they would share valuable combat intelligence in the Pacific and gave him assurances that the United States would be granted use of Soviet bases in the Far East for its final assault on Japan. Stalin had called the ambassador in to personally reveal the decision to allow American bombers to use airbases in the Ukraine for shuttle bombing of eastern Europe.

Kathleen Harriman thought her father had taken unrealistic optimism to Moscow with him. As a reporter in London, she got around, and she had acquired a picture of Stalin quite different from Averell's. British and American intelligence experts and refugees from eastern Europe, she told her sister, Mary, "distrust him and fear him, and figure he's doing a good job of out-smarting the Americans and the British. . . ."[3] Kathleen was not alone.

In Moscow, Archibald Clark Kerr, the British ambassador, thought Harriman a weathercock whose views shifted with the winds. Other colleagues felt he was too willing to take Stalin at his word. Unlike the salty old Standley, Harriman was unfailingly respectful in talking about Stalin. Even in the relaxed atmosphere of the boozy parties thrown by members of the military mission, he epitomized discretion.

His early cables from Moscow were uplifting. Roosevelt wanted an enduring relationship with Stalin; and when there was a glimmer of good news, the boss got it. Harriman wrote Churchill in a similarly cheerful vein, confessing to the doggedly skeptical Prime Minister, however, that he saw strong likelihood "we can get knocked back on our heels" unless there was a prompt follow-up to the successful Moscow foreign ministers' conference. "The essential quality of our relations with the Russians," he told Churchill, "is still patience and forbearance," and he worried that those were traits that were not his own "long suit."[4]

After the promising start, both his forbearance and patience were put to the test. Moscow was uninterested in a political partnership on anything but its own terms. On the simplest matters of military cooperation, Harriman and Deane began meeting contrived obstacles that dwarfed accomplishments like the orchestrated escapes of the interned flyers. Officials refused to provide American and British pilots flying into Moscow the location of the city's radio navigational beacons, making foul-weather arrivals in the Soviet capital unnecessarily dangerous. It took months to negotiate even an exchange of weather data. More galling than mere pettiness was the accumulating evidence that the Soviets were using Lend-Lease to hoard equipment for civilian use after the war was over. During a trip to Siberia, Averell found a dredge that had been provided to deepen a military harbor on the Pacific being used to mine gold. Diesel engines, urgently needed for amphibious assault vehicles being readied for the invasion of France, were rusting in freight yards. American bombers that had crash-landed in Soviet territory were secretly taken apart for examination by Soviet engineers.

There were times, as in the days following the Teheran summit, when the atmosphere improved, but the quarrelsome confrontations always resumed. Within months of his first upbeat reports, Harriman was treated more like an enemy than like the representative of the Soviet Union's principal benefactor.

What troubled Harriman more than Kremlin intransigence was evidence that his views were no longer getting real consideration, because Hopkins was out of the picture. Harry and Louise had left the White House for a home of their own, and on New Year's Day of 1944 he had suddenly fallen ill. He wound up in Mayo Clinic for another operation on his chronically ailing stomach, and it was nearly seven months before he was regularly back at work. The illness marked an important change in Hopkins's relationship with Roosevelt. Thereafter, the President's closest confidant was no longer the driving force in war policy. There was no falling out; but as Hopkins's biographer Robert Sherwood said, "There was simply an admission that while the friendship continued and Hopkins would still be useful in various ways, particularly on the domestic political front, he was no longer physically fit to share the burden of responsibility for the big decisions of the war."[5] Although Harriman had his direct link to the White House through military communications channels, the Hopkins absence left him for the first time under control of the State Department.

When Harriman took over the embassy in Moscow, the Soviet Union had already broken off relations with the Polish exile government, using the London-based Poles' demand for an international investigation of the Katyn Forest massacre as an excuse. The break dramatically increased the danger that Moscow would impose a puppet regime on postwar Poland rather than accept a "friendly" coalition government as it had promised. Equally vexing was the issue of Poland's postwar national boundaries.

After their pact with Hitler in 1939, the Soviets' attack on Poland occupied seventy thousand square miles of territory with a population of a million. Moscow now proposed to reclaim the area after the war and compensate Poland by advancing her western border to take in thirty thousand square miles of German territory, inhabited by some six million Germans. "Curzon and Compensation" the formula was called, a reference to the Curzon Line, where Poland's eastern border had been fixed following World War I, and approximately where the Red Army's encroachment ended in 1939.

Harriman thought it was imperative to get an agreement on a postwar government for Poland before resolving the issue of boundaries. Unless there was an independent government, the territorial issues would become moot as soon as the Red Army recaptured the country from the Germans. His recommendation was for the Allies to resolve to restore an independent Poland and postpone the territorial dispute until war was over—when a free Poland could be party to the resolution.

On January 4, 1944, the Red Army rolled across the 1939 Soviet-Polish border, retaking the territory it had first overrun as an ally of Hitler. The next day, the desperate exile government in London offered Moscow the cooperation of its Home Army underground if the Soviets would resume diplomatic relations.

Harriman went to Molotov several times to plead the case of the London Poles, but the foreign minister was unbending. Moscow would have no dealings with the exile government until it got rid of all of its anti-Communist ministers. With Roosevelt avoiding the problem and Churchill declining to pressure the London Poles to take ministers acceptable to Stalin, the ambassador was in no position to bargain.

The quid pro quo relationship he had hoped to create was a pipe dream. He saw a chance to use the Soviets' request for a $5 billion loan to pressure Stalin on Poland and demand more military cooperation. Instead of granting a huge long-term loan, he proposed offering the Soviets credits, requiring that they be used for purchases in the United States; but the protocol committee working on the matter was unprepared to risk offense. The recommendation was sloughed off, as was his call for closer scrutiny of Lend-Lease requests.

He could see nothing but a debacle ahead in Poland, the Soviets installing a regime led by Communists who had sat out the war in Moscow and ignoring the exile government in London. Sitting by the fireplace in the middle of the night, he drafted cables haranguing Washington and London. But the stern calls to toughen up and move before it was too late usually went into the fire rather than the cable office. The issue of Poland did not come to a head until the Warsaw uprising, which sharply altered Harriman's view of Stalin, the Soviet Union, and American policy.

As the Red Army's summer offensive rolled into range of Warsaw at the end of July 1944, wretchedly equipped partisans answered a call to arms broadcast from Moscow over the Soviet controlled radio, launching their heroic insurrection against the Nazi occupation. Fighting in the city broke out in the late afternoon of August 1 with the boom of Red Army guns echoing across the Vistula River, Russian planes controlling the skies above the capital, and Soviet troops holding the streets of villages just a few miles away. But Soviet troops made no move to cross the river, Russian planes disappeared, and the partisans' pleas for help went unanswered. Captured Poles were marched off to forced labor or executed.

In Moscow, Stalin had ridiculed the insurrection, expressing doubt that the Poles in Warsaw had the courage to fight the Germans, even questioning whether any real fighting was going on. The only assistance came from the British, who dropped supplies from bombers flying over partisan positions at night. That had done little good, because most of the parachutes floated into areas held by the Germans. In Washington, plans were made for daylight bombing runs on German antiaircraft positions, followed by a supply drop, while Harriman pressed the Kremlin to allow American planes flying the missions to land at Poltava. His written request was summarily rejected; and when he demanded to see Molotov, he was received by his deputy, Andrei Vishinsky, who only reiterated what he had been told in a formal message: that the uprising was "a purely adventuristic affair to which the Soviet government could not lend its hand."[6] Furious, Harriman attacked the Soviets for leaving the Poles fighting hopelessly without tanks or air support. It was, he later recalled, "the toughest talk I ever had with a Soviet official."[7] "It's a dirty business," he wrote Ira Eaker after the exchange. "The only satisfaction I have gotten so far is that they know in no uncertain terms how the Americans feel about it."[8]

Two nights later, he and Deane did see Molotov. When they renewed pressure for permission to land supply planes at Poltava, the response was a threat to close the shuttle-bombing bases. Both Americans were stunned. Averell had at first believed that the Red Army did not smash into Warsaw because its offensive had outrun the logistics required for a crossing in force. But it had become obvious that the Soviets were calculatedly allowing the Germans to wipe out the anti-Communist underground and massacre the Polish Home Army loyal to the exile government in London.

George Kennan was waiting for them when they returned from Molotov's office long after midnight, and he could see from their faces that the meeting had been a disaster. "There was no doubt in any of our minds as to the implications of the position the Soviet leaders had taken," Kennan recalled. "This was a gauntlet thrown down, in a spirit of malicious glee, before the Western powers."[9]

Backed by Kennan, who agreed it was time for a showdown, Harriman pleaded with Washington to tell the Soviet government flatly that its behavior was unacceptable, but the State Department demurred. Harriman was pressing too hard, it suggested, and if he continued he might endanger the shuttle-bombing collaboration.

Harriman, no longer able to see much hope for Poland's future being peacefully settled, drafted a cable, telling the President his view. What was worse, he feared that Poland only foreshadowed "similarly ruthless policy in other directions."[10] Like so many others, the cable was never sent. In the light of morning, he stuck it in his files instead.

The Warsaw disaster accelerated the disintegration of the political atmosphere. Military and diplomatic cooperation had reached their zenith in June when the shuttle bombers hit Hungary and eastern Germany, but the operation had begun to come apart almost immediately. A German fighter followed the Flying Fortresses on a subsequent run and located the base at Poltava. That night German bombers wiped out fifty-one American planes on the ground.

Determined to continue the shuttle raids, Harriman and Deane put before the Soviets a detailed plan to continue missions through the winter; but there had been no reply, nor was there any positive response to a host of other military requests. Permission for American reconnaissance planes to fly over Soviet-held territory was denied, as was a request for a bombing survey team to assess damage from the attack on the Ploesti oil refinery in Romania. The Kremlin response was again negative when Harriman asked that five hundred U.S. Army trucks be allowed to drive from Iran across Soviet territory to China with supplies for American flying squadrons.

Three months after the invasion of Europe, Harriman warned Hopkins that relations with the Soviets had taken a serious turn for the worse:

> They have held up our requests with complete indifference to our interests and have shown an unwillingness to even discuss problems. The general attitude seems to be that it is our obligation to help Russia and accept her policies because she has won the war for us. I am convinced that we can divert this trend but only if we materially change our policy toward the Soviet government. I have evidence that they have misinterpreted our generous attitude toward them as a sign of weakness, and acceptance of their policies. Time has come when we must make clear what we expect of them as the price of our good will. Unless we take issue with the present policy there is every indication the Soviet Union will become a world bully wherever their interests are involved. This policy will reach into China and the Pacific as well when they can turn their attention in that direction. . . .[11]

He wanted to go home and lay out his views in full, but permission was denied.

For the first time in years, his ulcers flared up. He lost weight, becoming a gaunt 160 pounds, smoked heavily, developed dark circles under his eyes, and grew churlish and gloomy. "It all adds up to a very bloody time for Averell," Kathleen wrote Mary in the midst of the Warsaw insurrection. "God knows it's been difficult before, but I gather the last bit has topped all, both unpleasant and worrisome. . . . Thank God I'm not ambassador to Russia."[12]

A month after Harriman's first request to help the Poles in Warsaw and three weeks after a direct appeal by Roosevelt and Churchill, the Soviets agreed to allow American supply planes sent over Warsaw to land in the Ukraine. The Soviets would also drop arms and ammunition to the Polish insurgents.

It was another five days before the weather cleared. By then it was too late. The territory held by the surrounded insurgents had so diminished that nearly all of the supplies fell outside their perimeter and into the hands of the Germans. On October 2, the last holdouts surrendered.

Another 250,000 Poles were dead, including a third of the underground army. The Germans counted ten thousand of their own dead, plus nine thousand wounded and another seven thousand missing. Bloated, unburied bodies lay in the streets when the Red Army finally crossed the river and entered the city unopposed.

Harriman put much of the blame for Warsaw on Vishinsky and Molotov. They were, he thought, "bloated with power," and, with Hilter's defeat only a matter of time, convinced that they could force their decisions upon Washington and London.

The only way to get cooperation out of the Soviets, Harriman told Hopkins, was "to make them feel their negative attitude will affect our willingness to cooperate with them on matters that have no immediate effect on the war."[13]

Unilaterally, he and Deane decided to take their own more firm and uncompromising course, letting the Kremlin know that it could expect to find American enthusiasm for military assistance dampened if every request for cooperation continued to be ignored. The stiffer attitude had an effect. Both the embassy and the military mission began getting action on matters that had long lain in limbo.

When Harriman and Clark Kerr saw Stalin on September 23 to give him a report on the just-ended Roosevelt-Churchill conference in Quebec, it was as though Warsaw had never happened. Stalin affably accepted the news of the meeting and praised the conduct of the offensive in France. Without Harriman even bringing it up, he turned to the war in the Far East, reiterating his intention to join the fighting against Japan once Germany was defeated. Though he was still unwilling to talk about American bombers' use of bases in the Soviet Union's easternmost

Union Station, Washington, D.C. Unlike his father, Harriman was endowed with an instinct for public relations. Days after the Union Pacific rolled its first streamliner onto the track, he had it brought to Washington, where he and U.P. president Carl Gray conducted FDR on a guided tour. Although dissuaded from making a record-breaking speed run to the nation's capital, Harriman soon raced from Los Angeles to New York, breaking a coast-to-coast record set by his father in 1906.

Little Mary. Harriman's sister, Mary Rumsey, was a powerful influence on him from childhood. A founder of the Junior League, she was a friend of the Roosevelts, a committed New Dealer, and one of the creators of the consumer movement. Her influence led her brother into the Democratic party and government service. In 1934 she was fatally injured in a hunting accident.

Sun Valley, Idaho. To publicize the Union Pacific passenger trains and stimulate traffic in hard times, Harriman created the Sun Valley resort in the Sawtooth Mountains of south-central Idaho and opened it for business in December 1936. Outside their new cottage, he and his wife, Marie, with his daughters, Mary (*left*) and Kathleen (*right*), prepare to head for the slopes early in Sun Valley's second season.

On Dollar Mountain. Expertly advised by Madison Avenue whiz Steve Hannagan, Harriman became a living advertisement for Sun Valley glamour. His scheme to use the ski resort to promote railroad business succeeded, but the larger impact of Sun Valley was to popularize downhill skiing all over the United States. After taking lessons while his Idaho lodge was under construction, he became an enthusiast of the sport, sponsoring championship competition, and hitting the slopes himself until he was nearly eighty.

The Young Churchills. Pamela Digby's 1939 marriage to Randolph Churchill had started to disintegrate even before Harriman's arrival in London in 1941. Divorced after the war, Pamela moved on to Paris, where she studied antiques, gave fashionable parties, and was courted by Italian auto magnate Giovanni Agnelli, among others. She moved permanently to America upon her marriage to Leland Hayward, but she became a U.S. citizen only after her marriage to Harriman.

Mission Accomplished. After his journey to Moscow in 1941 to work out Lend-Lease arrangements with the Soviet Union, Harriman was greeted in London by his daughter Kathleen and Brendan Bracken, Britain's minister of information. His first negotiations with Stalin set a pattern of alternating cordiality and bitter contention.

Levity in the Kremlin. In August 1942 Harriman joined Churchill, who had felt compelled personally to advise Stalin of the Anglo-American decision against an early second front in Europe. Roosevelt turned down Averell's request to join the mission, but relented in the face of Churchill's urging. The meetings were marked by some of the war's bitterest words with Stalin. When this photograph was taken, the mood seems to have been lighthearted. Joining Churchill, Harriman, and Stalin is Averell's nemesis, Foreign Minister V. M. Molotov.

Bound for the Crimea. Before the last leg of their journey to join Stalin at Yalta, American and British delegations to the climactic allied summit of World War II gathered for brief talks at Malta. With presidential adviser Harry Hopkins, Harriman boarded the British cruiser HMS *Orion* for a chat with Prime Minister Churchill.

Summit in the Crimea. Behind Churchill, Roosevelt, and Stalin are gathered the principal civilian aides who took part in the Yalta negotiations, setting the stage for the Cold War. *From left:* Charles E. Bohlen, the President's interpreter; Lord Leathers, Britain's Minister of War Transport; Foreign Secretary Anthony Eden; Secretary of State Edward R. Stettinius; Sir Alexander Cadogan, Britain's Undersecretary of State; Soviet Foreign Minister V. M. Molotov; Harriman, filling in for the ailing Harry Hopkins, who spent much of the meeting confined to his bed.

Atop Lenin's Tomb. Along with General Eisenhower, Harriman joined Josef Stalin in the place of honor to view Moscow's victory parade in 1945. His first meeting with the Soviet dictator came in 1941, when he was dispatched to the Kremlin to determine what the Red Army needed to survive Hitler's invasion. Though he regarded Stalin as supremely brutal and warned Washington of postwar trouble ahead, Harriman admired the Kremlin boss's technical and detailed direction of the war effort.

The Brothers. Celebrating Averell's return from Moscow after the war, the Harriman brothers went to the Stork Club on one of their rare nights on the town together. Their relationship was one of profound affection but of ever-diverging interests. Roland was relieved when his brother decided to stay with the Truman administration rather than return to the Union Pacific and the New York business scene.

Fueling the Recovery of Europe. President Truman, signing legislation authorizing another $5.5 billion for the Marshall Plan, handed out pens to the key figures in the recovery program. *From left:* Harriman, the program's field general in Europe; Paul G. Hoffman, head of the Economic Cooperation Administration; Texas senator Tom Connally, chairman of the Senate Foreign Relations Committee; and Secretary of State Dean Acheson.

Troubleshooter. In the White House Rose Garden, Truman announces Harriman's departure for Iran in an effort to ease the 1951 Anglo-Iranian oil crisis. The presence of Secretary of State Acheson and Secretary of Defense George C. Marshall emphasized the gravity of the new confrontation in the Middle East.

Oil Crisis. Iran's nationalization of Britain's Anglo-Iranian Oil Company in 1951 propelled Harriman into difficult, and ultimately fruitless, negotiations with the fiery nationalist Prime Minister Mohammad Mossadeq. Often the talks took place at Mossadeq's bedside. Always the interpreter was Vernon Walters, the Army officer whose language skills became legendary.

The People's Choice. With the outcome still in doubt, Harriman claimed victory in the one election triumph of his life—his 1954 triumph over U.S. Senator Irving Ives to become Governor of New York. With him and his wife, Marie, are state Democratic chairman Richard H. Balch (*left*) and Carmine DeSapio, the Manhattan Tammany Hall leader, who played a major role in the victory. Four years later DeSapio would be the chief instrument of Harriman's political destruction.

provinces, he reversed the earlier decision and agreed that American trucks could cross Soviet territory from northern Iran into China.

Poland was more than ever the supreme test of Allied solidarity; but the White House did not share Harriman's and Kennan's view that it was the issue and the time for a showdown, nor was it happy when Churchill announced plans to return to visit Moscow to discuss Poland and other political problems. To Roosevelt, Churchill's talks with Stalin could be nothing more than a preliminary to the long-anticipated Big Three summit, to come after the presidential election. But the Prime Minister thought it was, perhaps, the last chance to create an independent Poland, and Harriman agreed with him. "The clock was ticking," he said. "Opportunity was slipping away."[14]

He was ordered to act as an observer at the Moscow meeting, but the President made it clear to both Churchill and Stalin that his ambassador was not to make commitments on behalf of the United States.

Under these circumstances, Harriman was included only in the larger meetings that took place during Churchill's week in the Soviet capital. He was, therefore, absent when the Prime Minister presented Stalin his notorious proposal for a sphere-of-influence arrangement in the Balkans. Scribbled on a half sheet of paper and pushed across the table at their first meeting, it was a brazen suggestion for Britain and the Soviet Union to divide up the region, settling upon the degree to which they would share postwar authority in Romania, Greece, Yugoslavia, Hungary, and Bulgaria.

The scheme was revealed to Harriman in bits and pieces by Churchill and Anthony Eden, but he did not learn that it had been reduced to writing until he called on Churchill at his dacha and found the Prime Minister preparing a letter to Stalin confirming it. It wasn't necessary to check for Washington's reaction. It would be flatly repudiated, he warned Churchill, by both the President and the State Department. Apparently as a result of the warning, the letter was never sent.

Churchill's strange initiative was not the only unsettling experience for Harriman during the week. From Molotov, of all people, Harriman found out that he knew much less than he thought he did about his own President's position on the Polish boundary issue.

Thinking he saw a propitious moment to break the stalemate on Poland, Churchill sent for Stanislaw Mikolajczyk, Prime Minister of the exile government in London, and put him under excruciating pressure to endorse a territorial settlement. Churchill was in accord with Stalin on the Curzon and Compensation formula, with the German territory given to Poland in compensation to be determined after Hitler's surrender. In any case, Churchill assured Mikolajczyk, the new territory would include "a nice outlet to the sea, a good port at Danzig, and the priceless minerals of Silesia." Postwar Poland, by Churchill's design, would be "a nice big country . . . a real solid new home in which the Polish nation can live and develop in security, freedom, and prosperity."[15]

As Harriman sat by, Churchill and Stalin pressured the leader of the London Poles to accept the arrangement then and there, but Mikolajczyk fended them off. Roosevelt, he said, had personally assured him in Washington that only Stalin and Churchill supported the Curzon and Compensation solution. With that, Molotov chimed in that, to the contrary, Roosevelt supported the new border. The American President, he said, had endorsed it at Teheran nearly a year earlier. Molotov did not ask Harriman for confirmation; and Averell stared at the floor, knowing anything he said could only make matters worse.

Roosevelt had in fact told him months before that he considered the Curzon Line a reasonable basis for settlement on the eastern Polish border, although he had reservations about the city of Lwów and the oil fields around it.

The Kremlin session lasted for six hours. When it was over, Churchill joined Harriman for a midnight dinner at Spaso House. Alone, the two of them went over their recollections of the Teheran conversations on Poland nearly a year earlier. Neither could remember Roosevelt having made the commitment claimed by Molotov. When Churchill told that to Stalin and offered his own recollection, the Premier dismissed it as irrelevant. He said he had heard Roosevelt's statement in a private meeting with the President. Harriman's check of Bohlen's Teheran notes showed that in a private talk at the Soviet compound on December 1, Roosevelt had, in fact, agreed to shifting Poland's border with the Soviet Union to the west, even if he did not specifically endorse the Curzon Line.

Already distressed at being pressured by Churchill and shocked at Molotov's assertion that Roosevelt agreed to the Soviets' taking the swatch of Polish territory, Mikolajczyk was angry at Harriman for failing to speak up and for trying privately to assure him that Roosevelt had been misunderstood at Teheran. The Prime Minister of the exile government made it plain that he had neither the authority nor the inclination to "partition" his homeland. Distraught after one loud finger-pointing exchange, he asked for Churchill's assistance so he could parachute into Warsaw and die fighting with the underground. He preferred, he told Churchill, "to die, fighting for the independence of my country, than to be hanged later by the Russians in full view of your British ambassador."[16]

Amidst the rancor, it was impossible to get anywhere on the border issue. Harriman still considered the government question more urgent, and on that score he thought there was a chance for the London Poles and the Soviet-supported Polish National Council, headquartered in Lublin, to reach accommodation.

Taking liberty with his instructions from the President, he urged the leaders of the two factions reach an accord while they were both in Moscow. Though Mikolajczyk insisted on returning to London without settling anything, he did talk with Boleslaw Bierut, the leader of the Lublin group, who conceded that Mikolajczyk could be premier of a new coalition government. The hitch was that Bierut demanded that his Lublin group get 75 percent of the cabinet seats.

The one glimmer of hope to come of the meeting was Mikolajczyk's grudging agreement to argue the case for the Curzon Line before his ministers in London. Though he felt betrayed, he promised that he would return to Moscow for further discussion of political issues with Bierut.

As soon as Churchill left for London, Harriman headed for Washington, arriving in time to buy fifteen minutes on network radio and make a speech urging Roosevelt's reelection for a fourth term. He used the trip home to argue personally with Roosevelt for a stiffer approach to dealing with the Soviet government, telling the President that all of eastern Europe was in danger of falling under Soviet-style regimes. The only realistic way of settling political problems was to keep up the pressure every day rather than postpone everything until a peace conference.

The talks were anything but reassuring. He saw Roosevelt five times, four of them after the election, but he never got him to focus seriously on Poland and eastern Europe. FDR, he noted after their first meeting on October 24, showed "very little interest in eastern European matters except as they affect sentiment in America."[17] When the subject was revisited in their next session, the President casually remarked that, aside from Germany, he preferred to stay out of the European entanglements. He was not opposed to the Curzon Line if the Poles, the British, and the Soviets could agree on it, but he wanted Averell to emphasize to Stalin that the United States would consider it a significant peaceful gesture if the Moscow would agree to an adjustment of the line leaving the city of Lwów in Poland.[18]

In London, meanwhile, Mikolajczyk's colleagues refused to buy the Curzon and Compensation formula without a commitment that Lwów and the oil fields would remain in Poland. When Harriman stopped off to see him on the way back to the Soviet Union, he found the dejected exile leader preparing to resign. His assurance that Roosevelt was renewing his effort to alter the Curzon Line so Lwów Province and rich oil fields would remain in Polish territory did not dissuade him.

Scarcely more than a month later, the Lublin Committee declared itself the provisional government of Poland; and Stalin, ignoring Roosevelt's entreaty to put off all political decisions until the Big Three met again, promptly recognized it. The scenario that had haunted Harriman had been played out. Unwilling to press for an early settlement on a new Polish government, Washington had squandered its influence. A government of Soviet puppets, the precise thing he had warned the President about, now controlled Poland, while the United States and Britain recognized the dispirited exiles in London.

Stalin's cordiality during Churchill's visit to Moscow and his friendly demeanor in discussions of the Far East did not extend to Harriman and Deane in their long-suffering efforts to get more cooperation on military matters. Time after time, the Red leader lent encouragement and made outright commitments, then did nothing. The promise to allow American use of Far Eastern bases for combined operations against Japan was renewed several times, but when American officers arrived to coordinate plans with the Red Army, the commitment was withdrawn. The Soviets had decided they would need all the air and naval bases in the Far Eastern provinces, the chief of the Red Army general staff told the leader of the American team. Therefore, "American air and naval forces will be unable to operate from there."[19]

"The truth is they want to have as little to do with foreigners, Americans included, as possible," Deane wrote General Marshall. "We never make a request or proposal to the Soviets that is not viewed with suspicion. They simply cannot understand giving without taking, and as a result even our giving is viewed with suspicion. Gratitude cannot be banked in the Soviet Union. Each transaction is complete in itself without regard to past favors. The party of the second part is either a shrewd trader to be admired or a sucker to be despised.

"Our files are bulging with letters to the Soviets and devoid of letters from them. This situation may be reversed in Washington, but I doubt it. In short, we are in the position of being at the same time givers and supplicants. This is neither dignified nor healthy for U.S. prestige."[20]

With the Soviets' failure to deliver on cooperative planning for the Far East, Harriman and Deane turned the Spaso House ballroom into a war room. Deane divided it into cubicles for fifty-odd officers who spent weeks developing scenarios and estimates of Soviet supply requirements and the burdens likely to be placed upon the United States. Even without Soviet participation, the exercise proved worthwhile. For one thing, it showed that it would not be necessary to keep open a U.S. supply line across the Pacific.

The Soviets were as uncooperative in coordinating the war against Hitler as they were in planning for action in the Far East. As winter slowed the Allied offensive on the western front, knowledge of Stalin's plans became crucial to General Eisenhower's strategy for the spring campaign, but Harriman and Deane could get no indication of Soviet intentions. Following his November call on Mikolajczyk in London, Harriman had visited Eisenhower's headquarters in France to get a close-up picture of the western front. Wearing Ike's overshoes, a tank commander's coveralls, and an infantry captain's helmet, he spent a day slogging through the mud with Lieutenant General George S. Patton, whose Third Army was nearly immobilized by the floodwaters of the Saar River. Back at headquarters that evening, he invited Eisenhower to Moscow with him to meet face-to-face with Soviet military leaders.

The Allied commander was intrigued, but the Combined Chiefs of Staff dismissed the idea of his leaving France. It remained to Harriman to give Stalin Eisenhower's assessment and to plead on behalf of the Allied commander for more information on the eastern front.

Russia's offensive in Poland had also been frustrated by the weather, but when Harriman returned to Moscow, Stalin assured him that as soon as he could confer with his staff he would provide the ambassador a more comprehensive picture. It did not surprise Averell that the details were never delivered.

Plans for the spring quickly became irrelevant anyway, for on December 16, thousands of German tanks and artillery pieces on the western front launched the last major German thrust of the war, the Ardennes offensive.

Roosevelt and Churchill personally urged Stalin to let the Allies know when the Soviet offensive would come, and he agreed to see a member of Eisenhower's staff. By the time Air Marshal Arthur Tedder, Eisenhower's deputy, arrived in Moscow, however, the push was already under way. It would continue, Stalin told Tedder, and it would keep the Germans from pulling men and arms away from the eastern front to reinforce their troops in the Ardennes. The belated assurances were of no great import, but Tedder's mission led the Combined Chiefs to grant Eisenhower authority to communicate directly with the Russians on military matters. Harriman was told nothing of the decision, and Churchill would later blame Eisenhower's increased authority for the Soviets' arrival in Berlin ahead of British and American troops.

Less than a week after Tedder's meeting with Stalin, with Red Army divisions a scant forty miles east of Berlin, Harriman boarded the train for Yalta worried that the President would arrive at the summit inadequately prepared for decisions on eastern Europe that could wait no longer. He had asked permission to join the party several days before the meeting so he could bring the President up to date on Stalin's likely demands, and Hopkins, Stettinius, and Roosevelt himself had all agreed it was a good idea. When they met at Malta, however, the President was spent and obviously in more need of rest than a briefing. And when they got to Yalta, Harriman was never included in the private talks on Poland, although he undoubtedly realized better than any other American present how seriously Poland threatened all of Roosevelt's postwar dreams.

Predictably, the Red Army's offensive through Poland had produced a de facto settlement. The territorial matter was closed, and as for Poland's postwar government, Moscow's recognition of the new provisional regime had left Roosevelt and Churchill in poor shape to negotiate.

The President renewed his proposal to modify the Curzon Line; and Churchill, acknowledging that Britain had already endorsed it, joined the appeal to Stalin's generosity. But the Prime Minister now agreed with Harriman that the more urgent task was to establish a government including representatives of the exiles in London. His advice was to set up an interim government which all could recognize until elections could be arranged.

Stalin heard them out and asked for a recess before responding. When they resumed, he declared the London Poles a military threat and, therefore, unwelcome in Warsaw. With that, the session ended. Nothing had been accomplished, and the maneuvering over Poland continued for the next three days.

Staking out a democratic argument for himself, Stalin ridiculed the suggestion of an interim Polish government being created by the Big Three without the presence of a single Pole. That was an opening for Roosevelt. The next day, he proposed that Poles from both factions come to Yalta. Caught by surprise, Stalin had no counterproposal to suggest. He agreed; but after an overnight delay, he returned to the conference table with the lame explanation that he had been unable to reach any member of the Lublin government by telephone.

Averell thought it the moment for the President to demand continued efforts to get Polish representatives to Yalta, but Roosevelt let the subject drop. The conversation turned instead to a Stalin compromise. The Soviets would agree to changes in the proposed borders, but rather than accept a new interim government, the Marshal insisted that the Lublin regime remain in place—it could be expanded to include representatives of what he called "émigré circles."

Harriman helped draft a U.S. counterproposal calling for leaders of the Lublin regime, representatives of the exile government in London, and members of anti-Communist underground groups within Poland to meet with Molotov, Harriman, and Clark-Kerr in Moscow. Together they would set up a temporary government that would arrange for election of delegates to a constitutional assembly.

Tacitly acknowledging Moscow's puppet regime, it called for reorganization "on a broader democratic basis with the inclusion of democratic leaders from Poland itself and from Poles abroad." The new Polish Government of National Unity would be "pledged to the holding of free and unfettered elections as soon as possible on the basis of universal suffrage and secret ballot." All democratic and anti-Nazi parties would have the right to take part and put forward their own candidates.[21] The accord became Harriman's marching order for his most difficult days in Moscow.

Although the presidential delegation began its homeward journey weary to the bone, it was, unlike Harriman's Moscow-bound party, exalted in spirit. Hopkins thought "the first great victory of the peace" had been won.[22] Even Admiral Leahy, the President's chief of staff, who was usually skeptical of any foreigner's motives, thought the secret Far East agreement alone made the trip worthwhile. There was some conjecture that Stalin had made more concessions than he otherwise would have because he was touched at the heroic effort the so-obviously failing American President made in order to attend the conference.

Harriman returned to Moscow prepared to refight the whole battle over Poland. When one dealt with the Russians, he told Chip Bohlen, "you always have to buy the horse twice."[23] But he was not as gloomy as some others. George Kennan, who remained back in Moscow during the conference, thought it was pointless even to have negotiated about Poland at Yalta. As far as he was concerned, the declaration was nothing but "the shabbiest sort of equivocation."

The ensuing deliberations among Harriman, Molotov, and Clark-Kerr proved to be only "hours of unreal, repetitious wrangling."[24] Kennan's own solution for Europe was to acknowledge the reality of the Red Army's conquests and simply divide the continent into eastern and western spheres of influence. Elbridge Durbrow, who came from the State Department's European Division to join the negotiations, agreed that the talks were useless.

With Molotov acting as chairman of the conference, Harriman and Clark Kerr consented to members of the Soviet-backed provisional government joining them in Moscow. But Molotov objected to every non-Communist Pole suggested by Averell and the British ambassador. He would accept no one disapproved of by the Lublin regime, notably Mikolajczyk, who was by all odds the country's most popular political figure.

The Yalta agreement, Molotov insisted, had mandated a government built upon the regime already in place. What this meant to him was that the Soviet-supported provisional government had the right to approve any new minister. The squabble, centered on Mikolajczyk, paralyzed the conference as soon as it began. Since the Soviet foreign minister would accept none of the representatives proposed by Harriman and Clark Kerr, there was nothing to do but cancel the invitation to the provisional government.

The Soviets not only sabotaged the agreement on elections and a new government but promptly broke their promise to expedite the repatriation of American war prisoners freed in Poland. A month after

Yalta, three U.S. Army Air Corps officers, who had been POW's in Poland, showed up at the American embassy in Moscow after walking and hitchhiking six hundred miles. Liberated when the Germans withdrew before the thundering Soviet offensive, they had been ignored by Red Army occupation forces. With hundreds of others, they had wandered behind Soviet lines, depending upon Polish peasants for food and shelter. Unknown numbers of other American ex-POWs were hospitalized.

Harriman was infuriated that their accounts so completely contradicted assurances that he had received from Stalin himself, and he now believed the Soviets had grossly understated the numbers of American prisoners liberated by the advancing Red Army. He went back to the Kremlin with a formal request to use American planes based at Poltava to pick up liberated prisoners; but Stalin rejected it and, for good measure, dismissed a request that U.S. officers be allowed into Poland to make contact with them.

When a single medical officer was at last given permission to enter the country, he was not permitted to go out of Lublin. Disabused of his notion that the Soviet leader only manipulated the truth, Harriman told Roosevelt Stalin was categorically lying to him about the prisoners while refusing to allow the evacuation of the sick or permit provisions to be sent to assembly points.[25]

Finally, the President himself appealed to Stalin to allow flights from Poltava to pick up stranded Americans, but his request was also denied. He protested that he knew a "considerable number" of American sick and wounded remained in the country, but he was not willing to keep hammering at the matter.[26] It did not seem appropriate to write Stalin anymore, he told Harriman. And without comment, he simply passed along to the State Department Averell's recommendation that the United States retaliate by having Eisenhower restrict movement of Soviet officers who had gone to France to assist Red Army soldiers liberated from German camps.

Harriman was fed up, and when he at last got a grand opportunity to repay the Kremlin, he joyfully took it. Recognizing the inevitable, General Karl Wolff, the ranking SS officer and the Nazi police chief of occupied Italy, had slipped into Zurich and met with Allen Dulles of the OSS to discuss the surrender of German forces in northern Italy. On instructions from Washington, Harriman gave Molotov a full account of Dulles's report. The Kremlin reaction was a demand to join the conversations. It named two generals as its representatives, and since it had no diplomatic relations with the Swiss, it appealed for American help in getting them to Bern, where another contact between Dulles and Wolff was to take place.

Harriman and Deane wrote separate cables to Washington objecting to any role for the Soviets in the meeting. There was nothing to be gained by giving in to the Russians again. They would only consider it a sign of weakness and add more untenable demands. Their presence would probably jeopardize whatever chance there was that the talks would lead to anything.[27]

For once during the contentious spring of 1945, the United States' Moscow outpost got unequivocal support. The contacts in Switzerland, agreed Washington and London, were purely of a military nature. They had not reached a political level in which Moscow could legitimately claim a right to participate. Through March and into early April, at the same time the Polish talks were deadlocked and American POW requests ignored, the exchanges concerning Zurich grew increasingly heated.

Molotov demanded that Dulles's contacts with the Germans be broken off unless the Soviets had a part in them. Deane was summoned by the Soviet general staff and handed the same demand in the name of General Aleksey Antonov, the chief of staff. Harriman found the reaction more revealing than anything that happened since Yalta. Having successfully ignored the Crimean declaration on Poland, he told General Marshall, the Soviets now thought they could force their view upon the United States on any issue. The confrontation over the surrender conversations in Switzerland, he said, revealed "a domineering attitude toward the United States which we have before only suspected. It has been my feeling that sooner or later this attitude would create a situation which would be intolerable to us."[28]

It was possible that the Soviets simply did not believe what the United States was telling them; but, more likely, they saw a chance to dominate decisions on the future of Germany slipping away. "They have contended to the world and their people that Germany has been defeated almost entirely through the efforts of the Red Army," Harriman reminded the State Department after receiving Molotov's boisterous demand that the contacts in Switzerland be terminated. "Inasmuch as their advance in the East may be bogged down for a couple of months with the advent of thaws, it may be that they wish to insure being full participants in any major surrender if there is a break in Italy leading to one in the West."[29]

Harriman's estimate of the situation was no exaggeration. During Roosevelt's last days, the quarrel provoked an exchange of unprecedented bitterness between the President and Stalin. After four years of accommodating and deferring to the Soviet dictator, Roosevelt was roughly accused of lies and deceit. The charge went to the quick. With anger never before revealed in his wartime exchanges, Roosevelt wrote Stalin on April 5, "It would be one of the great tragedies of history if at the very moment of the victory, now within our grasp, such distrust, such lack of faith should prejudice the entire undertaking after the colossal losses of life, material and treasure involved.

"Frankly I cannot avoid a feeling of bitter resentment toward your informers, whoever they are, for such vile misrepresentations of my actions or those of my trusted subordinates."[30]

Stung, Stalin moderated his tone; and, on the last day of his life, Roosevelt reciprocated. In his final message, from Warm Springs, the President accepted Stalin's explanation, dismissing the whole matter as a "minor misunderstanding" now behind the two great powers.

To Harriman, it was a serious mistake to let Stalin's accusation pass so easily. Instead of delivering the message to the Kremlin, he held it, and wired the President a suggestion that he not minimize what had happened. "In the event you are willing to reconsider the wording of your message," he told Roosevelt, "may I respectfully suggest that the word 'minor' as a qualification of 'misunderstanding' be eliminated. The use of the word 'minor' might well be misinterpreted here. I must confess that the misunderstanding appeared to me to be of a major character."[31]

Roosevelt's reply was pointed. His last message to Harriman was another rejection of a stiffer approach to Stalin. "I do not wish to delete the word 'minor,'" the President cabled his ambassador, "as it is my desire to consider the Bern misunderstanding a minor incident."[32]

That night came word that FDR had died.

Though it was after two o'clock in the morning, Molotov insisted on coming to Spaso House to express his condolences. Later, Harriman went to the Kremlin and saw Stalin, who seemed still shaken. He greeted the ambassador in silence and grasped his hand for a long time before waving him to a chair. He wanted all the details of the President's death, but more than that he wanted to know anything Averell could tell him about Harry S Truman and his attitude toward the Soviet Union.

Certainly it was nothing Harriman wished to emphasize, but he had never met the new President. What he knew about the former senator from Missouri came from newspaper accounts of the Truman Committee investigation of waste in defense spending. But he had been concerned enough by the President's condition at Yalta that he had asked Roosevelt's political pal Edward Flynn about Truman. Flynn had expressed unusual confidence in the plain-spoken man Roosevelt had picked to replace Henry Wallace. Shaken as he was at the President's death, Harriman also saw the change of administrations as a potential opportunity. Poland could be discussed anew, as could Soviet disregard for freed American war prisoners, the nasty exchanges over the German surrender in Italy, and Moscow's requests for postwar assistance.

Harriman was alarmed that his warnings were not being understood in Washington. He had twice proposed going home to try to make the President realize what was happening in the aftermath of Yalta, but on both occasions he had been waved off by the State Department. With Roosevelt's death, he suggested it again—and once more the State Department told him his presence was required in Moscow.

Unhappy with the American and British opposition to UN charter membership for both the Ukraine and White Russia and deadlocked over the proposed voting rules for the Security Council, the Soviets had decided to downplay the UN conference in San Francisco. Molotov, the Kremlin announced in late March, would not attend the meeting.

Stalin's anxiety about the new President provided Harriman an opening to broach the subject of the UN again. At a critical moment of transition, he told the Marshal, the meeting would provide an opportunity for the Soviet government to show its intention to join in peacetime world leadership by sending Molotov to San Francisco. En route he could stop in Washington and meet the new President. Harriman offered to provide a plane—he would, he said, even paint a Red Star on the tail. Molotov was unenthusiastic, but Stalin agreed.

For Molotov served Harriman's purpose. With the Foreign Minister about to depart for Washington, the State Department reversed its order for Harriman to stay at his post; and the ambassador prepared to fly to Washington and put before the new President the whole unhappy account of what had happened since Roosevelt and Stalin met in the Crimea.

Molotov turned down his invitation to join him for the trip, but he did accept the use of an American C-54. While Averell had decided to travel via southern Europe, the Mediterranean, North Africa, and the Azores, Molotov insisted on going via Siberia and Alaska. Both parties took off four days after Roosevelt's death. Averell was in Washington a little more than forty-eight hours later, his modified Liberator bomber having set a new record between the two capitals. By the time Molotov got there, Harriman had already met with the President.

The Soviets were proceeding on two tracks, he told Truman. While cooperating when it suited their interest, they were also moving to brutally impose their authority across eastern Europe. He saw no great risk in the United States driving a harder bargain in every arrangement and negotiation in order to stem what he considered a "barbarian invasion."[33]

To Harriman's surprise, Truman had not only read the recent weeks' cables from Moscow, he had acutely understood what Harriman had been trying to convey, and he intended for his relations with Moscow to be firm.

On the following day, Molotov called twice at the White House. The first session was mainly a courtesy call during which Truman affirmed his intention to carry on with Roosevelt's policies. The two genially agreed that the two governments would adhere to the Yalta declaration in resolving the future of Poland.

In a later meeting at the State Department, however, the battle that Harriman had been fighting for two months erupted again. Molotov insisted that the provisional government in Warsaw would have to approve any other Poles added to it in preparation for elections. He was unmoved by American warnings that the stalemate over Poland threatened the United Nations organization. The conversation set the stage for Molotov's second visit to the President's office, and the famous Truman tongue-lashing—to which Molotov finally protested, "I've never been talked to like that in my life," and Truman replied, "Carry out your agreements, and you won't get talked to like that."[34]

Harriman was shaken by the vehemence with which Truman sailed into "Old Ironass," and he feared his new boss had overdone it and given Molotov an excuse to tell Stalin that Roosevelt's policy toward the Soviets was being abandoned. It was the first time he had thought the White House too tough on the Kremlin, and he would later consider it the precise moment that marked the beginning of the Cold War.

Averell stayed in the United States for another three weeks. Hard behind the opening session of the United Nations in San Francisco came the war's end in Europe. The rush of events threw American opinion into turmoil. Even in the flush of Allied victory, Averell found that a growing number of advisers—Stettinius, Undersecretary of State Joseph Grew, and Navy Secretary James Forrestal—shared his skepticism of Soviet motives. Under the circumstances, their message was not a popular one.

At San Francisco, he had invited several correspondents to his suite at the Mark Hopkins Hotel to hear his views on the Soviets' record since Yalta. When he asserted that long-term American and Soviet objectives were "irreconcilable," columnist Walter Lippmann and radio broadcaster Raymond Gram Swing walked out.

He had gained, and rather enjoyed, a reputation as a principal figure in a "get tough with Moscow" circle around the new President. Although he insisted that the United States had scrupulously to honor every commitment it had made to the Soviets, he was not for doing more; and Truman agreed, issuing a directive requiring full justification of new aid requests.

When it came to putting the new instructions into effect, however, the Protocol Committee went beyond what either Harriman or the President had in mind. Orders went out stopping the loading of ships and for vessels already bound for the USSR to return to American ports.

Harriman was flabbergasted, as was the State Department. He went to the President and got the instructions clarified, but the damage had already been done. Coming after Truman's upbraiding of Molotov, it looked like more evidence that Roosevelt's policies had died with him.

Concerned about that very thing, Averell and Chip Bohlen had proposed sending Harry Hopkins to see Stalin again. Truman had reservations about the idea. He had nothing against Hopkins; but Harry was obviously a gravely ill man, and the new President believed in conducting diplomacy through conventional channels. His instinct was to leave the task of communicating with Stalin to his ambassador, but Harriman pressed. Stalin fully understood the importance of the Roosevelt-Hopkins relationship, he told Truman; and if Hopkins returned to Moscow, Stalin would recognize that "he's speaking for Roosevelt as well as you." Should the United States and the Soviet Union head onto a dangerous new course, he argued, the country and the world should know that it was Stalin who parted from the course Roosevelt had advocated.[35]

Hopkins restored some of the diplomatic gentility that had faded from the U.S.-Soviet dialogue. During the two weeks that he and his wife remained in Moscow, Hopkins had six long meetings with Stalin. They reaffirmed the sanctity of the Yalta agreements and laid out once again each side's roster of grievances. Where Poland was concerned, Hopkins assured Stalin, the United States was not opposed to a government friendly to the Soviet Union; it simply wanted a government acceptable to the Polish people. After hours of fencing, Stalin agreed on a list of non-Communist Poles who could be invited to Moscow for the talks on the new Government of National Unity, thereby clearing the way for the Commission on Poland to meet again for the first time in weeks.

Harriman sat through all of the meetings but said little, except at Hopkins's invitation. The effort, he thought, had improved the atmosphere for the Big Three meeting planned for the Berlin area in mid-July, but the Polish problem was as imposing as ever.

"Stalin does not and never will fully understand our interest in a free Poland as a matter of principle," he cabled the President. "He is a realist . . . and it is hard for him to appreciate our faith in abstract principles. It is difficult for him to understand why we should want to interfere with Soviet policy in a country like Poland, which he considers so important to Russia's security, unless we have some ulterior motive."[36]

During the interim between Hopkins's departure from Moscow and the gathering of the Big Three at Potsdam, the bitterly divided Poles agreed on the makeup of a new government. Under pressure and pleading from Harriman, Mikolajczyk accepted the post of vice-premier in a government dominated by Moscow's puppets from the Lubin regime. Though he expected little of the new government, Harriman recommended that the United States accept it, and the Truman administration officially recognized it on July 5. Britain did the same, Churchill sadly giving up on the London government in exile.

Going home to Warsaw as vice-premier, Mikolajczyk considered himself as much a prisoner as a leader. Leaving Moscow, he told Harriman he feared they would never meet again. "It was clear to me that he went to Warsaw with a heavy heart," Harriman said, "fully aware that once the government was established—and to some extent strengthened by his participation—he might be arrested and executed."[37]

Although his admiration for Truman soared, Harriman was not at home in the new administration. Hopkins, after his trip to Moscow, left government service altogether and moved to New York. At the State Department, Stettinius was replaced by James F. Byrnes, a former associate justice of the Supreme Court and a former senator from South Carolina. Frances Perkins, the only Cabinet member to serve the Roosevelt administration from the first day to the last, left the Labor Department.

Without an open line to the White House, Harriman was working for a secretary of state for whom he had little personal or professional regard. He had joined Hopkins in pushing Byrnes for secretary when poor health drove Cordell Hull into retirement in 1944; but his view of Byrnes changed when, at Yalta, Byrnes childishly threatened to go home because he was left out of a military strategy discussion.

As arrangements were made for the Big Three summit at Potsdam, Harriman got no indication from Byrnes that he was even expected to attend. Seeing that he was about to be left out, he took the humiliating expedient of writing the secretary and more or less asking to be included. Byrnes's reaction was patronizing—of course Averell was to be a part of the American delegation.

It was obvious that he was not to be a consequential player, but the flight across Germany made going worthwhile. On his last trip home, Harriman had been assigned a new Liberator, luxuriously outfitted as an executive transport. It was sufficiently posh that no general or admiral would dare use it for fear he might get the attention of a congressman or a journalist. It had comfortable bunks, a galley, and huge picture windows offering a panoramic view. Bound for Potsdam, Harriman was riveted by the ravaged landscape of eastern Europe.

Poland had been relatively spared, but the Red Army's devastation of Germany had been complete. Its villages appeared lifeless, and heavily loaded trucks and herds of cattle could be seen moving eastward— reparations already being exacted by the Russians without any formal arrangement. In Berlin, industrial equipment in the Russian occupation zone had been stripped and hauled away. Even from the air, it was evident that survival would be a struggle.

At Potsdam, Harriman was as impressed as he had been in Washington by Truman's grasp of the presidency. Unlike Roosevelt, who was inclined to wander into unmapped territory, orchestrating positions as he went, Truman stayed crisply on the points staked out in advance. It was a negotiating style that Harriman admired. But he had to admire it from the fringe of the American delegation.

At the conference table, it was unmistakably Harry Truman who spoke for the United States; but away from it the American delegation was run by Byrnes, who neither shared his information nor delegated authority. Harriman thought he behaved as though he expected the Potsdam negotiations to be like a clubby Senate debate, and thought of himself as a mediator between Stalin and Churchill.

Averell lived in a bungalow in Babelsberg with Bob Meiklejohn and Eddie Page; and since he was taken into none of the President's private deliberations, he had time to idle away. He spent several hours with Secretary of War Henry Stimson, sitting in the sun outside Stimson's house, talking about the war in the Far East, the future of relations with the Soviet Union, and the atomic bomb.

Two months earlier in Washington, Stimson had brought him up to date on preparations for the first test. As they chatted at Potsdam, the secretary was anxious for news from Alamogordo, New Mexico, where scientists were at last ready. He was gloomy over the implications of the ghastly new weapon, and over Harriman's picture of an expansionist Soviet Union. Could the United States' monopoly on the atomic bomb be used to encourage the Soviet Union to back off its suppression of the countries it "liberated"? Harriman thought not. The Soviets would consider any suggestion of the kind overtly hostile.[38]

The conference leaders made a show of camaraderie, but they were split over the question of what German territory would be ceded to Poland in compensation for its eastern territory taken by the Soviet Union. Truman and Byrnes were willing to go along with Stalin and postpone the matter again, leaving it to be taken up at the fall meeting of the Council of Foreign Ministers. But Churchill thought it was time to put the long-suffering territorial issue to rest. Harriman staunchly agreed.

The solution was to invite representatives of the Polish government to Potsdam. Eight of them, led by Bierut and Mikolajczyk, arrived in Berlin on July 24. For once, non-Communist members of the new government agreed with Stalin. They wanted to reach west, taking as much German territory as they could, and they were abetted by the Soviets, who had already placed a portion of their zone of occupation under Polish administration.

Truman and Churchill disagreed with them. The Prime Minister saw Poland's reach into Germany as dangerously like her move eastward at the end of World War I. In the face of the deadlock, Truman's and Byrnes's senatorial instincts produced a compromise—another postponement. Until a new western border could be formalized at a peace conference, the United States would recognize Polish administration of the territory from the Soviet occupation zone. But since there was no peace conference, the boundaries of the new Poland were, with the minor concessions to Roosevelt at Yalta, as drawn by Moscow.

Depressed at the decline of his personal role and his incompatibility with Byrnes, Harriman went to Truman before the conference was over and told him that he was anxious to leave his post in Moscow. He would continue until the surrender of Japan. Then he wanted to "get out and go home."[39]

His biggest remaining job was to ensure that there was no upset in the plan for the Soviet Union to join the war against Japan, but even that looked much less important than it had in earlier days. The American offensive in the Pacific had brought the Japanese home islands within range of American bombers, making Soviet air bases in the Far East less than crucial. Indeed, the entire Far Eastern offensive by the Red Army was less vital than it had seemed a year earlier, when Roosevelt thought the fighting against Japan might go on until 1947. Harriman was among a growing number in the American government beginning to doubt that the Soviets would be needed in the Pacific at all. He had urged Washington to prepare for the possibility of a Japanese surrender before the Red Army moved.

On March 9, more than three hundred American bombers had hit Tokyo in history's most destructive air raid. Incendiary bombs set off a conflagration that wiped out 267,000 buildings and 18 percent of the city's industrial area. In April, May, and early June, similar attacks hit Nagoya, Kobe, Osaka, Yokohama, and Kawasaki. Forty percent of Japan's urban centers were in ruin, millions of her people were homeless. American bombers could range over cities of the empire unmolested.[40] The Japanese Navy was being systematically wiped out.

Two days after he arrived in Germany, Truman got word that the first atomic test had been a complete success. Thereafter both he and Churchill questioned whether there was any longer a role for the Russians in the Pacific.

The secret predawn explosion was followed by a public political upheaval. To the dismay of the world, Churchill's coalition government was turned out of office, and after a recess at Potsdam Clement Attlee and Ernest Bevin arrived to replace Churchill and Anthony Eden. Only Stalin and Molotov, among the principals of earlier meetings of the uncertain alliance, remained.

Of all the Americans at Potsdam, it was Harriman who was best acquainted with the leaders of the new British government, but he was a lonely figure in his own delegation. When the conference ended, he flew to London to offer his condolences to Churchill, who, at seventy-one, again seemed to have come to the end of his political road. Averell's diplomatic career was ending as well. Leaving Churchill, he flew back to Moscow, looking forward to winding up his affairs and going home.

He was back at Spaso House on August 5, the day the atomic bomb struck Hiroshima. The announcement, which set off celebrations in the United States, got only brief mention in the Soviet press; and, oddly, it produced little reaction in the American diplomatic community. Still afoot was Stalin's determined attempt to extract additional concessions from the Chinese. Two days after Hiroshima, he again pressed for full control of the Dairen seaport on the Yellow Sea and asserted a Soviet right to Japanese property in Manchuria. Under these circumstances, Harriman concluded, the Soviets would be happy enough to see the war in the Pacific go on for a while longer.

Molotov advised Harriman and Clark Kerr that the Soviets would declare war on the Japanese on August 9. Averell flashed the word to the President. "It was clear," Harriman said, "that the bomb had forced Stalin's hand."[41]

On the same day that the Red Army rolled into Manchuria, the atomic devastation that had struck Hiroshima was visited upon Nagasaki. Two days later, Japan was ready to surrender, and the United States was ready to accept.

Then, in a brazen attempt to make the Soviet Union a full partner in settlement of the war it had just joined, Molotov asserted that Moscow was entitled to participate in selection of Allied representatives to accept the surrender and to share in the Allied command in the Far East. For Harriman, it was a moment of immense satisfaction. There was no need even to consult Washington.

The United States would accept the surrender, he coldly told Molotov. There would be no joint command, no Soviet veto of the President's choice. It was unthinkable that the Supreme Commander would be anyone but an American, when the United States had been fighting the Japanese for four years and the Soviet Union all of two days. He stalked out of the Foreign Ministry to cable Washington and advise what he had done.

Word of Japan's surrender produced an outpouring of Soviet goodwill. Eisenhower was visiting Moscow; and in an unprecedented gesture of comradeship, Stalin had invited him, Harriman, and Deane to join him atop Lenin's tomb to review a huge sports parade that went on for hours. Appearing later at a soccer stadium with Marshal Georgy Zhukov, who had led the Red Army offensive to Berlin, Ike received a thunderous, standing ovation from Soviet citizens.

A huge party in the general's honor was under way at Spaso House when Harriman received official word of the Japanese surrender. After a cable conference with Byrnes in Washington, Hurley in Chungking, and Foreign Secretary Bevin in London, he dashed from the embassy telegraph office to the party where Zhukov and the top brass of the Soviet military had joined the salute to Eisenhower.

When he was able to speak above the din, Averell read President Truman's official announcement of the end of the war. The last part of it was lost in an uproar set off when Marshal Semyon Budenny, who had spent most of the war at the rear after being defeated by the Germans at Kiev, let out a derisive hoot at the announcement's reference to "his Imperial Majesty, the Japanese emperor."[42]

The war over, Harriman regarded his assignment as finished. The Council of Foreign Ministers, established at Potsdam, was about to convene in London to take up peace arrangements with the Axis satellites; and since he would be there to brief Byrnes on his Far East negotiations since Potsdam, Harriman cabled the secretary that he also wished to discuss his resignation as ambassador.

Byrnes's reply was a brushoff. Harriman, it made clear, was not expected at the conference. In any case, the secretary indicated that he would be too busy to see the ambassador during the first ten days of the meeting. If he wished to discuss the personal matter, he could come to London after that.

Steaming, Harriman wired the President. He had fulfilled his commitment to Roosevelt, he reminded Truman, and now he wished to return to private life. Acknowledgment came, not from the President but in a form message signed by his old Yale rowing friend, Dean Acheson, who was acting secretary of state since Byrnes had already set out for London. Instead of being offended by the bureaucratic reply, Harriman broke into laughter at the absurdity of being relieved with a form letter from his former schoolmate.

"I have never seen such a frank and healthy exhibition of merriment on his part," Meiklejohn wrote in his diary. "He howled for Kathleen and gave her the cable to read, then phoned Miss Jacoby [a secretary] and asked her if she wanted my job in Moscow. I am not entirely clear of the reason for the merriment, but it was doubtless compounded of: 1) thankfulness to get out of this God forsaken hole; 2) relief that the course of the future is fairly clear (no mention was made of a new government job)[;] and . . . 3) amusement at the clumsiness of Acheson's cable which, to my mind, looks like a form cable to be sent to any reasonably satisfactory ambassador who happens to resign. Nowhere, except in the address, does it mention Moscow or Harriman. It could have just as well been used to accept the resignation of the ambassador in Venezuela."[43]

Averell made his leisurely way to London by way of Frankfurt and the French Riviera, where he spent two days sitting in the sun playing bridge with Eisenhower, Kathleen, and Kay Summersby, the general's WAC chauffeur. Still he arrived three days before Byrnes expected him, and he took some secret satisfaction in finding that, with Byrnes and Bevin getting their first real experience with Molotov, the conference was aground. The ministers had accomplished nothing on treaties for Italy, Romania, Bulgaria, and Hungary; and Molotov and Byrnes were at loggerheads over the Soviets' demand for an Allied Control Commission to manage the occupation of Japan. In the course of discussions, Bevin had likened Molotov's behavior to Hitler's tactics, and Molotov had headed for the door, turning back only when the British minister apologized.

Byrnes had so firmly opposed Molotov's Far East position that Old Ironass accused the United States of trying to make itself the world dictator. The secretary had also managed to offend Bevin, who tattled to Harriman that Byrnes wasn't bothering to consult with the British delegation.

Toward the end of the meeting, Harriman at last got his chance to discuss his departure from Moscow. But instead of concluding his plan to go home, he had his tour in Moscow extended. It was up him, Byrnes declared, to untangle the mess left by the three disputatious weeks in London and "get the train back on the rails."[44]

Harriman's instinct was to put the matter into the laps of Stalin and the President; but when he got back to Moscow, he found Stalin had gone to the Crimea for a rare vacation. After a two-week effort, he managed to get approval from Stalin's office to visit the Marshal at his villa on the shore of the Black Sea. Armed with a message from the President, he set forth. Accompanied only by interpreters, he and Stalin held long talks on successive days, ending with the Marshal's agreeing for the foreign ministers to gather once more in Moscow and again consider peace terms for the Axis allies. He would not retreat, however, on his demand for a role in the occupation of Japan.

It took a month for arrangements to be worked out with Molotov and for Byrnes and Bevin to return to the Soviet Union.

In the end, the United States had its way in the Far East. After the long period of demanding establishment of a commission to oversee occupation policy in Japan, Molotov acceded to the United States' offer of an Allied Council that would advise General MacArthur but have no authority to countermand his decisions.

Such was not the case in Europe. Byrnes's and Bevin's appeals for free elections and broadened representation in the Balkan governments were fruitless, though Stalin finally agreed to send a tripartite commission to Romania to arrange for the Soviet-supported government to bring in representatives of dissident political parties.

Harriman's work in resurrecting the Council of Foreign Ministers after the debacle in London elevated his standing with Truman, but it did not diminish his resolve to get out of Moscow and sever his ties with the State Department. The egocentric Byrnes was, in the ambassador's view, disastrously misplaced as secretary of state. He arrived in Moscow with his mind made up to conclude the second foreign ministers conference before Christmas. He ignored Harriman's advice to send the President regular progress reports, and he only reluctantly coordinated anything with other departments of the government. During eleven days in Moscow, he sent only one cable back to Truman. Members of his delegation were unhappy with him, as were his former colleagues on Capitol Hill. Worse, Harriman thought, Byrnes's manner was doing substantial harm to relations between the United States and the new Labour government in London.

"Byrnes is letting the British slip away from us," he said in a memorandum shortly after the Moscow conference, "not because of any disagreement on policy but purely by offending them through his unwillingness to consult and what Bevin considers his somewhat overbearing attitude."[45]

Harriman finally left Moscow at the end of January 1946, but nothing was easy in Moscow, even to the last minute. His call for a farewell appointment with Molotov was returned after he had gone to bed on January 20. As he had done on occasion during the war, he arose, dressed, and headed for the Foreign Ministry in the middle of the night.

Three days later, he paid a last call on Stalin. Then, aboard *Grandpappy*, his modified bomber loaded with seventy-eight pieces of baggage and more than six hundred pounds of secret documents, he headed home by way of the Far East.

Accompanied by Kathleen, Meiklejohn, Eddie Page, a military aide, and his secretary, he flew south to Abadan on the Persian Gulf, then eastward to Karachi, and on to New Delhi, where he stayed overnight as guest of his old friend Field Marshal Archibald Wavell, now viceroy of India. In Chungking, he spent two days with Chiang Kai-shek and General Marshall, the latter in China trying to effect a peace between Chiang's nationalists and the Communists in the north.

He found little to make him optimistic in spite of Stalin's insistence that the Chinese Communists did not represent an extension of the Soviet system.

Chiang was weaker than he had thought, and he was further disturbed to hear T. V. Soong, the Nationalists' preeminent diplomat, relate a conversation in which Stalin warned that China would soon face a choice of allying itself with either Washington or Moscow. More than ever, he felt the United States was making a mistake by trying to play the mediator's role. From Chungking, he moved on to Shanghai and Seoul, detouring to dip down through the clouds for a look at the ruins of Hiroshima and Nagasaki. Only the most modern structures of Hiroshima still stood, and in the harbor, seventeen submarines rusted.

The party was in Tokyo when a White House message was delivered, telling him that Harry Hopkins had died. Nothing else made the end of his government service seem so final. He could think of no adequate way to respond. "I send you all my love and sympathy," he wired Louise Hopkins. "Harry's friendship has been a vital inspiration to me. His place can never be filled."[46]

They arrived in Washington just after daybreak on St. Valentine's Day, five years after he had taken the flying boat for London. The next day, Byrnes presented him the Medal of Merit at the State Department.

Chapter XVI

TRUMAN
Field General at the Talleyrand

For the first time since he faced his choice between shouldering a rifle or staying at home in World War I, Harriman was in early 1946 distressed about his future. Remaining at the State Department was out of the question, because he couldn't abide Jimmy Byrnes. He had no desire to go back to the bank, and he had in recent months fully realized that he could not push Roland aside at the railroad.

He was still chairman of the Union Pacific board, and he had until late in the war expected to go back and resume the duties that his brother had carried out for him since 1941. But Roland had presided over the company during a tough time. Aside from the disruption caused by thousands of employees going into wartime service, there had been severe morale problems in the executive offices in Omaha. Averell's man, the aging and ailing William Jeffers, had retired as Union Pacific president and had been replaced by George Ashby, who had risen from the accounting department to become executive vice-president. Averell had not liked the choice of Ashby and he had thought his brother's management tentative, which was all the more reason not to return and reclaim the chairmanship.

His own explanation was that he simply did not want to walk over his brother, who had been his loyal junior partner and friend. The truth was somewhat more complex. Roland had not aspired to the chairmanship. But after nearly six years, he had developed an agenda of his own.

He had paid his dues; he had helped make possible Averell's public career; and he had a wife who was much opposed to his stepping back to play in Averell's band. The ambassador knew all of this, and he also knew that his conventional, unpretentious, unassuming brother was better loved in the business community. The financial district was now Roland's turf.

Even before leaving Moscow, Averell, realizing he could not go back without causing wounds in the family, had pointedly hinted that he would be available for another presidential assignment, but the administration had done nothing to discourage his departure. Although he and the President shared a huge mutual respect, they had nothing personally in common. They were as different as the rocky hills on the Hudson and the plains of western Missouri. Harry Truman, the onetime county judge and unsuccessful haberdasher, represented the average man in America as vividly as Harriman personified privilege. There was no croquet lawn behind the Truman White House. There was no Harry Hopkins.

But Harriman lingered in Truman's Washington, unable to disengage when problems with the Soviets were potentially explosive, Europe was in shambles, and the United States' postwar foreign policy was still in search of itself. He reported on his trip through the Far East, visited with Churchill, who was vacationing in the United States, and went to Capitol Hill to give secret testimony on the ominous behavior of the Soviet Union since Yalta. At a hotel downtown, he spoke to his old comrades at the Business Advisory Council in such alarmed tones that Henry Wallace accused him of dangerous meddling and warmongering.

The Harriman litany of broken Soviet promises, the alarmed commerce secretary and erstwhile Vice-President predicted, would incite firebrands to "go out over the country and spread the word that we are going to get tough with Russia even though it means war."[1] The speech came a week after Churchill's "Iron Curtain" oration at Westminster College, which Harriman fully embraced, although the White House carefully avoided endorsing it. His own speech hardly had the repercussions Wallace feared, but several members of the audience, including Studebaker president Paul Hoffman, whose views bordered on pacifism, recommended that he go on the road with it.

A bit later, before one thousand business and professional people at a testimonial dinner sponsored by the American Society for Russian Relief, Harriman and Wallace argued face-to-face. The Soviets were merely trying to secure their borders against "capitalist encirclement," the commerce secretary contended. A relief affair for Russian war victims was no place to debate Kremlin behavior, Averell replied, but neither was it any time to "minimize the differences that have arisen between our two governments since the war."[2]

To point out his own differences belabored the obvious. In Washington, he had put in circulation a passionate six-thousand-word cable from George Kennan, assessing the expansionist forces at work in the Soviet Union. Its analysis was compelling, and its conclusions close to Harriman's own. After reading it, Averell commended it to Navy Secretary James Forrestal, who gave it wider distribution, saving it from burial in the State Department. Kennan's famous "long cable" thus made containment of Soviet expansion a touchstone of American policy. Even as it was circulating, the first postwar crisis with the Soviets was producing alarming headlines.

The deadline had passed for Moscow to withdraw its troops from northern Iran, as it had pledged to do in a 1942 treaty with Britain. For more than a year, there had been escalating Communist mischief-making in Iranian affairs, and it continued as Red Army troops remained in the Iranian province of Azerbaijan, adjoining the Soviet Union. Soviet agents were propagandizing against the government in Teheran, stirring up trouble among Kurdish tribesmen and providing arms to the pro-Communist Tudeh party, which was agitating for separation of Azerbaijan from Iran.

American and British interests included much more than principle and firmness against Kremlin adventurism. Western oil companies were anxious to conclude leases with the Iranian government and get on with exploration. And for Britain, Iran's independence was of strategic concern because of its location between the British Isles and the fading empire's interests in India and the Far East.

Harriman had given Washington good reason to expect trouble in Iran. Two months before leaving Moscow, he had delivered a message reminding the Kremlin that the United States took seriously the Allies' commitment to withdraw their troops. Byrnes had further emphasized the point to both Molotov and Stalin, as had Foreign Secretary Bevin. American and British troops withdrew on schedule, but Stalin had pressed the Iranian government for an agreement to develop oil in the northern provinces and threatened to leave Red troops in the country until Teheran granted autonomy to Azerbaijan.

Heading for a full-blown crisis, the Truman administration needed somebody in London who knew both the British and Soviet governments, not to mention the Iranians. John Winant was still there as ambassador, but he was a troubled and brooding figure, no longer appreciated in Washington as he had been during the Roosevelt administration.

Harriman was living out of a suitcase, back and forth between Washington and New York, when Byrnes broached the London assignment to him. Although the situation was urgent, the secretary, who had obviously not judged Harriman well in their previous encounters, suggested London was a little sinecure, an appropriate expression of appreciation for all Averell had done during the war. Harriman was offended by the inference, but he agreed to discuss it with the President.

Truman was blunt. Unless something was done, he said, the circumstances in Iran could even "lead to war," and he needed somebody he could trust in London. Harriman could again consider himself the President's man, not an ordinary minion serving Byrnes and the State Department; and when the crisis was resolved he would be expeditiously brought home, if that was what he wanted. With these assurances, he was on his way back to London as ambassador to the Court of St. James's, six months after he had arrived from Moscow.

As it turned out, his stay in England was even more brief than he expected. By the time he arrived, the crisis had already eased, the Soviets advising the Security Council that an agreement had been worked out for its troops to withdraw by mid-April. So the tour lasted but six months, just long enough for him to be properly welcomed, renew his friendship with Pamela Churchill, and get the croquet court at Great Enton, Robert Sherwood's country house in Surrey, into condition for weekend play.

Without urgent business before him in London, he joined Byrnes in Paris, where the wartime allies were finally concluding peace treaties with Germany's satellites. He worked so enthusiastically with the Labour government that Beaverbrook threatened to have Churchill denounce him in Commons for involving himself in Britain's domestic politics. He enjoyed the ambassadorial privileges, but his interests were back in Washington, even though he was no longer the insider he had been during the war. Embassy staff members, unlike old Lend-Lease-mission colleagues and Moscow subordinates, thought him reticent, aloof, distant, and not altogether engaged.[3]

To be sure, it was an uncomfortable interlude for him. He had to be especially discreet about his friendship with Pamela, since she was now divorced from Randolph and since Kathleen was not along to prevent the relationship from being obvious. Moreover, his responsibilities as ambassador made him much more a public figure than he had been as the Lend-Lease expediter. Largely at the instigation of Paul Felix Warburg, a family friend and embassy staffer who was nervous that talk would start about the ambassador and Churchill's former daughter-in-law, plans were put in place for Marie to move to London and take up her role as hostess of the American embassy. Her eye condition was now sufficiently improved that her doctors did not object, and she was weary of continuing problems with her own children, including Nancy's drinking and dropping out of college.

Before she could join him, however, Averell was called home, Truman needing him to help quell an eight-day uproar that made headlines in Europe as well as across the United States. Henry Wallace, whose sympathetic view of the Soviet Union had been tolerated although it was egregiously out of step with the view of the rest of the administration, had finally made the mistake of venting it at the very moment the United States was stiffening its posture toward Moscow, announcing to his Madison Square Garden audience that his remarks had the endorsement of the President.

Angry and embarrassed, Byrnes demanded that Truman either accept Wallace's resignation or put an end to the free-lance family criticism. Truman at first tried to explain it all away, but he couldn't because the truth was that he had scanned Wallace's text and offered no objection. So, to quell the political storm, he asked for Wallace's resignation and turned to Harriman to take over the Commerce Department.

Averell and Pamela, who was recharting her future after ending her hopeless marriage to Randolph, were at Great Enton when the BBC broadcast the news that Wallace had been sacked. Although Averell had been expecting it, his immediate reaction was gloomy and self-pitying. He had lost his big chance to be in the Cabinet because he was out of position, doing ceremonial duty in London. He would have been an obvious choice, he said, if he had only been at home. As it was, he was going to lose his chance because he had been talked into going off to deal with an emergency that never was.[4]

Still bemoaning his unfortunate luck, he had gone off to have lunch with Churchill when a White House operator called Great Enton in search of him. The call caught up with him at Chartwell within the hour, and both he and Churchill guessed what it was about before the President came on the line. When the offer of the Cabinet seat came moments later, he accepted it so casually that the President thought there had been a misunderstanding. "You don't seem to understand, I want you to be Secretary of Commerce," Truman repeated. "Yes, sir, I understand and I'll be only too glad to do it," Harriman replied, asking the same question he had asked Truman six months earlier, "When do you want me there?"[5]

He needed only enough time to inform his partners at the bank before the White House made the announcement.

Back home, he cut the business connections that he had left in place throughout his wartime absence. He resigned his active partnership in Brown Brothers Harriman and gave up his seat on the board of the Union Pacific and the Illinois Central, and moved into a $30-a-day suite in the Shoreham Hotel. With the embattled Truman administration facing its first congressional elections, he was for the first time in his life viewed as a political asset. Because of his background on Wall Street and in the railroad industry, he was a visible conduit to the business community, and his work throughout the war made him a powerful reminder of the Roosevelt legacy. All the insiders from the thirties—

Ickes, Morgenthau, Perkins—were gone, as were Roosevelt's lieutenants from the war years, all replaced by Truman loyalists.

His selection was not universally acclaimed by the Democrats, however. As the divided party faced the first postwar congressional elections, voters were in a sour mood over strikes, shortages, and the Red Menace. Liberals looked askance at his ties with the Union Pacific and his prominent history with Wall Street, not to mention his outspoken criticism of the Soviet Union. At a White House reception soon after his return, Walter Lippmann, who had grandly walked out of Averell's press conference in San Francisco, upbraided him for being "a goddamned pathological anti-Communist."[6] But among progressive, internationalist, politically flexible businessmen, he was deemed a highly suitable choice. In spite of his identity as a New Dealer, he retained his standing as a capitalist.

He "did not break with Mr. Roosevelt over social-economic experiments of which he strongly disapproved," Arthur Krock advised *New York Times* readers. According to Krock, he simply believed the world situation made it "too risky."[7]

His old friend and employee Raymond Moley predicted a new day at the chronically troubled Commerce Department, which, he observed, had been falling apart for nearly fourteen years. "The first Roosevelt appointee, Daniel C. Roper, was a weak man; the second, Harry Hopkins, was a sick man; the third, Jesse Jones, was a busy man; and the fourth, Henry Wallace, was, to many businessmen, a wild man."[8]

Harriman did not regard himself as the business representative in the Truman administration. To the contrary, he was the President's liaison to the business world. He rejuvenated the Business Advisory Council, which had fallen from influence during Wallace's administration, and recruited Republican businessman William C. Foster to take over the number two Commerce job and the day-to-day running of the department. But he made no move to sweep out the Wallace loyalists; and when the former secretary came back to Washington for speeches scalding the administration, he insisted that his predecessor's old lieutenants go to hear him.

His defense of one Wallace holdover against anti-Communist zealots on the House Un-American Activities Committee provoked a confrontation with an enduring animosity toward Richard M. Nixon. In its quest for Communist-tinged bureaucrats, the committee zeroed in on National Bureau of Standards chief Edward U. Condon, who made himself a detectable target. The Princeton mathematician, who had been brought in by Wallace, had encouraged scientists who worked for him to join the American-Soviet Friendship Society and had feuded with Lieutenant General Leslie Groves, who had headed the Manhattan Project, about a Moscow meeting with Soviet scientists.

A year after Averell arrived at Commerce, the departmental loyalty board looked into allegations against Condon; and the Atomic Energy Commission conducted a special review of his security clearance. In the course of the departmental investigation, Averell received a letter from J. Edgar Hoover disclosing Condon's acquaintance with purported spy Nathan Gregory Silvermaster, going on to say that there was no evidence that the Bureau of Standards director knew anything of Silvermaster's activities.

Several months later, the Nixon subcommittee cited the Hoover letter in attacking Condon as a weak link in U.S. atomic security, neglecting to mention that the FBI had failed to find any evidence that he was aware of Silvermaster's espionage activities.

When Nixon demanded the files of the Commerce Department Loyalty Board, Harriman refused, and the congressman threatened to subpoena him to be examined under oath. A formal demand for a copy of the Hoover letter was answered by Truman's having the letter locked in a White House safe.

Although Nixon would later acknowledge that the scientist had been treated unfairly, Harriman despised Nixon forever after. One night three years later, columnist Joe Alsop inexplicably invited Nixon to dinner with a little group of Georgetown friends who got together at one of their houses every Sunday evening for a meal and freewheeling political and social gossip. Nixon showed up early and was holding forth in the living room of Alsop's brother, Stewart, when Averell and Marie arrived. A step inside the door, Harriman spied him and wheeled to leave. He was intercepted by Mrs. Alsop and shamed into joining the rest of the group; but he sat through dinner without uttering a word, and as soon as the meal was over, he left.

At Commerce, undaunted by the experience of the unfortunate Wallace, and unmindful of his own public pledge not to dabble elsewhere, he took on not only the conventional topics of trade and commerce but the political transgressions of the USSR and the dangers of its foreign policy. The latter irritated the State Department, where the criticism of the Soviet Union was subdued. The bureaucracy in Foggy Bottom did not appreciate his poaching, but it seldom tinkered with his speeches—mainly because he ignored the protocol of offering an advance look at his texts.

The Truman administration watched with alarm as famine threatened Europe in the wake of consecutive winters of extraordinary severity. Industrial production was wrecked, transportation at a standstill, farmers barely feeding themselves. Tens of thousands of Germans still lived in cellars and beneath houses leveled by bombs and artillery shells. Coal production lagged because miners were weak from hunger. In

Holland, daily rations provided no more than six hundred calories a day.

In England, the war's victors suffered scarcely less than the vanquished. Offices were lighted by candles. Factories were closed down so coal could be used to prevent families from freezing in their homes. Spring and summer brought severe drought. "Europe was as close to destitution as a modern civilization can get," said Theodore H. White. "She could not grow enough food and she could not find the money or goods to buy food elsewhere."[9]

To help out, distillers in the United States were ordered to reduce their use of grain; good citizens observed "meatless Tuesday" and "eggless Thursday" and reduced their bread consumption by a slice a day. At the Waldorf in New York, the hotel bulletin advised guests that wheat bread would be served only upon request, and Washington's venerable Occidental Restaurant gave out a recipe for bread pudding, suggesting it as a way to use bread gone stale. Beef and pork were not to be found in the markets of major cities. Poultry prices shot up to $1 a pound, and a thriving black market for horse meat developed. Harriman was photographed dutifully enjoying a cafeteria lunch of bell pepper stuffed with rice, and newspaper ads featured him pleading with American housewives to save used fats for recycling to meet shortages overseas.

In the November '46 election, mounting frustrations against shortages and high prices were vented against the Democrats. Denounced by Republicans for appeasing the Communists and attacked by liberals for provoking tensions and risking war with Moscow, Truman's party was swamped. For the first time since 1928, the Republicans took control of both houses of Congress.

It was not easy for Harriman to settle into this postwar America. His business ties cut, he no longer felt at home in New York, and he had not yet found his niche in the Truman administration. While he was formally a part of the President's team, he was not at ease among the cronies who drank bourbon and played poker aboard the presidential yacht and in the sun at Key West's Little White House.

When he retreated to the gilded ghetto of Hobe Sound, north of Palm Beach, where he had bought a seaside house to make amends to Marie for his indiscretion with Pamela, he was surrounded by Republicans gloating over Truman's problems. There old acquaintances from Wall Street and the New York social establishment regarded him as an amusing and misguided leftover from the New Deal, consorting with another generation of Democrats, a tacky lower order whose moment had also passed, supporting an unelected President who was, they were certain, only serving out Roosevelt's term.

Waldemar Nielsen, a Commerce Department aide who often traveled with him, later recalled a visit to Florida on Marie's birthday. "As usual, there were six or eight or ten Long Island aristocrats around. Here was a guy who had been Ambassador to Russia, Ambassador to Great Britain, and was Secretary of Commerce, a truly big shot to those of us from Washington. But they didn't give a damn about him. What the hell was secretary of commerce? Nothing but a stupid political appointment by the goddamned Democrats. He was a formidable figure in Washington, but in that social circle, he was regarded not as an outcast, but as a strange kind of fellow—a jerk."[10]

Hobe Sound would remain a winter retreat for the Harrimans for more than twenty years, but increasingly they brought along their own friends, even Democrats, who had the boldness to meet Averell on his croquet lawn and the resilience to play bridge with Marie until dawn was breaking over the Atlantic. To the end, Marie boycotted the Jupiter Island Club, the community's social hub and nerve center, because it had turned away Eddy Duchin the first time he was a guest at the Harriman house. The sole reason for the slight, she was sure, was that he was Jewish.

By the spring of 1947, the United States had poured $9 billion worth of loans and relief aid into Europe, but the continent was still flirting with catastrophe. Americans were just beginning to understand that the war had destroyed not only homes and factories and transportation networks, but Europe's whole economic system. Long before the fighting ended, it was obvious to Harriman that ad hoc relief to one country after another would never put Europe back on its feet. He had, as far back as 1943, begun urging the British government to start systematic planning for the restoration of its economy. Later he had proposed extension of the Lend-Lease program in Europe. But in their yearning for normalcy and the comforts of peacetime, Americans had not permitted the war's economic devastation to penetrate their conscience. It was now indisputable that structural rehabilitation on a continental scale was necessary if there was to be a return to self-sufficiency.

Once home, he had talked about the deepening crisis with General Marshall, Acheson, Bob Lovett, and a host of others in and out of the government; and in March 1947 he joined officials of the War Department and Budget Director James E. Webb in endorsing a controversial recommendation by Herbert Hoover that Germany be made the engine of industrial and economic recovery for all of Europe.[11]

Nowhere was the war's destruction so complete, the recovery task so staggering, or policy issues so divisive. Averell was as touched by the plight of the Germans as by the condition of the British and the Poles. Old friends and business associates had been brutalized by the Nazis, impoverished by the war, and degraded by Hitler's mass murders of European Jews. Some had begun writing to him again, and he regularly sent them care packages.

The issue of Germany's future was a poisonous complication in relations between the Western powers and a source of rising anxiety among Americans. At the State Department, there was deep revulsion against restoration of so recent an enemy. But, as an old-line believer in open trade who had profited handsomely from German investments in the twenties, Harriman saw it as the key to Europe's economic recovery. More than that, it was the place where Soviet expansion had to be contained.

The crucial moment for European recovery came even before Hoover submitted his report recommending that Germany receive priority in the rebirth of Europe. With Britain's economy exhausted, the British Empire began its breakup. His Majesty's forces withdrew from Egypt and Palestine, and London announced the end of British reign in India. Three days after the news of Indian independence, Britain's ambassador to Washington notified the Truman administration that Britain could not continue its assistance to Greece and Turkey. The former was on the verge of collapse, its treasury nearly empty, the government's control of the countryside threatened by Communist insurgents. If Greece fell, it would only be a matter of time until Turkey and Iran followed. With control of the Dardanelles, the Soviets would have unimpeded access to the eastern Mediterranean, North Africa, and the Middle East.

Truman's historic request for $400 million for Greece and Turkey, a watershed in his presidency, was delivered to a joint session of Congress on March 12, couched in a declaration so unequivocal that it compelled politicians and the press to anoint it the Truman Doctrine. It would thenceforth be the policy of the United States, he declared, "to support free peoples who are resisting attempted subjugation by armed minorities or by outside pressure."[12]

From the intense discussions that produced the Greek-Turkish aid decision and the Truman Doctrine came a keener appreciation of the polarization Harriman had recognized with the end of the war. The crisis reached beyond Greece and Turkey to Western Europe and involved much more than military security. Harriman was not a participant in designing the Greek-Turkish aid package, but he embraced it when it was presented to the Cabinet, and he worked to drum up support for it in the business community.

By early April he had on his desk proposals for the Commerce Department to take the lead in an American program to rebuild the economy of Europe and secure it against the Communists. But the job obviously belonged to the Department of State, and there Acheson already had plans in motion.

To the general public, the necessity of moving away from piecemeal relief to massive structural restoration was first proposed by Acheson himself, who stood in for the President in a May 8 speech at Cleveland,

Mississippi. With Truman's authorization, he laid out in general terms thinking that had crystallized in the two months since presentation of the Greek-Turkish aid package. Ten days later in Los Angeles, Harriman sounded the same themes, stressing the need to restore European productive capacity in a coordinated fashion. The rebirth of economic vitality, he declared, could only come through American "ingenuity, technique, medical science, and capital" deployed to enable European countries to trade with one another again. And like Acheson, he stressed the imperative of restoring Germany's economic health.[13]

General Marshall's historic Harvard commencement speech proposing the recovery program that Acheson and Harriman had generally described came a month later. "It would be neither fitting nor efficacious for this Government to undertake to draw up unilaterally a program designed to place Europe on its feet economically," he said. "This is the business of the Europeans. The initiative, I think, must come from Europe. The program should be a joint one, agreed to by a number of, if not all, European nations. The role of this country should consist of friendly aid in the drafting of a European program and of later support of such a program so far as it may be practical for us to do so."[14]

With the general's speech, Harriman was swept into a torrent of events putting the recovery program in motion. What emerged was not an attempt to rebuild what had been there before the war but to create an economically integrated Europe, free of rivalries and trade barriers and capable of being an equal trading partner with the United States. It was what Harriman had dreamed of since his days traveling Europe after World War I. It was not without altruism; but to politicians and Harriman's progressive business friends, the obvious appeal was to use American resources to create new overseas markets dwarfing anything they had ever seen.

Politically, the business community was crucial: if corporate leaders opposed the program, getting it through the Republican Congress would be impossible. The key responsibility fell to Averell.

Two weeks after Marshall's speech, the President put him in charge of a committee bringing powerful corporate leaders together with labor officials and academics to assess both Europe's needs and the U.S. capacity to meet them. Popularly known as the Harriman Committee, its members included Studebaker president Paul G. Hoffman, an unabashed advocate of an expanded foreign-aid program, Owen D. Young, the former chairman of General Electric, Hiland Batcheller, president of Allegheny-Ludlum Steel, and John L. Collyer, president of B. F. Goodrich. Another member, National City Bank vice-president W. Randolph Burgess, was part of an institution with close ties to Harriman throughout his business career, and yet another member, Procter and

Gamble president R. R. "Rich Red" Deupree, had been an important customer of Brown Brothers Harriman.

To give the panel credibility, the White House had taken pains to avoid the appearance that Harriman was presiding over a rubber-stamping exercise. Deupree was "out of sympathy with the whole Marshall Plan concept," as was Batcheller, and it was Harriman's job to keep them and less noisy skeptics from obstructing the course of the majority.[15] At the suggestion of Senator Arthur Vandenberg of Michigan, a once-militant Republican isolationist reborn in January 1945 as a champion of bipartisan foreign policy, Truman added Bob La Follette, a former senator from Wisconsin. It would be politically helpful, Vandenberg knew, for the committee to have a member of a noted isolationist political family from a part of the country where isolationist sentiment was still robust. La Follette became one of the group's activists.

While the committee's membership was important politically, it was the professional staff that would ultimately shape its findings. To head it, Harriman recruited Richard M. Bissell, a brilliant, autocratic economist he had first known in London in 1942 when Bissell was on the staff of the War Shipping Administration. Leaving to him the collection and organization of data and management of the massive study, Harriman made himself the recovery program's principal pitchman, presenting it to the skeptics as a counter to Soviet expansionism and a requisite for a stable domestic economy. The rapid restoration of Europe, he told business groups, was the only way to avoid the folly of World War I, when the United States tried to withdraw from Europe's problems.

His staunchest ally was Hoffman, who shared a conviction that the program had to proceed without regard to political objectives, supporting, if necessary, governments that Washington found altogether distasteful. The surest way to drive Europe to the left, they agreed, was to delay the program any longer.[16]

In essence, the plan was to use American tax money to rebuild European markets for American products, generating jobs and corporate profits in the process. The alternative to full engagement in the affairs of Europe, both told business friends across the country, was an isolationist, fortress America that would wind up with its economy sapped by staggering costs of military security.

Before he brought his committee together, Harriman spent a month touring the capitals of Western Europe with Agriculture Secretary Clinton Anderson. By the time he returned in mid-July, Foreign Minister Molotov had already taken the Soviet Union—and Eastern Europe—out of participation in the plan, and representatives of sixteen countries in the West had met in Paris and organized the Committee for European Economic Cooperation.

Averell returned depressed over what he had seen in Germany, and to a lively debate between the United States and the Europeans over German reparations, the level of industry to be permitted in the country, and the future of the Ruhr Valley and its vast coal resources.

It was time, he advised Truman, for Washington to do more to support German recovery. The United States was "putting in too little too late," he said, and as a result, its effort was being largely wasted. "We shall face one crisis after another unless steps are taken promptly to turn the downward trend upward. . . . We cannot attain our basic objectives unless we are ready to move rapidly to reconstruct German life from its present pitiful and chaotic condition. The recovery of Germany in feeding and in industrial production has lagged far behind western Europe. We cannot revive a self supporting western European economy without a healthy Germany playing its part as a producing and consuming unit."[17]

The Harriman committee began hearing testimony in the commerce secretary's conference room on July 23. Kennan was among the first witnesses, and he kept the businessmen riveted for a full day with his analysis of expansionist Soviet policy and the imperative for a mighty U.S. response to shore up Western Europe. Panel members met regularly through the rest of the summer and fall, and Harriman and Bissell drove the staff into the night week after week.

The only time the committee chairman took a break from constructing the plan for Europe's recovery was the week in early October when he went to Arden for the wedding of his younger daughter. Having been pursued through the war by journalists, diplomats, and military officers, including Franklin D. Roosevelt, Jr., Kathleen had become engaged to Stanley Mortimer, Jr., who had grown up at Tuxedo Park, just down the road from the Harriman estate. A naval officer in the Pacific during the war, he had earlier been married to Barbara Cushing, who had since become the second wife of Averell's old friend William Paley.

In November, the Harriman committee's findings and recommendations—*A Report on European Recovery and American Aid*—reached the President's desk, following a marathon editing session that had sent it to the printer at four A.M. Three inches thick, it called for a U.S. commitment of $12 billion to $17 billion for Europe's recovery, spread over five years. In spite of the whopping expenditure proposed for American taxpayers, the case was made compellingly enough that Truman decided to release it on November 17, when Congress convened in special session to take up a $642 million White House request for aid to get France and Italy through the coming winter.

Its introduction, whose authorship was proudly claimed by Paul Hoffman, echoed Marshall's admonition that Europe's future was in its own hands. The Studebaker executive's stirring call for American action had been extemporaneously delivered at the last full meeting of the committee and had so moved Bissell that he urged Hoffman to commit it to paper.[18]

The document was unusual in its candor. Marshall had carefully not excluded the Soviet Union and Eastern Europe from the invitation to join in the reconstruction, but the committee made clear America's aim to eliminate the "misery and chaos" wherein communism could thrive. But at the same time, the report declared that it would be "an unwarranted interference with the internal affairs of friendly nations" to demand that participants adopt the model of American capitalism. It dismissed as nonsense the assertions that the Marshall Plan was mainly a device to save the United States from a postwar depression. "On the contrary, we are convinced that the immediate economic danger to the United States is inflation, which means, among other things, a shortage of goods in relation to demand. We believe that our goal should be to bring about a condition where exports from this country are more nearly balanced by a return flow from abroad of services and materials essential to our own economy. We also believe that the European nations desire to achieve such equilibrium in the interests of their self respect and prosperity. To make this equilibrium possible should be a major objective of any program of aid."[19] It could all be done, the committee concluded, without inflation or increased taxes. Government spending would invigorate the American economy, create jobs, boost tax revenues, and keep the budget in balance.

Averell did little of the report writing himself, leaving that to Bissell and others while devoting himself to maneuvering the conclusions past committee members who thought the $17 billion figure outrageous. In the end he got it to Truman's desk without a recorded dissent. When the time came to take up the cost figures, Bissell employed such stupefying detail and deadening economic jargon that Rich Red Deupree and other skeptics were rendered glassy-eyed. In the rush to meet the deadline, Averell persuaded members to sign off on their own subcommittee findings, with an understanding that there would be a later vote on the full report. The document was dispatched to the printer with only a few of the nineteen committee members ever seeing the whole thing. When it was released at the White House, the favorable reaction snuffed out any chance of a revolt.[20]

Cables from embassies up and down Massachusetts Avenue relayed the findings to Europe before they could be digested by diplomats, but Britain's ambassador quickly concluded that the recommendations of the Committee on European Economic Cooperation had stood up well under the scrutiny of the Harriman panel. Of more immediate moment to the Truman administration was the assessment of Senator Vandenberg, now chairman of the Senate Foreign Relations Committee, which would have first responsibility for seeing the program through Congress.

Happily, the senator was more than pleased with what Harriman had produced and was prepared to defend the program before Republicans across the country.

"Only a Hollywood press agent could do justice to it," he cabled Harriman after receiving a copy rushed to him in Michigan.[21] Privately, however, the senator was not excessively confident about prospects for congressional approval. Despite the likelihood of freezing and starvation in Britain and France before winter was over, there was strident opposition to the President's emergency aid bill. "If the resistance which is showing up to the little short-range European relief bill is any criterion, our friend Marshall is certainly going to have a helluva time down here on the Hill when he gets around to his long-range plan," Vandenberg wrote in his diary. "It is going to be next to impossible to keep any sort of unpartisan climate in respect to anything. Politics is heavy in the air."[22]

The selling of the Marshall Plan was well advanced before Harriman produced the hard figures. One delegation of congressmen after another was escorted across Europe, asking questions, and taking in the sights— the theory being that firsthand knowledge would generate support. After working on business executives during the early weeks of his committee's deliberations, Harriman hit the road to stir up grass roots support. He traveled in a government-owned DC-3, logging eighteen-hour days, which typically included a speech at breakfast, another at lunch, and a third after dinner, with three long flights in between. Along the way, there would usually be airport press conferences, interviews as he was driven in and out of town, and quick stops at newspaper offices and radio stations.

Night after night, Waldemar Nielsen, his speech writer and tour director, fell asleep aboard the plane as they sat together scratching over speech texts, making minuscule changes that, to Harriman, always assumed major importance. Occasionally the plane wallowed through thunderstorms and bucked weather fronts, leaving Nielsen nauseous and exhausted while the unperturbed Harriman squinted through his half-moon glasses and tinkered with his text.

Crossing the Rockies late one night on their way from Spokane to Omaha, they hit a storm that Nielsen was sure would tear the wings off the plane. "It was raining and the lightning was flashing and the plane was bucking violently up and down," he remembered. "We were strapped in our seats, holding Army oxygen masks on our faces because we were up there in the clouds and there was no pressurization in the cabin. Averell sat there going over papers, checking figures and changing a word here and there, preparing his speech for the next day—as if we were sitting in a quiet office at some reasonable hour."

With his portable typewriter bouncing in his lap, the speech writer was getting nowhere trying to type the changes in the Omaha text between gulps of oxygen. "Averell, for Christ's sake, can't we knock it off?" he finally pleaded. Harriman was taken aback by the plea for mercy. "Oh, certainly. Are you tired? Of course. Of course. Let's call it a day." Then as Nielsen turned his full attention to the storm buffeting the plane, fearful that he would never see Omaha, Harriman pulled a blanket over himself and went to sleep.[23]

No matter how carefully labored over, the speeches came out the same: careful, earnest, detailed—and paralytically boring. Hopelessly bound to his text and his figures, Averell was incapable of humor or repartee. His voice did not project well, and he sounded a bit condescending no matter how mightily he tried to be folksy. His speech writers despaired. "If I wrote a joke or a little something that I considered a nice phrase, he always edited it so that it wound up limp and ass-backwards," said Nielsen. "I would sit in the back row and just die because he murdered every speech."[24]

Nielsen's frustrations were shared by generations of writers who worked for Harriman, though few were as brave as Alfred Friendly, who told him after one botched joke, "God strike me dead if I ever feed you another gag. I will campaign for you if you run for President of the United States; I will press agent for you when you are an author on croquet, skiing, international economics, personnel, or personal relations. I'll be chief tout for you when you expound on horses, democracy, communism, or what goes on in Russia, and the Russian mind. But I'll never plug you as a gagster."[25]

In Washington, Harriman arrived at his office while the huge Commerce Department building was still empty in the morning, and often remained until after midnight, oblivious of the time. Except for the weekends on which he went to New York, he was at his desk on Saturdays and Sundays, and he was often there on holidays—as were aides such as Nielsen. In his apartment at the Shoreham, he often summoned an assistant or two to join him for work after dinner, and at dawn he was frequently on the telephone in excitement over something in the morning papers. There was no predicting how he would receive any of the speeches and congressional testimony churned out for him during the selling of the recovery program. "Goddamn it, I am the secretary of commerce," he would thunder—in the accent that made it come out "secretry of commus." "I am a member of the President's Cabinet. How in hell can I can present this *gahhhbage* to the United States Congress?"[26]

He was equally apt to find an offering wonderful. In either case, a luncheon invitation—as an apology or as a reward—often followed. And without fail, the bill found its way into the hands of the guest, for he had never acquired the habit of carrying pocket money.

His inability to inspire Rotary clubs was not a serious problem in the grand scheme of selling the European recovery program. Because of his long experience in dealing with the Soviets, he commanded the attention of citizens who saw the program as a bulwark against the spread of communism. He also had the ear of businessmen whose humanitarian impulses were more than matched by their desire to see vigorous European markets for American products.

Although the report of his committee provided the foundation for the debate in Congress, Harriman himself was not one of the major witnesses in the long round of hearings. As his friend Charles Bohlen, who put together the witness list, well knew, he was as uninspiring as a witness as he was on the banquet circuit. Before a congressional committee, he was as careful and fastidious as he was in a stand-up speech. Adrian Fisher, the Commerce Department's top lawyer, had watched him at congressional witness tables and thought that he "looked like a man trying to lie his way out of a traffic charge. . . ." He worried so much that he might give the wrong impression that he indeed gave the wrong impression.[27]

Altogether, ninety witnesses were called, making the hearings one of the Senate's most thorough studies of a foreign policy initiative. When they were over, the committee sent the authorizing bill to the Senate floor without opposition. There, it was adopted by a vote of 69–17 on March 14, 1948, Vandenberg successfully turning back an effort by Senator Robert A. Taft to reduce it by $1.3 billion. But respecting the strength of the opposition and Taft's standing in the Senate and the Republican party, Vandenberg orchestrated a compromise wherein the administration request for $6.8 billion for the first fifteen months was reduced to $4.6 billion over a period of twelve months.

Congress finally completed work on the authorization measure on April 1, and Truman signed it into law two days later.

Not surprisingly, approval of the Marshall Plan's first and largest appropriation aroused envy in economically distressed governments of Latin America. The United States, leaders felt, had arrogantly ignored its hemispheric neighbors and responsibilities in favor of rebuilding countries on the other side of the Atlantic. They could foresee little benefit coming their way from the reconstruction of Britain and the European continent.

The issue would come to a head at the Ninth International Conference of American States, and the Truman administration did not take lightly the potential for a serious backlash. General Marshall was named head of a blue-ribbon delegation that included Harriman, Treasury Secretary John Snyder, and Federal Reserve chairman William McChesney Martin. They planned to take the offensive and show how $1.5 billion in Marshall Plan funds would be spent in the hemisphere. Marshall himself intended to remain for the duration of the month-long meeting.

In Bogotá, the delegation moved into a red brick house in the city's wealthy Chapinero neighborhood and made the rounds of social engagements preceding the opening session. They arrived amid rumors that the Communists would try to break up or disrupt the conference, but for a week the meeting took place in relative serenity. Then on April 9, while Harriman was having lunch with Marshall, Martin, and several others at the residence of the American delegation, Jorge Eliécer Gaitán, the leader of Colombia's opposition Liberal party, was gunned down as he left his office in the middle of the city.

The assassin was caught by a mob and beaten to death with shoeshine boxes taken from small boys on the street, and the body was dragged to the entrance of the presidential palace. Rioting broke out and grew into a leftist insurrection. Revolutionaries with guns and machetes set fires, looted, overturned trolley cars, and smashed windows in the presidential palace, finally capturing the city's eight radio stations and demanding the resignation of President Mariano Ospina Pérez.

Members of the U.S. delegation were given protection by the Colombian Army, and the conference was suspended. Gunfire rattled into the night, and the death toll mounted into the dozens. With the city under curfew, some delegations departed for home, although Marshall urged them to stay and resume the conference when order could be restored.

The street fighting continued into the weekend, and on Sunday Marshall and the rest of the delegation were astonished to find Harriman preparing to go to lunch with Ospina Pérez at the presidential palace. There was still shooting in the neighborhood, and even Marshall, who had watched the disruption with composure appropriate for a five-star general, was incredulous.

"Harriman," he asked, "do you have any reason to believe that this lunch is still on?"[28]

There had been no notice of cancellation, Averell replied, and until there was, he would consider the command performance on schedule. With that, he summoned Major Vernon Walters, who had been sent to Bogotá to interpret for General Marshall, and departed.

They drove through empty streets to the palace, arriving to find the doors closed, sentries absent, and no sign of other guests. Harriman ordered Walters to knock, and they waited. After a long delay, the heavy door was slowly opened by a wide-eyed butler in formal attire and armed with a submachine gun. Harriman handed the speechless servant his hat and walked in.

The President was no less surprised than his butler. Snipers in adjacent buildings had riddled the windows of the presidential office at the top of the palace with bullet holes. Only in the recent hours had the neighborhood been quiet enough for the president to return to his desk. It hadn't seemed necessary to cancel the luncheon, and except for

Harriman and Walters no one else showed up. So they dined at the President's desk, served by Colombia's First Lady, since all of the servants, save the butler, who was at his post by the door with his submachine gun, had disappeared.[29]

The Army gradually regained control of the streets, and the conference resumed, but Averell was ordered home. Paul Hoffman had been named head of the new Economic Cooperation Administration, created to run the Marshall Plan. The President's first choice had been Dean Acheson, who had left the government for private law practice; but Vandenberg insisted on a Republican, and Harriman had recommended Hoffman.

Vandenberg, who did not know Hoffman well, had asked business friends for their views on a director, and fully half of them had put Hoffman at the top of the list. Truman personally questioned whether Hoffman had the toughness for the job, but he detected among Washington insiders the same kind of support noted by the senator.

Hoffman was then fifty-six, an ebullient, uncomplicated Midwesterner, well liked by politicians on both sides of the aisle. He had started in business as an automobile salesman, and eventually founded his own company. He was a millionaire by the time he was summoned to take over the ailing Studebaker Company, which he guided out of bankruptcy. Like Vandenberg, he was a former isolationist, convinced by two world wars that "there was no way we could insulate ourselves against the impact of these new world forces."[30]

With Hoffman at the ECA's head, the post of European representative had to go to an identifiable Democrat, and the new director asked the President for either Harriman or Lewis Douglas. Early on, the European job had been envisioned as that of roving ambassador who would serve as the eyes and ears of the Washington headquarters. That concept had changed. The appointee, it was decided, would direct operations on fronts across Europe in the manner of an army field commander. Hoffman would retain final authority in Washington, but the field general in Paris would engage the Europeans on the problems of trade restrictions, competing currencies, and national rivalries that stood in the way of the recovery and the economic integration of Europe envisioned by the Marshall Planners.

Douglas, a four-term congressman from Arizona and FDR's first budget director, didn't want to give up the ambassador's post in London, where he had only recently succeeded Averell. Truman was reluctant to let Harriman leave the Cabinet, and suggested Will Clayton, the undersecretary of state, who was another of the plan's architects.

Since the President had to have a Democrat in the position, Hoffman thought "there were probably not more than five men in America equipped for that job."[31] Unless he could have Harriman or Douglas, he told the President, "we just can't get done what you want to get done."[32] Averell's acquaintance with scores of important officials across Europe would give the American organization instant credibility and authority. Like Eisenhower, he personified the United States to millions. Some Britons thought of him as almost one of their own.

The new ECA chief insisted upon Harriman, although he knew they had fundamentally different perceptions of America's mission. To Averell, economic recovery was but an element in a Western security strategy to contain Soviet expansion. As far as Hoffman was concerned, there was no objective in American policy as urgent as restoration of Europe's economic health. He did not share Harriman's conviction that recovery also had an equally legitimate military dimension.

On matters of immediate moment, however, they were altogether in accord, especially on the need for moving without further delay. Unless there was economic rejuvenation in countries such as France and Italy, they might swing precipitously to the left. They also agreed that the program had to be kept above politics. Attaching political objectives or overselling the U.S. contribution would be foolhardy.

For a man prone to prompt decisions, Truman labored over the appointment. He consulted Marshall in Bogotá and Undersecretary Bob Lovett, who was in charge at State while the secretary was out of the country. He sounded out William Foster at Commerce, and was assured that Averell would take the job after making a pro forma protest against the offer.

Lovett was privately enthusiastic, but he remained discreetly silent. "I have kept strictly out of this in order to avoid embarrassment to Harriman, to Department, and to myself because of personal relationships," he cabled Marshall in South America, "but I think Hoffman's recommendation is right."[33]

The matter was resolved while Harriman listened to gunfire in the streets of Bogotá. When Truman's call came, he departed for Washington in such haste that he left most of his clothes behind.

He made a perfunctory protest against going overseas again, as Hoffman had predicted. Relishing his place as a Cabinet member, he was already looking forward to Truman's election campaign, but he was privately certain the Republicans were going to recapture the presidency in 1948. In anticipation of a return to private life, he had already bought a big house on East Eighty-first Street in New York.

Truman assured him he would be more valuable as Hoffman's partner in the Marshall Plan than in the Cabinet and the election. The President did not have to remind him of the recovery program's priority. "The Marshall Plan was, after all, the hottest game in town," said Richard Bissell, "which the Commerce Department emphatically was not."[34]

Fortuitously, the Harriman and Hoffman personalities fit the roles that political necessity bestowed. Hoffman was at home in the company of politicians. Talents perfected as an ace car salesman made him a devastating witness before committees, and his after-dinner speeches stirred audiences as quickly as Harriman's lulled them off to sleep. Averell was, on the other hand, attuned to European ambitions and rivalries and was ever willing to throw blunt American demands on the table and to pressure aid recipients. "Once Harriman was wound up and pointed in the direction his government told him he must go," said Theodore H. White, then a young reporter for the Overseas News Agency, "he was like a tank crushing all opposition. From America, he expected nothing in return except recognition, for he was [as] vain for honor as he was wise in experience. They made a fine pair. Hoffman trusted people. Harriman distrusted them."[35]

With Hoffman at his side, Harriman was sworn in as Special Representative of the Economic Cooperation Administration by Chief Justice Fred M. Vinson on April 27. The ceremony, at the ECA's headquarters across Lafayette Park from the White House, exemplified the frantic pace with which the program was being thrown together. When the moment for the oath arrived, there was no Bible; Harriman's official commission had been misplaced at the White House; and nobody had thought of a flag for a photographic backdrop. A messenger retrieved the commission, borrowed a Bible from a bookstore, and appropriated a flag from the Budget Bureau. The oath was administered barely in time for Vinson to get to the Supreme Court and open the fall session on schedule.

As the ceremony took place, the freighter *John H. Quick* was already bound for Europe from Galveston, its cargo hold filled with Marshall Plan wheat. It was the beginning of a new lifeline that would eventually see 150 ships loading, unloading, or crossing the Atlantic with Marshall Plan cargo every day.

Harriman's technical and political challenges were as daunting as the task of rebuilding the bombed and shelled cities. He faced divided Europeans and a deluge of special pleadings from American politicians and businessmen who fancied him their sales representative. Canners wanted him to buy rutabagas for European tables. Arkansas chicken farmers pushed frozen, full-breasted birds wrapped in cellophane. Hearing that Holland preferred Carolina and Virginia tobacco to Kentucky burley, Senator Alben Barkley demanded that Harriman encourage Dutchmen to smoke fewer cigarettes and more cigars. Congressman Lyndon B. Johnson, representing a constituent in Marble Falls, Texas, urged the Marshall Plan to provide Europeans shipments of mohair instead of wool.

The war had been over for nearly three years when Harriman arrived in Paris, and almost a year had passed since Marshall's speech at Harvard. Europe's cities still lay in darkness and factories in silence. The broad boulevards of Paris were vacant. With nothing to export, governments were gripped by critical shortages of gold and dollars. Tariffs and import restrictions throttled trade within the community, circumstances that made political unrest unavoidable.

Europe "was not only incapable of resistance to the Russians, but was engaged in a desperate ordeal of survival that had nothing to do with the Soviet Union," wrote Theodore White. "The tides of trade in which Europe lived had vanished. Like a whale left gasping on the sand, Europe lay rotting in the sun."[36]

Harriman's advance party set up headquarters on the second floor of the U.S. embassy annex and began arranging for office space wherever it could be found. His first contacts with the new Organization for European Economic Cooperation told him there was going to be trouble from the beginning.

What he and Hoffman had in mind was a powerful central organization with finance ministers of all the participating countries regularly present at the OEEC's Paris headquarters. Instead, the Europeans opted for operational responsibility in the hands of civil servants, keeping political authority at home and frustrating the Americans' push for an integrated European economy. In Paris, the ministers were represented by an executive committee of civil servants, presided over by Britain's Sir Edmund Hall-Patch.

At fifty-one, Hall-Patch was a well-seasoned bureaucrat with impressive service in both the Foreign Office and the Treasury. He was an accomplished musician, a talented linguist, a theatrical dresser, and an enigmatic personality who relished and encouraged the mystery and rumor that followed him. What characterized him more than anything else, however, was abiding pessimism and suspicion. He took Harriman's insistence upon dealing with Cabinet ministers as nothing more than personal vanity. The American envoy, Hall-Patch wired London, "thinks himself to be such a swell that he cannot have any truck with anyone unless they are Ministers."[37]

It was the beginning of a dispute that lasted as long as Harriman remained the Marshall Plan's ramrod, relentlessly pressing the Europeans to strengthen their organization. To move toward integrated economic planning, the recovery program required direction, not by bureaucrats but by foreign ministers and finance ministers who could speak for their governments with authority.

The technical delegations themselves were of uneven quality. Robert Marjolin, a deputy finance minister from France, was named secretary-general, putting him in nominal charge of the OEEC's bureaucracy. The selection, Harriman first suspected, "was the British doing," designed to keep Hall-Patch in control, although he was later pleased and surprised by both Marjolin's competence and his independence.[38]

In his first personal encounter with Hall-Patch, Harriman had made clear his displeasure over the level of representation in the OEEC. If heads of government could not regularly confer at the new organization's headquarters, they could at least arrange for frequent conferences of their transportation and interior ministers as well as foreign ministers and finance ministers, depending upon the agenda.

What Hall-Patch first took as excessive ego was a typically direct Harriman assault upon the recovery program's profound political dilemma—Britain's determination to have a dominant role and preserve sterling as an important world currency. In the Lend-Lease days when Roosevelt had sent him to help save Britain, Harriman had been an unabashed Anglophile, now, trying to save Europe and contain communism, he sometimes indelicately sounded taps for the empire.

In Paris, Harriman set up shop in the Hôtel de Talleyrand, across the Place de la Concorde from the American embassy. He knew that the old mansion, where Napoleon's foreign minister had carried on both official and personal intrigues, had been coveted by Stalin. At Potsdam, the Soviet dictator had suggested that he would like to have it for the use of Soviet diplomats—a reminder that the Red Army had diplomatically equaled Czar Alexander's westward thrust in pursuit of Napoleon in 1814. For no purpose but one-upmanship against Stalin, Averell had taken the initiative for the United States to acquire the use of the building. Now that it had become his headquarters to dispense aid to secure Europe against Communist expansion, he savored his private little victory. He moved into a corner suite furnished with antiques and trimmed in green and gold, its floor-to-ceiling windows affording a panoramic view of La Place. Carpenters divided the rest into cubicles for staff members who filled the landmark to overflowing.

As soon as he was settled, he began to worry about the appearance of his lavish accommodations. Surrounded by the antiques, oil paintings, and wine-colored silk cushions, he sat beneath a huge bust of Benjamin Franklin, the United States' first representative in Paris. He did not find it hard to imagine accusations of personal extravagance in a country where shortages of necessities were rampant. His personal wealth, his roots on Wall Street, even his reputation as a playboy in times past had already made him a target of the Communists.

At the United Nations meeting at Lake Success, Soviet delegate Andrei Vishinsky had labeled him a "warmonger." *Pravda* said he was a plutocrat, representing a ruling circle bent on "world political and economic supremacy of the United States," a capitalist whose goal was "ex-

ploiting the grave conditions in Europe for purposes of self-enrichment."
Specifically, the commentary went on, the ambassador was interested in
"the transformation of western Germany into an anti-Soviet beachhead
of the United States because this would secure a strong position in that
area for Brown Brothers Harriman and Co., as well as for other of
Harriman's concerns."[39]

The Soviet harangue began months before Averell got to Paris, and
upon his arrival, it was picked up by the leftist press all across Europe.
He was accused of dumping inferior American coal on Europeans, destroying the orchards of the Netherlands, and exploiting European governments at every turn.

His worries that somebody like columnist Drew Pearson would dis-
cover his posh surroundings were put to rest by Alfred Friendly, the
mission's press officer. Friendly's simple expedient was a preemptive
strike. He leaked to Pearson a description of Harriman's appointments in
rich detail—along with the explanation that the luxurious appointments
belonged to the French government and had fallen to Harriman because
the hotel was a national monument. The tactic worked. From the Talleyr-
and, Harriman conducted relations with the Economic Cooperation Administration's European counterpart and oversaw sixteen Marshall Plan
mission offices across Europe. He installed a lunchroom to discourage
the staff from going out to lunch, kept them into the evening, and after
work led them to the bar of the Hôtel Crillon, where Europe was rebuilt
and communism contained nightly.

The electrically charged atmosphere brought young professionals
to Paris and the Marshall Plan, just as Pearl Harbor had rallied boys
from the farms to enlistment offices. With the opening of Harriman's
command post, the American community burgeoned to more than three
thousand—economists, engineers, agricultural scientists, bureaucrats,
and war veterans with wide-eyed young wives seeing Europe for the first
time.

Harriman lured William Foster away from the number two job at
Commerce to be his point man in dealing with ECA headquarters in
Washington. A Republican, Foster had been successful enough that he
became the youngest member of the Business Advisory Council, where
he formed a close friendship with Hoffman. He had no interest in a
government position, and when Harriman first called him in the fall of
1946, he turned down the invitation to come to Washington for a talk.
But for days thereafter, Averell continued to call every morning. Finally,
Foster agreed to go to Washington for a face-to-face meeting; and before
he got out of town, he was talked into an interim appointment as undersecretary and sworn in. It was the beginning of a distinguished public-
service career that lasted the rest of his life.

To fill the role of shop foreman in dealings with the Europeans,

Harriman recruited Harvard law professor Milton Katz, whom he had known since New Deal days, when the professor was his counsel at the National Recovery Administration. Katz also turned down several overtures from Harriman to join the Department of Commerce, but he was finally talked into taking a leave of absence to assume the job in Paris.

For mission posts across Europe, Averell had in several cases leaned upon old friends, such as David Bruce and Louisville *Courier-Journal* publisher Barry Bingham, to drop what they were doing and take up the cause. Through such contacts and his sharp eye for young talent, the European organization was put together with a dispatch that surprised and gratified Hoffman, who completed his Washington organization at the same time.

Katz's opposite number at headquarters was Dick Bissell, who had been the ramrod of the Harriman Committee during the recovery program's creation. Impatient, stubborn, and sometimes lacking diplomatic touch, he was, in the eyes of many, the driving intellectual force in the Marshall Plan's eventual success. Years later, with the Central Intelligence Agency, Bissell would be a key figure in reconnaissance of the Soviet Union by the U-2 spy plane, and receive an inordinate share of the blame for the 1961 Bay of Pigs fiasco in Cuba.

From the Marshall Plan's outset, incipient rivalries between Washington and Paris generated tensions that could have jeopardized Truman's bipartisan construction. Accountable to a big new bureaucracy, Averell missed the authority he had enjoyed in London and Moscow. "Your staff must recognize that we are not branch offices, but that I and the country mission chiefs have a responsibility to you similar to that which the Ambassadors have to the Secretary of State," he reminded Hoffman after a run-in during the fall of 1948.

> We are part of the policy-forming group on a top level. I know this is your conception. You should not have asked me or the fine men who are heads of the country missions to serve it if had not been so. . . . I am not referring to the minor misunderstandings that are inherent in the inadequacy of communications by cable, or of the normal mistakes a new, widespread organization makes during the period of growing pains, but I am referring to the basic concept which I feel your subordinates on the staff in Washington have as to their authority and the manner in which they are attempting to exert it without full consultation with you, myself or the mission chiefs. We are not engaged alone in a financial undertaking, but also in carrying out a broad and most enlightened American foreign policy affecting the organization and lives of 260 million people.[40]

As had so often been the case in Moscow, the outburst wound up in the files rather than the mail pouch. With their surrogates, Katz and Bissell, defending their interests in the trenches, Harriman and Hoffman remained above the fray.

For the Americans who served in the Office of the Special Representative, and for Harriman himself, it was a time of rare fulfillment. Young Americans with dollars lived in a Parisian style never possible again. They had hard currency, social status, priority at gasoline pumps, favoritism in housing, and the gratitude of Europeans. They could see the result of their work in Europe's dramatic recovery.

The stay in Paris was a time of reconstitution for Harriman himself. He was joined by Marie, their dogs, and her favorite Gauguins, Derains, Picassos, and Walt Kuhns from her gallery, now closed. Averell moved out of the Crillon, leased an apartment on the Left Bank, and the two settled back into a marriage that had been a formality since the beginning of the war.

His liaison with Pamela had not been the extent of his roaming. While he was commerce secretary and Marie was still in New York, he spent free evenings with Kay Halle, a spectacular blond wartime employee of the OSS turned reporter and commentator. The daughter of a Cleveland department-store owner, she was also a friend of the Churchills'. Randolph had fallen in love with her during his travels in the United States before the war, and by some accounts had begged her to marry him. Halle also had connections with important Democrats around town, starting with the Roosevelts, and Averell had sometimes seen her during wartime trips home. Their friendship resumed as a matter of course when he was back in Washington to stay.

On weeknights, the commerce secretary's limousine was frequently parked at Halle's house in Georgetown. Aides who went to see Harriman with urgent business after hours sometimes found her at his apartment at the Shoreham. To close friends she suggested that the secretary might shed his wife in New York and marry her. The proximity—and Halle's high visibility and earnest intentions—made the matter more irritating to Marie than the wartime affair with Pamela had been.

With Marie's arrival in Paris, the Harriman apartment became a gathering place for bridge and canasta parties, afternoon cocktails for visiting mission chiefs, and even occasional press conferences. In spite of years of dealing with reporters, Averell had never been comfortable with the press, even when questions were uniformly gentle. In Paris, Al Friendly found that in the social atmosphere provided by Marie at home, Averell could unbend and talk with correspondents much as he did with anyone else. Reporters were tamed by cheeses and vintage wines and an opportunity to see the Harriman paintings.

Among the new acquisitions was a Matisse, *Lady with a Hat*, which

Averell bought at a charity auction he arranged on President Roosevelt's birthday. It was contributed to the crippled children's benefit by the owner of a Paris gallery; and while Harriman wanted it badly, he wouldn't bid for it—knowing that his interest would inflate the offers. So, he had instructed Vernon Walters to buy it for him. As the bidding opened, Walters enthusiastically joined in—to the astonishment of his mother, who lived with him and knew his Army major's pay was too meager to invest even hundreds, much less thousands, of dollars in art. But as the offers passed his annual salary, he casually continued to raise his bids. By time the competition was silenced, the price approached $20,000, and his mother was frantically looking about the ballroom of the Hôtel George Cinque for help.

Harriman's determination to keep the recovery program on course took him into incessant conflict with Europeans who concluded that he was out to usurp authority that properly belonged to their own organizations. None held to their national interests as doggedly as the British, who commiserated among themselves over their "Harriman problem." It especially irritated them that he demanded American admission to deliberations of the OEEC just as he had been admitted to the meetings of the British War Cabinet's committee on the Battle of the Atlantic. An ensuing test of wills on the issue dragged on for nearly a year.

Hall-Patch and Stafford Cripps, the latter now chancellor of the exchequer, led the resistance, with Hall-Patch accusing Averell and the U.S. Marshall Planners of trying "to enjoy power without responsibility . . . to take a complete part in the organization without being members of it."[41] Harriman complained of being "humiliated" and took his case to Marjolin, who counseled the British without much success to treat the American more gently.

After a particularly contentious exchange in March 1949, Britain relayed its grievances to Washington, sending Ambassador Oliver Franks to call on Hoffman and Dean Acheson, who had succeeded General Marshall as secretary of state. Both sympathized with the OEEC's sensitivity to Harriman's attempts to look over its shoulder all the time, but not enough to call him off. The British insisted that personal vanity was involved as much as desire for results, but Hoffman, with his Midwestern country-boy amiability, would not be drawn into any second-guessing of Averell's style. It was a little difficult, he conceded, for an outsider like himself to fathom "why those who had spent time in diplomacy attached importance so often to questions of prestige."[42]

In the end, compromises saved face. Averell accepted Hall-Patch's offer for him to join the Executive Committee meeting each Wednesday afternoon. Eventually the ministers' deliberations in the Consultative Group were opened, too—but only by invitation.

More than anything else, the struggle over access was Harriman's device to keep up pressure to strengthen the European organization and dampen the nationalistic rivalries. He had already prevailed on the issue he considered most crucial of all, that the Europeans themselves take the responsibility for dividing up the aid from Washington. It was the only way for the United States to avoid being presented a shopping list from every country in the program. If that happened, he saw the dread prospect of all the European ministers "with their front feet in the trough" quarreling with each other and quarreling with Washington.[43] There would be interminable one-on-one negotiations and rampant dissatisfaction, the United States making itself an archvillain by making choices between old rivals like the Greeks and Turks. Harriman put the proposition before the ministers on June 5, the first anniversary of the Marshall speech, calling upon the OEEC Executive Committee to assess each country's requirements and produce a plan for distributing the first year's appropriation. Not surprisingly, the proposal was greeted without a trace of enthusiasm. Expecting to deal with the United States on a one-on-one great-power basis, the British found the idea especially offensive. They had not been defeated in the war, and they hardly expected to lay details of their economic plight before the governments of defeated Europe. They were as intent upon limiting the authority of the OEEC as Harriman was to promote it.

In spite of the objections, members formally agreed on July 16 to take on the task of dividing the first $4.9 billion. It was an unavoidably brutal process: every time one country asked for a dollar it did not need, the dollar was, in effect, taken from its neighbors. It required two months, but ministers finally approved the allocations by a vote of 9–6.

To Averell, the successful negotiations put the Marshall Plan over its greatest hurdle. Had the OEEC failed at distributing the resources for the first year, the concept of mutual assistance might have been destroyed. But while the principle was established, the fight over details was even more difficult. For a while it even threatened to break up the OEEC and shook the recipients so profoundly that they agreed in advance to an arrangement in which all members presented their requirements and mutually made allotments, thereby avoiding a perilous showdown against each other.

With that explosive problem out of the way, Marshall Planners still had to contend with excruciating challenges. Governments were hesitant to contemplate dependence upon each other. Trade barriers defied all the nudging toward economic integration, deficits with the United States worsened, and Britain and France contested for OEEC leadership.

Hoffman conceded that European countries were individually putting forth the maximum effort they had promised, but cooperation was anything but satisfactory. He and Harriman threatened to tell Congress that nothing had been accomplished to stimulate European trade, and they warned that a prompt cut in appropriations would follow.[44]

While he was inveighing against tariffs and trade barriers and promoting production and exports, Harriman found himself with responsibility for restricting shipment of strategic items to the Soviet Union and the East. The list of forbidden items included not only steel pipe and oil drilling bits, but, inexplicably, frivolous items such as duck feathers and wooden toilet seats.

Harriman was in the middle. He implored the Defense Department to be reasonable in what it defined as strategic, then pleaded with Europeans, who desperately needed exports, not to sell listed items, even if the claim to strategic importance was tenuous. The exercise was time-consuming and ineffective, and shortly the Marshall Plan nations set up a committee that met three times a week in Paris to act on requests for export licenses.

The problem threw Harriman into more conflicts with the autocratic, excitable General Lucius Clay, the U.S. military governor in Germany known with a mixture of admiration and exasperation at the Talleyrand as "the Kaiser." At the same time Clay battled for more aid to Germany and an equal standing in the European community, he succumbed to narrow interpretations of strategic materials, often ignoring a list that proscribed items when Soviet and Eastern markets beckoned to Germany.

It was in the ruins of the Third Reich, where postwar disaster had at first appeared most imminent, that Harriman found resurgent confidence in European determination to rebuild. The prospect of full reconstruction was, to many, outright fantasy, but Harriman was ever certain that Germany would drive the comeback. On a trip to Essen in the summer of 1948, he and Vernon Walters visited with a family living in a basement beneath the rubble of a destroyed building. After they left, Walters wondered aloud whether there could ever be recovery. There could be, and there would be, Harriman curtly replied. Proof enough had been right there before them in the family's room beneath the wreckage—a bowl of flowers. "Any people who will, in the midst of this desolation, think of putting flowers on the table," he said, "will rebuild the ruins."[45]

At the Talleyrand, members of the staff thought Harriman had begun to lose his intensity once he had settled the dispute over the first year's division of aid. He was preoccupied with the Truman-Dewey campaign as the election approached; and like most people, he expected that Dewey would be the new President and John Foster Dulles would be secretary of state. He therefore anticipated that he would be replaced in Paris. His resignation to the Republican victory was so complete that he responded without enthusiasm when fund-raisers came for his contribution to the Truman campaign coffers. Around the office, staffers thought that he suddenly looked tired and gray.

On the night before the election, with the outcome seemingly ordained, he invited a few of his aides into the office, pulled a bottle of scotch from his desk, and presided over a sad little wake for the Truman presidency.

It was midday on Wednesday in Paris, and most of the Marshall Plan mission was gathered around Al Friendly's shortwave radio when California's votes concluded the political upset of the century. The news of Truman's election reignited Harriman's spirits with a burst that echoed through the Talleyrand. He would not be needing the house he had bought in New York. John Foster Dulles, the presumptive secretary of state, who had not long before called and invited Harriman to join him for a chat at the Crillon, would have to come to the Talleyrand instead. "There ought to be enormous opportunities open to you in the new dispensation created by Tuesday's unexpected victory," Herbert Swope advised Averell from New York. "I believe you should be thinking of your destiny."

Swope had picked up rumors that General Marshall was about to retire, and he concluded, "I don't see why you shouldn't be the Secretary of State."[46]

Marshall, now sixty-eight, had been ailing for several weeks. In early December, surgeons removed a kidney, and it was obvious that he would not be returning to the Cabinet. When speculation over a successor began in earnest, Harriman was high on the list. Friends with connections in the administration volunteered their services to lobby for him. Some took his appointment for granted. "Wild Bill" Donovan wrote to wish him "all good luck in anticipation of the new responsibilities that are going to be placed upon you."[47] Swope, who credited himself with much of his friend's success in public affairs, relayed continuing rumors circulating among insiders in New York.

Harriman desperately wanted the job; and when Truman announced the appointment of Dean Acheson in January 1949, he was crestfallen. Friendly got the news from a reporter who watched the bulletin tapped out on a United Press wire machine. He relayed the word to Harriman's office, but neither Hildy Blanken, the ambassador's personal secretary, nor Colonel Charles Bonesteel, his executive officer, wanted the chore of telling him. So Friendly trudged through the maze of cubicles to the boss's suite with a copy of the bulletin in hand. He handed the story to Harriman without saying anything and watched his face collapse in disappointment. He mumbled a few words that were hard to follow and turned back to some papers on his desk. It was the first time Friendly had fully realized how much Harriman had wanted to be secretary of state.[48]

Before Harriman left the office that afternoon, he sent a cable of congratulations to the new secretary's home in Georgetown. It was gracious, but it hardly exuded the warmth or excitement that one might have expected from appointment of a schoolmate and fellow oarsman. "Warmest congratulations. Looking forward keenly to working with you again."[49]

Even though ministers of the OEEC nations eventually accepted the idea that it was useful for them to meet monthly, Harriman and the Americans were still not satisfied with the OEEC organization. Robert Marjolin was more effective than Harriman dreamed he would be, but he was still hamstrung by Hall-Patch and, indirectly, by Stafford Cripps.

Harriman lobbied for selection of a permanent director general, who would have authority to speak and make commitments for the entire community, loosening Britain's grip. The concept was anathema to the British, who saw it as another case of Harriman's seeking control. After one early meeting, Hugh Gaitskell, then Britain's minister of fuel and power, recorded in his diary that he had taken an immediate dislike to the American, finding him "much over-rated." Even Cripps, Gaitskell said, had "for the first time agreed that Harriman was rather a stupid man and exceedingly vain."[50] On further reflection, Gaitskell later concluded that Harriman was not dull but exceedingly single-minded.

Averell's attention was always focused on bringing Britain into line. His candidate to become OEEC's director general was Prime Minister Paul-Henri Spaak of Belgium, who shared the U.S. commitment to economic integration and agreed that the OEEC ought to be an instrument of change rather than a conveyance for American largesse. He had been allied with Harriman on most of the major issues that had arisen in the first months of the recovery program—among them OEEC distribution of aid and ministerial representation, in addition to transcendent economic issues.

As far as Britain was concerned, the Spaak-Harriman alliance was far too close. Making the Belgian an OEEC superman, thought Hall-Patch and his colleagues, would have the effect of putting Harriman himself in control. Even Foreign Secretary Bevin, regarded by the Americans as the most reasonable and dependable of all European officials, was convinced that "neither Spaak nor the Americans had thought through what a political figure at the head of the OEEC was going to do."[51] European integration, Bevin thought, would have to come through direct cooperation between nations, not through the OEEC.

More than once, British officials, squirming under Harriman's relentless pushing to integrate them into the European community, tried to deal directly with Hoffman. Tension was sharpest with Stafford Cripps, the director of British economic policy. The chancellor was stubborn, austere, self-righteous, and brilliant. Harriman was not his match as an economist, but he was more than the Englishman's equal as a tactician.

During one standoff when Hoffman and Bissell were visiting from Washington, Cripps slipped a note to Hoffman suggesting that the two of them get together that evening and settle the disagreement without Harriman. Hoffman passed the note to Katz, who eased it over to Averell. That evening, when Hoffman showed up for the meeting, he was accompanied by Katz, who Cripps knew was Harriman's eyes, ears, and chief troubleshooter.

On trade, Harriman was as stubborn as he was on division of aid and access to deliberations of the OEEC ministers. He took bitter issue with Britain's attempts to enhance the world position of sterling. With Hoffman, he fought against dual pricing policies and agitated for reduced import quotas. Restrictions were gradually lifted, but the real hope to invigorate trade was a proposed European Payments Union. Plans had been drawn in the fall of 1949 for such a mechanism for uniting the economies of Europe with a common currency supported by Marshall plan funds. Months of haggling followed, most of it over ways of protecting the value of sterling and Britain's position as leader of the sterling bloc. By the time the European Payments Union came into being, Harriman was gone from Paris. He departed for home as the Cold War with the Soviet Union was intensifying by the week.

The Soviets and Communist China signed a mutal defense treaty; Truman ordered development of the hydrogen bomb; and the Soviets shot down an unarmed Navy patrol plane over the Baltic, claiming the plane had violated Soviet airspace. Harriman's interests had shifted from Europe's economic recovery to its military security. It was another two years before the recovery program was finished, but in the spring of 1950, the economic reconstruction faded from its place as the centerpiece of American foreign policy.

Harriman and Hoffman had overestimated how long the recovery would take. They had gone into the Marshall Plan with a goal of restoring European production to 1938 levels by the time the program ended. But after only two and a half years, Europe's industrial output would be 40 percent ahead of 1938, and agricultural production 20 percent ahead.[52] The program outlined in 1947 was substantially completed six months ahead of schedule and at a cost nearly $5 billion less than the Harriman Committee's high estimate.

Averell's growing restlessness was obvious at the Talleyrand. He relied more and more upon Katz, eased his pressure on Hall-Patch, and looked for excuses to get out of Paris. In April, he abandoned his political nonpartisanship and went home to address the annual dinner of the New York State Democratic Committee.

It was an occasion for florid rhetoric, and Harriman rose to the occasion. Before 1,500 Democrats, including Eleanor Roosevelt, the cream of the New York party, and the chairman of the Democratic National Committee, he sailed into the Republican party for timidity and vacillation. The GOP was "terrified of progress," he said, and was led by men "looking fondly backward for safety." He denounced Joe McCarthy and called Governor Tom Dewey, the two-time presidential candidate, a man with no program "except unity and Dewey for President."[53]

Harriman had publicly expressed no interest in running for office, but friends had written to him in Paris suggesting a future in New York politics. Although he professed to be surprised and uninterested, the speech at the Democrats' big event of the election year was an obvious audition before party officials in search of a gubernatorial nominee. His reception was warm, but he hardly brought down the house.

A month afterward, as Katz prepared to fly from Paris to Washington for a short visit, Harriman called him into his office and asked him to deliver a personal letter to the President. It was a request for permission to come home.

"I wanted you to know that I am most anxious to come home and do not want to tackle another job in Europe," he told Truman. "I feel that things are in such good shape here that I can leave with conscience. The OEEC has been vitalized . . . and I am confident that within a few weeks the European Payments Union will be agreed to. We have a good organization in Europe to carry on."[54]

The President read the letter with more amusement than surprise. There was no denying Harriman's interest in building the military preparedness of the new North Atlantic Treaty Organization, but Truman thought Harriman had not mentioned his real motive. "I think Averell wants to be Governor of New York," he told Katz.[55]

On June 16, the White House announced that Harriman would be coming home in early August to become Special Assistant to the President.

Chapter XVII

KOREA
Helping Dean

Even before Milton Katz handed the President Harriman's request to come home from Paris, Truman had been thinking about a new assignment for his Marshall Plan ambassador. Europe's economic crisis had eased and Washington's priority had shifted to the Soviet military threat that had preoccupied Averell all the while he was working on the recovery program.

Al Friendly had seen Harriman's passion for the Marshall Plan wane once the Europeans accepted responsibility for the division of aid. "He was still interested in the recovery program," said Friendly, "but he started to concentrate on security. All the time he was seeing prime ministers and heads of state on the recovery program, he was beating the drum for military security."[1]

Within weeks of his arrival in Paris, Averell was urging Washington to send used planes and Army hardware to the French, reminding Marshall and Forrestal of the huge psychological lift given the British Army by early American support in 1940. He saw in European leaders a sharpened awareness of Soviet armed forces and an appreciation that military security was crucial to full recovery. "They recognize only too well that as things stand today, they would be overrun, and when their countries were again liberated, the life of their people would be irreparably destroyed," he told the Senate Foreign Relations Committee after the signing of the NATO treaty in the spring of 1949.[2]

Still, on NATO's first anniversary, European military security had not appreciably improved. Seven skeleton divisions confronted 200,000 East German security police in the Russian zone and a potential Soviet Army of 175 divisions. Still, alliance partners resisted U.S. pressure for a West German role in their defense.

When NATO ministers met in London in May 1950, however, they adopted the policy that Harriman had been touting in all of his extracurricular sorties into military matters, agreeing to an integrated defense establishment. Facing the Soviet threat together, Western European countries would no longer go their lonely way with expensive independent military establishments tailored to narrow national needs.

Harriman hailed the arrangement, largely the handiwork of Dean Acheson, as the step that finally put the *O* in *NATO*.[3] The integrated force and its Supreme Allied Commander would answer to a Council of Deputies, chaired by the representative from the United States. Acheson wanted either Bob Lovett, who was back at Brown Brothers Harriman, or Averell for the job, but another tour in London was not what Averell had in mind. He didn't consider the new NATO post a promotion, and after two years as field general of the Marshall Plan, he was weary of dealing with Europe's national rivalries and fears of integration.

Acheson's suggestion was, therefore, what had moved him to write the President, asking to come home. The letter reached the President at a moment when Truman needed help. The political harmony that had launched the Marshall Plan was gone. Officials of the Navy and Air Force were feuding over roles, missions, and new weapons. Senator Joseph McCarthy was throwing gasoline on flaming anti-Communist fanaticism; and both liberals and conservatives were carping about budget deficits arising from the surge in military assistance to the Europeans. In terms of raw politics and the cascade of events upon him, 1950 was what biographer Robert Donovan would call Truman's "savage year."[4]

Before spring, he had given the go-ahead for development of the hydrogen bomb, approved rearmament of conventional U.S. forces, and committed the first American aid to Vietnam. No matter how much he relied upon his Cabinet and the conventional instruments of executive authority, the pace of national security policy brought decisions to his desk with increasing frequency. "Mr. Harriman's long experience in international affairs," said the White House announcement of his appointment as Special Assistant to the President, "will be of great value in helping him [Truman] deal with these matters."[5]

The main reason Truman wanted Harriman in the White House, however, was to help Acheson, who was in the center of the administration's most intense internal debates and its most difficult public trials. A year after taking office, the secretary of state had not only policy problems, but blood enemies in the Congress, the press, and the administration. For many of his headaches, he had himself to blame: he exerted no apparent effort to control his sharp tongue, or to conceal his lack of regard for ordinary intellects. To go with his haughtiness, he had a trip-wire temper. Once when he was being badgered by Senator Kenneth Wherry of Nebraska, Acheson had angrily demanded that the cranky old isolationist stop shaking his "dirty finger" at him. When the senator persisted, Acheson leaped to his feet and wound up to throw a haymaker at the lawmaker's jaw. Providentially, a State Department aide interceded, else history—certainly Acheson's—might have been different.[6] On another occasion when the secretary was exasperated at a pointless cross-examination by Senator Bourke Hickenlooper, he had fixed his tormentor with a withering stare and replied, "That is a pretty stupid question, Senator."[7]

When Truman brought Harriman to the White House, Acheson was feuding with Defense Secretary Louis Johnson, who had moved into the Pentagon after the tragic mental and emotional collapse of James Forrestal. He was hounded by the China bloc in its search for the culprit who "lost China," and he was being condemned by apoplectic anti-Communists for his declaration after the Alger Hiss perjury conviction that he would not abandon his friend and former aide. And with the Hiss case fresh in the background, he was put in an uncomfortable spotlight by McCarthy's claim to have the names of more than fifty Communists in the State Department.

Both the President and Acheson realized that Harriman would have to be eased into the White House job with care to keep his appointment itself from causing an additional problem for the secretary. At home and across Europe, he had accumulated immense prestige. He was now the country's best-known diplomat and, in the estimation of some, its best informed. But he was also a man whose ambitions, including his desire to be secretary of state, were widely known. If he was suddenly called home, the press would take it as the first step toward his replacing Acheson, whose enemies would be encouraged to bore in even harder.

Though agreeing that tongues would wag, Acheson certainly felt no threat. He had "forty-five years of confidence in Averell's integrity and honor" which would not be easily undermined.[8] Immediately after the appointment was revealed, Acheson called a press conference at the State Department and warmly welcomed Averell's return. There could not have been a happier choice, he said, than his old schoolmate. Averell's arrival at his new post was set for August 1, six weeks after the announcement.

As it happened, the concern and precaution were for nothing. Nine days later, as Harriman began winding up his affairs in Europe, the Korean War broke out.

* * *

Just before dawn on a rainy Sunday morning, artillery barrages, bursting mortar shells, and rumbling Soviet-built tanks accompanied a massive thrust of Communist troops across the 38th parallel into South Korea. Despite provocations and recurrent rumors of invasion, the Army of the Republic of Korea was taken by total surprise. It was hours before officials in the South Korean capital of Seoul, in General Douglas MacArthur's Far East headquarters in Tokyo, and in Washington comprehended that it was a real invasion rather than just another border probe.

Averell was in London when news broadcasts carried the first word of the fighting; and by the time he got back to Paris on Monday, the South Korean Army had been overrun in its defensive positions all along the border and was rapidly falling back. There was still no word on how the United States would respond. Getting none of the Korean cables in his office, he left the Talleyrand and joined Chip Bohlen at David Bruce's embassy office, where he could read the cables from Washington as soon as they reached the ambassador's desk. The massive scale of the North Korean attack had become evident, but there was no news from Washington, and the three old friends speculated on the gloomy consequences of what they feared would come next—an American decision to do nothing. But what came was a dramatic announcement that Truman was ordering the Air Force and the U.S. Navy to take the steps necessary to keep the Seoul–Kimpo Airfield–Inchon area from being overrun while Americans were being evacuated. The Air Force was ordered to prepare contingency plans for destruction of Soviet air bases in the Far East, and the Seventh Fleet was being sent north from the Philippines. After a National Security Council meeting on Tuesday, Truman ordered the fleet to prevent any attack on Formosa and called upon Chiang Kai-shek to cease raids against the mainland. Then, pledging that "the United States will uphold the rule of law," he waited for the U.N. Security Council to take the next step.[9]

Harriman couldn't bear to sit in Paris waiting for August; but in the first day after the invasion, no one sent for him. Finally, he called Acheson and announced he was on his way home, asking the secretary of state to "square it with the boss."[10] Then, deciding it was prudent to have direct authorization before flying across the Atlantic to present himself, he placed a personal call to the President.

"You must be a bit short handed," he said. "Do you want me to come home a bit earlier?"

Under the circumstances, replied Truman, he would be pleased.

"Well, if you want me," said Harriman, having invited himself, "I might as well come right away."[11] He left Marie to host a dinner party alone, and accompanied by Bohlen and Vernon Walters, all using assumed names, he caught a flight to London. There, he boarded an Air Force plane for Washington. He was home in time to join the National Security Council meeting at the White House on Wednesday afternoon.

The war was by then three days old. Seoul had fallen and Syngman Rhee's government had fled south to the port city of Pusan, but so far only one other member of the United Nations had agreed to join the effort to keep the country from being overrun—Britain had put its warships in the Sea of Japan at the disposal of the U.S. Navy. Washington had the same concern that Harriman had felt sweeping Europe when he departed, a fear that the invasion of South Korea was but a prelude to something worse—a Communist attack on Formosa, an action in the Middle East, or even an offensive against Europe itself. But Averell reached Washington with a shred of good news. The President's prompt action, he reported to the National Security Council, had brought "a general feeling of relief" to Europeans who "believed that disaster would otherwise be certain."[12]

Between urgent meetings from early morning until late evening, Harriman moved into the Executive Office Building, which had in earlier times housed the State, War and Navy departments, and now provided quarters for the growing executive office of the President. It was a sharp disappointment, for he had expected to be literally at Truman's side in the west wing of the White House. Neither he nor Vernon Walters, a resourceful aide-de-camp as well as a whiz at languages, could dislodge anybody from an office in the executive mansion. In the adjacent building, however, Walters laid claim to an exquisitely ornate suite once occupied by General John J. Pershing.

Separated from the White House by only a driveway, Averell was two minutes from Truman's desk, and his window provided an unobstructed view of all the comings and goings; but symbolically, the driveway was a moat. To presidential aides with large ambitions and fragile egos, it was the boundary which separated the serfs from the castle. Harriman's disappointment at being consigned to the huge neo-Gothic annex was diminished when he realized that he had space for several secretaries and a platoon of assistants, which he had started to line up even before he left Paris. He enlisted Marshall Plan economist Lincoln Gordon, who was on leave from Harvard, and drafted Sam Berger, who had been his labor adviser at the Talleyrand. On the recommendation of Louis Johnson, he hired as his chief of staff Theodore Tannenwald, Jr., a gregarious little New York lawyer, who had worked for James Forrestal on the reorganization of the armed forces and the creation of the Department of Defense. Russell Deane, who had headed the wartime military mission in Moscow, flew to Washington from retirement in the California wine business and set up the new shop before escaping Harriman's

clutches to go back West. Harriman replaced him by arranging a promotion to major general for Colonel Frank Roberts, Deane's Moscow deputy, coaxing him out of retirement to be his military adviser.

The ignominy of his assignment to the Executive Office Building
was only one indication that his station in the administration was less
exalted than he had expected it to be. No matter that he had been a
Cabinet member, friend of Roosevelt, the country's most visible ambassador, and one of the creators of the Marshall Plan, he was now a staff
man. John Steelman, jealous of his own title as Assistant to the President,
considered him a rival in the hierarchy of underlings. While Averell was
Special Assistant to the President, Steelman remained, in his own mind
anyway, The Assistant, and that amounted to more than a nuance of
title.

Sidney Souers, a onetime Missouri businessman who had risen to
the rank of rear admiral during World War II, remained executive
secretary of the National Security Council. While it was only a clerical
job, Harriman saw it as a potential power base, as did Louis Johnson,
and earlier, James Forrestal. Afraid that Acheson would get control of
the NSC, Johnson encouraged Souers to build a staff and make himself
a source of influence on national security policy. Harriman had much
the same in mind for himself when he had headed for home, but Truman
was not disposed to convert the NSC into a super Cabinet agency in the
hands of a White House bureaucracy. Congress, he said, had made its
wishes known by creating an executive secretary and not a director of
the council.[13]

To further clarify his own view, Truman, in one of his first assignments for his new assistant, had Harriman draft a presidential order
limiting attendance at NSC meetings to members, plus others explicitly
invited by the President himself.

Nonetheless, a new power center in Washington would over the
years evolve from Harriman's circumspect beginning as the first presidential assistant for national security affairs. It could hardly have been
otherwise once lightning communications put a hair trigger on global
crises. Beginning with McGeorge Bundy in the Kennedy administration,
the national security assistant became adviser, conduit, arbitrator, interpreter, and more. There would be moments, as in Henry Kissinger's
controversial reign, when the staff man would supersede members of
the Cabinet, including the secretary of state.

What Truman most wanted from Harriman in lifting some of
Acheson's burden was for him to manage the destructive feud between
his secretary of state and secretary of defense. Political considerations
aside, it was a situation which the President found personally distressing.
Acheson was one of the people Truman most admired in public life, and
Louis Johnson was a man to whom he owed considerable gratitude. His

instructions to Averell were typically cryptic. "Dean's in trouble," he said. "I want you to help him."[14]

"Dean's in trouble" required no explanation, but the President's summation distilled a host of problems. The United States' nuclear monopoly had vanished. The Communists controlled mainland China. The Soviet threat in Europe had come into clear and alarming focus. In the spring, the administration, having capped defense spending at $13 billion, undertook a massive study of Western defense posture. The review concluded that, in light of the continuing buildup by the Soviet bloc, Western defenses had to be drastically shored up. Budget estimates were not included, but it was implicit that the U.S. defense spending would have to receive a stupendous increase—to about $50 billion a year.

Walter Lippmann, who had criticized Harriman as a reflexive anti-Communist at the end of the war, hailed his appointment as a step up from policy management by quarreling Cabinet officers, and an important moment in Truman's presidency. The decision to have a special assistant in foreign affairs was "wise," the oracle concluded, and Harriman was "well-suited to the post."

> Mr. Truman has been learning the hard way that the President cannot delegate the conduct of foreign affairs, no matter how eminent and able the Secretary of State may be. Only the President in the White House has the power, can bear the responsibility, and exert the influence which the shaping of high policy requires. But the man who is the President has not the time and the energy to do all that himself directly. So he must have within the White House someone whom he trusts absolutely. His relations with that man have to be personal rather than official. For that man must be able to speak for him, to do a lot of the thinking for him, and indeed to get a lot of thinking, which could not pass through a bureaucracy, done for the President.[15]

The expected rumors that Harriman would replace Acheson did sweep Washington and they did not easily die no matter how forcefully Truman rejected calls for the secretary's resignation, or how often Harriman took occasion to support him. When Averell was asked about them at a newspaper editors' convention, he responded with a passionate defense of Acheson as "one of the wisest and most courageous Secretaries of State that this country has ever had," pointing to the secretary's role in the formation of the Truman Doctrine and the Marshall Plan, and his taking charge of the Korean crisis in the first hours after the invasion while the President was still out of town.

"I don't believe we have had in our history many Secretaries of State with the guts to deal so forcefully with issues with which he has been faced. The President has faith in Acheson, and there is good reason for it." He spoke for ten minutes, and he made certain that a transcript of what he had said was put on the President's desk.[16]

His public defense was matched by private loyalty, especially in the running conflict with Johnson. Harriman was at the State Department every morning when Acheson presided over his 9:30 meeting with top department officials. If the President had him otherwise occupied, an assistant was dispatched. "Averell was always incredibly careful," said Tannenwald. "Anytime he went to the President on a matter where he disagreed with Acheson, he was meticulously sure that Acheson knew exactly what he was doing."[17]

Although they had known each other since they were boys, Harriman and Acheson were not intimate friends. In Averell's case, as in Acheson's, truly intimate friends were few. Acheson's ascendancy at the State Department had been difficult for Averell to swallow. Not only was Acheson a bit younger, but he had been only a minor figure in the Roosevelt administration and, in fact, had not personally liked FDR. Even now, he was aloof from Truman politics no matter how fiercely he fought for the President's foreign policies.

While the secretary admired Harriman's energy and tenacity and respected him for his integrity in dealing with the President, he was never in awe of Averell's intellectual gifts, nor was Harriman especially impressed by the great bearing, confidence, and presence that made Acheson an effective negotiator and the physical prototype of the modern world statesman. Indeed, Harriman suggested that his fellow Bonesman might improve his relations with conservative American congressmen by getting rid of the haughty grenadier's mustache that was his trademark. Socially, the two had little in common. While Averell despised the thought of a meal or an evening alone, Acheson was happy spending solitary evenings with a book and retreating on weekends to the quiet of his farm at Sandy Spring, Maryland. Certainly, their wives did nothing to bring them together, for Alice Acheson, a demure, Wellesley-educated daughter of a Michigan railroad lawyer, was put off by Marie's New York manner and privately offended by her humor.

What overcame their differences and bound Harriman and Acheson more than Groton, Skull and Bones, and the Yale boathouse was the reverence each had for Truman and the presidency. "Acheson thought the presidency had a halo around it," said William P. Bundy, who was married to Acheson's daughter. It was even more true of Harriman, who would serve other presidents as eagerly as he worked for Roosevelt and Truman even when he couldn't muster the same personal admiration or fully embrace their policies.

Positioned in the White House hierarchy where he had easy access to Truman, and interposed between two huge State and Defense bureaucracies, Harriman could not have avoided the Acheson-Johnson conflict if he had tried, which he did not. He was on Acheson's side and was constantly in touch with several of the secretary's lieutenants, led by Undersecretary James E. Webb, who were conspiring to hasten Johnson's departure.

At the same time, he took pains to stay on good terms with the Pentagon chief. Like Truman, Johnson had been a captain of infantry in World War I. They had become acquainted thirty years earlier, when Johnson was a national leader in veterans' affairs. Johnson had served as undersecretary of war from 1937 to 1940, aspiring even then to be in the Cabinet. He had been helpful to Truman in the Senate, and most importantly, he had been at the President's side in the desperate 1948 presidential race.

When the campaign seemed a lost cause and the hands of discreet givers were slow to open, Johnson had been an indefatigable fund-raiser. Harriman was obviously among the important targets, but he was also one of those whose 1948 generosity was tempered by Truman's poor prospects. Campaign fund-raisers who called on him in Paris left disappointed, and some of his intimate friends would later believe that he had then grievously damaged his chances of ever being Truman's secretary of state.[18] Johnson's willingness to take the fund-raising job after three or four others had turned it down had earned him Truman's profound appreciation and the Cabinet appointment. With great enthusiasm he accepted his assignment to hold the line on the nation's military budget. Throughout the capital, it was accepted that Johnson was seeking to replace Acheson as the dominant figure in the Cabinet and hoping to use the Pentagon as a springboard for a presidential campaign in 1952.

The ugliest moment in the whole Johnson-Acheson affair had come early in 1950 at a meeting the secretary of state arranged to review the landmark defense reevaluation the President had ordered. Angrily shouting that he would not be summoned and presented conclusions by another Cabinet member, Johnson stormed out, leaving Acheson and officials of both the Defense and State departments embarrassed and astonished. Truman's tolerance continued even after that, but Johnson's behavior grew so consistently unreasonable that Acheson began to wonder whether he was mentally ill.

Harriman, Truman hoped, could make the situation bearable even if it remained unpleasant for everybody concerned, and he brushed aside Averell's first suggestion that Johnson simply be dismissed.

Although he was located beyond the walls of the White House, Harriman's job made him a fixture both in the group Truman gathered around him at times of crisis and the friends he took along when he escaped to Key West or boarded the 240-foot presidential yacht, *The Williamsburg*, for a weekend cruise.

The President liked to play eight-handed poker and Averell was often among the seven invited to sit in, the others being members of Cabinet and Congress, including freshman Texas senator Lyndon Johnson. Standing rules put a ceiling of $900 on any participant's losses. As the party cruised down the Potomac, each player received a $500 stack of chips, which could be replaced if he lost them all. But White House aide Clark Clifford, who arranged the outings and served as banker for the game, collected a 10 percent tax on each pot, building a bank which he kept in a silver "poverty bowl." A loser who exhausted his second $500 stack turned to the poverty bowl for funds to keep him in the action. On none of the journeys on *The Williamsburg* or games at the Little White House at Key West was Harriman ever remembered to have landed in poverty. At bridge with his friends in Sands Point or Hobe Sound, he was aggressive and supremely confident, but he sat down at the less-genteel poker table across from the President as grimly as he had faced Stalin in the Kremlin. "The agreed description for him as a poker player," said Clifford, "was that he was very tight-arsed."[19]

The loyalty Harriman had for Roosevelt was supplanted by genuine personal devotion to Truman. Especially after the 1948 victory against all odds, there developed a personal bond that had never existed between Harriman and his fellow aristocrat from New York. Some things about Truman were reminiscent of E. H. Harriman. They were both small, combative men with quick tempers, bantam-rooster confidence, and fierce family loyalties. Tempered by their challenging upbringing, they made fateful decisions quickly and stuck with them defiantly. When Averell spoke of his father, it was with admiration; but of Truman, he spoke with affection, and it was reciprocated. " 'I'm just a little fella, lucky in politics, from Missouri,' " Clifford recalled Truman saying once. " 'But there is one great man in this town. He comes in, after all he has done for the Roosevelt administration, and says, "I'd like a desk somewhere if you have room. In any way I can, I'd like to help the United States." ' " Clifford told the story many years later at a Harriman birthday party; while it was undoubtedly apocryphal, the sense of it was not inaccurate.[20]

The analysts who predicted that Harriman would be Truman's Hopkins knew neither Averell nor the President very well, however. Truman was not a man to share his burdens as Roosevelt had with Hopkins, nor was Harriman one to assume authority not explicitly granted to him. Truman's personal esteem for him notwithstanding, he was relegated to a staff man's role; and except for times when he was called into crises, he found it unsatisfying. After a few months, it was obvious to White

House insiders that he was becoming increasingly restive, anxious to get away to Sands Point or to Hobe Sound or Sun Valley.

He was happiest when on presidential missions for Truman as he had been for Roosevelt, and in that he was fortunate that the American commander in the Far East was Douglas MacArthur.

Besides keeping the North Koreans from overrunning the South and bringing the entire peninsula under a Communist regime, Truman's objective in Korea was to prevent a conflict between the Chinese Communists and the Nationalists that might trigger World War III. That had been the reason for his quick decision to send the Seventh Fleet, then consisting of only one carrier and a dozen other vessels, to the Formosa Strait in the first hours of the Korean War.

The move boldly risked junking the U.S. policy against using arms to defend the Nationalists against the Communists, even though the purpose was also to make sure that Chiang Kai-shek did not attack the mainland. With that decision, the United States had thrown itself back into the China conflict, a position it had profoundly hoped to escape, and it had started trouble between the President and the most famous American in uniform.

More than five years after becoming President, Truman still had never met MacArthur. Twice he had invited the great warrior home for a talk, but on both occasions the general had replied that his presence was required in Japan.

On July 31, a little more than a month after the outbreak of the war, MacArthur showed up on Formosa, surrounded as always by the press. Although the retinue filled two transport planes, no diplomatic representative was included. In an explosion of flash bulbs, he dramatically embraced Chiang, whom he had never met before, and Formosan governor K. C. Wu, who declared MacArthur's arrival on the island a demonstration to the world that the forces fighting communism were united. With that, MacArthur and the Chinese Nationalist leader closeted themselves for several hours of private meetings that generated dramatic headlines.

The general had been explicitly authorized by the Joint Chiefs of Staff to assess Chiang's defense requirements, but his unexpected appearance at Chiang's side brought Truman and his top aides out of their chairs. The tone of the reports beneath the headlines suggested a political connotation that Truman did not like—especially after follow-up reports out of MacArthur's Tokyo headquarters that the general believed communism was to be fought wherever it was found in Asia. To compound it all, there was a suddenly famous picture of MacArthur gallantly kissing the hand of Madame Chiang.

During the early days of the war, Truman had no complaint about the way MacArthur had responded to the crisis, but it was inevitable that the general's personal airs and his posturing as a demigod would raise the hackles of the old Missouri National Guardsman. Truman was aware that MacArthur's political sympathies lay with the Republicans and that the general had gone so far as to allow his name to be entered in the 1944 Republican primary in Wisconsin. Yet as much as the trip to Formosa irritated the White House, Truman and his aides tried to avoid any hint of an alarmed public reaction.

The day after MacArthur flew back to Tokyo, Harriman had a dinner party at the house he had just moved into on Foxhall Road in northwest Washington. Major Walters, after securing Pershing's old office, had scored another coup by arranging for his boss to lease a house that once belonged to Daisy Harriman, former envoy to Norway and widow of Averell's cousin, J. Borden Harriman. A short drive from the White House and set on a hill with a terrace looking out toward the Potomac, it met the Harrimans' entertainment needs perfectly, and Averell began having guests in while Marie was still packing in Paris. He invited congressmen to breakfast, went home for working lunches, and entertained at dinner nearly every night when he was not otherwise occupied. On Sunday night, September 2, his guests included Lieutenant General Lauris Norstad, the deputy chief of staff of the Air Force, who was about to go to Tokyo to visit General MacArthur.

In Korea, the Eighth Army was valiantly defending the seventy-by-sixty-mile Pusan Perimeter in order to protect the vital seaport and avoid being pushed into the sea. Laying plans for the United Nations' counteroffensive, MacArthur was watching the North Koreans extend their supply lines and increase their own vulnerability even as they threatened to crush the American defenses. In the precariousness of that position, he found his strategy to reverse the direction of the war, a landing behind the enemy forces, cutting them off. Although General J. Lawton Collins, the chief of staff of the Army, and General Hoyt Vandenberg, the chief of staff of the Air Force, had been to the Far East for face-to-face talks, the Pentagon wanted to know a lot more about the plan and about MacArthur's troop requirements. Even after the 1st Marine Division had been sent to the Far East, troop requests continued. In Washington, there was reluctance to give the general everything he requested, because of the chilling possibility that the Soviets might strike in Europe if they saw American reserves overwhelmingly committed to Asia. It was to further evaluate MacArthur's continuing requests that Norstad and Lieutenant General Matthew B. Ridgway, the deputy chief of staff of the Army, were going to Tokyo for still another conference.

After the dinner that Sunday, Norstad casually welcomed Averell to join the party, and he jumped at the invitation. It was a chance to see the war firsthand and clear the air about MacArthur's visit to Formosa, but he doubted that Truman would allow him to leave Washington at the moment. Relations between Acheson and Johnson had so deteriorated that some influential Democrats, such as J. Percy Priest, the House whip, were joining Republicans in saying that both of them should quit.

Nevertheless, Truman found Averell waiting for him when he returned from his Monday-morning walk. The President bought the idea without a blink. Harriman could accomplish two things. He could assure MacArthur that the President would do everything in his power to meet his troop requirements, and he could make it clear to the Far East commander that Chiang Kai-shek was not to be permitted to start a war with the Chinese Communists. Word of Harriman's trip was sent to MacArthur a few hours later, and that afternoon Truman announced it at his weekly press conference.

Of all the people around Truman, Harriman was the most logical one to have a serious talk with MacArthur at a delicate moment. He could speak with the full authority of the White House, and he was in Truman's view the administration figure best prepared to discuss Formosa and Far East policy in the context of the administration's concerns about Europe and overall national-security requirements. Although he did not count himself a close friend of the general's, they had known each other since the early twenties, and he was one of the few people in Washington—or anywhere else—who was at ease addressing the proconsul as "Doug." Back when MacArthur was a lieutenant, his ever protective mother, believing that he was unhappy in the Army, had approached E.H. Harriman about a position for young Douglas with the Union Pacific. E.H. had dispatched a personnel man to interview Lieutenant MacArthur, only to find that the young officer had no desire to leave the Army.

Many years later, while he was superintendent of the U.S. Military Academy at West Point, MacArthur had been Averell's guest at Arden "duck drives"; the Military Academy bought its milk from the Harrimans' dairy; and its polo players regularly rode their ponies over to Arden to play against Averell's early Orange County team.

Harriman and MacArthur had hit it off well when their acquaintance was resumed after World War II. Averell had taken his trip through the Far East on the way home from Moscow primarily to warn MacArthur what he could expect in dealing with the Soviets. The general had been grateful. He and his wife had entertained the visitors in style, and Averell had sent Jean Marie MacArthur a large bouquet as soon as he got home.

The proconsul was not in the habit of meeting visiting dignitaries at the airport, but he was waiting at the ramp when Harriman, Norstad, and Ridgway arrived on August 6. The presidential envoy and the general rode into the city together; and in the following three days, they talked for more than eight hours, several of them alone. On the second day, Harriman flew to Korea, where he met with MacArthur's officers, conferred with South Korean president Syngman Rhee, and visited an exposed 1st Cavalry command post on the Naktong River. While he was there with Norstad, Ridgway, and Lieutenant General Walton Walker, the commander of the Eighth Army, the quartet watched American artillery pieces lob shells across the river into enemy territory. The front, where there had been bloody fighting in recent days, was otherwise quiet; but officers at the outpost feared the visitors might all be killed by a sudden mortar barrage. There were huge sighs of relief when the jeep convoy departed for the rear, Harriman caked with dust and riding in the first vehicle with Walker.

Back in Tokyo the next day, the mission heard the details of MacArthur's planned counteroffensive. Harriman, like Norstad and Ridgway, was spellbound for the entire two and a half hours that the general took to lay out his daring plan to ambush the North Koreans from the sea.

As the Communist forces had driven south, MacArthur had watched them expose themselves to encirclement, just as they had encircled the American Eighth Army at Pusan. The Joint Chiefs were well aware of the plan's outline, but some of it troubled them. The approach to Inchon was so narrow that one disabled ship might cripple the whole operation. There were broad, sticky mudflats when the tide receded, and the Marines might be exposed to murderous fire. If they successfully got ashore they could not be resupplied, reinforced, or rescued until the next high tide, about twelve hours later.

MacArthur did not dwell on the innumerable ways a landing could go wrong. Instead he employed all of his theatrical skills to describe his strategy—"supported by every logical military argument of his rich experience, and delivered with all of his dramatic eloquence," Ridgway noted.[21] Pacing, his voice falling to a whisper, then rising to a commanding baritone, MacArthur roamed from the beach at Inchon into philosophy and the contrasting Western and Oriental perceptions of death. Along the way, he folded his arms and sighed in a demonstration of the way Oriental soldiers met death.[22]

"I cannot believe that a great nation such as the United States cannot give me these few paltry reinforcements for which I ask," MacArthur intoned after reviewing his troop requests. Then coming to his grand finale, he urged Harriman to "tell the President that if he gives them to me, I will on the rising tide of the fifteenth of September, land at Inchon and between the hammer of this landing and the anvil of the Eighth Army, I will crush and destroy the enemy armies of North Korea."[23]

Far less clear-cut than the Inchon plan were the general's private reassurances that he understood the administration's political views and Formosa policy. He couldn't see where he had exceeded the boundaries of military leader, but he would, he promised, abide by the policy laid down in Washington, chapter and verse. Still, Harriman went home with the nagging feeling that there had not been a real understanding between them despite all the hours of talk.

Although the general acknowledged that Chiang's ambition to return to the mainland was unrealistic, he would not accept Harriman's assessment that the United States would suffer gigantic consequences if the Generalissimo tried it. "I explained in great detail, why Chiang was a liability," Harriman noted, "and the great danger of a split in the unity of the United Nations on the Chinese Communist–Formosa policies; the attitude of the British, Nehru, and such countries as Norway, who, although stalwart in their determination to resist Russian invasion, did not want to stir up trouble elsewhere. . . .

"For reasons which are rather difficult to explain, I did not feel that we came to a full agreement on the way he believed things should be handled on Formosa and with the Generalissimo. He accepted the President's position and will act accordingly, but without full conviction. He has a strange idea that we should back anybody who will fight Communism. . . ."[24]

MacArthur in turn came out of the meetings with the impression that "there was no fixed, comprehensive United States policy for the Far East." From Harriman, he said later, he had got only a message that "President Truman had conceived a violent animosity toward Chiang Kai-shek, and that anyone who favored the Generalissimo might well arouse the President's disfavor. He left me with a feeling of concern and uneasiness that the situation in the Far East was little understood and mistakenly downgraded in high circles in Washington."[25]

Harriman's flight home was timed to get him back to Washington in the early morning, when he would have an immediate chance to see the President and get his undivided attention. More than MacArthur's comments on Formosan policy, he was anxious for the President to hear in detail the plans for the Inchon landing.

The plane took off from Tokyo at midafternoon on August 8, crossed the international date line, stopped for two hours in Anchorage, and landed at Washington National Airport at 6:59 A.M. the next day. Minutes later, Harriman was at the White House, and found the President alone in his office.

Truman listened intently as he recounted MacArthur's plan to put the 1st Marine Division ashore as September's highest tide rolled into the shallow harbor at Inchon. Dramatic as the scheme was, Harriman later recalled that he was careful to give the President full appreciation of its dangers, although he had already signed a memorandum with Ridgway and Norstad recommending that the operation go forward. Truman listened without much comment, then ordered Harriman to give the same briefing to the secretary of defense.

Two hours later, after a shave and shower and a fast breakfast at home, Averell got to Louis Johnson's office to find that not only had the secretary already spoken to the President but that Truman was calling back to ask Johnson what had been decided.

With planning for Inchon going forward and Harriman having delivered MacArthur's assurance that he would hew to Truman's policy on Formosa, the administration tried to put the flap over the visit to Chiang behind it. Everybody concerned worked to scotch rumors that Averell had gone to Tokyo with a presidential wrist slap. Harriman himself assured the press, inaccurately, that the White House, the State Department, and the Pentagon had all known of MacArthur's Formosa trip in advance, and that the talks with Chiang had been entirely on military matters. Truman himself told a press conference that he and the general were now in complete agreement.

But the matter did not long rest. Before the month was out, MacArthur again plunged into the delicate subject of Formosan policy. In a speech prepared for delivery in his behalf at a Veterans of Foreign Wars convention in Chicago, he railed against appeasement and defeatism in the Far East, and called attention to the strategic importance of Formosa and to the mighty offensive potential of Chiang's Nationalists. A direct slap at the President and the administration, it shattered his pledge to Harriman.

Much of it was what MacArthur had said privately before promising to confine himself to military affairs. The speech was not an outright call for the use of Chiang's forces, but it made the idea sound powerfully attractive to the old warriors. There was on Formosa, he said, "a concentration of air and naval bases which is potentially greater than any similar concentration on the Asiatic mainland between the Yellow Sea and the Straits of Malacca."[26]

Advance copies of the text had been sent to the VFW and to publications with a record of reverence for the general's views. On Friday, August 25, the Associated Press transmitted a story on the speech, for release upon delivery on Monday. No longer could the differences be brushed aside.

A State Department press officer who read the story on the news ticker alerted Acheson at his Maryland farm. About the same time, the dispatch reached Lucius Battle, the secretary's personal assistant, who alerted Harriman, hoping to keep his own boss from becoming involved. Averell immediately took the news to the Oval Office, and when the President called a meeting including Acheson and Johnson, he advised that MacArthur be ordered to withdraw the speech, even if it provoked the general's resignation. Truman agreed and told Johnson to send the message directing that the speech be pulled back.

The simple matter of transmitting a point-blank presidential order quickly became complicated. Johnson was hesitant to send such a bare-knuckled directive to the country's most renowned military officer. There was no doubt that MacArthur was out of line, but the speech had already been spread across the country, and the damage was done. Instead of sending an order, Johnson talked again with the chiefs and concluded it would be better to send MacArthur a warning that the speech would be repudiated by the White House if it was not withdrawn.

Acheson, meanwhile, called Harriman to confirm his understanding that the President had issued a clear order. About that, Averell had no doubt—Johnson was to call MacArthur and advise him of the decision. White House press secretary Charles Ross was in Averell's office when Acheson called, and listening to Harriman's end of the conversation, he realized that the matter was too controversial to be handled with a telephone call. The order to MacArthur had to be put in writing.

Acheson thought it advisable to have another meeting. If Johnson was doubtful about the order, then the Defense Secretary should ask the President to bring them all together again. Acheson phoned Johnson and made the suggestion; but before Johnson could call the White House to recommend another meeting, Truman, who had by then talked with Ross, telephoned the Pentagon and dictated the cable he wished sent: "The President of the United States directs that you withdraw your message for the National Encampment of the Veterans of Foreign Wars because various features with respect to Formosa are in conflict with the policy of the U.S. and its position in the U.N."[27] Johnson and the Pentagon made one last futile try to get the order reconsidered, but Harriman talked with Truman again and confirmed that the President indeed wanted the message sent just as he had dictated it. At long last, the message went out; MacArthur complied, but the damage was done.

Three weeks later, as he had promised, MacArthur sent Marines ashore on the high tide at Inchon, launching a monumental offensive that drove the North Korean Army from the South and brought the United Nations command within reach of total victory. At the Pentagon, the chiefs breathed a huge sigh of relief that it had worked; but the crowning moment of MacArthur's long military career left a bitter aftertaste with his superiors, particularly Joint Chiefs' chairman Omar Bradley.

MacArthur had contrived for the messenger delivering the final operational plans for the landing to reach Washington after it was too late for the Joint Chiefs to do anything about the operation they regarded as a huge gamble and insisted upon monitoring in detail. It was, Bradley said in his memoirs twelve years later, "an act of arrogance unparalleled in my military experience."[28]

On the advice of Harriman and White House political adviser

Charles Murphy, Truman flew to Wake Island in October to meet MacArthur face-to-face at last. The atmosphere exuded cordiality, and Averell felt confident the bitter feelings were behind them. Truman added a fourth oak-leaf cluster to the general's Distinguished Service Cross; and MacArthur, looking to the end of the war, assured the President that, rumors and sporadic Chinese activity in North Korea notwithstanding, there was no chance of Communist Chinese intervention in Korea.

While withdrawal of the VFW speech, the success at Inchon, and the brightened picture in Korea muted the dispute over Far East policy, Louis Johnson's reluctance to relay Truman's order hastened the conclusion of his stormy career in the Cabinet.

It was Harriman who brought the President to his painful conclusion that he had no choice but to fire his longtime friend. He had taken seriously Truman's injunction to help Acheson, and through the summer he watched the Pentagon chief become more and more reckless in sniping at his Cabinet colleagues.

Johnson himself finally presented the necessary ammunition. In mid-August, just after Harriman's trip to Tokyo, the defense secretary appeared before a closed session of the Senate Foreign Relations Committee, and Averell sent Tannenwald to Capitol Hill to hear what he had to say. Most of the hearing concerned military assistance and defense spending. But when the controversy over MacArthur's visit with Chiang was raised again, Johnson told the committee that the President, Harriman, and Acheson all well knew about it in advance. He blamed the whole controversy on a State Department official, who, he said, had taken too much to drink and had "talked too much."[29]

When the session was over, Tannenwald introduced himself, and the secretary offered him a ride downtown. As they rode down Pennsylvania Avenue, Johnson began telling Tannenwald of all the troubles he was having with Acheson. In this difficult time, he said, he was happy to have Harriman back in Washington as an ally. He was depending on Averell for help in protecting himself against "that terrible man in the State Department."[30] By the time they reached the Executive Office Building, Johnson had vented so much venom toward Acheson that Tannenwald felt compelled to report it Harriman.

The defense secretary was obviously sincere in his inexplicable belief that Harriman was on his side against Acheson. Some weeks later, with Averell sitting in his office, he made the fatal mistake of attacking Acheson during a telephone conversation with Senator Robert A. Taft of Ohio, the Republicans' chief critic of Truman foreign policy, whose voice was always prominent in the chorus for Acheson's resignation. When he hung up the telephone, he proceeded to solicit Harriman's help in forcing Acheson out of office, promising that, in return, he would see to it that Averell was named secretary of state. As soon as he could get back across the Potomac, Averell reported the entire conversation to Truman. At last, Johnson was called in and forced to write a letter of resignation in which he also called upon the President to name George Marshall as his successor.

With Johnson gone and Marshall back in service as his replacement at the Defense Department, Harriman was working with the three men he most admired in public life—the President, Acheson, and the general who had been his mentor and confidant since early in World War II. Together, they shortly rode out Truman's stormiest days in the White House, when the President sacked Douglas MacArthur.

Just days after leaving the President at Wake Island, MacArthur alarmed the chiefs by sending U.S. Army outfits into the northernmost provinces of North Korea, in violation of explicit orders to use only South Koreans when the UN drive neared the Manchurian and Soviet borders. Although MacArthur disputed the interpretation, JCS chairman Bradley thought the action "came very close" to insubordination and found MacArthur's responses to questions "evasive, if not untruthful."[31] And there was more. To seal off infiltration from Manchuria, MacArthur was planning to bomb the Korean end of bridges across the Yalu River, which divided North Korea and Manchuria. When word got back to Washington and Truman ordered him to stop, MacArthur cabled alarming reports of his forces being threatened by arms and troops flowing across the bridges from the North.

Ignoring serious Pentagon concerns, he deployed his two principal commands, the Eighth Army and X Corps, into the far north with a mountain range separating them. Then, after Chinese regulars battered South Korean divisions and put them to flight on October 26, he grossly underestimated the enemy force and went ahead with what he envisioned as a war-ending drive to the Yalu. He continued to talk of having American soldiers home for Christmas.

On the day after the offensive began, his forces were ambushed by massive numbers of Chinese, who had come south and hidden in the hills even before the bombing of the Yalu bridges. When the harrowing situation was clarified, his response was to recommend accepting Chiang Kai-shek's long-since-rejected offer of troops and to launch another bristling public criticism of the administration's limited war policy.

The upshot of the new dispute was a presidential order drafted by Harriman, stopping MacArthur and other officials from making foreign policy speeches without approval. The directive was obeyed until spring; but in March, as Truman was about to launch a personal initiative for a political settlement to end the fighting, MacArthur issued a communiqué

in Tokyo, challenging the policy of limited warfare and offering to negotiate personally with the commander in chief of enemy forces. In response, Truman sent the general a stinging reminder of the December
directive, and further ordered him to report immediately to the JCS for
instructions if he received any feelers for an armistice.

If there was any chance for the incident to blow over in the fashion
of the earlier clashes, it was swept away on April 5. On the floor of the
House, Republican leader Joseph Martin, who was calling for Chiang's
troops to open a "second front" against mainland China, released a letter
from MacArthur, endorsing the use of Nationalist troops against the
Chinese Communists. Martin's idea of a second front, said the general,
contradicted neither logic nor the tradition of meeting force with coun-
terforce.

With the bombshell on the House floor, Truman sent for Acheson,
Marshall, Harriman, and Bradley. For an hour, they discussed this new-
est effrontery, with the President giving no indication of his intentions.
It was Harriman who volunteered the recommendation that MacArthur
be dismissed. In retrospect, he said, the President should have fired
MacArthur five years earlier when the general twice turned down a
presidential suggestion that he return to the United States for a talk.
The others did not disagree, but they were cautious.

Marshall was worried that the firing would provoke such a furious
political backlash that the administration would have trouble getting its
military appropriations bill through Congress. In Acheson's mind the
question "was not so much what should be done as how it should be
done." Certainly the Joint Chiefs had to be unanimously behind it.[32]
Bradley agreed. He doubted, however, that MacArthur was technically
guilty of insubordination "as defined in Army regulations," and before
making any recommendation, he wanted to talk with all the members of
the Joint Chiefs.[33]

That same afternoon, the four advisers met in Acheson's office
to cover the ground again. Marshall raised the possibility of ordering
MacArthur home for consultation before a final decision by the President. Acheson, Harriman, and Bradley all disagreed. Such a step, Averell
said, would invite MacArthur to create a national uproar, perhaps even
launching a political career for himself.

After another short session with the President on Saturday, each of
them mulled it over alone through the weekend. On Monday all agreed
it was time for MacArthur's recall. Marshall had gone back and read all
the cable traffic that had passed between MacArthur and the JCS since
the beginning of the war. Bradley had held a long conference with the
Joint Chiefs.

MacArthur's behavior, going back to their own talks about Formosa
the previous year, still baffled Harriman. "I can find no rational explana-

tion for his motives," he wrote Eisenhower after the decision was made. "Aside from insubordination, he is now making statements which the record shows are just not true. And all of this after Truman stood squarely back of him when he made his blunders in Northern Korea. Anyway, thank God for Ridgway—and the President. Action will be taken by the time you get this letter."[34]

On Tuesday, April 10, Harriman spent the day preparing what Truman wanted to be a finely orchestrated announcement. The President would go on the air with it at the same time reporters were given the full background of the decision and as the order was personally delivered to MacArthur in Tokyo.

The plan was to cable the order to U.S. ambassador John Muccio in Korea on Wednesday and to have it hand delivered to MacArthur in Tokyo by Army Secretary Frank Pace, who was on a visit to the Far East. But late Tuesday, the *Chicago Tribune* began inquiring at the White House and the Pentagon about a major announcement in Tokyo, and the Mutual Broadcasting System made preparations for an important news development from the Far East. There was also a hitch in getting Truman's order delivered. Pace could not be reached because he was on a visit to the front.

Concerned that MacArthur would get wind of what was happening, Truman prepared for an immediate announcement. By ten P.M., his statement had been drafted and he went over it with Harriman, Acheson and Marshall. Three hours later, the White House rousted reporters from bed and alerted them to get to the pressroom. MacArthur himself received the news from his wife, who heard it on a radio broadcast in Tokyo.

None of the four who recommended the firing was surprised by the hysterical reaction that followed. The White House was deluged with denunciations surpassing anything in living memory. Amidst cries for Truman's impeachment, thousands of MacArthur worshipers awaited his plane when he returned to the capital in the middle of the night to be formally greeted by Marshall and the Joint Chiefs. There followed a ticker-tape parade up Broadway, a heart-rending farewell to a joint session of Congress, and a rambling, massive Senate investigation lasting through much of the summer.

The show on Capitol Hill wandered far from the dismissal of MacArthur and into the nooks and crannies of Far East policy. As it delved into the "who lost China" morass, Harriman expected to be called as a major witness. Not only had he been involved in firing MacArthur, whose criticism of limited warfare and Truman Far East policy was being aired day after day, he was also the last major Yalta participant in government, and he had been intimately involved in the secret Roosevelt-Stalin agreements on the Far East. Anxious to testify, he labored for weeks, going through his files to reconstruct what had happened in the Crimea. When he left the White House in the afternoon, he would round up Tannenwald and Hildy Shishkin, his secretary, and take them home with him to work into the night on his testimony.

To his disappointment, he never appeared before the Senate hearings. He was sent to Iran to deal with a crisis touched off by the government's nationalization of the Anglo-Iranian Oil Company, by which time senators had decided not to call him anyway. After the emotional uproar, the MacArthur controversy quickly died. Both investigators and the public were tired of it.

But while he was away, Tannenwald finished a five-thousand-word treatise on Yalta disputing the continuing assertion that a sellout to Stalin in the Crimea had led to the loss of China to the Communists. When he returned, Harriman pored over the paper for days, editing and rewriting and, in the view of Tannenwald and other aides who saw the draft, weakening it. Even so, it was compelling, weaving Harriman's recollections with the official record. Truman found it "a most important document" and circulated it with the note that Harriman had brought together the facts of the Yalta summit "more clearly than they have ever been stated before."[35]

With the departure of Louis Johnson, there was no longer any need for an intermediary between Foggy Bottom and the Pentagon. Although he was at Truman's side, Harriman could not forget that he was on a rung far below the Cabinet rank he had held four years earlier. State and Defense, under Acheson and Marshall, dominated foreign policy, Walter Lippmann's advice that the President take more personal control notwithstanding.

Averell's perception of his role had come quickly into focus in the first days of the Korean conflict. Seeing an unavoidable political backlash down the road, he urged the President to get the Congress on record with a resolution endorsing his commitment of American armed forces. Without hesitation, Truman dismissed it, accepting Acheson's advice that it would set a troublesome precedent. Some future President might be unable to respond to a crisis until Congress gave him the same endorsement.

The Truman administration's larger nightmare was always the specter of a Communist move in Europe. It had an inviolate commitment to put flesh on the NATO skeleton, but European security had to compete with Korea for Washington's attention. Helping out with Europe and NATO became Averell's prime function.

Before departing for the Wake Island rendezvous with MacArthur, Truman called General Eisenhower and offered Ike the job as NATO's first Supreme Commander. The imperative of shoring up NATO was discussed around the table at Wake. With the tide of the Korean War running heavily for the United Nations forces, MacArthur assured the President and the Joint Chiefs that one of the infantry divisions then in Korea could soon be moved to Europe. But when the Chinese sprang their massive ambush, that hopeful prospect went out the window. It was a moment of acute anxiety in NATO. If the Soviets intended to probe in Europe, their opportunity was at hand.

A war warning flashed to American theater commanders advising them that the JCS believed that "the current situation in Korea has greatly increased the possibility of general war."[36] On December 15, the President went on radio and television to declare a state of national emergency, and three days later the NATO council formally asked him to name Eisenhower to lead NATO forces.

The military situation in Europe was not much improved over that in 1948, when Harriman had gone to Europe to represent the Marshall Plan. Now, the most pressing military question was whether American troops could be successfully withdrawn from Europe in the event of a Soviet invasion.[37]

When Eisenhower assumed command, the Truman administration was enveloped in a bitterly partisan debate with Congress over the President's authority to send troops overseas. Harriman became the link between the President and the new NATO commander, going out of his way to cultivate the promising friendship between them. He passed compliments back and forth and shared letters and bits of gossip.

On the imperative to rearm Europe, the general and the President were warm allies against the Taftites. But even as Eisenhower arrived in Europe, the move to make him the 1952 presidential nominee was building in both parties. Thomas E. Dewey, having twice lost White House races for the Republicans, had already endorsed him as the new GOP standard-bearer. Polls showed he had the support of Democratic governors and members of Congress.

Although the general was publicly coy with his political suitors, Harriman knew he had been thinking about running for the presidency for years. During the war, they had talked politics on occasions, and Eisenhower had been quick to appreciate public idolization after the invasion of France. He was torn, he told Averell, between running for President and taking a place on the sidelines as an elder statesman.

After the war, when Eisenhower left active service and became president of Columbia University, they had continued their casual friendship. Upon assuming the university leadership, the general promoted the idea of a Columbia University–sponsored forum where political figures and labor, government, and industry leaders could gather for long, uninhibited discussions of world affairs. Averell was anxious to help, and he was able to provide the perfect setting.

The Arden mansion had been vacated early in the war; and, like the Sun Valley Lodge and Challenger Inn, it had become a Navy convalescent hospital. Members of the family now had their cottages on the estate, and E.H.'s mansion was a cold, empty tax burden which Averell was anxious to shed. For what Eisenhower had in mind, it was ideal. Within easy reach of Manhattan, it still remained serene and remote; it was comfortable and it was large enough to accommodate dozens of scholars, government officials, and business people. It thus became the seat of Columbia's American Assembly, but by the time it was turned over to the university in May 1951, Eisenhower had resigned the Columbia presidency and returned to uniform as NATO commander. Averell was on hand for the inaugural event—a five-day consideration of U.S. relations with Western Europe.

One of the keynote speakers, as it happened, was Robert Taft, the nemesis of administration foreign policy, who naturally laid into the administration for pressing European rearmament. The administration was refusing to adopt a strategy to win the war in Korea, he charged, "but in Europe we have not hesitated to risk a third war over and over again."[38] Taft, Averell wrote Eisenhower, "thinks we made a great mistake in taking the responsibility of an American Supreme Commander in Europe, so maybe you ought to pack your grip and come home."[39]

A year after creation of the integrated force in Europe, Eisenhower commanded a paper army supported by nations under renewed duress and uncertain of their commitments. Inflation was on the loose. There were shortages of coal and steel, heavy trade deficits with the United States, and, in the case of Italy, stupendous unemployment. Eisenhower had to be concerned about morale. "It could be fatal," he wrote Harriman, "if the workmen of Italy, France, and Germany came to believe that workmen in Poland, Czechoslovakia, Hungary and so on were as well or even better off in their daily lives as are they, themselves.

"Yesterday, I was visited by a World War II officer, now a French businessman. He has been mayor of the same village in France for twenty-six years. He knows every man in it, and he told me that this is the first year in which many of these old friends of his have voted Communist in the sincere belief that conditions under any other kind of system would be better than they now are."[40]

Harriman did not have to be convinced. He was already cautioning the President against putting undue pressure on Europeans whose military budgets had doubled. Since the war had broken out in Korea he said, the United States had "pressured only for expansion of military effort, without due attention to equally vital economic stability."[41] Acheson agreed that rearmament was being pushed faster "than economic realities would permit."[42]

Hugh Gaitskell, Britain's chancellor of the exchequer, and René

Mayer, the French minister of finance, crossed the Atlantic with the same message for the American government. Britain's alarming balance-of-payments problem was getting worse. Cutting domestic programs to make ends meet, Clement Attlee's government was risking a potent political backlash. France, saddled with worsening shortages, was fighting its own war in Indochina.

The problem was that the rearmament objectives were being set by military men with little regard for political or economic concerns. With the North Atlantic Council about to meet in Ottawa, the French planned to call for a complete reassessment of member nations' economic ability to achieve rearmament goals. The idea received Washington's quick endorsement. "It made no sense," Acheson said later, "to destroy them in the name of defending them."[43] Before Mayer left town, Harriman, State Department policy planning chief Paul Nitze, and Pentagon officials took up the subject with the President, and Harriman was made the point man for the United States. "You have probably noticed the demand for a committee of so-called 'Wise Men,' to deal with the political and economic capabilities of Europe in the defense effort," he wrote Eisenhower after the talks with the French and British visitors ended. "Should this plan be adopted in Ottawa, I gather that I am to be hooked. I must confess that the work would be for me intensely interesting, an analytical job, which, as you know, I think should have been done some time ago."[44]

Indeed, he was hooked within hours. On September 19, the same day he wrote to Ike, the NATO ministers formally established a Temporary Council Committee, with a representative from each of the twelve member nations, to reconcile security objectives with economic output. The real work fell to the "Wise Men" of the three-member executive committee, chaired by Harriman, with Jean Monnet of France, and Britain's Gaitskell, who was shortly replaced by Sir Edwin Plowden, as its members. Under orders to report at the council's Rome meeting just two months later, Averell flew to Paris and launched a study that put the cohesion of the alliance to its first real test.

Under a crushing deadline, he had to obtain extraordinarily sensitive economic information which governments had never before released. He was acquainted with the difficulties of getting them to subordinate national prerogatives to regional authority, and his approach was as hard-nosed as he had been in pressuring the Europeans to agree on the division of Marshall Plan assistance.

Even though the French government had planted the idea for the undertaking, Monnet thought it hopeless. As principal architect of the Schuman Plan for the integration of the European coal and steel industries, he was more interested in the struggle to see that through than he was the Harriman-led study of NATO burden sharing. He was as outspoken as Averell, and not disposed to defer to the American chairman. Eric Roll, who was Plowden's deputy, would later recall with studied understatement, "There was some quite hard talking between them from time to time—on several occasions in the middle of the night."[45]

During the last days of converting country statistics into charts and graphs supporting the Wise Men's conclusions, work went on nearly around the clock. Exhausted and depressed, Plowden pleaded for an occasional day off "to relax and reflect," but the chairman ignored him.

The immediate problems before the alliance were so staggering that it seemed impossible to think seriously of the longer-range concerns that had brought it together.

There was no doubt that present commitments were inadequate, Plowden told Harriman, but most of the members were unable to do any more. "In short, the near term situation, both as regards the burden on national economies and the state of military preparedness, is worse than anything I expected."[46] Averell was scarcely less pessimistic. The dollar shortage in Europe was far more acute than he had imagined, and it was aggravated by a continuing coal shortage which paralyzed both industrial expansion and defense production.

In the end, the seven-hundred-page final report proposed a heavier burden for everyone: a total of fifty divisions—instead of the thirty-six previously planned—by the end of 1952, with an eventual force of ninety-five divisions to meet the Soviet threat.

The recommendations were not unexpected, but the details compelled serious attention. NATO members and Germany, the report concluded, needed to collectively spend $16 billion a year for three successive years to put NATO's crisis behind it.

Bitter as they were, the findings were adopted at the February meeting of the NATO ministers in Lisbon. The smaller countries, with Belgium most outspoken, took exception to several of the conclusions and stoutly maintained that the Wise Men had paid scant attention to the other nine members of the commission. The French said the goals were economically and politically impossible.

Harriman promised to expedite $250 million worth of American purchases of French military hardware and supplies as part of a procurement program designed to underpin all of the stressed allies by paying them to build what would in turn be given them.

Finally, Prime Minister Edgar Faure agreed to the Wise Men's call for fifteen French divisions for NATO, but he told Harriman it would cost him his head politically. And it did. His cabinet refused to raise taxes to support the commitment, and he was forced to resign.

European criticism of the goals as fanciful were not shared by the Pentagon. Joint Chiefs chairman Omar Bradley, who headed the American military delegation at Lisbon, balked when the recommendations were put to him for endorsement and insisted upon language stressing the urgency of meeting the targets. He and Harriman fell into a heated argument, which Harriman clearly could not win.[47]

At a delegation meeting, Acheson listened until "it seemed to be getting out of hand," then adjourned and sought a compromise. It took two more days of negotiations to find language acceptable to both the Wise Men and Bradley. In the end, the general still did not give flat endorsement to the proposed force levels, but he did agree to acknowledge that they would pose a powerful deterrent—in conjunction with the American nuclear arsenal.[48]

As Harriman expected, NATO would never meet the goals. But the existence of ambitious, politically agreed targets gave the alliance a momentum and political resolve that had been missing. For the first time, European defense had credibility. Said Plowden: "It broke the wartime practice of the military saying what they needed and the politicians setting out to meet it—if they could."[49] It put forces in a broader national-security context with military doctrine adapted to resources.

Even before Harriman went to work on the Wise Men's report, Congress passed a bill placing the expanding foreign-aid programs under the tent of a new agency and a single boss.

Earlier, Truman had considered turning the obscure National Security Resources Board, created by the 1947 National Security Act, into a powerful vehicle for mobilization of resources and delicately balancing priorities between Korea and NATO. Averell was his choice for the job, which would have made him a full-fledged member of the National Security Council. But at the last hour, Truman had decided against the shuffle and Averell remained Special Assistant to the President, still feeling that he was serving no critical purpose.

But with the creation of the new Mutual Security Administration, in the autumn of 1951, he became the czar of American foreign aid, taking responsibility for the Pentagon's Military Defense Assistance Program and the not-so-old-but-nevertheless-obsolete Economic Cooperation Administration, as well as for the Marshall Plan and the Point IV Program of technical assistance to underdeveloped countries. At last he held the equivalent of a Cabinet post and was in a position to exert heavy influence in the shaping of administration foreign policy and carrying through the rearming of Europe.

But a month after NATO ministers adopted the report of the Wise Men at Lisbon, Truman announced that he would not seek reelection. Averell, like the President, was suddenly a lame duck.

Chapter XVIII

IRAN
Oil, Mullahs, and Mosaddeq

The Fourth of July, 1951, was one of the rare days when Harriman stayed at home alone. Marie had gone to Paris, where her daughter Nancy was about to deliver a baby; the servants, the office staff, and the rest of Washington were celebrating the holiday. The White House, the State Department, and the Pentagon were deserted. Before noon Congress met in pro forma session to hear the traditional reading of the Declaration of Independence, and Chief Justice Fred Vinson addressed the nation over a radio hookup from his chambers at the Supreme Court. In spite of a threat of one of Washington's notorious summer thunderstorms, a quarter of a million people began gathering on the Washington Monument grounds to hear President Truman speak on the 175th anniversary of the Declaration.

The uproar over the MacArthur firing had abated; and on this lazy holiday afternoon, the administration was entertaining encouraging prospects of imminent cease-fire talks in Korea.

There was, however, rising alarm over another crisis in Iran, where oil, politics, and strategic location provided conditions for a collision between the Soviet Union and the West. The problem in the summer of 1951 was the doing of neither the Russians nor Iran's home-grown Communists, but a long-coming confrontation between the Iranian government and Great Britain. Four months earlier, a pro-Western prime minister, Ali Razmara, had been assassinated; and the caretaker government, intimidated by nationalist fanatics, had taken over the Anglo-

466

Iranian Oil Company and its great Persian Gulf oil refinery at Abadan. As a result, Britain's most prized overseas asset, remaining testament to its status as a world power, was seized without compensation. When authorities asked the assassin why he committed the crime, the twenty-six-year-old gunman's only reply had been, "Why do you give the country to foreigners so I must do this deed?"[1]

Undersecretary of State George McGhee, a Texas-born geologist who had long labored to head off the crisis, rushed back to Teheran days after Razmara's death and found the caretaker prime minister, Hosein Ala, unable even to recruit a cabinet. All of his candidates were of a moderate stripe and terrified of being killed. The fiery Mohammad Mosaddeq and his aroused National Front spat at any suggestion of accommodation with the British. Going on to London, McGhee had then been stonewalled by the British, who thought he was meddling and exerting unseemly pressure. In Teheran, Mosaddeq, a wealthy land-owner and former finance minister, replaced Ala at the head of the government.

Fearing imminent violence, the families of three thousand British production workers had been evacuated from Abadan, and several British warships, including the cruiser HMS *Mauritius*, had taken up positions offshore. The output of the world's largest refinery, capable of processing 500,000 barrels of oil a day, had already slowed drastically; under Britain's threat to withdraw all of its technicians, the plant faced a shutdown. Iran, meanwhile, refused to load tankers waiting in port and turned back sailors from the *Mauritius* who went ashore for supplies. Nationalist militants warned that a single shot from the British would start World War III.

"We have about ten days in which to get some action before the catastrophe of closing down of the plant takes place," U.S. ambassador Henry Grady cabled on July 1. "If the British think they can, as some directors have said, bring the Iranians to their senses by having the plant closed down, they are making a tragic mistake. Those who are making the policy on the oil question in London evidently are counting on Mosaddeq falling if the plant closes. This is very doubtful. In any case it is my opinion there is no chance of any reasonable Prime Minister succeeding him. It is all too likely that the country will quickly fall into a status of disintegration with all that implies."[2]

During the last week of June, Truman had called a National Security Council meeting on the situation and personally presided over the discussion, after which a declaration was issued setting down restoration of stability, support of the Shah, prevention of Communist subversion, and settlement of the oil dispute as U.S. national-security objectives.

But despairing over the weakness of Iran's moderates and the British government's deference to the unbending oil-company management, the administration found itself with only limited and unsatisfactory options. Certainly Washington was not inclined to take Iran's side against its own most important ally, but neither could it encourage British intransigence. If it did nothing, on the other hand, it might well see armed British intervention with Iran driven into the arms of the Soviet Union.

Under these circumstances, Dean Acheson and British ambassador Oliver Franks arrived at Harriman's door in midafternoon on the Fourth. They were shortly joined by McGhee, Deputy Undersecretary of State Freeman "Doc" Matthews, and Paul Nitze. Sipping drinks, listening to the occasional crackle of fireworks, and watching the holiday crowds along the Potomac, they talked until dusk.

Preventing armed intervention, they agreed, was the most urgent priority. Military action at Abadan would provide the Soviets the excuse they needed to move back into northern Iran to take oil fields where they had been denied a concession. But if violence broke out against British workers still at the refinery, London would have little choice except a military response. Acheson could even envision Mosaddeq inviting the Russians to come in order to prevent the British from moving on the refinery and the oil fields. It could end with Britain out of Iran altogether and the Soviet Union in control of the country's oil, not to mention a port on the Persian Gulf and a toehold in the Middle East. Almost as dangerous, in the secretary's mind, and probably more likely, was Britain's threat simply to remove its technicians and close the refinery responsible for 80 percent of Iran's oil revenues. Already in desperate economic straits, Iran would be plunged into chaos just as Grady had warned; and rather than being starved out of its belligerence, it might well see a Communist coup. Averell reiterated what he had been telling the President for weeks—that nothing could be accomplished unless the hand of Iranian moderates could be strengthened.

With extensive experience in both capitals, the imprimatur of the White House, a long-standing acquaintance with the young Shah of Iran, and the personal confidence of the President, Harriman seemed to stand a chance, if anybody did, of having some impact. He had been keeping the President abreast of the situation in Iran, and he had been at the National Security Council meeting when Truman had codified the United States' interest in the issue. When Acheson had called and asked to have the gathering at his house on the Fourth, Averell knew he would shortly be on his way to Iran, and, for once, he was not enthusiastic about a presidential mission. He was busy with European rearmament, the foreign-aid bill struggling through Congress, and a reorganization of the United States' foreign-aid bureaucracy. And still hoping to testify in Senate hearings on MacArthur's dismissal, he had been working overtime on his long account of what happened in the Far East negotiations back at Yalta.

He could see little chance of accomplishing anything in Teheran; and even if he did, he did not relish the thought of negotiating with Iranian radicals on one side and his friends in Britain, who fully shared responsibility for the crisis, on the other. The United States' own relations with the Iranian government were sliding downhill, with the nationalists convinced that Washington was moving in lockstep with the British government and the oil company. He did not have to go to Teheran to know that the Shah was in a poor position to influence Mosaddeq and the National Front.

Furthermore, as McGhee had found, both the Labour government and Anglo-Iranian company officials regarded U.S. policy as "aggressive" toward Middle Eastern oil.[3] In fact AICO officials blamed the new militancy in Iran on a deal the U.S.-controlled Arab-American Oil Company had made with the government of Saudi Arabia. Concerned over Saudi unhappiness, ARAMCO had the previous year torn up its seventeen-year-old agreement with the kingdom and had written a new one providing a fifty-fifty split of profits. Britain's refusal to do the same in Iran had inflamed nationalist sentiment and made an unlikely political hero of the seventy-year-old Mosaddeq.

The Anglo-Iranian Oil Company had been taking lopsided advantage of the Iranians for as long as it had held the concession on the world's most productive oil fields. The agreement, dated six days before the outbreak of World War I, had been urged upon the British government by Winston Churchill, who realized that oil would soon power all of the naval vessels in the world. Government officials in London had long acknowledged the unfairness of the arrangement; years earlier, Foreign Minister Ernest Bevin, who died three months before the Razmara assassination, had suggested a fifty-fifty profit split with Iran, but oil men had scoffed at the idea.

After Franks reported the possibility of Harriman's going to Teheran, Foreign Secretary Herbert Morrison warned the State Department that the American's appearance there would cause Mosaddeq to believe that serious differences existed between the U.S. and British governments and that the United States would side with Iran in order to keep the Russians out of the country. Instead of a presidential troubleshooter in Iran, Britain preferred a strong U.S. endorsement of a World Court recommendation that the oil company's management remain in place, operating under an international board of supervisors.[4]

But by the time Morrison's warning arrived, Truman had already accepted the plan to send Harriman to Teheran as his special emissary. After meetings with Averell and Acheson, he had cabled Mosaddeq to emphasize the gravity of the dispute and urge him to consider the World Court finding, concluding by offering Averell's services: "I have discussed this matter at length with Mr. W. Averell Harriman, who as you know is one of my closest advisers and one of our most eminent citizens. Should you be willing to receive him, I should be happy to have him go to Teheran as my personal representative to talk over with you this immediate and pressing situation."[5]

Morrison was not the only skeptic. When Francis Shephard, the British ambassador in Teheran, whom Acheson found an "unimaginative disciple of the 'whiff of grapeshot' school of diplomacy," heard about it, he declared it pointless.[6] American ambassador Henry Grady disliked the prospect of a big gun from the White House coming into his territory to take over a problem. And Mosaddeq's reaction to Truman's cable was a burst of laughter at the President's endorsement of the World Court recommendations. He followed with such a profuse denunciation of U.S. policy that Grady didn't bother calling attention to the Harriman mission suggested at the end of the message.

Infuriated at the response, Acheson ordered Grady to see the Prime Minister again. The Harriman mission, he said, was "the one new positive element contained in the President's proposal and is the step to which the President and I attach greatest significance. I cannot believe that Mosadeq's [sic] initial reaction will, upon reflection, be his final one. Considerations of courtesy will lead him, I am convinced, to take no hasty or abrupt action, to give President's message full consideration, and to receive President's personal rep who can give both you and Mosadeq the benefit of great thought which President has put to this matter and receive any suggestions which Mosadeq may have. Therefore request that you see Mosadeq again as speedily as possible and in tactful way, which I know you will employ, urge these considerations upon him."[7] After Grady's return visit, Mosaddeq relented, and Harriman began putting together his team.

The task before him was to convince the Iranians that taking over the oil company was foolhardy for technical reasons alone. Although he was not a stranger to the oil business, he proposed to put the argument into the hands of an expert. Within an hour of Mosaddeq's acceptance, he had lined up Walter J. Levy, who had been the top oil analyst for the OSS during World War II. In the intelligence community, Levy was remembered for having pinpointed the location of Hitler's synthetic fuel plants by analyzing German freight routes and schedules. During the development of the Marshall Plan, he had taken off from his oil consulting business in New York to serve as the petroleum expert on Harriman's Committee of Nineteen.

With Levy aboard, the team was completed with the addition of Deputy Undersecretary of State William Roundtree, who had worked for Grady in Greece; Vernon Walters, who had been promoted to lieutenant colonel and returned to Europe as Eisenhower's interpreter; and Brigadier General Robert Landry, the ranking Air Force aide at the White

House, sent along by the President to take care of security and administrative work.

Ten days after the meeting at his house, Averell was escorted before cameras in the Rose Garden of the White House, patted on the back, and sent on his way by Truman, Acheson, and Marshall. As he departed, the situation was still deteriorating. During a brief stop in Paris, where he collected Walters and Marie, who was going along to shop for rugs and provide a demonstration of her husband's confidence in Teheran's security, he got an even gloomier assessment from Chancellor of the Exchequer Hugh Gaitskell. If tension was rising between London and Teheran, it was also increasing between the Iranian Communists and Mosaddeq's followers in the right wing National Front. Gaitskell was afraid that factional fighting might break out at any moment and set the stage for Soviet intervention or an outright Communist takeover. If that happened, British lives would be endangered and Attlee would have no alternative but military intervention.

When the party arrived in Teheran twenty-four hours later, Gaitskell's gloomy assessment proved to have been unexaggerated. Ten thousand demonstrators milled around the American embassy shouting "Death to Harriman," and riots broke out as the party was whisked away from the airport to Sahebgaranieh Palace in the foothills of the Elburz Mountains north of the city. As Averell signed royal guest books and paid his courtesy calls, thousands of protestors pressed into Majlis Square carrying banners denouncing the mission, the United States, and Great Britain. There, the leftists were confronted by members of the National Front, and pitched battles with sticks, stones, and fists broke out. Police rode into the melee on horseback and Army troops arrived in trucks and armored personnel carriers, clearing the square with tear gas, only to see the rioting spread. As the Americans dined in their palace garden late on their first evening in Iran, the chatter of gunfire echoed sporadically through willow trees and across the lily ponds.

The next morning, as Averell prepared for his first meeting with Mosaddeq, the city remained on the verge of an explosion. Authorities counted two dozen dead and scores injured from the previous day. Government police closed the Communist newspaper and raided party headquarters; and when demonstrators again took to the streets, demanding the bodies of the rioters killed the day before, martial law was imposed.

Everywhere he went, Harriman was preceded, surrounded, and trailed by heavily armed security forces, but in spite of the uproar, he rode in an open car with Marie, wearing a Panama hat, which, she kept reminding him, made them an unmissable target. The danger, he insisted, was not from an assassin but from a wild shot from one of the obviously frightened security men.

The disorder provoked by his arrival was scarcely more unsettling than his meetings with Mosaddeq. Neither his briefing books nor travels around the world had prepared him to do business with the new leader of Iran. The Prime Minister was a cartoonist's dream. A tiny, birdlike man with black eyes, a slick bald head, and an enormous beak of nose, he could produce copious outpourings of tears in an instant, or fall into a dead faint, as he had at crucial moments during debate in Parliament.

Caught in a deception, as he often was, he would respond with disconcerting, childlike laughter or a heart-rending confession, often followed by a repeat of the devious tactic with an ill-concealed new twist. He projected helplessness; and while he was obviously as much a captive as a leader of the nationalist fanatics, he relented on nothing. Under pressure, he would take to his bed, seeming at times to have only a tenuous hold on life itself as he lay in his pink pajamas, his hands folded on his chest, eyes fluttering, and breath shallow.

At the appropriate moment, though, he could transform himself from a frail, decrepit shell of man into a wily, vigorous adversary. He would arrive at the entrance of Harriman's guest palace shuffling slowly along while leaning heavily on his cane; but once inside, he would throw the cane aside and sometimes forget where it was. The first time he was presented to Marie Harriman, he took her hand and didn't stop kissing until he was halfway to her elbow. Later, he could be caught stealing glances at her, sometimes losing his train of thought altogether.

Although the Abadan nationalization and his vehemence against the British made him a hero to the Iranian masses, Mosaddeq lived in fear of assassination. In the presence of his countrymen, he would say nothing of consequence about the crisis; and in his negotiations with Harriman, he declined to use an Iranian interpreter. Alone with Averell and Walters, he would speak in a whisper whenever they came to a matter he regarded as sensitive, which was anything to do with Abadan, oil, the British, the Communists, or the Americans.

In their first meetings, he refused to yield an inch on any of his demands. His quarrel, he insisted over and over, was with the oil company; and he would speak to no British official unless the Attlee government first accepted all points of the nationalization law without reservation. The demand, Harriman told him over and over, was out of the question, for it would set a precedent that might be applied when any British possession was taken anywhere in the world. Mosaddeq was, nevertheless, glad to have a third party try to help find a way out of the crisis, and that was some small encouragement.

Though the old man was politically skillful, it was obvious that he truly knew nothing about the international oil business. So, finding uncustomary patience, Harriman and Levy spent hours trying to acquaint him with the stupendous challenges before his country if it tried to go it alone without Britain's technical expertise. Iran had no transportation or marketing system, and no prospect of operating Abadan with other foreign experts. None of the considerations appeared to have occurred to Mosaddeq.

He was, nevertheless, unmoved by their warnings of the economic chaos that would follow loss of the refinery and of the $27 million in yearly royalties. Nor did he seem impressed by the United States' nightmare of Iran falling under Communist control. If there was real danger of that, he told Harriman, it would be up the United States and Britain to prevent it. On that score, he was offered no comfort. A Communist takeover, Harriman acknowledged, would be undeniably "unfortunate for the Free World," but for Iran, "it would be the end."[8]

Day after day, the conversations went nowhere. Walters thought the Prime Minister had an upside down version of Lenin's maxim that it was sometimes necessary to take one step backward in order to take two forward. "Dr. Mossadegh" he said, "had learned to take one step forward in order to take two backward. After a day's discussions, Mr. Harriman would bring Mossadegh to a certain position. The next day when we returned to renew the discussion, not only was Mossadegh not at the position where he was at the end of the previous day, he wasn't even at the position where he had been the day before that. He was somewhere back around the middle of the day before yesterday."[9]

Since he had not been invited to mediate, Harriman's objective was to promote direct talks that would ease the danger of British military intervention. The problem was that the Prime Minister himself had created an atmosphere that made negotiation nearly impossible. Under the circumstances, his extremism was as much a requirement of practical politics as a product of emotion or conviction. Members of Parliament were in the same trap. After thirty-five senators and a dozen members of the Majlis listened to Harriman and Levy argue the economic folly of driving Britain from the Iranian oil industry, several came around and privately agreed that their government had made a grave mistake but stated that nothing could be done to change it because of Mosaddeq's popularity with the masses.

Nor was any consolation to be found in the Iranian press. It had naively expected Harriman to embrace Iran's argument the moment he saw the situation for himself. When he called a news conference and opened it with an appeal for "reason as well as enthusiasm," the session collapsed. An Iranian reporter jumped to his feet and shouted that Harriman must understand that "we and the Iranian people all support Premier Mosaddeq and oil nationalization." With that, the reporter turned and walked out, followed by the rest of the Teheran press corps.[10]

As Washington already knew, the Shah could do nothing. Besides being frightened and politically paralyzed, he was recovering from an appendectomy, made far more serious than it would have otherwise been because it was delayed for the arrival of an American surgeon. The Shah encouraged Harriman to keep trying to reason with Mosaddeq's government, but he confessed that he could no more back away from the nationalization law than could Mosaddeq.

Harriman resorted to the pallid argument that the Iranians needed to make some public relations gesture to prevent the world from seeing them as the culprit in the crisis. Meanwhile he urged Washington to keep pressure on London to postpone a full-scale debate in Parliament and to hold off announcing a schedule for withdrawing its technicians from the refinery and oil fields.

After days of wrangling, Mosaddeq suddenly sent word through an intermediary that he was prepared to receive a minister from the British government. Harriman and Walters rushed to the Prime Minister's bed-side, and to the surprise of neither, they got an entirely different story. The situation was the same. Iran would receive a British emissary only if the Attlee government first accepted all nine points of the nationaliza-tion law.

As long as Mosaddeq refused to budge, making it impossible for the Shah or moderates on the government oil commission to do anything, Harriman figured he had nothing to lose by taking his case to the only influential Iranians with freedom to move—the fundamentalist clerics fanning hatred of the British and keeping the irresistible heat on Mosad-deq. The idea got no support from Iranian contacts or members of Harriman's own party, but he was not dissuaded. Furthermore, he had decided to take his case to the most extreme mullah of them all, the Ayatollah Sayed Abolghassem Kashani. "The Black Eminence," as Ka-shani was known, controlled the mobs that had greeted Harriman's ar-rival in Teheran, and it was widely believed that he had had a hand in the assassination of Razmara.

Accompanied by Walters, Harriman went to Kashani's house unan-nounced, knocked on the door, and asked to see the holy man. They were received in a small, dimly lit room where thick carpets and heavy curtains exaggerated the stifling afternoon heat, deadened sounds and seemed to soak up the oxygen.

Kashani ignored ordinary courtesy. There would be no help from him in easing the pressure on Mosaddeq. He would speak to none of the British "dogs," whether they represented the oil company, the govern-ment, or the press. He had no interest in Harriman's presence in Tehe-ran. As far as he was concerned, the United States was only conspiring with London to perpetuate colonialism, add to Iran's misery, and steal its natural wealth.

It gave him personal satisfaction, he said, that the late prime minis-ter, Ali Razmara, who had been nothing but a lackey for the British interests in Iran, had paid with his life. Furthermore, he wanted to assure Harriman that the blood of Mosaddeq would also flow if Mosaddeq attempted a retreat from the requirements of the nationalization law. Coming from Kashani, Averell took the vitriol as an outright threat on the Prime Minister's life, which Kashani no doubt expected him to repeat. The face-to-face encounter better than anything explained Mosaddeq's behavior and the Shah's paralysis. Without the assent of Kashani and fundamentalists like him, Mosaddeq's popularity brought him nothing.

Beyond his hatred of the British, Kashani despised anything that smacked of Western modernism. As far as he was concerned, Iran's black gold could stay in the ground. It was just as valuable there. Indeed if exploited, even by Iranians, the wealth it would bring into the country would lead to modernization and the subversion of religion. He wished Harriman to repeat that view to President Truman, and to advise the President that Iran wanted none of the U.S. aid that was being talked about.

The atmosphere was as intimidating as the threats. Heavily bearded and wearing a black turban, the ayatollah sat on a sofa directly in front of his visitors, never removing his gaze from Harriman's face or looking at the heavily perspiring Walters. After a while both Averell and the colonel were sure that the draperies were moving, that someone was listening behind them.

Although he was on the defensive from the moment he sat down, Harriman managed to reply to a few of the assaults without anger. But then Kashani, stroking his beard and assuming an almost theatrical air of intimidation, suggested that Harriman should not take even his own personal safety for granted. Another American, a Major Embry, had come to Iran early in the century, he said, and "dabbled in oil, which was none of his business, and aroused the hatred of the people."[11] One day when he was walking on the street in Teheran, he was attacked and shot down. The authorities rescued him and rushed him to the hospital, but a mob followed, burst into the operating room, and butchered him on the operating table.

Harriman saw the point of the story long before Kashani got through the details. The ayatollah had overplayed his role, and Harriman was suddenly furious. Threatening Mosaddeq was one thing; threatening a representative of the President of the United States was quite another. Walters watched Harriman's eyes narrow and his lips tighten as Kashani finished the tale and then asked whether he understood. There was dead silence. Harriman returned the mullah's stare without blinking. Walters could see that he was seething with anger rather than frightened. When he spoke, his voice was cold and even.

"Your eminence, you must understand that I have been in many dangerous situations in my life," he said, "and I do not frighten easily."

The ayatollah was not a foolish man, he went on. Therefore, the ayatollah knew that any harm to an envoy of the President would not be without heavy consequences. Besides, he would be worth nothing to Iran if he were dead. Kashani was taken aback, and, Harriman thought, showed a flicker of humor. "Well, at least," he said, "there was no harm in trying."[12]

In their own way, Harriman found the British as difficult as the extremists in Teheran. Where oil and Iran were concerned, the colonialist mindset survived. Neither the Labour government nor the Conservative opposition revealed much understanding of the nationalist sentiment underlying the crisis.

"In spite of the fact that the British consider oil interest in Iran their greatest overseas asset, no minister has visited Iran as far as I can find out, except for Churchill and Eden on wartime business," Harriman cabled Acheson and the President after he had been in Teheran for ten days. "Oil company directors have rarely come. Situation that has developed here is tragic example of absentee management combined with world-wide growth of nationalism in undeveloped countries. There is no doubt Iranians are ready to make sacrifices in oil income to be rid of what they consider to be British colonial practices. Large groups are in mood to face any consequences to achieve this objective. It is clear that British reporting and recommendations from here have not been realistic, and it seems essential that member of British government find out for himself what is going on here."[13]

By the last week of July, Mosaddeq was showing signs of relenting. The Shah had gently encouraged him to seek a settlement, as, apparently, had the government's chief oil adviser, who confessed to being shaken by what he had heard from the American experts. Between his talks with Harriman, Mosaddeq had increasingly lengthy sessions with his cabinet and members of the oil commission. From them, there finally emerged a draft of conditions under which the Prime Minister would agree to discuss renewal of oil operations with the British.

They were, Harriman immediately saw, unacceptable from the British viewpoint, but the draft nevertheless represented a remarkable turnaround for Mosaddeq. From it, Harriman was able to work out language that provided the Prime Minister cover from accusations that he was retreating from nationalization while allowing the British to deny bowing to Iranian demands. "In case the British government on behalf of the former Anglo-Iranian Oil Company recognizes the principle of nationalization of the oil industry in Iran," said the key paragraph, "the Iranian government would be prepared to enter into negotiations with representatives of the British government on behalf of the former company."[14] Mosaddeq had abandoned his position that his fight was solely with the oil company. More significantly, he had dropped his demand that all nine points of the law had to be accepted in advance.

On July 24, Harriman told Washington that opportunity was at hand. "With all the increasing difficulties and grave danger involved in delay, I believe the sooner a member of the British government with appropriate advisers, including representatives of the AIOC, comes to Teheran, the better it will be."[15] Given the magnitude of the Iranian concessions, Harriman hoped that Attlee would agree to send Gaitskell, or even Foreign Minister Morrison.

The next communication to reach the Iranian government from Britain was not a response to the Harriman formula, however, but a four-point demand that Iran accept the ruling of the World Court and take steps to end the harassment of British oil workers.

The message had been discussed before Iran's revised position had been sent; and now with Mosaddeq awaiting a response to his concessions, British ambassador Shephard delivered the demands, telling the Iranians that they had been read and approved by Harriman.

Averell demanded an explanation, and Shephard could offer only a mixup in timing, but over the next two days he continued to tell Iranian officials that their proposal would not be accepted unless the conditions contained in the British cable were first met. At the same time, Harriman was prevailing upon Mosaddeq to disregard Shephard's efforts to negotiate on a different track and to say nothing until Britain's formal reply was forthcoming.

For psychological reasons, he had hoped to remain in Teheran while the answer was shaped in London, fearing if he went to Britain his credibility with Iranians already suspicious of secret Anglo-American collaboration would be undermined. But with Shephard's efforts to exert pressure, it had become necessary to follow at close hand the formulation of London's reply. Accordingly, he took off from Teheran just before midnight on July 27.

With the rest of the American contingent from Sahebgaranieh Palace, he arrived on Saturday morning, and spent most of the day in meetings with Attlee, Morrison, and other officials of the Cabinet at 10 Downing Street. That night, he sent Grady the formal response that Britain was prepared to make. The reply made no mention of the World Court, and it specifically noted the government's recognition of "the principle of nationalization." If Mosaddeq found the answer acceptable, a British mission would be prepared to leave for Teheran within twenty-four hours.[16]

Even before the Iranian answered, though, British officials had decided that their emissary would not be Gaitskell or Morrison, as Harriman had hoped, but Neville Gass, who had been chief negotiator of the hated existing agreement between the oil company and the government in Teheran. Walter Levy, who had remained in London while Harriman was spending the Sunday with Attlee at Chequers, knew that Gass was detested in Teheran and that Iranians remembered him as a haughty and imperious man who had told their negotiators he had no interest in "rug bargaining."[17]

When a Sunday-afternoon strategy meeting was called at Gass's house, Levy declined to go, since he would have been compelled to argue against the the host's selection. The meeting was then shifted to the Foreign Office; and in front of Gass, Levy warned that his presence would wreck any chance of resolving the crisis. Sending Gass to negotiate with the Iranians, he said, would be like sending a Jew, such as himself, to deal with the Saudis. If Britain insisted on making Gass Britain's special negotiator, Levy declared, Harriman would refuse to go back. Gass listened without any sign of anger, and when Levy had finished, he volunteered to leave the meeting so the choice of a negotiator could be reconsidered.

The threat by Harriman's oil expert worked. With Gass out of the room, the ministers agreed to replace him with Sir Richard Stokes, a millionaire industrialist and former Lord Privy Seal. By the time Harriman returned from Chequers, the minicrisis was over; and on Monday, Morrison announced in Commons that Stokes would go to Teheran.

The press declared the crisis settled. "W. Averell Harriman has worked a miracle in Iran," *Business Week* magazine declared. "He's averted an explosion over the Iranian oil issue, which three weeks ago threatened to blow the West out of the Middle East." With that glowing conclusion, it went on to report that now it was "just a question of who gets what and who does what"—as if those were piddling matters.[18] Truman's troubleshooter was also on the cover of *Newsweek*, the subject of a full-scale profile tracing his business career and political conversion and recording his triumph in Iran under the headline, "How Harriman Swung the Truce Deal."[19]

The reports were as erroneous as they were optimistic. Indeed, Harriman had to rush back to Teheran on July 31 for additional stroking of Mosaddeq and some minor amendments to Britain's statement before the invitation was formally extended, and it was not until August 4 that Stokes and his delegation arrived.

Although there was no deal at all, Harriman still thought there was a chance of getting one. Stokes brought with him proposals that Averell considered within the formula that he and Mosaddeq had agreed upon. British experts immediately went to work with Iranian negotiators, and Mosaddeq and Stokes jointly asked Harriman to remain in Teheran while they deliberated.

Having made the concessions necessary to get the talks started, Mosaddeq again became as unbending and unreasonable as he had been when Harriman arrived. In his first meeting with London's emissary, he inquired whether his visitor was Roman Catholic. When the nonplussed Stokes replied in the affirmative, Mosaddeq gravely pronounced this a serious obstacle to meaningful negotiations. The problem, he said, was that Catholic faith did not recognize divorce. Muslims, on the other hand, did accept divorce, and Iran had merely divorced the Anglo-Iranian Oil Company. The crisis was nothing more than the dissolution of a bad marriage. With that, he broke into his familiar cackle, which Harriman finally overcame by promising to pass the clever observation along to President Truman.

Stokes appreciated neither the analogy nor the humor. Divorce of a wife might be acceptable, he stiffly conceded, but neither Muslims nor Catholics would condone her murder, and that was what had happened to the oil company. The riposte threw the Prime Minister into another convulsion of giggles.

After the first meeting, Harriman wanted to bow out and leave Stokes and Mosaddeq to talk alone and off the record; but to placate the Prime Minister once again, he had to fly to Abadan and join Stokes in an inspection of the refinery and a tour of Iranian workers' housing. Carefully protecting his neutrality, he made a point of flying in his own plane and taking several Iranians with him rather than traveling with the British party. The refinery was shut down, its storage tanks filled to the brim; and with nothing to do, British technicians either remained in their homes or busied themselves with construction projects.

Iranian officials were less interested in talking about the idled refinery, waiting tankers, and lost revenue than in conducting Harriman through the village where the oil company's twelve thousand Iranian employees lived. Escorted by Hussein Makki, an ambitious nationalist politician who had taken over the refinery manager's comfortable, air-conditioned office, Harriman tramped through the workers' quarters hovel by hovel. All the while, Makki railed at the evils of the British and their cruel subjugation of the workers. Harriman conceded nothing, but when he returned to Teheran, he cabled Washington that all the complaints about company housing were fully justified. The slums around Abadan were "typical of the Middle East," he reported to the President, but, nevertheless, "shocking for housing of employees of a large western oil company."[20]

When the negotiations at last began, Britain offered to transfer the refinery and the rest of Anglo-Iranian assets to a new National Iranian Oil Company, with another British company to market Abadan's products. Profits would be divided fifty-fifty with the Iranian government, and British technicians would continue to oversee oil field and refinery operations.

Not even refinery ownership and the even profit split was enough, however. Mosaddeq would accept no arrangement leaving management in the hands of the British. Iran would be disposed to accept a British organization that would market Iranian oil, he told Harriman, but he would never be able to sell his people on allowing the foreign organization to run the refinery.

With August, Teheran's heat was debilitating even in the guest palace on a hillside outside the city. The novelty had worn off. The physical discomfort and the futility of the negotiations made Harriman snappish and anxious to get back to Washington. The only antidote for the tedium and frustration was Marie's whimsical view of security, diplomacy, and the great and small men who plied the trade, especially her husband and the leader of Iran.

Her repertoire included hilarious allusions to Averell's legendary parsimony and observations on Mosaddeq's sex appeal. In spite of all precautions, including shipments of food and bottled water from the embassy, Averell fell victim to the dread "Teheran Tummy"; and while the veteran globe-trotter was confined, treating himself with paregoric, his wife conducted a successful search for quality Persian rugs. When he recovered, bounding down the stairs of the palace saying, "I feel like a million dollars," she cracked, "Oh, I'm so sorry you're still not feeling well, Ave."[21]

On Fridays, the Muslim sabbath, they took flying trips around the country so they could escape the heat in the air-conditioned *Constellation*. Evidently thinking no one had guessed why they flew about with no destination, Harriman bristled at Walters's suggestion that it was an unseemly indulgence to cool off in an airliner burning eight hundred gallons of fuel an hour. "If you had seen my income tax returns over a period of years," he growled, "you would know that I have bought a number of these for the United States government."[22]

Although attention had turned to the talks between Mosaddeq and the British minister, Harriman's security continued to cause acute concern, even after the anti-American demonstrations and the "Death to Harriman" chants had subsided. Plots were still whispered about by tipsters, and threats were regularly delivered to the embassy.

Hours after he had retired one night, the CIA's Teheran station chief, a small, nervous, round-cheeked man Marie had named "Chipmunk," arrived at the palace in a state of alarm. Agency sources in Paris had reported that Iranian Communists had dispatched an assassin for Teheran with Harriman as his target. The station chief's instructions were to notify the presidential envoy immediately. Failing to understand why her husband could not be told of his imminent death when he awoke in the morning, Marie ordered Chipmunk back into the sultry night, warning him that he, too, would be in danger of termination if he awakened Harriman with a story of an assassination plot in Paris.

Mosaddeq and Stokes tried for days to find an opening on refinery operating arrangements, but everything offered was deemed British interference in the eyes of Mosaddeq or outrageously impractical in the view of Stokes. Like Harriman, the British negotiator adapted to Mosaddeq's weeping, illness, and hysterical laughter at unpredictable moments, but Stokes made a serious blunder in offending Hosein Ala, who was Averell's most useful contact and one of the few moderates with any influence on the Prime Minister.

After three weeks, Harriman and the British negotiator agreed there was little chance of accomplishing anything. Whenever Mosaddeq had no other objection to Stokes's proposals, he fell back on his excuse that he could not sell them to his people. Exasperated, the British emissary presented him with an ultimatum—prepare to negotiate seriously within twenty-four hours, or the delegation would go home to London. That, too, was a mistake, for it angered moderates like Ala who were sympathetic to a negotiated settlement. Harriman's patience with the Prime Minister had run out, too. It was impossible to deal with him. "In his dream world," he told Washington, "the simple passage of legislation nationalizing the oil industry creates profitable business and everyone is expected to help Iran on terms he lays down. He appears to ignore all of the information and advice Levy and I have been trying to give him and his associates during the past weeks."[23]

The next day, Stokes began preparations to go home, and Harriman declared the negotiations suspended. He, too, was leaving, he told Mosaddeq, because he had other things to do. The Prime Minister hobbled out of the palace garden to a cluster of reporters waiting outside. "The result is nothing," he wailed. "It is no good. Everything is finished."[24]

Before leaving, Harriman made a last call on the Shah, and for the first time, they talked about the possibility of removing Mosaddeq from office. Trying not to sound alarmist, Harriman suggested that the Shah get Mosaddeq before Mosaddeq got him.[25] But the ruler of the Peacock Throne was still far from ready to challenge the Prime Minister. Unless Mosaddeq resigned, he could see no chance of naming a moderate to lead the government.

Resignation, Harriman was sure, was out of the question, and even if Mosaddeq did somehow leave office, his departure in itself would not restore stability. A weak successor, the Shah agreed, would fail. A satisfactory solution would require exiling or imprisoning "the trouble makers of both extremes—the Communists and the fanatical Nationalists," and in Harriman's opinion the Shah was not up to the task. He was "high minded," but "lacking in decisiveness in dealing with critical situations."[26]

Word trickled out that Mosaddeq planned at last to "open his heart" when Averell paid his final call. But "he did nothing of the sort," Harriman recorded in a note on their final meeting, he only "returned to his original hazy thoughts."[27]

After all the humoring and pampering, Averell did have one small triumph before his departure. If the British oil concession was an affront to Iranian sovereignty, he told Mosaddeq, so was the Soviet Union's caviar concession. The Soviets were taking the world's finest caviar from Iran, packaging it in the USSR, and exporting it all over the world with Russian labels. Mosaddeq found the logic impeccable, and when the caviar concession expired some months later, Iran refused to renew it.[28]

Aside from lowered tensions, Harriman left the situation as he had found it. The prospect of a settlement was no worse, but it certainly was no better. Still, the mission was not the failure that he labeled it in his bitter disappointment. It had prevented the crisis from slipping out of control, bringing military intervention and, perhaps, even a war over Iran.

Determined to salvage something more, Harriman had arranged a stop in Yugoslavia to see Marshal Tito on the way home and encourage him in his brash course of independence from Moscow. The renegade of the Communist bloc was anxious for his flirtation with the West to stay on the minds of the Kremlin, and Harriman was happy to help. When Tito had first broken with Stalin in 1948, Harriman had made hurried plans to fly in from Paris to confer with him; but the cautious State Department had waved him off. Now, however, Washington was ready to give a symbolic show of support.

Because of the unpredictable schedule in Teheran, there was little time for arrangements for the stop in Belgrade. For two hours, Harriman's plane flew in circles over Greece while the crew awaited a landing clearance, which never came. Finally, running low on fuel, they went on without it, touching down as their fuel tanks registered precariously close to empty.[29]

Averell spent five hours at Tito's summer palace near Bled before going on to London to give the British government his view of the breakdown in Teheran. His advice to Attlee and the Cabinet was merely to let Iran simmer for the time being. The atmosphere was still dangerous, but agreement with Mosaddeq was out of the question and the Shah had nowhere to turn. In the long run, however, the situation was not lost. Iran was in steep economic decline, and the Prime Minister would eventually suffer the political consequences. If Britain and the United States kept themselves at a distance, Iranians would be more likely to blame their plight on Mosaddeq's failure than on foreign interference. For the immediate future, the West's best hope was to encourage the Shah without pressuring him.

Politically, this cautious approach was hardly the most popular for Attlee, and he warned that he could not allow the standoff to drift indefinitely. He urgently wanted the United States with him if circumstances forced him to move, but he agreed that Britain and the United States "should take an independent though closely coordinated line on the situation as it develops."[30]

Soon after Harriman returned to Washington, Mosaddeq upped the ante. In a letter to Harriman through the Iranian embassy, the Prime Minister announced that he would cancel the residence permits of all the remaining British refinery workers unless Britain came to terms in two weeks. Attlee's response to the threat was to send more warships to stand off the coast as the technicians, jeered by Iranian crowds, were expelled from the country. Against the United States' advice, Britain then took its case to the United Nations Security Council, and Mosaddeq flew to New York to direct Iran's argument personally.

Appearing more ailing that ever, he arrived with his physician-son and his nurse–daughter-in-law at his side. He checked into a hospital suite, where he received a procession of diplomats. While his lieutenants successfully turned back the British resolution condemning Iran, he captivated the American press, traveling down to Washington and checking into the presidential suite at Walter Reed Army Hospital for further medical treatment. There, the Truman administration tried once more to sell him on accommodation with the British. Acheson, Paul Nitze, and Harriman all sat at the bedside and accomplished nothing. After a four-hour visit, Acheson felt he had been "walking in a maze and every so often finding [himself] at the beginning again."[31]

Unlike the secretary and Leon Henderson, who had replaced Grady in Teheran, Harriman thought talking with Mosaddeq any more was a waste of time. Britain fared no better. London compounded its mistake of going to the Security Council, in his view, when it tried to pressure the Shah into moving against the Prime Minister. To make it worse, it had pushed Sayed Zia, whom moderates regarded as a shameless Anglophile and Harriman considered incompetent, as Mosaddeq's successor. When Herbert Morrison came to Washington for talks in September, Harriman warned that Britain was on a course that "would render the situation yet more explosive." It was an approach, he said curtly, that was "calculated to worsen rather than improve matters."[32]

Two months after the Prime Minister departed Washington, the Truman administration ceased its military aid to the Iranian government and sharply trimmed economic assistance. But ever concerned over the ultimate danger of Iran being swept into the Communist orbit, it continued efforts to establish negotiations even after Iran severed diplomatic relations with London. As time ran out on the Truman administration,

Acheson tried to arrange a deal in which the United States would advance Iran millions of dollars against future oil deliveries while the issues of the AIOC's canceled concession would be settled by international arbitrators.

In the end, the crisis was resolved, not by negotiation but with the expedient Averell had discreetly suggested to the Shah—the ouster of Mosaddeq.

The Shah signed a decree dismissing the Prime Minister, only to see the royal messenger put under arrest when it was delivered. With that, the Shah fled into exile in Iraq, but in the turmoil that followed, the Army rallied behind him, and the Eisenhower administration used the CIA to provide the "stiffening" Harriman had found missing. With ease, CIA operative Kermit Roosevelt helped organize pro-Shah demonstrations, and General Fazollah Zahedi, the erstwhile interior minister, emerged from hiding to take over the government.

After being put on trial, convicted, and sent to prison for three years, Mosaddeq returned to his estate—and lived another twelve years under house arrest. With the Shah in control of the country, Britain agreed to join a consortium to market Iranian oil, Iran receiving the same fifty-fifty split the Saudis received from ARAMCO. Harriman and the Shah remained friends over the years, the ruler visiting Sun Valley to ski, and Harriman calling on him in Teheran in later troubleshooting journeys around the world.

Nearly thirty years later, the same forces that produced the oil crisis overthrew the once-hesitant Shah, who had come to rule as well as reign after Mosaddeq was deposed. His fall produced the disintegration that Harriman had feared and plunged President Jimmy Carter into a crisis that cost him the White House. Harriman was by then an old man anxious for diplomatic bit parts. But he was never called as the United States and Iran entered a long era of bitter hostility.

Chapter XIX

POLITICS
Truman's Choice?

March 29, 1952. It was hands down the biggest political dinner Washington had ever seen, more Democrats than any hotel in the city could hold. Excited by the prospect of the first knock-down, drag-out fight for the presidential nomination in twenty years, lobbyists, patrons, and party activists shelled out $100 for each of five thousand tickets and filled the floor of Washington's cavernous National Guard armory for the annual Jefferson-Jackson Dinner.

The burgundy was cheap; the salads were wilted; and the filets were cold. In spite of the aroma of food and the pungent odor of cigar smoke, the hall reeked of petroleum, moth balls, and sweeping compound. The air was stifling, and ice cream donkeys' legs were gone by the time they were put on the tables. None of that mattered, though. The Democrats were tossed on a sea of political gossip. Around every table, the chief subject was whether Harry Truman would try to repeat the miracle of '48.

Estes Kefauver, an ambling senator from Tennessee, had thrown the party and political commentators into a swivet by challenging the President in the New Hampshire primary and defeating him with an astonishing display of endurance and determination. The maverick in a coonskin cap had knocked on the door of nearly every known Democrat across the state, shaking hands until his fingers bled and changing American politics more than he ever dreamed. Truman had not campaigned, but he had allowed his name to be put on the ballot, and the outcome shook the timbers of the White House and the party establishment. Kefauver won all twelve of the delegates to the Democratic National Convention, while General Eisenhower, still in Paris and in uniform, thrashed Robert Taft.

The Kefauver insurgency was not the only rumbling in the Democratic ranks, however. Richard Russell, the much respected Georgia senator, stepped forward to lead loyalist Democrats in the Deep South, bidding to bring home the hardheaded segregationists who had bolted to become Dixiecrats in '48. Robert Kerr of Oklahoma had announced a conditional campaign to continue only as long as Truman did not declare for reelection. In spite of their eagerness, none of the avowed candidates stirred as much interest as Illinois governor Adlai Stevenson, who insisted that he had no intention of running for the nomination, although liberals, the press, and party pros across the country were clamoring for him.

The huge dinner turnout included so many dignitaries requiring recognition that two head tables had to be set—one at the north end of the armory floor and one at the south, the President dividing his time between them.

Truman was back from three weeks at Key West; and at sixty-seven, he looked more fit than he had on the day he was sworn into office seven turbulent years earlier. He was tanned, a little thinner, and obviously invigorated by the huge partisan bash.

He and Bess had just moved back into the White House from Blair House, where they had lived during a long-overdue facelift of the executive mansion. Now that they were in the official presidential quarters, said vice-chair India Edwards in a warmup speech, they owed it to the country to stay for another four years.

Typical of political dinners, the rhetoric from the podium was lost in the din of a thousand table conversations echoing up to the high, arched roof. Not until Truman himself was introduced for the climactic speech of the evening did the crowd become interested in the oratory and start cheering, whistling, and urging him on. It was the perfect occasion for him to give the GOP a proper Missouri tongue-lashing.

Republicans, he said, were nothing but "dinosaurs," a lot of "loud talkers," who peddled "phony propaganda." On domestic policy, they were "against all the advances the country has made since 1932." On foreign policy, they had never understood that "the hardest and bravest thing in the world is to work for peace—not war." But the campaign ahead would be tough, he warned. The Republicans would have the support of "most of the press and most of the radio commentators." They would also have plenty of money, professional polltakers, advertising experts, and few scruples.[1]

His bombshell was saved for the end. After a little summation of his record in the White House, he pulled a handwritten paragraph from his pocket and concluded, "I shall not be a candidate for re-election. I have served my country long, and I think, efficiently and honestly. I shall not accept renomination. I do not feel it is my duty to spend another four years in the White House."[2]

Harriman had known since the previous November that Truman would not run again, for the President had confided his decision to his inner circle. But he had no inkling that an announcement was imminent. There was scattered, confused applause and then a rolling chorus of "No, No," but much of the crowd appeared not to have realized that the President had just announced his retirement. As a buzz crossed the hall, he sped through his concluding sentences and was gone, swept out a side entrance by the Secret Service.

Moments later, when Harriman stepped down from the head table, he was collared by New York State Democratic chairman Paul Fitzpatrick. "You've got to run to keep New York together," he said, "you've got to run." Instinctively, the chairman was already moving to position his delegation for the convention in July. The challenge was always the same when the nomination was up for grabs, to keep the party's biggest delegation in step and make its role decisive. Fitzpatrick had therefore been touting Harriman for second spot on the ticket with Truman. But Averell, knowing of the President's decision, had been mulling over the idea of running for the White House itself.

The President's choice of a successor, he knew, was Stevenson. Two months earlier, the Illinois governor had been invited to Washington and privately offered the chief executive's support, but he had insisted he was not interested. He had reiterated his position in a second conversation with Truman just two weeks before the armory dinner, and had left the meeting thinking that the incumbent might yet decide to make the race himself.

Before the armory affair, Averell had asked Stevenson and Arthur Schlesinger, Jr., the Harvard historian and liberal gadfly, to his house for a nightcap, but instead they decided to meet at the Metropolitan Club, around the corner from the White House. By the time they got there, however, the bar was closed and they retired to an empty upstairs lounge.

Stevenson was already under siege. He was to appear on the NBC television program *Meet the Press* the next morning; and he knew that the pesty moderator, Lawrence Spivak wouldn't take no for an answer. The host would drive him to the wall for a sign of deception in his claim not to be interested in the nomination. He was intensely uncomfortable about his situation, and Harriman made it worse, urging him to go for the nomination without delay. He could be the candidate of Truman loyalists as well as party liberals like Schlesinger, who had little enthusiasm for the President and his administration.

Stevenson listened with his head in his hands. He had a rotten cold; and at that moment, he hardly cared what happened to the Democratic party. His own solution was for Averell to run. He would see to it, he said, that the big Illinois delegation voted solidly Harriman when the roll was called in Chicago.

With that, he went off to bed. Harriman and Schlesinger went on to Averell's house, where they poured a drink and resumed their talk. If Stevenson stood by his refusal to run, Schlesinger said, then Averell could indeed be the candidate of the liberals. Harriman feebly demurred. Nominating a man for President who had never been a candidate for any public office would be "idiotic," he said, but Schlesinger could tell that his suggestion had not been unappreciated.[3]

Although the symptoms had been suppressed, Averell had suffered a low-grade political infection for a long time. It secretly pleased him to be included in speculation. Vernon Walters had discerned political aspirations in Paris, and Walter Levy had come back from Iran thinking that Harriman had his eye on the White House in 1951. Truman himself had sensed it as early as anyone.

The ambition had been fed by friends who found his name a potentially powerful political resource. He had long been Herbert Swope's candidate for secretary of state; and after the job went to Acheson, Swope began encouraging him to seek the presidency. "You could not reenter the national scene at a more propitious moment," Swope wrote him when he came back to Washington to join Truman's White House staff. "How does Mr. President sound?"[4] Before that, Tammany Hall wheelhorse Ed Flynn had sounded him out about the 1950 gubernatorial nomination in New York. After Truman confided his retirement, the prospect of running for President had become real.

On the way to Hyde Park, where he spoke at ceremonies on Roosevelt's birthday on January 30, he had broached the idea of running for President to White House aide George Elsey, but received no encouragement. It was already late to start the prodigious preparations necessary for a national campaign, Elsey advised, especially for a man trying it for the first time.[5]

Actually, Harriman had thought of himself as a political figure for years, but the idea had occurred to few others until 1950, when he made a venomous attack on Senator Taft in a speech in Houston. Ted Tannenwald, who wrote the draft, was astounded at the personal and grossly partisan language that Harriman penciled in, and they argued over it for the better part of an afternoon. Harriman would change nothing. He went before the national convention of the American Federation of Labor and accused the senator of espousing foreign policies that would please Stalin and advance the cause of communism. "Actions which further the designs of the Kremlin cannot be forgiven on the ground that they are taken unwittingly," he declared. "The most charitable thing one can say about Taft is that he knows not what he does."[6]

The attack had the obvious approval of the White House, which issued a text of the remarks in advance. All across the country, the attack got front-page play, analysts taking it to be the opening shot of an administration crusade to unseat Taft in the Senate, or at least damage him as a presidential threat. It brought an avalanche of abusive letters from Taftites and angry conservatives across the country. Harriman, said the *Washington Star*, had "forfeited any claim to respect or support as an instrument of bipartisan foreign policy."[7]

On Capitol Hill, Democratic politicians who had always referred to him as Mr. Harriman or Mr. Ambassador began calling him Ave, clear evidence that the speech had served its personal purpose as well as the wishes of the President. It had given him a political identity of his own, making him one of the boys for the first time in nearly twenty years of off and on public service. He personally answered many of the furious Republicans who wrote him, and when they questioned his traveling at government expense on his journey to Texas to attack Taft, he forwarded the $156.80 for his airline ticket.

At the Mutual Security Administration, he began to enlist lieutenants whose true forte was politics, starting with James Lanigan, an Iowa-born Harvard law graduate who had briefly worked on Wall Street before moving to Washington to become a congressional aide. Lanigan wrote speeches, developed lists of contacts, and arranged meals and cocktails at Averell's house, where the chieftains of obscure political empires mingled with the members of Foreign Relations and Appropriations committees who came regularly to Foxhall Road to talk about foreign-aid and national-security matters. From his political guests, Harriman collected gossip and occasionally wisdom. "It was a worthwhile educational process," Lanigan later recalled, "both for them and for us."[8] It cast Averell in a stronger light in the eyes of Democrats, who only knew him from afar and found him politically stiff and awkward.

Without revealing his political plans, he talked Charles Collingwood into taking a leave from CBS and joining him as his press secretary. The correspondent was also put into service as speech coach; but when it became obvious to him that Harriman was about to become a candidate, he made a hard-eyed assessment of Averell's prospects and his own future, and returned to network news.

A few days after the midnight talk at the Metropolitan Club, Harriman flew to Chicago to meet with Stevenson again, hoping in private to get a final answer. They met alone in a suite at the Conrad Hilton, and the governor again assured him that he intended to run for reelection in Illinois and nothing else. He would shortly end the speculation, he said, with an unequivocal formal statement.

That was assurance enough for Averell to edge toward his own open candidacy. He gave his friends in New York the go-ahead to arrange a favorite-son movement, and the first Harriman for President Committee went into business in Orange County.

True to his word, Stevenson publicly reinforced his resolve to stay out of the race. A formal statement issued in Springfield, Illinois, on April 16, seemed a categorical rejection of a draft. "In view of my prior commitment to run for Governor and my desire and the desire of many who have given me their help and confidence in our unfinished work in Illinois," it said, "I could not accept the nomination for any other office this summer."[9] The whoops of excitement in Harriman's office could be heard across the driveway at the White House.

Stevenson's statement came the day before a huge fund-raising dinner in New York at which Averell was to be guest of honor and put on display with the avowed candidates for the nomination. It was his great opportunity to shine—Stevenson's withdrawal having elevated his candidacy to something much more than a favorite son's holding action. He was to be joined by Kefauver, Kerr, and Russell, plus Vice-President Alben Barkley, who was emerging as a potential candidate in spite of his seventy-four years.

Unfortunately, Stevenson also showed up. He had at first declined the New York invitation on grounds that his appearance would be taken as confirmation of his availability. But since his Springfield statement had removed him as a candidate, he decided he could attend. He proceeded to steal Harriman's show, delivering a philosophical talk with eloquence that thrilled New York liberals and made Averell's stiffness all the more obvious. The truly important decision before the party and the country, he said, was not who won the presidency but "what ideas, what concept of the world of tomorrow, what quality of perception, leadership, and courage."[10] He received an ovation accorded none of the others.

Unable to compete with that, Harriman stuck to his own more ponderous themes—the inseparability of foreign and domestic policy and the Republicans' persistent habit of voting "against everything that has made this country strong in the last 20 years."[11] He sat down to polite applause, having missed his chance to light a fire in his campaign. "Probably the trouble was that he tried too hard," Joseph and Stewart Alsop wrote in their syndicated column, "for he is conscious of his peculiar problem, and he works over his major speeches so endlessly and painstakingly that he tends to go stale before delivering them. In any case, it is generally agreed that the great triumph of the New York dinner was scored by Gov. Stevenson, the man who had just said he could not 'accept the nomination this summer.' "[12] Stevenson agreed that Harriman's performance "had not pleased the politicians." Averell, he thought, "would make a very good President" but he probably could beat neither Eisenhower nor Taft.[13]

When forty-five of New York's sixty-two county Democratic chairmen gathered at the Waldorf the next morning and formally declared Averell their favorite-son candidate, it was a huge anticlimax. There was only a murmur of protest from Stevenson admirers that the decision should be put off until the convention delegates had been selected.

With Stevenson on the sidelines, Averell had high hopes of Truman's all-out support at the convention. If he got it, he had a grand chance to win the nomination, no matter what Kefauver did on the long road through the primaries. As he began his campaign in earnest, he thought he was Truman's man.

Following a meeting in the Oval Office a few days after the New York dinner, he came out and told Tannenwald he had gotten "the blessing." Franklin Roosevelt, Jr., the Harriman campaign's national chairman, had his own meeting with the President about the same time and also came away convinced that the President was aboard. In the following weeks, nearly everybody assumed that Truman would drop his neutrality and publicly step into Harriman's corner at Chicago.[14]

Further encouragement came from Stevenson, who told a dinner audience in Chicago at the end of May that, of all the candidates, Harriman was "strong enough, brave enough, and wise enough—and most of all, humble enough" to be President. Introducing him at a Roosevelt College dinner, the governor added, "If Presidents are chosen for their vision, their courage and conviction, for their depth of understanding of the meaning of this revolutionary era and the mission of America, you will find them all in our honored guest, Averell Harriman."[15] Privately, Stevenson renewed his promise to deliver the Illinois delegation, but to Arthur Schlesinger he confided growing doubt that Harriman could get anywhere.[16]

The political pros didn't think Harriman had it. "Honest Ave, the Hairsplitter," he was called. Years in public life hadn't dented his ingrained aloofness. One morning after he and Collingwood had talked politics over breakfast at the house, they headed for the office; and as Collingwood slid under the steering wheel, Harriman absentmindedly got into the back seat with his *New York Times*.

His formal announcement confirmed how much he had to learn. With the word long since spread that he was running, he scheduled the ritual press conference to make it official, and capital's political reporters climbed the broad stairs to his second-floor office. The candidate was nowhere to be seen. His door was closed, and he was said to be dealing with an urgent foreign-aid matter on the telephone. After half an hour, the correspondents were handed a four-paragraph statement and advised that Harriman did not have time to see them. The announcement read, and was handled, "like a diplomatic aide memoire," *New York Times*-man James Reston later recalled.[17]

On this uncertain note, the sixty-year-old neophyte began an unlikely political odyssey that would see him seek office in four consecutive elections, trying twice for his party's presidential nomination, winning the governorship of New York, and then losing it just when it seemed he had reestablished the Democratic grip that Al Smith, Herbert Lehman, and Franklin Roosevelt had so long held on the state house in Albany.

Harriman's hope of proving himself as a credible alternative to the reluctant Stevenson in 1952 did not take wing—in part because party stalwarts who encouraged him were less interested in his success than in using him to prevent the disliked and mistrusted Kefauver from absconding with the nomination. As long as they could see a long-shot chance of Stevenson changing his mind, the governor was their choice.

"With the exception of Harriman's close personal friends, practically all of the people supporting Harriman are primarily pro-Stevenson," White House political aide Charles Murphy concluded in May.[18] Unless Harriman's movement took hold, Murphy warned, there was real danger that Kefauver's populist campaign would develop so much support that he would be unstoppable at the convention.

But outside New York, Averell's only backing was along the routes of the Harriman railroads, where the name still held some magic. In the South, his image as a liberal made him anathema. He had no field organization; and, oddly, he had campaign financing problems. As much as he lusted for the nomination, his prospects were not bright enough to encourage heavy personal investment.

Members of the family, including Roland, pitched in $5,000 each, as did a few wealthy friends, but still there was less than $50,000 in the treasury when the campaign got under way. Because local committees and every campaign supplier assumed that a campaign by Averell Harriman would be awash in money, fund-raisers found it nearly impossible to successfully solicit small contributions.[19] When they called on Senator Lehman of New York, Harriman's own national cochairman agreed to double what Averell had given the last Lehman campaign. After consulting his records, he wrote out a check for $200.[20]

With what local campaign managers described as ice cream and cake money, he reluctantly entered his only direct contest with Kefauver—in the Washington, D.C., primary. Terrified at the thought of a head-to-head joust, he accused his advisers of jeopardizing his support in the South by putting him into a popularity contest for the city's Negro vote. Their reply was brutal. He had no support in the South, nor would he ever. His whole public life identified him as a liberal. Not only did he have to enter the D.C. primary, he had to run to the left of the liberal Kefauver.

So, with an army of black volunteers working out of five offices in the city, he billed himself "a rich man's son, who took the poor man's side," and asked for votes for the first time in his life.[21] He was chauffeured about the city in a well-worn Plymouth by his press secretary, former Reuters correspondent Joe Laitin, knocking on doors and shaking hands as single-mindedly as Kefauver had campaigned in New Hampshire. Marie arrived from New York and joined the effort with gusto, riding about town with him, handing out the "I Crave Ave" buttons that she had dreamed up, and leading the singing of the campaign song parroting George M. Cohan's "Harrigan." "H, A, double-RI," it went, "MAN spells Harriman." The borrowed campaign song would be remembered when the rest of Averell's political career had been forgotten.

The value of Laitin, who joined the campaign on orders from Senator Lehman, went beyond driving cars and writing press releases. He was a constant source of both solicited and unsolicited advice in creating an image of Harriman the politician. He headed off a plan to produce a poster of Harriman as a straphanger on the New York subway—voters, he said, knew that Averell had never been on a subway in his life. He and Marie also sabotaged a plan for publicity pictures of her cooking bacon and eggs for the candidate's breakfast. "Are you kidding?" she asked. "I don't know how make bacon and eggs."[22]

Still in search of a common touch, the New York office went to work on a brochure exploiting the candidate's prowess as an athlete. There were pictures of him rowing at Yale, playing polo at Meadow Brook, wielding his croquet mallet at Sands Point. Blair Clark, a former CBS correspondent who was handling campaign publicity, looked at the collection a little sadly and dumped the project. He would trade every picture of all the triumphant moments, he said, for one lousy shot of Harriman sliding into second base. Kefauver was a formidable campaigner in Washington, as everywhere else, but he could not overcome his southern origins nor an unequivocal Harriman civil rights stand, expertly embellished by his campaign manager.

Black neighborhoods were blanketed with flyers crediting Harriman with single-handedly desegregating the rest rooms and dining rooms of the government-owned Washington National Airport just across the Potomac in rigidly segregated Virginia. That was enough to make him a hero to blacks and a radical to white conservatives.

Harriman could not remember whether he had desegregated the terminal or not, and he was terrified that his supposed heroics as secretary of commerce would be exposed as a fraud. Claiborne Pell, a campaign handyman who would rise to become chairman of the Senate Foreign Relations Committee thirty-five years later, was detailed to investigate. What he found was that Harriman had sent Congress proposed legislation in 1947 that would have given the commerce secretary authority to desegregate the federally operated terminal, but the bill was ignored. When the Justice Department, moved by a lawsuit filed by a member of the Civil Rights Commission, notified Commerce that segregation at the terminal should be ended, Averell had been in Paris with the Marshall Plan. The campaign quietly dropped its claim and tiptoed past a serious embarrassment.

Washington residents, not then permitted to vote in federal elections, poured out for the party primary. Balloting was particularly heavy at polling places in black neighborhoods, where ministers urged their flocks to support Harriman, some of them hailing him as a "second Abe Lincoln." The Reverend Smallwood Williams of the venerable Bible Way Church, whom Harriman had assiduously courted, personally led four hundred voters to ballot box. "I want you all to vote for Honest Ave," he counseled his flock in the days before the vote. "He's not going to steal any cabbage, he's already got all the cabbage he can use."[23] In some of the city's all-black neighborhoods, Harriman's margins exceeded ten to one.

He campaigned until the last moment. After discussing his race with President Truman in the morning, he went on the radio to underline his commitment to civil rights one last time. "There is a lot of talk about states' rights," he declared. "Actually, they should be talking about states' responsibilities, for the fight against discrimination is everybody's responsibility." With that, he went off to vote at a Washington firehouse in his own all-white neighborhood and make a last tour of the city. Laitin, noticing scores of limousines arriving at voting precincts in poor neighborhoods, investigated and discovered that black chauffeurs working for the government had created a shuttle service for Harriman voters.

When it was over, Averell tallied 14,075 votes to just 3,377 for Kefauver, taking all but four of the city's forty-five precincts, and winning its six convention delegates. It enabled Kefauver's opponents to claim that Kefauver had been in only three meaningful contests, and had lost two of them—to Richard Russell in Florida, and to Harriman in Washington. Averell's victory hardly derailed the Tennessee senator, though, and it did nothing to blemish the party's fascination with Stevenson.

Thrilled by his triumph, Harriman, accompanied by Lanigan, set out on his second foray into the West, showing signs that he was getting the hang of campaigning. He had dropped the W. from his name and had taken to wearing red suspenders and a Teamsters Union tiepin. He shed some of his inhibition about back-slapping and hand-shaking, now downed any food thrust in his face, and allowed himself to be photographed in any manner of headgear handed to him. There were moments when he even appeared to enjoy ordeals such as a Utah buckboard ride, escorted by cowboys and Ute Indians, who declared him an honorary chief.

He still failed to remember the names of people crucial to him, and in his speeches he was stricken by recurring attacks of stammering—which Kathleen attributed to the pressures E.H. had put on him in his formative years. On the stump, he adopted the habit of swinging his arms and rocking on the balls of his feet as he spoke. Walter Reuther, president of the United Auto Workers, started calling him "Hup Hup Harriman" because his arm-swinging and his peculiar cadence made it look as if he were about to leap into the air with a "Hup Hup Hooray!" Before he finished his third long swing across the West in his chartered DC-3, the *Harriman Express*, he was gaunt and pale. In Montana he had to undergo emergency surgery for hemorrhoids, and although the doctor ordered him to stay off his feet for a few days, he was on his plane again within hours, bound for Denver.

Still in pain and with only a handful of delegates to show for all his travels across the West, he gave the best speech of his campaign at the Colorado state party convention, clearly upstaging Kefauver. He renewed his memorable Houston attack on Taft, labeling the Ohio senator the candidate that Stalin would like to see elected. "If Senator Taft is nominated, we will show that his policies can only help Stalin. We'll make Taft Stalin's candidate before we are through with him."[24] That brought Colorado Democrats to their feet; and when he sat down, delegates gave him a long, standing ovation. As he departed for Washington, surveys showed him easily ahead of both Kefauver and Russell, although the Colorado delegation would go to Chicago officially uncommitted. His chief supporter in the state, former congressman John Carroll, was chosen delegation chairman.

But as he went home to prepare for the convention, Harriman still did not know what Truman would do—nor was he going to find out. A week before the Democrats were to gather, the President checked into Walter Reed Hospital with a virus infection and became unreachable. He had, however, given up on Averell's slim chances.

Harriman still took heart from friends and advisers, who told him the nomination was possible in spite of his failure to excite public interest as the keeper of the New Deal and Fair Deal flame. Arthur Schlesinger continued to think Stevenson would stay out and Averell would get the President's full support. "It is my guess," Schlesinger told him, "that the President will support you and that you will have enough votes to keep Adlai from entering seriously. I do not think Adlai wants the nomination if he has to make a real fight for it; I think he means it rather literally when he talks about a draft. So I am tempted to think that he may not yet become a really serious candidate."[25]

At the same time, however, the professor counseled Averell to position himself to be a kingmaker, in case events made Stevenson's nomination inevitable. "If the moment should come when it seems certain that he will be nominated," he added, "perhaps you ought to consider coming out for him. I suggest this reluctantly but for two strong reasons: (1) If you do it early enough to bring a large number of delegates over, you will be the logical candidate for Secretary of State; (2) by coming out for him, you will avoid a situation where all the conservatives get behind Stevenson and claim his nomination as a conservative, Southern victory."[26]

Harriman hit Chicago with all the trappings of a contender, although he could count only seventeen and a half delegates outside New York. His consolation was that he was the second choice of many. If the fight got to a second ballot and Stevenson stayed out, there was a good chance that the governors' supporters would switch to Harriman to head off Kefauver. Many of Kefauver's backers also listed Averell as their second choice. So if a Harriman-Stevenson deadlock somehow developed, Averell's strategists saw the Kefauver people switching to Harriman in order to block Stevenson. But unbeknownst to all but a few men at the White House, Truman had decided just before going into the hospital that he would support Alben Barkley. Harriman had shrugged off the Barkley rumor at first; but by the time the delegates arrived, it was clear that Truman had, in fact, decided to back the veep. While Averell concealed his disappointment, his campaign leaders were livid, feeling the President guilty of outright betrayal.

By the tally of the Alsop brothers, Truman could personally swing 400 delegates to any candidate generally favored by the convention, or 200 to one whom the delegates personally disliked.[27] Under the circumstances, the Vice-President's advisers thought they could get 225 votes on the first ballot and perhaps 360 on the second, enough to put a bandwagon in motion.[28]

Harriman's victory scenarios were no more farfetched than Barkley's. The convention was certain to be the most open, freewheeling one since Roosevelt was nominated in 1932. With a chance that the battle would go eight or ten ballots, anything could happen. Although the Dixiecrat movement fizzled after the 1948 southern walkout, there was a good possibility that six states from the Confederacy might bolt again. Barkley's emergence and the prospect of another southern rebellion threw the Harriman campaign into a necessary alliance with Kefauver. They were scorpions in a bottle, but it was to their advantage to cooperate in getting recognition of loyalist Texas and Mississippi slates being challenged by states' rights delegations.

In spite of Truman's support, Barkley's rally collapsed. Labor leaders decided that Barkley was too old, and that was the end of it.

With his natural allies divided with Kefauver, Harriman saw his support erode from the first day. His failure to generate national enthusiasm undercut him in New York; and by the time the convention was called to order, powerful delegation members, such as Herbert Lehman and Robert Wagner, Jr., were agitating to move to Stevenson at the first opportunity.

Although Stevenson told members of the Illinois delegation that he considered himself unsuited for the presidency and urged them not to nominate him, he personally set the draft movement ablaze with a welcoming address that would be remembered as a classic in convention oratory, compared in its effect with the Cross of Gold speech that led to William Jennings Bryan's presidential nomination in 1896.

Returning to the theme he had used four months earlier at the Harriman dinner in New York, he reminded Democrats that "what counts now is not just what we are against, but what we are for. And who leads us is less important that what leads us—what convictions, what courage, what faith—win or lose."[29] It was the kind of eloquence that Harriman, Kefauver, Richard Russell, or even Harry Truman could not approach.

The noncandidate governor was not only in a class by himself as an inspirational speaker, but he was also in the great middle ground of the convention. Richard Russell, hoping to avoid the disaster of another Dixiecrat revolt, held the Deep South. Kefauver owned a national following with the fierce commitment of cultists. Averell's only hope, if Stevenson was put in nomination, was that some issue would split the convention into liberal and conservative blocs and force Stevenson to take one side or the other. The fight over the rival delegations from Texas and Mississippi, which spread to include Virginia, was potentially such an issue.

In five days of acrimonious committee meetings, offstage arm-twisting and massive confusion on the convention floor, Harriman and Kefauver failed to force the seating of the loyalists from Mississippi and Texas, but they extracted a price. Harriman's camp offered a loyalty pledge requiring delegations to attest that the convention's nominees for President and Vice-President would be placed on their state ballots in November. Put before the convention on Monday night, the pledge threw the southerners into an uproar that went on into Tuesday morning.

As Truman followed the convention proceedings from the White House and Stevenson settled into the brownstone town house of his friend William Blair on Chicago's North Side, Harriman fought a hopeless battle to scotch a Stevenson bandwagon. With FDR, Jr., directing strategy in the loyalty-pledge struggle, Harriman courted delegates at their convention hotels, promising a campaign and a presidency carrying on the policies of Roosevelt and Truman. Escorted from hotel to hotel in a three-car motorcade, trailed by a station wagon filled with reporters, he was a picture of futility. He looked more wan than ever. His double-breasted suits were too large. There were huge bags under his eyes; and in the clamor of the crowded hotel room, his soft mumble was hardly audible. And as his campaign made its stand on credentials and liberal planks in the party platform, the middle of the polarized convention opened wider for Stevenson.

On Tuesday, the day after the governor's welcome ignited the convention with draft talk, Averell sent Schlesinger to see him, ostensibly to reconfirm Stevenson's old promise to vote Harriman on the first ballot. Schlesinger found Stevenson unhappy about the spectacle on the convention floor the previous night and concerned that the South might be driven out by a loyalty pledge. He was disappointed at the showing Harriman had made and worried that Averell had gotten into a position where he was becoming a divisive figure. Stevenson still did not want the nomination, but he confessed that he did not want to slam the door on an honest draft either. Schlesinger took it as an indication that he was becoming resigned to running.[30]

With this evidence of Stevenson's drift into the race, there was a brief effort to forge a Harriman-Kefauver ticket. The two met in Averell's suite just long enough to determine that taking the second spot was unthinkable to both. After the session, Harriman slogged on, insisting that the nomination was still up for grabs. But it was obvious that he was finished. Columnist Murray Kempton wrote a graceful appreciation as the quixotic campaign approached its ordained conclusion.

"Of all men, the good Lord gave Averell Harriman nearly the least of the natural equipment of a campaigner," Kempton said, looking back at the campaign across the West. "That trip cannot have been easy for him; the rising at six, the press of strangers; the business of learning every step of the way. But Harriman came home with something that he had won himself and that neither his father nor his party had given. He had held aloft the lamp of the New Deal; and in every state he visited, someone had listened and believed in him."[31]

On Thursday afternoon, Harriman watched on television in his convention-hall dugout as his name was put before the convention by FDR, Jr., who hailed him as the "great trouble shooter in a troubled world."[32] He did not know that Stevenson had called the President a few hours earlier to let Truman know that the governor had decided get into the race. But there was no longer any doubt that Stevenson was actively seeking a draft. The final confirmation came when word leaked to the press that the President had instructed Thomas J. Gavin, his alternate in the Missouri delegation, to vote for Stevenson on the first ballot.

Before the nominating speeches were finished, a new floor fight over the loyalty pledge hastened Harriman's end. The major candidates had been nominated, and many of the delegates had left the hall for dinner when Governor John Battle of Virginia got the floor and questioned whether his delegation was, in fact, in the convention. The ruling from the chair was that Virginia had not complied with the loyalty pledge, and neither had South Carolina or Louisiana.

The ruling threw the hall into an uproar, exposing a raw nerve that had been covered by the convention's preoccupation with the nominations. There was a motion to seat Virginia in spite of its failure to comply with the pledge, and a furious debate lasted for more than two hours. At the end of the roll call, the vote was 462½ against seating Virginia to 351½ in favor. The party was suddenly face-to-face with 1948 again. If Virginia walked out, other delegations from the Deep South would follow.

Where Averell's feeble chances were concerned, a southern walkout could do nothing but help. New York weighed in with 90 votes to anchor the liberal-bloc voting against seating, and Stevenson's Illinois voted against Virginia 45–15, suggesting that Stevenson, too, was prepared to see the South walk out, although it was crucial to him.

But with the end of the first reading of the roll, leaders of the Illinois delegation rushed back from dinner, and the state's vote was switched. It was the decisive moment of the convention. From 45 to 15 against, the Illinois vote was changed to 52 to 8 in favor of seating Virginia. A torrent of similar switches followed. When it was over, the new count was 615 to 529 in favor of the motion to seat. Skirmishing continued until two A.M., as Harriman and Kefauver forces tried to prevent South Carolina and Louisiana from being seated on the Virginia precedent; but it was no use.

Stevenson had won. He was within reach of the nomination; the South was in the convention and ready to vote for him when the moment came. With no chance of an alliance with Kefauver, Harriman was finished.

Northern liberals and Kefauverites made a last-gasp search for some way to stop the Stevenson steamroller. Harriman again met briefly with Kefauver, joined by Hubert Humphrey, Senator Paul Douglas of Illinois, Governor G. Mennen Williams of Michigan, and Walter Reuther. None saw a plausible way to go on, and Harriman went off for a few hours' sleep, the others to one more gathering of liberals at the Congress Hotel. There, FDR, Jr., made an angry speech accusing Stevenson of pandering to southern reactionaries, and there was more talk of a Harriman-Kefauver or Kefauver-Harriman ticket. That obviously going nowhere, holdouts kicked around the possibility of a Kefauver-Roosevelt lineup.

Walter Reuther pulled Roosevelt aside and suggested he could have the second spot on the ticket with Stevenson, if he would persuade Harriman to give up and throw his support to Stevenson before the first ballot. Roosevelt bristled at the suggestion of cutting a deal for himself behind Harriman's back. He gave Reuther a frigid no and walked away.[33] With dawn approaching and everybody exhausted, Humphrey made a fraternal appeal to reason. Stevenson was, after all, a liberal, he said, and it was time to get on with the business of the liberal agenda. With that, the quarrelsome Democrats made their first step toward conciliation.

A few hours later, Harriman and Stevenson slipped away from their aides, evaded reporters and, with Schlesinger joining them, had breakfast at the home of Mr. and Mrs. Ernest Ives, Stevenson's sister and brother-in-law. Averell was still miffed about the Illinois delegation's switch on seating Virginia. Because of that, he said, Stevenson had identified himself with the worst of the Democratic party, including the Dixiecrats and the bosses. He was not prepared to drop out, he continued, but when and if he decided to quit, he would support the governor.[34]

Shortly after noon, four days after Stevenson's memorable welcome, delegates convened to nominate their candidate to face Dwight Eisenhower, who had been nominated by the Republicans two weeks earlier. In the Harriman dugout, Marie, Kathleen, Schlesinger, Michael Forrestal, Jim Lanigan, and several others gathered with Averell to watch. For nearly three hours, the pageant played out before a national television audience unaware of how neatly the outcome was now scripted.

At the end of the first ballot Kefauver led with 340 delegates. Stevenson followed with 273, the most important of which was Thomas J. Gavin of Missouri. Russell captured 268, nearly all from the Deep South, and Averell trailed them with 123½. He was followed by only a few nominal candidates with a smattering of favorite-son votes.

New York held firm, although Jim Farley had challenged Fitzpatrick's control of the delegation and worked all day to get the Stevenson supporters to leave Harriman and join Stevenson at the end of the first ballot as soon as their favorite-son commitment was discharged. With Stevenson certain to be the nominee, Farley argued, New York risked being left behind by waiting for Averell to withdraw. As the balloting began, Harriman, Roosevelt, and Fitzpatrick held to the slim hope that Stevenson might fall short of a majority through three or four ballots. If he did, he would be forced to turn to the South. That would give liberals grounds for a switch to Harriman.

But Averell also had to consider a role for New York to play in a Stevenson nomination, as well as the risk of the personal embarrassment

of having the delegation defy Roosevelt, Fitzpatrick, and himself. Moreover, New York friends were already coming to him anxious to nominate
him to run against Republican Senator Irving Ives when Democrats
gathered for their upcoming state convention.

As the second ballot got under way, he took a legal pad and a stubby
pencil and wrote his three-paragraph concession:

> I am deeply grateful for the support given me and the principles
> for which, I stand both before and during this convention, by
> my friends in the Democratic party.
>
> I came to this convention to fight for my nomination and
> for a liberal, progressive platform true to the higher traditions
> of Franklin Delano Roosevelt and the fighting policies of Presi-
> dent Harry S Truman. I am proud that this convention has
> adopted such a platform. At this time in the deliberations of
> this convention, I withdraw as a candidate and urge my support-
> ers to cast their votes for my old friend, Governor Adlai E.
> Stevenson of Illinois. I have asked my alternate, sitting in the
> New York delegation, to do so.
>
> I want to make it perfectly clear that I am governed by no
> other motivation than that the Democratic party unite behind
> the fine liberal candidate who will lead our party to victory in
> November.[35]

The second roll call moved faster than the first, ending just after six
P.M. Harriman held steady with 121 votes, but all of the other consequential candidates gained, as Kerr and several favorite sons dropped by the
wayside. Kefauver and Russell picked up a handful; but Barkley gained
30 votes, and Stevenson added another 50, giving him 324½.

With that, the convention recessed for dinner, and Harriman called
Paul Fitzpatrick on the convention floor to let him know that he was
pulling out. He would throw his support to Stevenson at the beginning
of the third ballot.

About the same time, Truman arrived in Chicago and was driven
to the Stockyard Inn. Unaware that Harriman had made up his mind to
drop out, the President had decided it was time to call him on their
understanding that Averell would fall in behind the party's choice when
the proper moment came. Charles Murphy was sent to deliver the word
as Truman sat down to dinner with Sam Rayburn, Chicago party leader
Jacob Arvey, Governor Paul Dever of Massachusetts, and Democratic
National Committee chairman Frank McKinney.

In the lobby of the convention hall, Murphy encountered Lanigan
and suggested that he deliver the President's message. Frayed from a
week of chasing delegates, Lanigan was in no mood to tell his boss it was

time to quit. "You want me to tell Averell Harriman that?" he asked incredulously. "You work for Harry Truman, that's your message, for Christ's sake. You tell him."[36] Lanigan walked away with no special place to go.

Murphy fought his way through the delegates returning for the third ballot. By the time he reached Harriman's dugout, he was trailed by reporters and photographers. Though his onerous mission was unnecessary, the press naturally concluded that Harriman's withdrawal minutes later was in response to an order from the President. In fact, the statement, written hours earlier, had secretly been mimeographed by Marie.

While Murphy was looking for Averell, Paul Fitzpatrick arrived at the President's dinner party to tell Truman of Harriman's decision. He arranged to be recognized by Rayburn to read the withdrawal statement to the convention before the next roll call began. Rayburn would first recognize Governor Dever, who would throw his Massachusetts favorite-son delegates to Stevenson, and then turn to Fitzpatrick for the Harriman statement to break the dam.

In his own room in the same hotel, Kefauver had no idea that Harriman had sealed Stevenson's nomination. He was watching television, waiting for the delegates to be called back to order, when Michigan's Governor G. Mennen Williams and Senator Blair Moody arrived with the news of Harriman's withdrawal. They wanted him to join in putting Stevenson over the top on the third ballot.

Angry that Harriman had not bothered to tell him what he was doing, the Tennessean rushed across the street to the convention hall, accompanied by Paul Douglas, surrounded by bodyguards, and trailed by a mob of reporters.

On the floor, the proceedings were already unfolding as planned. Dever withdrew. Then, as Harriman watched from the mezzanine, Rayburn recognized FDR, Jr., who introduced Fitzpatrick, who then read Harriman's concession statement. As the third roll call marched on, Arkansas switched to Stevenson, as did Harriman's Colorado delegates. Just as Colorado was being polled, Kefauver pushed his way through the mobbed aisle to the front of the hall, trying to get recognition so he could withdraw and throw his support to Stevenson, too. At the steps to the rostrum, he encountered a scowling Rayburn, who advised him that nothing would be permitted to interrupt a roll call once under way. It took nearly three hours for the third ballot to be completed, while Kefauver sat steaming.

When it was over, the governor was still two and a half votes short of the nomination, and Kefauver was finally recognized. Saying he had "fought the hard fight" and "done the very best that we could," he capitulated, as did Russell. As he walked from the hall, his delegates in the Utah delegation, one of Averell's western enclaves, switched four and a half votes, making Stevenson the 1952 Democratic presidential nominee.

Neither Chicago nor the widely held view that he was out of his element in electoral politics dissuaded Harriman from his new calling. The exhilaration of his primary triumph in Washington, the drama of the convention floor, and new public recognition seduced him. Nothing in his poor showing escaped rationalization: he had been late starting; he had begun without an organization; he had been poorly advised.

In the fall, he threw himself headlong into the Stevenson campaign, traveling the western states for the ticket and lending money to state campaign committees when they were pinched for cash. He worked enthusiastically enough, in fact, that he wrecked his friendship with Eisenhower, who proved surprisingly thin-skinned.

While he reserved his criticism for Taft during the primaries, he spared Eisenhower nothing once the general was the Republican nominee. "Governor Stevenson is being opposed by a General who has shown clearly that he doesn't know the first thing about our problems here at home," he told a Democratic rally in Madison Square Garden. "He gets a briefing on economics from Herbert Hoover and a lesson on labor from Robert Taft. When it comes to political decency, he clasps the hand of Joseph McCarthy."[37]

Before 1952, Harriman's politics had been defined mostly by his personal loyalty to Roosevelt and then Truman; but once he had carried the Democratic banner, he was no less a party man than union workers and precinct captains. He did not take the Eisenhower landslide easily. When Marie's sister, Frances, and her husband, William Lord, arrived for dinner at Eighty-first Street with Lord sporting a large "I LIKE IKE" button in his lapel, Harriman plucked it away and threw it into the fireplace. Fortunately there was no fire, because Marie demanded that he retrieve it, which he did, shamefaced at his loss of temper.[38]

In spite of his poor showing with his presidential campaign, New York party leaders were prepared to make Harriman their candidate for the Senate, figuring he would not only stand a strong chance of taking the seat from Irving Ives but give the national ticket an especially needed boost to offset Stevenson's choice of Senator John Sparkman of Alabama as his running mate. Averell, in turn, had trouble seeing himself as a junior member of the Senate club, and he waffled too long before agreeing to make the race. By the time he made up his mind, the leaders had committed themselves to Brooklyn borough president John Cashmore. Averell was not interested enough to challenge the decision. Besides, as long as there was the chance that lightning might strike and put Stevenson in the White House, he had hopes of being secretary of state.

Eisenhower's landslide left him at loose ends. He toyed with ideas for international financing projects and made the bank his headquarters for the first time in more than a decade. The partners saw little of him, though. He took long vacations at Sun Valley, Hobe Sound, and Sands Point. He whipped his croquet game back into shape and puttered at preparations for writing his memoirs.

He regularly turned up at political speeches and fund-raisers, wrote magazine articles, and spoke to labor union conventions, chastising the Republicans and denouncing Joe McCarthy. When friends inquired about what he was doing, as they often did, he merely replied, "Public service; some people call it politics."[39]

Although Democrats held city hall, party leaders had decided to find an alternative to Vincent Impellitteri, the incumbent. Harriman was an obvious possibility, first promoted by David Dubinsky, the powerful president of the International Ladies Garment Workers Union. The concept of running for Gracie Mansion after first trying for the White House was novel, but he was interested. He discussed the race with veterans such as Sam Rosenman, who had been an adviser to Roosevelt and Truman, as well as with Carmine De Sapio, the boss of Tammany Hall. Both looked favorably on Harriman's potential as a New York political power, but when they got down to the specifics of a race for mayor, they found problems.

While he now lived on East Eighty-first Street—the house he had bought when he thought Truman was headed for defeat in 1948—he still used the Arden estate as his official residence and voted in Orange County. So instead of running himself, he jumped into the campaign for Robert Wagner, Jr., the Manhattan borough president, who became the choice of Tammany Hall. He contributed substantially to the Wagner campaign coffers and paid the rent on Wagner's headquarters for the first weeks of the race.

The job that interested him much more was the governorship. Ever since returning from Europe, and even before getting into the race for the presidential nomination, he had had an eye on Albany and 1954. Thomas E. Dewey was nearing the end of his third term, and Democrats saw their best chance in a dozen years to recapture the state executive mansion.

Historically, the Republicans controlled the legislature, but Al Smith, Franklin Roosevelt, and Herbert Lehman had made the governor's office a Democratic stronghold until 1942, when it was captured by Dewey, the crime-busting New York City district attorney. Like Smith and Roosevelt, Dewey had used the office to mount a challenge for the presidency. He was still popular in the state and under pressure from his party to seek a fourth term.

On the advice of Julius Edelstein in Senator Lehman's office, Harriman hired a political handyman. Milton Stewart, a thirty-year-old New Yorker on the staff of the Budget Bureau in Washington, had started his political career as a volunteer in New York campaigns while he was still a teenager. Afterward, he had worked for Americans for Democratic Action and for the mayor's office before moving to Washington when FDR, Jr., was elected to Congress in 1948.

By 1953, he wanted to get out of politics and learn the bond business on Wall Street. With Averell's assurance that he had no intention of running for another political office, Stewart jumped at the chance to become his assistant at Brown Brothers Harriman. Soon after he got there, however, he realized that he hadn't got out of politics at all: he spent less and less time learning about bonds and banking, and more and more writing political speeches and sitting in Harriman's office talking politics, gradually realizing that he "had been conned more than a little."[40] Before he knew it, he was putting together a Harriman gubernatorial campaign, pitting him against his friend and former boss, FDR, Jr., whose chief operative, ironically, was now Jimmy Lanigan, Averell's political right hand in '52.

While Harriman had dabbled in the Wagner mayoral campaign and worked at establishing himself as a New Yorker again, young Franklin was well along the way to locking up the gubernatorial nomination. He was quietly courting Democratic chairmen upstate, lining up commitments from the men who would control county delegations at a state party convention still more than a year away. He campaigned in the honored New York tradition, denying that he was a candidate but conceding that he would be available if the public called. The strategy of building momentum upstate had been recommended by Carmine De Sapio as a way for him to avoid the appearance that he was the candidate of the New York City machine.

Roosevelt had a lot of his father's personal charm, a solid base in Dutchess and Erie counties, a big following of energetic young liberals, and the admiration of upstate politicians because he had defeated the city organization in being elected to Congress on Manhattan's West Side.

Once he got to the formality of making himself an avowed candidate, he already had campaigned in nearly every county in the state, drawing impressive crowds everywhere he went. His goal was to assure himself of 350 delegates before the convention opened; and by all appearances, he was succeeding marvelously.

Harriman, on the other hand, was hesitant when the time came for serious commitments to a race. He was not sure where he stood with party power-brokers. While he was eager, he worried about embarrassing himself. Having gotten nowhere in his try for the presidential nomination, he would end his political career if he lost to Roosevelt. Whenever the question arose about his plans to seek the nomination, he evaded it with the excuse that it was still too early to make a decision. Privately, he was afraid that Roosevelt's name and head start were too much to overcome.

On June 10, he had lunch with Liberal party leader Alex Rose and assured him that he was interested in running. He urgently needed the party's support, but as far as Rose was concerned, any of three Democrats being mentioned—Harriman, Roosevelt or Wagner—was acceptable. Choosing among them was the Democrat's problem.

But Harriman's interest caused Rose to take a closer look at the field, and to his surprise a poll of his members showed Roosevelt had serious problems in the liberal community. Catholic voters were unenthusiastic about him because his mother had feuded with Francis Cardinal Spellman over federal aid to parochial schools. Jews had strong reservations about him as well. He also had a record of absenteeism in the House; there was gossip about his personal life; and he was hurt by the much-publicized divorce of his brother James. Successful as he had been, there was still a widespread notion that he was a playboy traveling on the reputation of his father. After the poll, Rose no longer believed Roosevelt could defeat the Republicans in the fall, and his doubts were taken seriously by influential friends such as Herbert Lehman's political maven, Julius Edelstein.

More important than Rose's misgivings was doubt in the mind of Carmine De Sapio. While the Tammany leader could see Averell's obvious shortcomings, he was impressed by Rose's argument that the Democrats' foremost need was a candidate whom no one was against. Too many people were against Roosevelt, but few had yet figured out reasons for being against Harriman.

Within a week of Averell's luncheon with Rose, the ground began to shift in the Democratic party. Edelstein's soundings convinced him that Rose was correct, and on his advice Senator Lehman retreated from a commitment to give FDR a public endorsement. Before leaving on a European vacation, he instead issued a statement saying he found either Roosevelt or Harriman acceptable. Privately, he urged Harriman to immediately declare himself a candidate.

To Rose's dismay, nothing happened. Harriman continued to spend hours with Milton Stewart analyzing the situation, and talking with Sam Rosenman, who was recommending caution. George Backer, his closest political friend and confidant, was in Europe. Finally realizing a decision could wait no longer, he sent for Backer to come home.

The two had been friends since the 1920s, neighbors at Sands Point, croquet competitors and bridge partners before becoming political allies. Backer was a novelist, playwright, and heir to a real estate fortune; and while married to *New York Post* owner Dorothy Schiff, he had been publisher of that liberal tabloid. Politically, he had strong ties with both

the city machine leaders and liberals in the Herbert Lehman–Eleanor
Roosevelt branch of the party. Where Harriman's political career was
concerned, Backer was selfless. He asked for nothing more than to serve
his friend's interests. Harriman appreciated the value of such commitment, and he rarely made a political decision of moment without Backer's
advice.

Even after Backer returned anxious to get started, Averell continued
to waffle; and Rose threatened to withdraw his support and find another
candidate. It was July 24 before Harriman finally acknowledged his
candidacy in a television interview, and it was hardly a ringing declaration. He was not prepared to start buttonholing convention delegates
and county leaders, he said, but he was available and he "would be proud
to lead the Democratic party." "When you go around asking for delegate
support, you have to make commitments, which I am not prepared to
do," he explained.[41]

The suggestion that he would have to be drafted was a transparent
admission that his only hope lay with the bosses of the city organization.
More than a month passed, however, before the Tammany leaders publicly made him their choice. In the interim, they professed neutrality,
and polls showed Averell, Roosevelt, and noncandidate Wagner nearly
even in popular support.

In spite of his declaration that he would not go out and buttonhole
delegates, Harriman traveled around the state lining up support and
putting together a savvy campaign organization. When Charles Van
Devander, a former director of public relations for the Democratic National Committee, was invited to New York for an interview, he was
shanghaied to Sands Point and put to work for a week before he was
released long enough to go back to Washington for his clothes.

Though damaged by Lehman's retreat and ominous signs that the
city organization was lining up against him, Roosevelt worked harder to
put together an overpowering upstate, liberal, and labor coalition.
Unions of the CIO pressured new state chairman Richard Balch to get
behind him and planned to turn their state convention into a giant
Roosevelt rally.

Concerned that such a show of force would seriously damage their
own candidate's chances, Tammany leaders dumped their pretension of
neutrality with a De Sapio announcement that Harriman was their man.
Delegates would make their choice at a free and open convention, he
said, but the leaders would "recommend a candidate who they feel repre-
sents the sentiment of the rank and file members of the party."[42]

Two days before the CIO convention, Harriman gained the support
of four of the five Tammany borough chairmen, plus that of Herbert
Lehman and Robert Wagner. Outmaneuvered CIO officials saw their
endorsement of FDR, Jr., buried by the news of the city organization's

move and of Senator Ives's emergence as the Republican candidate following Dewey's final refusal to run again.

The only question was whether Roosevelt would go quietly or make a futile and damaging fight on the convention floor. He chose not to disappoint his loyalists, although he knew a floor fight was hopeless. When the stacked conclave opened at the 165th Infantry Armory in Manhattan, it would have appeared to the uninitiated that Roosevelt owned it. His partisans drowned out Harriman supporters among the two thousand delegates and alternates on the floor, as well as in the spectators' section, where another 2,700 Democrats crowded in for the show. A brass band and a sea of Roosevelt streamers and banners gave the armory the air of a huge Roosevelt rally, as his managers launched a last-ditch attempt to stampede the convention. The show of force produced fistfights with Harriman supporters, and every mention of Roosevelt's name set off a new demonstration. Furious at De Sapio, Roosevelt delegates and spectators booed unmercifully when the Tammany chief went to the platform to speak.

At times the scene resembled a riot more than a convention. Raiders from each side stole the other's placards. Power to the elevators was shut off several times; the public address system went dead; and the floor swarmed with boozy, argumentative Democrats with balloons, banners, funny hats, and phony credentials.

Insofar as the pandemonium was controllable, it was directed by Roosevelt himself, who was in a hideaway behind the platform with his mother, communicating with floor leaders by telephone. When he was nominated, the demonstration went on for nearly an hour.

Through it all, Harriman, Marie, and their retinue cooled their heels behind the podium. It was after eleven o'clock before Syracuse attorney John J. Young began his nominating speech. When he concluded, Harriman delegates launched their own demonstration and more fistfights broke out, ending with police hauling off several Roosevelt supporters who tried to break into the Harriman delegations with huge Roosevelt posters. The roll call at last got under way after midnight.

Still trying desperately to break the grip of party chiefs, FDR's floor leaders demanded roll calls of the big Harriman delegations, and Averell's managers returned the favor. In spite of the disorder, the organizations' ranks held firm. It was 1:10 A.M. when the votes of Onondaga County put Averell past the 509 votes he needed for nomination.

Dejected at the scene he knew was inevitable, Lehman had skipped the convention and gone to Sun Valley on vacation. At four A.M., he telephoned De Sapio to urge that Roosevelt be offered the nomination for attorney general as the best way to make amends to the people who had been trampled. Harriman was all for it.

For Roosevelt, it was a chance to salvage his career, to show that he truly had more popular support in the state than Harriman, and he took it. The rest of the slate emerged from the usual exercise in ethnic ticket-balancing: Italian Catholic George DeLuca, the Bronx district attorney, for lieutenant governor, and Jewish Aaron L. Jacoby of Brooklyn for comptroller. Jacoby would shortly resign from the ticket when there were allegations of involvement in an old scandal; Arthur Levitt would replace him. The only problem was that the ticket had no upstate representative. It was all New York City.

Given the battle of the previous night, Harriman accepted the nomination in an atmosphere of surprising calm and civility, pledging to make "the dead hand of Republicanism" the preeminent issue of his campaign against Ives.

The next day, the entire ticket, with the exception of one nominee for the Court of Appeals, received the endorsement of the Liberal party convention. Harriman appeared before five hundred delegates with his battered hat on, bringing laughter and warm applause, for Alex Rose was president of the Hatters' Union and often complained of modern politicians' habit of going bareheaded.

But those who feared that Harriman could never break out of his aristocratic shell had their doubts promptly validated. In his first appearance as the nominee, Harriman gave his running mate a rousing buildup—and forgot his name. "George DeMumba . . . DeMuu . . . DeLumba . . . ," he sputtered, looking stricken. Roosevelt, sitting behind him, came to the rescue with a stage whisper loud enough to reach several rows into the audience, "DeLuca, De LUCA, DE LUUUUUKA, DE LUUUUUUUU-KAAAAH."[43]

Chosen by the machine, Harriman was now thrown into the elemental politics of city streets, county fairs, and upstate political clubs. When it was all over six weeks later, Alex Rose would conclude that he would have won more handily had he not campaigned at all. His name and reputation brought him much, his campaign style, little.

As he hit the road, Ted Tannenwald asked the bank for $5,000 in cash, which he presented to Harriman with a gentle suggestion he use it for tips, meal tabs, and contributions to useful causes that publicly presented themselves. Four months later, when it was all over, more than $4,900 of it was returned, and Tannenwald noted that the bills were the same ones he had given the candidate at the beginning.

Averell's journey through the autumn took him across a New York he had never really known. He stumped Harlem, traveled upstate country roads by bus, went into the subways, slums, and tenements. President Truman and his daughter, Margaret, came to help out, and occasionally Marie joined the tour; but usually he was accompanied by Bernard Ruggieri and Joe Tepper, his streetwise young advance men, who along the way taught him to campaign. Harriman loved it. Riding in an open convertible with his lucky hat that had been with him since Moscow days, he was preceded by Tepper and Ruggieri in a car with a loudspeaker, playing the campaign song and bellowing, "Here's your next governor, ladies and gentlemen. Here's Averell Harriman."

When he stopped to speak, Tepper and Ruggieri would fade into the crowd; and as soon as he got started, they would whistle and clap and cheer him on. "Attaboy, Ave. Give 'em hell, Ave." Harriman would pick up the tempo, and sometimes get a crowd behind him. In New York City, he demanded the rollback of rents; and upstate he lambasted Vermont entrepreneurs for buying New York maple syrup and taking it home, and then selling it back to New York as Vermont syrup. He delighted in going after the Dewey administration, but he was still prone get off into the swamp of great national and foreign policy issues; and when he did, audiences could not be awakened by any amount of pump priming by Tepper and Ruggieri.

Tepper, who had grown up on the Lower East Side, could take the pulse of a crowd on sight, and was prone to make policy through his bullhorn as he prepared an audience for the candidate's speech. Campaigning at subway stops during one rush hour, Harriman noticed that his advance man was announcing that there would never be an increase in subway fares in a Harriman administration. Aside from the fact that it was a city matter, the subway fare was something the candidate had never thought about. He admonished his hucksters against making state, local, or national policy; but otherwise in his journey through the hustings, he put himself in their hands.

Arriving an hour late for an October speech at a Fourteenth Street Union Hall, they found an angry union member before the microphone denouncing Harriman as an "arrogant millionaire keeping us waiting and insulting us." As Averell hesitated outside, embarrassed and uncertain what to do next, the advance men raced into the crowd and disconnected the microphone, shutting the troublemaker off. Tepper took the floor with his bullhorn, and Ruggieri led Harriman forward to rousing cheers.[44]

So went the campaign into the fall. Irving Ives had never lost an election, and the polls showed him leading again. But once the Democrats' ugly convention faded from the public memory and the party realized it was within reach of state government control for the first time since World War II, Harriman pulled ahead. To his campaign headquarters on Park Avenue South rallied state party pros and a new generation of activists, including Jonathan Bingham, Daniel Patrick Moynihan, and others who would become powerful figures in New York politics years later. With them came closet Democrats from Long Island, platoons of old New Dealers and Fair Dealers from Washington, labor leaders, and functionaries of the Tammany Hall machine.

Although Dewey remained personally popular, the Republican administration in Albany had been tainted by a racetrack scandal; and it appeared Harriman and the Democrats were on their way to a rout—until the Republicans decided to make Harriman himself and his selection by the machine the central campaign issue.

The Democratic nominee, said Dewey, was a man who had left the state for twenty years and returned only to get the best job $40 million could buy. Once branded a reckless Cold Warrior by liberals in his own party, Harriman was now indicted by the Republicans for being soft on communism, Ives's waving the the old bloody shirt of the Yalta agreement.

In mid-October rumors began circulating that the Republicans were about to explode a bombshell that would turn the race upside down. On the 18th, Ives suddenly canceled the next day's schedule of upstate appearances and rushed back to New York City, leaving a campaign spokesman to announce dramatically that he would have an earthshaking statement in the city. When reporters piled into his state headquarters in Manhattan hours later, Ives announced that he would go on a statewide television hookup that night to disclose "a startling and shocking situation involving the Tammany-Democrat candidate for governor."[45]

Harriman was upstate on his campaign bus when the papers came out with headlines on Ives's promise of a bombshell. Without knowing what the senator was going to say, he and Charles Van Devander, his press secretary, stopped the bus in Watertown long enough to compose an all-purpose statement accusing the Republican candidate of turning away from the issues.

At campaign headquarters, a move to discredit Harriman personally had been anticipated from the beginning, and Tannenwald had been assigned to prepare responses to anything that presented trouble. Given the soft-on-communism theme, he expected Ives to drag out Harriman's old business dealings with the Russians. But Tannenwald guessed wrong. What Ives resurrected was a long-forgotten scandal involving not communism but Harriman shipping interests and a Brooklyn judge jailed years earlier in a mail-fraud scheme.

In the course of a much publicized investigation of Judge Bernard Vause in 1930, there had been headline charges that Harriman's United American Lines paid Vause what amounted to a $250,000 bribe to secure piers for Harriman ships. The payments came to light years after they were made, when Vause, a prominent Tammany Democrat, his brother, and several others were indicted in a phony banking operation. In the course of that investigation, the U.S. attorney came across documents showing that a $250,000 payment had been made by Harriman's shipping company to the law firm where Vause had practiced before he was appointed to the bench by Al Smith. There was evidence that the money eventually got to Vause and that Vause continued to take a hand in the lease negotiations after he was appointed to the bench.

Harriman had appeared before a federal grand jury and sworn that he knew nothing of the payments. Richard H. M. Robinson, Averell's business associate going back to his shipbuilding days in the Delaware Valley, acknowledged that he was aware of payments to the Vause law firm, although he said he was surprised at the amount.

Displaying twenty-four-year-old newspaper headlines, Ives ridiculed the possibility that Harriman might have known nothing of the transaction. The whole thing had happened, he accurately noted, when United American Lines' business was going badly and Harriman needed pier leases so he could sell his unprofitable passenger ships. The political utility of the old case was that it gave Ives his chance to hammer on Harriman as a tool of Tammany Hall. Vause was a Tammany man, and Harriman was now Tammany's candidate for governor. Said Ives: "I can tell you that you can't trust the business of the state to a man who says he didn't know what happened to a quarter of a million dollars of his own company's money paid to a corrupt judge. . . . You can be sure that if he is elected, Tammany Hall will make away with everything in the state except the steps of the state capitol."[46] Harriman was embarrassed and angry, but he didn't see his lead threatened. The charges confirmed the Republicans' desperation.

Dewey followed with a second televised "chapter," charging that Harriman had been responsible for American investors' losing $5 million in his Polish mining venture started in 1925. The attacks continued almost until election day, Ives claiming there was a clear pattern revealing Harriman to be unfit for public office.

Harriman's closing of Arden Farms' milk-processing plant in 1947 when employees were demanding higher wages was offered as proof that he was a union-buster. And the case of a defunct title company, where Harriman had served as a director, was resurrected with the allegation that he had been party to deception about its financial condition. Investors had been assured the venture was Depression-proof, Ives charged, but lost $60 million when it collapsed.

Jacob Javits, the GOP's candidate for attorney general, looked at Ives's material and refused to have anything to do with the scandal charges. The Teamsters Union, which had represented Harriman's Arden Dairy employees, and American Federation of Labor president George Meany ridiculed the notion that Harriman was a union-buster. More damaging to Ives and Dewey, Senator William Langer, a conservative, unpredictable North Dakota Republican, declared the pier bribery charges against Harriman baseless. Three years earlier, Langer had held up Harriman's confirmation as Mutual Security director while he looked into the Vause case and United American Lines' pier leases. He had, he said, found Harriman "entirely innocent of wrong doing."[47] For days, Harriman could not bring up the charges in public without sputtering with frustration. The Republican campaign was now one of desperation, he said over and over, and the governer and the senator had stooped to a personal smear with distortions and outright lies. But not until nine days after resurrection of the Vause case did he respond in detail. Accusing Ives and Dewey of stooping to the Communist and Fascist big-lie tactic, he struck back in a speech delivered in Queens and broadcast statewide. The payments to Bernard Vause, he said, had been for legitimate legal and engineering services. Vause's indictment, conviction, and imprisonment had resulted from later activities that had nothing to do with the piers or the shipping line. Perjury charges filed against the judge in that matter had been dropped.

While Harriman's aggressive investment activities through the twenties and thirties indeed invited investigation, the Ives campaign's excesses swamped its own credibility. In the case of the Silesian mining venture, Ives claimed that Harriman had been ready to do business with Hitler to save his investment after the Nazis overran Poland. To the contrary, Harriman had pulled out of the venture four years before the invasion of Poland ignited World War II.

Harriman pounced on the implied criticism of his patriotism. At the time Hitler tried to buy out the mining company through Swiss banks in 1941, he declared, he was already in London. "I was there as the personal representative of the President—Franklin D. Roosevelt," he reminded voters. "It was during the bomb-blitz days when Britain was standing alone against the full force of the Nazi power. I was Lend-Lease administrator and held vital responsibilities in the conduct of the war. I was involved deeply in the struggle against Nazi Germany."[48]

The speech was his most important of the campaign. But after his aides spent more than a week searching archives, running down participants in the ventures, and writing and rewriting, Harriman's counterattack fell flat. His advisers well knew that he lapsed into stammering and mumbling when he was tired, yet they scheduled no time for him to rest before he went on the air. And because of the importance of the speech, they decided to have him use a TelePrompTer. He had never used the device before and the result was that he not only stammered but got lost in the text in front of him. At his headquarters on Park Avenue, his campaign workers watched in horror. De Sapio turned his eyes from the screen, held his head in his hands, and cursed Harriman under his breath.

The campaign ended with little evidence that cynical New York voters had been massively disturbed by old business deals transformed into political fodder. Polls indicated the bombshells were having no telling effect. Milton Stewart looked at all of them, took his own soundings and concluded that Harriman would win by 150,000 votes. More trouble-some than the personal attacks was an education issue used by the Repub-licans upstate. It produced few headlines, but it was getting results. Averell had endorsed a platform plank, written by Mayor Wagner, call-ing for more money for New York City schools. Afterward, the Republi-can campaign discovered a study done in the mayor's office, suggesting a reallocation of state education funds. What that meant, the Ives cam-paign said, was that Harriman was planning to take money from upstate schools and give it to the schools of New York City. In late October, they pinpointed how much every upstate town and county stood to lose. Preoccupied with the "bombshells," the Harriman campaign was slow to deal with the controversy or the Republican assertion that Averell's elec-tion would mean a certain tax increase.

Fortunately election day brought a heavy tide for Democrats across the country; and in the first hours after the New York polls closed, Averell appeared to be riding its crest. In a third-floor suite at the Bilt-more, he was surrounded by the men who made him the candidate and delivered the victory—De Sapio, Rose, Lehman, Backer, Balch, Julius Edelstein, David Dubinsky, and campaign manager John P. McGrath. As they dined, Democrats began their celebration in the ballroom down-stairs and across the city. It looked as if he would bury Ives under an avalanche of 300,000 votes or more. Two hours after the polls closed, the senator prepared to concede and head back to Washington, while the Harrimans began a triumphant tour of all the Democratic candidates' headquarters.

The celebration was grossly premature. Both sides had badly under-estimated the Republican turnout in upstate counties where the educa-tion issue had swept school districts. Only wise old Herbert Lehman voiced a word of caution. He had been in politics long enough to know that there would be a penalty for Harriman's three weeks on the defen-sive. The early lead, he warned, might not withstand the late upstate count.

When Ives territory began to report after midnight, Averell's huge lead vanished. Roosevelt, who had kept his distance from the Harriman campaign, quickly went down to defeat before Republican congressman Javits from Manhattan. Harriman watched, seemingly immobilized by the turnaround; and campaign officials, seeing a recount coming, began rousing lawyers from bed and sending them upstate to watch out for vote thievery. Dewey ordered the ballot boxes impounded to prepare for a recanvass. By two A.M., Harriman's lead was down to twelve thou-sand and dropping. Exhausted, the candidate left the Biltmore and went home to Eighty-first Street at three A.M., the outcome anything but certain.

The recount took the rest of the week. While the probable new governor awaited the outcome at Arden, his slim lead dwindled but finally held. Of the more than five million votes cast, the final tally showed him elected by a margin of slightly more than eleven thousand. The landslide had ended in the closest gubernatorial election in the state's history, Harriman saved only by a heavier-than-normal turnout in the city. Still, he and the party reacted as if they had been given an indisputable mandate. If the entrenched Republican legislature was obstructive, Harriman warned, he intended to go over its head and take his programs directly to the people.

On New Year's Eve, 1954, as Democrats converged to reclaim the Executive Mansion in Albany, two railroad cars filled with the special friends of the governor-elect pulled out of Grand Central Station. Aboard were the Swopes, the Sherwoods, the Backers, friends from polo and New Deal days, the De Sapios, the Roses, and the politicians who had delivered Harriman into his first elective office. Of the one thousand celebrants on the train, nearly a hundred were invited to the Executive Mansion for the Harrimans' first dinner there. Several, including Margaret Truman, were to stay overnight. On the train to the capital, around Sands Point bridge tables, and in mobs of Democrats checking into Albany hotels, conversations already turned toward 1956. Perhaps, said friends of the governor-elect, the Executive Mansion in Albany was but a way station on a journey to the White House.

Surrounded by members of his family and a conglomeration of old friends and pols invited to dinner on his first night in the Executive Mansion, Harriman was sworn in as New York's governor at one minute after midnight on January 1, 1955. The lights were dimmed for thirty seconds at the stroke of midnight and then turned back on as Albert Conway, the new chief judge of the Court of Appeals, read the oath.

Downtown Albany swarmed with politicians celebrating the first hours of the new year and what they took to be a new era. It was the first time a Democrat had taken the reins from a Republican since Al Smith succeeded Nathan Miller in 1923.

At ten A.M., the Assembly chamber was opened an hour ahead of schedule to accommodate the crowd surging into the capitol for the inauguration ceremony. It immediately filled, and hundreds of Democrats who had come from across the state with personal invitations were unable to get even a glimpse of Harriman as he took the oath, his hand on his mother's Bible. Some moved over to the Senate chamber and listened to the proceedings on the public address system. Outside, 105-millimeter howitzers boomed a nineteen-gun salute as the new governor, dressed in formal morning attire, stepped to the podium to deliver his inaugural address.

Chapter XX

GOVERNOR
Tammany's Choice

Harriman promised New York a "bold adventurous administration." He would, he said, "reject no approach because it is unorthodox, and no answer merely because it requires a radical revision of present machinery or prevailing prejudices."[1] To the Democrats overflowing the capitol, the rhetoric evoked FDR and Al Smith, but the new governor came to office severely handicapped in spite of his legendary name and vast national and world experience. His victory margin had been the slimmest in the history of state gubernatorial campaigns. He bore the onus of being Tammany Hall's handpicked candidate; he was faced with a reactionary Republican legislature doggedly clinging to the power it had shared with Dewey. More seriously, he had no sharply honed agenda and, in some ways, knew little about his state.

He had truer instincts for the opposition politics of Europe than the perversity of the Republicans in Albany. And while he had been comfortable exercising authority on behalf of Roosevelt and Truman, he was hesitant when New Yorkers handed him the whip and reins for his own.

His challenge was all the more daunting because he followed a long succession of progressive governors: Roosevelt, Smith, Lehman—and Thomas E. Dewey. In private, many of his supporters acknowledged that his Republican predecessor had given the state a dozen years of truly effective administration.

Dewey had loyally recited the conservative litany and launched the usual assaults upon liberalism and big government, but he had not been afraid to ignore Republican party orthodoxy. On important matters, he shocked reactionary party brethren from rural upstate counties, calling for reapportionment of the legislature, agreeing with Democrats on public ownership of the huge Niagara hydroelectric-power project, and pushing antidiscrimination legislation. In broad respects, his internationalist views were wholly compatible with Harriman's. He supported the Marshall Plan and NATO; and when Douglas MacArthur came home to his hero's welcome in Manhattan, he discreetly absented himself from the state.[2]

But Averell, nevertheless, took office with a promise "to put a little atomic bomb under the myth that Dewey was a good administrator." The Republicans, he said, had for years been hiding the truth about the state's unemployment and concealing grave financial problems with bookkeeping tricks.[3]

For help, he turned to friends from the New Deal days, entrusting the state budget to Paul Appleby, who had served Democratic presidents from the grim banking crisis of March 1933 to the last day of Harry Truman's term, and the Labor Department to Isador Lubin, a liberal economist regarded by the right wing as a fellow traveler, if not worse. A friend and college classmate of Harry Hopkins, Appleby had got his start under Henry A. Wallace at the Agriculture Department; but he had spent much of his career working on the federal budget, and he was deputy director of Truman's Budget Bureau when he left Washington. By inauguration day, he and the governor-elect had already been planning the New York budget for six weeks, and to no small degree they had already set the Harriman administration on the course it would follow for the next four years.

It was a far cry from anything imagined by Republicans, who expected them to unleash a deluge of New Dealish tax-and-spend projects. Harriman instead stepped before the legislature on opening day with a stern conservative lecture to the state for living beyond its means. New York had over the years drifted into a financial crisis, he said, and the moment of reckoning could no longer be postponed. Rather than priming the pump in the fashion of FDR, he ordered pencils sharpened in the budget office.

The decision wasn't easy, but the eight weeks between the election and his inauguration had brought him face-to-face with a kind of choices that had never reached his desk in Washington, at Brown Brothers Harriman, or in the boardroom of the Union Pacific. He responded by adopting economic policies more reminiscent of Hoover than of the New Deal. He was unwilling to ask for a general tax increase or accept a budget deficit, and consequently his progressive social agenda had to be put on hold.

As he and Appleby were looking into the ledgers of the Dewey administration in November, he had George Backer, Thomas Finletter, a pillar of Manhattan's liberal establishment, and Julius Edelstein working on a blueprint to make New York a beacon of progressive social policy in America. Using proposals from the Democratic and Liberal party platforms, borrowing from the Lehman administration, and developing ideas from Harriman's own campaign, they proposed "to renew the leadership that New York once enjoyed" and "plow new ground in social and economic matters as well as in the general level of governmental administration."[4] It was the kind of agenda that could easily be polished up as the centerpiece of a 1956 campaign for the Democratic presidential nomination.

The hitch was that Averell was so rocked by what he found in the state's budget books that his blueprint for a new era was reduced to a fuzzy outline devoid of schedules, hard numbers, and serious commitments before he ever got to Albany. He was stuck with both inherited budget problems and firm and costly campaign commitments to increase unemployment compensation, expand disability benefits, raise the minimum wage, improve conditions for migrant workers, tighten rent controls, and enhance highway safety. The innovations he and his brain trusters envisioned as the hallmark of his administration were, therefore, left unfunded. "He talked a good liberal line, until somebody showed him a deficit," said Backer. "At that point, he became a conservative."[5]

Thus, four days after he was sworn in, Harriman set a course that was cautious and awkwardly out of phase with the bold new era that he and his progressive advisers had set out to create. Because the state was in such a fiscal mess, he solemnly told the legislature after the inaugural festivities were over, "many services and projects, which our state government should undertake and our people want, must be postponed."[6] Republicans were indignant. Dewey had left touting a healthy budget surplus of $142 million.

That was in fact the case. The trouble was that the surplus was in a special fund created long ago to balance the budget in emergencies. Dewey had deftly avoided either tapping the emergency fund or increasing taxes by dipping heavily into yet another kitty—a special account that had been set up to pay for postwar construction projects. It was a sleight of hand made possible because the state had adopted budget habits resembling a housewife's stashing spare cash in mattresses and sugar bowls.

The construction fund had accumulated during World War II, when state revenues boomed and construction projects were deferred because the able-bodied were in the military or working in war plants. Within a few years, it soared past $500 million, enabling the state to adopt a practice of "forgiving" half of individual taxpayers' obligations and collecting only half of what they actually owed.

When state spending overtook and exceeded tax collections, Dewey cut the "forgiven" portion of personal taxes from 50 percent to 40 percent, and then to 10 percent—in effect getting two tax increases that were, politically, relatively painless. Then, when still more revenue was required to keep the budget in balance, he had started tapping the flush construction fund. On Harriman's inauguration day, the account still had $287 million in it, but two thirds of that was already obligated to projects on the drawing boards or actually under way. To balance the first Harriman budget, civil servants in the state budget office told Appleby after the election, the new governor would have to find an additional $100 million.

Averell's options were grim. He had vowed there would be no income-tax increase; but if he continued Dewey's practice of bleeding the construction fund, the fund would soon be exhausted and the long list of bridge and highway projects already deferred would grow longer.

Republicans who had crowed loudly about the dozen years of balanced Dewey budgets took the offensive. Harriman, claimed GOP state chairman Judson Morhouse, was laying the groundwork to ask for new taxes "to finance a socialistic welfare state planned by his left-wing, poverty-crying advisers, who consider the average American incapable of making his own decisions."[7] Before Harriman and Appleby could issue their first spending plan, the legislature passed one bill slashing taxes and another increasing state spending on education for the next five years.

Harriman vetoed both. To keep his promise against raising the state income tax, he sent the assembly a plan for a $750 million bond issue to save the construction fund and cover the first year's deficit. At the same time, he asked for an additional two cents a gallon tax on gasoline, and canceled the last 10 percent of forgiven taxes. This, plus a one-half percent increase on corporate franchise taxes, and a 1 percent addition to taxes on unincorporated businesses, would produce $127 million and balance the budget.

So much for bold social progressivism. It was the beginning of a game of chicken with Republican lawmakers, who regularly passed appropriations far exceeding his requests for his favorite projects, forcing him to veto them in order to hold the line on the budget. In other cases, they made brutal cuts so he had to ask for more money and give them a chance to label him a profligate spender. At times legislative leaders were willing to flirt with state bankruptcy to keep the political pressure on.

The governor and Appleby came out of the first budget battle looking clumsy and inept because they had been excessively cautious. The national and state economy didn't falter as they expected, and revenues, therefore, exceeded their projections. When the legislature convened for its second term, the problem before it was not a tax increase but to design a tax cut.

Although Harriman had come to pride himself as a liberal, he looked on the governor's office as a boardroom in which he was called upon to defend the returns he produced on stockholders' investments. His budget, he thought, was the instrument to build his support, and he spent weeks explaining his management of it to businessmen, newspaper publishers, labor union officers, and local government officials who were invited to the mansion to be briefed. Before each session of the assembly, he held "budget school" and more or less compelled Albany correspondents of New York newspapers to wade line by line through the document, with Appleby and himself as their guides.

House rules for the evening sessions at the governor's mansion required reporters to address questions to the chief executive, who rephrased them to suit himself and put them to Appleby. Harriman was growing quite deaf, but he refused to wear a hearing aid for fear that it would make him look old. His budget director's hearing was even worse, so the sessions in the reception room filled the first floor of the house with shouting. Harriman couldn't hear reporters' questions and Appleby often missed the governor's translations. The answers that made their way back often had nothing at all to do with inquiries. Confusion was rampant. More than briefings, recalled Jack Germond, the correspondent for the Utica papers, budget school resembled the child's game "Sounds Like."[8]

When all was said and done, Harriman slipped through his term with his pledge against a general tax increase intact, saved by tight budgets, bond issues, and fingers gingerly put into the diminished construction-fund sugar bowl that had been so successfully raided by Dewey. The price for his stolid, conservative handling of the New York purse was an unremarkable record as a leader.

In spite of the haggling with the legislature and his eye toward bigger things in Washington, Harriman was a different man in Albany. He loved being governor. "The Guv," he called himself. He was up at the crack of dawn to peruse *The New York Times* and shake his minions awake with news and their first assignments for the day. First on the list was always Jonathan Bingham, his executive secretary and chief lieutenant. "This is the Guv," he said cheerily to Jonathan Bingham's wife, June, when she was awakened from a sound sleep before a winter dawn in 1955. "What are you doing?" "We were having intercourse," she replied sleepily. Thereafter, the Guv's wakeup calls to Bingham came later, but only by a few minutes.

He worked at the residence until midmorning, then walked the three quarters of a mile to the office with his white Labrador retriever, Brum. Usually he was back at the mansion with luncheon guests, returning to the office at midafternoon. The routine agreed with him so thoroughly that he soon gained fifteen pounds, and for the first time in years looked positively robust.

Unlike Dewey, he made a point of being an Albany resident. He decreed that all the members of the administration family would live in the capital as well, stopping the practice of commuting from Manhattan, as many preferred. Although he was often in the city two or three times a week, he nearly always made it back to Albany, even if he arrived at two or three A.M.

When Marie was away, he got on the phone and tried to get a dinner invitation, which he usually was able to do with unconcealed hints that he was available for the evening. But if no invitation was forthcoming, he would invite guests to the mansion for a swim in the heated pool that had been installed for Franklin Roosevelt. His home telephone number was listed in the Albany directory; and for the first time in his life, he sometimes answered calls himself, listening to constituent complaints and dispatching a snowplow to rescue a stranded farmer or alerting the highway department to a dangerous pothole or a damaged bridge.

He hadn't been so satisfied with life since he was in the prime of his polo career. He had "tasted the pure unalloyed joy of self discovery," said his friend Teddy White, and he had become "a warmer, more gregarious person."[9] He was an incessant booster of his state, serving New York wine at dinner, touting Long Island ducks and potatoes, and glorifying New York maple syrup and Genesee beer. Depending on the circumstances, he proclaimed himself a fan of the New York Yankees or the Brooklyn Dodgers, and occasionally took in a fight at Madison Square Garden. Living at Arden had been good training for the fortress on Eagle Street in Albany, where governors had lived in varying states of discomfort since 1877. Some of the Harrimans' early predecessors had found the old house so cold in the winter they had passed hours in the kitchen to stay warm. The Lehmans had been there for nearly a decade and had never bothered to explore all of it. Later, the Deweys had undertaken to redecorate it, but the public rooms had a depressing, institutional, shrinelike quality, and the outside, with its gables, turrets, and towers, had the look of something from Edgar Allan Poe.

"Early Halloween," Marie called it as she undertook to brighten and modernize it the way she had enlivened the drab interiors of the Union Pacific railroad cars. The government colors left behind by the Deweys were replaced with lively pastels, and inevitably the now famous paintings followed. The house where the Deweys had taken refuge from his office became under Harriman an extension of the executive suite, and operated in the manner of an American embassy. Their entertaining far exceeded what the state provided, and they dipped into their own pocket, mainly to replace the silverware, which Democrats kept carrying away as souvenirs. They also entertained friends from stage, screen, world diplomacy, and New York commerce. The composer Richard Rodgers and his wife, the latter one of the governor's vicious croquet rivals, dropped in occasionally, as did the John Steinbecks and Oscar Hammersteins. Robert Sherwood fell ill and stayed for days, being nursed back to health by Averell and the "Governess," as Marie styled herself. "You took in a wretched cadaver at a time when you had other problems to worry about," Sherwood wrote gratefully, "and you fed and pampered and returned him to some semblance of living humanity. I must confess it was pretty damned embarrassing to have the Governor of New York bringing me pillows for my back and baked macaroni and cheese for my frayed tissues."[10]

Marie had detested the self-importance and company-town mentality of Washington, and she had expected Albany to be worse. "Albania," she would mutter, "Albania. Jesus Christ, can you imagine me milking cows in Albania?" Once she was there, however, she adored it, and defended it against the gibes of her friends in the city and at Hobe Sound. Once a week, she had ladies from the community in for tea; and like the legislative wives, they loved her absence of pretension, her habit of calling everybody "dahling" in her Miss Spence baritone, telling little stories out of school, making irreverent jokes about "Ave," and winking about the great statesmen of both parties. When friends remarked how splendid Averell looked, her side of the mouth reply usually was, "He should, he didn't do anything but play polo until he was 50."[11]

Albany, the old Democratic stronghold, gloried in the change from the ascetic Deweys, who had regarded the capital as if it were a military hardship post. The lights on the hill now blazed into the wee hours of the morning, Marie's bridge games keeping them burning on nights when the state was not entertaining. During the summer, passersby could see the Harrimans, their relatives, their dogs, and their out-of-town visitors out on the wraparound porch. Marie was often about town in charity work and activities at the Albany Art Institute. When there was an idle evening, they occasionally showed up unannounced for drinks and dinner at the Ten Eyck Hotel, where legislators congregated, or even at Yenties, the frayed restaurant and bar, which journalists regarded as their domain.

Harriman worked harder than he ever had before. As a businessman, and even in Washington, he had been notorious for launching projects and promptly dropping them into lap of hired help, but in Albany he felt compelled to operate the state himself. He ordered detailed reports of all fatal automobile accidents sent to his desk so he could decide whether state action was called for. He set up an alert system to flash him word of a forest fire, jailbreak, train wreck, or wildcat strike. Cabinet and staff members were ordered to make their whereabouts known around the clock, on weekends, and during their vacations. Any legislation that had to do with horse racing, state parks, or development of skiing in the Adirondacks was personally handled.

By no means were all of his duties so stimulating. He had been in office scarcely a week when he received his first clemency petition from death row, a plea from one Norman Lee Horton, a former college student who had hitchhiked home, broken into his family's residence and stabbed his sleeping father to death. The motive had been the son's anger that he had less money than his friends at school. The state Court of Appeals reviewed the jury's verdict and upheld it by a vote of 6–1, and Horton's electrocution was set for January 17, 1955, at Sing Sing. The more the governor read about the case, the more seriously he wondered about the young man's sanity.

Before acting on the clemency petition, he ordered the prisoner brought to the capitol for an interview with Daniel Gutman, his legal counsel, who was a former judge. Since psychiatrists disagreed about Horton's sanity, Harriman left the question to the judgment of Gutman. Pale, trembling, and effeminate, the condemned prisoner was barely able to speak when he was led in, and Gutman concluded after trying unsuccessfully to question him that he was "in a fog." Harriman commuted the death sentence to life imprisonment, saying he couldn't allow the execution of a man "whose mind undoubtedly is befogged," even if he was considered legally sane.[12]

Eighteen executions were carried out during his administration, however, and he found allowing them to proceed the most distasteful duty of his public life. He was always terrified that something would go wrong on execution night, that a court reprieve would fail to get through in time, as once happened in California when a condemned man died two minutes before lawyers with a stay order could reach Governor Goodwin Knight on an ocean liner.

On the night of his first execution, he sat at his desk and waited until it was over, looking at his watch and refusing to talk. When the warden called from Sing Sing and Averell's secretary handed him a note that the sentence had been carried out, he walked out into the night without a word. After that, he arranged for Gutman and an assistant to wait in the governor's office, with two telephone lines open to the warden, and a third reserved for lawyers and relatives of the condemned. At the mansion, another line was kept open for Harriman himself.

As execution dates approached, he would call Gutman in and agonize over the clemency petitions and requests for stays. "I don't like this," he would complain. "I can't understand how any civilized man can like the death sentence. But what can I do?"[13] It was, he later said, quoting Al Smith, "the Governor's private Gethsemane." The night of the eighteenth electrocution was as difficult as the first. Sending men to die, he said, had made him realize "how backward our system of correction is."[14]

Convinced after the Horton case that legal grounds for the determination of sanity were inadequate, he ordered an updating of the hundred-year-old guidelines being followed by New York courts and doubled the number of psychiatrists and psychiatric social workers on the Governor's Prison Commission to ensure more thorough examination of prisoners on death row.

Although he lived in the house and worked in the office once occupied by Roosevelt, Harriman's role model was Harry Truman, from his combative style and command of budget detail to his balancing of liberal ideals and practical politics. The trouble was that many of the lessons of Washington and the Fair Deal, particularly as they applied to members of the legislature, were irrelevant. Unlike Congress, the perpetually Republican legislature could be organized into monolithic opposition to anything the administration attempted. It was dominated by a conglomeration of party professionals from upstate, reactionary country lawyers, farmers, small businessmen, and a few wealthy Manhattanites. After twelve years of Dewey, they were sour over their lost patronage and of no mind to meekly surrender power in the state, or concede another long Democratic run in the governor's mansion.

Democrats, on the other hand, had been out of control for so long that they had become a defeatist, downtrodden, permanent minority. Good men in his own party, Harriman thought, had come to resemble burned-out racehorses; the best of them became fed up and moved on—to lifetime judgeships if they were lucky—and those who remained accepted whatever crumbs the Republicans swept their way.[15] Outnumbered ninety to sixty in the Assembly and thirty-four to twenty-three in the Senate upon Harriman's arrival, the Democrats mainly contributed to the administration by sustaining his vetoes of the bills the Republicans passed. Their ineptitude was not the party's sole problem, though. Because New York Democrats had been out of power so long, Harriman did not inherit the usual legion of staff people to provide the institutional memory and infrastructure of government.

The chief remaining links back to the Lehman years were Charles Poletti and Julius Edelstein. Poletti had been Lehman's lieutenant governor and had briefly served as governor after Lehman resigned to join the State Department's wartime foreign relief work in 1942. He was one of the few people around who would argue with Harriman publicly or privately. Averell recognized the value of somebody who would challenge him, but he couldn't entice Poletti into another tour in Albany. Nor could he recruit Edelstein away from Lehman's Senate staff in Washington.

The real obstacle to a reincarnation of the Truman administration in Albany, however, was the governor himself. He used his veto power with a heavy hand and occasionally astonished his aides with his stubbornness—as when he offered to accept the resignation of Robert Moses during a dispute with New York's autocratic master builder over contracts for power from the Niagara hydroelectric project.

But his instinct was for compromise, and he usually did whatever necessary to placate the godfather of New York's dams, bridges, and freeways. He acceded to Moses' insistence that their business be conducted in New York City rather than Albany, murmured no protest when he was excluded from ground-breakings or dedications, and saw to it that a dam was named in Moses' honor.

He got along well with Assembly speaker Oswald D. Heck, the most important Republican in Albany, who had sufficient standing to break party ranks occasionally and help the administration. Speaker since 1937, Heck had often found himself taken for granted in the Dewey years, and he was flattered by Harriman's attention. Averell invited him to the mansion, sent aides around to brief him, solicited his views, and said nice things about him to the press.

While compromise was possible with Heck, no amount of goodwill worked for very long with Senate leader Walter Mahoney, who tied up crucial legislation, delayed Harriman's important appointments, and refused to cooperate even on routine matters in his own interest. He was rigid, obstructive, blindly partisan, strongly tied to the insurance industry, and, Harriman thought, personally and politically untrustworthy.

For six weeks, Mahoney held up Averell's nomination of Isador Lubin to be commissioner of labor just because he did not like Lubin's New Deal pedigree. It was hardly surprising that the Republicans opposed the choice, for Lubin was a member of the Roosevelt brain trust and a longtime U.S. commissioner of labor statistics. The Senate Labor Committee in Albany put together a dossier filled with evidence of what it regarded as Lubin's damning leftist associations; then, having made its point, recommended approval of the nomination.

Mahoney refused to bring it to the floor, however. When the twenty-day period for approval of nominations had passed, Harriman responded by putting Lubin to work anyway, inviting a showdown. Nothing happened until Irving Ives, knowing that Harriman would eventually win the fight and perhaps split the legislature in the process, warned Mahoney to back off.

In some ways Harriman was fortunate that his arrival in the governor's office coincided with the Republicans' return to the White House. Eisenhower's election to the presidency meant that young Democrats who would have otherwise been working in Washington were available for service in Albany. With a few notable exceptions, such as Gutman and De Sapio, most of Harriman's first team had already done time in the nation's capital. They were backed by a corps of professionals and civil servants held over from the Dewey administration. Altogether, they would make the Harriman administration remembered as much as anything for the people it brought to state government.

Given that the governor had been the candidate of the party bosses, it was natural to assume, as the Republicans did, that the fingerprints of Carmine De Sapio would be everywhere in the Harriman administration. As secretary of state, Democratic national committeeman, and the power behind both the mayor of New York City as well as governor of the state, Manhattan's Tammany leader had modernized and redefined the image of the big city's political boss, giving it a respectability the organization had never enjoyed before. Rather than operating in back rooms, he made public speeches and gave television interviews, expressing his opinions not only on New York politics but on the nation's economy and Eisenhower's foreign policy. His ambition was to move Harriman from Eagle Street in Albany to Pennsylvania Avenue in Washington. Since that goal would hardly be served by a hovering presence in patronage or administration policy, De Sapio kept a discreet distance.

Instead, it was George Backer who cleared important nominees for staff jobs, provided personal political advice, and molded the administration's personality. And it was Backer who recommended that De Sapio himself be made New York's secretary of state. While Backer held no official post in the administration and refused even to have a desk in Albany, his influence was everywhere, although day-to-day state business was in the hands of Gutman and Jonathan Bingham, with help from Milton Stewart, whose portfolio was state politics and patronage matters.

A key figure in FDR, Jr.,'s campaign and a principal author of the 1954 Democratic party platform, Bingham, as executive secretary, was at the crossroads of the administration. Although he was twenty-five years younger than Harriman, his credentials—Groton '32, Yale '36, and Truman administration '51–'53—qualified him as both Harriman's top aide and effectively as the backup governor, who ran the office anytime Harriman was away.

Gutman, who had been brought to Averell's attention by Mayor Wagner, was a competent lawyer, a former judge, and a onetime member of both the state senate and the assembly with strong ties to the Tammany organization. He worked well with the Republican leaders, insofar as anyone from the administration could. Along with Bingham, he had a hand in shaping nearly every piece of legislation the administration proposed, as well as Harriman's veto decisions, dealings with the legislature, and party politics. He assured cabinet members that they could appeal his decisions to the governor, but aside from the irrepressible consumer adviser, Persia Campbell, few ever did.

With the Bingham-Gutman team discharging the routine business of running state government, Harriman spent an increasing portion of his time with James Sundquist, an aide whose responsibilities lay beyond the borders of New York. Before hiring either Bingham or Gutman, Harriman had, on the advice of Ted Tannenwald, recruited Sundquist from the staff of the Democratic National Committee. A former Truman speech writer, he was given the title of assistant secretary to the governor, and moved into the executive suite. His duties were not outlined in any detail. He was simply told to look after Harriman's national political interests, and that, he assumed from the beginning, meant preparing for a Harriman campaign for President.

The state's financial bind and Harriman's terror of deficits and taxes left him with less than half of 1 percent of his budget to make his mark as heir to the Roosevelt and Lehman legacy. That came to about $6 million, not enough to begin underwriting the agenda drawn up in the first weeks after his election. He was, however, beneficiary of one extraordinary piece of good luck, and he capitalized on it, revolutionizing the state's care for the mentally ill.

New York's mental hospitals in 1955 were overflowing warehouses, and new patients were being admitted faster than space could be found for them. When he was inaugurated, 94,000 New Yorkers were confined to state hospitals. Admissions were running at more than 2,500 a year and rising, making the Department of Mental Hygiene the fastest-growing, most-expensive, most-hopeless department in state government. It had not opened an up-to-date mental hospital in twenty-five years.

Something had to be done for political reasons alone, but Harriman had an interest beyond the developing emergency. Mental health had been one of his family's causes going back to his mother's decades of work in the field and her support for eugenics research. And because of one of the family's own tragedies, he had acquired much more than an ordinary layman's knowledge of the subject. His niece and namesake, Mary Averell Harriman Rumsey, had once seemed headed for permanent institutional care. And had the Harriman family been one of ordinary means, she might well have wound up in one of the crowded custodial wards of a state hospital as a result of the serious breakdown following her mother's death.

Averell consulted doctors from New York to London, Moscow, and Paris. Her course led through counseling, dozens of shock treatments, brief recoveries, long relapses, and eventually a lobotomy. The long, unhappy experience gave him a personal revulsion toward custodial management and the resignation with which mental health was viewed in public policy.

While he had quickly settled on the rest of his cabinet choices, he

ordered a search for a nationally recognized authority to be commissioner of mental hygiene, someone whose interest lay in research instead
of custodial care. The hunt, organized by Backer, took weeks and led
administration scouts into public health departments, private clinics, Veterans Administration hospital wards, and university laboratories around
the country. Ironically, it ended in one of the state's own facilities in New
York City.

One prospect who declined an interview sent Backer to the New
York State Psychiatric Institute and a slight, Hungarian-born psychiatrist
named Paul Hoch. The doctor was getting encouraging results treating
patients with Thorazine and reserpine in combination with psychotherapy; and after long personal interviews with him, Backer was convinced
that the fifty-two-year-old Hoch was their man. The problem was that
he had never headed an organization of more than eight people, and
state law required the commissioner to have no less than five years'
experience as head of a large institution.

Nearly all of Harriman's other advisers, Appleby, Bingham, and
Senator Lehman among them, thought the choice unwise. Running the
state's aging hospitals, overseeing the department's expansion, and trying to invigorate research would be a daunting management assignment.
Even more than technical expertise, the job would require uncommon
political skills.

Mahoney and Senate Republicans would attack the nomination because Hoch lacked the requisite experience. Even if the doctor could get
past that, he hardly seemed the person to work the legislative corridors
and sell the Republicans on new programs that Harriman wanted. But
after two long talks in Albany, Harriman offered Hoch the job, ignoring
advice to give him the number two position instead. Getting the nomination past Mahoney and his troops in the Senate promised to be far more
difficult than finding Hoch in the first place.

Harriman first had to have the help of Jacob Javits and a formal
opinion that Hoch was legally qualified for the job despite being short
of the management experience required by law. As the Republicans' top
elected official in the state, the attorney general was in a delicate position,
so rather than risk a direct approach to him, Harriman went through
their mutual friend Lester Markel. An editor on *The New York Times*,
Markel took a special interest in mental health and gladly interceded
with Javits. Before Mahoney could organize his attack, the attorney general issued a formal opinion that the doctor's experience was sufficient.

Hoch was, as it turned out, the most successful appointment of
the Harriman administration. His heavy Hungarian accent, unflagging
optimism, and political neutrality charmed the Republicans into supporting nearly anything he asked.

It was summer before Hoch even started to work. He arrived in

Albany ready to expand his small experimental program to depressed and psychotic patients in hospitals across the state. Harriman and the legislature provided the money, doubling the budget for drugs and tripling the outlays on psychotherapy and intensive care. As a result, the patient population of the state's mental hospitals turned downward for the first time in half a century.

From custodial care, Hoch swung priority to intensive outpatient care and community services. New York was not alone in moving away from giant, warehouse mental institutions. The revolutionary impact of psychotropic drugs swept the country and in time contributed to the tragedy of homelessness in America; but Harriman, Hoch, and the mental-health community could not foresee that in the dazzling new light of the mid-fifties.

With more foresight but less to show for it, Harriman planted the seeds of other initiatives as showpieces of his administration. He installed Persia Campbell in his own office to represent consumer interests the way Mary Rumsey had in Roosevelt's NRA. He set out to address systematically the special problems of the elderly, and he directed the first local skirmishes of what Lyndon Johnson would later proclaim a national "War on Poverty."

The underlying work for his more modestly styled "Attack on Poverty" had been started under Lubin's direction at the Roosevelt Foundation, which Harriman had helped bankroll. Before his election, Averell decided to transplant both Lubin and the antipoverty research to Albany, thinking of it not so much as an innovation as a continuation of work started in the New Deal.

Roosevelt's recovery program had touched millions of impoverished Americans, but as Lubin regularly emphasized, it had not dented the issue of the chronically poor. Uncounted Americans were nearly destitute before the Great Depression, and many of them were even poorer after the rest of the country recovered. New York, like less affluent states of the South and the West, had its own pockets of permanently poor who politically remained invisible. The state's long-term goal, Harriman and Lubin agreed, was to attack the underlying causes, hoping someday to concentrate on prevention instead of supporting generation after generation of the afflicted. In the end, however, the attack was mostly rhetorical. Over four years, less than $2 million was put into a program that tried to reach chronic welfare families, the indigent elderly, and former mental patients. Pilot projects were started to rehabilitate welfare cases and provide scholarships for trade-school training, but that was as far as the program got. It made no inroads, because Harriman was saving the real offensive for a second term.

The story of the administration's help for the elderly was much the same. Philip Kaiser, a forty-two-year-old economist, former Rhodes scholar, and assistant secretary of labor under Truman, was assigned to organize the problems of the elderly into a coherent agenda. Averell delivered a special message to the legislature and called a statewide conference which produced a "Charter for the Aging." Job counselors in the Department of Labor were assigned to specialize in problems of the unemployed over forty-five. A Bureau of Chronic Disease and Geriatrics was set up in the state health department. A tax amendment increased exemptions for the elderly, and public-housing legislation required future projects to include units designed for them.

The Republicans quickly recognized the towering political potential. Realizing they were in danger of being viewed as obstructing worthy social initiatives, they cooperated in adopting statutes limiting the authority of insurance companies to cancel hospital-care policies of the elderly and to prohibit discrimination based on age. They refused to go along with Harriman's proposal for a $50 million low-income-housing project for the elderly, however, and rejected his plan to set up a permanent State Commission on Aging. Within the administration, the failure to accomplish more was blamed on Kaiser as well as on the legislature.

The governor's expert on aging was interested in a foreign-service career, and his colleagues complained that he wasted the governor's time talking about foreign policy and Washington politics rather than the issues he was supposed to be addressing. Such was not the case with Persia Campbell and her consumer program. Making full use of her mandate, she demanded support as did no other member of the cabinet. Bingham, Gutman, Appleby, and even Harriman preferred to avoid her rather than tell her no. With the governor's approval, she launched a crusade against bait-and-switch advertisers, excessive interest rates, and chemical food additives. Her pursuit of fraudulent repairmen was sabotaged by Harriman's friends in the International Brotherhood of Electrical Workers, who pressured Democrats to join Republicans in killing the administration's own bill. Publicly Campbell kept silent, but she privately blamed Averell for his unwillingness to tangle with the union.

Otherwise she was successful enough that Republican leaders began producing consumer initiatives of their own. When the administration offered a bill to regulate chemical food additives, they countered with a substitute, causing a deadlock resolved by withdrawal of both. They also substituted their own bill for Campbell's plan to control "bait" advertising, moving enforcement authority from her office to the office of the attorney general.

When they also adopted legislation putting all responsibility for consumer protection under the attorney general, Harriman vetoed it. The legislature retaliated by defeating his plan to set up a cabinet-level Consumer Protection Department, which the aggressive Campbell would undoubtedly have headed.

Though underfinanced, the initiatives all had promise, and it was no accident that they addressed national problems. When it came to matters of interest solely to New York, aides often found it difficult to keep Harriman's attention, even on the volatile issue of rent control, which theologically divided Republicans and Democrats. He liked to ruminate on the implications of the population explosion, but he thought of it in global terms; and his advisers could never get him to connect with an urgent need for massive expansion of the state university system. While he labored for hours over his speeches on national issues, he gave drafts of addresses on state matters only a cursory review.

Because Republicans hardly ever broke ranks, Harriman vetoed more than 1,200 of the nearly 5,000 bills sent to his desk, most of them in a thirty-day orgy of bill signing and rejection following adjournment. Tannenwald and Poletti would come to Albany for the exercise and closet themselves with Gutman and the imposing stack of legislation. For days, they would work their way through it, jotting down their recommendations to Harriman and drafting veto and approval statements for him.

In this way, scores of bills shouted through without hearings or debate and bereft of any purpose but the governor's political embarrassment were killed. Among those left behind and routinely vetoed was one requiring New York secondary school students to salute the flag and recite the Pledge of Allegiance each day. The Republicans made nothing of it, for Dewey had also vetoed a nearly identical bill. But more than thirty years later, the same issue would be used to provoke a national uproar and help elect George Bush President of the United States.

Constant use of the veto was not a satisfactory substitute for policy. Given the chronic budget problems, Appleby pleaded with Harriman to concentrate his resources on a few programs where he could make impressive strides and hold them up as hallmarks of his administration, but the governor was unwilling to choose.

His first reaction to new ideas was nearly always negative; he would ridicule proposals that did not have obvious precedent in the New Deal or Fair Deal—and often the people who brought them. To some extent, it was a tactic to bring forth the best case for an initiative, and it was not unusual for him to turn around and accept a recommendation just as he had finished denouncing it. Where his own ideas were up for discussion, he was easily peeved by questions and he would shop around until he found unbridled enthusiasm.[16] Eager as he was for approval, he was strangely reluctant to claim credit for actions that he might have converted to political support. He passed up, for example, an obvious chance to capitalize on his refusal to extradite blacks wanted under dubious circumstances in the Deep South. Nor would he allow his press secretary to issue regular news releases on his vetoes of mischievous legislation. In such ways, opportunities to present himself as a forceful leader were frittered away.

The 1955 legislature had just gone home when federal authorities announced approval of Jonas Salk's polio vaccine. Sundquist, Stewart, and Daniel Patrick Moynihan, Bingham's deputy, pleaded with him to dramatically promise New Yorkers that the vaccine would immediately be made available to every child in the state regardless of families' ability to pay. Instead, he hesitated, assigning Dr. Herman Hillboe, his commissioner of public health, to convene a committee to coordinate distribution. It was weeks before Harriman announced that the Department of Public Health would make the vaccine available to all children in the state. In other states, meanwhile, assurances were quickly given. By the time he moved, another opportunity to demonstrate forceful leadership was gone.

Harriman's instinctive caution was undoubtedly magnified because every move he made was assayed for national implications. With a Republican in the White House, he was, by virtue of being governor of the nation's largest state, a de facto candidate for the Democratic presidential nomination. The question of another presidential race had first been thrown at him on election night in 1954, and he brushed it aside with a matter-of-fact reply that he was for Adlai Stevenson. But from that night onward, the question was asked every time he talked with the press. For months, he ritually dismissed the queries by renewing unequivocal support of Stevenson. He had stayed in touch with the 1952 standard-bearer after the Eisenhower landslide, offering advice when Stevenson took a long tour of foreign capitals and joining a group of liberals organized by Thomas Finletter to explore issues for another race in 1956.

Inexorably, the position changed once Harriman was in the governor's chair. After a while he quit repeating his unequivocal commitment to Stevenson and started responding to questions about his own plans with the pat answer that he was not an "active" candidate.

By the time he and George Backer went out to Libertyville, Illinois, to talk national politics with Stevenson in the summer of 1955, it was obvious to the host that Harriman was still infected by the presidential bug. Before they left for New York, Stevenson pulled Backer aside and asked him point-blank what Harriman planned to do. Averell's friend still couldn't say, but he promised to let Stevenson know the moment a decision was made.[17] The Illinois governor was sure what the answer would be. Harriman, he noted in a letter to his friend Barbara Ward, had been fairly "panting with anxiety" during the visit.[18]

The new evidence of presidential aspiration should have come as no surprise. Harriman had used his first gubernatorial press conference for a caustic critique of Eisenhower's economic policy. He had barely put his cabinet together when Democratic national chairman Paul Butler came to Albany and went out of his way to talk about Harriman support across the country. In July, De Sapio went to Washington and, on NBC's *Meet the Press*, challenged the wisdom expressed by Senator Clinton P. Anderson of New Mexico that Stevenson would "have to fight off the delegates" once he announced. The nomination was not in the bag, De Sapio advised. The New York delegation, for one, would be solidly for Harriman.

Averell and Marie, meanwhile, set off on a transparently political "vacation," going to London to see Churchill and Harold Macmillan, to Rome for a call on the pope, and to Israel, stopping off for a chat with the Irish president and foreign minister on the way home.

He was so obviously preoccupied with foreign affairs and everything that went on in Washington that members of the Albany press corps and some of his own staff sometimes thought he had no interest in being governor—beyond the possibility it presented for a presidential candidacy. State political reporters dared not broach foreign policy, for if they did, they invited a discourse on U.S.-Soviet relations, often coming around to familiar stories about his late-night visits to the Kremlin and eyeball-to-eyeball negotiations with Stalin.

With Taft out of presidential politics, his favorite Republican target became John Foster Dulles. Eisenhower's secretary of state was a disaster, he argued, because Dulles had not understood the significance of the Soviet Union's turn to "peaceful coexistence" as the hallmark of its relations with the West. The Eisenhower administration, in his view from Albany, was failing to deal with the Communist problem in any substantive manner except to prepare for military conflict with the USSR.

Still, after a year of acting like a candidate, he had given Sundquist no go-ahead to organize a campaign for the White House nomination. Doing nothing became a strategy. He would avoid primaries, where he might be damaged by Stevenson or Kefauver; and he would wait for Stevenson to falter. But Backer secretly set up a "boiler" room in the penthouse of the Berkshire Hotel in Manhattan, hiring a small staff to clip newspapers, track the activities of Stevenson and Kefauver, and keep account of the delegates. He saw no chance of Harriman winning the nomination, and he was actually opposed to his friend's making another race for it; but he knew that in the end Harriman would run, if only as a favorite son to invigorate the state party.

But contrary to what Backer thought, Theodore White concluded after making an early survey of the national scene for *Colliers Magazine* that 1956 held realistic promise for Harriman. White's friendship with the governor went back to Marshall Plan days in Paris, probably explaining why his assessment was undeservedly optimistic. With nearly a year to go until the convention, the reporter found more Harriman support than he had seen in 1952. While Stevenson's camp was mainly concerned about another Kefauver challenge, White wrote, "the whole weight of American history makes Harriman the more formidable threat."[19]

De Sapio was eager to play kingmaker. After visiting Washington and announcing that his goal was to head off a first-ballot Stevenson nomination, he flew to California to take soundings of Averell's prospects and see if there was any anti-Stevenson sentiment to be exploited. The trip proved to be of no help to Averell's prospects and demonstrated that De Sapio had much to learn about politics when he was beyond the territory of Tammany Hall.

Ignoring Democrats who counted, the Tammany chieftain contacted only his cronies. His audacity set state party officials on edge and stirred supporters of Stevenson, who was yet to declare his candidacy, to launch a draft movement. Attorney General Edmund G. "Pat" Brown, California's ranking Democratic official, wired Stevenson, urging him to announce his candidacy at once, then staged a press conference and trotted out a galaxy of California notables endorsing the Illinois governor. The reverberations flashed back to New York. Sundquist complained to Backer that De Sapio had caused an unnecessary fiasco. Thereafter, the Tammany leader stayed closer to home.

Harriman himself went to California three months later and made major speeches in San Francisco and Los Angeles, taking the occasion to announce that he would not authorize his name to be put on the ballot in any state Democratic primary. That revealed nothing about his real plans, because he obviously was in no position to start challenging Kefauver for grass roots support. State Democratic chairman Michael Prendergast, meanwhile, was confidently predicting announcement of an active Harriman candidacy, and Averell's friends were calling Stevenson a demonstrated loser who would have no chance in a second rerun with Eisenhower.

For a time, the inactive campaign strategy seemed inspired. Kefauver stunned the experts by upending Stevenson in the March Minnesota primary, even though the Illinois governor had the solid backing of the entire party leadership in the state. It didn't matter that massive numbers of Republicans had crossed over to vote for the Tennessee liberal with the intention of creating just such an upset. Kefauver suddenly had a chance to stay in the contest all the way to the convention.

On April 21, Harriman was in Washington for the annual convention of the American Society of Newspaper Editors and a party fundraising dinner featuring Alben Barkley and House Speaker Sam Rayburn. He had also dropped in on a rally for Stevenson, who was again being treated as the party's presumptive nominee—once the Minnesota shock had worn off. During the day, both the President and Stevenson spoke to the editors, and Stevenson made headlines by suggesting that the United States consider a unilateral suspension of hydrogen-bomb tests.

That night when Harriman and Sundquist walked into their hotel after dinner, the morning *Washington Post* was already out with a huge headline: "PEACEFUL ERA CAN EMERGE, IKE SAYS; STEVENSON CHARGES U.S. LOSES INITIATIVE." Harriman read the beginning of the story on Stevenson's speech and threw the paper aside. "That man can't be President," he growled. "He has no earthly idea of how to deal with the Russians."[20]

The remark reflected a bottom-line opinion of Stevenson, which Harriman had been unwilling to state publicly. His problem with his fellow governor was not that the 1952 nominee could not beat Eisenhower; the truth was that he thought Stevenson simply did not deserve to be President.[21] Doubts about Stevenson's fiber had been gnawing at him all along. He couldn't forget the night of Truman's withdrawal announcement in 1952 when Stevenson had sat with his head in his hands at the Metropolitan Club, wishing he could hide from the pressure; and there had been other conversations when Stevenson had shown a bothersome lack of enthusiasm for leadership.

Once, after a small dinner in Albany, Averell had steered the conversation around to Quemoy and Ma-tsu, the small islands in the Formosa Strait, where it periodically appeared that war between Chiang Kai-shek and the Communist government on the Chinese mainland might erupt. This was an issue, Harriman insisted, where the Democratic party had to have a strong position, and he suggested that Stevenson was obliged to stand up as the leader of the Democrats and assert American determination to prevent the islands from being taken by the Communists. The Quemoy–Ma-tsu problem, Stevenson kept insisting, was something for the chairman of the Senate Foreign Relations Committee to handle.

The next morning the subject came up again in a chat with Ted Tannenwald. Frustrated, Stevenson said he wished he was sick or out of the country so he wouldn't be hounded about it. Tannenwald repeated the conversation to Harriman, who scowled with contempt but said no more.[22]

The campaign organization that was at last put together in the spring of 1956 deployed Sundquist on a belated search for people willing to be state leaders for Harriman. Meanwhile, De Sapio courted the big-city organizations, and Backer took charge of fund-raising and speech writing.

Although Stevenson recovered from the Minnesota stumble and was from all indications within a whisper of having the nomination locked up, Harriman was inexplicably optimistic, even when friends such as Schlesinger, Lehman, and Wagner told him they would have to remain with Stevenson. John Carroll of Colorado, who had led the Harriman western campaign four years earlier, would no longer help, because Averell had shown his gratitude with a mere $250 contribution to the 1954 Carroll for Senate campaign.[23]

Because he had been coy while Kefauver drove through the primaries and Stevenson lined up the party establishment, Harriman found it nearly impossible to enlist supporters of stature. He was left with the people who had lost party primaries and were now willing to become Harriman leaders because the victors had all come out for Stevenson. As usual, the South was the Democrats' cross. Divided and self-destructive, it was inflamed over the Supreme Court's 1954 decision holding segregated schools unconstitutional. In Dixie, Harriman was viewed not so much as an architect of the postwar foreign policy as the epitome of the race-mixing northern radical liberal. He had blasted the Eisenhower administration for reacting too timidly when Autherine Lucy, the first black student admitted to the University of Alabama, was driven from the campus by a white mob. Following that, he had endorsed an amendment by Adam Clayton Powell, the flamboyant black congressman from Harlem, calling for denial of federal school aid to segregated schools. And in a radio interview, he left open the possibility that he would use federal troops to enforce court-ordered desegregation.

The South was hardly the only place where he was out of contention. He had no delegation in any of the primary states, because he had ducked all of them. In several others, he was precluded because incumbent Democratic governors were either favorite-son candidates or already pledged to Stevenson. When all were added up, there were only seventeen states where he had any opportunity to pick up delegates. Altogether, these accounted for just 378 of the 600-odd delegates required for nomination.[24] In the whole country, only one governor was an avowed Harriman supporter—Oklahoma's Raymond Gary.

Keeping his year-old promise, Backer went back to Illinois to privately inform Stevenson that Harriman was about to become an avowed candidate. The front-runner received the news with characteristic grace. He didn't feel betrayed, but he was disappointed, he said, that he wouldn't have Harriman's advice and help as the convention approached. He had hoped, he added a little wistfully, to have him as his secretary of state, a remark hinting that Averell's candidacy would disqualify him from a Stevenson Cabinet, if there ever was one.[25]

To avoid pressure to face Kefauver in the primaries, Harriman withheld his announcement until the last one, Montana, was past, traveling the West, meanwhile, under the aegis of the Democratic National Committee, raising money for the party and reestablishing himself in the territory where the Harriman name was legend but Democratic voters few—Cody, Wyoming; Missoula and Butte, Montana; Idaho Falls,

Idaho; Reno, Nevada; Spokane and Pullman, Washington. There followed a swing through the Midwest, hoping that somewhere, somehow he could start a prairie fire.

After four years in politics, he had not developed the campaign skills of Kefauver or Stevenson. His exuberance was obviously manufactured, his grin was frozen, and his glad-handing mechanical. He still regularly forgot names, faces, and places important to him, and never mastered the trick of acting as if he remembered everybody and everything. Even in Albany, people had to be introduced to him repeatedly, and he took to using a greeting of "Hello, Stranger," as a means of familiarity relieving him of pressure to remember names. "After a while people thought my name was Jack Stranger," said Jack Germond, one of the better-known members of the capitol press corps.[26]

No amount of help could hide the problem. After appearing before Midwestern party leaders at a Des Moines fund-raiser, Harriman stationed himself in his suite at the Fort Des Moines Hotel to make personal pitches to potential supporters. Sundquist roamed the lobby, spotting prospects and sending them up one by one. While they were on the way, he called Harriman to tell him who they were. Forewarned, the governor warmly greeted the visitors by name. During one sweep, Harriman's scout encountered Democratic national committeeman Bernard Boyle and gave him the pitch in whispered confidentially, "Bernie, the governor is up in his suite, and he asked me to come down and tell you that he'd like to see you." Boyle flushed. "The hell he did, he doesn't care about me. I went up to say hello to him when he got off the plane this morning, and he walked right past me without even speaking. I was all out for him in '52. I ran all over Nebraska trying to sell him, and I delivered the damn state. Now he doesn't even see me when I'm three feet from him." If Harriman wanted to see him, he said, Harriman could call himself.

That night as they flew back to Albany, Sundquist told Averell about the embarrassing slipup, and the governor was mortified. He remembered Boyle only vaguely, but obviously he had to make amends. The opportunity soon came on the next trip west. The Nebraska committeeman showed up at another party gathering where Harriman was hustling delegates. This time Sundquist instructed Bernice McCray, the governor's secretary, to call Boyle's room and put Harriman on the phone for a personal invitation for a chat. With that, Sundquist went about his errands. When he returned, he was horrified. Emerging from Harriman's suite was not Bernie Boyle, but former Democratic national chairman William Boyle of Missouri, who had in 1951 been forced out of the party leadership under accusations of influence peddling in Washington. "The governor just called out of the blue and invited me up to see him," said the obviously pleased visitor. "We had a wonderful talk about the party and the campaign, which I enjoyed immensely. It was a little peculiar, though, because he seemed preoccupied with Nebraska. He kept going back to it and asking me all about the situation out there."[27]

Although Harriman acknowledged that he would be a favorite-son candidate, he did not declare his active national candidacy until June 9, three days after Stevenson completed his recovery from the Minnesota mishap by smashing Kefauver in California. The leader's resilience caused Liberal party vice-chairman David Dubinsky to plead with Averell to stay out of the race so liberals could go to the convention united behind Kefauver. But it was too late for that. Before the convention of the United Hatters, Cap, and Millinery Workers Union, Averell announced he was going to Chicago "fighting for the principles of Franklin Roosevelt and Harry Truman. . . . I am going back and, as long as I can stand on my feet, I am going to fight for those principles. The Democratic party isn't going to compromise on them."[28]

He had planned to make Governor Gary of Oklahoma director of his national campaign, bringing it a direly needed common touch. Gary was a former schoolteacher, a red-faced, rough-hewn country boy who delighted in talking about his dear friend "Arabel Hairman." Over the past two years, they had become good friends at governors' conferences, and Gary had visited Albany months earlier and volunteered his support. His admiration was not without practical considerations, since he had significant rivals within the party in Oklahoma, all of whom were rabid Stevenson people.

When it came to putting the campaign into gear, however, Gary decided that he was too busy to run it. He turned it over to Oklahoma state chairman Loyd Benefield, with himself as honorary chairman and manager. Harriman's quest for the White House therefore wound up in the hands of an Oklahoma lawyer who had no national political experience and barely knew him.

Once it was openly under way, the campaign was an echo of 1952. His advisers again wanted him to position himself to the left of Stevenson and force the front-runner to take a stand on civil rights. Because he was comfortably ahead, the Illinois governor had been able to duck the school desegregation issue and woo southerners while keeping himself in the good graces of liberals by merely saying that school desegregation shouldn't be a campaign issue.

Instead of forcing Stevenson's hand, however, Harriman sent mixed signals of his own. Before a garment workers' convention, he called for "zeal not moderation in the struggle for civil rights."[29] Moderation, he told a black fraternal organization, was "the counsel of timidity, stagnation, and defeat."[30] But when he went to the party establishment and into the West, his tone was different; and for reasons his strategists did not understand, he persisted in believing that he could stir up support in the South. They suspected that the obvious attempt to stay in the middle of the road was being privately urged upon him by Truman.

Wherever it originated, the notion of Harriman getting southern support was hopeless. Aside from Gary and Benefield, his advisers were staunchly opposed to his trying to transform himself into a moderate; but he ignored them, and at crucial moments echoed the notes sounded by Stevenson, his semantical squirming becoming embarrassing. At a rally of western supporters in Denver, Governor Gary assured everyone that the man who had declared himself a zealot on civil rights really held moderate views—"like Oklahoma's"—on school desegregation. Averell arrived shortly thereafter and passed up all invitations to take issue with the characterization. Then realizing he was caught in a blatant contradiction, he called reporters in and instead of disassociating himself from an Oklahoma-like civil rights posture, he aggravated his problem by claiming that "some scoundrels" were "trying to make me out the wild man on civil rights. That's simply not true."[31]

Backer, who was in charge of speech writing, kept steering him toward a staunch antidiscrimination posture. As the campaign moved to North Carolina, he and Sundquist saw the perfect opportunity for Harriman to crystallize an image as the fighting liberal running on principle. For a rally at Asheboro, they wrote a speech making an unequivocal stand against discrimination. After outlining what he had done for the cause of civil rights in New York, it proclaimed, "Tonight in North Carolina, I am the same man I was yesterday in New York." With regard to court rulings on school desegregation, "Government authorities— federal, state, and local—have the obligation to go forward in accordance with these decisions and, through normal procedures, see that the law is complied with."[32]

Backer wrote the passage, intending it to put Harriman in sharp contrast with Stevenson, but it was delivered in a mumble and missed much of the audience. Backer was crushed.

With Stevenson's triumph over Kefauver in California and Harriman's failure to make any inroads, the Illinois governor appeared invincible. On July 21, Kefauver withdrew and threw his support to Stevenson. It was a broadside to Harriman's dim chances and a surprise to the Stevenson camp, which had passed around rumors that Kefauver was being kept afloat by Harriman money. There had, in fact, been discussion of Harriman's slipping financial support to the hard-pressed Kefauver, but it always deteriorated into jokes. If Averell was offered the nomination on a platter for $10,000, Tannenwald said, "he would have to weigh it carefully and then sleep on it."[33]

As the New York delegation departed for Chicago, there still had been no public indication of Truman's choice. Given his well-known feelings about Stevenson, it was generally supposed that he was for his good friend Harriman; but without any real news to be had, the "mystery" of the former President's choice became the headlines of the convention buildup. Everybody played it straight. Harriman and Stevenson were earnestly hopeful; and Truman, enjoying the spotlight after three years in Independence, teased reporters while keeping mum on his endorsement.

With the New York and Oklahoma delegations as his only blocs, Harriman's sole chance was to try to drive Stevenson into the arms of the South on civil rights. His problem was that there wasn't much difference in their positions, and Stevenson had moved to shore up his support among liberals by finally coming out for a plank endorsing the '54 Supreme Court decision.

Sundquist, Backer, Gutman, and Sam Rosenman had already been in Chicago several days following the platform subcommittee's work on the plank. With Stevenson's belated support for it, casually announced in a sidewalk interview, Harriman liberals saw a new opportunity. Averell's principal advisers wanted to attack Stevenson for being two-faced—playing it cozy with southern segregationists for months and then switching when he thought it was safe. They wanted Harriman to come off the plane in Chicago "with the bit in his teeth," launching an offensive to put the Democratic party on record as not only supporting the court decision but demanding its enforcement. It was a way for him to make himself a candidate running on principle.

Instead of arriving prepared to lead a civil rights charge, however, he focused on the Truman endorsement as the key to stopping Stevenson short on the first ballot. Sundquist, who made a last try at persuading him to make desegregation the issue, was summarily dismissed. The Harriman civil rights position, said the candidate, was well known.[34] Not even Backer could get him to listen.

As soon as he got to Chicago, Averell called on his old boss. "I didn't ask him his decision," he said, "and I didn't expect him to tell me."[35] Rumors circulated around delegations' headquarters that Truman was under intense pressure to endorse Stevenson for the sake of party unity, and Stevenson himself predicted that Truman would wind up giving a blessing to no one.

At last, on Saturday afternoon, the man from Missouri strode into the overflowing Crystal Ballroom of the Sheraton Blackstone, prepared statement in hand, and endorsed Harriman as "the man best qualified to be the next President of the United States." He made no direct mention of Stevenson; but in his observation that Harriman would be a "fighting candidate," there was a sharp dig that was not lost upon anyone.[36]

In his suite upstairs, Averell watched with his retinue and a few minutes later bounded two flights up the back stairs to Truman's suite to express his thanks. De Sapio and other campaign people hailed it as the breakthrough that would bring Harriman the nomination on the second ballot. Had it happened in 1952 while he was still in the White House, Truman might well have been able to make Harriman the nominee, but it was soon obvious that Democrats no longer cared much about his endorsement. In spite of the contrived suspense, the announcement surprised nobody and there was no flood of new support. The switches came in scattered ones and twos; and before the afternoon was out, Harriman knew it was all over. "Let's not kid ourselves," he told Gutman. "We can't win this thing."[37]

The harshest, but obviously expected, moment came the next day when Eleanor Roosevelt, the godmother of party liberals, arrived and added her blessing to the power brokers and southern segregationists behind Stevenson. Truman, she suggested, had reached an age when he should leave party decisions to the younger generation. And Averell, she suggested, was overrated on foreign policy. He was facile where Europe and the Soviet Union were concerned, she conceded, but she was not impressed with his competence about Asia and Africa.

It was her bitter way, Harriman thought, of squaring accounts for Franklin Junior and the gubernatorial nomination fight. Its main effect was to encourage Stevenson supporters in the New York delegation to ignore their favorite-son commitment to Averell and jump to Stevenson on the first ballot.[38]

Benefield and De Sapio's public claims that Harriman would get five hundred votes on the first ballot were absurd; and when they were scaled down by a hundred, Stevenson vote counters still scoffed. Nothing stood in the way of Stevenson's nomination. His campaign organization had the Democratic National Committee and the convention apparatus under such tight control that Harriman supporters and staff members found it impossible to get floor passes and parking spaces. A New York delegate had to fly home to print bogus floor passes, and Joe Tepper had to pay the Teamsters Union $700 for a few parking spaces.[39] De Sapio, as chairman of the New York delegation, was under increasing pressure to release members to vote as they pleased. As he and everybody knew, the count of 95½ votes for Averell to 5½ for Stevenson didn't remotely represent delegation sentiments. On the other hand, hundreds of delegates bound to vote for Stevenson personally favored someone else. Had there been a secret ballot, Sundquist would always argue, Harriman might have won.

Under the unhappy circumstances, the strategy changed. The important objective gradually came to be an exit from Chicago without damage that would follow him back to Albany. Benefield was kept busy trying to squelch rumors that Harriman would withdraw before the first ballot. Sundquist and Stewart, concerned that the floor demonstration would be embarrassingly feeble, took on the task of making sure there was enough commotion and noise to give television viewers the illusion of a serious candidacy. Stewart lined up union members and Sundquist made a deal with Governor A. B. "Happy" Chandler of Kentucky, who had designs on the vice-presidency. Chandler's people would demonstrate for Harriman and Harriman's meager forces would take up balloons and posters for Chandler.

Down in the New York delegation on the floor, a "NEW YORK DELEGATES FOR STEVENSON" banner was hoisted as though announcing the end of the Harriman campaign. Seeing a chance to have a role in Stevenson's nomination, governors Mennan Williams of Michigan and Robert Meyner of New Jersey dropped their favorite-son candidacies before the first ballot, destroying Harriman's last flickering hope of surviving for a second roll call. Still he refused to concede, pleading with delegates to "hold this thing a couple of hours, and you'll see a change."[40]

His plodding pursuit made friends and staff around him wonder whether he even realized that it was all over. Finally, seemingly oblivious to everybody around him, he watched Gary's speech putting his name in nomination on Thursday night and savored the floor demonstration—augmented by Happy Chandler's ranks from Kentucky—as though it were wholly spontaneous.

The roll call brought him only 210 votes, a better showing than had been expected. When polling of the delegations reached Pennsylvania, Stevenson had the nomination, and delegates in the states yet to be called began clamoring for release so they could join the bandwagon. Some were released by Gary and others jumped without seeking permission. By end of the ballot Stevenson had 905½—300 more votes than he needed. Backer turned to Averell and got permission to call Rayburn on the podium and ask him to recognize Gary for a motion to make the nomination unanimous.

Harriman walked out of his hideaway to meet the press. He would, he said, campaign for Stevenson wholeheartedly—and in 1958, he would run for another term as governor of New York. He expected, he said, to remain in Albany for "many, many years."[41]

Chapter XXI

LOSING
A Million Votes in Buffalo

While he was working the West in his futile effort to spark a presidential prairie fire in 1956, Harriman unwittingly lit an altogether different political fire back home. Oblivious to implications that should have been obvious to a precinct volunteer, he invited Nelson Rockefeller to get into New York politics, appointing him to chair a state commission to prepare for a monumental convention at which New York's 180-year-old constitution would be brought up to date. Under the existing document, voters were given the opportunity every twenty years to call another constitutional convention. Their chance was coming around again in 1957, and Harriman entrusted to his friend Nelson the assignment of laying the groundwork for the referendum.

Nothing the administration had undertaken had more profound implications for New York's future. A convention appeared to be the only way—except the courts, which eventually resolved the problem for all the states—ever to break the rural and upstate domination of the legislature and vault Albany into the twentieth century.

In Harriman's mind, the convention was so supremely in the public interest that it transcended personal ambition, partisanship, and State House politics. And who was there in all New York better suited to lead a great civic movement for political reform than the most public-spirited and energetic of John D. Rockefeller's five grandsons?

Nelson was then forty-eight years old. Like Averell, he was politically liberal, enthusiastically internationalist, and ambitious. And like Averell,

543

he had found in public service something far more satisfying than tending to his personal fortune. He had served in the Roosevelt and Truman administrations as well as Eisenhower's. In 1950, Truman made him chairman of an advisory panel to recommend strategy for implementing the Point IV Program's assistance to underdeveloped countries. His chief recommendation was to bring all overseas economic assistance under a new agency with a single administrator, reporting directly to the President. The plan got no further than Harriman, who was then Truman's special assistant for foreign policy matters and of no mind to see his own role diminished.[1]

Over the years, Harriman and Rockefeller had always been on affable terms. Rockefeller had been invited to become a charter member of the Sun Valley Ski Club. They had served together on various committees in New York, and they had been neighbors on Foxhall Road in Washington. Technically, Rockefeller had worked for Averell at the end of the Truman administration when the Point IV Program fell under Harriman's new Mutual Security Administration. Socially and professionally, the governor enjoyed Rockefeller's company, as, it seemed, did everyone.

The families had collaborated for years. E. H. Harriman and old John D. had become friends when the former was on the way up. Thereafter, both E.H. and Averell had maintained cordial ties with the Rockefeller financial empire and the men around John D. in Standard Oil. Nelson's Uncle William had helped E.H. get control of the Southern Pacific. His cousin Percy had invested in several of Averell's ventures during the twenties. His father, John D., Jr., had been a dependable supporter of civic work undertaken by Averell's mother.

With Eisenhower's election, Nelson had become a presidential assistant on foreign policy matters, but he had never been pleased with his circumstances. He did not have very close ties with the President, and he was often at odds with the tightfisted treasury secretary, George M. Humphrey, and the undersecretary of state, Herbert Hoover, Jr. Frustrated, he quit in December 1955 and moved into the Rockefeller brothers' softly lit suite on the fifty-sixth floor of the RCA tower at Rockefeller Center.

The idea of making him chairman of the constitutional commission originated with Republicans in the legislature; and one day while it was being talked about in the corridors of the state capitol, Jonathan Bingham encountered Rockefeller at the airport in Washington, giving them a chance to chat on a flight to New York. Friends since the days when both worked in the Point IV Program, they gossiped about Washington, Albany, and the gestation of Harriman's still unacknowledged presidential campaign. When Bingham mentioned preparations for the referendum on the convention, Rockefeller's antenna snapped to enthusiastic attention. Like Harriman, he saw an opportunity to scrape the barnacles off the machinery of state government. When he got back to Albany, the governor's executive secretary was convinced that Rockefeller was the man they were looking for.

Ordinarily, Harriman didn't look to Bingham for political advice. Small patronage belonged to Milton Stewart, the large to George Backer. But since the governor didn't think of the commission job as a political operation, and since Bingham took everything Rockefeller said to mean that he was all for a convention, Harriman saw no need for a full-scale review. The choice was compelling. It would get around a lot of haggling with Heck and Mahoney and avoid the appointment of some compromise figure who could never match the stature of Rockefeller. What was more important to Harriman was that he saw Rockefeller as assurance of a commission majority in favor of a convention. The legislature had authorized a panel of fifteen members, seven to be named by the legislature, seven by the governor, with the chairman, the fifteenth, to be mutually agreed upon.

There were raised eyebrows when the idea became known around the gubernatorial suite, but not much more. The only real objection came from Milton Stewart, who insisted it was political folly. He saw in Rockefeller an obvious hot commodity in a party short of attractive statewide candidates. In spite of Rockefeller's professed nonpartisan interest in a constitutional convention, Stewart was convinced from the beginning that the gregarious young millionaire had notions of running for governor. For the first time since he had been working for Harriman, he bluntly challenged his boss's political judgment. Rockefeller, he warned, was "the very sonofabitch we are going to have to beat. The guy is not anybody to fool around with."[2]

Indeed, Rockefeller had come home from Washington convinced that he could play an important role in public life only by holding elective office. He had already broached the subject of a gubernatorial campaign to Dewey, but the former governor half-seriously ridiculed the idea, suggesting that an appointment as New York City postmaster would be more realistic. Rockefeller had not been put off. He was, he said, going to "try for Albany" anyway.[3]

Unfortunately for Harriman, the commission chairmanship came up when Backer and De Sapio were preoccupied with stopping Stevenson. Stewart had nobody to support him. His warnings were greeted with more amusement than concern by both Harriman and Bingham. The governor, Stewart recalled, "sort of looked down his patrician, aristocratic nose at me as though I was, well, maybe OK, but that I had standards lower than one should have."[4] Ironically, Averell had forgotten the most useful advice he had received from the departing Dewey—that *every* decision he made in Albany would be political. If he didn't keep that in mind, his predecessor had told him, it would be at his peril.

Remarkably, the July 8 announcement of Rockefeller's appointment didn't cause a ripple, Democratic party leaders evidently sharing Harriman's belief that Rockefeller was accepting the job as a nonpartisan civic duty. After only a few weeks, all of them realized that they had been played for suckers.

Rockefeller took on the Constitutional Convention Commission with all the enthusiasm Harriman had expected, but he mostly used it as a vehicle for a crash course in state politics and government, which he absorbed like a sponge. Almost overnight, he developed connections with Republican organizations in every county of the state; and as he held perfunctory hearings on convention issues, he acquired a personal following that grew far more dramatically than support for constitutional reform.

Harriman had unwittingly given New York Republicans their own Eisenhower; and when he realized what had happened, there was nothing he could do. Milton Stewart had been right. Harriman's and Bingham's friend had been no gentleman. He had taken advantage.

With the referendum still five months away, Rockefeller announced that, since he was under no legal requirement to do so, he would make no recommendation on calling a convention. It was a supremely political move, keeping him on good terms with both sides of the issue in his own divided party.

When the referendum came, a low turnout in New York City helped Republicans and upstate Democrats reject the convention by 100,000 votes. Averell, angrily blaming the defeat on Rockefeller, pointlessly proposed to set up a permanent nonpartisan commission with a staff of experts who would work steadily on constitutional modernization. Getting rid of Rockefeller, however, was not as easy as bringing him aboard. Besides his name and fortune, Rockefeller was blessed with the raw political talent that Averell lacked. Suddenly, with the gubernatorial election still a year away, talk of a Rockefeller campaign was rife, and within weeks of the referendum a Manhattan office was opened by volunteers organizing a draft movement.

Since they had been served so well by it, Republicans refused to accept the demise of Rockefeller's temporary Constitutional Convention Commission. They responded to Harriman's idea for a permanent panel by passing a bill creating one that would be selected by the legislature. When the governor vetoed that, they merely established a legislative committee with the same function, making Rockefeller its executive director.

The long episode opened a Democratic tragicomedy, Rockefeller emerging to rescue the Republicans just when the party might have ripped itself to bits over the choice between Walter Mahoney and Oswald

Heck for governor. By creating Rockefeller, Harriman did more for the GOP than the party was capable of doing for itself.

For a long time, he still didn't understand his peril. Just as he had believed the people who told him he could beat Stevenson, he believed polls that now showed he could beat any Republican on the gubernatorial horizon, Nelson Rockefeller included. At the 1958 dinner of the New York Legislative Correspondents Association, the early spring rite in which newspaper people lampooned and satirized politicians, he went out of his way to put Rockefeller in the spotlight. Once the reporters had done their little songs and skits, Harriman stepped up for the governor's traditional closing. The show, he said, had touched on all of the potential Republican gubernatorial nominees except "the most likely of all, Nelson Rockefeller—stand up and take a bow, Nelson." Rockefeller did, to warm, prolonged applause. Mystified Democrats shook their heads as Harriman acknowledged he expected a challenge from the man who had profoundly embarrassed him already, giving him a boost before the best political audience of the year.[5] The governor had reason to be confident, though, quite apart from the polls. For four years, he had courted upstate New York as had no state Democratic official in memory. A National Guard airplane took him to festivals, plant inspections, and cornerstone layings in every county; and wherever he went, he shook hands with people who had never seen a Democratic governor in the flesh. By all indications, he had made an important impact. Mike Prendergast's books showed that upstate Democratic registration had increased a full 40 percent, while equally astonishing strides had been made in the Republican suburbs of Nassau, Suffolk, and Westchester counties.

De Sapio predicted he would be returned to office by a margin of 375,000 to 400,000 votes, maybe even 500,000, "if the international climate persists."[6] The Tammany boss did not toss out such predictions lightly. Harriman had not only campaigned throughout his term and tried to please every known Democratic pressure group, he had given the state four years of clean, fiscally conservative, socially progressive government. When there were hints of scandal, he had acted with dispatch.

He had moved too quickly, some of his aides thought, when he saw a potential political damage from a parole-board controversy based on innuendo. Without waiting for explanations, he sacked a parole-board member after it was disclosed that a hood named Joseph "Socks" Lanza, who had connections with Tammany Hall, had been mysteriously released from jail after being pinched for a parole violation.

Once known as the "Czar of the Fulton Fish Market," Lanza had, during the 1930s, done time for extorting protection money from merchants, truckers, and fishing vessels around the market in lower Manhattan. When he got out, he went back into his old game, and in 1943 he and four of his musclemen were convicted of shaking down members of a Teamsters Union local. Upon his second conviction, he got a seven-and-a-half-to-fifteen-year sentence. After he was paroled in 1950, he stayed out of sight and out of trouble for nearly seven years. Then, on February 2, 1957, he was picked up for violating parole by spending far in excess of his explainable income, and by consorting with known criminals.

Although his career hardly qualified him as a significant racketeer, he had kept company with such criminal heavyweights as Frank Costello and Charles "Lucky" Luciano. More interesting to Harriman was the fact that Lanza's brother-in-law, Vincent "Duke" Viggiano, was a Tammany district leader, and his brother, Harry Lanza, had a courthouse job as an assistant clerk in Municipal Court.

So, when word got around that parole commissioner James R. Stone had reinstated Lanza's parole two weeks after he was rearrested, Republicans thought they had the makings of another Tammany scandal, particularly after they discovered that Stone was a distant relative of Congressman Charles Buckley, the Democratic boss in the Bronx.

The legislature's "watchdog committee" was ordered into action, and the telephone began ringing beside Averell's croquet lawn at Hobe Sound, where he had gone to take the sun. Gutman wanted to dump Stone immediately, but Stewart counseled against panic. As far as Stewart could tell, the commissioner was guilty of nothing more than a lapse in judgment, if that. Furthermore, Stone was not even a political appointee, but one of the hundreds of career officials who remained in the state government from the Dewey administration. He had been a parole officer for a decade, and when there was a vacancy in the summer of 1955, Harriman had made him a commissioner.

But the governor had a gnawing fear of the very thing the Republicans insinuated—underworld access to the government through contacts in the Tammany organization. So, before the legislature could get the committee investigation rolling, he put Arthur L. Reuter, the administration's commissioner of investigations, on the case, and accepted Stone's resignation.

He ordered the Parole Board to tighten its procedures, requiring approval of all five commissioners before dropping charges of violations. And to make sure that he hadn't missed anything, he launched a long-range review of the state's whole parole system. A month after being freed by Stone, Lanza was rearrested and sent back to Sing Sing to finish his term.

The reaction was obviously out of proportion to the problem, a demonstration of the governor's sensitivity to his relationship with the

Tammany organization. The legislature's probe dragged on for weeks anyway, a fishing expedition winding up with hearings in Manhattan. There it was easier to generate headlines; and the committee did, revealing surreptitiously recorded jailhouse conversations in which Lanza and visitors talked about his release being expedited by "the guy with the glasses." That brought the spotlight squarely down on De Sapio. His dark glasses, required because he suffered from iritis, had helped make his face as familiar to New Yorkers as Averell Harriman's and Tom Dewey's.

Smarting at the insinuations against De Sapio, Harriman invited reporters to the Executive Mansion for a background session and, with ground rules preventing his being quoted by name, suggested that "the guy with the glasses" was really Lee B. Mailler, the Dewey-appointed Parole Board chairman and former leader of the Assembly. Republicans were furious.

After two months, the case faded away, but crime as a political issue was about to emerge in a big way. Thanks to a state cop suspicious of strangers with fancy cars, fat cigars, and pointy-toed shoes, a national gathering of mobsters was uncovered in the hamlet of Apalachin, twelve miles from Binghamton. Among the sixty-five "delegates" were underworld figures from as far away as California and Puerto Rico.

Because Apalachian was too small to have a police force, its law enforcement was provided by Sergeant Edgar Croswell of the state police, who regularly stopped by to keep abreast of anything out of the ordinary, which was usually nothing. But in the late autumn of 1957, he got a tip that every room in the community's only motel had been reserved by Joseph Barbara, who lived reclusively in a stone mansion outside the village. Barbara made a point of assuring the manager that the cost of the accommodations was "no object." He had also gone to the grocery store and had the owner order special cuts of meat never seen in Apalachin.

Croswell kept an eye on Barbara because he had once been picked up, though never convicted, on a homicide charge. Although he had been around for years, the locals knew nothing about him except that he was a soft-drink bottler and beverage distributor in Binghamton. By the appearance of his house, the cars he drove, and the suits he wore, business was good.

All the guests for his big party arrived at the motel in black Lincolns and Cadillacs, and the next day proceeded to his house en masse. Early that afternoon, as smoke began drifting up from the barbecue grill, Croswell, backed by reinforcements from the state police barracks and the U.S. Treasury Department, blocked all the exits and began taking down license numbers.

Spotting the uniforms, the guests tried to flee, some jumping from windows and running into the woods, losing their hats and snagging their expensive overcoats. Others headed for their cars, and found themselves hemmed in. All were quickly rounded up, searched, and found to have pockets full of cash and long criminal records. Among them were Vito Genovese, Carlo Gambino, and Joseph Bonanno, who would gain national notoriety as kingpins of the principal Mafia "families" in the United States. Only days earlier, several of them had been questioned in the slaying of Albert Anastasia, a professional executioner, who had been riddled with bullets while getting a haircut in midtown Manhattan. Nine of them, it developed, were fresh from appearances before a federal grand jury investigating racketeering in the garment and trucking industry in the New York City area. None was armed, and neither the state police nor Treasury Department agents could come up with a reason for holding any of them. The officers had struck without benefit of a warrant, and after several hours, they had no choice but to release those arrested with a warning to get out of town.

Harriman was driving from New York City to Albany when he got the first brief reports of the raid. By the time he reached his office, his alert network had already produced the guest list with enough detail to call for several investigations. Investigations Chief Reuter was put on the case, as were Croswell's superiors at the state police, plus the State Liquor Authority, the Parole Board, and the Department of Taxation.

District attorneys from across the state were summoned to a meeting at the governor's office, and Gutman was ordered to have legislation ready for the Assembly the day it returned. The "watchdog committee," just finished with the Socks Lanza affair, prepared for hearings and a special grand jury was impaneled. The investigation quickly spread as Barbara's guests were examined by a federal grand jury and by investigators in Washington.

Of more concern to Harriman than the known hoods at the Apalachin convention were Utica businessmen Joseph and Salvatore Falcone, and John C. Montana, a former city councilman and "Businessman of the Year" in Buffalo. The Falcones' presence triggered an exposé of their hometown in central New York as a "Sin City," where prostitution and illegal gambling were protected through political payoffs. It was also a Democratic stronghold. When the legislature reconvened, the Sin City investigations in Utica were under a full head of steam.

For the first time, Harriman's relations with Republican lawmakers became personally acrimonious. Mahoney demanded that he appoint a special prosecutor in Utica and create a new state crime commission, or else the legislature would do it for him. The "watchdog committee" called for New York to form its own "little FBI" and promised to air all of the sordid details of Utica.

With Mahoney vowing to make feeble administration efforts against organized crime the Republicans' foremost campaign issue in '58, Harriman could not afford to let the "watchdog committee" get ahead of him anywhere, certainly not in exposing Utica. Besieged by state investigators, the town's police chief acknowledged he knew of brothels and gambling establishments operating in his city and then resigned. So did the deputy chief, who was unable to explain his "financial practices." The acting chief was then indicted for lying to a grand jury about his own business interests, and evidence was disclosed that private communications between the city police and the district attorney were winding up in the hands of the Falcone brothers. Harriman called for a new three-man crime commission as the supreme state instrument against the underworld, and the legislature responded by creating a commission of four members, dooming it to partisan splits and immobility. The governor signed the bill anyway, named four former prosecutors as members, and sent them into the Utica investigation as their first assignment.

With Democrats in both the Assembly and the Senate ready to break ranks and jump aboard anything advertised as tough on crime, it was a time when Harriman might have capitulated to legislative witch-hunting. But he didn't. When lawmakers sent him a bill giving the attorney general authority to carry out criminal investigations anywhere in the state without the governor's concurrence, he vetoed it. Then he killed a bill that would have opened union books to state investigators. Republican sponsors claimed it was designed to curb racketeering, but Harriman took it as a political threat to organized labor. Mahoney did not pass up the chance for demagoguery, calling the veto the most disgraceful act of Harriman's term in office.

Before it was over, the Republicans' eagerness to portray Harriman as soft on crime got so out of hand it damaged their own credibility and devalued the issue's worth. In a speech reminiscent of the 1954 barrage against Harriman's business "scandals," Irving Ives astonished even a whooping fund-raising dinner audience by claiming that the governor had vetoed the Republican bill to open union books because "one of his closest pals is one of the leading racketeers in the United States."[7] He was, he said, thinking of having the Senate rackets investigators look into the friendship between New York's governor and the racketeer, whom he tactfully declined to name.

Around Harriman, the salvo was greeted with amusement. Backer and Stewart thought Ives had done the governor a favor by making the Republican crime campaign look silly. As far as they were concerned, they were happy to let Ives's blast go without the dignity of a serious answer, since no one else in the GOP, not even Mahoney, would have anything to do with it.

The "pal" Ives had in mind was Robert Bernard Baker, a three-hundred-pound Detroit Teamsters Union organizer and friend of union president James Hoffa. Stewart remembered that Baker had shaken hands with Averell at the 1956 Democratic Convention, when the union had been supporting him for the presidential nomination. Baker had later bragged among his friends that he knew the governor.

Harriman was not inclined to let the matter pass. After first brushing it aside with a "no comment," he called reporters to his house in Manhattan, identified Baker, and recounted what Stewart remembered. By late spring, the crime issue had fizzled. Without a rallying point for an attack on Harriman, the Republicans relied on the polemics of Harry O'Donnell, who cranked out daily broadsides characterizing the governor as a New Deal–Fair Deal retread—"living in the political past, dreaming of a political future, and ignoring his responsibility to the people in the political present."[8]

Although the months of harping over crime and Harriman's handling of the budget never escalated into the issue the Republicans needed for their battle to reclaim the old house on Eagle Street, they were handed devastating ammunition by Harriman himself.

With Ives retiring, the Democrats had a marvelous chance to regain a Senate seat. The Republicans were about to nominate Congressman Kenneth Keating of Rochester, a less than awesome campaigner who was not very well known and not especially anxious to run. The trouble was that Harriman and party leaders had not decided on the Democrats' candidate, and Averell was even muttering about shuffling the ticket for state offices.

He wanted to drop George DeLuca, and he would have been happy to replace Comptroller Arthur Levitt as well. DeLuca had adequately performed his ceremonial chores of lieutenant governor, but Harriman offered him no important responsibilities and no one had ever thought of him as a potential successor. When the slate-makers had selected him four years earlier, they thought they had taken care of gubernatorial succession question by getting FDR, Jr., to run for attorney general. Roosevelt's loss to Javits had taken care of that.

The possibility of dumping DeLuca arose in Harriman's mind because he was already looking ahead to 1960 and the possibility that he would not finish his second term in Albany. Although he was sixty-six years old and had twice fallen flat on the national stage, Averell hadn't ruled out still another try for the presidential nomination. Obviously, 1952 and 1956 provided no grounds for optimism, but 1960 would be different. Eisenhower would be out of the way, and so would Stevenson. More likely than his getting the Democratic nomination was the possibility that the new President would make him secretary of state. He would have to be considered, he thought, by any Democrat who might be elected.

He shuddered at the thought of leaving the governor's office to DeLuca. The reins of state government might as well be handed over to Charley Buckley, the Bronx boss being the lieutenant governor's chief supporter.[9] Harriman had no reason to dislike Levitt. He merely had no relationship with him. The comptroller had been a substitute acceptable to everybody when Aaron Jacoby withdrew from the ticket in 1954, but there were plenty of potential Jewish candidates who could bring more to the ticket.

Averell was not disposed to start a fight over DeLuca or Levitt, nor start one for the candidate for attorney general. Whenever the question of the ticket arose, however, he replied that, except for himself, it was wide open. The attitude did not go over well with the Liberal party, which was staunchly committed to Levitt, and it produced pious Republican observations that Harriman was insensitive to the feelings of his running mates. It also troubled De Sapio. So without even consulting the governor, the Boss summarily announced that both DeLuca and Levitt would be renominated. Harriman let the affront pass. To have disagreed would have created a needless issue. But had he stopped to think about it, the high-handedness might have given him cause to consider his own relationship with the Tammany leader.

Instead of heading for Hobe Sound when the legislature adjourned in that election-year spring, the governor began traveling the state to get things in shape for November. He didn't want just reelection: he wanted to win big. He needed to win big, and the prospect for that looked good. The administration had held the line on taxes and prepared the ground for his deferred social agenda to flower in his second term. As Truman had run against a do-nothing Congress a decade earlier, he tore into the legislature for killing bill after bill he had sent to them.

Backer had begun giving the campaign serious attention with more than a year to go, hiring media consultants and putting Harriman on the air with a series of chatty reports designed to make him at home in living rooms across New York. He talked about his travels, his visitors, and his plans, touching only lightly upon contentious politics. It was the campaign of a man comfortably ahead.

He was not the only Democrat on the hustings early. So was Tom Finletter, the choice of Eleanor Roosevelt, Herbert Lehman, and the New York Stevenson crowd as the party's candidate for the Senate. Averell was not ecstatic about Finletter's chances, but he emphatically was not opposed to him. So when Admiral Alan Kirk, chief of the state Civil Defense Commission, went to Europe on a long vacation and business trip, Finletter was made acting director. That gave him an opportunity to conduct an unannounced campaign in inimitable New York fashion.

Before his tour as Truman's air force secretary, Finletter had served

well as head of the Marshall Plan office in London. After the 1952
Democratic convention, he had taken it upon himself to organize a liberal
brain trust to analyze issues for Stevenson, and in 1956 he had been
chairman of the second Stevenson campaign. He was, like Stevenson,
urbane and articulate, but he was also dull, given to wearing brown suits
and brown shoes, and speaking in a soft monotone. He had been a party
stalwart for years, though, and he was deeply admired by liberals who
looked askance at Tammany Hall, Carmine De Sapio, and the New York
city organization. To ordinary Democrats, he was unknown.

Harriman doubted that he could ever generate any excitement
among voters. But as the governor himself had been encouraged by
Truman in 1952, he encouraged Finletter to take his wares on the road.
Reports that came back confirmed what he had feared. Finletter was
leaving no tracks as he traveled the state.

Liberals, remembering how the bosses had handled the 1954 convention, could now see the Tammany machine taking control of the
Senate nomination. Already, they were grousing about De Sapio's domination of the party. Roger Tubby, Truman's last White House press
secretary, issued a warning that De Sapio would select a Senate nominee
"who might be a less fortunate choice" than Harriman had been. The
control of "patronage, political power, and preference," by De Sapio and
the Tammany bosses, he said, was hardening the party's arteries. "Let's
not again have a candidate for high office in this state maneuvered in
such a way as to keep him from campaigning in New York City before
the convention and then at the convention facing a monolithic block, an
impervious legion of De Sapio stalwarts, many following not the dictates
of their own consciences or even the wishes of their own constituents,
but rather the dictates of one man."[10] Because Tubby was a friend,
Harriman was stung by the public candor. He reported the remarks to
Truman, and the former President sent Tubby a typical dressing down.
"I thought I had succeeded in impressing upon you that you cannot win
in politics if you don't stay with your friends," he said. "Averell and I
were your friends when you needed us, and it might be a good thing for
you to sit down and ponder your past position and what Averell and I
have done to try to help you."[11]

In spite of his wounded reaction to Tubby's observations, Harriman
privately shared them. To make party politics more democratic, he had
called for selection of its nominees in primaries rather than the state
convention. And long before Tubby's public warning, he had regularly
heard friends express private concerns about De Sapio. Though the
Manhattan boss had behaved with unassailable discretion in Albany, he
remained a concern, especially after an episode that evoked a Tammany
image of old. One morning in July of 1957, De Sapio hailed a taxi near
his apartment on lower Fifth Avenue and took it uptown to the Biltmore

Hotel. Moments after he got out, the cabbie noticed on the passenger seat a white envelope, which turned out to be filled with $50 and $100 bills amounting to $11,200. He turned the money in, along with a description of the swarthy passenger in dark glasses. As soon as the description circulated, De Sapio acknowledged that he was the passenger in question; but when he denied any knowledge of the cash, political insiders hooted.

Their guess was that he wouldn't admit that the money was his because he would then have to explain what he was doing with a stack of musty bills. Although the episode emphasized De Sapio's vulnerability, Harriman was convinced of his personal honesty. As the state Democratic convention approached, the governor's problem with the Tammany chief was not his reputation or heavy-handedness, but De Sapio's hesitation on the issue of a candidate for the Senate. Averell had wanted to get the matter out of the way in January; but when spring came, De Sapio still showed no inclination to resolve it.

It was Harriman's chance to take the initiative, but he did nothing. He gave different people different views, never being fully candid. Backer was all out for Finletter and thought Harriman was, too. State chairman Prendergast was under the impression that the governor favored Thomas Murray, a former member of the Atomic Energy Commission, who had the support of the upstate Irish.

Periodically, Harriman also talked with Milton Stewart and Charles Van Devander about Mayor Wagner, usually winding up uncertain whether Wagner would be a boost or a drag on the ticket. He had a passing notion that the answer was Edward R. Murrow, the CBS correspondent who had attained the status of a demigod in the broadcast business after taking on Joe McCarthy. His willingness to consider Murrow was evidence that the newsman's candidacy was being seriously taken, inasmuch as Murrow had eclipsed Averell in the affections of Pamela Churchill back in London. This time, the broadcaster was untempted.

Of one thing Stewart was sure. Harriman was being advised by too many people, pulled in too many directions, and for that he had himself to blame. He had let four years go by without consolidating his power and assuming party leadership. Old pro Charley Poletti had fervently tried to get him to declare his independence of Tammany Hall and establish himself with the liberals and reformers who were his natural allies. Instead, he had allowed himself to go on being the quintessential organization man. Even when he traveled on official business having nothing to do with politics, he still hooked up with local party chiefs.

It was not his style to challenge the establishment. It never had been. From the time Jim Ten Eyck taught him to row, he had succeeded by entrusting himself to experts. And where elective politics was concerned, his expert was Carmine De Sapio. After he left office, *New York Post* publisher Dorothy Schiff would lament that "he had bowed to the city machine more often and more abjectly than any Democratic governor of our time."[12] Robert Wagner could have been the consensus Senate candidate. Although he had just been elected to a second four-year term at City Hall, it was assumed by everyone that his real ambition was to claim his father's old seat in Washington. Although he had been the Democrats' unsuccessful candidate against Jacob Javits in 1956, he had run a powerful campaign. Afterward, it was accepted that he had first call on the 1958 nomination for the open Ives seat if he wanted to try for the Senate again.

But in another colossal blunder, Harriman decided early that he did not want Wagner on the ticket. Scandals in the city, he told De Sapio, would make the mayor a burden. New York City's problems would be superimposed on the state ticket and his own campaign. In rather more genteel terms, he told Wagner the same thing when the mayor stopped by for a talk at Sands Point one Saturday afternoon in May. While he was still undecided about his choice, he had concluded that the timing for Wagner was wrong. As Wagner remembered the conversation, Harriman simply "thought I was at one of those dips in popularity that we all go through. He just thought that I couldn't be helpful to him."[13]

Both knew there was more to it. Wagner had made a try for the vice-presidential nomination when Stevenson left the choice to the convention in 1956. In the Senate he would be an obvious possibility as a running mate for the Democratic nominee in 1960. Such a possibility could complicate Harriman's own plans and might even hurt his chances of being secretary of state.

De Sapio was not unhappy about Harriman's position, since a chill had descended upon his own relationship with Wagner—in part because of the mayor's support of Stevenson in 1956. Besides, the organization had done nothing to prepare for a successor at City Hall.

Under these uncertain circumstances, seventy-year-old former postmaster general James A. Farley became the first announced Senate candidate, followed by Finletter, and then by Edward T. Dickinson, Averell's commissioner of commerce. Publicly neither Harriman nor De Sapio was showing his hand; but, disappointed at Finletter's tryout, Averell began encouraging Tom Murray to get into the race.

A wealthy electrical engineer, inventor, and industrialist, Murray had served on the AEC for seven years, acquiring a reputation as its conscience on the political aspects of nuclear-weapons policy. Harriman liked that, and he also liked the fact that Murray was an upstate Irish Catholic. He would fit nicely on a ticket with himself, a Protestant, DeLuca, an Italian Catholic, and Levitt, a Jew, although he was frail and had little charisma or instinct for politics.

Just as he had provided Finletter the opportunity to work the state, Harriman arranged for Murray to be introduced around Albany, and asked Wagner to bring him together with city leaders. The mayor obligingly invited the five borough chairmen to sit down with Murray in the secretary of state's office across the street from City Hall. Murray handled the politics well enough, but the meeting was disastrous for his Senate ambition. "The guy looked like death on vacation," Wagner later recalled. "He was so pale and thin that all of the leaders came out saying, 'Jesus, he won't live through the convention.' "[14]

De Sapio evaded questions about his own choice, falling back on platitudes about democratic process and producing a list of acceptable candidates, including everybody running or thinking about it. His own sympathy, however, was for Manhattan district attorney Frank Hogan.

Unlike Finletter and Murray, the DA had appeal on the stump. He had been the Democrats' first choice for attorney general in 1954, and he had been a good soldier when the leaders found it expedient to push him aside and give the nomination to FDR, Jr. At times, he had been courted by both Republicans and Democrats as a potential candidate for mayor. The son of a factory worker, he had been Dewey's assistant when the future governor was making his reputation as a crime-busting prosecutor. After Dewey entered politics, Hogan succeeded him, and he had been district attorney ever since. Dewey's unconcealed admiration for him caused acerbic Jim Farley to label him a "Dewey Democrat."[15] As far as the 1958 Senate nomination was concerned, though, the liberal Democrats had no interest in him solely because their hearts belonged to Finletter.

August came with nothing resolved, and it became obvious that Wagner was the only candidate who could bring the party together. He was a strong campaigner, and while the organization had supported him, he was still in good standing with the liberals who favored Finletter. When the party convened in Buffalo, the first order of business might well have been an effort to draft him.

But now it was his turn to repay Harriman and De Sapio for their rebuff. With the convention barely more than two weeks away, he firmly closed the door on the Senate race. When reporters cornered him at his summer house at Islip, he told them he would refuse a draft by the convention. And to make sure there was no doubt about his sincerity, he had his remarks transcribed and telephoned to his press secretary for dissemination in the city.[16]

With that, both Murray and Hogan declared themselves candidates; and on Backer's advice, Averell decided to show his hand. It was yet another unfortunate mistake.

As he was flying home at the end of a long day upstate, he talked about his options with Warren Weaver, a *Times* correspondent in Albany,

who raised the subject fully expecting to get the usual runaround. But
Harriman started to talk, and Weaver was so astonished that he took no
notes, thinking it might cause Harriman to put his words off the record.
Finletter, the governor said, was still his first choice. He clearly had the
most solid experience, especially in the area of foreign policy. But months
of campaigning as an undeclared candidate had produced little Finletter
support. While it wasn't yet time to give up on the former secretary of
the Air Force, Murray was an entirely acceptable second choice. Back in
his seat, Weaver worked furiously to reconstruct the conversation. His
exclusive, published August 15, was the most revealing story of the entire
campaign, and it set the stage for a disastrous Democratic convention.
Though the story did not identify its source, *Times* editors were informed
that it came from Harriman himself and put it above the fold on the
front page:

> Gov. Harriman is supporting Thomas K. Finletter for the Dem-
> ocratic nomination for the U.S. Senate, but is prepared to settle
> for Thomas E. Murray. The Governor has told friends and
> close political associates that he feels Mr. Finletter, a former
> Secretary of the Air Force, is the best qualified candidate and
> would make the strongest running mate with him on the party
> ballot this fall.
>   The Governor has been under considerable pressure from
> the Liberal party to persuade other Democratic leaders, notably
> Carmine De Sapio, that Mr. Finletter should be the unanimous
> choice of the party's nominating convention. Thus far, Mr. Har-
> riman has not been successful in this move, and he has told
> advisers that the political situation may force him to shift his
> support to another of the five Senate candidates if the Finletter
> cause bogs down. He does not feel that time has arrived.[17]

The story sent the anemic Finletter campaign reeling and publicly
saddled Murray with the onus of second choice. Eleanor Roosevelt wrote
the governor a blistering letter, demanding that he stand up to De Sapio.
She could not publicly oppose him for governor, she said, but she threatened to sit out the campaign if it was run by the Tammany boss.

> You know as well as I do that you can control Mr. De Sapio if
> you make up your mind to do so. I know it is hard for you to
> do, but the man you decide to have for the US Senate will be
> nominated. You say that the Liberal party has put pressure on
> you. I would suggest that the Liberal party is the least important
> factor in the pressures exerted at the present time. It is the

liberals in the Democratic party that are going to be upset if
they think, as many of them do, that what you have done by
permitting this article to be written is to give "the kiss of death"
to Mr. Finletter's nomination, because the moment you say you
will accept an alternative you imply that you are subservient to
the bosses.

Many liberal Democrats in this election are weighing the
question of whether they will vote for you or for Nelson Rockefeller—both of you suffer under the same difficulty, that of not
really knowing the game sufficiently well to play it on the level
of the bosses. You have the advantage because many people
feel that you have learned something about this game during
your time in office and this is a Democratic year, but from what
I hear it might be quite possible that Democratic liberals, not
wanting to vote for the Democratic candidate for the US Senate,
will shed also the Democratic governorship because they will
think the responsibility is yours.

I am afraid I am being rather brutal, but I would rather
tell you now what I hear than wait until after the race is over.
I told you a long while back that I thought you would win and
I still think so, given a feeling among liberal Democrats that you
can control De Sapio and the other leaders and that you will
stand and work for the candidates that you really think are the
best for the job for which they are nominated.

There is considerable criticism just now of Nelson because
people have felt that he is compromising on principles in order
to get the support of the organization in his party. If this be-
comes equally true in both parties, then where do the Liberals
put their trust?

I hated to have to fight you for the nomination in Chicago
but I believe that Adlai was actually the best fitted for that
nomination. I certainly will not fight you openly in this state but
it would be hard to work for you if I felt that the party was
guided by De Sapio and not by you.[18]

In the last days before the convention, Hogan's campaign also faltered, and Backer and Liberal party chairman Alex Rose pleaded with
De Sapio to put the organization behind Finletter. They came out of a
meeting with him thinking they had at last succeeded. But on the night
before going to Buffalo, Harriman's dinner with Gutman and Van Devander was interrupted by a call from the leader. De Sapio had consulted
the borough chairmen and they'd decided they couldn't go along. Finletter had never been elected to public office; his success in politics resulted

solely from his personal association with Adlai Stevenson; he was a tool
of the Liberal party and the Stevenson Democrats who looked down
upon the state party organization.[19]

The stage was set for a calamity.

The convention was carefully arranged to get maximum exposure
across the state. Delegates arrived on Sunday and killed Monday with
routine business before nominating Averell for a second term on Monday night. His acceptance speech on a statewide television hookup was
set for prime time. After more preliminaries during the day on Tuesday,
the grand finale would come in the late evening with the nomination of
the Democratic candidate for the Senate.

Buffalo was draped in bunting and swinging to the Harriman campaign song as state police escorted the governor's motorcade into town
on Sunday afternoon. Accompanied by Marie, his two daughters, and
his grandchildren, he worked his way through the crowded Statler-
Hilton lobby ignoring reporters' shouted questions about the Senate
nomination. Tan and fit, he looked a good ten years younger than his
nearly sixty-seven, and in the organized fanfare he was able to hide his
distress over the showdown that could no longer be postponed.

In the sitting room of his twelfth-floor suite, he and De Sapio finally
met to decide on a nominee for the Senate. Prendergast and Wagner
joined them, along with Alex Rose, who had come to collaborate with
them before going back to Manhattan for the Liberals' own convention.
Other party leaders and Harriman's political aides drifted in an out, but
all except Averell, De Sapio, and Wagner were basically spectators. In a
faceoff with the organization that had put him in office, Averell was
without George Backer. The one man he most needed was in New York
City with an ailing wife.

Having ruled Finletter out the previous night, De Sapio professed
to have an otherwise open mind on the matter, but when Harriman
steered the conversation around to Tom Murray, it was obvious that the
organization wouldn't support the former AEC commissioner either.
The obvious solution was still the pudgy, balding mayor of New York
City. Prendergast relieved them of the embarrassment of having to eat
crow by several times suggesting Wagner as a consensus candidate. Harriman was all for it, but De Sapio was noncommittal, and Wagner himself
was silent. Since the mayor didn't say no, Harriman got the impression,
as did Rose, who had met with him earlier, that he could still be persuaded. The session broke up at four A.M., the room littered with food,
warm half-drinks, overflowing ashtrays, and nothing resolved.

Later on Monday, Harriman and Gutman holed up in the governor's
suite while the convention dragged through its opening session and
delegates awaited the word. But nothing happened because Wagner had

gone off to Niagara Falls with his wife and two sons. When he returned in the late afternoon, he told Harriman he had not changed his mind. Careful not to push him into an unequivocal refusal, Averell pleaded with him to think about it overnight and discuss it one last time at breakfast on Tuesday.

The answer, the mayor assured him, would still be no, but he would consider it once more. Desperate, Harriman tried to make it easier for the mayor to say yes by getting Hogan out of the way. He had Milton Stewart find the district attorney and slip him up the back stairs to the gubernatorial suite. But it was another blunder. First, Stewart and Hogan were intercepted by reporters; and when Harriman suggested that Hogan stand aside, the candidate was incredulous. Dropping out was unthinkable. He was in position to win the nomination, and if he pulled out, it would be obvious to all the reporters lurking outside that Harriman had jerked his string. He would put a gun to his head, he told the governor, before he would be forced out under naked pressure.

Under these dismal circumstances, Harriman drove the block and a half to the convention hall on Monday evening and accepted nomination for a second term. Because of the tide of rumors and gossip about backroom deals, the convention was consumed with the Senate nomination fight. Not surprisingly, the nominating speeches and Averell's acceptance were all flat.

Still, his people performed admirably. Joe Tepper, the ace advance man of 1954, who had been elevated to the state Athletic Commission, was back in his element, leading the floor demonstration after the nomination. When enthusiasm flagged, he pushed the Harriman grandchildren into the spotlight with their blond, long-stemmed nanny Gretchen Cooper, and the delegates whooped it up as though their man were bound for the White House.

On the tick of 9:30, the outpouring of enthusiasm ended. Delegates fell into their seats; Harriman lashed into the Republican leadership in both Washington and Albany, focusing his attention on the obstructionist legislature. His words were sufficiently incendiary, but the hall was a huge echo chamber. Speakers couldn't make themselves understood beyond the first two dozen rows. As the governor sounded the trumpet for a second term, delegates in the back wandered around exchanging rumors about the Senate fight and news from the Republican convention under way in Rochester.

After midnight, the wrangling at the hotel resumed for several more hours. It was time wasted, since Wagner's final answer was still to come.

At the private breakfast, Harriman got the word he dreaded. "It's still the same," said the mayor. "It's no." He would live with his promise to complete his full term at City Hall. He had run in three successive campaigns, for mayor in 1953, for the Senate in 1956, and for mayor again in 1957. He didn't wish to have a reputation for running for every open office. Moreover, his family didn't want him to run for the Senate again. His elder son had told him that if he broke his promise to finish his term in City Hall, the boy would be ashamed to go back to school at Exeter.[20]

Harriman was beaten. Because he had ignored the advice of Wagner and Tannenwald and accepted the nomination before getting the Senate issue settled, he had no leverage left. De Sapio, who had been quietly lining up support for Hogan all along, openly declared the DA the organization's choice.

Hogan was unquestionably the strongest candidate. He was attractive, clean, and widely known. He was also Catholic. Had Harriman supported him at the beginning and not allowed him to emerge as De Sapio's choice, he might have even become a consensus nominee. But the governor had needlessly trapped himself by publicly announcing for either Finletter or Murray. Now he could not switch to Hogan without the world seeing him abjectly bow to Tammany Hall, and he had no chance of defeating the organization in a floor fight.

Between them, the Tammany leaders, De Sapio, Buckley in the Bronx, Joseph Sharkey in Brooklyn, Joseph Crissona of Queens, and Joseph McKinney of Richmond, controlled 601 votes; only 572 were required for nomination. For insurance, however, De Sapio and Buckley made a deal with Erie County chairman Peter Crotty. In exchange for his support of Hogan, the Buffalo leader was promised the nomination for attorney general.

That was another personal insult to Harriman. He had given the leaders a list of three acceptable candidates, and Crotty was not among them. The governor's first choice was Dan Gutman, his own counsel. At last, he was left the option of suffering his humiliation quietly or making a stand for Finletter on the convention floor and going down with flags flying. Neither alternative suited his style, and with Finletter beaten he looked at the possibility of getting behind Murray. Wagner could make a rousing nominating speech, and then they would demand a slow roll call. That would require delegates to individually declare themselves and provide them a chance to break with the machine and vote as they wished. If a miracle happened and the tide began to turn, Averell could go to the floor and try to turn it into a bandwagon.

Wagner was willing, but when Finletter's people heard about it, they were livid. Their man was still in the running; and they were prepared to lose, and see Harriman lose, for their principles. Furthermore, they assured Wagner he would never again have the support of liberals in the Democratic party if he joined in any such scheme.[21]

The string had run out. As certainly as they had presided over Harriman's nomination in Manhattan four years earlier, De Sapio and the Tammany powers watched delegates follow the choreography in Buffalo. The Boss was on the platform on Tuesday night when the last suggestion of rebellion was snuffed out—a Prendergast attempt to circumvent the deal with Crotty by opening the floor to nominations for attorney general.

For a time, Averell refused even to go to the convention hall; and when he finally did, he balked again in his hideaway in a hockey team's offices. It took a shaming from Marie to move him into the hall, where he finally joined the delegation from Orange County just before midnight.

Murray was nominated by Mayor Erastus Corning of Albany and Finletter by his own campaign manager, former New York City police commissioner Francis W. H. Adams. When it was over at 1:59 A.M., Hogan had amassed 772 votes, to 304 for Murray, and 66 for Finletter. In what he would later call the lowest moment of his life, Harriman stood before the convention and raised Hogan's hand in victory, but he could scarcely bring himself to look at De Sapio.

The Boss's motives for what happened were never explained. Harriman's own theory, in long and bitter retrospect, was that De Sapio wanted the district attorney out of office, not because he feared action from the aggressive prosecutor but because he saw an opportunity to expand Tammany's stable of incumbents.[22] He was no doubt looking toward 1960 and another presidential campaign as well. Except in Averell's mind, another Harriman campaign was out of the question. De Sapio had his own role at the national convention to consider. "When he set about creating the coalition of county bosses who would control the Senate nomination of 1958, he intended to maintain it as a unit which would decide whom New York backed for President at the next national convention," former New York Times reporter Warren Moscow concluded in his De Sapio biography.[23]

Harriman's glowing reelection prospects disintegrated with the Buffalo debacle. On the morning after the convention, the telephone in his suite was silent. No one waited to see him. He was drained of enthusiasm for the campaign ahead. The fight had cost him no less than a million votes, he told Gutman, and he wouldn't be able to make them up. He would lose by 500,000 votes. It was going to be up to Gutman to tend the office through the fall. Meanwhile, he was going to hit the road and "do everything that I am supposed to, and everything I can do."[24]

He and Marie faced a long drive back to Albany. Unlike Averell, she had not been surprised by De Sapio's ruthlessness. She had disliked and distrusted the man all along, no matter how much Averell admired his political instincts. The deception, she thought, was the very kind of thing they should have expected. "Yeah," said the First Lady as the team vacated the suite where her husband's political career had been dismembered, "they gave ole Ave a real Philadelphia rat fucking."[25]

That was only part of the problem. In Rochester, the bunting was being taken down after a Republican convention that had given its nomination to an ebullient Nelson Rockefeller.

Harriman made a poor effort to conceal his anger.

Ignoring the leaders, he announced that upon Hogan's election to the Senate, former police commissioner Francis Adams, who had been Finletter's campaign manager, would be named district attorney. It was an intended olive branch to the liberals, but it was also a slap at the organization, which he now depended upon more than ever. Gutman rushed to the city from Albany, hoping to head off the announcement. It was "going to get the leaders excited," he warned, but Harriman refused to discuss the matter. He didn't give a damn, he said, how they felt. "The press is expecting an announcement, and I'm going to make it."[26]

Later, when his rage subsided, he perfunctorily tried to restore peace, supporting Hogan and citing the DA's record to counter Republican claims that Democrats were soft on crime. On several occasions, he campaigned with De Sapio himself.

But the "bossism" issue created in Buffalo meshed perfectly with the long-term Republican strategy of portraying Harriman as complacent, compliant, and ineffective. Judson Morhouse, the state GOP chairman, set the tone, denouncing Harriman's failure to protest the public display of Tammany bossism. "If a Governor obviously has so little power and influence in his own political organization, it is not difficult to judge how little power and influence he must have in the administration of the state government itself."[27] Rockefeller talked bossism every day. When Averell appeared with De Sapio in the city, the Republicans portrayed him as a tool of the machine. When he kept his distance from Tammany, he was accused of hiding from his friends. The Boss's appearance anywhere offended liberals. Arthur Schlesinger even wrote Averell suggesting that something be done to keep De Sapio from speaking—"Every time he gets a headline, he identifies the Democratic party all the more with bossism and thereby plays into Rockefeller's hands."[28]

From the convention onward, Harriman was on the defensive. Rockefeller blamed him for a flight of industry from New York, and credited him with taking the state into the worst fiscal crisis in a generation. Administration laxity, he said, was responsible for a "steady march of crime" in the state.

The issues were hardly new, but New Yorkers had never seen a campaign quite like this one. The princes of eastern capitalism, heirs of the fortunes that had shaped the city and the country, slogged through the Garment District, the Lower East Side, and Harlem. They patted sweating seamstresses, squeezed grubby hands at loading docks, solicited the votes of derelicts, and shouted themselves hoarse. They commiserated with farmers from the potato fields of Long Island to the dairy barns of the north country, and rushed through schoolhouses, firehouses, and courthouses in the clutches of aides who pushed them in and out of motorcades and on and off airplanes until the hours and days and townships became a blur. In communities like Painted Post and Horseheads, from Lackawanna on the shore of Lake Erie through the Adirondacks, voters clucked at being personally courted by a Harriman and a Rockefeller.

In the city, Averell revisited the sidewalks he had traveled with Joe Tepper and Bernie Ruggieri four years earlier, making walking tours in Brooklyn, Queens, and the Bronx, dropping in at nursing homes, schools, and ground breakings. He still campaigned by the numbers, with little humor and less spontaneity, but he had improved. He had acquired useful tricks that included a little ethnic lingo and a few serviceable phrases in foreign tongues.

Back in the wreckage at Buffalo, some Democrats had naively consoled themselves in the Republicans' nomination of a political novice. But on the campaign trail, Rockefeller was a duck in water. No politician in the country, with the possible exception of Hubert Humphrey, exhibited as much joy playing the game. He wisecracked, brushed insults aside without a waver in his grin, and disarmed skeptics with a wink, a "Hiya fella," and a hearty slap on the back.

He was seventeen years younger than the governor, and his vitality called attention to Averell's age, while his easy embrace of strangers created an appealing contrast to the Harriman reserve. Men admired his earthiness and children besieged him for his autograph. Women were flattered by his appreciative eye—a blow to the ego of Harriman, who was not unaware of his own stature as a ladies' man on more than one continent.

As flashy as Rockefeller was, and as heavy as the bossism issue weighed about Harriman's neck, the campaign was not a Republican cakewalk. The "soft on crime" refrain did not take hold, and Rockefeller's alarm bells about the administration's fiscal policy alarmed hardly anyone.

Truman arrived in Manhattan and joined Harriman and Hogan in a motorcade from the city up through White Plains, Yonkers, Spring Valley, and Newburgh, to Albany. At every stop the three of them used a bullhorn to rally crowds around their open car. Averell was so energized by Truman at his side that he jumped from the car and chased a bunch of small boys who showed up carrying a sign saying "Harryman for Ex-Governor." But there was tension even on the best days. Averell resented Hogan because he had been imposed. While Truman was campaigning with them, the governor and the Senate nominee fell into an argument over a triviality within earshot of both Truman and embarrassed staff men. It continued until it could no longer be ignored, and the former President shamed them to silence.[29]

All indications pointed to a Democratic autumn across the country. Arriving from California, where Attorney General Pat Brown was leading in the governor's race, Hubert Humphrey reported, "The sun is rising in the West," adding with unintended gallows humor, "I hope it is not setting in the East."[30]

Since Rockefeller had no record to defend, Harriman aimed his attack on the lame-duck Eisenhower administration and Richard Nixon, belittling Rockefeller for "going around the state trying to cover up the Eisenhower recession," and for hiding from the Republican party.[31] Rockefeller did skillfully distance himself from Republican conservatives. When Eisenhower denounced Democrats as "radicals" and made blanket attacks on labor unions, the candidate gingerly parted ways with his President.

In truth, not much separated the millionaires philosophically, and their criticism of each other was more of style than of substance. The Rockefellers, Harriman said, were "all fine boys," but Nelson had a problem of wanting to be everybody's friend. Running behind, he challenged Rockefeller to debate, and Rockefeller accepted—but only on condition that the exchange be limited to state issues. Obviously, said the Republican nominee with a dig at Averell's preoccupation with Washington, they were not running for national office.

The worst day of the campaign came on October 15, when *The New York Times* endorsed Rockefeller. *Times* editors had not endorsed Harriman in 1954, but they had appreciated his work in Albany and had often commented on it favorably. Even in relaxed times, the tone of Harriman's days as governor was set by the paper. He could be massacred elsewhere, but if he was well treated in the *Times*, he was happy. Often it seemed that the object of his service was to please the gray eminence of American journalism. When the *Times* ignored him or treated him badly, his aides were in for hours of sulking, bellyaching, and recrimination. When coverage was favorable, no adversity fazed him.

By the time he arose at the Mark Twain Hotel in Elmira that morning in October, political lieutenant Milton Stewart had already seen the editorial, bought out the newsstand, and swept every copy of the paper from sight. But Harriman demanded and got a copy, and for the rest of the day he was depressed and disagreeable.

Rockefeller, said the editorial, had "the qualities of character, the breadth of business, administrative, and governmental expertise, the vigor, and strength of conviction to make a good chief executive of New York State, and possibly a great one." But what cut Harriman to the quick was not the fawning over Rockefeller as much as the judgment of his own four years as governor. The Harriman record, the *Times* found, was "barren of sufficient major accomplishment to recommend a second term. Instead of fulfilling his inaugural promise of a 'bold adventurous administration,' he has given the state a pedestrian performance, disappointing in achievement and, we believe, unpromising of improvement in the future."[32]

Although Harriman's attention to upstate precincts was paying off, there was an unsettling disinterest in the Democratic wards of Manhattan as the campaign entered its last weeks. Liberals were sitting on their hands or, like Eleanor Roosevelt, supporting the Democratic ticket grudgingly. Independents were flocking to Rockefeller, as were other Liberals already seeing him as a potential rival to Richard Nixon for the 1960 presidential nomination. In New York City, pollsters found middle-aged and elderly black and Jewish voters planning to vote Republican for the first time in their lives.

Capable as he was of self-deception, not even Averell could ignore the dark clouds. With Rockefeller cutting away at the Democratic base in New York City, he trimmed his statewide schedule and worked the wards, where it was imperative to build huge margins to offset suburban and upstate deficits.

The campaign's end was as bizarre as the beginning at Buffalo. During a press conference at Port Jervis at the end of October, Harriman took Rockefeller and Eisenhower to task on American policy in the Middle East. On the advice of muckraking columnist Drew Pearson, who warned him of a wholesale defection of Jewish voters, he accused Rockefeller of being a part of the White House's wavering in America's commitment to Israel during the 1956 Suez Crisis. "As far as I know," he said caustically, "Mr. Rockefeller was in the White House when we supported Nasser and the Arab nations. We are committed to Israel and we must make it plain to the Arab nations that we intend to stand by that commitment."[33]

The comments were briefly reported, but they faded without causing a ripple. Harriman still thought it was a useful issue, and he raised it again five days later. Interviewed on a late-night radio talk show, he repeated what he had said at Port Jervis—that Rockefeller had been Eisenhower's foreign policy adviser at the time "when the first appeasement of President Nasser of Egypt took place."[34]

This time, the reaction was stunning. On election eve, *New York Post* publisher Dorothy Schiff withdrew her paper's endorsement. In a front-page column, she said Harriman's "snide insinuation that Nelson Rockefeller is pro-Arab and anti-Israel" could not be condoned. She urged voters who agreed with that not to vote for Harriman.[35] In terms of influence, Averell had never regarded Schiff's paper as very important, but her switch added to an impression that the governor's campaign was fading at the finish line.

Averell was shaking hands in Queens when he learned of the publisher's turnabout. Rather than his remark about Rockefeller, he suspected that her real reason for embarrassing him was her unhappiness at being excluded from social affairs at the governor's mansion—she had been routinely left out because she was inclined to put private comments at such occasions into public print.

After the paper hit the streets, he convened the campaign's last crisis meeting in Backer's headquarters office. He didn't remember the precise words he had used on the radio show, but he would not back down. The room practically stood and cheered—the defiant captain of the *Titanic* was prepared to go down with his ship. The next morning Rockefeller workers were outside polling places with thousands of copies of the *Post* carrying the Schiff column.

Harriman was swept away in a landslide, losing by more than half a million votes, and running far behind Hogan. Not even the most optimistic Republicans had dreamed they could win so easily in the face of a national Democratic resurgence.

Early in the evening, leading briefly on the strength of the first New York City returns, he and Marie and a party of old friends went to dinner at the Waldorf. But he couldn't sit still long enough for the first course to arrive. The returns were too slow to reach him there, and he went back to the Biltmore, arriving just as the avalanche broke. By 10:45, it was all over. He called Rockefeller and congratulated him; and then, mustering a smile, he stepped before the cameras and conceded defeat. He pledged to "cooperate fully in the transfer of responsibility of the state government to the men whom Mr. Rockefeller may choose as his associates."[36]

As expected, Crotty, who had been denied the Liberal party's nomination, was also buried. Hogan held on until after midnight before bowing to Keating by 160,000 votes. Levitt held a thin lead through the night and emerged the Democrats' only statewide survivor.

Harriman's political career was obviously finished. Though the outcome would take longer, the disaster was also the beginning of the end for De Sapio, whose slide from power would eventually land him in jail. If any Democrat, save Levitt, could be said to have won, it was Wagner. Instead of a new Democratic dynasty in Albany, Harriman had presided over the return of the executive mansion to Republican control, where Rockefeller would hold it for sixteen years.

The last weeks in Albany were excruciating. As Averell went through the motions of fulfilling his last obligations, Jonathan and June Bingham moved into the mansion to keep him and Marie company. All four were miserable. Averell was blaming everybody but himself for his loss. Bingham stood high on the list of the culprits because he had recommended Rockefeller for the Constitutional Convention Commission in the first place. "He was like a wounded animal," June Bingham remembered, "flailing, snarling, snapping at everybody."[37] Even Marie got the blame, and on several nights she was left downstairs in tears as Harriman went off to bed, an angry, suddenly old, man, raging at the world.

Chapter XXII

NEW GENERATION
Days of the Crocodile

On a crisp autumn afternoon soon after his election to the presidency, John F. Kennedy went to Harriman's house in Manhattan for lunch with British Labour leader Hugh Gaitskell. The governor, as the host still preferred to be called after his dismissal from Albany, had been a good friend of Gaitskell since Marshall Plan days, and Gaitskell always visited whenever he was in the United States. In late 1960, Gaitskell entertained hopes of becoming Prime Minister, and he was naturally interested in meeting with the President-elect. He needed only to mention his wish to Averell.

For Kennedy, a meeting with a leader of the British opposition before seeing Prime Minister Harold Macmillan presented a sensitive problem of protocol, but Harriman was able to arrange it in strict confidence and he was eager to do it because it gave him a chance to do a bit of logrolling in behalf of his own career. He had not handled the 1960 election well; and being seventy years old and the man who had lost the New York state house for the Democrats, he could not be certain of an invitation to join the new administration in Washington. Through the early months of the presidential campaign season, he had dillydallied while the Massachusetts senator captured the imagination of Democrats across the country, and by the time the governor recognized the obvious and scrambled aboard the bandwagon, it was heavily loaded.

Since the election, Averell had flooded the political network with hints that he was available to serve once more, and his name had ap-

peared in the newspapers as a possible secretary of state or secretary of
the treasury. But where it counted, he was being ignored. He had heard
nothing from the President-elect, the Kennedy family, or the headhunt-
ers filling the ranks of the new administration.

At lunch, Kennedy and Gaitskell hit it off easily, chatting about
trade, NATO, and politics. Averell, who was having trouble hearing,
occasionally exercised the interlocutor's prerogative and brought the
conversation around to Nikita Khrushchev, the Soviet Union, tensions
between the great powers, and the problems the Eisenhower administration would leave behind in Foggy Bottom. Michael Forrestal—both a
Kennedy pal and a Harriman protégé—and Jonathan Bingham were
there to fill the table, though they were not much needed to keep the
conversation moving.

During dessert while the principals were having a casual exchange
about Soviet meddling in the Congo, Gaitskell murmured a two- or three-
word dissent from one of the host's observations on the Khrushchev
mindset, and Harriman bristled, thinking the challenge had been uttered
by Bingham. As Gaitskell looked into his coffee cup and Kennedy stared
into space, Harriman upbraided his erstwhile executive secretary for a
display of ignorance which he attributed to an obvious lack of experience.
The storm passed as suddenly as it had arisen. Later, as Harriman and
Gaitskell were saying farewell, Kennedy whispered to Forrestal, "I have
to talk with you privately for a moment," and pulled him into a powder
room in the foyer. "Jesus," thought Forrestal as the door was closed,
"this is it. He's going to make Averell secretary of state."

"Now, this is very serious," said the President-Elect, starting to laugh
at the thought of Harriman's assault on Bingham. "Averell's hearing is
atrocious. If we're going to give him a job, he has to have a hearing aid,
and I want you to see that he does."[1]

A hearing aid was very nearly the only thing Harriman had overlooked. Preparing for a return to Washington all the time he was in
Albany, he had tracked foreign policy issues as carefully as he had monitored the state budget. When traveling notables such as Gaitskell, the
Shah of Iran, Israel's Golda Meir, or nearly any visiting Russian found
it inconvenient to call on him in Albany, he drove down and entertained
them in the New York City. For touring statesmen, a visit with him was
as much a part of a New York City schedule as a call at City Hall or
Gracie Mansion. Since 1953, Harriman's house had been one of the
places where foreign leaders maintained contact with the American
power structure.

When he turned the state over to Nelson Rockefeller on January 1,
1959, he had already made plans for personal foreign missions that
would take up the better part of a year and prepare him to join a new
Democratic administration in Washington. Although his White House

ambition had at last been extinguished, he still wanted as much as ever
to be secretary of state. That was the job he had coveted more than he
had ever wished to be President, he confessed to his secretary on the
melancholy day he cleaned out his desk in Albany.[2] With hope resurgent,
he began preparations on the farfetched chance that the elusive opportunity might yet come.

He first headed for India, which had escaped his close attention
over the years, and then returned to Moscow for the first time since he
left the American embassy in 1946, itching to size up Khrushchev and
take the measure of the nuclear-armed, post-Stalin Soviet Union. After
an absence of more than a dozen years, he badly needed to get back to
the territory to revalidate his cherished reputation as an authority on the
Kremlin.

For a month, he traveled the subcontinent from Jaipur to the slums
of Calcutta and from the Himalayas to the shores of the Arabian Sea, all
the while sampling the political winds for every hint of Soviet influence.
He shook hands with local politicians, took in the sights of the Taj Mahal,
trudged through sprawling construction sites, and interviewed Russians
working on new factories and power plants. When he was recognized by
Soviet officials overseeing the building of a steel mill, his spirits fairly
soared, the humiliation of the Rockefeller defeat behind him. In Bom-
bay, he encountered a horde of American tourists just off a cruise ship
and greeted them with more gusto than he had summoned on the campaign trail—until one traveler squeezed his hand and exclaimed, "I'm
from New York, and I voted for you because I'm a great friend of
Carmine De Sapio."[3]

After a month, he came home confident that India was still pro-
Western at the grass roots in spite of its official flirtation with the Soviet
Union. But he sensed that there could be serious trouble at almost any
moment on the border between India and China. A series of newspaper
articles ghosted for him by *Look* magazine editor William Attwood got
front-page play across the country. "The best news out of India today is
that her leaders are finally aware of the menace of Communist China,"
began the first. "Impressed by communism's achievements but repelled
by its methods, they are now facing up to the fact that the world's
most populous democracy is in crucial competition with the world's most
populous dictatorship. Either they or the Chinese will become the model
for Asia's awakening peoples."[4] It was a highly satisfactory beginning to
his campaign for the State Department, even though the Democrats'
field of presidential contenders hadn't begun to sort itself out.

With a supply of clean shirts, he then set off for the Soviet Union
on a mission that extended through June and July. It was crucial to his
hopes to return to diplomacy; and much to his satisfaction, he found he
was not as out of date as he had feared. He was still recognized by

ordinary Russians grateful for his wartime work, in spite of his subsequent career as a Cold Warrior. When he arrived at a Zil automobile plant, workers left their jobs to crowd around him. And when he went back for his first appointment at the Kremlin, he was received by Deputy Premier Anastas Mikoyan, whom he had first met in 1941, in the same office where he, Lord Beaverbrook, and Molotov had signed the Lend-Lease agreement.

Accompanied by Charles Thayer, a Russian-speaking foreign service officer recruited as his $1,000-a-month ghostwriter, adviser, advance man and tour director, he filled one notebook after another with statistics on automobile production, corn harvests, and housing construction, and interviews with bureaucrats, factory managers, and workers. Day after day, he arose before dawn and traveled and interviewed into the night, working out of the suite in Moscow's National Hotel, where Beaverbrook had stayed when they came to the besieged Soviet capital in 1941.

With Marie and Mary Russell, a Russian-born friend from Washington, he took in *Swan Lake* at the Bolshoi, laid a wreath honoring the heroes of Stalingrad, and went steamboating on the Volga. At Yalta, he escorted Marie through Livadiya Palace, which had become a sanitorium for ailing Soviet workers, who lounged in the rooms where Roosevelt's entourage had lived during the meeting that set the stage for the Cold War. The conference room itself was a dining hall; Roosevelt's private dining room, a lounge for Soviet nurses. Down the corridor in the bedroom where Averell himself had stayed, four sickly coal miners were confined to their beds.

In late June, he got what he had really come for—an appointment to sit down face-to-face with Nikita Khrushchev. His first meeting with the former miner and factory worker who had emerged from the collective leadership as the clear successor to Stalin began at the Kremlin, but after an hour and a half moved on to dinner and several more hours of talk at the Premier's dacha. Khrushchev was as earthy, rough-edged, and quarrelsome in private as he was in public, yet more approachable than the inscrutable Stalin. In the course of the evening, he ruminated over Soviet agriculture, boasted about his seven-year economic plan, talked fondly of his grandchildren, and recalled the last days of his predecessor.

But Harriman was most interested in the repeated references to the Soviet atomic arsenal and in his demand for an agreement permanently legitimizing the division of Berlin. Unless an agreement was forthcoming, Khrushchev said he would act unilaterally and terminate the Western powers' rights in the divided city. If it became necessary, he warned, the Soviets could swallow the eleven thousand American troops in the city with "one gulp." Within five to seven years, he told Harriman after dinner and several cognac toasts, "we will be stronger than you. . . . If we spend 30 billion rubles on ballistic missiles, we can destroy every industrial center in the U.S. and Europe. Thirty billion rubles is no great sum to us." Not only could the Soviets lay waste the industrial centers of the United States and Europe, he went on, the Chinese could wipe out Formosa with Soviet rockets already in place. "Your Seventh Fleet will be of no avail. Fleets today are made to be destroyed. If the Chinese decide to take Formosa, we will support them, even if it means war."[5]

Some of his ranting was reminiscent of Hitler's; and while Harriman believed the statements to be shrewdly calculated, they disturbed him, nonetheless, because Khrushchev also revealed a profound ignorance of the West. Unlike Stalin, the Kremlin's new leader displayed little comprehension of America's politics, its economy, or the roots of its foreign policy. That being the case, Harriman judged him to be a greater concern than the tyrant he had succeeded—he was unsophisticated enough to be vulnerable to dangerous miscalculations.

Altogether the meeting lasted for ten hours, and even then Harriman had difficulty bringing it to an end. It was past midnight when he and Thayer got back to their hotel, and they worked until nearly dawn on their notes. He slept only briefly before going to the embassy to give Ambassador Llewellyn Thompson a minute-by-minute account of the most extensive conversation Khrushchev had held with any American. Combining Averell's observations and Thayer's near-verbatim account of the exchange, Thompson cabled the State Department a six-thousand-word report, including Averell's characterization of Khrushchev's remarks as "terrifying" and his observation that Khrushchev was potentially a more dangerous man than Stalin.[6] It took only days for the secret cable to leak in Washington. In a copyrighted story by Joseph Alsop, the New York *Herald Tribune* reported that the State Department was in a state of alarm over the Soviet leader's "Hitler-like" outbursts.

By the time Averell got back to New York, the political right wing was in full cry, accusing him of allowing himself to be used by the Red propaganda machine. His use of the word "terrifying" in reporting the meeting to Thompson was the chief problem, causing his critics to claim the meeting had served the very purpose intended by the wily Khrushchev, who was shortly to receive Vice-President Nixon.

It had beautifully served Harriman's purpose as well. Like other Soviet officials before and after him, Khrushchev was as fascinated by Harriman as a pillar of capitalism as he was interested in him as a reliable emissary of the American government. When he visited the United States for talks with President Eisenhower three months after the marathon conversation in Moscow, he went to Harriman's house on the first day of a tumultuous tour of the country.

Averell had left the Soviet Union as much disturbed by Khrushchev's acceptance of every Marxist bromide and cartoon image of American capitalism as he was by the bravado and boasting about the Soviet nuclear arsenal. So, with the announcement that Khrushchev would tour the country, he invited him to stop by the Harriman house in Manhattan. It was a perfect opportunity to show him that American industrialists and businessmen did not have pig noses and wear silk top hats and diamond stickpins.

In his second-floor drawing room, Harriman gathered leaders from mining, manufacturing, oil, chemicals, banking, and insurance industries, including John D. Rockefeller III; General David Sarnoff, chairman of RCA; Frank Pace, chairman of General Dynamics Corporation; W. Alton Jones, chairman of Cities Service Corporation; and John J. McCloy, chairman of Chase Manhattan Bank. By his estimate, scribbled on a yellow legal pad before Khrushchev arrived, they represented assets of some $38 billion. Among them, as witnesses to history, were a few men of ordinary means, former ambassadors, educators, and, notably, Rockefeller Foundation president Dean Rusk and Harvard economist John Kenneth Galbraith, the latter having invited himself as a "representative of the proletariat."[7]

Surrounded by Picassos and Derains, their voices muffled by Persian carpets, the capitalist Titans greeted the Communist chieftain one by one, then sat in a semicircle savoring caviar and sipping champagne and New York wine as Averell conducted his exposition of capitalism, war profits, and American politics. No one present, nor any of their friends, he and the others assured the guest of honor, favored world tensions. The assembled war profiteers, said the host, were men who would champion disarmament the moment it became safe for the United States. There was not a hint, however, that mingling with the millionaires did anything except reinforce Khrushchev's belief that he was then in the presence of the men who controlled America far more than Eisenhower and the members of Congress he had met in Washington. One testimonial to free enterprise followed another. And when the Soviet leader reasserted his stubborn belief that the men present composed the country's ruling circle, Galbraith later tattled, "Somebody demurred, but in perfunctory fashion."[8] After it was over, Harriman insisted that the Soviet leader had gained insights of "real importance."[9] But more to the point, the meeting, coming after Averell's well-chronicled visit to Moscow, had reasserted the governor's claim to a continued place in U.S.-Soviet diplomacy.

Politically, Harriman had not positioned himself nearly as skillfully as he had revalidated his diplomatic credentials. As the struggle for the 1960 presidential nomination unfolded, candidates were hardly knocking down the door in search of his support. After his humiliation by Rockefeller and De Sapio, his personal political stock was nearly worthless. And, largely because of his clumsiness, New York Democrats were split by open warfare between bosses and reformers. An ineffectual campaigner and known to be a modest contributor, Averell could no longer sway the New York delegation.

Early on, Truman had prevailed upon him to join supporters of Senator Stuart Symington of Missouri. It was clear to him that Symington would get nowhere, but in deference to Truman, he didn't tell Symington no. He was not interested in Senate majority leader Lyndon Johnson, because the Texan had the millstone of the South around his neck. Although Hubert Humphrey had the experience and the right instincts, Averell was sure he was too liberal to generate national support. Adlai Stevenson was damaged goods.

He was not convinced that John Kennedy was the candidate with a future either. The senator had started early and, as expected, had easily won the New Hampshire primary. With money, instinctive political savvy, his enormous family, and a volunteer army raised by Ivy League believers, he had picked up where Kefauver left off in perfecting the strategy of winning primary campaigns. He scored a huge Wisconsin triumph over Humphrey in April, then followed it with West Virginia in May. With that, Humphrey was finished.

Three months before the Democratic National Convention, a Kennedy juggernaut was rolling. Still, Harriman was ambivalent. His experience in New York campaigns had made him more than a little sensitive to ethnicity and religion in politics. He had not thought of that when he broke with his Republican roots and voted for Al Smith in 1928; but thirty-two years later, he was listening to Truman argue that it was still too early for a Catholic to have a chance at the White House, and he took the argument seriously.

He was also preconditioned to be skeptical about the young Kennedys because he had over the years acquired an active dislike for Joseph P. Kennedy, the family patriarch, who Harriman would privately complain was now determined to buy the nomination for his son. He had known Joe Kennedy since the twenties. He had watched him wheel and deal in the stock market, and he regarded him an unprincipled marauder. As a diplomat, he found Kennedy's London performance during the early days of Britain's war against Hitler indefensible, and his disloyalty to Roosevelt shameful. He had first met Jack Kennedy when the senator was fresh out of the Navy and attending the 1945 United Nations Conference in San Francisco, but he had not paid him much attention until Kennedy tried to get on the ticket with Stevenson in 1956.

What distressed him in early 1960 was not Kennedy's flaws, but the fact that no one from the candidate's camp had asked for his help or even his endorsement. Too proud to go to them hat in hand, Averell assumed the posture of a man surveying the field, a poor tactic consider-

The Governor. Fiscally cautious and politically unsure of himself, Harriman lost to Nelson Rockefeller in his race for reelection as New York's chief executive. Although he failed to reach the heights of illustrious predecessors Al Smith, Franklin D. Roosevelt, and Herbert Lehman, he made a mark with mental-health, consumer-protection, and anti-proverty initiatives. For the rest of his life, he wished to be referred to as Governor.

A Run for the White House. Twice Harriman bid for the Democratic presidential nomination. In 1952 he launched his campaign thinking that he would have the support of President Truman, who finally endorsed Adlai Stevenson. Here, he is greeted by supporters at the 1956 Democratic National Convention in Chicago. This time he did get Truman's endorsement, but it was to no avail.

On the Hustings. This reelection campaign picture in 1958 showed a happy side of a race that really had few happy moments. With the governor are grandchildren Robert Fisk, the wheelman, with David Mortimer, Averell Harriman Fisk, and Kathleen Lawrance Fisk in the rumble seat.

The Last Campaign. Harriman's defeat by Nelson Rockefeller was made nearly inevitable when Tammany Hall chieftains ignored his wishes and made Manhattan District Attorney Frank Hogan the Democratic nominee for the U.S. Senate. As a result of the clash at the party's state convention, "bossism" became a damaging campaign theme and created a split between reformers and establishment Democrats that persisted for years. Not even former President Truman, campaigning here with Harriman and Hogan, could help.

Allies. Robert F. Kennedy was skeptical of bringing the sixty-nine-year-old Harriman into the New Frontier, but he became his booster and confidant. Harriman, in turn, helped Kennedy begin a new career in New York politics. The friendship endured to RFK's death, in spite of Harriman's loyalty to Lyndon Johnson and differences with RFK over Vietnam.

In the Better Days of the Shah. From the time the young Shah of Iran succeeded his father on the Peacock Throne in World War II, he was among the leaders Harriman regularly called upon during missions for five presidents. During visits to the United States, the Shah skiied at Sun Valley and dined with Harriman at Georgetown. More than a decade before the regime was deposed in the Islamic revolution, Harriman was troubled by the Shah's heavy spending on western military hardware.

To Moscow for Kennedy. Almost bypassed by the Kennedy administration in 1961, Harriman established himself with his new boss by doggedly pursuing negotiations on the neutralization of Laos and eagerly accepting the relatively low-level appointment as Assistant Secretary of State for Far Eastern Affairs. After this conference with JFK on July 10, 1963, he headed for Moscow, where he negotiated the landmark treaty banning nuclear weapons tests in the atmosphere. By the time of Kennedy's death, Harriman, at seventy-two, was the number-three ranking official in the State Department.

Loyalty Put to the Test. The Johnson years were the hardest. Approaching the end of his career, Harriman was increasingly unhappy over government policy in Vietnam and being left out of important policy debates. He held on in large measure because he wanted a role in negotiating an end to the war. Substantive negotiations were about to begin when LBJ's term ended. On the night before Richard Nixon's inauguration as president, Harriman went to the White House to give Johnson his final report on his efforts. This photo was taken several months earlier, during a trip home from the Paris talks.

Preparing for Paris. At Camp David on April 9, 1968, President Johnson chauffeurs his top Vietnam advisers to a meeting to prepare for the first meeting with representatives of North Vietnam in Paris. In the front seat with LBJ is Ellsworth Bunker, the U.S. ambassador to Saigon. In the back, Secretary of State Dean Rusk, Harriman, and Secretary of Defense Clark Clifford. Rusk and Bunker were for sharply limiting Harriman's authority in the upcoming talks, and the President agreed.

The Peace Team. After getting their final instructions from the President, Harriman and Cyrus Vance are escorted from the Oval Office on their way to Paris in May 1968. Vance, who had become LBJ's favorite troubleshooter, was included in the delegation because Johnson was concerned that Harriman was too eager to conclude a peace agreement. As it happened, the former Defense Department official was in full accord with Averell rather than with the White House and the State Department.

Reunion. Months after Marie's death, Harriman was reunited with the former Pamela Churchill, who had charmed him in London in the midst of World War II. Divorced from Winston Churchill's son, she had subsequently married the legendary theatrical producer Leland Hayward, who had died in spring 1971. Nearing eighty, he married Pamela the following September.

Elder Statesman. Unenthusiastic about Jimmy Carter as a candidate for president, Harriman eagerly offered his services to his fifth Democratic chief executive. Although Harriman was eighty-five when Carter took office, there was talk within the new administration of giving him another tour as ambassador at large. But, apart from the burden of age, he had a chilly relationship with National Security Adviser Zbigniew Brzezinski. His service to Carter was, therefore, limited to ad hoc assignments and enthusiastic lobbying for the SALT II and Panama Canal treaties.

Changing Guard at the Kremlin. Fifty-seven years after going to the Soviet Union to confer with Leon Trotsky, Harriman became one of the few Americans to meet Uri Andropov during Andropov's brief tenure as the Soviet leader. He was accompanied by Pamela and Soviet protocol chief Nikolai Forov. The interpreter was Viktor Sukhodrev.

ing that the Kennedy firebrands took account of endorsement dates in their loyalty assessments. Unlike her husband, however, Marie Harriman was an early Kennedy fan. She liked the senator's good looks, his Irish humor, and all the young people with unbridled energy around him. She was also out of patience with the stiff-necked pride that kept Averell from calling Kennedy and enlisting, and she could see the train leaving without them.

So, unbeknownst to Averell, she opened her own line to the Kennedy campaign, calling William Walton, a Washington painter and longtime social friend of Kennedy's, who had been a *Time* magazine correspondent when Averell was Lend-Lease coordinator in London. After the war, when Walton took up his new career as an artist, Marie had made him one of her pets, helping him with contacts and encouraging his work. In turn, Walton had become devoted to her, finding hilarity in her exaggerated cynicism, her tongue-in-cheek ridiculing of Averell's wealth and stodgy habits, and her comic view of herself, politics, and New York society.

In the winter of 1960, Walton had put aside his brushes and joined Kennedy volunteers who went to Wisconsin and on to West Virginia. He was packing his bags for the primary in California when Marie reached him. "Bill, you simply have to do something about Ave," she said in her Tallulah Bankhead voice. "He's making a goddamned ass of himself. He has sat around talking about supporting Stuart Symington just because Harry Truman wanted him to, for Christ's sake, and pretty soon it's going to be all over. You've got to do something about it, or he's going to lose absolutely everything."[10] Walton thereupon became the Kennedy campaign's self-appointed liaison to Harriman, assuring him of Kennedy's desire for his support and dropping his name within the organization whenever there was an opportunity.

After West Virginia, Averell no longer needed to be convinced, but the truth was that the Kennedys could see nothing for him to do. He was an old man, and they were riding a youth movement.

In New York, Robert Wagner, who had completed his break with Tammany Hall, was leading the fight to wrest control of the convention delegation from De Sapio and the organization. Under the circumstances, Harriman was occasionally useful for ceremonial duties, so he was allowed to introduce Kennedy when the senator came to New York for a Democratic Club luncheon and to present the victor when Kennedy won 87 of the state's 105 delegates at the Democratic party caucus. A week before the convention, however, he got another chance to be helpful when Truman called a press conference in Independence and resigned as a convention delegate, saying it was pointless to go to Los Angeles when there was "no opportunity for a democratic choice." For

the first time, Harriman publicly crossed swords with his political hero. Truman was not always right, he told his own press conference, gently putting down the former President's grumpy protest.

Kennedy was grateful, though he couldn't have appreciated that even a small public disagreement with Truman was for Harriman a wrenching experience. In Los Angeles, he asked Averell to second his nomination, using the governor's brief presence in the spotlight to provide a missing touch of maturity to a campaign whose candidate was only forty-three and surrounded by men in their thirties.

Still, when it came to running against Richard Nixon, the Kennedy organization had no need for his services. When a huge New York City rally was planned for Kennedy, Tammany leaders arrogantly excluded the revered Herbert Lehman from the speakers' platform, and a furious Robert Kennedy had to come in and impose order, extracting from the organization an agreement to give all Democrats a full role in the campaign against Nixon.

Appreciating the futility of his situation, Harriman flew off to take the pulse of Africa—where independence movements could potentially explode into important campaign issues, not to mention long-range foreign policy problems for the new President.

Having fumbled the civil rights issue in his own bids for the Democratic nomination, Harriman saw black Africa's implications for Kennedy with remarkable clarity. The dramatic emergence of black nations in western Africa would demand the attention for a new administration faced with a rapidly developing civil rights struggle at home. Having a high-caliber senior statesman traveling Africa would not only help with the black vote, it would call attention to a foreign policy issue that Kennedy had already made his own.

In 1957, the senator had sharply criticized France for its armed suppression of nationalists in Algeria, and had chastised the Eisenhower administration for taking refuge in neutrality. He had, as a result, been accused even by fellow Democrats of causing needless trouble with an ally and undercutting the North Atlantic alliance. But with thirteen new African countries now about to enter the United Nations, his early encouragement of nationalism suddenly seemed prescient.

The Congo's independence from Belgium in June 1960 had also presented the specter of a civil war. Fighting had broken out among Congolese factions, requiring Belgian troops still in the country under a friendship treaty to restore order. Leftist Prime Minister Patrice Lumumba appealed to the Soviets for help, setting off tremors in the Eisenhower administration and bringing in United Nations troops to keep the peace. Of even more grave concern was the secession of the newly independent country's mineral-rich Katanga Province under the leader-

ship of Congolese politician Moise Tshombe, who was backed by Western mining interests and an army of mercenaries.

As Kennedy and Nixon slugged it out on the campaign trail in the fall of 1960, Harriman traveled to Senegal, Guinea, Liberia, Ghana, Nigeria, the Ivory Coast, and the Congo. With the Soviet Union egging on the fiery Lumumba, the Congo was boiling. After spending an hour and a half with Monsieur Patrice, Averell concluded that he probably was not a Communist but a no-less-dangerous rabble-rouser who would accept help anywhere he could get it, even if it meant inviting the Soviet Union into Africa. The best hope for preventing a civil war in the Congo, Harriman advised Kennedy, was not to choose sides between factions but to prevail upon the Soviets to channel their aid through the United Nations.[11]

For the first time, Africa became important to an American presidential campaign. Using Averell's reports, Kennedy skillfully denounced the Eisenhower administration's ignorance and neglect of African policy, a nimble way to appeal to American blacks without alienating southern whites. Harriman encouraged the Kennedy campaign to be more direct, and "comment on the damage to our position in Africa by the reports of discrimination and injustice that still exist in our country."[12] But that was advice the Kennedy campaign chose not to heed.

Harriman got home just in time to make a few solitary campaign stops which he personally planned, naturally heading for Union Pacific territory where Democrats were, as usual, being left to fend for themselves while the party concentrated on the mother lodes of the industrial states.

Before he got away, though, Bill Walton, who was working as a New York coordinator for the Kennedy-Johnson ticket, was on his doorstep looking for money. The campaign had to have a million dollars in a hurry, Walton said, and the word had come down from the Kennedy family to "hit everybody you know, starting out with Averell."[13] While no figure was suggested, Walton knew the Kennedys were expecting a substantial offering, and he also knew they were apt to be disappointed. Harriman bellowed in anguish. The whole African mission had been paid for out of his own pocket, he protested, and he considered that a quite substantial contribution. Before he started writing checks, he wanted to know how much people like David Bruce were kicking in. He was not impressed by Walton's statistics of hefty expected contributions nor his expression of the Kennedys' gratitude for the African mission. Finally, he offered $10,000, but Walton braced himself and replied, "Averell, I really don't think that will do." There was another fit of grumping about the cost of the Africa mission, and Walton played his last card. If that had to be the answer, he said dejectedly, he would just

go back and tell the campaign people that the answer was no. Perhaps they would understand.

That, obviously, was unacceptable to a man hoping for a call back to Washington in January. He snatched the telephone and called William Pemberton at Brown Brothers. He would give $30,000, $3,000 in each of ten crucial states.[14]

With Kennedy's victory, Harriman's campaign for a job began in earnest. He sent the President-elect long "Dear Jack" letters of congratulation and advice; and when the crisis in the Congo worsened, he rushed to Palm Beach at Kennedy's invitation to discuss the plight of the arrested Patrice Lumumba. Officials of the Soviet Union clearly expected him to be a significant figure in the new administration. Alexander Korneichuck, a member of the Soviet Communist party Central Committee, called for a long talk in New York, quizzing him at length on Kennedy's foreign policy views and suggesting the Soviets were ready to turn a new leaf in dealing with the administration. From the "spirit of Camp David" days in late 1959, relations between Washington and Moscow had collapsed in the wreckage of the CIA's U-2 spy plane shot down over the Soviet Union on May 1, 1960.

Three days after Korneichuck's visit, Soviet ambassador Mikhail Menshikov came with a personal message from Khrushchev along the same lines. The government in Moscow had been contemplating a return to the kind of relations that had existed in the Roosevelt era, a situation that the message called "not only desirable but possible."[15] Harriman detailed his contacts with the Russians in letters to Kennedy, sharpening his hints that he was available: "I would like to have an opportunity to talk with you about our relations with the Soviet Union, and other parts of the world. I would be glad to come to Palm Beach for a brief chat, if that would suit your convenience."[16] Nothing happened. After the visit to Florida to talk about the Congo, they saw each other two or three times in Washington and New York, but there was no hint of an assignment. Averell waited, his anxiety increasingly obvious.

Even after the lunch with Gaitskell, there was no inkling of an appointment. For all his preparation, traveling about the world and cultivation of his global contacts, Harriman was not in the running to be secretary of state, and he received only passing consideration for secretary of the treasury. He was a possibility as ambassador to the United Nations, but since speaking eloquence and skill in public debate were requisites, it was not Harriman's kind of assignment. Once Adlai Stevenson was available, Averell was hardly in the competition. Arthur Schlesinger discreetly reminded both John and Robert Kennedy of the governor's record, but such hints produced nothing. The insiders thought Harriman "old hat"; and to bring him into the administration,

Robert Kennedy thought, would be nothing more than "an act of sentiment."[17]

The prospect of being left out hurt most because Kennedy had offered to Bob Lovett the choice of being either secretary of state or secretary of defense. Although Averell's lifelong friend and Brown Brothers Harriman business partner had been Truman's undersecretary of state and secretary of defense, he remained a Republican. When Lovett declined, Kennedy considered Stevenson and Senator J. William Fulbright of Arkansas for State, before settling on Dean Rusk of the Rockefeller Foundation. Rusk had not supported Kennedy at the convention and had even sent Averell a note advising him to "stop being a damn fool" and get behind Stevenson. With his lucrative Rockefeller job, Rusk was ambivalent about joining the administration. He asked Harriman whether he could refuse Kennedy's offer, and Averell told him no.[18]

As December marched on and the opportunities rapidly disappeared, Harriman reconciled himself to the possibility that nothing would be offered. "People have to be given big jobs when they are young," he told Arthur Schlesinger, "or else their minds become permanently closed. The men who work their way step by step to the top in business are no good for anything in big government."[19]

Schlesinger and Galbraith, mindful of the symbolic value of having a Roosevelt stalwart in the new Washington, told the President-elect they found a Democratic administration without Harriman unimaginable. He was, after all, not a discredited New York politician but an embodiment of the administration's New Deal roots, a repository of insiders' wisdom from the Depression, two shooting wars, the Cold War, and the reconstruction of Europe. After making his pitch, Galbraith thought that Kennedy had at last "sensed that he had made a slight mistake."[20]

In any case, intermediaries began to sound the governor out. Walton, who, with Marie's collaboration, finally undertook the hearing-aid assignment that Kennedy had given Forrestal, brought word that Kennedy indeed wanted him on the diplomatic team, possibly as a roving ambassador. Since that was in effect an invitation to think up a job for himself, Harriman went to Rusk, and together they kicked around the notion of having a minister of state who would represent the State Department at international conferences, freeing the secretary for more urgent business.

It sounded grand—perhaps a little too grand, because it would require an act of Congress, which, Harriman was sure, would cause "a lot of fuss and feathers" and lead to complications that no one could foresee. In the end, he would still be a servant of the State Department bureaucracy. He much preferred the notion of being ambassador-at-large, working directly for the President. That solution, Galbraith

thought, was ideal—"sufficiently honorific and sufficiently ambiguous."[21] The precedent for it went back to Benjamin Franklin, and it solved Kennedy's Harriman problem. Without specific responsibility, Averell could take advantage of his contacts with far-flung world leaders and his experience in all manner of diplomatic crises. It was a job that could be as large, or as small, as he made it. If it became necessary, he could be eased into retirement gently and quietly.

On December 30, wearing his new hearing aid in his right ear, he arrived at the Kennedy compound at Palm Beach. The villa was swarming with visitors, and the President-elect was trying to get in a round of golf between appointments. He spent only a few minutes closing their deal. The appointment was announced immediately. When not on special missions, the White House said, Harriman would be "working closely with the President's policy advisers, particularly the Secretary of State."[22]

Having nothing on his desk after he was sworn in, Harriman packed his bags in mid-February and went on a tour of world capitals. He was on the road for more than a month, stopping off to offer personal reassurances about the new man in the White House wherever he knew the people in power. He called on Harold Macmillan in London, General Charles de Gaulle in Paris, Konrad Adenauer in Bonn, Willy Brandt in West Berlin, then went on to see leaders in Rome, Teheran, New Delhi, and Karachi. In the middle of his planned itinerary, he detoured to Rabat to represent Kennedy at the funeral of King Muhammad V of Morocco.

Back home, he could see that he was still regarded more as a New Deal and Fair Deal icon than a consequential player on the new team. Officially he was told nothing about the brigade of anti-Castro Cubans being secretly trained in Guatemala for the Bay of Pigs invasion. But the White House shortly found that he was needed for much more than window dressing.

The Congo and the nearly complete Bay of Pigs plan were not the worst of the problems the Eisenhower administration left behind. Kennedy immediately faced the prospect of having to send American troops into combat in Indochina. In Laos, the United States had set out to turn a remote mountain and jungle kingdom inhabited by gentle Buddhists and illiterate farmers into a bastion of anticommunism bordering mainland China and North Vietnam. It was, Kennedy concluded, no place to fight a war. Instead of continuing a policy headed for confrontation, he opted for a course designed to create a neutral Laos "tied to no outside power or group of powers, threatening no one, and free from any domination."[23]

About the same time the President was privately settling on the new policy, Harriman was in New Delhi on his long tour, having tea with

Laotian Prince Souvanna Phouma, who had for years been trying to establish a neutralist government in his country, incorporating representatives of both the Communists and the U.S.-backed conservatives. The Eisenhower State Department had regarded him as much too cozy with the Communists, if not Red himself, but Harriman came home with a different impression and encouraged Kennedy to back him.

In the mid-fifties, Souvanna had succeeded in setting up a neutralist Laotian regime which included the Communist Pathet Lao, led by his half-brother Prince Souphanouvong. The Eisenhower administration reacted by throwing its support behind Major General Phoumi Nosavan, staunch anti-Communist and dubious warrior, who wanted to wipe out the Pathet Lao and make Laos a firm ally of the United States.

Toward the end of 1959, Phoumi deposed Souvanna and installed a new government headed by the anti-Communist Prince Boun Oum, with himself as the minister of defense. With that, Souphanouvong fled to North Vietnam, and Souvanna into exile in Paris.

Within months, however, a five-foot four-inch paratroop captain named Kong Le led a countercoup, ousting Boun Oum; and Souvanna was invited home to form another government. In Washington, the chagrined State Department agreed to drop its objections to Souvanna, as long as he did not oppose continued U.S. military support to Phoumi. For his part, the general promised to fight only against the forces of the Pathet Lao, but he promptly broke his word, surrounded the capital at Vientiane, and forced Souvanna to flee the country again. In response, Kong Le's neutralists joined an alliance with the Pathet Lao, and for help they turned to Moscow. Supplied by a massive Soviet airlift, Kong Le and the Pathet Lao together were more than a match for Phoumi's Royal Laotian Army, and it appeared that the Communists were ready to take control of the entire country.

The Eisenhower administration made contingency plans for intervention by modest American forces, but military leaders were either for sending no troops at all or making a large commitment to action on a regional scale. Modest intervention, they feared, might bring in overwhelming numbers of North Vietnamese or Chinese troops, in which case the United States might be forced to use tactical nuclear weapons to prevent its forces from being massacred.[24]

In April 1961, when it appeared that the Laotian capital might fall to the Pathet Lao within hours, the Soviet Union joined Great Britain in calling for a cease-fire and the convening of a fourteen-nation Geneva conference on Laos. Reeling from the Bay of Pigs fiasco just ten days earlier, the Kennedy administration was thus spared a decision on intervention. Three days later, aboard a plane bound for Turkey and a meeting of the Central Treaty Organization, Rusk turned the crisis in Laos over to Harriman. As soon as they landed, the roving ambassador

went to a PX in Ankara where he found one tropical suit that more or less fit, and flew off to engage in his first crisis for Kennedy.

He spent eleven days chasing down key players in the drama, sleeping on airplanes, consulting the feuding princes, conferring with the Laotian King, and receiving briefings by old foreign service hands in seven Southeast Asian capitals. At the end of his tour, he compared notes with General Lyman Lemnitzer, chairman of Joint Chiefs of Staff, in Saigon. Finding that neither had much hope for a cease-fire taking hold, the two of them cabled a recommendation that the President send enough troops to Laos to "make the Pathet Lao stop, look, and listen."[25]

By the time Harriman got home to report fully to the President, however, the cease-fire had gone into effect and the Geneva conference scheduled. His hasty troop recommendation was mercifully forgotten, but he was, nonetheless, embarrassed that he had made it.

Rusk led the U.S. delegation to the opening of the conference in May, but after the first round, he turned the negotiations over to Harriman, advising the President that he did not see much chance of success. Averell was not so gloomy. With Kennedy's marching orders to negotiate a neutralist settlement, he dismantled the U.S. delegation of 126 State and Defense Department experts, sending home Phoumi sympathizers, military aides, and the top State Department official, Deputy Assistant Secretary John Steeves. His choice to replace Steeves was William Sullivan, a prematurely gray, exceedingly bright foreign service officer who had written an analysis of the Laotian conflict, concluding that there could be no satisfactory military solution. But when word of his plan to make Sullivan his deputy reached the State Department, it was rejected on grounds that Sullivan was still a class-III foreign service officer and outranked by a number of FSO I's and II's in the delegation. Harriman responded by sending the I's and II's home.

Once negotiations resumed, they were as complex as the relations between the Laotian princes themselves, remaining mired in procedural disagreements through the summer with the cease-fire regularly breaking down. Harriman proved uncharacteristically patient, coddling Laotians of the left, right, and center, holding daily talks with Soviet negotiator Georgi M. Pushkin, an amiable adversary who became an occasional collaborator. Through May, June, and July, and thirty-six plenary sessions, nearly nothing was accomplished, even after Kennedy and Khrushchev agreed at their Vienna summit to support creation of a neutralist regime.

In spite of his presidential mandate, Harriman remained on a short State Department string in Geneva. Long after the departure of Rusk and Foreign Minister Andrei Gromyko of the Soviet Union, Foreign Minister Chen Yi of China was still at the conference representing a government looming over the future of Laos and Southeast Asia. To

Harriman, he presented irresistible prey, an avenue to explore the ideological fault between China and the USSR. After Rusk had greeted him at the outset of the Laos conference, the United States and China had spoken only in the stiff formality of speeches in the plenary meetings. When Harriman notified the State Department that he intended to arrange a meeting with Chen through the British, he was sternly waved off by Rusk. Word of the meeting would leak, the secretary said, enhancing China's prestige and making the United States appear "weak and anxious." Averell was instructed to maintain a "correct attitude" toward the Chinese both inside and outside the conference room.[26]

Outraged, Harriman threatened to pack his bags and go home. He was not a State Department serf, he told Chester Cooper, a CIA officer who had become one of his favorites in the delegation. He could get along fine without a penny-ante government job. Who the hell did Rusk think he was?[27]

The fact was, he was not about to quit, nor was he yet prepared to ignore the Chinese. He shortly suggested bringing them into more intimate discussions with the conference's Big Four—the United States, France, Great Britain, and the Soviet Union. The time was at hand, he told Washington, to initiate formal contacts with Chinese officials, time for the "serious phase of horse trading and compromise." He planned to interpret his instructions in a manner that would enable him to talk with the Chinese directly "and, if necessary bilaterally."[28] This time his mistake was to refer to a "Big Five," an inference of equal status for the Chinese, and the State Department again fired back a firm rejection.

With that, he complained to Galbraith and Schlesinger, knowing they would pass his complaints along to Kennedy. In short order, Galbraith wrote to Kennedy from New Delhi, Schlesinger took it up at the White House, and the President passed the word that Harriman could speak with whomever he saw fit.[29] By then, though, Chen had left Geneva and gone home.

Three weeks after Kennedy and Khrushchev's Vienna summit and a meeting of the minds on Laotian neutrality, the Laotian princes had their own summit in Zurich and agreed to a coalition government for their country, but they adjourned without deciding who would be prime minister or how the cabinet positions were to be allocated. All seemed prepared for those questions to rest indefinitely. But with the Communists holding the upper hand on the battlefield, Washington, following suggestions from Harriman, turned up the heat. Kennedy ordered additional military training teams to support government forces, stepped up aid to Meo tribesmen ready to resist the Pathet Lao, and sent photo reconnaissance missions over the country to photograph Pathet Lao positions. Meanwhile, Averell flew back to Southeast Asia to personally twist the arms of the three princes.

In Rangoon, he spent two days with Souvanna, who was insisting that his neutralists get eight of the cabinet ministeries, warning the neutralist prince that more representatives of the Phoumi–Boun Oum faction would have to be included before the United States could support him. In Vientiane, he made it clear to Phoumi and Boun Oum that the administration's patience with them was at an end; and in Luang Prabang, he got assurances from the King that Souvanna would be appointed prime minister if the Boun Oum and the Communist prince Souphanouvong agreed to it. While he did not hint it to any of the Laotians, Harriman was prepared to see the United States bring about Phoumi's removal as the anti-Communist military strongman if he stood in the way of an agreement between the princes any longer. Before leaving Washington, he had talked with CIA director Allen Dulles about the possibility of finding "a substitute general," and after his meetings in Laos, he told Rusk he had not changed his mind. "The more I see of Phoumi, the less I trust him as U.S. chosen instrument to carry out faithfully our agreed policies and objectives now or later," he cabled Rusk after leaving Vientiane. "Recommend this subject be pursued further urgently to analyze alternatives and be prepared to act promptly if need be. We will simply have to determine for ourselves whether Phoumi is in fact negotiating in good faith."[30]

The American pressure was beginning to pay off, however. Three weeks later, the princes convened at a crossing on Nam Lik River near the village of Ban Hin Huep to take up the division of cabinet posts and the selection of a prime minister. Boun Oum, arriving in his American helicopter, declined to meet on the north side of the river belonging to Souphanouvong and the Pathet Lao. Souphanouvong, in turn, refused to journey over to the south bank. A tent on the bridge at midstream was suggested, but with the river rising, the structure was considered unsafe. A raft anchored in midstream was thought about, but there seemed a real possibility that it would be swept away. Eventually, all swallowed their pride and agreed to alternate sessions on each side of the stream.

When the conference ended late on a Sunday afternoon, October 6, Souvanna stepped from a candy-striped tent with the news that he had been selected to head the government. "Prince Boun Oum and Prince Souphanouvong have agreed to our selecting my name and presenting it to his majesty the King as prime minister of a provisional coalition government."[31]

With the turn of events in Laos, there was also movement in Geneva. The Soviets agreed to take responsibility for all the Communist states' compliance with the neutrality declaration and accepted language declaring that Laotian territory would not be used in the affairs of neighboring

states—meaning the North Vietnamese could not use the trails through Laos to support the insurgency in South Vietnam.

At times it was easier for Harriman to agree with Pushkin than with Washington. When the conference turned to arrangements for an International Control Commission to monitor violations of the accord, he collided with State Department officials, who insisted that the commission be given authority to travel the country at will. Freedom to move about the country, Rusk told the President, was critical "especially on the routes for present [North Vietnamese] infiltration into South Vietnam."[32]

Harriman insisted that ICC authority was one issue where the United States would have to compromise. Unless all three Laotian factions got a right to approve movement of the commission, the conference would collapse. From Rusk down, the State Department disagreed. Undersecretary Chester Bowles, Deputy Undersecretary U. Alexis Johnson, and Walter McConaughy, the assistant secretary for Far Eastern affairs, went to the White House to make their case with the President, and afterward Johnson joined Kennedy on the telephone to Harriman in Geneva. With the President listening, Harriman and Johnson argued their way over the familiar ground again, Averell urging that the point be conceded so the conference could act while the situation in Laos was still salvageable. Johnson was in no mood to budge, but neither was Harriman. In the end, Kennedy gave Averell the go-ahead to endorse the restrictions on the ICC and move on.

With that concession, neutrality would amount to a partition of the country beneath the sophistry of coalition government. Harriman's critics, even those who argued partition was the solution, would always point to the concession as a fatal mistake that opened the way for North Vietnam to use the jungle trails through Laos for its invasion of the South—the Averell Harriman Highway, some would call it. At the State Department, John Steeves acerbically suggested that the next cable from Harriman's Geneva mission would probably be signed by Pushkin.

The longer-term implications aside, Harriman was relentlessly bearing down on the objective Kennedy had assigned him, and the President watched with growing admiration. When the impetuous Prince Norodom Sihanouk quit the negotiations in frustration and left Geneva, Harriman went after him. Learning that the Cambodian leader was driving to Rome, he took a plane, checked into the prince's hotel, and waited while an aide stood watch in the lobby. Cornered when he arrived hours later, the weary Sihanouk agreed to talk for fifteen minutes, but the well-rested Harriman hammered at him for two hours, lecturing, cajoling, and flattering, until the prince agreed to send his ambassador back to the meeting.

* * *

Harriman was still involved in his Laos assignment when, less than a year after his inauguration, Kennedy decided that he had to make major changes at the State Department.

Chet Bowles, a good friend and early ally with valuable political assets, proved to have been a poor choice for the number two post. The former Connecticut governor was loyal and widely admired as a man of unshakable principle, but despite his rich experience, he was a bust as an administrator. He did not take the reins of departmental management as Rusk wished. As a result, he was soon bypassed by the secretary and left isolated and increasingly ineffective. Out of frustration, he had made the unfortunate, self-serving, and ultimately fatal mistake of leaking a memorandum showing he had opposed the Bay of Pigs operation.

When Kennedy concluded that Bowles had to be replaced, he decided on several other changes at the same time, including a new assignment for Harriman in place of his formless role of ambassador-at-large. His first thought was to make him assistant secretary for European affairs, and he and Harriman briefly discussed the possibility when Averell returned from Laos in September.

Two months later, when the shake-up—promptly dubbed the "Thanksgiving massacre"—put George W. Ball in Bowles's position, Harriman was in Geneva haggling over the language of a draft of a neutrality agreement and trying to wrestle the Laotian princes into dividing up cabinet positions for their coalition government. The President didn't want to relieve him, and by then he had decided he also needed a new assistant secretary for Far Eastern affairs. Walter McConaughy, who was in the post, was a professional foreign service man, but he had not become accustomed to the pace and the intensity of the Kennedy administration, nor did he share its political views. As a result, not much had changed in the Bureau of Far Eastern Affairs since the Eisenhower administration.

Given the new policy in Laos and increasingly troublesome conflict in South Vietnam, FE—as the bureau was known at State—was a place where Kennedy wanted an assistant secretary in tune with his policies. So instead of giving Harriman the European job, he instructed Rusk to call him in Geneva and offer him the post of assistant secretary for Far Eastern affairs.

Averell readily accepted, but, after hanging up the phone, he was not sure what he had accepted. He had been expecting the billet as the State Department's European expert, and a poor connection had compounded his bad hearing. He thought he heard something about the Far East, but was certain only that he had accepted a new job as an assistant secretary for something. A little embarrassed, he had to call back and ask Rusk what he had agreed to do.

Becoming an assistant secretary, he gave up a job created to provide him prestige befitting his experience in exchange for one that offered constant pressure and grubby detail work in ranks filled by upward-bound professionals who were a generation younger. Colleagues were astonished that he would take what seemed to them a demotion. It wasn't as though his personal ambition had been vanquished, however. He had "started as a private with Roosevelt," he told *New York Times* correspondent C. L. Sulzberger in the spring. He had started all over with Truman and that was what he intended to do again.[33]

The President hardly expected him to recede into the State Department bureaucracy no matter how modest his post. Therefore, as part of the same shakeup, he called Mike Forrestal to make good on a year-old promise to come to work at the White House. He would be the National Security Council's specialist on Far Eastern affairs, the President explained, and that meant serving as "emissary to that special sovereignty, Averell Harriman."[34]

In the new job, Harriman's first priority remained getting the administration out of the bind in Laos. "Our job is not to confront the President with a situation requiring a decision on whether to permit Laos to be overrun by the Commies, or introduce American combat forces," he reminded Ambassador Winthrop Brown in Vientiane. "A President cannot be asked to make such a decision in advance. We have to start skating, even though we don't know how firm the ice may be in the center of the pond. The problem is to work out how—and not whether—a coalition government under Souvanna's leadership with a reasonable chance of success is formed."[35]

For months after the princes agreed on Souvanna as prime minister, the dispute continued over the cabinet, with Phoumi demanding that his faction get the all-important interior and defense ministries, which Harriman and the State Department insisted should be given to the neutrals. From Washington at the end of January 1962, Harriman sent Phoumi an ultimatum. Unless he cooperated, Washington's purse might be closed. Indignant, the general left Geneva for home; and when he got there, he found that Harriman had already suspended the State Department's $3 million in monthly economic assistance.

Again backed by the President, Averell followed up with a demand that every American agency involved in Laos replace any official with personal ties to Phoumi. That put him at even sharper odds with the Pentagon and the CIA and left the administration in the peculiar position of refusing economic assistance to Phoumi and the government while backing them militarily.

Among the experts, there was growing doubt that the Soviets were genuinely interested in neutrality, and as concern that Harriman's cutoff

of economic assistance was about to push the country into economic collapse rather than force Phoumi into line. Averell himself was beginning to have second thoughts. "I don't know if it is going to work," he told Kennedy, "but I am going to suggest that you leave this one to me. If it doesn't work, you can fire me, but don't take the responsibility for doing it yourself. Leave it to me."[36]

Early in 1962, Laos plunged into its most severe crisis in ten months. Phoumi continued to make provocative thrusts against the Pathet Lao; and with military advisers withdrawn from the field on Harriman's advice, the Communists launched a major attack on the government's northern stronghold at the village of Nam Tha, only twenty miles from the Chinese border. Using tactics reminiscent of those the North Vietnamese employed against the French at Dien Bien Phu, the Communists captured Phoumi's defensive outposts and kept the town under siege for several weeks.

Harriman put the blame on Phoumi as much as on the Pathet Lao. By trying to improve his battlefield position, the general had undermined the Geneva conference and had deliberately tried to provoke American intervention. Ignoring advice from the Pentagon, he had flown reinforcements to Nam Tha, bringing his force to five thousand men and obliging the United States to support him or risk a disastrous defeat. With his best battalions being chewed up in the northern fighting, more and more of the countryside was falling under Pathet Lao control.

In March, Averell sent Sullivan and Forrestal to Laos, then flew to Bangkok himself to work on Thailand's Marshal Sarit, who was Phoumi's idol. Under pressure, the Thai strongman agreed to accompany him to a meeting with Phoumi in the village of Nong Khai on the bank of the Mekong. There, Harriman bluntly told Phoumi that his forces were finished unless he got behind Souvanna and the coalition government. There were varying accounts of what transpired, but Forrestal, who served as Harriman's French interpreter, remembered Averell telling Phoumi, in so many words, that if the fighting continued, "You bastards will have to swim that river out there, and not all of you are going to make it."[37]

In May the Communists resumed their offensive, overrunning Nam Tha, and as Harriman had warned, Phoumi's defenders were driven to the banks of the Mekong, with more than two thousand of them scrambling across into Thailand on rafts and in small boats. At Harriman's urging Kennedy sent ships of the Seventh Fleet into the Gulf of Siam and two Marine battalions into Thailand, after which the Communist offensive ground to a stop.

Discredited by the performance of their troops and strapped for

funds after the United States cut off of economic assistance, Boun Oum and Phoumi agreed to join the coalition.

By the time the Geneva conference turned to final consideration of its neutrality declaration, Souvanna had been installed as prime minister. Continued quarreling over arrangements for the withdrawal of foreign forces sharpened Harriman's doubts that the military agreements would be honored, but there was no turning back.

Although the North Vietnamese never made anything more than a token withdrawal, the United States pulled its advisers out on schedule, determined that the onus of failure would fall on the Communists.

The country entered into a de facto partition, with two thirds of its population living in areas under the control of the Souvanna's new coalition government. The jungle trails along the border with Vietnam were still held by the North Vietnamese and their Pathet Lao supporters.

Harriman had carried out his marching orders, averting American military intervention and getting a neutralist coalition government. But the agreement was frail. "Laos," he wrote Ambassador Alan Kirk in Taipei a few months later, "is going about as badly as I expected."[38] Although the North Vietnamese ignored the agreement from its first day, Harriman would never concede that he had misjudged the Soviets in accepting their promise to ensure Communist adherence to the pact, nor in urging the President to accept the restrictions on the International Control Commission. The failure of the agreement to stem the Communist push on Laos, he always suggested, might have been a result of the untimely death of Pushkin not long after it was signed.

In March 1963, five months after the Cuban missile crisis and the most dangerous showdown in history of the nuclear age, Kennedy appointed Harriman undersecretary of state for political affairs. After two years of diplomatic odd jobs and concentrating on the Far East, Averell was, at the age of seventy-one, in the top echelon of the State Department hierarchy. Making it to the seventh floor at Foggy Bottom had not been easy, nor did his elevation bring him into a partnership with Dean Rusk and George Ball.

From the beginning, he had been generally excluded from matters concerning the Soviet Union and the overarching superpower issues that made everything else a sideshow. For that, he blamed Rusk, but the secretary was not alone. Ball, National Security Adviser McGeorge Bundy and others, including the President at the outset, thought him over the hill and out of date.

When Kennedy summoned Soviet experts to brief him on Khrushchev not long after the inauguration, Averell was left off the exclusive list of George Kennan, Charles Bohlen, and Llewellyn Thompson. He

was crushed, believing with some justification that he knew the Soviet leader better than any of the three. So he called Bundy, mentioned the upcoming session, and asked point-blank whether his exclusion hadn't been an inadvertent mistake.

He was promptly invited; and when the meeting took place, he somberly advised Kennedy that people who knew Khrushchev personally could best deal with him. No one present, said Bohlen, could have any doubt whom he had in mind.[39]

But when Kennedy headed for his June summit with Khrushchev, Harriman was again excluded. It was the first time a Democratic president had ever gone into a meeting with a Soviet leader without Harriman's being in the party. Remembering other summits when he had gotten aboard at the last minute, he boarded a plane in Geneva and intercepted the presidential party during its overnight stop in Paris. There, he appeared at a reception hosted by Kennedy and was barely able to say hello. But not dissuaded, he picked up an invitation to a private dinner that followed and got a seat one place removed from the President. During the evening, he talked so earnestly about the upcoming meeting that Kennedy's sister, Eunice Shriver, turned to her brother and told him, "Averell wants to talk to you about Vienna and the government." Irritated at being pursued, Kennedy let him know he was in no mood to be briefed. With that Harriman meekly observed that Khrushchev's gruffness should not be taken too seriously, and the next day gloomily slunk back to Geneva while the summiteers proceeded to Vienna.

His subsequent advice on Soviet matters was shrugged off as casually as he had been dismissed in Paris. When he recommended that the administration reconsider its plan to make Foy Kohler, whom he regarded as unimaginative, ambassador to Moscow, he heard nothing. Nor was there any response when he urged the administration to undertake a worldwide propaganda campaign against the Soviets' explosion of a fifty-megaton nuclear device in 1962. During the Cuban missile crisis, he had been included in none of the momentous meetings in which the President considered an air strike against the Soviet missiles in Cuba before finally settling on the less drastic option of a naval embargo against Fidel Castro's island.

Embarrassingly, the only thing he was asked to do was to serve as a decoy to throw the press off the scent of crisis while the President and the Excomm, the National Security Council's crisis panel assembled by Bundy, debated the administration's course. Before emergency meetings on Sunday, October 21, members of the crisis committee slipped into the White House through a tunnel from the Treasury Department. Harriman, Martin Hillenbrand of State's German Affairs Office, and Phillip Talbot, the assistant secretary for Near Eastern affairs, arrived at

the front of the White House and hurried into the west wing to make any
suspicious reporter think that the activity around the executive mansion
concerned China, India, or Berlin.[40]

But as he had before, Harriman stubbornly put forward his advice,
unrequested. On October 22, the day that discovery of Russian missiles
in Cuba was made public, he sent Attorney General Robert Kennedy a
memorandum suggesting that the Kremlin had been long embarrassed
because the United States had intermediate-range Jupiter ballistic missiles across its border in Turkey. During his visit to the Soviet Union in
1959, Harriman had been asked about the weapons over and over. Now,
he surmised, Khrushchev was under heavy pressure to do something
about the nuclear-armed missiles in both Turkey and Italy. "I have felt
from the first time it was proposed that the placing of our missiles in
Turkey and Italy was counter productive," he told the President's
brother, "both in our relations with the Soviet Union and domestically.
This is especially so because the missiles can be destroyed so easily, but
beyond that, they have been humiliating to Soviet pride in that they had
to permit such a threat to exist so near."[41]

Knowing Khrushchev, Harriman was sure the premier was looking
for a face-saving way to get out of the confrontation, and as U.S. warships
formed a picket line around Cuba, he thought he saw clear signals from
the Kremlin. "We must give him an out," Averell told Schlesinger, who
was in New York helping Adlai Stevenson prepare to put the United
States' case before the UN Security Council. "If we do this shrewdly, we
can downgrade the tough group in the Soviet Union which persuaded
him to do this. But if we deny him an out, then we will escalate this
business into a nuclear war." He had not raised these thoughts with the
State Department, because, he said with some bitterness, the department
never consulted him on anything except the Far East.[42] Schlesinger
passed them all along to both Stevenson and the President.

Five days after Harriman's message to Robert Kennedy on the missiles in Turkey and Italy, Khrushchev made withdrawal of the Jupiters
a condition for his pulling the Soviet missiles out of Cuba. Khrushchev's
demand, couched in invective escalating the palpable tension, arrived as
Kennedy and his advisers were preparing a response to a more moderate
letter received twelve hours earlier. In one of the key decisions of the
crisis, Kennedy decided to go ahead with a response to Khrushchev's
first letter, which had made no mention of the Jupiters, ignoring the
more threatening second message.

Thereafter, the Jupiters disappeared from the communications between Kennedy and Khrushchev; but the missiles in Turkey, targeted
on Soviet territory, had become hostages in the Cuban standoff. The
superpowers stepped back from disaster with their agreement when
Soviets withdrew their missiles in exchange for a U.S. pledge not to

invade Cuba. Subsequently, the Jupiters were quietly removed, as Robert Kennedy had secretly assured Soviet ambassador Anatoly Dobrynin they would be.

Although he was never brought into the crisis, Harriman's freelance advice from the perimeter shored up his Soviet credentials and cemented his friendship with Robert Kennedy, who became an increasingly important figure in administration foreign policy. It was Averell's relationship with the younger partner in the Kennedy team that brought his elevation from the Far East bureau to the number three job in the State Department.

Two weeks after he was sworn in as undersecretary, Harriman departed for Moscow on his first Kremlin mission for Kennedy. His chief objective was to call the Soviet government's attention to wholesale violations of the year-old Laotian neutrality agreement by the North Vietnamese and the Pathet Lao. But he also saw his junket as the beginning of the road back from the close call in Cuba, which was still not fully understood by either side. When he reminded Khrushchev of the Soviet promise to ensure the adherence of other Communist powers to the Laos agreement, the Premier threw up his hands. He suggested that he and Harriman make a million-dollar wager on whether the North Vietnamese were still in Laos. The United States and China could fight over all of Southeast Asia, he said. The Soviet Union wanted none of it.[43]

But where nuclear weapons were concerned, he was ready to be seriously engaged. Two months after the missile crisis, he had written to Kennedy telling him the time had come "to put a stop to nuclear tests once and for all," and suggesting the possible locations within the Soviet Union where America might place black boxes to monitor for underground test activity.[44]

Kennedy was cheered by the message, but while two or three inspections were a huge concession for Moscow, there was no chance that Congress would approve anything with less than seven or eight annual on-site inspections. He had answered Khrushchev with a wholly new proposal of his own—to send an American delegation to Moscow for direct negotiation of a test-ban treaty rather than waiting for something to come of the eighteen-nation disarmament conference in Geneva.

The Soviets were still studying the President's suggestion, Khrushchev told Harriman, and an answer was forthcoming. But he wanted to make it clear that the Soviet Union would accept no "espionage inspections—ever."[45]

In the end, the session produced as much comedy as diplomacy. Khrushchev, still impressed at Harriman's millions, at one point offered Averell a job as his economic adviser. As the American party was de-

parting, Harriman dropped a key to his briefcase. It couldn't be found because it had gone into the cuff of his trousers. The meeting concluded with Khrushchev, Sullivan, and Forrestal on their hands and knees beneath the Soviet leader's desk in search of the missing key.

Ten days after Harriman's visit, however, Khrushchev, as promised, sent Kennedy a message on arms negotiations—he was prepared to receive an American delegation for nuclear-test-ban negotiations in Moscow. However, he waited until June 8 before sending word that the Soviets would be ready to begin negotiations on July 15.

On June 10, in an internationally acclaimed American University commencement speech looking beyond the Cold War, the President announced plans for the talks. The United States, he said, would again refrain from atmospheric tests so long as other nuclear powers did the same.

Serious efforts to achieve some restraint on nuclear arms went back to 1958 and the Special Geneva Conference on the Discontinuance of Nuclear Weapons Tests, which continued through 353 meetings over nearly four years before expiring in January 1962. Thereafter, the subject was taken up in the eighteen-nation disarmament committee at Geneva, where the United States and Great Britain submitted two proposed treaties—one banning all nuclear weapons tests, the other outlawing testing in the oceans, the atmosphere, and in space. Both were rejected by the Soviets, and testing went ahead at an accelerating pace. The Soviets exploded a fifty-megaton device—2,500 times the power of the Hiroshima bomb—in the atmosphere; in response the United States began a series of forty explosions in the Pacific.

The prospect of limiting tests seemed fanciful because of the deadlock over inspections. Moscow contended that on-site inspections were no longer necessary, because black boxes could distinguish between earthquakes and underground nuclear tests. In Washington, a comprehensive test ban without provision for several on-site inspections was unthinkable.

Harriman's selection to lead the U.S. team was announced by the White House on June 11, the day after Kennedy's acceptance of Khrushchev's invitation.

Sensing that the moment was at hand for a historic decision, Averell put together a small team whose members had open lines to the National Security Council, spurning a large support staff of scientists, engineers, and weapons experts. From the National Security Council staff, he took former Harvard professor Carl Kaysen to report directly to Bundy and the President; from the Pentagon, John McNaughton, the Defense Department's general counsel and McNamara's top arms-control expert; from the Arms Control and Disarmament Agency, Adrian Fischer, whom he had first hired in Harry Truman's Commerce Department;

and from the State Department, William Tyler, the assistant secretary of state for European affairs. Only two scientists, Franklin Long, the Arms Control and Disarmament Agency's technical chief, and Frank Press, a seismologist from the California Institute of Technology, were put on the team as consultants.

Kennedy's instructions were as simple as they had been in the Laos negotiations. He was "to get an agreement and come home."[46] Ideally, the administration continued to prefer a comprehensive ban, but if that was impossible, it was ready to accept the next best thing, namely, an end to tests in the atmosphere, in space, and in the oceans. Kennedy also wanted him to sound out the Soviets on China's nuclear development. Otherwise, Harriman was free to talk about anything the Russians wanted to bring up. He flew to the Soviet Union uncertain that anything would come of the negotiations after the great buildup of expectations. In a speech on July 2, Khrushchev took the offensive against on-site inspection, and in Washington concern grew that the Soviets would demand a moratorium on underground tests as a price for signing a treaty banning explosions in the oceans, in space, and in the atmosphere. Such an arrangement, the administration knew, would be bitterly opposed by military leaders and have nearly no chance of being approved by the Senate. Furthermore, there was new tension in the political atmosphere arising from Kennedy's much-publicized visit to the Berlin Wall, where he delivered his famous "I Am a Berliner" speech ringing with belligerence.

More serious was the possibility that test-ban talks could be thrown off track by Khrushchev's insistence upon discussing an East-West non-aggression pact, a matter which the Americans and British were resolved to keep off the agenda.

Harriman went to his first private meeting with Khrushchev expecting an opening attempt to put him off balance, and it came in a peevish attack on U.S. ambassador Foy Kohler. The American envoy, Khrushchev complained, was carrying on economic warfare against the Soviet Union by advising Washington to deny an export license for oil pipe the Soviets wanted to buy in America. Harriman replied that he had come not to discuss pipelines but a test ban.[47]

The cloud passed as quickly as it had gathered. Khrushchev joined the opening session and remained through the first three hours of deliberations. He was ready to talk about Soviet agriculture and make jokes with Harriman and Lord Hailsham, the unctuous barrister who headed the British delegation. "Since we have agreed to have a test ban, let us sign it now and fill in the details later," Khrushchev bubbled as they sat down to their first meeting. Harriman pushed a legal pad across the table in the Premier's direction. "Fine," he replied, "you sign first."[48]

When Harriman delivered a letter from Kennedy, emphasizing that

the United States preferred to outlaw all testing, Khrushchev announced that the Soviet government would agree to no on-site inspection, "not even the two or three we had proposed before."[49] On-site inspection, he argued, would provide the United States an opportunity to spy on the Soviet Union. Harriman denied the charge, but to no avail. "You're trying to tell me that if there's a piece of cheese in the room and a mouse comes into the room, that mouse won't go for the cheese," Khrushchev replied. "You can't stop the mouse from going for the cheese."[50]

There was then no point in talking about a comprehensive treaty. The Senate would never buy it. It was, said Harriman "really appalling to realize what a missed opportunity we had."[51]

After the first day, the deliberations took place around a table on the second floor of Spiridonovka Palace, a yellow pseudo-Gothic monstrosity erected as the home of a wealthy merchant in czarist times. Before joining the Russians each morning, Harriman and Hailsham assembled their teams at the British embassy for a strategy session. In the afternoon, they repaired to the "tank," the secure room at the American embassy, where, carefully protected from Soviet eavesdropping, they reviewed the session and their communications with Washington and London.

At the White House, Rusk, McNamara, CIA director John McCone, and their aides convened in the Cabinet Room each evening to study Harriman's detailed cables. Kennedy himself usually joined them in drafting replies and instructions. The President, impressed and amused at Averell's meticulous reporting, needled him for more detail; and when it came, he twitted him to dispatch the reports more quickly.[52]

The jocular atmosphere of the first days soon vanished. Gromyko renewed the Soviet demand for a nonaggression treaty between the Warsaw Pact and the NATO countries, a treaty which Khrushchev had proposed the first day. It was a matter on which the United States' position had been firmly set before the delegation left Washington. Discussion of that, Harriman insisted, would have to come in another forum; it could not be allowed to complicate the test-ban talks. In Washington, some Soviet analysts believed that a nonaggression pact and not the test-ban agreement might be Khrushchev's real objective in the negotiations, and Harriman was briefly concerned that the test agreement might be held hostage. He promised he would discuss the nonaggression treaty in detail when he returned to Washington, and he proposed that they make reference to it in the meeting's final communiqué. Gromyko gloomily gave in.

That obstacle behind them, they fell into another dispute, however. Harriman insisted upon explicit language stating the right to withdraw from the agreement, but the Soviets contended it was unnecessary. On this point, Harriman could not relent, so he decided to make a trade. Before leaving for Moscow, he had talked with presidential science ad-

viser Jerome Weisner about research on the use of nuclear explosives for excavation in huge construction projects. Such a capability, Weisner assured him, was years in the future at best. After double-checking with the White House, Harriman offered, therefore, to ban peaceful explosions in exchange for Soviet acceptance of the withdrawal clause. But then they disagreed on language, Gromyko refusing to have the words "nuclear explosion" in the article. Fuming, Harriman challenged the Foreign Minister's sincerity, swept up his papers, and prepared to lead his negotiators out the door before all agreed it was time for a night's rest. The exchange so unnerved Hailsham that he cabled London his concern that Averell was about to break up the meeting with his hard-headedness. Overnight cables between the White House and Harriman's team produced a solution. Washington agreed to a text referring to "extraordinary events" instead of "nuclear explosion." The rationale was that "event" had, over the years, become synonymous with "explosion" in U.S. nuclear test jargon.

After ten days' work, the conference was suddenly all over. In a late-afternoon meeting on July 25, Harriman, Hailsham, and Gromyko agreed on the last outstanding issue—procedures for governments not recognized by the three powers to sign the pact banning nuclear tests in the atmosphere, in space, and underwater. The conclusion came so suddenly that Harriman was caught unprepared. He needed not only Washington's nod on the oral understanding but authority to initial the text.

Because it would take another day for the exchange of cables, Kaysen suggested simply picking up the telephone and calling the President. Minutes later, with the help of the Russians, they got through to the White House on an ordinary telephone line. Bundy and the President were in the situation room, where Kennedy was about to talk with Macmillan in London. Britain was concerned about the cables from Hailsham warning that Harriman was being too hard-nosed, and the Prime Minister had called to discuss the matter with the President. Bundy relayed the message from Moscow as Kennedy held another phone waiting for Macmillan to come on the line. The President nodded his assent for Harriman to close the deal.

Two hours later, three leather-bound copies of the treaty were put on the table in Moscow; and, surrounded by reporters who had waited outside for hours, Harriman, Hailsham, and Gromyko initialed the Limited Test Ban Treaty.

Averell flew home in triumph, stopping in London to see Macmillan. He arrived at the President's home in Hyannis so rumpled and haggard from the flight that he was escorted upstairs and given one of the President's clean shirts before he was sent out to describe the negotiations to the press. It was dark by the time he got home to Georgetown; and as

soon as he arrived, his neighbors from up and down the street collected in front of his house to applaud him. When he stepped out to thank them, they sang, "For He's a Jolly Good Fellow," and his old campaign song, "H, A, Double-R I, M A N Spells Harriman."

It was his finest moment as a New Frontiersman. He had at last fully established himself with John Kennedy—so solidly that his Georgetown neighbor, Dean Acheson, growing grumpy in retirement, was soon complaining that Averell was using the test ban to campaign for secretary of state.

VIETNAM
Backing Strong Men

Although John Kennedy staffed the top of his State Department with men of Cabinet quality and experience, the hulking bureaucracy in Foggy Bottom was a source of frustration and dissatisfaction almost from the day he entered the White House. It was slow to react to crises, of which the new administration had aplenty, and to understand great events such as the rift between the Soviet Union and Communist China and the emergence of neutralism in world politics. Neither Dean Rusk nor his top lieutenants moved to modernize the machinery and weed out the old attitudes as the President wished. Kennedy was not certain that he knew what went on in the department, or who did what.

In this context, Harriman was a pleasant surprise. Brought aboard as a symbol of continuity and a gesture to the Democratic party's past, the old man of the administration became the State Department's foremost New Frontiersman. More than any other Kennedy appointee, he sensed opportunities to shed the moss of the fifties. He understood and cheered the thrust of Kennedy's foreign policy. His blend of liberalism, old-fashioned anticommunism, and eagerness to engage Moscow on global issues were easily compatible with the view of a resurgent America described in the President's ringing inaugural speech.

It no longer mattered very much to him that he was down in the administration's ranks, as long as he was on the team. He had a political and social constituency that spanned decades and stretched around the world. When it suited him, he could ignore bureaucratic protocol and

600

use his personal channels into far-flung governments, not to mention the White House and the inner circles of Kennedy's advisers. Before it was widely noticed, he had acquired his own coterie of career officers and Kennedy appointees to whom he was leader and mentor. He looked out for them, and they looked out for him.

Mike Forrestal and Carl Kaysen provided an avenue to the Oval Office through the National Security Council staff. Arthur Schlesinger, a longtime friend with vaguely defined responsibilities and constant access to the President, kept Harriman's views on politics, the Soviet Union, the condition of the State Department, and anything else that occurred to him before the President. Even before he was sworn in as Kennedy's ambassador-at-large, his advice, thanks to Schlesinger, was already landing on Kennedy's desk.

He thought, for example, that Mennen Williams's plan to head for Africa in February 1961 was a trifle premature; and Schlesinger passed the word along to the President a few days after the inauguration, adding a glowing observation that "Averell has never been more relaxed or more full of wise counsel than he is at the moment."[1]

His alliance with Robert Kennedy, solidified as the attorney general moved into the foreign policy and national-security picture, became as effective as his friendship with Harry Hopkins had been in the Roosevelt administration. Unlike Rusk, who personally and professionally resented the attorney general, Harriman courted the President's brother, serving as a contact, adviser, and sounding board. Though the collaboration was at the start calculated and self-serving on the part of both, they were natural allies, impatient, intolerant, sometimes ruthless, and consummately loyal to the President. All this made it possible for Bobby to forgive Averell's having consorted with Carmine De Sapio and the New York bosses, and for Averell to lay aside his contempt for Joe Kennedy.

As faithfully as any of the young lawyers at the Justice Department, Averell wore a badge of loyalty to the attorney general, particularly after the Cuban missile crisis. The Robert Kennedys were regulars when the Harrimans entertained in Georgetown, and the Harrimans were often among the Kennedys' guests at Hickory Hill. Bobby and Ethel and their brood went skiing at Sun Valley, and Averell and Marie went sailing at Hyannis.

The home base of the Harriman–Bob Kennedy team was eventually established in a high-powered National Security Council committee created to coordinate the United States' response to Communist-backed "wars of liberation." Set up in early 1962, Special Group (CI)—the "CI" for *counterinsurgency*—included the President's national security adviser, the chairman of the Joint Chiefs, the directors of the CIA, the Agency for International Development, and the United States Information Agency, and a representative of the State Department.

Headed by General Maxwell Taylor until the President's special military adviser went back into uniform as chairman of the Joint Chiefs of Staff, and then by Undersecretary of State U. Alexis Johnson, Special Group (CI) was dominated by the attorney general. It was Robert Kennedy's command post in the national security establishment. Like Rusk, Alexis Johnson thought the President's brother excessively arrogant, prone to cruelly browbeating subordinates, and bent on acting as a shadow secretary of state. Consequently, after only a few months, Johnson asked to be relieved as CI chairman, and upon the younger Kennedy's recommendation, the President replaced him with Harriman.[2]

Unlike his predecessor, Averell embraced his friend's tactics and agenda. "On nearly every issue that came up, whether it was getting walkie-talkies for Venezuelan police or diesels for troops in Thailand," said Mike Forrestal, "Averell and Bobby were always together, often a minority of two. When the others came in with reasons why things couldn't be done, they rammed right ahead. Bobby was brutal, and although Averell was a little quieter, he was just as firm. They didn't want to hear excuses, they wanted the job done, and they wanted it done promptly. Bobby thought Averell was wonderful because he liked and understood the concept of supporting counterinsurgency and he was more receptive to new ideas than any of the others who belonged to the group."[3]

Like his brother, the President developed an appreciation for Averell's curmudgeonly assaults upon policy he considered wrongheaded and his willingness to speak up with advice when the State Department quibbled. He watched with amusement as Averell turned off his hearing aid to shut out irrelevant arguments and then turn it back on when he was ready to sail into the fray himself.

There were embarrassing moments, though. During a meeting on Laos, the governor launched into an assessment of Phoumi Nosavan at the same time the President started to speak. Seated three chairs away on the same side of the table, Kennedy cleared his throat and raised his voice, but Harriman lumbered on, and the President relented. In another session, Averell was railing against "goddamned generals" anxious to intervene in hopeless places like Laos when he looked across the table into the somber face of General Earle Wheeler, the Army chief of staff, four stars sparkling on his shoulders. He was unsettled for only a moment. "Oh, excuse me, Wheeler," he muttered and charged on.[4]

He realized the seriousness of his hearing handicap, and so he began having Hildy Shishkin, his longtime personal secretary, or one of his other assistants monitor his telephone conversations, particularly when the President called. One day when he was under full throttle, telling Kennedy about his problems with the Laotian princes, Shishkin rushed

into his inner office stricken, holding a hand-lettered sign: "THE PRESI-
DENT IS TRYING TO SPEAK."

His episodes of impatient snapping in the genteel atmosphere of the
White House caused McGeorge Bundy to liken him to an old crocodile
arousing from a feigned doze with flashing jaws. Stories like the Wheeler
episode made the rounds of Georgetown dinner parties, where they were
embellished. With the help of Joe Alsop, who had firsthand experience
with the crocodile phenomenon, Bundy's label stuck. Harriman was,
Alsop declaimed, "quiescent looking, even somnolent seeming, until the
dictates of common sense or the great interests of the United States are
attacked. Whereupon the great jaws open and another fool finds that he
is figuratively missing a leg."[5]

Harriman loved the image because it enhanced a reputation for
toughness which he had valued and long cultivated by sprinkling cables
and memoranda with references to how "blunt" or "brutal" or "tough"
he had been with one foreign official or another. So, when he was showered with crocodiles of brass, crystal, silver, and cloth, he put them on
display in his office and his various residences, and sometimes used
Crocodile as his code name in secret cables from abroad.

No longer considered a mere political adornment after he dug into
the Laos assignment, he became Kennedy's busiest troubleshooter. His
bags were always packed; and whether he was bound for Luang Prabang,
Rangoon, or Rawalpindi, he clamped on his old hat and set out with all
the urgency of a trip to a superpower summit. In less than two years, his
passport was also stamped in Prestwick, Ankara, Bangkok, New Delhi,
London, Paris, Geneva, Rome, Beirut, Vientiane, Saigon, Cairo, Manila,
Baguio, Phnom Penh, Taipei, Tokyo, Seoul, Hong Kong, Zurich, Vienna, and Karachi. He was in several of the capitals on repeated occasions, including six stops in Paris and ten visits ranging from hours to
weeks in Geneva.

When Indonesia and the Netherlands spoiled for a war over West
New Guinea, he took on the assignment of pressuring the Dutch to
negotiate while the attorney general sought to undo President Sukarno's
dalliance with the Communists. After Chinese Communist troops swept
across India's borders, he was sent to New Delhi to calm Prime Minister
Nehru and on to Rawalpindi to reassure President Mohammad Ayub
Khan, lest Pakistan misread American aid to neutralist India and move
toward an alliance with the Chinese.

Although China's move across the rugged border on two fronts
appeared designed to secure its direct route to Tibet, a more ominous
interpretation was that the aggression was a move to discourage India's
relations with Moscow. Verging on panic, Nehru appealed to Moscow,
Washington, and London for help. The Soviets declined, unable to see

themselves supporting India against the world's other great Communist power, no matter how sharp their doctrinal feud with Mao Tse-tung. Neither could they overtly support the Chinese, even if they wished. To do so would risk driving India into the arms of the West.

Washington's choices were equally unsatisfactory. In the immediate aftermath of the Cuban missile crisis, the Kennedy administration was in no mood to rush into another foreign policy crisis, certainly not a border dispute with Soviet and Chinese interests at stake.

But a month after the first border skirmishing, China destroyed a brigade blocking the main avenue into India, and New Delhi was swept by rumors of an invasion. Nehru's strident plea for help from American bombers so concerned Dean Rusk that he insisted on going to the White House for a late-evening meeting with the President, where it was decided to rush Harriman to the scene.

Averell was less alarmed than the secretary because he saw it as a case where U.S. and Soviet interests coincided. Moscow needed to see the fighting stopped and Indian neutrality left undisturbed, and the Chinese had no rational reason to invade. By the time his emergency mission was airborne, the Chinese had in fact declared a unilateral ceasefire; and by the time his plane landed in New Delhi, Nehru was again a picture of tranquillity.

Kennedy's envoy, nevertheless, stayed for a week. With the ceasefire holding, he steered the talks around to the Kashmir dispute with Pakistan, taking the opportunity to inform Nehru that the Kennedy administration had no intention of arming two of its friends to fight each other.

Concerned by the ease of China's operations in the mountains and sobered by Harriman's warning, Nehru agreed for the first time to sit down with Ayub Khan. Harriman flew to Karachi and got a similar promise from the Pakistani president before heading for home, having come on one mission and accomplished another.

On such occasions, the long haul across the ocean was made in windowless, uninsulated aerial tankers, outfitted with portable passenger seats with bunks above them in the upper half of the fuselage. The "McNamara Specials," as the flying torture chambers were called, subjected passengers to brain-deadening jet noise and temperatures rising and falling by sixty degrees. To traveling companions, Harriman seemed strangely immune to the gross discomfort. Indeed he could hear better than anyone else when it was necessary to have shouted conversations. He seemed to even enjoy Air Force box lunches, and when he climbed into a bunk, he fell asleep in minutes. After journeys halfway around the world, he would return to his office and wade into his mail and waiting appointments, while companions came off the plane deafened,

exhausted by the alternating heat and cold, and disoriented from hurtling across time zones.

His durability became a point of macho pride and Washington folklore. Years later, when he and Dean Rusk arrived in Saigon from Washington and the secretary of state, who was eighteen years younger, headed to his room for a nap, Harriman departed for his first meeting. "You young fellows get your rest," he said, making sure that all the young embassy officers heard him. "I have to get to work."[6]

When he was named assistant secretary for Far Eastern affairs, Harriman became a key player in a Vietnam "conflict" looming larger in the galaxy of American entanglements as the quarreling princes in Laos edged toward an accommodation. He would in later years embellish his reservations about the United States' most unpopular armed conflict; but he did not, in fact, disagree that, after Laos, South Vietnam was the place to engage the Communists.

There, Washington's allies were more willing fighters than the peaceful Laotians; the country had a location that bestowed some strategic value and it had a functioning government—one, Harriman concluded, that was no more democratic or likely to provide long-term security than the faction the Eisenhower administration had supported in Laos.

As the conference on Laos came to an end, the only faint hope he saw to escape a continuing struggle in Indochina was a regional settlement that would include Vietnam. If the Soviets were willing to vouch for other Communist states' respect of Laotian neutrality, it could be argued that they might accept regional neutrality. Before leaving Geneva at the end of the conference on Laos, he got Kennedy's personal approval to meet secretly with Hanoi's delegation leaders to see whether there was a flicker of interest from North Vietnam. Through Burmese diplomat James Barrington, he and Bill Sullivan, who had become his special assistant for Southeast Asia, arranged a rendezvous early on a Sunday morning when they could meet representatives from Hanoi without attracting attention. Parking their car on a side street near the Geneva railroad station, they wound their way through back alleys to a small hotel used by the Burmese, entered a service door, and climbed the back stairs to the suite where two North Vietnamese officials, Foreign Minister Ung Van Khiem and Colonel Ha Van Lau, awaited them.

Harriman sipped tea and inquired about the health of Ho Chi Minh, then slipped into a well-developed spiel that the tragedy in Vietnam might have been avoided had Roosevelt lived longer. During the war, he said, he had personally heard FDR express strong opposition to the return of the French to Indochina, and afterward the United States had

been in position to prevent it; but the new administration in Washington had raised no objection. Khiem replied that he had heard that, too. Indeed he had been surprised when the United States had acquiesced in the return of the French to their former colonies.

When the conversation turned to the future, the congeniality was over. Even in private, Khiem refused to acknowledge that North Vietnamese forces were present in either Laos or South Vietnam, except for a few "trainers," who had been invited by Souvanna Phouma. When Harriman demanded to know whether they would be withdrawn in compliance with the neutrality arrangement, he would only reply that North Vietnam would do nothing "contradictory to the agreement." As far as Vietnam was concerned, there was no aggression from the North, he insisted, only a popular southern uprising against the puppet regime of Ngo Dinh Diem.[7] The conversation got nowhere. The North Vietnamese obviously had no authority to do anything except recite their usual litany against Saigon. In the middle of it, Harriman got up, thanked Barrington and, towering over Khiem, warned there would be no peace until the North ended its aggression. With that, he stalked out. It would be six years before he talked with the North Vietnamese again.

He was hardly more patient with Washington's ally in Saigon than he had been with the minister from Hanoi. When he first went to Saigon in the spring of 1961, he found President Diem rigidly opposed to Souvanna Phouma and to the Kennedy administration's support for a neutral Laos. Diem not only backed General Phouma, he wanted the United States and its allies in the Southeast Asia Treaty Organization to occupy Vientiane and towns along the Mekong River in southern Laos to stop infiltration from the north. That was not an unreasonable position considering Diem's situation, but the South Vietnamese leader was personally vexing. He groped for words to explain his policies and was comfortable and articulate only when he got into long discourses on Vietnam's history and its future. He had a fascination with minutiae, which suggested to Harriman that he was not a decisive personality. On at least one occasion, Averell dozed while listening to Diem hold forth, and an American embassy official took it as calculated rudeness to demonstrate his disdain for him.

Harriman's skepticism was heightened when he returned to the South Vietnamese capital in the fall. In spite of Washington's increased aid and the hundreds of additional military advisers sent to the country after a visit by Vice-President Johnson, there had been a serious escalation of fighting without any gains by the government.

Diem had lost public confidence, Harriman wrote Galbraith when he got back to Geneva. The United States was in the same boat it had been in when the Eisenhower administration had supported Phoumi in Laos—hardly on the side of democracy. It was time, he said, "to get away

from Dulles's policy of backing 'strong men' regardless. . . . Our present stable of strong men are not winners for the long pull, at least in Southeast Asia."[8]

Kennedy's response to the escalating warfare was to send Maxwell Taylor and National Security Council staffer Walt Rostow to Vietnam for a broad assessment of the situation. They brought back a foreboding glimpse of a protracted struggle and a lengthy list of recommendations, including a proposal to send eight thousand American troops to South Vietnam under the guise of flood-control workers.

While the administration ignored the advice, the Taylor-Rostow mission was an early milestone in the United States' slide toward its huge stake in Vietnam. Once the military commitment was made, Harriman would support it publicly and privately, staunchly opposing a "cut and run" policy while arguing that political reform in Saigon was needed as urgently as the military opposition to the Communist insurgency. Throughout his travels in Asia, he told the President, he had been hearing stories over and over about "the dictatorial regime of Diem, its palace guard, his family, and their corruption. . . . I want to add my voice to those who believe that we should give more consideration to the political situation, which cannot be cured alone by military preparation or assistance."[9]

He also urged use of the United Nations to spotlight the Communist aggression and called upon Britain and the Soviet Union as co-chairs of the 1954 Geneva conference on Indochina to reconvene the major powers to consider new accords. "The best any international settlement can do is to buy time," he acknowledged, but on the other hand the Diem government was on a disastrous course. "The country will not long retain its independence. Nor can the United States afford to stake its prestige there. We must make it clear to Diem that we mean business about internal reform. This will require a strong ambassador who can control all U.S. activities (political, military, economic, etc.), and who is known by Diem to have the personal intimacy and confidence of the President and the Secretary."[10]

Kennedy was getting much the same advice from Galbraith. After a visit to Washington from his post in New Delhi, the ambassador stopped off in South Vietnam to make a personal report to the President and left with an assessment of the South Vietnamese President that was even harsher than Averell's. "The only solution," he counseled, "must be to drop Diem." Shedding him, Galbraith advised "will neither be difficult nor unduly dangerous."[11]

Trying to support the government militarily and simultaneously encourage reform, Kennedy was no more prepared to dump Diem than he was to buy the Taylor-Rostow recommendation to send in American troops as flood-control workers. Instead, he split the difference: he urged

Diem to make political and social reforms, but at the same time he agreed to a vague military commitment—which led to the dispatching of sixteen thousand Americans to South Vietnam rather than eight thousand.

The administration was only beginning to look at Vietnam as a first-order problem when Harriman took over the Far Eastern billet at State, inheriting a staff that was divided and, more than other bureaus of the department, still imprinted with Eisenhower-Dulles views. As holdovers at FE considered Phoumi Nosavan the answer in Laos, they believed Ngo Dinh Diem to be the instrument for victory over communism in Vietnam. Among survivors of the old order, the seventy-year-old assistant secretary was regarded as a dilettante and resented for his open lines to the White House and his lack of regard for channels. But with Rusk conceding Vietnam to the Pentagon, Harriman became the leader of a small State Department circle that held the solution to be in political reform and civic action as much as in firepower.

During the first months of 1962, the conflict seemed to have taken a turn for the better. With U.S. advisers accompanying main units of the South Vietnamese Army throughout the country, there was a drop-off in the number of battalion-sized Viet Cong attacks. Fifty troop-carrying American helicopters shuttled government soldiers to engage guerrillas, and American pilots in World War II trainers and Liberator bombers flew missions against concentrations of Viet Cong strength. There was a rice surplus and the Saigon government reported that construction of strategic hamlets, providing security for peasants in the countryside, was booming.

In a search for a strategy for winning the war against the insurgents, the hamlets became the centerpiece of a plan to separate the Viet Cong from both the people and the provisions required to sustain them. The grand design was to gather peasants into compact enclaves protected by barbed wire and bamboo spikes and provided with radio transmitters for constant contact with government forces. Borrowed from Britain's experience in Malaysia, the hamlets were supposed to create an ever expanding secure zone, attracting peasants from old villages vulnerable to tax collection, pillaging, and coercion by antigovernment guerrillas.

Harriman doubted the upbeat military reports and dismissed General Paul Harkins's assessment that defeat of the guerrillas was in sight. He was dubious about what he heard from the American embassy because he considered Ambassador Frederick Nolting too close to Diem.

In April of 1962, five months after taking the Far East job, Harriman had three long talks with Galbraith. Although the economist-turned-diplomat was more outspoken, he and Harriman held the same basic distrust of the Saigon regime. The South Vietnamese were making undeniable gains, they told Kennedy, but the United States' growing military commitment was risking "a major, long drawn out, indecisive military

involvement." As far as Diem was concerned, they saw evidence that he was already "beyond the point of no return." They counseled a lowered American profile, a policy that focused on political solutions, and a backing away from association with the strategic hamlet program and its burning of old villages.[12]

In a talk with the President the day after Galbraith gave their memorandum to the White House, Harriman told Kennedy he simply considered Diem "a losing horse in the long run." Unlike the ambassador, however, he cautioned against a move to oust the South Vietnamese president, because he could see no plausible candidate to replace him.[13]

The real problem in Saigon, all agreed, was Diem's brother, Ngo Dinh Nhu. The chief of the secret police and head of the strategic hamlet program, Nhu fancied himself an intellectual, espoused a curious political philosophy of "personalism," and exerted unchallengeable influence over his brother's presidency. His spitfire wife, the country's self-styled First Lady, antagonized American officials with her intrusion and self-promotion, and earned the hostility of the South Vietnamese with high-handed dictates.

The warnings from Harriman and Galbraith in early 1962 led to nothing, which was not surprising. Robert Kennedy had just visited Saigon and promised that American troops would stay until the defeat of the Viet Cong. Robert McNamara, supported by an avalanche of statistics, was telling the President the war was going well, and Rusk agreed.

Harriman nevertheless kept urging Ambassador Nolting to keep up the pressure on the Diem government to reach out to the opposition. He had little success, for Nolting had arrived in May 1961 at a period when the administration was trying a soft-sell approach to getting the Diem regime to reform itself. The strategy suited the ambassador's easy-going style and the genuine affection that he developed for the South Vietnamese president. An affable Virginian, Nolting was a career diplomat who had once served as a special assistant to Dean Acheson. He was far ahead of most of his contemporaries on the career ladder, having already been offered the embassy in Vientiane and wisely turning it down before being selected for Saigon.

Nolting was caught in a clear contradiction between his instructions from Rusk to do everything he could to help the Saigon government and Harriman's determination to bring about reform. He could not reconcile the objectives of inspiring confidence in the government while supporting the opposition.

Nolting also felt, as did Ngo Dinh Diem, that Harriman had traded away too much in Geneva. He could see the North Vietnamese using the trails through neutral Laos at will, and he found Averell's defense of the Laotian neutrality agreement surprisingly naive. "He had what he called

a 'fingertips feeling' that the Russians were going to cooperate in policing the agreement," Nolting later recalled. "He thought it was in their interest, too." When the ambassador expressed his doubts about the future of Laos, Harriman sharply cut him off. President Kennedy had ordered him to get an agreement on Laos, he told the ambassador, and he had gone to Geneva determined that the President was "damn well going to get it."[14]

In spite of their differences, Harriman and Nolting closed ranks to keep American interests in Saigon under civilian control as the military numbers mounted and the Pentagon established the new Military Assistance Command. Seeing his prerogatives threatened by the military escalation, Nolting flew to Washington to establish that he, and not General Paul Harkins, the first MACV commander, would exercise overall U.S. authority in Saigon. Rusk shrugged off his concern with an assurance that he would find it easy to get along with the general, but Nolting took his problem to Harriman. It was something Harriman had written the President about months earlier. He telephoned the White House, made an appointment for Nolting to see the President, then went along with him. The President agreed and, on the spot, ordered Taylor to draft language for the order creating the Military Assistance Command, making it clear that overall U.S. authority in South Vietnam resided with the ambassador.[15]

For months after becoming assistant secretary, Harriman held his fire on the issue of Ngo Dinh Nhu, more or less accepting Nolting's argument that Diem couldn't get along without his brother. But by the spring of 1963, he had become convinced that the regime was past saving as long as Nhu remained in Saigon.

What troubled him as much as Nhu's psychological hold on his brother, the brutality of his secret police, and his repression of the Buddhists was the mess made of the strategic hamlet program. The enclaves had not been located in a manner to create an expanding secure zone. Instead, they had been set up at breakneck speed across the country, many of them no more secure than the old villages whose inhabitants had been uprooted and driven into the hamlets as virtual prisoners. But there was no dissuading Nhu, because he saw the program as a way to solidify the regime's own political control of the countryside. A close look at the program showed the figures on the numbers of hamlets, their populations, and the areas under government control to be figments of Nhu's imagination.

Harriman resurrected an old idea of sending Nhu to South Vietnam's Paris embassy, and Nolting put it to Diem as a friendly suggestion; but it got the same icy rejection it had earlier received when Elbridge Durbrow, Nolting's predecessor, had suggested it. The brothers were as

fiercely loyal as John and Robert Kennedy, causing Americans in Saigon to call South Vietnam's junior partner "Bobby Nhu."

Harriman had been doing the blue-collar work of statecraft for two years when he was promoted out of his day-to-day responsibility for Vietnam and to the seventh floor of the State Department as undersecretary for political affairs.

The move was not taken to get him out of FE, or to move him along in his career, but to complete what Bob Kennedy considered the unfinished business of the "Thanksgiving massacre" five months earlier. When Chester Bowles was ousted and George Ball was elevated to the number two spot as principal undersecretary, Ball had been replaced by George McGhee, the department's counselor and an old friend of Rusk's, who had been the only department official personally chosen by the secretary when the administration took office.

Since the reorganization, State had been less of an irritation to the President, but the attorney general had soon thereafter begun to agitate for McGhee's replacement, complaining that he was bland, long-winded and ineffective. "It all sounded good and it came out in the right order, but he just said nothing," Robert Kennedy later complained. "He wouldn't do anything, and he'd get nothing done, and he wouldn't follow anything up."[16]

Finally given the President's go-ahead, the attorney general strolled into the secretary's office with his dog one Saturday morning and laid it on the line. He wanted McGhee to go. Rusk obviously didn't like the ultimatum and suggested that Kennedy's motives were personal, but there was nothing he could do. He agreed to let McGhee go, but with the understanding that he would be given an ambassadorial appointment.

Harriman's choice for a successor at FE was William Bundy, the brother of the President's national security adviser and son-in-law of Dean Acheson. But McNamara objected to Bundy's being moved from the Pentagon, the Far East job went to Roger Hilsman, another friend of the President and the attorney general, who had been director of the department's Bureau of Intelligence and Research. The Kennedys liked Hilsman's work because he was willing to challenge conventional wisdom and speak up when tough issues were on the table. As far as nearly everybody else was concerned, though, the new assistant secretary challenged too much and spoke up too often.

Hilsman was in the little circle that had come to make up Harriman's Vietnam team—Forrestal, Bill Sullivan, Vietnam-desk officer Joseph Mendenhall, experienced Saigon hand Paul Kattenburg, and Asia scholar James Thomson. All regarded the conflict as a civil war and a political problem more than a battleground against world communism

or a domino whose fall would trigger the capitulation of all Southeast Asia. All had grave doubts about the Diem government.

The new assistant secretary had become close to Averell on Vietnam matters because Harriman refused to listen to Walt Rostow, who had become chief of the department's plans and policy staff. Rostow was for moving the war north, and after a few days of reading his memos, Harriman ignored them. The word got to Kennedy; and the President let Hilsman know that, where the Far East bureau was concerned, he was to be Harriman's man on matters that would ordinarily belong to the Policy Planning staff.

A graduate of West Point and a Yale Ph.D., Hilsman had been a lieutenant with Merrill's Marauders in Burma during World War II, and he was not bashful about recounting how he had been wounded, how he had recovered to take command of a battalion operating behind enemy lines, and how he had rescued his own father from a Manchurian POW camp. That he was exceedingly bright no one denied, but his cocksure attitude and his conspicuous lack of awe for general officers infuriated many people.

He was known to correct high-ranking military briefers in the presence of the President, the secretary of state, and the secretary of defense, using their maps and charts to launch soaring military and geopolitical expositions that left his superiors with jaws set and gripping the arms of their chairs. Once he stepped up and took the pointer from the hand of General Lyman Lemnitzer, the chairman of the Joint Chiefs of Staff, and more or less preempted his presentation. Taylor and McNamara stiffened at the mere mention of his name, and even the monumentally patient Dean Rusk could not conceal his dislike for the assistant secretary's impertinence. Lyndon Johnson, who usually said little in Vietnam meetings, took a simmering dislike to him because of the way he excoriated Diem and asserted himself in matters Johnson considered in the province of the military. One night, when Hilsman held forth on counterinsurgency after one of Harriman's dinners, which included the Vice-President and General Lemnitzer, Johnson looked at him through narrowed eyelids and ordered, with barely controlled anger, "Goddamnit, Captain Hilsman, shut up and let the general talk."[17]

While the promotion of Harriman and Hilsman strengthened the voice of Diem critics, Averell was the odd man out on the seventh floor. Rusk and George Ball enjoyed an extraordinary personal and professional compatibility, and Harriman was close to neither of them. In all the months the three served as a troika at the top of Kennedy's State Department, the secretary and his deputy never left town at the same time, even on weekends, and Averell was sure that it was deliberately planned so he would not be left as as acting secretary.

Ball had been an early and devout Stevensonian, serving as one of

the Illinois governor's closest advisers during Averell's two contests with him for the Democratic nomination. His demeanor was tinged with the self-satisfied intellectual superiority that Harriman found irritating in many of Stevenson's true believers. Ball considered Averell a valuable public servant, but he did not have great regard for his intellectual acuity, finding him still holding to every worn shibboleth of the New Deal and Fair Deal. Ball, as a Europeanist, was not eager to have Averell on that turf again; and he had also taken a keen interest in Africa, where Averell had come to regard himself as a bit of an expert as well.

Like Harriman, Ball was uncomfortable about the Diem regime in Saigon, but more than that, he was doubtful about South Vietnam's importance to the United States. In time he would become the foremost inside dissenter on Vietnam policy, playing a role that would have logically been Harriman's except that Averell's objections became more muted as the military commitment increased and he found himself on less certain grounds with John Kennedy's successor in the White House.

Rusk was studiously deferential to Harriman, solicitous in staff meetings, thoughtful in sending appropriate congratulations, and tolerant of his political connections and disdain for the rules. It was not an act, for in private conversation the secretary would speak admiringly of him as a figure of historic stature. Harriman was equally the gentleman, but there was a chronic tension between them because Rusk knew that Harriman considered himself better equipped to be secretary of state.

Fred Dutton, the State Department spokesman, recalled a Rusk staff meeting at a time when Britain's Harold Wilson was on a personal visit to Washington. When Rusk expressed an interest in talking informally with him and wondered aloud where he might be staying, since he was on a personal visit, no one at the table, including Harriman, seemed to know. Ball went to find out. When he returned, he whispered to the secretary that Wilson was in fact a guest at Averell's house. Harriman never blinked and never spoke, and Rusk went on to another subject.[18]

From time to time, Averell made efforts at friendship, having the Rusks to dinner on a wedding anniversary and sending the secretary notes of congratulation. About to take off for the Moscow test-ban talks in July 1963, he saw a front-page story in *The New York Times* reporting a sharp exchange between Rusk and segregationist Senator J. Strom Thurmond of South Carolina over legislation banning discrimination in public housing. The Communists, Rusk told Thurmond, considered racial discrimination in the United States one of their most valuable propaganda assets. He refused to allow Thurmond to lead him into denunciation of civil rights demonstrations sweeping the country. To the contrary, the Georgia-born secretary assured Thurmond that he would himself be demonstrating in the streets "if I were denied what our Negro citizens are denied."[19]

Moved by such a display of courage, Harriman telephoned congratulations from the plane before it took off. Taken by surprise, Rusk was instinctively defensive. Apparently taking the praise as sarcasm from one who still liked to parade his liberal credentials, Rusk reacted coolly. Harriman, expecting a warm reception, put down the phone sorry that he had even made the call. "I will never understand the man," he said. "I don't understand him at all."[20]

The cultural gap between them was too wide. Rusk was the son of a down-on-his-luck Presbyterian minister. In his formative years, he had lived precariously near railroad tracks once controlled by the Harriman empire, working as a delivery boy and appliance salesman while attending high school. At a similar stage in his own youth, Averell was already traveling the world. Both had been imprinted by those years.

They had first met at the Potsdam summit, when Rusk was an Army staff officer. Later, Rusk had worked on the Greek-Turkish aid program and the crisis over Soviet troops in Iran. He had established himself as a favorite of President Truman, who appointed him assistant secretary of state for Far Eastern affairs. During the years Harriman was in Albany and Rusk was at the Rockefeller Foundation, they had stayed in touch and Rusk was occasionally on the guest list when foreign visitors were entertained.

The secretary still had the personality and habits of a professional staff man. He could brilliantly distill convoluted policy debates into their purest expression and strip arguments clean of rhetoric. He made discretion and integrity a fetish, striving always to emulate his hero, George Marshall. Personal differences made him uncomfortable; and if there were differences, he had a habit of keeping his opinion to himself as long as a matter remained unresolved. He held back when sharp exchanges arose in the presence of the President, preferring to remain after all the others had been heard and give his own recommendations in confidence.

It was a style that made Harriman boil, as it did Robert Kennedy. Averell blamed Rusk in good measure for the Bay of Pigs debacle because the secretary had remained silent when the President had offered his advisers a last opportunity to dissent. Rusk, the attorney general said, habitually went into meetings without a position on the issue at hand. "He was tremendously influenced by what the President wanted to do," the President's brother recalled. "He didn't have any strong point of view."[21]

The starkly different Harriman and Rusk outlooks were manifest in the issue of Vietnam. Averell was the godfather of the anti-Diem band; Rusk was the faithful ally of the Pentagon school that spoke in the same breath of defeating the Communists and supporting the government in

Saigon. Kennedy lent encouragement to both, accepting the McNamara-Pentagon advice to up the ante militarily while encouraging Harriman and the Diem critics to keep up the pressure for reforms.

The conflict was managed by a proliferating legion of American military agencies employing no less than twenty-two generals in Vietnam by 1963. Coordination with the Saigon regime did not improve with the buildup. Although the government in South Vietnam came to view the strategic hamlet program as a panacea, little effort was made to coordinate it with U.S. strategy or the government's political and pacification efforts.

At the end of 1962, Hilsman and Forrestal visited South Vietnam and came home with a mixed report on the Diem government; but while they were there, the illusion of an improving combat picture was shattered. Learning that a full Viet Cong battalion was near the village of Ap Bac, forty miles southwest of Saigon, the government sent three Ranger battalions to trap them in a fight that would heavily favor the government forces with their new helicopters and American weapons. It was the opportunity for the large-scale engagement that the South Vietnamese and American advisers had awaited. But the guerrillas stayed in hiding until the airlifted battalion was nearly all on the ground, then opened fire on the last wave of helicopters, shooting five of them down and killing three American pilots. At the same time, they surprised the two government battalions moving in from the other direction. When it was over, sixty-one government soldiers had been killed, and the Viet Cong, outnumbered four to one, had faded into the jungle. The debacle was compounded when Lieutenant Colonel John Paul Vann, the American adviser, bitterly chastised the South Vietnamese, suggesting that the Diem government wanted the war to go badly so the gusher of American aid would continue to flow.

Forrestal and Hilsman concluded that the war against the guerrillas was being won, though more slowly than had been expected. Diem, they reported, was in more firm control of his government and professing concern for the plight of South Vietnamese peasants.

The big problem remained Nhu. Never failing to unnerve Americans with his lack of contact with reality, the President's brother seriously put before the visitors from Washington a plan to defeat communism on an apocalyptic scale. In essence, it called for the United States to draw Communist China into war in Laos.[22]

Harriman's lieutenants were barely back home when disaffected South Vietnamese pilots attacked Diem's palace, flying low over it in a strafing run that seemed to concentrate on the wing occupied by Nhu and his wife. It was the second serious assassination attempt, and Nhu's reaction was to turn the screws tighter against dissent.

The crisis that turned the course of the war for the Kennedy admin-

istration came in the spring of 1963. When several thousand Buddhists who were gathered in Hue to celebrate the anniversary of Buddha's birth refused a police order to disperse, troops surrounded them and orders were given to fire. Panic ensued, and when it was over, nine of the Buddhists were dead, either killed by gunfire or trampled. Diem, Nhu, and their government, dominated by Catholics, plunged toward civil war with the country's huge Buddhist majority.

Demonstrations quickly spread from Hue to Saigon, and the government reacted by bringing troops in from the countryside. Day after day, the tension steadily escalated, the Buddhists taking clever political advantage of Diem's use of increased force.

After two weeks, however, the crisis eased, and Ambassador Nolting and his wife left Saigon on a long-planned sailing vacation in the Aegean Sea. The affable diplomat from Virginia was nearing the end of his tour. He had, in fact, suggested early in the spring that a successor be named, but Averell had asked him to remain indefinitely, suggesting that he get away for a vacation. Believing the repercussions from Hue had passed, the Noltings flew from South Vietnam to Greece on May 23, leaving William Truehart, the embassy's political officer, in charge in Saigon.

Two weeks after they departed, the Buddhist problem took a dramatic turn for the worse. An elderly monk burned himself to death in a busy Saigon intersection as chanting monks and nuns looked on. An Associated Press photograph of the tiny bonze, stiffened grotesquely inside an orange fireball, created worldwide revulsion. Nhu's wife scornfully called the Buddhists dupes of the Communists; and when more suicides by fire followed, she referred to them as "bonze barbecues" and suggested that some American reporters follow suit.

Within hours of the first self-immolation, on June 11, Harriman and Hilsman dispatched a top secret cable to Truehart, in effect ordering Diem to meet the Buddhists' demands. Otherwise, they warned, the United States would withdraw its support of his government. It was an implied threat of a coup. At the same time, Truehart was told to discreetly advise Vice-President Nguyen Ngoc Tho that should Diem become "unable to act as President" the United States would back him as the constitutional successor and that Washington "would assume he would need military support."[23]

Unlike Nolting, Truehart shared Harriman's view that the way to resolve the crisis was to hound the government until it addressed the Buddhists' demands to punish those responsible for the demonstrators' deaths in Hue. He enthusiastically carried out his instructions to exert pressure, seeing Diem every day, and, in terms seldom used with the head of a government, insisting over and over that the regime respond to the Buddhist demands. Finally, Diem agreed to sign a promise of

religious freedom and to compensate the families of the victims of Hue, but he then tried to keep the pledge secret because he thought it acknowledged guilt. In the long run, the tough U.S. tactics accomplished little, because they were reported in the press, infuriating Diem and stifling whatever chance Truehart had of getting him to change. Soon, the South Vietnamese President would barely speak to the American representative.

In the midst of the crisis, Harriman had to turn his attention from Vietnam to the Moscow negotiations on the nuclear-test-ban treaty. But before he left for the Soviet Union, he received a visit from Henry Cabot Lodge. The former senator, who had been Richard Nixon's 1960 vice-presidential running mate, was a major general in the Army Reserve, and he had spent his annual active-duty stint the previous summer working on a paper on Vietnam. He was interested in helping out with the war.

Harriman had not been impressed by Lodge's period as Eisenhower's ambassador to the United Nations, where he had engaged in loud confrontations with the Soviets, but he found that Lodge shared his serious reservations about the Diem government.

It didn't occur to him that Kennedy might make Lodge ambassador; and when the appointment was announced, he was not happy about it. Although a conspicuous Republican would provide the administration political cover, he thought the real need was for somebody with close and well-known personal ties to Kennedy so that both the Diem government and the U.S. military command in Saigon would understand that the ambassador spoke authoritatively for the President. Lodge obviously didn't have that qualification, though he did offer an aura of bipartisanship. In addition, he spoke French fluently, and his background gave him credibility with the military.

Once the decision was made, Averell tried to hasten Lodge's arrival in Saigon. He suggested that the President immediately announce the new ambassador's nomination, summon Nolting back from vacation, and make the change immediately; but because Kennedy was leaving on a trip to Europe, the matter was allowed to drift. Nolting, meanwhile, continued his vacation. Stopping at an Aegean island, he saw the newspaper photograph of the first self-immolation in Saigon, but when he checked for messages from the embassy, there were none. When his vacation was over, the ambassador and his wife took an ocean liner from Genoa to New York, and then a train to Washington for a last round of consultations before going back to Saigon to conclude their tour. At sea, they learned of the continuing crisis in South Vietnam and heard of Lodge's appointment as the new ambassador. Arriving in Washington, Nolting found Harriman surly and uncommunicative, raging against the Diem administration, and disinterested in Nolting's return to Vietnam.

But even while Truehart was energetically carrying out Harriman's mandate to keep the heat on the Saigon regime, the White House hoped that Nolting's friendship with the South Vietnamese President might still count for something. After talking with Kennedy, Nolting flew back for one last attempt to make Diem understand the gravity of the Buddhist crisis and his problems in Washington. He succeeded in getting a few small conciliatory gestures to the Buddhists, but the government extended them with such bitterness and ill grace that they only made the situation worse. Police threw barricades around Saigon's largest pagoda, refusing to let anyone enter or leave, and in Nolting's sad last days in the capital, four more monks committed flaming suicide.

The ambassador left Vietnam on August 5, still bitter at Harriman for not getting him back from vacation. He was convinced that Averell had compounded the disaster by leaking the details of Truehart's pressure on the South Vietnamese president in an effort to generate public pressure on Diem to follow directions from Washington. "He thought things could be done as they were done in Europe," Nolting said after the war. "He thought you could drive a hard bargain and make it stick, that you could get things done efficiently. Well, the South Vietnamese government was not an efficient government, and that made him want to get rid of it."[24]

Nolting told himself that had he come back from his vacation earlier in the crisis, he might have persuaded Diem to make peace. But he was convinced that "Harriman didn't want me back, because he thought that I might be able to get a reconciliation, that I might persuade Diem to come to terms with the thing. They could have easily gotten me back in eight or ten hours."[25]

The ambassador departed Saigon with Diem's personal word that there would be no further violence against the Buddhists. But, even before he got to Washington and before Lodge reached Saigon, the promise was shattered. With the South Vietnamese capital under martial law, Nhu cut off the telephones to the homes and offices of American officials and sent his security forces dressed in uniforms of regular army troops rampaging into pagodas in Saigon, Hue, and other cities. Amid the sounds of gongs and exploding grenades, they beat and arrested monks and nuns, destroyed religious icons, looted and sacked sanctuaries. Word of the violence first reached Washington in news bulletins filed by wire-service reporters who witnessed the last minutes of the attack on Saigon's Xa Loi Pagoda.

Awakened at his hotel in Tokyo, Lodge took off for Saigon immediately and arrived late that night. Awaiting him were threats against his life, a warning from Nhu's wife that he was on probation, and urgent cables from Hilsman and Harriman. Washington no longer knew who

was in control of the government in Saigon. "Regardless of who is running the show," one of the cables from Hilsman and Harriman advised,

> we should continue to seek the same objectives. These are [(1)] acceptable solutions to the Buddhist problem and [(2)] a more responsive and representative government capable of carrying on the war effectively. GVN [government of Vietnam] must show own population and world that improvement in Buddhist position will be eventual outcome of evolving situation. If we impress this need on both civilians and military at all levels [of the] GVN, we may be able to achieve some progress not only on immediate Buddhist problem (with all implications this has for U.S. and world opinion) but also on longer range objective of broadening regime and limiting Diem's exercise of arbitrary power. As situation develops, we may deem it useful to throw our influence toward reducing or eliminating the power of the Nhus [sic]. However, we will welcome your fresh reading of this and other aspects of the situation.[26]

The secret message was a clear signal that Washington was ready to involve itself more deeply in forcing change.

Lodge's reply requesting guidance reached Washington on a Saturday morning that found nearly all of the Kennedy administration's top-ranking national security officials out of the city, an unusual circumstance even for sultry late August. The President himself was at Hyannis. Rusk, just back from signing the limited test-ban treaty in Moscow, was spending the weekend in New York. McNamara was hiking in the Tetons. CIA chief John McCone was away, as was McGeorge Bundy. At the State Department, Harriman went to work early—to read the cable traffic from Saigon and to talk with Hilsman, who only hours earlier had returned from Hawaii, where he had met with Nolting and Lodge as their paths crossed.

Forrestal was at the nearly deserted west wing of the White House. After talking with Harriman and Hilsman, he sent a top secret cable to Kennedy, indicating how fast the situation in Vietnam was changing. "It is now quite certain that Brother Nhu is the mastermind behind the whole operation against the Buddhists and is calling the shots," Forrestal advised the President. "This is now agreed by virtually everyone here.

"Agreement is also developing that the United States cannot tolerate a result of the present difficulties in Saigon which leaves Brother Nhu in a dominating position. There is disagreement on whether Diem has any political viability left, and on whether he could ever be brought to acquiesce in the removal of his brother.

"Averell and Roger now agree that we must move before the situation in Saigon freezes. I am pressing them to get John McCone's endorsement of one of several courses of action which can be presented to you at the earliest opportunity. We are still trying to keep all of this as closely held as possible."[27] Early in the afternoon, Hilsman drafted and Harriman approved a reply to Lodge's request for guidance. In the most blunt language the administration had ever used concerning the government of South Vietnam, it all but sanctioned a coup against the Diem regime. Diem was to be given one last chance to remove his brother's influence.

"U.S. government cannot tolerate situation in which power lies in Nhu's hands," began the most famous cable of the Vietnam War. "Diem must be given chance to rid himself of Nhu and his coterie and replace him with best military and political personalities available. If in spite of all your efforts, Diem remains obdurate and refuses, then we must face the possibility that Diem himself cannot be preserved."[28]

Forrestal had been especially anxious to get fresh guidance to Lodge; but when he saw the draft, his instinct was that it should wait until Monday when it could be fully discussed. Harriman dissented. Lodge wanted an answer, he said, and it was time for Washington to bite the bullet.

The cable went on to tell the ambassador that he and his team "should urgently examine all possible alternative leadership and make detailed plans as to how we might bring about Diem's replacement if this should become necessary.

"You will understand that we cannot from Washington give you detailed instructions as to how this operation should proceed," it concluded, "but you will also know we will back you to the hilt on actions you take to achieve our objectives."[29]

Forrestal called the President and read him the draft. Kennedy also questioned whether it shouldn't be talked out the following week, but when Forrestal told him that Harriman and Hilsman were insistent upon a prompt reply, the President told him to proceed with getting the necessary clearances. So Forrestal joined Averell and Hilsman in finding officials who could endorse it for the CIA, the Defense Department, the Joint Chiefs of Staff, and State. Precisely what happened after the first call to Kennedy would be disputed as long as the participants lived. The message and the way it was handled split the administration and riveted Kennedy's attention on Vietnam as it had never been.

While Forrestal was making the calls, Harriman and Hilsman drove out to Bethesda, Maryland, and found Ball, who was acting secretary since Rusk was out of town, on the ninth tee of the Falls Road golf course. The undersecretary scanned the draft; and after Harriman made his

pitch for sending the cable, they moved on to Ball's home to review its contents. Ball agreed with Averell that the time had come to deal with the Nhu problem. "We had," he later said, "really run our course with the Diem regime. Unless he got rid of the Nhus and straightened up, it was impossible to go forward." After making a few changes that somewhat "watered down" the language, he discussed it on the phone with Rusk. The amended text was then cabled both to the secretary and the President.[30]

Forrestal, meanwhile, telephoned Richard Helms, the deputy director of the Central Intelligence Agency, who listened to the contents of the message with satisfaction and approved it on behalf of McCone. With McNamara unreachable, Forrestal then tracked down Deputy Defense Secretary Roswell Gilpatrick at his farm in Maryland. Maxwell Taylor, now chairman of the Joint Chiefs of Staff, could not be reached, but Forrestal located Victor Krulak, a Marine major general and special assistant to the Joint Chiefs. Krulak dropped by the White House, read the message, then went in search of Taylor. Forrestal's recollection was that Krulak called back in the late afternoon with word that Taylor had approved the message.

With that, it lacked only the President's final authorization, which came in the early evening. Kennedy again wanted to be assured that his team was agreed. Once more he asked the young White House aide, "Are you sure you are all right?" Forrestal had no doubt. At 9:36 P.M., the message was dispatched. Averell went home to Georgetown satisfied that the administration was on its way to resolving one of its fundamental problems in Vietnam.

On Monday, Kennedy returned to the White House to find an uproar on his hands. McCone and McNamara were furious because they had not been directly consulted. Taylor, insisting he had not seen the message until after it had been sent, thought Harriman, Hilsman, and Forrestal had taken advantage of the principals' absence at a crucial moment to change administration policy.

No one was blameless. Kennedy had told Ball it was all right, if Rusk and Gilpatrick agreed. Rusk said he would not object, if it was approved by the President, Ball, and Harriman. Gilpatrick contended that he took it as a State Department matter, that he thought he had only been informed as a courtesy to the Defense Department. Krulak denied telling Forrestal that the message had been cleared by Taylor. Taylor's version was that he had first heard of the message in a telephone call from Gilpatrick and did not see it until sometime after ten P.M., half an hour after it had been dispatched. The chairman of the Joint Chiefs was decidedly not for encouraging a coup in Saigon. He thought the message "a helluva poor cable," which, he said, he had difficulty even understand-

ing. Its weekend clearance, in his eyes, amounted to an "egregious end run" taking advantage of the absence of the President and his senior advisers.[31]

Although it was Harriman who had applied the main pressure to get the cable out and Forrestal who bore the responsibility for the disorganized clearance process, it was Hilsman who received the brunt of the anger. He was, after all, the author, and his name at the bottom of it gave McNamara, Taylor, and McCone their chance to put him in his place before the President. But after days of finger-pointing and recrimination, nobody was prepared to vote for the recall of the cable. As long as the Nhus were aboard, support of the Diem government was "impossible to contemplate," said Ball. "It put America in an odious position quite inconsistent with the principle on which we had based our Vietnam intervention in the first place."[32] Only Taylor and Nolting, who arrived in Washington just in time to be invited into the fracas by the President, were for withdrawing the message.

Lodge would later claim to have been shocked by the suggestion that he involve himself in a coup against a government yet to receive his credentials. The fact was, he responded without hesitation and with enthusiasm. There was virtually no chance of separating Diem and Nhu, he replied. Even to approach the President with a demand to get rid of his brother was hopeless. Lodge instead proposed going straight to the generals plotting the government's overthrow. He would tell them, he suggested, that Washington was "prepared to have Diem without the Nhus but it is in effect up to them whether to keep him."[33] His approach was approved.

The tense White House meetings over five days produced the angriest exchanges heard in the Oval Office during all of Kennedy's administration. Hilsman defended the cable's content with as much determination as Harriman fended off the critics of their haste. Averell stormed at Krulak and accused Taylor of being wrong on everything since World War II. He sailed into Nolting for being too cozy with Diem. And when the former ambassador tried to defend himself, Harriman snapped that he should keep his mouth shut because no one cared what he thought. With that, Kennedy curtly interrupted. He was fond of Nolting, and he told Harriman that the President, for one, was interested in hearing what Nolting had to say. Forrestal, distraught because his staff work had been the target of ridicule, told Averell he was going to resign and go back to being a lawyer in New York. They had grievously failed the President. Averell's response was peremptory: it was time, he said, for his young friend to "quit being a goddamned fool" and get back to work.[34]

When fresh opinions were solicited from Saigon, the answer from General Paul Harkins was sharply at odds with the opinions of Lodge

and CIA station chief John Richardson. The military commander did not see any urgency and was not optimistic at the chances of a coup installing a new government.

Harriman did not like the smell of it, and offhandedly mentioned to the President that he thought Harkins's answer odd. His curiosity aroused, Kennedy sent for copies of the outgoing cables soliciting the views and found that Taylor had carefully suggested the answer he wanted from Harkins. The August 24 cable had been sent to Lodge without the approval of the Defense Department or the Joint Chiefs of Staff, Taylor advised Harkins, and "authorities are now having second thoughts."[35] It was a careful attempt to line Harkins up with Taylor and the coup opposition, and Harriman had caught it. He was, said Kennedy, one "shrewd old SOB."[36] The President was nonetheless surprised and disappointed at Harriman's overly emotional behavior in the episode.

It was a time, Robert Kennedy later recalled, when "the government was broken in two in a very disturbing way."[37]

Saigon, it turned out, was not as ripe for a coup as the Harriman faction believed, but the policy laid down in the Harriman-Hilsman cable stood. Kennedy himself publicly stated it in less blunt language in an interview with Walter Cronkite a week later. The war against the Communists was "their war" in Saigon, he said, and it could not be won unless the Diem government regained the support it had lost as a result of its treatment of the Buddhists, a goal that could be accomplished "with changes in policy, and perhaps with personnel."[38] The reference to "personnel" could not have been lost upon Ngo Dinh Diem, or the generals who had been involved in the coup planning.

After the violence against the Buddhists and the uproar over the green-light cable, Vietnam became the top item on Kennedy's agenda. And in the President's intensive effort to understand the tactical situation as well as the political morass, Harriman was conspicuously missing. His advice had become suspect in the course of the cable dispute.

Paul Kattenburg returned on August 31 from a trip to Vietnam and long talks with Diem, whom he had known for years. The major cities of South Vietnam were "living under a reign of terror," he reported to the National Security Council. And while Vietnamese citizens blamed the Nhus for most of their problems, they were increasingly coming to associate Diem himself with arrests of students and abuse of the Buddhists. A growing number of students, he said, viewed the Viet Cong as a "preferred alternative to existing government." It was time, he suggested, for the United States to "get out with honor."[39] The suggestion brought stern rebukes from McNamara, Rusk, and Lyndon Johnson.

To follow up, Kennedy dispatched Krulak and Joseph Mendenhall for another on-the-spot assessment, but they returned in total disagreement, the Marine general having seen progress in the war, while

Mendenhall found a South Vietnamese government teetering on collapse. Kennedy sardonically asked whether they had gone to the same country. With that useless assessment and with Lodge and Harkins on separate tracks, the President then sent McNamara and Taylor to Saigon to do the job all over again. They were accompanied by Bill Sullivan. The military picture was anything but as bright as Krulak had found it; and to their surprise, they discovered that the South Vietnamese generals were again laying plans for a coup.

To Sullivan's dismay, Taylor began writing another report infused with optimism, proposing the withdrawal of one thousand American troops by year's end and looking toward removing most of the rest by the end of 1965. Furious, Harriman's man argued that "anything as phony as this" couldn't be given to the President, and Taylor agreed to take out the troop-reduction language. On the way home, the debate started all over again, with Taylor arguing that a withdrawal target would put pressure on the Vietnamese to fight harder.[40]

Sullivan went to Harriman's house for breakfast the morning after their return, and together they proceeded to the White House, where they were joined by Rusk, John McCone, and several others for the mission's oral report to the President. Harriman was prepared to take up the argument where Sullivan had left off, but after an hour the meeting broke up with no indication that anything would be said about troop withdrawals in 1965.

Rusk, McNamara, and Taylor remained behind with the President; and when the White House issued its statement on the mission later in the day, it announced that America had turned the corner in Vietnam and suggested that troops would be coming home in 1965.

Feeling personally deceived, Sullivan demanded to know what had happened. McNamara claimed the reference to troop withdrawals had gotten into the statement by mistake, but shortly afterward went to Congress and made the same statement himself. Although Sullivan was outraged at the defense secretary's duplicity, Harriman blamed Rusk for talking Kennedy into a commitment that had no chance of fulfillment.

Watching the situation deteriorate, Kennedy was looking toward another shake-up once he got past the election, perhaps replacing Rusk with McNamara.[41] He was already thinking of replacing Lodge in Saigon as well.

Some of Averell's friends, including Hilsman, who had heard Bob Kennedy muse about the possibility of Harriman as secretary of state, thought there was still a chance that Averell might yet get the Foggy Bottom job he had so long coveted.[42] But that had been before the notorious coup cable.

Though the President had avoided criticism of Averell in the episode, Harriman knew Kennedy's confidence in him was shaken. After

working his way to the seventh floor, he was suddenly viewed as a problem. Almost overnight, he looked ten years older. Privately, the President and the attorney general talked of finding a way to rehabilitate him, to find a job that would get him out of the Vietnam business. There was a need to put more emphasis on hemispheric matters, and the President thought that one way to solve two problems might be to create a new post of undersecretary for Latin American affairs for him.[43]

As deeply as the administration had involved itself in the machinations against Diem, Kennedy still appeared stunned when the long-anticipated coup ended with the assassination of Diem and Nhu on November 1. The United States could technically claim that it had been a Vietnamese affair; but the administration had conditioned the atmosphere, beginning with the Harriman-Hilsman cable to Lodge.

By that time, Averell was already turning more attention to hemispheric problems. The afternoon of November 22 was set aside for a meeting with oil company executives about the future of their contracts with the government in Argentina. Beforehand, he went to a Hilsman luncheon for a delegation of politicians from the Philippines. He was finishing his dessert and talking with Senator Frank Church of Idaho about extremism in American politics when Church was called to the telephone. A minute later, the senator rushed back into the room, his face ashen. The President had been shot, he said, and was feared dead. There was a moment of silence, and then turmoil, shouted questions, and people getting up from the table to head for telephones. Averell hadn't heard; and when Church repeated the news, his reaction was that it couldn't be true. "No, Sir, I'm not joking," said Church.[44]

Averell heard the shattering confirmation of Kennedy's death in George Ball's office moments later. So undone that he could think of nothing else to do, he convened his oil meeting, but it lasted for only a few minutes. When an executive tastelessly suggested an urgent approach to the new President to write the government of Argentina in behalf of American oil interests, he adjourned in disgust.

He spent the afternoon helping Ball, who was, if anyone truly was, running the United States government, since Rusk and several other Cabinet members were airborne, coming home after turning back from a flight to the Far East. As darkness fell, Averell drove out to Andrews Air Force Base with Ball and Alexis Johnson, joining the official mourning party standing silently on the floodlit ramp as the President's casket was lowered from the rear door of *Air Force One*.

The following days were a blur of meetings and trips to airports to greet delegations arriving from all over the world for the state funeral. While Rusk and Ball attended to ceremonial duties, Harriman sat down with visitors who brought urgent diplomatic problems with them—an insurgency developing against the government in the Dom-

inican Republic, intelligence warnings of political upheaval in Brazil, and signs of new trouble between India and Pakistan over Kashmir. He met with Turks, Romanians, Cambodians, and Indonesians, going to embassies to receive messages they had hoped to present to Lyndon Johnson and finally saying good-bye to the dignitaries as they departed after the funeral.

At a State reception following the President's burial on the hillside in Arlington, he took Deputy Premier Anastas Mikoyan of the Soviet Union aside and warned that the United States government had not taken kindly to the Soviet news agency's propaganda broadcasts attributing the President's assassination to right-wing extremists.

Later, as the new President prepared to occupy the White House, the Harrimans packed their own bags and moved into a hotel on Wisconsin Avenue. Jacqueline Kennedy and her two small children had no obvious place to go, and Averell had sent her word that his home was hers.

Chapter XXIV

AMBASSADOR FOR PEACE

An Uncertain Mandate

Dear Mr. President,

I am anxious to have a talk with you about how I can be of most assistance to you and your administration. I am keen to continue to work for you, as I have for previous Presidents in whatever way seems most useful. I am not looking for any decisions but would like your guidance and judgment. If you could spare me a few minutes before the end of the year, either here or in Texas, I would be most grateful.

Sincerely,
Averell[1]

It was a month after the 1964 election, and it was the second such message that Harriman had sent Lyndon Johnson since he had won the White House in his own right. The first, which had gone unanswered, had been a desperate attempt to establish himself with a President and an administration that increasingly considered him irrelevant.

"With a new administration, a President has an unusual opportunity for a few months at least . . . to establish a fresh image, to get out of certain rigidities and dead ends, to take new tacks, and give new inspiration to world leadership," he said in the plaintive first memorandum to Johnson.

I would like to play a part if you care to have me. Fortunately, I chose my ancestors well, and I am still able to outpace some of the younger men.

During the past year, I have had a seven-day-a-week job, much of it doing details which I think others could handle as well, while I have not been consulted on many of the major issues. Presidents Roosevelt, Truman, and Kennedy used me as a pinch hitter for special negotiations, in addition to my regular duties. By luck or good fortune, my batting average has been surprisingly good.

In recent years, it is perhaps because I have been around a long time and people associate me with Roosevelt and other historic periods, I am continually struck by my personal acceptance on the part of leading personalities wherever I go.

In Russia, Khrushchev treated me with respect, because I sat next to Stalin when he was at the lower end of the table. Kosygin met me first when he was an assistant to Mikoyan at a time when I was negotiating with Stalin. I know Harold Wilson from his days as a rising civil servant when I was dealing with Churchill and the British War Cabinet as President Roosevelt's personal representative. Erhard knows me from 1948 when we brought the Germans into the Organization for European Economic Cooperation against the opposition of Clay and others who wanted Germany to be represented by the Military Government. The Latinos seem to associate me with Roosevelt. To mention a few.

As a result of my experiences over the years, I feel that I can be of value to you in some of the tough negotiations ahead and also in advising on some of the difficult problems we face.

I think that my work for you during the past year has shown that I am not looking for honors and am ready to take on any work. I would like, however, to be in a position to come to you on matters where I feel my past experience has a contribution to make. I had this relationship with Presidents Roosevelt, Truman, and Kennedy, and never misused it.[2]

The Kennedy team had long since started to break up, but Harriman was hanging on. He had no cachet with the Johnson people. If he were younger, he had told Roger Hilsman a few months earlier, he would have quit. But he was seventy-three years old and it was no longer possible for him to walk out on the Washington game. He knew it and Marie knew it. If he quit government, she told friends, he would turn into an old man and he would soon be dead.

Harriman had known Johnson since the thirties. They had met in

Sam Rayburn's office when LBJ was a skinny, hustling secretary to Texas congressman Richard Kleberg and Averell was in Washington keeping an eye on the New Deal's securities reform bill. Theirs was a typical politicians' relationship. All they had in common were party loyalty, a few mutual heroes, and a lot of identical mementos and autographed pictures from the New Deal, the Fair Deal, and the New Frontier. But when circumstances called for it, either would claim the other as an intimate in the Democratic party's great struggles for noble causes.

When Johnson squeaked into the Senate in 1948, Harriman was overseeing the Marshall Plan in Paris. He fired off a congratulatory cable to Johnson City, assuring the Texan that "all of your many friends and admirers in Paris cheered when we heard of your election. It is a great thing for the country."[3]

Afterward, when he was back home working for Truman, he would sometimes include Johnson among breakfast guests he invited to receive the administration slant on crises in Korea and NATO or on the problems with General MacArthur and Louis Johnson. The sessions helped Democrats on Capitol Hill prepare for trouble before Republicans got the bit in their teeth. LBJ hadn't been much engaged in foreign policy at the time, but Harriman found it worthwhile to stay in touch with him because Johnson had an acute sense of congressional moods—as evidenced by his rise to the Senate's Democratic leadership in 1953.

Later, while he was governor, Averell had been active on a panel that advised the Democratic National Committee on policy and political strategy. Johnson considered the committee an infringement on the prerogatives of the party's congressional leaders and its members a nuisance. These views were made known in "blunt and heated" fashion, but Averell went right ahead with his advising, considering himself at least Lyndon Johnson's equal in the party and his insights on national issues no less useful than the senator's.[4]

Neither LBJ nor Texas did anything to advance Harriman's presidential ambitions in 1952 and 1956, and New York returned the favor when Johnson made his own 1960 bid for the nomination. Unlike so many of his friends, however, Harriman applauded Kennedy's selection of Johnson as a running mate. It was nothing but smart ticket balancing, he thought, giving Kennedy a shot at holding the border states, if not the Deep South. As far as Johnson was personally concerned, he told his friend C. L. Sulzberger soon after the inauguration, he had no use for him.[5]

Candor of that sort was reserved for a few intimates, though. Seeing Johnson fretting in the vice-presidency, left out of decisions, and suffering imagined and innocuous slights by Kennedy men, Harriman had been studiously attentive to him. He made it a point to brief him after missions for the President, to seek his advice, and to stay in touch with

him socially. After Johnson arrived from Dallas with Kennedy's body, Averell had been one of the first to see him and offer to stay as long as he was wanted and serve wherever he was needed. The postelection letters came after a largely unsuccessful campaign of flattery and self-promotion through the entire year that Johnson had been President.

The decline of Averell's fortunes began when Thomas Mann was made the President's Latin American specialist less than a month after Johnson moved into the White House. Appreciating the problems created by his age, membership in the Eastern establishment, and close friendship with Robert Kennedy, Harriman courted Johnson more earnestly than he ever had Roosevelt, Truman, or Kennedy. Seldom did he return from a mission abroad without a little gift. In Iran, he picked up the best caviar to be had. In Afghanistan, he bought a handsome antique musket. Everywhere, he found something to send along to the Oval Office with a little note of praise and admiration. There were flowers for Lady Bird's birthday, congratulations on anniversaries, get-well notes, and faithful applause in moments of triumph. Later, when the Johnson daughters, Lynda Bird and Lucy Baines were married, each was given a huge party where members of the diplomatic corps, the President's Cabinet, and the other leaders of official Washington spilled out of the drawing room into a huge tent on a terrace beside the Harriman pool.

When the 1964 presidential campaign had rolled around, he eagerly volunteered to go on the hustings for LBJ and Hubert Humphrey. Rusk was happy to keep his distance on grounds that foreign policy had no place in partisan politics. It was a gospel that Harriman had long preached, and still did, but easily ignored when it suited him. Barry Goldwater was going after the State Department and administration foreign policy with gusto; and though he was not doing much damage, Harriman went to White House aide Douglass Cater and urged that somebody from the State Department get out and answer the broadsides. "If Rusk is unwilling," Cater told the President, "Harriman says he would like to have this job. He doesn't feel the Department should be a eunuch incapable of defending itself."[6]

With a green light from Johnson, he hit the road, hopping commercial flights out of Washington National Airport at dawn, taking dogleg connecting routes and long drives to reach South Fulton, Kentucky, Worthington, Minnesota, Ames, Iowa, or familar towns of the Illinois Central and Union Pacific. With the Johnson campaign mercilessly portraying Goldwater as a man not to be entrusted with nuclear weapons, Averell's mere presence as the negotiator of the Limited Test Ban Treaty made a powerful point for the Johnson-Humphrey ticket.

He returned from campaign swings with glowing after-action reports, detailing favorable receptions and a strong tide running for the Democrats. "I underlined the need for a bipartisan approach in arriving

at foreign policy, referring to Arthur Vandenberg and your own role," he told Johnson after a stump appearance in Kentucky, adding with a rare attempt at self-deprecating humor, "For some reason the speech went better than usual—standing applause after, as well as before, I spoke."[7]

The lobbying didn't end with the campaign. He lathered Johnson with praise for the way the administration steamrolled the Kennedy civil rights program through Congress and launched its own "war on poverty." "Marie and I join the many who were deeply moved by your historic speech last night," he wrote Johnson the morning after his address to a joint session of Congress unveiling the 1965 Voting Rights Act. "It was one of the greatest speeches ever made in the halls of Congress. The simplicity and eloquence of your words will surely carry around the world and offset the malicious propaganda that is being spread. I was interested to hear when I was in Afghanistan and India that people were beginning to say that while opposition to discrimination was talked about in many countries, the United States under your leadership was the only country that was at last doing something effective about it."[8]

Old friends, who had watched him give the treatment to other Presidents, thought he was finally overdoing it with Johnson. They winced at his egregious efforts to curry favor with public gestures such as the parties for the Johnson daughters. "His tendency to get behind the President no matter what must have been exacerbated by age," said Mike Forrestal. "It became really undignified, self-deceiving, and embarrassingly partisan."[9] Said Chet Cooper, who worked with him as closely as anyone through the Johnson years, "I wouldn't want to use the word *grovel*—but I guess I just did."[10]

An insecurity had been there all along, but never readily discernible as long as he was doing vital work. Overtaken by age and sidelined by the administration, he betrayed his hunger for approval. "He had a sense that he really didn't belong," said Milton Katz, who had known him since the spring of 1933 and worked at his side through the Marshall Plan years. "Separated from his role in important affairs, he had a horrible feeling that he had no personal significance as a human being. There wasn't an independent, defining sense of who he was. When you got down to the inner core, you found that it wasn't filled. There was a vacuum, and he sensed it himself. He was at his best when he had a big job, as he had in World War II, the Marshall Plan, and NATO days, and in a sense he was at his worst when he didn't have a big job, because he was fleeing the vacuum inside him."[11]

No amount of obsequious attention could make Averell a Johnson man the way he had been a Truman man and a Kennedy man. He had his own political persona; he had his own following, a following that

included too many people who neither personally nor politically admired LBJ. Harriman's best friends were gone from the administration before Johnson completed the last months of Kennedy's term. Arthur Schlesinger departed almost immediately. Hilsman left, with Rusk and Ball vying for the pleasure of personally firing him. Mike Forrestal moved from the White House to the State Department and, shortly, back to New York to practice law. Carl Kaysen had returned to Harvard even before Kennedy's death.

With tensions between Johnson and Robert Kennedy becoming the talk of Washington, Averell was suspect to Johnson no matter what he did. He grabbed an opportunity to serve the President and himself by encouraging the attorney general to run for the Senate in New York, once it became obvious that Kennedy could not continue in the administration.

While McGeorge Bundy stayed on as Johnson's national security adviser until March 1966, he was less and less inclined to involve Averell. Walt Rostow, Bundy's successor, simply ignored him altogether. The Counterinsurgency Committee, which had provided Harriman Cabinet-level work and access to the national security machinery, continued to exist in name only.

As Johnson shaped his Great Society with a blizzard of domestic legislation reminiscent of Roosevelt's first weeks in office, foreign policy decisions settled back into the traditional channels that had fallen into disuse with Kennedy's hands-on style and deployment of special envoys like Harriman. For a change, there was genuine rapport between the White House and Rusk, and the secretary of state began to exert himself as he never had in Kennedy's days, particularly on administration policy in Vietnam. Harriman was more isolated than ever at the top of the State Department, and his messages to Johnson after the election made it clear that he preferred to get out as undersecretary for political affairs.

A few weeks after Thomas Mann had become Johnson's trouble-shooter for Latin America, the State Department's dealings with the embassy in Saigon, the Pentagon, and the South Vietnamese government were put into the hands of a special working group reporting directly to Rusk. Even though the group was headed by his protégé, Bill Sullivan, Averell himself was cut out of the communications loop. He no longer saw the important cable traffic between Washington and Saigon or got his daily briefing from the assistant secretary for Far Eastern affairs. When he went to Bill Bundy—who had moved over from the Pentagon to succeed Hilsman at FE—and demanded to know why he was being bypassed, he was told only that Rusk had ordered it.

As usual, he was left out of dealings with the Soviets by the secretary, and out of European issues by Ball. A few months after Johnson moved into the White House, he was "exiled to Africa," as he put it, sent back

to the area where he had auditioned for Kennedy during the 1960 campaign.[12] It remained a job that commanded Washington's attention only when there seemed to be danger of the Russians making a move.

After having high visibility in Kennedy's campaign and the 1961 Congo crisis, Africa was again in the news when Johnson assumed the presidency. His announcement in March 1964 that Averell was being put in charge of African affairs was an easy way to make an emphatic statement of American interest. Not only was Harriman a conspicuous figure of American diplomacy whose decline was not yet perceived abroad, he knew most of the new leaders of Africa and had a personal civil rights record which endowed him with credibility.

Harriman was sent to Africa on his first special mission for Lyndon Johnson—after being given all of three minutes for a photo session with the President before he departed. As he left, the White House was already fending off reporters asking the obvious question of whether the United States' most seasoned diplomat had been demoted.

In Ghana he spent two hours counseling President Kwame Nkrumah about the country's flirtation with the Communists. The mercurial Nkrumah had grandiose notions of leading the whole continent, and Harriman caught him at a heady time. He had just received Premier Chou En-lai of China, and he appeared ready to take his country leftward in spite of huge sums—including the $25 million Volta hydroelectric project—lavished upon it by the United States. Washington was not opposed to neutralist regimes, Harriman told him, but communism was quite another matter. As a result of Nkrumah's equivocation on the matter of private investment in Ghana, Kaiser Aluminum Company, to mention but one American firm, was having second thoughts about a huge plant it had planned to build. In the end, Nkrumah agreed to issue a statement that he was anxious to have capitalist enterprises invest in his country. That was fine for the moment, but Harriman told Johnson that Ghana would require the administration's constant attention "to prevent too many and too deep relapses."[13]

The crisis that took Harriman back to Africa was not Ghana and Nkrumah, however, but the rising threat of tribal and civil warfare in the Congo four years after its independence. Newly independent from Belgium, the Congo had presented Kennedy with the first full-blown crisis of his administration, and violence threatened to erupt again in the spring of 1964. United Nations troops had forcefully put down the secessionist movement in Katanga Province after its leader Moise Tshombe had reneged on promises to cooperate with the central government. With the last five thousand UN troops preparing to end their four-year peacekeeping hitch in the country, the Johnson administration wanted to know whether the Congolese Army could be trusted once the UN troops were gone. In the capital, there was euphoria over the UN's

imminent departure, but resistance to the central government still burned in the countryside, where tribesmen neither understood nor liked the concept of national unity.

The Congolese Army had huge equipment needs, especially for vehicles to move government troops about a country the size of Western Europe. Its troops were poorly trained, possessing only rudimentary infantry skills, and a long-planned international training program was still nothing more than an outline on paper. But what concerned Averell more than that, after his spending hours with Prime Minister Cyrille Adoula, was that nearly nothing had been done to forge ties between the national government and the provincial capitals. In Léopoldville, the government knew dangerously little about the activities of Tshombe, who had gone into exile in Spain after his secessionist movement was put down, or about the possibility of his again trying to take control of Katanga.

As feared, the Congo shortly plunged into a new crisis, which was just as bad but altogether different from the last. Tshombe did not try to retake Katanga, but returned from exile, and to Washington's considerable chagrin, President Joseph Kasavubu named him Prime Minister. Harriman could suggest no alternative to continued military aid to the government, in spite of its unsavory new leader, and the administration agreed, following his recommendation that it be provided "quietly" and with the clear understanding that it was not "unqualified."[14] In July, Tshombe began assembling another army of white mercenaries, including elements of the force he had used in Katanga, but this time his objective was to put down a Chinese-supported rebellion by Simba tribesmen in the northern reaches of the country.

When the rebels captured Stanleyville in August, Tshombe asked for three battalions of American paratroopers to help retake the city, but the request was summarily denied. Instead, he was provided four C-130 transport planes, five B-26s equipped with reconnaissance cameras, and a few T-28s to fly air cover. The crisis deepened through autumn as the insurgents of the "Congo Peoples' Republic" rounded up more than three thousand white hostages from nineteen countries.

Harriman had pressed the administration to make contingency plans for the emergency evacuation of foreigners; and with the taking of the hostages, he was for preparing for a quick rescue operation. George Ball, who stepped into the picture as crisis loomed, was insistent that the United States stay out of a lead role, and he was backed by Rusk. Having been assigned to look after Africa, Harriman felt humiliated at seeing matters taken out of his hands the first time priority attention was required. The administration, he complained, was merely aggravating matters and making the hostages more valuable by repeated public expressions of concern for their safety. "I can only think of how I would

feel if I were there," he told Deputy Defense Secretary Cyrus Vance. "I would want everything done to get out of there before I got butchered. It seems I was told to take care of Africa, and then every important decision is taken out of my hands."[15]

Another month went by before the government of Belgium, with the help of American transport planes, finally launched a rescue mission. At dawn on the morning of November 24, American C-130s dropped six hundred paratroopers over Stanleyville as infantrymen struck rebel strongholds where hostages were held. For fifty of the captives, it was too late. Priests and nuns, having no valuables with which to ransom themselves, had been hacked to death, mutilated, and cannibalized by the Simbas. Just minutes before the planes appeared, rebels adorned in feathers and monkey fur began herding 1,700 foreigners, including 55 Americans, into Patrice Lumumba Square, preparing to shoot them.

Army chief of staff Earle Wheeler gave Harriman the credit for getting the mission approved. It was, he said "a shining example of the use of military force to achieve a worthy political and humanitarian end."[16]

Harriman finally got his answer from Johnson in February, 1965. For the second time in his career, he was named ambassador-at-large. He was out of the State Department and the isolation on the seventh floor and once again working directly for the President.

He thought it was his opportunity to get back into the diplomatic jetstream as he had never able to do in the number three post at Foggy Bottom, to be involved once again in issues between the great powers. He especially wanted to explore the rift between Moscow and its Communist Chinese ally.

Johnson had nothing so important in mind. He was less tolerant than Kennedy of Averell's deafness, and he was less appreciative— perhaps even jealous—of his stories about Roosevelt, Churchill, and Stalin. And, above all, he considered Harriman too much of a Bobby Kennedy man.

The only Johnson men Averell could count on to help him in the Oval Office were Bill Moyers, the White House press secretary, and presidential assistant Jack Valenti. The latter tried, even after leaving the President's staff, to ease him into the second circle of advisers. Harriman was able, wise, and good "armor plate" against liberals rumbling against the administration's policy in Vietnam, he kept telling Johnson, but to no avail.[17]

Harriman later complained that he was "shut out day by day, squeezed and squeezed and never allowed to see the President."[18] Some of the slights seemed blatantly calculated, as when the White House omitted him from the U.S. delegation to Churchill's funeral in January

1965. Crushed, he wrote Johnson a note begging to be included. Aside from Bernard Baruch, he said, he was Churchill's oldest friend in America. "It would mean much," he said, "if I could go to the funeral as a member of your party."[19] He was added to the list and sent along with Rusk and General Eisenhower to represent the United States.

His reaction to being ignored was to try harder than ever to be a Johnson man. As the administration waded deeper into Vietnam, he defended positions that he personally abhorred. He was sometimes sad, sometimes angry, but he was publicly unwavering. He had never set a pace more demanding than the one of his first year as Johnson's roving ambassador. In January, he went to Paris. In March, he was in Jerusalem, Tel Aviv, London, and New Delhi. In May, he called in Bogotá, Lima, Buenos Aires, Rio, Brasília, Santiago, Montevideo—and Addis Ababa. In July, he visited Moscow, Bonn, and Belgrade. In August, he was back in London; and in November, he was off to Helsinki and Copenhagen. At the end of the year, he returned to Belgrade, making his second stop on a thirty-thousand-mile mission that included Warsaw, Paris, Cairo, New Delhi, Canberra, Bangkok, Vientiane, Saigon, Manila, and Honolulu.

On the journey to South America, he had the unenviable chore of explaining Johnson's armed intervention in a political crisis in the Dominican Republic. With no instructions except to clear up any misunderstandings, he briefed eight chiefs of government in seven days.

As Harriman departed Washington on his emergency mission, fourteen thousand U.S. Marines and paratroopers were in Santo Domingo, with more arriving every hour. What had begun as an operation to protect American lives had expanded to one of maintaining political stability. Ordered by the President without consultation with the Organization of American States, the military intervention outraged Latin America, where it was widely taken as an action to prevent the return of deposed president Juan Bosch. Within hours of the Marines' landing, there were attacks on U.S. embassies, consulates, and American-owned businesses.

In private, the leaders visited by Harriman were more sympathetic than they were in public. Humberto Castelo Branco in Brazil and Marco Robles in Panama were firmly behind the U.S. action and were willing to back an OAS peacekeeping force. When Peruvian officials suggested that distinguished statesmen instead of Marines should have been dispatched to the Dominican capital, Harriman grumpily replied that moral force would have been as effective against the Communists supporting Juan Bosch as it was against Lenin and Trotsky in the October revolution of 1917.

Two days after his return to Washington, the hemispheric peace-

keeping force that he had been promoting was approved, legitimizing Washington's first intervention in Latin America since 1927.

The same week Harriman became roving ambassador, Viet Cong guerrillas slipped into an American outpost near Pleiku in South Vietnam's central highlands and launched an attack killing eight Americans, wounding more than one hundred, and destroying ten fighter planes. In retaliation, Johnson ordered air raids against barracks and staging areas in the southern part of North Vietnam, beginning a new phase of the war. The U.S. policy of using air strikes for retaliation was replaced by systematic bombing designed to drive the North Vietnamese to the conference table.

Having seen how the German bombing had stoked defiance in World War II England, Harriman doubted the policy's effectiveness and feared it was drifting toward "applying the stick without the carrot."[20] But while he was consulted on none of the big escalation decisions in 1965, he was found useful in publicly supporting them. Mindful of Valenti's observation that Averell could provide armor plate against the liberals, Johnson put his roving ambassador on the road.

Regardless of his feelings about the bombing, he welcomed the daily opportunity to demonstrate his loyalty to the President and the team, and perhaps worm his way toward the inner circle of the presidency yet one more time. He went out and vigorously justified the air raids and expounded the administration gospel on preventing a Communist conquest. Allowing South Vietnam to fall, he told a newspaper interviewer, "would be like letting Hitler march into the Rhineland in the 30's. It would be as if President Truman failed to act in Korea in 1950."[21]

As Kennedy's men had brought the White House favorable war news from their early trips to Vietnam, Harriman brought LBJ good news from across America, emphasizing his favorable receptions and his positive press coverage as evidence of staunch support of the war. Even from his most intimate friends, he would stand for no criticism of Lyndon Johnson or his policies. At a Georgetown cocktail party, he upbraided Arthur Schlesinger for contributing to the death of American soldiers through his war opposition. When Mark Chadwin, a young historian who had joined his personal staff, condensed seven or eight paragraphs of fawning praise of the President in a speech draft, Harriman exploded at the impertinence of an upstart slighting the President. And when Waldemar Nielsen, a lieutenant from the Truman days, criticized the escalation of the conflict, he got a scorching Harriman letter of reprimand.

Sensitive to Johnson's paranoia about leaks, he scrupulously followed orders to report every contact with the press. Even if his neighbor

Joe Kraft strolled across the street for a dip in the pool, Harriman reported the contact to the White House.

But with 75,000 Americans in South Vietnam and the war going no better, the administration's Indochina policy became harder and harder to sell. For the first time in his life, he was shouted down by an audience. The experience rattled and unnerved him because it came on the stately campus of Cornell University at Ithaca, New York—not in some union hall or at a street-corner rally. He got through his prepared remarks, but his answers to questions were drowned out by boos and catcalls from demonstrators wearing masks representing the face of death and questioners who made him defend the bombing and the possibility of more troops being sent to support the government in Saigon. He was still shaken when he got back to Washington, but in his report to Johnson, he glossed over the incident: A small minority had kept him from completing a few answers, he told the President, but otherwise the meeting had been "clearly useful." The interest stirred by the antiwar activists in fact "provided a unique opportunity for the Administration to send out speakers to provide the necessary information to those who want to support you and rebut the opposition."[22]

When there was any kind of a peace initiative, he was always among the first to jump behind it, as he did in April 1965 when Johnson offered Hanoi a part in a regional economic development plan in exchange for peace. The idea was rejected less than a week after LBJ dangled a $1 billion carrot, but Harriman loved it because it had a resonance of the New Deal and included a role for the Soviet Union in the economic development of Southeast Asia. The key to peace in Southeast Asia, Harriman kept insisting, as he had since the Geneva conference on Laos, lay in Moscow. But his new job produced no presidential assignment to get him to the Soviet capital, so he decided to vacation there. Ostensibly, he was going to take in an international film festival, although he hadn't entered a movie theater in years and had seen few films since Stalin's screenings after Kremlin banquets. But since he was going to be in Moscow anyway, he told Ambassador Dobrynin, he might as well see Aleksey Kosygin and party chairman Leonid Brezhnev. There had been no top-level contact between the U.S. and Soviet governments since Khrushchev's ouster nine months earlier, and Harriman had been horrified to learn that Kosygin had been in Hanoi sounding out the North Vietnamese on possible peace negotiations when heavy air strikes hit in February 1965.

Thus, in July, while Johnson contemplated the troop commitment that led him into a land war in Asia, Harriman was in Moscow, killing most of his "vacation" meeting government functionaries while he waited for Kosygin to return from a trip. When the Premier got back, Harriman pressed to find whether he might quietly help get the North Vietnamese

to the conference table. Moscow had no authorization to negotiate for Hanoi, Kosygin replied, but he emphasized that his Vietnamese comrades did not exclude a political settlement, "even one bypassing the Chinese."[23] Averell went home certain that the Soviets wanted to see the war ended but were in no position to deny support to Hanoi for fear of pushing the North Vietnamese into close alignment with China.

A week later Johnson made his fateful announcement that fifty thousand additional American troops would be sent to South Vietnam, with more to follow if necessary. Averell was in Yugoslavia seeing Marshal Tito when he heard the news, and the Yugoslav President echoed Kosygin's claim that Hanoi would negotiate if the United States would stop bombing. The White House was hardly in a mood for the messages that Harriman brought home, but by the end of the year Johnson's secretary of defense, Robert McNamara, had developed serious doubts that bombing was the answer.

With air strikes suspended for the Christmas holidays, McNamara persuaded Johnson to keep the planes grounded for a while longer to see if a favorable reaction might be forthcoming from Hanoi. Then, against the advice of Rusk and Ball and an array of others, the President also decided to launch a highly visible "peace offensive" reaching around the globe. Portrayed as a mighty quest for some diplomatic opening, the gaudy demonstration of Johnson's commitment to peace was just the kind of exercise where LBJ found Harriman useful.

Averell was in his office at State when Johnson called him on December 28. "I want to get negotiations started," he said, "and I want you to go and see some of those friends of yours in Eastern Europe, and I want you to put pressure on Hanoi to get negotiations going."[24] More importantly he wanted Harriman to come back prepared to tell Congress that Lyndon Johnson had sent him "the last mile" in search of a peace settlement.[25] A plane was waiting at Andrews—the sooner he could leave, the better. Eight hours later, he was off for Warsaw on the first leg of a journey that would last three weeks.

His was far from the only mission getting under way. United Nations Ambassador Arthur Goldberg was sent off to see Pope Paul VI, Charles de Gaulle, and Prime Minister Harold Wilson. Assistant Secretary of State Mennen Williams was ordered to Tunisia, Ethiopia, Morocco, Algeria, Kenya, Tanzania, Uganda, Nigeria, Ghana, the Ivory Coast, Liberia, Guinea, and Senegal. McGeorge Bundy was sent to Canada, and Vice-President Humphrey to South Korea, Taiwan, Japan, and the Philippines.

Ball, who was summoned from a Florida vacation to brief key senators and handle coordination, thought it was "futile and unbecoming," as did Rusk, although he finally joined in the recommendation to extend the pause.[26]

The flying circus was launched with no preparation. Harriman was crossing the Atlantic before the American embassy in Warsaw was even advised that he was coming. Ambassador John Gronouski, at a trade fair in Poznań, had to be rousted from bed and rushed back to the capital. Jerzy Michalowski, Poland's undersecretary of the foreign ministry, was shaken awake by a phone call before dawn, advising him that Harriman's plane was approaching Polish air space and needed a Warsaw landing clearance.

In spite of the helter-skelter beginning, Averell was able to go at once into a meeting with Foreign Minister Adam Rapacki and Communist party chairman Wladyslaw Gomulka, who was rarely seen by Western diplomats, including the American ambassador. His pitch was that the United States was prepared to go more than halfway to reach a diplomatic resolution of the war. He was armed with a fourteen-point proposal drawn up weeks earlier putting down all the conditions for getting to the conference table, and he found Rapacki and Michalowski attentive listeners. Gomulka responded with a tirade that the bombing was uniting North Vietnam just as Poland had been united by the brutality of the Nazis. The United States was going to lose in Vietnam, and Poland was prepared to help Hanoi accomplish that end.[27] As Harriman departed Warsaw for Belgrade the next morning, however, Michalowski was secretly leaving for Moscow on a mission that would wind up in Hanoi encouraging the North Vietnamese to negotiate.

The President had first suggested Averell make stops in Warsaw and Belgrade, then return by way of Paris. But that, the emissary concluded, would hardly prepare him to tell Congress that he had gone the last mile in search of peace. He had two full flight crews and sleeping accommodations aboard his executive jet, so the possibilities were unlimited.

On New Year's Day, he saw Tito and, on his advice, decided to call on Gamal Abdel Nasser in Cairo. The Egyptian leader had good connections with the Chinese, and there was a chance he could shed light on the state of relations between Hanoi and Peking, as well as on Hanoi's perception of the war. The idea was appealing, especially since Nasser was one of the big names in world politics he had never met. Thereafter, a long schedule began to unfold.

Before it was over, he wound up in eleven countries, passing through Bangkok on three different occasions, talking not only with Gomulka, Tito and Nasser, but Prime Minister Sato in Tokyo, Ayub Khan in Pakistan, the Shah of Iran, Foreign Minister Thanat Khoman in Thailand, and Souvanna Phouma in Laos.

While Harriman was on the wing, Michalowski spent two unfruitful weeks in Hanoi. All of the traveling generated no movement toward peace; and in diplomatic circles, the widely held view was that it was counterproductive showboating at a time when secret contacts were indi-

cated. By the time Averell got to Vientiane, Souvanna Phouma had already been visited by Michalowski, who had reported that Hanoi saw the peace offensive as nothing but an American ultimatum.

Harriman returned worried that renewed air raids after the great peace offensive would leave the United States in worse shape than ever in the eyes of the world, and that the failed exercise would be used as an excuse for further escalation.

The North Vietnamese made new attacks certain by taking full advantage of the suspension. A surge of men and equipment had moved into the South, and Ho Chi Minh had denounced the peace offensive as a fraud.

After thirty-seven days, Johnson ordered the planes back into the air. Harriman entered only a mild dissent through Rusk—urging that the attacks be limited to the southern portion of North Vietnam "to convince the world that our bombing is for the purpose of interdicting traffic, not to inflict punitive damage on North Vietnam."[28] On Johnson's orders he went to antiwar Democrats in the Senate, explaining and defending all the scurrying around the world. The mission to Capitol Hill was as futile as the global extravaganza—most of the senators had already issued press releases denouncing resumption of the air raids.

Foreign Relations Committee chairman J. William Fulbright was preparing to hold televised hearings featuring Rusk and Maxwell Taylor, now ambassador in Saigon, as the principal witnesses, but Johnson did not wait to be skewered. As suddenly as he had launched the peace offensive, he announced a Honolulu summit with South Vietnam's Premier Nguyen Cao Ky and chief of state Nguyen Van Thieu to emphasize South Vietnam's struggle for a democratic social revolution. He flew to the meeting two days after it was thrown together, taking with him an entourage that included his secretary of agriculture, Orville Freeman, and secretary of health, education, and welfare, John Gardner, as well as Harriman. Borrowing heavily from Johnson's own messages, Ky rose to the occasion with a speech glorifying economic development, rural electrification, and low-income housing.

After the meeting ended with the signing of a ringing "Declaration of Honolulu," Harriman was ordered to join Vice-President Humphrey on a tour of the Pacific to brief America's allies. The Vice-President hadn't been at the meeting and had to meet Johnson in Los Angeles to be filled in on South Vietnam's social revolution before going on to Honolulu to pick up Averell and the rest of the traveling party, including Ky and Thieu, who hitched a ride to Saigon.

Beginning with an inspection of pacification programs, civic projects and troop installations in South Vietnam, the trip stretched out to two weeks and eight countries, taking the entire delegation to the brink of exhaustion. Fulbright, meanwhile, held the television spotlight with his hearings, and Robert Kennedy captured headlines by calling for the Viet Cong to be included in the postwar government of South Vietnam. Anxious to please the boss, Humphrey grew stridently anti-Communist, talking until his voice was a wheeze, taking an increasingly hard line and overreacting by calling Kennedy's suggestion the first step toward Communist control of the South.

Harriman, uncomfortable traveling with a crowd and seeing his own behavior reflected in Humphrey's feigned enthusiasm for a policy about which he had grave doubts, was crotchety, irritated by Kennedy's remarks and resentful at the Vice-President's response. Toward the end, when Humphrey called the delegation together to consider a report proclaiming the mission's great success, he stomped out, loudly announcing that he was going to bed. "I never attend meetings after midnight," he said. "You write your report, and I'll sign it blind." Humphrey was furious, and Averell mumbled under his breath that the Vice-President knew nothing of foreign policy and properly belonged back in Minneapolis.[29]

Once home, however, he was not to be outdone by Humphrey in praising the President for his handling of the summit, sending Johnson a memo lauding him for masterfully handling the Fulbright hearings and for hanging tough in Vietnam. "I wish Fulbright and Company could understand that if we quit in Vietnam, the props would be pulled out from under most countries in the East," he said. "Even in such countries as Japan and India, the Peking appeasers would get the upper hand. Your Honolulu meeting has had a profoundly beneficial effect in the area, not only because of the far-sighted substance of the declaration, but also for the much-needed prestige you gave the Saigon government."[30]

Harriman was, by the middle of 1966, frustrated and unhappy. He hadn't gained the confidence of the President, and he knew it. His differences with Rusk, who had become the dominant force in Vietnam policy as McNamara lost his taste for the war, stayed just beneath the surface, suppressed by the secretary's unfailing southern courtesy and Averell's own desire to remain on the team. The Vietnam policy was not working, but publicly Averell supported it 110 percent, passing up chances to privately urge a more moderate course on the President. When he did protest the decision to take the bombing campaign into the Hanoi and Haiphong areas, Rusk ignored him. He stayed on the job because he was sure that someday the war would have to end at a conference table, and he wanted to be there for the United States.

Only to his closest friends did he at last acknowledge his unhappiness at the steadily increasing commitment to military options without commensurate attention to a diplomatic strategy. But staying on and working

from the inside was the only way to accomplish anything, he told such confidants as Schlesinger and Galbraith, and there his new soul mate was McNamara.

When he was in the State Department building, McNamara would drop by Harriman's office and occasionally on weekends they would get together at Averell's house. The same thing was always on their mind—finding some way to get negotiations started. McNamara urged him to go to Paris secretly and see Ambassador Mai Van Bo of North Vietnam, or even talk directly with the Viet Cong in Algeria. He had become convinced that the Saigon government would only grow weaker with time. If the public in South Vietnam would accept it, he now thought the United States should accept a coalition government with Viet Cong participation in Saigon.

Neither would put his cards on the table with Johnson, though. "There were two Harrimans and two McNamaras," said Chester Cooper, who resigned from the National Security Council staff and left government in the spring of 1966, fed up with the determination of National Security Adviser Walt Rostow to bomb Hanoi into suing for peace. "At the White House, neither would express his deep reservations and doubts. Since they were reluctant to speak aloud, they would meet and try out their ideas on each other, using each other as an escape valve in a sense. In Harriman's case, the White House didn't trust him, but they couldn't fire him, because he was who he was, and he wouldn't quit because power and access to power, influence, and knowledge were his mother's milk."[31]

As always, Harriman wanted to engage the Russians in bringing about direct negotiations, and McNamara urged the President to send Averell to Moscow for another try in the summer of 1966. Plans for the trip were put in place, but there was no response from the White House.

Johnson himself had a better idea. Harriman had already been given the unenviable responsibility for all matters concerning the growing list of American prisoners of war in Vietnam, so Johnson simply declared him to also be the President's "ambassador for peace." Harriman never received his assignment in writing, and his mandate was never spelled out by the President. He professed to prefer it that way because he was left to define his own responsibilities. The title had a splendid sound, and he took it to mean that he was free to pursue any diplomatic route to peace. He recruited Cooper to join him as his chief of staff, confidant, adviser, and traveling companion and opened what was somewhat derisively called the "peace shop."

The "marching and chowder society," as Cooper called the group, assembled for a weekly brainstorming session, included Bill Bundy; Benjamin H. Read, the State Department's executive secretary; Asia specialist James Thomson; Tom Hughes, State's chief of intelligence and research;

Joseph Sisco, the assistant secretary for international organization affairs; and various others. Every Tuesday, they went over hints of signals
from Hanoi, possible channels for secret messages, and openings for
some new initiative. Their first project was to develop a response to four
points that Hanoi had been publicly using as conditions for peace, and
send it along to U Thant, the secretary general of the United Nations.
Nothing came of Thant's desire to provide a channel, nor did anything
come of dozens of other suggestions for transmitting messages. Finding
ways to get secret communications to Hanoi had never been a problem
anyway. The trouble was that neither side had anything to offer. Even
though he was ostensibly in charge of Vietnam diplomacy, Harriman
was never included in operational meetings where policy was shaped,
nor was he invited to the President's Tuesday luncheon, where targets
were approved and decisions were made. For a year, he and Cooper
grasped every flickering hint of an opening, "dreaming up ideas, chasing
will o' the wisps, pushing, cajoling."[32]

Governments, professional diplomats, and well-meaning amateurs
were all ready to help, but the bombing issue was Johnson's Tar Baby.
The harder he hit, the harder he was stuck. Hanoi refused to negotiate
unless the bombing stopped unconditionally, and Johnson refused to
stop unless the North Vietnamese assured him there would be some
form of reciprocation.

In November, with congressional elections at hand, Johnson staged
another public relations blitz. At the instigation of the White House,
President Ferdinand Marcos of the Philippines invited leaders of all the
countries with units in South Vietnam to a summit where Johnson sat
around the table with them as an equal. Focusing on negotiations and
looking toward postwar withdrawal of American troops, the Manila conference ended with a declaration calling for a phased departure of U.S.
troops as Hanoi ended its infiltration and pulled its forces back. It provided for removal of all foreign troops from the South within six months,
but it did nothing to resolve the bombing impasse or move toward a
peace settlement.

Before taking off on a visit to South Vietnam, where he delivered his
famous exhortation for troops to nail the coonskin to the wall, Johnson
summoned Harriman, who did not have to be told that another long trip
was ahead of him. This time the assignment was to visit important figures
who had not been at the table in Manila. "You know what I want," the
President told him. "Peace. You can quote me in any way that you think
would be useful. I will support anything you say."[33] Johnson offered no
itinerary.

Accompanied by Cooper, State Department spokesman Robert
McCloskey, and Hildy Shishkin, he visited eleven countries in two weeks,

keeping a killing schedule because he had to see the leaders before the summit was forgotten. In the course of his journey, he met with not only allied and neutralist political leaders but influential Buddhists and Pope Paul VI. Before landing back in Texas to give Johnson his report, he visited Singapore, Indonesia, Ceylon, India, Pakistan, Iran, Italy, France, Germany, England, and Morocco. On one numbing day, he had break- fast in New Delhi, lunch in Rawalpindi, afternoon tea with the Shah in Teheran, and still made it to Rome in time for a late-evening television interview.

Despite Johnson's dramatic pledge to get American troops—now approaching 400,000—out of Vietnam six months after a cease-fire, the bombing was still the first topic raised everywhere the mission landed. In New Delhi, the Indians as usual urged stopping unconditionally. In London, Foreign Minister George Brown warned that more escalation "might well lose you the support of all your friends in Europe, like me, who are trying to help."[34]

Unexpectedly, in Rome, however, Harriman and Cooper tapped into a promising line to Hanoi. Giovanni d'Orlandi, the Italian ambassa- dor to South Vietnam, had some months earlier introduced Henry Cabot Lodge to Janusz Lewandowski, a Polish diplomat who made regular trips between Saigon and Hanoi as a member of the International Control Commission. The three had been meeting informally through the spring and summer, and Lewandowski was anxious to be helpful.

While Harriman was talking with Foreign Minister Amintore Fan- fani, d'Orlandi told Cooper that he was returning to Saigon and thought it a propitious moment for the United States to pass Lewandowski a substantive message to take to Hanoi. Later, he took Harriman aside and repeated the suggestion; and once they were back in Washington, Averell and Cooper pressed the new initiative.

Lewandowski flew to Hanoi, taking with him the same points that Harriman had put before leaders around the world after the Honolulu summit ten months earlier. But he was also authorized to raise a new wrinkle in the bombing issue. The Phase A–Phase B Formula, as it was known in Washington, had been drafted before the Manila meeting, and one of its principal authors was Cooper.

Under the plan, the United States would announce an ostensibly unconditional bombing halt, while Hanoi would give secret assurances that it would stop sending reinforcements into South Vietnam. Although the plan would be fine-tuned and emerge in a number of different versions, it was basically the only plan the Johnson administration ever produced for stopping the air attacks.

Hanoi showed no interest in the proposal when it was relayed by Lewandowski, but hinted that it might be prepared to talk about other matters. With that flicker of interest, Johnson slapped such sharp restrictions on information that even Harriman and Cooper were briefly cut out of access to cables.

Although Washington insisted on clarifying its position further, it still appeared that a late-November face-to-face meeting between the North Vietnamese and Ambassador Gronouski would take place in Warsaw. The ambassador was preparing for a session on December 5.

Meanwhile, American bombing plans called for strikes on the outskirts of Hanoi itself, and Harriman and McNamara were commiserating over the consequences. Both felt that Johnson had come back from the Manila conference with a mistaken belief that he had the world behind him in Vietnam. McNamara had already argued against the new targets recommended by the Joint Chiefs, but Johnson himself had put them back. The secretary urged Averell to go to the President and protest the new attacks, but again neither of them would step forward and tell Johnson what they were telling each other.[35]

On December 2 and December 4, American planes carried out two raids on Hanoi, which had been delayed by sloppy weather since November 12. Unfortunately, the skies cleared at the moment when the last obstacles to a Warsaw meeting were being tackled, and with the raids, the secret initiative, code-named Marigold, died.

After his conversation with McNamara on November 26, Averell flew to Paris for a meeting recommended by Henry Kissinger. The Harvard professor had arranged for him to see Jean Sainteny, a former French intelligence officer who had served in Vietnam after World War II and retained high-level contacts in Hanoi. Sainteny said he had been told in the presence of Ho Chi Minh that North Vietnam would make an important gesture if the United States stopped bombing. He was willing to return as an intermediary and try to pick up a thread of that conversation.

Given the hopes raised by the Marigold discussions, it seemed a time to keep the diplomatic track open, but Sainteny's trip was vetoed by Charles de Gaulle. What was even more disappointing was the failure to get Aleksey Kosygin to try out a version of Phase A–Phase B in Hanoi. On February 6, the Soviet premier arrived in London for talks with Harold Wilson. Vietnam was at the top of their agenda, and Hanoi seemed to be sending signals. In January, the Russians had passed word that the American embassy should contact Hanoi's chargé d'affaires in Moscow. Accordingly, American chargé John Guthrie had knocked on the door of the North Vietnamese embassy and had been invited in, starting a series of strained and eventually useless meetings.

Again Harriman thought it a moment to demonstrate restraint in bombing the North. "I realize there is ever constant pressure for new targets," he told Rusk before Kosygin's arrival in London, "but I earnestly hope that restraint can be exercised."[36]

By the time the Premier got to London, Cooper was already there to brief the Prime Minister on the Phase A–Phase B proposal, and he remained to serve as Washington's unseen participant in the meetings. When Wilson and Kosygin got down to business, the Prime Minister orally spelled out the formula to the Soviet leader; and afterward, Cooper drafted a formal version of it for Wilson to hand to Kosygin before the Russian left for a visit to Scotland.

That night, an emergency telephone call from the White House summoned Cooper from a London theater. Unbeknownst to him or Harriman, the White House had drastically changed the U.S. position. A new text cabled to London turned the formula upside down. Instead of a bombing halt, followed by a secret agreement to cease outside reinforcement, it called for Hanoi to first give assurance that infiltration had ended. Then, the United States would announce a bombing halt.

There was a final effort to salvage something. U.S. planes were grounded in observance of the Tet holiday in Vietnam, and Wilson pressed Washington to extend the stand-down in exchange for a North Vietnamese halt in troop movements immediately to the north of the 17th parallel. The deal was to be passed to Hanoi by Kosygin.

Harriman had for weeks been urging an extension of the Tet pause. It was an opportunity, he said, for the President "to show again that he is in the lead in seeking a peaceful settlement. If Hanoi abuses the pause, it will strengthen the President's hand in the prosecution of the war."[37]

Washington's answer to Wilson arrived on Sunday night. It would agree to a continuation of the bombing hiatus, but it had to have Hanoi's acceptance on Monday morning. Obviously, there was not time, yet when the deadline passed, nothing happened for several hours. Then, in the middle of the afternoon, Hanoi broadcast a letter from Ho Chi Minh to the Pope, again demanding an unconditional bombing halt. About the same time, the American planes struck.

Acutely conscious of his limited influence with Johnson, Harriman was now more than ever unwilling to take risks in behalf of his peace initiatives. Twice, when he and Cooper were arranging to get messages to the North Vietnamese through diplomats traveling to Hanoi, Cooper pleaded with him to go to the President and demand changes in bombing schedules, but he refused. He had to preserve his political capital, he said, and wasn't going to squander it by arguing about something that was hopeless.

That autumn Cooper flew to Oslo to arrange for a Norwegian envoy to take a peace feeler to Hanoi. Getting agreement on the message was simple enough, but it took days and several contentious telephone talks with Washington before he could give the emissary his word that Hanoi would not be bombed while he was there.

When he got home, however, he was horrified to see that a truck park just outside the Hanoi airport was scheduled to be hit on the very day of the Norwegian envoy's arrival. "The goddamned trucks have been there for months," he told Averell. "They will be there next week, and they will be there in two weeks. We've committed ourselves that we wouldn't bomb, and here we are hitting the bloody airport on the day the guy arrives. You've got to go over and convince Rostow to call this off."[38] Again Harriman refused. Cooper had made the agreement, he said; and if Cooper wanted to argue for canceling the strike, he should do so, but Harriman would not personally take it up with Rostow. Fuming, Cooper went to the White House alone; as expected, Rostow turned him down. Mercifully, however, clouds settled low over Hanoi on the day of the Norwegian's arrival. They stayed for several days; and while the unsuspecting messenger was there, the fighter bombers never came.

Obviously, the "peace shop" was only for show. All the action on the dual track was on the military side, but Harriman held onto what he thought was probably his last presidential assignment. He spurned McNamara's urging to go to Johnson with his case against the bombing; but on at least two occasions, the defense secretary put him in a position where he had to disagree with the President. Trying to get the target list whittled down, McNamara telephoned from the Oval Office and asked Harriman to repeat what he had told him in private conversation, then handed the telephone to the President.

While Harriman had always chosen lieutenants willing to argue with him, none would presume to explore his relationship with Lyndon Johnson or suggest he was being duplicitous on Vietnam. In these matters, even Robert Kennedy was kept at arm's length. Averell snappishly accused the senator of taking Hanoi's side by endorsing a coalition government for South Vietnam and calling for a bombing halt in exchange for nothing more than negotiations.

Indeed, the younger men around him tried to keep him from knowing how far he had slipped. Jack Valenti continued to do what he could to keep him involved, and Cooper and Ben Read at the State Department stayed alert for a careless slight, working behind the scenes to have Averell included in obvious places where he was about to be left out.

When Johnson and Kosygin arranged to meet for two days of talks at Glassboro, New Jersey, during the Premier's visit to the United Nations, Harriman was left off the list of officials to accompany the President. Even Kosygin assumed that Harriman would be involved; and during the negotiations over a meeting site, he suggested the old Harriman mansion at Arden would be the ideal venue.

Averell, too, took it for granted that he would be going and peppered Johnson with unsolicited memoranda on what to expect from the Soviets. Telling the President that he had "a unique opportunity for progress towards negotiations for a peaceful settlement" in Vietnam, he urged Johnson to deescalate unilaterally by limiting the bombing to south of the 20th parallel "without any commitment as to the length of time this restraint would hold."[39] There was no response to his advice, and it was only through the deft intercession of Cooper and Ben Read that the White House eventually included him in the presidential party.

Cooper finally decided that the peace shop was, as much as anything, a device to occupy Averell and keep him out of the way. He was sure that, in his heart of hearts, Harriman felt the same way. So in the fall of 1967, barely more than a year after he had come back, Cooper left the government again. "It was quite clear," he said, "that my views were not unlike his. The difference was that Harriman felt that he still had a toehold."[40]

Others in the marching and chowder society had long since come to the same conclusion. Early on, Joe Sisco had begun to attend committee sessions only sporadically. "It was largely a mechanism to make it very sure that it could never be said that Averell wasn't getting his oar in."[41]

Harriman's efforts on behalf of American flyers in captivity in North Vietnam were as unproductive as his pursuit of peace talks—and more disappointing in their own way, for he was later accused by some of their families of being insensitive and making the prisoners' plight worse by keeping knowledge of their circumstances secret. It was certain that American flyers were being brutalized in captivity, but the White House and the State Department opted to keep silent, and Harriman did not quarrel with the decision. Admiral James Stockdale, who spent seven and a half years in captivity after being shot down in 1965, and his wife, Sybil, were the most outspoken. In his preoccupation with peace negotiations, Stockdale later charged, Harriman had throughout shown "a callous lack of concern."[42]

If the Harriman operation was not on the cutting edge of Vietnam policy, there were moments of hope for diplomacy. Kissinger learned that a French doctor of his acquaintance had a friend who was a friend of Ho Chi Minh. The Frenchmen, Herbert Marcovich and Raymond Aubrac, were anxious to put the connection to use, and the State Department accepted Harriman and Kissinger's suggestion that the two go to Hanoi. The Frenchmen returned believing that Hanoi was prepared to hold secret talks with the United States if the bombing stopped. The State Department proposed a return trip with the Frenchmen to tell Ho Chi Minh that the United States was prepared to stop bombing for a commitment to hold negotiations. It was an initiative that President Johnson would make public two months later as his "San Antonio Formula," but the connection was suddenly broken off in Hanoi. North Vietnam declined to issue the necessary visas. The message was relayed through the North Vietnamese representative in Paris, but there was no reply.

Although he wasn't on the payroll anymore, Cooper still dropped by to help out occasionally at the peace shop. Like McNamara, he took any chance he got to encourage Averell to stiffen up. If anybody had a chance to push Johnson onto the peace track, it was Harriman, but he wouldn't press. On at least one occasion, Cooper even drafted the language for him. "I'm not going to say that," Harriman replied, shoving a draft back at him. "Maybe you can say it, and maybe you will say it. But I won't, and that's why you are out on the street, and I'm still here."[43]

Chapter XXV

PARIS
Peace and Politics

American intelligence expected something big from the enemy in early 1968, but it foresaw nothing like the monumental Tet Offensive unleashed in the darkness of January 31. With clockwork precison, Viet Cong guerrillas materialized in simultaneous, coordinated attacks from the Demilitarized Zone all the way to the South China Sea, hurling suicide attacks against the fortresslike American embassy, the presidential palace in the center of Saigon, and the Citadel in the imperial capital at Hue. American outposts were taken under rocket attack. Government buildings were assaulted by squads armed with satchel charges; public officials, ordinary workers, and peasants loyal to the regime were kidnapped and murdered wholesale. General William C. Westmoreland, the U.S. commander who had in the previous autumn assured Americans that North Vietnamese and Viet Cong strength was on the decline, was forced into an underground command post. Ambassador Ellsworth Bunker was whisked from his residence near the embassy to a secret CIA hiding place.

By the time the bold but doomed operation was spent weeks later, the counterattack by superior U.S. and South Vietnamese firepower had killed and wounded more than fifty thousand men. Militarily, it was a colossal failure, but the operation designed to terrorize South Vietnamese loyal to the Saigon government was like gasoline on the flames of opposition to the war in America. While the enemy had made an "incredible miscalculation" and failed in every one of its military objectives, the

CIA concluded, it had made "an impressive display of strength that netted a psychological victory."[1] That was to put it mildly.

The spectacle of Communists roaming the country and attacking heavily defended installations of the mighty American military machine had made a mockery of the administration's argument that the war was gradually being won. Public confidence in Lyndon Johnson's leadership, slipping ever since the escalating war had superseded the initiatives of the Great Society, rapidly dissolved. Deep divisions split the administration; even the President's firmest Vietnam supporters in Congress and the Democratic party faltered.

As the fighting raged across South Vietnam, "Ambassador for Peace" Harriman was sorting through the ruin of another failed diplomatic initiative, one which had momentarily seemed more promising than anything since the Marigold contacts more than a year earlier. As shepherd of the State Department's secret cable traffic, Ben Read had given the latest initiative the tongue-in-cheek code name Green Bay Packer, adopting the name of the professional football powerhouse. It turned out to be the last attempt by Harriman and the Johnson administration to use secret intermediaries to bring about negotiations to end the war.

It had begun in November of 1967, when Averell led an American delegation to the dedication of Pakistan's huge new Mangla Dam, a project built in substantial part with American aid. On the way home, he made a stop in Belgrade to see Marshal Tito, as he always did when passing through that part of the world. Then, without attracting any attention, he added a stop in Bucharest. He hadn't been in Romania since 1946, he said, and just wanted to see it again.

The fact was that Prime Minister Gheorghe Maurer had been on a visit to Hanoi during the fall and had returned with the impression that the North Vietnamese were not altogether averse to negotiations. Their position had been couched in the usual rhetoric, but Maurer thought it possible that they would now agree to negotiations in exchange for a halt in American bombing. Since they had just rejected that formula, the prospect hardly seemed likely, but Maurer's report was precise and intriguing enough that Harriman urged him to go back to Hanoi to try to pick up the conversation where it left off.

The swap of a bombing halt for "productive discussions," publicly offered by President Johnson in his San Antonio Formula in September had one caveat: that North Vietnam would not take military advantage of a bombing suspension. It was the same offer secretly handed to the North Vietnamese by Henry Kissinger's friends in Paris a month before the President's speech in San Antonio. Although Hanoi had rejected Johnson's offer four days after his address, Averell thought there was a chance that a more considered response could be obtained through the Romanians. After hearing his rationale and his insistence that the President had to know more before he could move further, Maurer agreed that the Romanian government would try its hand as an intermediary. As Harriman set out for home, Deputy Foreign Minister Gheorghe Macovescu was ordered to Hanoi.

Of all the intermediaries who made the journey to Hanoi, the Romanian diplomat proved the most skillful in sensing nuances that had developed in the continuous fencing between the two sides. Hanoi's reception of the renewed contact was tantalizing enough that Macovescu flew directly to Washington to see Harriman. The State Department fine-tuned the feeler, expanding on what was meant by the "no advantage" proviso, and the Romanian returned, only to be told that the San Antonio Formula was unacceptable.

With that Harriman went back to the Soviets, who were hinting that there might be a response from Hanoi if the United States would unilaterally limit its bombing to the area just north of the Demilitarized Zone instead of pounding targets all the way to the Chinese border and around the fringes of the North Vietnamese capital itself.

Under the circumstances, any possibility seemed worthy of serious consideration. A presidential election campaign was about to begin, and unless something was done soon, the White House would be in danger of capture by the Republicans. For several months, Averell had been discussing the coming race with Washington lawyer James Rowe, a party stalwart he had known since Roosevelt days. Rowe was convinced that, with the exception of Ronald Reagan, any Republican on the horizon would beat Johnson unless real progress was made toward settlement of the war before summer. In Harriman's view, negotiations were still not out of the question in spite of Hanoi's rejection of the San Antonio Formula.

There was still a chance of getting Vietnam to the negotiating table before autumn, he told Johnson a month after Tet, if Hanoi could be made to understand that November's elections in the United States would amount to a referendum on a "tougher U.S. position." The military course being followed—Westmoreland's war of attrition—was getting nowhere. In spite of the impressive body counts, the North Vietnamese and the Viet Cong were prepared to accept their current rate of losses indefinitely.[2]

The Romanian contact having produced nothing, Harriman turned to the Soviets with a proposal that they try yet another wrinkle on the San Antonio approach. Although it had gained surprisingly little recognition, the administration had significantly clarified the President's formula just days before Tet, providing an opening for a new contact through Moscow. Appearing before the Senate Armed Services Committee considering his nomination to replace Robert McNamara at the Pentagon, the President's stalwart kitchen cabinet adviser Clark Clifford had acknowledged that Washington expected North Vietnam to continue infiltration, even if there was a bombing halt. The San Antonio Formula merely required that Hanoi not increase its normal flow of men and supplies into the South, he explained. That did not mean that Hanoi would be expected to stop all military activity.

There had been no indication that the North Vietnamese were interested or even understood that there was a new U.S. position. On March 10, Harriman invited Anatoly Dobrynin to lunch and proposed that the Soviets explain to Hanoi the significance of Clifford's answers to the Senate. By May, he argued, it would be obvious to Hanoi that its offensive had failed, and that would be the moment for a diplomatic initiative with the Soviets as the key player. The ambassador was unmoved.[3] Hanoi would have to put the bitter experience of Tet behind it before there was any chance for a diplomatic opening.

At the time, neither the State Department nor the President fully appreciated the earthquake Tet had triggered in American politics. But Johnson shortly got an inkling of the mood Harriman and Rowe had been discussing. Senator Eugene McCarthy of Minnesota, running on a peace platform and a shoestring budget, came within three hundred votes of winning the New Hampshire Democratic primary. Then, seeing Johnson perhaps mortally wounded, Robert Kennedy jumped into the race for the nomination four days later.

It was an acutely distressing moment for Harriman. He was stuck with Johnson, stuck with Vietnam, and getting nowhere in his effort to induce the President to relent on the bombing and commit himself to a negotiated settlement. If in unguarded moments, he would rage to intimates about the "goddamned cowboy" in the White House and the hopeless campaign to bomb North Vietnam to the peace table, publicly he never wavered. His gloom intensified when McNamara, who had seen the light, had been replaced by one of the principal opponents of every effort to limit the bombing. He wasn't willing to quit, so he couldn't dissent. He had never been as uncomfortable in public life, especially after RFK's decision to run against the President. Long before New Hampshire, Harriman had tried to dissuade the senator from getting into the race on the grounds that he would be another divisive force in their divided party. But after McCarthy's showing in New Hampshire, that argument was clearly moot. Knowing Averell's predicament, Kennedy didn't even consult him on his decision to get in the race, and four days went by before there was a personal call from the younger man. When he did get in touch, neither had anything to say, and the conversation lasted only seconds. "I don't expect to have a press conference soon," Harriman said, "but if it does come around I'm going to support the President."[4]

Clifford moved into the expansive defense secretary's suite a week after Joint Chiefs of Staff chairman Earle Wheeler had visited Vietnam and submitted a request for another 206,000 troops, forcing Johnson to confront once again the politically volatile decision to order a massive mobilization of the military reserves. When the request hit the new secretary's desk, it ignited a long-deferred review of the war's objectives and an unflinching look at its prospects. Rather than simply ratchet up the stakes once again, it was time to ask whether and when the war could be won and at what cost. From briefings by military officers and intelligence experts on the immediate issue of the troop request, Clifford looked outside the government to men who had shaped American policy and advised presidents through the Cold War and every national security crisis for more than a generation. Within weeks of joining the Cabinet, he was turning administration policy in the direction advocated by Harriman and the doves. Although he had known Clifford since the Truman days, Harriman had never been especially close to him. In the Johnson White House, the courtly Washington lawyer was one of the insiders of whom the President asked advice on nearly any issue of political import. It was a circle to which Harriman had never been admitted.

Averell had never realized that Clifford's opposition to bombing pauses had been based on his certainty that resumption always brought escalation. Clifford had been more perceptive of Harriman's position, sensing the tension between the President and the old man of the administration. In November 1967, the President had summoned the elders of the American foreign policy establishment—in and out of government—for briefings and several hours of discussion of war strategy. Averell had been on the long list provided to the President by Clifford and Walt Rostow, and Johnson had included him among the dozen he invited. With the war going reasonably well at the time, the session ended with Johnson's determination reinforced by the support of stalwarts, including Acheson, Bob Lovett, General Omar Bradley, and John McCloy. Through it all, Harriman sat stone-faced, saying nothing. Toward the end, when there was discussion of possible negotiations, Clifford noticed that he perked up and weighed in by advising the President that negotiation with the Communists was both "inevitable and necessary."[5]

When the Wise Men were again called in in the wake of Tet and Wheeler's request for the huge troop increase, Harriman was not included—ostensibly because the meeting was limited to nongovernment advisers. But he had sensed a change in the views of some of his contemporaries, especially Acheson, since the November meeting, and he had already been encouraging the former secretary to unburden himself thoroughly to the President.

On March 25, Clifford convened at the State Department basically

the same group which had met with the President in November—
Acheson, John McCloy, McGeorge Bundy, Douglas Dillon, retired ambassador Robert Murphy, generals Bradley, Taylor, Ridgway, and Earle
Wheeler, plus Rusk, Ball, Rostow, and UN Ambassador Arthur Goldberg. Tet had dramatically changed things. Instead of more optimism
from Clifford's briefers, they heard estimates that the war might well
continue for another five or ten years. A gloomy assessment from Philip
Habib, a plainspoken Vietnam expert just back from a trip to Saigon,
disturbed all of them more than anything else.

As the session resumed the next morning, Harriman squirmed in
his office, and when the group moved to the White House for lunch with
the President, he could sit still no longer. Just as he had taken it upon
himself to intercept Kennedy on JFK's journey to meet Khrushchev
seven years earlier, he walked into the luncheon uninvited. Except for
the head waiter, who scrambled for another place setting, everyone there
evidently assumed that he had been invited by the President, who, perhaps, thought he had been invited by Clifford.

Being an interloper, he held his tongue, listening in silence as one
Wise Man after another revealed deep misgivings at upping the ante in
Vietnam. Although Acheson had been in for a private lunch days earlier
and had told the President of his profound doubt that the conflict could
be successful, Johnson was surprised and shaken by their turnaround.
As the session broke up, he took Rusk and Clifford aside and bitterly
demanded to know who had "poisoned the well."[6] After lunch he ordered a repeat of the same briefing the others had heard, out of the
presence of Clifford, Rusk, and others in the administration. Later in the
afternoon, Harriman learned from Henry Cabot Lodge that all present
except Wheeler, Taylor, Bradley, and Murphy now wanted to disengage
in Vietnam.

Even Rusk, who had only a month earlier called suggestions of a
bombing halt "almost obscene," favored restricting strikes to the area
south of the 20th parallel. Seeing policy about to fundamentally change
for the first time since the beginning of the bombing in 1965, Harriman
argued for a halt to the bombing of all North Vietnam by mid-May. It
wasn't working; and continuing on a more limited scale, he told Rusk
the day after the luncheon with the President, was "unlikely to be effective and could be counter-productive."[7] A total suspension would provide
a strong basis to press for the Russians' help. One possibility was to follow
a bombing suspension with a request for Moscow to cut back its arms
shipments to Hanoi. If a full bombing halt produced no movement
toward negotiations and the North Vietnamese again took military advantage of U.S. restraint, then the President would have popular support
for resumption.

By the time a memorandum from them was in Rusk's hands, a major presidential speech to the nation, which had been a driving reason for the policy review, was nearing its final form. On Sunday evening, five days after his meeting with the elders, Johnson went on television from the Oval Office with his announcement that he was stopping the bombing over 90 percent of North Vietnam. "Now as in the past," he said, "the United States is ready to send its representatives to any forum, at any time, to discuss the means of bringing this ugly war to an end. I am designating one of our most distinguished Americans, Ambassador Averell Harriman, as my personal representative to such talks."[8]

Not until the end did he drop the bombshell that he was taking himself out of the presidential race. Harriman watched the telecast in Hobe Sound, where he was winding up the weekend. He had received a telephone call from Rusk to let him know officially that the President would be announcing his appointment as the American negotiator—in case there was any answer from Hanoi; but, like the rest of the country, he was dumbstruck by the conclusion. While he thought the President's retirement would help the chances of reaching an agreement, he nevertheless doubted that Hanoi would accept the invitation to talk. They had demanded a total unconditional end to the bombing for too long. The presidential election was too near. Back in Washington, he continued to argue for further steps to deescalate, causing Maxwell Taylor to suggest to the President that Clifford replace him as negotiator if the North Vietnamese accepted the invitation.

Surprising everyone in the administration as much as Harriman, Hanoi took only three days before agreeing to meet. Harriman had the assignment he had coveted and awaited ever since he realized that his ambassador-for-peace assignment had been a public relations ploy; but in spite of Hanoi's quick acceptance, it seemed in the days that followed that the opportunity might slip away. Johnson hadn't quite meant it when he said the United States was ready to go anywhere to sit down face-to-face with the North Vietnamese. There were a great many places, it turned out, where the President was not willing to go. There followed a full month of jockeying over a site. When the United States proposed Geneva, Hanoi countered with Pnompenh, which Washington rejected on grounds that communications facilities were inadequate. Washington suggested Vientiane, but Hanoi found the transportation connections unsatisfactory. Indonesia offered to anchor its navy's only cruiser, a Soviet-built vessel of dubious seaworthiness, for negotiations off the coast of Vietnam as a floating conference site. That was acceptable to the United States, but North Vietnam concluded that the vessel lacked adequate press and communications facilities.

Hanoi continued to insist upon Pnompenh or Warsaw, while Washington offered more than a dozen other possible sites. Harriman wanted to accept the Polish capital and called the White House to ask Rostow to urge the President not to reject it. When Rostow told him a statement had already been dictated refusing to go there, Averell telephoned the President himself, finding Johnson surly and impatient with the whole subject. Warsaw, he said angrily, had been rejected "outright, flat, all the way." The United States was not going to negotiate there as long as Lyndon Johnson was President; what was more, he didn't intend to approve any other Eastern European capital either. He was unimpressed by Harriman's rejoinder that putting the peace talks in Eastern Europe would eliminate the Chinese Communists from the politics of Vietnam peace.

"I would like to be able to tell you how I feel," Harriman persisted.

"You did, you see," Johnson snapped and hung up the phone while Harriman was apologetically trying to recover, assuring him, "I am a soldier. I obey orders."[9]

Paris was an obvious possibility; but Johnson was afraid that de Gaulle would interfere, and Rusk worried that the very suggestion of it by the United States would bring an automatic rejection from Hanoi. It was therefore left for Hanoi to propose the French capital. On May 3, the North Vietnamese advised William Sullivan, who had become U.S. ambassador in Vientiane, that they would send a delegation to Paris on the 10th. The word reached Johnson after midnight, and he announced it in the East Room of the White House at ten A.M.

Averell's loyalty had once again paid off for him. Friends who had spoken their dissents too openly were gone. But while he was the consummate American negotiator, and again of great symbolic importance to the President, he did not have Johnson's trust as he had enjoyed Roosevelt's and Truman's—and even Kennedy's.

At the same time he named Harriman to lead the negotiations, Johnson had also picked Llewellyn Thompson, his ambassador to the Soviet Union, to be a full partner. During the month of maneuvering over a meeting site, however, the President had decided to leave Thompson in Moscow to work on arms-control negotiations and to send Cyrus Vance with Averell instead.

Vance's selection was calculated to ensure against Harriman's over eagerness. A former secretary of the army and deputy to McNamara at the Pentagon, he had returned to his New York law practice, but he had become Johnson's favorite troubleshooter. He had been sent to restore peace when race riots swept Detroit in 1967. On a few hours' notice, he had taken on a crisis in Cyprus that same year, and he had flown to Seoul in January 1968 to steady the South Korean government after North Korea had captured the U.S. Navy spy ship *Pueblo*. Four days after Johnson's announcement of the bombing restriction and his withdrawal from the presidential campaign, the assassination of civil rights leader Martin Luther King, Jr., set off urban riots from coast to coast, and the

President again sent for Vance. The former Pentagon official was staying at the White House, working with the President to restore domestic peace when Johnson drafted him for the Vietnam negotiations.

But if the President was looking for a Harriman watchdog, as was widely believed within the administration, he got the wrong man. Vance had developed a close friendship with Robert McNamara, and he had watched at close range as McNamara became depressed and disillusioned with the war and administration policy. He had attended the conclave of Wise Men in March; and like most of the others, he had been deeply affected by the Tet Offensive and its aftermath. Although his answer had surprised Johnson when he was asked for his views during the luncheon, the President retained as much confidence in Vance as in anyone who had served him, and he fully trusted him to keep an eager Harriman within the confines of their negotiating instructions, though Vance was far more in accord with Harriman than he was with the President.

Johnson's announcement of the bombing limitation muted the debate, but the continuing strikes in the panhandle still sharply divided hawks and doves. In his speech, the President ended raids into North Vietnam except in the area north of the DMZ. Harriman tried to get him to spell out more specifically that the air raids would be confined, but to no avail. Administration hawks were not enthusiastic about Paris.

Ellsworth Bunker flew home from Saigon to help prepare for the meetings, contending that it would be better to delay negotiations five or six months, when the Saigon government would be stronger. With Rusk insisting that the team be kept on a short leash, Harriman's negotiating instructions gave him almost no latitude. He was to seek substantive negotiations, respect of the Demilitarized Zone, machinery to oversee a cease-fire, and an assured future role for the South Vietnamese government. Restrictions would have been tighter had Clifford not intervened against Bunker and Rostow during a long meeting at Camp David.[10]

Rusk said nearly nothing at the meeting, but clearly he and Rostow held the upper hand in a policy debate. On the day before the negotiating team finally departed for Paris, he called Harriman and Vance to his office to warn them about leaks and to emphasize that the talks were not to become a source of pressure on the President for concessions. In short, their mission in Paris was only to find out what the North Vietnamese were prepared to do in response to the bombing limitation already in effect. There was to be no discussion of a fallback position.

Barring capitulation by Hanoi, it was obvious that nothing would be done toward a political settlement until the bombing was stopped, and that still appeared to be out of the question. "I'm glad we're going to talk," the President told them, "but I'm not overly hopeful. I think it is going to be tough going, very tough. . . ."[11] Nothing the President did was designed to inspire the delegation. Several members were told their responsibility was to keep an eye on Harriman, and within the team the word quickly went around that the real role of press spokesman William Jorden was to be the eyes and ears of the White House—reporting the inner workings of the team back through his own channels.

The White House had its ways of subtly emphasizing its limited expectations. When it was time to go, Harriman's assistant, Peter Swiers, who was handling the logistics, was informed that no government plane would be available to take the team. There was, after all, a war on. The Harriman-Vance operation would have to pack up its gear and make its way to Paris on a commercial flight. It was pointless to argue at the very outset about something that was comparatively so small; but Harriman mentioned the slight to Clifford, and the defense secretary ordered the bunks removed from his plane and made arrangements to deliver the peace team to Paris on his way to a meeting in Brussels.

They departed with minimal official fanfare and reached Paris on the twentieth anniversary of Averell's arrival to take charge of the Marshall Plan. There, the mood was dramatically different from that of Washington. In spite of mass student demonstrations in Paris and several days of heavy rain, the atmosphere around the conference was electric. Fifteen hundred journalists and technicians from around the globe, including the anchormen of all the American television networks, were waiting. Ever accommodating, Clifford adjusted his schedule so Harriman could walk off the plane and into the klieg lights of the evening news broadcasts.

For days thereafter, the story captivated Paris, the United States, and the world. Throngs of reporters awaited Harriman and Vance's comings and goings outside the U.S. embassy, and French police sirens brushed aside Parisian traffic for their motorcades. Press spokesman Jorden and Nguyen Thanh Le, his counterpart from Hanoi, daily went before auditoriums filled with journalists with their versions of what passed between the negotiators at the old Majestic Hotel. So completely did the Americans take over the venerable Crillon next door to the embassy that the North Vietnamese investigated to find out whether the United States government had bought it.

The talks were as unfruitful as Harriman and Vance had feared, nothing but twice-a-week exercises in polemical posturing and propaganda. Averell's speeches, sweated over for hours, were so laden with boilerplate quotations of LBJ that he sounded more like a mouthpiece of a totalitarian regime than the ambassador of a democracy. Sitting across the table from Xuan Thuy, a second-level party official, backed by Colonel Ha Van Lau, a veteran of the 1961–62 Geneva conference on Laos, he delivered hour-long reviews of North Vietnamese aggression. Thuy replied with longer, more doctrinaire denunciations of American aggression. When the sessions ended, the action moved to press conferences. While Jorden's briefings were the circumspect, low-key presentations expected at sensitive diplomatic meetings, the North Vietnamese provided a circus, complete with photographs of bombing casualties and displays of captured American weapons.

Thuy, whose chubbiness and reflexive smile gave him the appearance of a man much younger than his fifty-five years, incessantly ridiculed the Harriman-Vance demand for assurances of reciprocity before a U.S. bombing halt. If reciprocity was what the United States required, he said at the opening session, then Hanoi would gladly comply—it would pledge not to bomb the United States.[12]

Harriman complained that the meetings, rather than being occasions for give and take, were exercises in "suggest and reject." Still, there were a few moments when eloquence transcended the bickering. After Thuy had delivered one particularly excessive tribute to the Viet Cong, Harriman replied, with his anger barely controlled: "You speak of the NLF as the worthy and true representatives of the people of South Vietnam, if I quote you correctly. On what basis do you make that assertion? What is the NLF worthy of? Terror and assassination, bringing hardship to the people, acting as an arm of aggression from the North. By whom where they chosen—by the terrorists? Who elected them—Hanoi? What peace do they seek—peace of terror?"[13]

Every Thursday the two sides trooped into the conference room at the once-grand Majestic Hotel, where the Gestapo had made its headquarters during World War II. There, they delivered speeches translated from English and Vietnamese into French, the working language of the conference. Halfway through, they broke for tea and cakes.

It was not the Harriman style of negotiation. It was not negotiation at all. To move toward serious business, he tried to get the North Vietnamese to agree to keep speech texts secret and pleaded with Washington for more latitude for talks during the tea breaks. But he could convince neither.

Each week was the same. As soon as the Thursday encounter was past and the cables filed, work on the next week's speech began.

Although the United States' bombing was officially limited to the 20th parallel, and in practice to the 19th, it continued to be almost as effective as when it had extended over all of North Vietnam. The North Vietnamese demanded a complete cessation without condition before moving on to substantive talks. Harriman and Vance had to first have assurance that Hanoi would accede to the "no advantage" proviso of the President's San Antonio Formula. In South Vietnam, meanwhile, the fighting only intensified. Two days after Hanoi accepted Paris as the meeting site, North Vietnamese and Viet Cong guns began shelling Saigon and continued to do so for six weeks.

Except for hard-core diplomatic correspondents, the horde of reporters soon grew bored with the repetition and started disappearing. The American delegation gave up the opulence of the Crillon and closed its press center. The North Vietnamese moved out of their hotel and into houses provided by French Communist friends. Marie arrived from Washington with dogs and paintings and rented the house where Gertrude Vanderbilt Whitney, her long-ago mother-in-law, had lived on Rue de Boileau. There were enough old cronies like Cyrus Sulzberger and Virginia Chambers, a New York friend whose late husband had worked for Averell in the Marshall Plan, to put together regular bridge parties. Office hours took on a routine, and Marie and Averell settled once again into a semipermanent Paris lifestyle.

Eventually Harriman was cleared to approach Thuy during the tea breaks on the subject of secret meetings. Thereafter, the carefully choreographed social conversations led to clandestine conferences between Vance and Ha Van Lau to arrange for secret negotiations to take place on another track. But like the tedious maneuvers that had finally brought them to Paris, the effort to arrange back-channel talks was excruciating.

Meanwhile, the Democratic presidential primary trail had already reached California and a crucial test for Robert Kennedy. On the night of the showdown in the West, Averell and Marie went out with CBS correspondent Charles Collingwood and his wife Louise to celebrate Collingwood's birthday, but they were back home and asleep long before the California polls closed. When Averell awoke several hours later, there was a message to call Peter Swiers. Still half asleep, he learned from his assistant that Bob Kennedy had been gravely wounded in an assassination attempt moments after he claimed the victory that might have catapulted him on his way to the nomination and the White House.

All day, Harriman went through the motions of his schedule while Hildy Shishkin followed news bulletins and gathered any information she could from the office of Ambassador Sargent Shriver, the senator's brother-in-law. The chances of survival were nearly nonexistent. Kennedy was on a respirator, a bullet in the area of the brain controlling the involuntary impulses, including breathing. The delegation was in its weekly plenary at the Majestic when word came that he had died. Harriman and Vance crossed the Atlantic as the body was flown back to New York from California; and the next morning at eight, Averell took his turn as a long list of the senator's friends alternated in a guard of honor beside his coffin at St. Patrick's Cathedral. After the funeral the following day, he traveled to Washington aboard a train with the family, and hours after nightfall helped other pallbearers take Kennedy to his resting place on a gentle slope near his brother in Arlington National Cemetery.

In spite of the tension between them brought on by the war, Harriman had no closer friend in political life. He had become a regular in the Hickory Hill Gang—a figure from another time who enjoyed the company of Bobby and Ethel's generation more than that of his own contemporaries. The Kennedys were among intimate friends welcome to show up at N Street in Georgetown unannounced with dogs and children and to stay long after other guests were gone from parties and dinners.

Understanding the animosity between Kennedy and Johnson, Averell had been among the first who urged Bobby to become a New Yorker and run against Republican senator Kenneth Keating. He had helped the former attorney general defuse the issue of carpetbagging by pushing a draft movement, which allowed Kennedy to present himself as a man responding to New York's call.

Limited as he himself had been as a politician, Harriman brought not only prestige but wisdom to a senatorial campaign that had problems in spite of the huge crowds and the orgy of national press attention. Unlike his older brother, Kennedy came across to television audiences as cold, aloof, and mechanical, and Averell urged him to abandon set speeches and use television to show himself in give-and-take exchanges with both supporters and critics. He accepted the advice, and it marked a turning point in his race against Keating.

When Averell came home from his long jaunt through Asia following the Manila summit in November 1966, he had arrived just in time to celebrate his birthday at Hickory Hill. It was number seventy-five, and the Kennedys turned it into a zany parody of the old television show *This Is Your Life*. Friends showed up wearing Yale crew shirts, carrying oars, skis, and polo mallets, pulling toy trains, and wearing Russian fur hats. After toasts filled with ribbing about Averell's money and procession of jobs were over, curtains on wide bay windows were opened and he stood face-to-face with life-sized figures of Roosevelt, Churchill, and Stalin. In the mist outside, they looked just as they had at Yalta, but for a Harvard beanie worn by Roosevelt in wax.

During the weeks of Kennedy's presidential candidacy, the Paris negotiations had provided Averell a haven. His heart was with Bobby, but, safely in Paris, he obviously could not involve himself in the primary struggle. His only opportunity to help out was to have his own Union Pacific railroad car made available for a short Kennedy whistlestop campaign.

On the day Kennedy was shot, the President had received an unusual personal message from Aleksey Kosygin suggesting a possible opening in the bombing debate. On the way to Paris to join the talks, Le Duc

Tho, a powerful elder figure in the North Vietnamese Communist party's central committee, had stopped off in Moscow, and he had given the Premier the strong impression that Hanoi was at last prepared for serious negotiation—again, if the bombing stopped.

Harriman had long been convinced that Kosygin personally wanted to see the war end, and Paris provided him a chance to be helpful without putting pressure on Hanoi. The straightforward language of Kosygin's letter to Johnson left no doubt in Averell's mind that the Soviet leader took Tho's comments seriously. Rather than merely paraphrasing Le Duc Tho's words, Kosygin said he and his Kremlin colleagues believed, and had grounds to believe, that a bombing halt would lead to a breakthrough. Harriman saw it as an opportunity for Washington to give the Soviets a stake in the peace effort, as he had long tried to do.

In a meeting in Rusk's office before going to the White House to discuss Kosygin's letter with the President, Harriman and Clifford recommended taking the Premier at his word and responding favorably. Harriman could not remember a Soviet cable being more direct than the message telling Johnson that Kosygin and his advisers believed "with good reason" that Hanoi was ready to talk. His and Clifford's advice was for the President to tell the Soviets that the United States would stop the bombing on the basis of Moscow's assurance of North Vietnamese good faith. Rusk asked a few questions but raised no objection, and the three drove to the White House.

In the President's office, however, the secretary uncharacteristically took the lead in the discussion. He brought up the Russian cable and firmly advised Johnson to ignore it. It was just more Soviet posturing, he said, offering nothing that they hadn't peddled before.

In earlier days, the Crocodile might have snapped. But aware as always of his position with Johnson and of the President's regard for Rusk, he didn't argue. Sabotaged, Clifford vainly made his brief for accepting the opportunity. Once his advice probably would have outweighed Rusk's, but after the defense secretary had joined the doves, he had forfeited his influence.

Although Averell told Johnson he agreed with Clifford, Rusk had won with his preemptive strike. With Abe Fortas, the associate justice of the Supreme Court who had worked in tandem with Clifford as a kitchen cabinet hardliner before the latter's defection, Rusk was ordered to prepare the President's answer to Kosygin. There would be no substantive response.

As much as he disagreed with Rusk on Vietnam, Harriman had always considered him above all else a gentleman. Now, he found the blindsiding of Clifford contemptible. Never had he seen one Cabinet member so brazenly undercut another, not even Louis Johnson in his guerrilla war against Acheson nearly twenty years earlier. Clifford's position was destroyed before the President even had a chance to hear it.

On the way back to the State Department with Rusk, he cryptically took exception to both the secretary's tactic and his judgment, suggesting that an extraordianry opportunity was being thrown away. Rusk naturally disagreed. The problem, he replied, was that Clifford had "lost his nerve" on Vietnam once he had gone to the Pentagon.[14]

Back in Paris, Vance finally succeeded in setting up secret negotiations with the North Vietnamese away from the weekly meeting at the hotel. In themselves, the arrangements had required settlement of minute details, down to Vance's formal assurance that he, Averell, and their aides would refrain from bringing weapons to the meetings. The sessions, to be called when either side had something to discuss, would alternate between three "safe houses," two belonging to the North Vietnamese, the third a residence rented by the Central Intelligence Agency in the Parisian suburb of Seaux. Among the requirements for each of them was an enclosed two-car garage, enabling the delegates to drive inside and enter the house unobserved.

Once the secret sessions got under way, the meetings at the Majestic continued chiefly because they provided cover, letting the world know that the sides were still talking, though getting nowhere. With press interest flagging, it was easy for the American envoys to slip away unnoticed, leaving their offices in the embassy annex by the back entrance to be separately picked up a few blocks away by an unmarked car. Sometimes, they left from home under cover of evening darkness, joining John Negroponte, their interpreter, and Philip Habib, the delegation's political officer.

One reason for sites other than the hotel was the certainty on both sides that the conference room was infested with electronic bugs. But at the first meeting at the American safe house, Harriman and Vance realized that their secret talks were already known to French intelligence. Outside the house, several workers—conspicuous because all were dressed in fresh new coveralls—spent the whole afternoon puttering around a fire hydrant.

Back at the office, Harriman telephoned the French Foreign Ministry in a fury. "You get those damned goons away," he told the minister's office, "and don't tell me they aren't security people. If this happens again, Mr. Vance and I will go home, and we will announce to the world community why it is impossible to negotiate here. We will not be bothered by this."[15]

Hopeful that he could at last get somewhere in a more relaxed setting, Harriman tried to create an ambience worthy of great negotiation. Before one Vietnamese call at the American house, he sent Negroponte for caviar. When the time arrived for the "tea break," the group stepped into the dining room where Negroponte's exquisite choice was offered with champagne. The hosts' illusion of momentous diplomacy dissolved in unconcealed horror when all the Communists spurned the caviar and champagne for ice cream and cookies. While they failed to get a suspension or reduction of the bombing in response to Kosygin's message to the President, Harriman and Vance did get Johnson's approval to offer North Vietnam one new enticement—a bombing suspension in exchange for a pledge to honor the Demilitarized Zone between North and South Vietnam. The proposition had repeatedly been sent to Hanoi through intermediaries, but always rejected or ignored. This time the offer was to keep Hanoi's assurance secret, allowing the North Vietnamese to claim that the American decision was unilateral. The North Vietnamese listened in silence, and in the meetings that followed, offered no response.

In July, however, there was an unmistakable lull on the battlefield. The shelling of Saigon stopped, and there was a slowdown of troop and supply movement into the DMZ. After talking with Undersecretary of State Nicholas Katzenbach and William Bundy, Harriman and Vance cabled the President recommending that the relative calm be taken as a signal of Hanoi's acceptance of the offer, suggesting that Vance fly home to discuss the possibility in detail. Unfortunately, their message arrived on the same morning that *The New York Times* called for an unconditional end to the bombing, and after the President had received a similar recommendation from Vice-President Humphrey. Johnson "went through the roof."[16] He vetoed Vance's return and ordered Rusk to hold a press conference in which the secretary warned that the North Vietnamese were preparing a huge new attack. As usual, Harriman and Vance suffered the setback in silence, although Averell privately complained that the ground had been cut from beneath everything they had tried to do since their arrival in Paris.

The split in the Johnson administration was obvious even to the North Vietnamese. Reading reports from Washington detailing the administration's warning of a new offensive, Ha Van Lau asked whether the American delegation in Paris any longer spoke for the President, a question perhaps more perceptive than the colonel realized. The administration was as deeply divided as the American public. Averell and Vance, along with Clifford, Ball, Katzenbach, and Ben Read, were for stopping the bombing. Rusk, Rostow, Bunker, Fortas, the Joint Chiefs, and the military advisers in Paris favored keeping the heat on until there was clear assurance of reciprocity.

At home, some of Humphrey's closest advisers, seeing his chances of winning the presidency as increasingly remote, recommended that he resign the vice-presidency as soon as he received the nomination—so he could run for the White House without the burden of every Johnson war decision. Averell was briefed on the plan and was willing to endorse it when it was put to Humphrey. One draft of Humprey's speech accepting the nomination had him dramatically resigning the vice-presidency at the same moment he became the party's 1968 standard-bearer. There was even an elaborate scenario for making the decision known to Johnson.[17]

But at the convention, the faithful Vice-President backed down from even submitting his own Vietnam plank and condemned himself to defend the administration policy that had fractured the party. Like Harriman, he found himself estranged from his natural allies because of his loyalty to Johnson. Antiwar liberals booed, and radicals fought pitched battles with Chicago police as Democrats bestowed upon Humphrey a nomination that looked nearly worthless.

Harriman followed the spectacle, sickened. With the war tearing the country apart and with Richard Nixon leading the Republican ticket, he wanted an agreement in Paris more desperately than ever. Although Nixon had moderated his anticommunism since the days of his congressional witch-hunting, Harriman detested him as much as he had in the days when Nixon was smearing Helen Gahagan Douglas, his Democratic opponent, as "the Pink Lady."

Ending the war was an urgent matter, he told Katzenbach, in the summer of 1968, but even that paled in comparison to the necessity of keeping Nixon out of the White House.[18] For that cause, he was, if necessary, willing to break with the President or even quit his effort to negotiate a Vietnam truce. More than once, he offered to come home from Paris and join the Humphrey campaign; but Humphrey, like Johnson, knew he could be helpful only in Paris. So he was left unable to influence anything, bound by his negotiating instructions and his commitment to a President who was determined not to let the campaign alter his position in Paris.

After the convention, there was a move to send Arthur Goldberg to Paris as Humphrey's representative for a publicized meeting with Harriman, but Averell headed it off with a warning that it would do more harm than good. He could tell Goldberg nothing that would be useful to Humphrey's campaign and publicity about the meeting would infuriate Johnson. After that there was talk of his coming back for a secret conference with the candidate, but he vetoed that, too. His own recommendation was that Humphrey demonstrate firm leadership by publicly asking the negotiators to come home to brief him on the talks and receive his ideas, but Humphrey demurred.

In September, Averell flew home with Marie for her mother's funeral in New York. Before they returned to Paris, he went down to Washington in a mood to tell the President that continued bombing would put Nixon in the White House. He let Clifford know what was on his mind, and was cautioned that such an approach would be useless. Everybody in politics realized that Humphrey wanted to distance himself from the President, and Clifford thought that Johnson's support of his Vice-President was now based upon necessity rather than shared commitments. That made Harriman wonder aloud whether Johnson might actually want Nixon to win the election. "If you agree it is just between you and me," replied the defense secretary. "I believe you are right. The President wants to see him defeated."[19] Harriman was furious to think that he was possibly put in the position of merely holding the line for Nixon in Paris. If he knew that to be the case, he said, he would quit.[20]

That night, Harriman and Rusk argued strategy again. There had been three long meetings with Le Duc Tho in recent days, and a scenario for a possible arrangement to stop the bombing had emerged. In exchange for an end to the air strikes, the North Vietnamese would cease their attacks on all cities in the South, but Hanoi was insisting that Harriman and Vance agree to a statement declaring the bombing halt to be unconditional.

Averell was for making a positive response to an intriguing situation on the ground. A substantial portion of the North Vietnamese forces had fallen back into Laos and Cambodia from the northernmost provinces of South Vietnam.

That presented an opportunity to pull American and South Vietnamese troops back in the hope of further disengagement. Rusk would have none of it, and Harriman angrily told him that he had no right to ask more Americans to die pointlessly in maintaining military pressure in the area. "The other side is beginning to disengage," Harriman told the secretary, "why the hell don't we?"[21] The answer was the same as it had always been: the North Vietnamese had to stop shelling South Vietnamese cities, the Demilitarized Zone had to be reestablished, and the Saigon government had to be represented when and if the Paris talks got down to substance.

Although an understanding on the first two matters seemed to be within reach, whenever Harriman and Vance brought up Saigon's participation, the Hanoi delegation was "totally unrealistic."[22] On that issue, the secret talks were snagged for much of the fall.

In late September, George Ball, who was about to leave the administration to become Humphrey's chief foreign policy adviser after a brief tour as ambassador to the United Nations, arrived in Paris to catch up on the state of the negotiations. The White House was keeping the Democratic campaign in the dark, but Harriman could find no hope to offer the candidate. The North Vietnamese were intransigent and Rusk was simply out of touch. The secretary, Harriman told Ball, was "on another planet." In spite of everything, including the near anarchy at Chicago, Rusk still thought that Johnson's policy of bombing North Vietnam to the negotiating table had the country's support. In his mind, the only thing Humphrey needed to do was stand behind the President.[23]

With scarcely more than a month remaining until the election, the Humphrey campaign at last prepared to move its man away from Johnson. A draft of an agonizingly debated and rewritten speech calling for a halt in the bombing of North Vietnam was flown to Paris for Harriman to see before Humphrey delivered it on national television. As much as he wanted to help, Harriman couldn't endorse anything that contradicted administration policy and remain in Paris, so he sent the speech back without either endorsement or disapproval. Still, when Humphrey delivered it on October 1, it was carefully calculated to be acceptable to the negotiators. Before calling for a bombing halt, he said, he would carefully consider whether the Communists showed evidence "direct or indirect, by deed or word" of reestablishing the DMZ.[24]

Ten days later, Xuan Thuy and Ha Van Lau suddenly indicated they were ready to discuss arrangements for the Saigon government to join the talks. Thereafter, a torrent of urgent cables between Paris, Washington, and Saigon turned the mission into an around-the-clock operation. A message from the Soviets the next day affirmed the new position taken by the North Vietnamese negotiators. In Saigon, Ellsworth Bunker received the endorsement of the South Vietnamese government.

Washington's instructions on what Harriman and Vance were to say on each point in their private conversations with the North Vietnamese were now delivered in excruciating detail. After each session, a summary of the exchange was rushed to the State Department, followed by transcripts of John Negroponte's copious notes.

At the White House, Johnson read the messages line by line, maintaining intricate defenses against the smallest leak. The most sensitive top secret cables, designated "Harvan Double Plus," were hand carried to the officials personally authorized by the President to see them. In the entire State Department, only four persons, Rusk, Katzenbach, Bill Bundy, and Read, could see them all. Under orders from Rusk, the delegation's cables were limited to a recounting of conversations. They were to include neither interpretation nor analysis. Communication of such material had to be conducted on telephones equipped with scramblers, and at State, Ben Read and Bill Bundy began taking turns sleeping by the secure phone.

In Paris, Vance, who suffered from a painful, chronic back condition, sometimes slept on his office floor as the delegation worked past midnight, and returned at eight A.M., when Harriman insisted on having a daily staff meeting. Arriving at the office one morning and learning that an important cable had come in after he had gone home, Averell reprimanded everybody in earshot for the failure to call him. Thereafter, he was aroused from sleep if an especially urgent message came in. More than once, he pulled on his clothes over his pajamas and rushed to the office to study a dispatch from Washington or sit by as Vance talked on the scrambler phone. Once or twice, when Vance went to a meeting alone, he returned after midnight to find Harriman prowling the office in a robe and bedroom slippers.

In late October, with Humphrey rapidly gaining ground on Nixon, a plan to begin negotiations on the political future of Vietnam was completed. First, the United States would announce a bombing halt, with the understanding that Hanoi would meet its demands to honor the Demilitarized Zone, desist from attacks on cities, and refrain from firing on American reconnaissance planes. The two sides would promptly enter into substantive negotiations, with both Saigon and the Viet Cong included.

When Washington demanded that the first expanded meeting take place on the day after the bombing halt went into effect, Xuan Thuy and Ha Van Lau maintained that their representatives could not get to Paris that soon. Moreover, they again insisted upon a secret U.S. statement saying that the bombing halt was unconditional.

The two sides haggled over the details in meetings of four and five hours at a stretch before the North Vietnamese abandoned their demand for the "secret minute." The first timetable, calling for the bombing to stop on October 30, with the peace negotiations to begin on November 2, passed with the parties still debating. When the details were cabled to Saigon, the government balked. President Nguyen Van Thieu announced that leaders of Parliament would have to be consulted, and that it might even be necessary to have a plenary meeting. Harriman angrily blamed Bunker for failing to keep the Thieu government in line.

The South Vietnamese government was disturbed, Thieu told the American ambassador, over a cable it had received from Pham Dang Lam, its representative in Paris, saying, "The US is not opposed to a delegation from the NLF distinct from Hanoi" in the talks. The South Vietnamese envoy also complained to Harriman that he had been left out of communications between Paris and Saigon, and now he was expected to represent his government in the first sessions of the broadened talks—until a delegation could get to Paris from Saigon.

It was clear, Harriman and Vance warned, that Lam did not fathom the "our side–your side" understanding that would allow the Communists to organize their delegation as they saw fit, as would Washington and Saigon. Twice during the crucial days of October, the South Vietnamese envoy came to the Americans with questions about the display of flags, the procession of negotiators into the room, and the arrangement of the doors they would use. The absurdities had to be addressed,

Harriman acknowledged, lest Saigon "balk at participation in the first meeting . . . on the grounds that procedural matters have not been worked out. . . ."[25]

Through late October, the press was filled with rumors of a deal, but Johnson stubbornly insisted that the looming election not be allowed to influence the negotiations. Then, with the polls showing Humphrey within reach of Nixon, Johnson ordered General Creighton Abrams, Westmoreland's successor as field commander, home from Vietnam to give his views on the effect of ending the bombing. With Johnson then ready to announce the suspension and a November 2 meeting of the North and South Vietnamese in Paris, Thieu balked on sending a delegation. Seeing the election slipping away, Harriman blamed Bunker.

It was too late for Humphrey, and it was too late for Harriman. On election day, Averell had lunch alone in his office, and that evening Marie had Irwin Shaw and Lauren Bacall to a small dinner party so he would not sit by and mope over a Nixon victory.

Almost another month of waiting, coaxing, and deliberation passed before Saigon sent its delegation to Paris. When it did, the meeting immediately became entangled in the same kind of trivia that Harriman had faced in October. The new obstacle was the shape of the negotiating table.

The debate was not as vacuous as it seemed, nor was it new. It was a fight over the status of the Viet Cong—South Vietnam's last stand against a forum in which the VC would enjoy the legitimacy of a government. The haggling went on for ten weeks. With Harriman grabbing an occasional doze, Vance took the lead for the United States, making his lawyerly way through variation after variation of square, rectangular, oblong, oval furniture. Parallelograms, semicircles, diamonds, and half-moons were tried. At the end of each day, the delegation now turned to sketching table designs rather than drafting cables. Richard Holbrooke, who took on additional duties as draftsman, suggested breaking the stalemate by putting a long table before a curved mirror, enabling each negotiator to see the conference from his own perspective.

This was hardly the way Harriman wanted to close his diplomatic career, in a long, sorry string of missed opportunities—Rusk's undercutting of Clifford on the Kosygin message in June, the President's refusal to stop the bombing when the fighting subsided in July, Washington's unnecessarily heavy hand on the delegation's every move, Johnson's tepid support of Humphrey, Humphrey's timidity about taking his own course, and Bunker's ineffective handling of the Thieu regime.

If all that and Hanoi's intransigence were not enough, Nixon's agents, alerted by Henry Kissinger, had gone to work on Thieu as soon as it appeared that a bombing halt might come before the election. With Anna Chennault, the Chinese-born widow of General Claire Chennault, leader of the World War II Flying Tigers in Burma, providing the conduit, the Nixon campaign encouraged the Saigon government to hold out. Once Nixon was in the White House, Thieu was assured, South Vietnam would have more steadfast support from Washington. A Nixon administration would give him a more sympathetic hearing than he was getting from Johnson and the Harriman delegation in Paris.

Everything would have been different, Averell wrote in a memorandum summarizing his seven months in Paris, if Johnson had only stopped the air raids in July. "There is no doubt in my mind if the President had taken this opportunity to stop the bombing about three weeks before the Democratic convention, the Democrats would have been united, without serious divisions. Humphrey would have been nominated without conflict over the plank on Vietnam, and . . . would have been elected comfortably."[26]

After the election, however, Harriman's contempt for Nixon went into temporary remission. Seeing himself at the end of the road, he momentarily entertained a fanciful notion that the new administration, too, might need and want him. Without telling anybody, he put out discreet signals that he would be available.

To Kissinger, who was becoming the new President's national security adviser, he offered his State Department office as well as the use of the house on Eighty-first Street during the transition period. In early December, he met with Nixon personally and was told by the President-elect that the White House would like to call upon him for occasional advice. "The Soviet Union, as well as Vietnam, was mentioned," he told William P. Rogers, Nixon's choice to become secretary of state.[27]

He wound up his affairs in Paris without much hope for the negotiations as Nixon put day-to-day war diplomacy in the hands of the men Averell considered among the most rigid and committed to a military solution—Bunker in Saigon, Henry Cabot Lodge as his own successor in Paris, and U. Alexis Johnson as undersecretary for political affairs in Washington. But he resolved to keep quiet and give the Republicans a chance to pick up the ball in Paris.

The great seating crisis persisted into January, long after resolution of the thorny question of how many entry doors there would be in the conference room.

Harriman was morose. Out of patience with Saigon's stalling, he wanted to give Thieu a deadline for arriving in Paris and then announce that negotiations would proceed with or without the presence of his administration. But where Saigon was concerned, Washington was patient, ignoring Averell's recommendation that Thieu simply be told to accept a round table, stop obstructing, and get down to business.

The struggle ended with the only possible solution—a big round table. Hanoi's representatives could claim they had succeeded in seating the Viet Cong as full-fledged, independent, equal participants. But with the peace table flanked on opposite sides by two small rectangular tables for members of the negotiators' staffs, Washington and Saigon could maintain that the conference was a two-sided affair—between the Communists and non-Communists. It was not an original solution. A similar expedient had been worked out to accommodate East and West Germany ten years earlier: while the United States, Great Britain, France, and the Soviet Union sat at a round table, the two Germanys sat at small side tables, separated from the main one by precisely six pencil widths.[28]

The final positioning of the two rectangular tables in Paris was an inspiration of the Russians. When the question of distance arose, they quietly suggested the width of the hips of Sergei Bogomolov, the skinny first secretary of the Soviet embassy. Given the history of the deliberations, the absurdity was appropriate. Harriman and Vance agreed. Bogomolov was measured, and the Vietnamese parties gravely accepted without knowing the basis of the proposal. It was one of the rare uncontested decisions of the meeting.

With the stage thus set to discuss peace in Vietnam, it was time for Harriman to go home. The mechanics of handing the negotiations over to Nixon's team would be left to Vance.

Averell spared himself prolonged farewells, pleading that he was too busy. The truth was, it was hardly an occasion for celebration. His hopes of negotiating the United States out of Vietnam had succeeded only in setting the stage for Nixon to do it. The White House didn't send a plane to bring him home, another slight that was unpalatable to Clifford, who dispatched a jet to get him. Vance and the whole delegation went out to Orly to see him off. With Marie, Hildy, Peter Swiers, his wife, Karen, and their young son, Thomas, he flew home to Washington on Lyndon Johnson's last day in the White House.

It was dark, and a raw wind was raking Andrews Air Force Base when they arrived. A crowd that had welcomed Richard Nixon, who had just arrived from New York to be inaugurated the next morning, was still drifting away. But along the fence outside the base operations building more than two hundred of Harriman's friends waited—Humphrey, McNamara, Dick Helms of the CIA, and dozens of others from an administration destroyed by the war. Most of them, though, were people who had never been directly involved in the struggles over Vietnam, people close to him who had come out because they knew it was his last hurrah. Roosevelt people, Truman people, Kennedy people. Chief Justice Earl Warren, former treasury secretary Henry Fowler, Art Buchwald with a huge sign, "Welcome Home, Sir Ave, Knight of the Round Table."

Dean Rusk, looking almost as old as Averell himself, was there to present him a permanent diplomatic passport. Although they had never understood each other, and seething disagreements had created palpable tension between them, they had been gentlemen. Now the man Harriman blamed more than anyone else for preventing a peace agreement in Paris was there to acknowledge the end of his career.

"We don't have a House of Lords, Privy Council, or Order of the Garter," the secretary said, "all we do is ask a good man to serve again and again as Presidents Roosevelt, Truman, Kennedy, and Johnson did."[29]

Averell arrived hoping, half-expecting, that the President would be there, too; but from Johnson there was only an invitation—an order, really—to come to the White House for a final report. In the Oval Office, Harriman found LBJ subdued, tired, strikingly older, expressing little joy that the peace talks could finally get started. More than forty years after they had met in Sam Rayburn's office, public life was ending for both of them. At the moment, neither had the stomach to reminisce, and after only a few minutes, the photographers were ushered in. It was the way nearly all of Johnson's meetings ended.

The next day, as Republicans celebrated Nixon's inauguration, Johnson spent his last hours in Washington among the men who had struggled for his soul at every Vietnam crossroad for the last year. Before going out to board *Air Force One* for Texas, he and his wife went to lunch at Clark Clifford's house; there, he presented the Medal of Freedom to both Clifford and Harriman. It was not a final concession to the old soldiers of the peace track, however, for he also awarded the medal to Rusk and Walt Rostow.

Chapter XXVI

GEORGETOWN
Dinner at Mrs. Graham's

Facing surgery for the third time in her long, losing struggle to preserve her eyesight, Marie Harriman went to New York to see her doctor in September 1970, and while she was there she came down with an overpowering chest cold. She might have taken to her bed at the house on Eighty-first Street, but since Averell was alone in Washington, she flew home, accompanied by her friend Ann Sardi Giná.

The next day, she was feeling no better. In the afternoon, she complained of having chest pains, whereupon Averell called Janet Travell, their neighbor, who had been the White House physician during the Kennedy and Johnson years. Knowing that Marie had suffered episodes of angina, Travell sent for a cardiologist, and shortly the mildly protesting patient was carried down the stairs on a stretcher, put into an ambulance and rushed to George Washington University Hospital.

Although she insisted there was nothing seriously wrong at the moment, Marie's health had been in decline for several years. Besides glaucoma, which had afflicted her since the thirties, she had cataracts, leaving her unable to see anything except when she looked downward. In addition, she suffered from high blood pressure, and because of her angina, she was under doctor's orders to carry nitroglycerin tablets in a locket around her neck, limit her exertion, and stop going into the pool alone. True to form, she had ignored advice she didn't like, continuing to smoke cigarettes, as she had for more than forty years—unlike Averell, who had given them up during his 1954 gubernatorial campaign.

In spite of her ailments, her ribald sense of humor was still in the pink of health, however, rescuing flagging dinners and pool parties with stage whispers and side-of-the-mouth one-liners that used Averell as her foil. "Cheap old bastard," she would murmur from the side of her mouth, throwing in some deftly timed line about his buying a cut-rate swimming pool, keeping an old car, or sleeping in woolen underwear his mother had given him. The gibes were never cruel; and being unable to trade one-liners with her, he sometimes seemed to go out of his way to set himself up. Once during a well-attended pool party, he had brought the merriment to a stop with a long exposition on the travails of de Gaulle's government in France. Sensing that the audience was growing glassy-eyed, she interjected, "Oh God, Ave, you know very well that de Gaulle doesn't know his ass from his elbow."[1]

Their longtime friend Donald Klopfer liked to tell a story about being in a Manhattan nightclub with them not long after World War II, when somebody at the table recognized Pamela Churchill across the room. An innocent in the party started to babble about Sir Winston's famous ex-daughter-in-law as Averell sat like a cigar-store Indian, pretending not to hear; Marie defused the embarrassment of the others by standing, whipping off her dark glasses and pretending an exaggerated stare across the room.

Their wartime estrangement had been pretty much forgotten, through efforts by both of them. If the subject of Averell's London romance ever arose, Marie treated it as though he had gone through a period of temporary insanity. For his part in the reconciliation, Averell had not only bought her the house at Hobe Sound but lobbied the Navy to give Eddy Duchin a medal for his wartime service, although he suspected that she had been in love with the widowed bandleader. Like Marie, he regarded Duchin's son, Peter, a part of the extended Harriman family, and at crucial moments he had provided Peter financial help for his own orchestra.

But while Marie made jokes about her husband's age, she confessed to bridge friends that she could no longer keep up with his pace. Her poor vision had long ago reduced her mobility; she had gained weight; and in addition to her angina, she had respiratory problems—all of which had caused her to age beyond her years. Because she had to constantly look downward, some who met her for the first time got the impression that she was drinking to excess. Averell, meanwhile, kept almost as trim as he had been in his prime, still putting on his skis and hitting the slopes at Sun Valley in his late seventies. He reveled in his friends' congratulations on his vigor and robust appearance. "Christ," Marie would say to his admirers, "you'd look good too if you'd done nothing but play polo until you were fifty." Although he was a dozen years older, it became increasingly obvious to her that he was going to outlive her. When she was gone, she told friends, he would have to find another wife, and a younger one, because he couldn't stand to be alone and he refused to act his age.

Her choice for him was their Georgetown neighbor, Mary Russell. Not long after Averell and Marie had bought their house on N Street, Russell's late husband, Ned, a correspondent for the New York *Herald Tribune*, had lain in a coma for many months after being injured in an automobile accident, and the Harrimans had been her constant support. Like Marie, Mrs. Russell was years younger than Averell, and she was an ideal prospect for a third wife, not only because she was a lovely woman with a fine appreciation for art, but because her parents had belonged to the prerevolution Russian aristocracy and she retained a lively interest in the Soviet Union. She spoke Russian fluently and had joined the 1959 Harriman expedition to Moscow as its interpreter.

Once she was checked into the hospital, Marie began feeling better and sent Averell home to get her a ham sandwich. After the scare, he was relieved that her crisis seemed to have passed; and as they raided the refrigerator, he told Ann Giná the patient would be home as soon as she had a thorough examination.

He was up early the next morning and read the papers for an hour before heading for the hospital. Henry Kissinger was off to Paris to try to talk Vice-President Ky of South Vietnam out of a Washington visit certain to provoke more antiwar demonstrations. The Nixon administration was venting its displeasure over construction of a Soviet submarine base in Cuba. About nine A.M., as he was on his way to the hospital to visit her, Marie suffered a massive heart attack and died without gaining consciousness.

Three days later, she was buried in the family cemetery behind St. John's Church at Arden, a place for Averell reserved beside her in the hemlock-shaded outcropping of rock on the flank of Tower Hill. "As perfect as Heaven used to be it will be so much more fun now that Marie is there," wrote a saddened Ethel Kennedy, who spent several hours at the funeral home with him before the wake. "I know that Bobby and Jack were with her from the very moment she left us and how they must have delighted in initiating her into The Everlasting Light, The Boundless Love and the Infinite Joys of Paradise."[2]

Harriman was distraught. Without thinking about it, he and Marie had become a team. Her failing eyesight had caused her to become dependent upon him, and his deteriorating hearing made him need her as well. More than that, he had come to realize that friends like the Kennedys were drawn to them because of her as much as him. The last years of their forty-year marriage had been the best. After initially spurning Washington, the New York girl had taken to it with characteristic gusto. She had especially loved to go to the White House during the

Kennedy administration because the President loved her wisecracks and gave her more attention than he gave Averell. She did not like Lyndon Johnson and the way he treated her husband, but she went along without objection when Averell proposed the big wedding parties for the Johnson daughters, doing what she could to help his futile effort to ingratiate himself with LBJ. After he retired, she found herself hosting dinner parties that had become even more important to him because they were one of his chief ways of staying in touch. With her death, said columnist Joe Kraft, the capital had lost the last of its witty grande dames.

Without her, Averell's zest vanished. He scarcely read the papers or watched the news, and took little interest in the friends who quickly mobilized to keep him company. He couldn't talk about her; he wouldn't let anybody into her room; and he seldom left the house. In that melancholy autumn, he looked and acted like an old man who had come to the end of the road. When he was coaxed to a dinner party at Llewellyn Thompson's house, he got into an angry argument with Edward Weintal, a former journalist and Nixon administration functionary, over the Soviet Union's postwar subjugation of Poland. When Weintal disputed the assertion that Harriman had warned Washington of the Soviets' intentions in Poland, Averell threatened to break his jaw and stomped off to the library, where the women were playing bridge. The next day, he telephoned Jane Thompson with an embarrassed apology and asked for the name of the chap involved in the fracas so he could invite him to lunch.

With winter coming, he went to Hobe Sound, where he could at least be warm while he was miserable. Peter Duchin and his wife, Cheray, moved in with him and arranged a procession of visitors, from grandchildren to political cronies, to keep him occupied with bridge and croquet. But old friends found him poor company. As if he expected to die himself, he went through a period when he was again preoccupied with thoughts of the Vietnam War, determinedly clarifying his early opposition to anyone unkind enough to remember how he had publicly stood with Johnson on the bombing of the North. He was bitter at Nixon because the new administration had not picked up the opportunity to carry on where the Harriman-Vance negotiation team had left off in 1969.

Not surprisingly, it was his old passion to be involved in U.S.-Soviet affairs that finally lifted him from the doldrums. Just as he had gone back to Moscow after his political career crashed on the rocks in New York, he went back to the Soviet Union to get rid of his loneliness, accepting Edmund Muskie's invitation to accompany him on a tour of the country and to join him in a meeting with Kosygin. He came home with his spirits much restored, ready to hold Nixon's feet to the fire on Vietnam and again interested in writing his memoirs. Rummaging through his papers and the accounts of his father's wars with James J. Hill and Teddy Roosevelt, he once again chafed at the picture of his father left by history, and he took on a private little mission to tidy up some of the old splotches on the reputation. Even to his close friends he had never talked much about the old man, and when he did it was usually about what the railroad king had done, and not what he was. Friends who had known Averell all the way back to the days when he took on his high-risk shipping, mining, and aviation ventures never doubted that E.H.'s somewhat unsavory reputation had been the motive force in the son's life. "He always spoke well of his father," Donald Klopfer recalled, "but he had a needle up his backside to be something bigger and better than his father had been."[3]

Across the years, the reputation rested on the family-commissioned 1922 biography by George F. Kennan's uncle, George Kennan. But in modern times, E.H. was better known through Matthew Josephson's book *The Robber Barons*, portraying him as one of the principal pirates in the heyday of American railroads.[4]

After weeks of looking for something authoritative to shore up E.H.'s reputation and pretty much giving up hope, he finally hit paydirt, turning up a faded manuscript by the great naturalist John Muir. The manuscript said everything he had wanted to believe about his father. "You have to read this," he told Peter Duchin with the biggest smile anybody had seen from him since Marie died. "It clearly shows that my father was a wonderful man."[5]

Muir, who had become a Harriman family friend during the famous Alaskan expedition in 1899, had written an unqualified tribute soon after E.H.'s death, and it had been buried in the files for more than six decades. The essay portrayed a warmhearted humanitarian to whom wealth was wholly incidental. The king of the Union Pacific, Muir said, was in truth "one of the rare souls Heaven sends into the world once in centuries, a man who seemed to regard the whole continent as his farm and all the people as his partners, stirring millions of workers into useful action, plowing, sowing, irrigating, mining, building cities, and factories, and farms, and homes."[6]

Since Muir was also a staunch friend of Teddy Roosevelt's, Averell considered his testimony irrefutable evidence of his father's sterling character. Some months later, he ordered several thousand copies of the eulogy printed in a pocket-sized booklet. For the rest of his life, he mailed them out, presented them to visitors, and took a supply with him whenever he traveled. He no longer had to explain his father. Whenever the subject of E.H.'s railroad career came up thereafter, John Muir was handy.

By the spring of 1971, he was approaching his old form. After Senator Fulbright called another round of hearings on the war in Vietnam and left him off the witness list, he wrote and demanded to be heard. The Foreign Relations Committee staff gave him several reasons for the omission, including the fact that his position was well known, but none of them satisfied him. Under siege, Fulbright agreed to have him speak for the record again.

He resumed inviting people to dinner, and occasionally resorted to his old trick of inviting himself out. He restored regular office hours, updated his will, tapped the Vietnam and political gossip circuits, and initiated negotiations with the National Gallery of Art to leave it his Federal-style house and his art collection as a memorial to Marie. He and his wife had bought the house when they moved to Washington at the beginning of the Kennedy administration. Built around 1805, it had long been the home of a Dr. Joseph Riley, who had his offices in a wing, which later came to house its kitchen. Averell and Marie acquired it, along with most of its furnishings, from the governor of Pennsylvania, William Scranton.

Divided between New York, Washington, and Hobe Sound, the Harriman collection included van Goghs, Picassos, Renoirs, Rousseaus, Toulouse-Lautrecs, and Matisses, the gem being van Gogh's memorable still life *White Roses*, painted shortly before the artist shot himself in 1890. Averell had bought it for himself and his mother while he and Marie were on their honeymoon, paying $72,000. His mother had promptly given her interest to him as a wedding present.

Since he had a New York residence less than a block from the Metropolitan Museum of Art, for which his mother had been a trustee, it had long been assumed that much of the collection would eventually go there, but both he and Marie had developed an affection for Washington's National Gallery. What most appealed to him was an arrangement that would make it possible for his paintings to be exhibited not only in the capital but in American embassies around the world and in cities such as Omaha and Salt Lake City, where the family had established enduring bonds through the Union Pacific.

Gallery director J. Carter Brown put the proposed gift of the house and collection before the board of trustees with a strong endorsement of domestic settings for the exhibition of masterpieces. Members were intrigued, but they could see severe problems arising from Georgetown's traffic congestion and the necessity of providing parking, access for the handicapped, and public restrooms. There was also the possibility that an economy-minded Congress might someday deny sufficient funds to operate it. What would happen to the paintings then? The trustees wanted an understanding that the works would go to the gallery. But negotiating as methodically as he had ever bargained with the Russians, Harriman insisted that in such an unhappy event the entire gift must revert to his estate.

In the midst of deliberations on this last big sticking point, Harriman suddenly lost interest. After a few days, no one had to ask why. The story swept Georgetown salons, gatherings of Democrats, and offices on Wall Street. One night in July, he went to a dinner party at the home of *Washington Post* publisher Katharine Graham, and among the guests he found the recently widowed Pamela Digby Churchill Hayward. It had been thirty years since he had first met Churchill's beautiful daughter-in-law at Lady Cunard's dinner party in London. The friendship had survived his move to Moscow and had resumed during his brief sojourn as America's postwar ambassador, but while he had seen her, briefly, only once or twice since then, he had never really got over her.

About the time he left London in September of 1946, she had taken a job with Lord Beaverbrook's *Evening Standard*. In part because of Marie Harriman's anticipated arrival in Britain and the awkwardness it would create, she had asked to be based in New York as a correspondent. When Truman called Averell home to become secretary of commerce, she had already made preparations to take up her assignment, and by coincidence, she reached New York two days after he did. Beaverbrook, perhaps at the suggestion of Paul Warburg, immediately dispatched her to Montego Bay, Jamaica, in the company of his friend Lily Ernst, an Austrian ballerina. She was infuriated at being, in effect, sent into hiding, but she stayed there for several weeks, writing a few travel articles from Jamaica and the Bahamas while Harriman settled into the President's Cabinet. She had returned to New York only briefly before giving up journalism and going back to Europe and starting a new career that invited comparison to that of her aunt, the celebrated Jane Digby.

Keeping company with men who were richer and more glamorous, though less important, than Averell, she led the life she had dreamed about as a teenager back in Dorset. She studied antiques and developed a reputation as an extraordinarily accomplished hostess, admired by men as much as she was envied by women, who were always in the distinct minority at her entertainments. Her uninhibited style caused discomfort in her conservative family back home; and when Averell saw her by chance, he had rather sanctimoniously blurted out that she was ruining her life.

After that uncomfortable moment in Paris he did not talk with her again for nearly fifteen years, although she stayed in touch with Kathleen. Then in 1965, he saw her at Churchill's funeral, and they sat together aboard the President's plane crossing the Atlantic on the way back to Washington. He was by then seventy-four; she was forty-five, happily married to theatrical producer Leland Hayward, and living just across the Hudson from Arden. It had been a memorable moment in Harriman's life, saying good-bye to the leader he idolized, and seeing the woman who still possessed him and talking with her for hours as they crossed the Atlantic.

The flight had also provided him a compelling opportunity to end his feud with General Eisenhower. The former President had headed the American delegation to the funeral; and while Averell and Pamela talked, he had come back and said hello. After a few minutes, Averell had gone forward for a long private conversation with him in the President's compartment.

It was the first time they had spoken to each other in more than a decade. When Harriman had gone through a White House receiving line at a reception for the nation's governors soon after his election in 1954, Eisenhower, remembering Averell's venomous attacks on him in the 1952 campaign, had shown him no sign of recognition, coldly addressing him as "Governor" and extending the perfunctory "welcome to the White House." They had not met since. Each had taken derogatory potshots at the other over the years, and in private Eisenhower had referred to Averell as a "nincompoop" and a "Park Avenue Truman."[7] In return, Averell ridiculed him for fawning over rich men. The nostalgic atmosphere on the plane made the whole affair seem childish.

Harriman had no inkling that Pamela was to be at Kay Graham's, nor had the thought of being a matchmaker occurred to the hostess. She had known Averell most of her life, and she had developed a friendship with Pamela through her daughter, who had been neighbor of the Haywards' estate in New York. If the reunion hadn't taken place at Mrs. Graham's dinner, however, it would have soon happened somewhere else, for Averell had been thinking about Pamela since hearing of Leland Hayward's death in March. Sometime in June, he had called Bill Walton, who had been a friend of both all the way back in the war days, and inquired where she was. Unfortunately, said the greatly amused Walton, recognizing a hint for him to become an emissary, she had just gone to England. The good news was that she would soon be back.

The idea of marrying Averell had never occurred to Pamela during their days together in London. His age alone was enough to make it unthinkable even if they'd been unattached and anonymous. But after he had gone off to Moscow in the autumn of '43, she had written to him nearly every week for most of the remaining months of the war, providing him graphic details of Hitler's buzz bombs and rocket attacks.

In June 1944, she described how one V-1 flying bomb narrowly missed the Churchill Club just after she arrived for work one Sunday: "I hadn't been there very long when we heard one of the creatures coming. It came louder and nearer and the flack poured down on the club and through the windows; then as it came over us, it cut out—and we waited for the bang. It came and everything shook, and we breathed again. It had landed on the guards' chapel—Wellington Barracks—and as there was a special service in progress, it killed a great many people, including several I knew well."[8]

She did not tell him that she sometimes watched the raids from rooftops with Ed Murrow as he described them with the doomsday voice that more than any other made the war real in homes across America. To her, Averell remained her special friend and supporter, but she wanted to marry Murrow once he could shed his wife, Janet, who had gone back to the States knowing that her husband was captivated. But the star correspondent was a man with some old-fashioned notions about marriage and fair play, and when he was at last confronted with a choice he had picked his wife, who after years of trying unsuccessfully, became pregnant as the drama unfolded.

In Paris, the banker Elie de Rothschild had been smitten by the beautiful redhead and had cared for her in exquisite style; but in the end, he had unceremoniously dropped her. The playboy Italian auto manufacturer Giovanni Agnelli had showered her with jewels and antiques and marriage seemed to shimmer on the horizon, but he instead chose to wed Princess Marella Caracciolo di Castagneto, though he remained Pamela's friend over the years just as Averell had.

In 1961, by which time she had achieved renown on both sides of the Atlantic, she had married Hayward, the suave, prodigiously successful film producer who was about to go to work on *The Sound of Music*, already having films such as *Mr. Roberts* and *The Old Man and the Sea* among his credits. For her, the legendary Hayward left his third wife, the glamorous Nancy Keith, who considered herself a victim of grand theft rather than desertion.

Over the ten years thereafter, Pamela moved comfortably in the international film and theatrical community, a happily devoted wife. For weeks before Hayward died in March 1971, she nursed him night and day, earning grudging admiration even from people who liked her least. She was left with a fifty-seven-acre hilltop estate in Westchester County and the enduring enmity of her stepdaughter, Brooke, who recorded the unhappy saga of the Hayward children in a best-selling memoir, *Haywire*, which suggested, among other things, that Pamela made off with jewelry belonging to her mother, Margaret Sullavan,[9] who had been Hayward's second wife.

She had just returned from London to the lonely Haywire House when she received Katharine Graham's invitation to come down to Washington for a dinner party the following evening. She was weary from the trip, and she would have declined, but the sky was overcast and in the empty house she was fully realizing that she was alone for the first time in her life. She accepted the invitation.

She had already arrived and was in Graham's garden when Averell came in. They spent most of the evening talking together, and before the dinner was over whispers and knowing smiles were going around. The old friendship had obviously exploded into instant bloom. Within days, he showed up for a visit at her house in the country. To make it more convenient to see her, he once more began staying at his residence on Eighty-first Street in New York rather than his house in Georgetown. "Since we were both suddenly free and alone," she said, "it just seemed the most natural thing in the world to kind of get together again."[10]

Not long afterward, the Duchins arranged a dinner in Averell's behalf at his house at Sands Point, inviting his neighbors, Edward and Marian Goodman, George and Evie Backer, and Mike Forrestal. When Cheray Duchin inquired whether he would also like to invite Mrs. Hayward, he agreed before the question was out of her mouth. Pamela arrived with luggage and settled into the guest bedroom.

Throughout the evening, Harriman sparkled as he hadn't in months; he was still excited over the leak of the secret Pentagon papers with their inside account of the Vietnam War, though distressed over the grievous breach of security. Pamela's presence inspired Churchill and World War II stories none of the others had ever heard.

After the Backers and the Goodmans had gone and Averell and Pamela had each said good night, Forrestal and Duchin talked past midnight. Because the weather was balmy, Peter and Mike sat with the doors and windows open, taking in a gentle breeze off Long Island Sound. One of them heard a thump beside the house, and when they looked out across the dimly lit garden, they saw a figure emerging from the window of the master bedroom. Dressed in a robe, the host stepped smartly across the garden and into the shadow of the opposite wing of the house. There was a light tapping on the window of the guest bedroom, and, momentarily, the faint sound of it opening. The figure disappeared from the garden; and inside there was a crash of something being overturned in the darkness, as the living room erupted in laughter.

Their engagement was announced in mid-September. At City Hall, surrounded by photographers, they lined up with twenty-year-olds to get their marriage license. On September 27, an hour and a half before 150 guests started arriving for an engagement party, they slipped out and drove eight blocks up Fifth Avenue to St. Thomas More Roman Catholic Church, where the Reverend Joseph Christie, Pamela's priest from London, assisted in performing the ceremony. Ethel Kennedy was the matron of honor. Marriage in the Church was not a problem, since Pamela had converted to Catholicism after her divorce from Randolph and since she also had gotten an annulment of the marriage, meaning that it had never existed in the eyes of the Church. The name, nevertheless, remained useful, and she chose to be, after her marriage to Averell, Pamela Churchill Harriman.

Before the engagement was announced, she had sent her son to deliver personally the news of her plans to eighty-six-year-old Lady Churchill. She had no idea whether or when her father-in-law and mother-in-law had ever learned the extent of her wartime friendship with the American envoy, and she was relieved by Lady Churchill's reaction relayed by young Winston: "My, my, an old flame rekindled."[11]

Having recently seemed old, spent, and ready to die, Harriman once again had spring in his step and his killer instinct on the croquet lawn.

He showed his bride the Union Pacific, rowed her out to the island in Forest Lake where he had camped as a boy, took her horseback riding at the railroad ranch and skiing at Sun Valley, where old-timers watched and gave each other knowing smiles as the newlyweds walked about hand in hand. He escorted her about his old capitol at Albany, took her out to Missouri to meet Harry and Bess Truman, and even down to Texas to spend the night at the LBJ Ranch. He presented her to Georgetown at a star-studded party unmatched in Washington since the heyday of Camelot and introduced her at Democratic enclaves as proudly as he had shown FDR his new streamliner. The old man was in love, maybe for the first time in his life. Unlike Marie, who had kidded and deflated him, Pamela petted and humored and stoked the still-robust ego. When he snapped, she could restore tranquillity with a wounded look. And when she moved about the room among their guests, he could be caught stealing admiring glances at her as though he were seeing her for the first time.

Old friends marveled that his tight grasp on his purse strings had been relaxed as if by magic. The furniture in the Georgetown house was replaced with French antiques; new pillows were adorned with the Digby family crest. A new chef and an expanded staff accompanied the pair as they moved from residence to residence with the changing seasons— Hobe Sound for the harshest weeks of winter, and to Yorktown Heights and Haywire House, rechristened Birch Grove, during Washington's stifling summer. His Manhattan residence, which she found gloomy, was sold, and eventually so was Hobe Sound. Barbados became their winter retreat; and when airline travel eventually became difficult for him, they acquired an Israeli-built Westwind executive jet.

As a wedding gift to him, she became an American citizen—so she could vote for Democrats, she said. She went along and listened whenever he was invited to lecture on U.S.-Soviet relations, took notes when visitors came to brief him, made their dinners and parties the talk of political Washington, and eventually became the Democrats' most spectacular fund-raiser.

He was more relaxed than anyone could remember; but some of his old-fashioned ideas persisted, even with the house being managed by

Pamela's legendary touch and his wife taking a part in all of his political and diplomatic interests. One was that ladies would withdraw after dinner, leaving the gentlemen to their brandy, cigars, and the manly subjects of money, politics, and diplomacy. It was a custom egregiously out of sync with the Pamela era, but she indulged him, escorting the ladies off to their own precinct when he deemed it the appropriate moment. But not even she could forever avert a collision between past and present.

It came on an evening when Senator Muskie was the honored guest and others around the table included *Washington Post* editor Ben Bradlee and Sally Quinn, a *Style* section feature writer who had personally charmed the boss as much as her catty profiles of Washington personalities had impressed him professionally. After dessert, Averell gave the nod. Pamela suggested that the ladies retire; but when Averell led the men up the stairs to his study, Quinn joined them. She was a reporter, she said, and she was interested in politics.

Harriman fumbled with his hearing aid, thinking that his ears had deceived him. Quinn repeated that she had no interest in joining the ladies. That being the case, the host growled, then she could get out of his damned house; and as the gentlemen gazed into their brandy snifters, Quinn marched down the stairs and out the door. Left behind visibly squirming, Bradlee excused himself, mentioning an important telephone call he needed to make. When he returned, he told Averell an emergency had arisen requiring his presence at the office. Quinn was waiting in the car.

In the early seventies, the major political topic at Harriman's table was defeating Nixon; and in 1972, Muskie was his choice for the assignment. Senator George McGovern of South Dakota was too willing to cut and run in Vietnam, and Humphrey had been fatally damaged by failing to stake out his ground on the war in 1968. In the late winter and early spring of 1972, Harriman and Pamela campaigned for Muskie, riding with the senator on a whistle-stop tour of Florida and working retirement communities heavily populated by elderly former New Yorkers.

Later, he hit the campaign trail to win a place in the New York delegation to the nominating convention. Party reforms, adopted in reaction to the Tammany Hall bossism, had made it impossible for him simply to be appointed. He had to be elected. To his amazement and disappointment, Muskie's chances had evaporated early, when the senator appeared to have cried in responding to attacks of William Loeb and his right-wing *Manchester Union Leader*. So instead of campaigning as a Muskie delegate, he ran as an independent against an entire slate committed to McGovern.

While state Democrats were in disarray, nearly anybody who pretended to know anything about politics assured him there was no way he could lose to inexperienced antiwar activists. Having heard similar forecasts when he was running for reelection as governor, he took no chances. With Pamela at the wheel of a station wagon, they logged a thousand miles a week crisscrossing Orange and Rockland counties through May and into June. They rang doorbells, worked community centers and union halls, and buttonholed voters in grocery stores, attracting curious crowds more anxious to see her than to hear him. In spite of the assurances from supporters, both realized they were bucking a landslide for McGovern. In the end, the effort netted him only a little more than three thousand votes, leaving him behind the entire slate of six candidates pledged to McGovern, including a nineteen-year-old from New Paltz with no previous political experience.

He would not be a delegate to the convention in Miami Beach. Considering that George McGovern was certain to be nominated, he did not really care. He was concerned, though, that his image and, perhaps, his future would suffer because of the loss. He asked several friends whether they thought he had been "damaged"; most, struggling to keep a straight face, assured him the setback was likely to be temporary.[12]

Left without any role to play, he went to the convention anyway and spent most of two days shaking hands around Muskie headquarters at the Americana Hotel in Miami Beach and sitting in the gallery with Pamela as the party nominated McGovern to challenge Richard Nixon. But on the night of his acceptance, the convention, under control of reformers and political neophytes, dallied until 12:38 A.M. before calling the roll to nominate Senator Thomas Eagleton of Missouri for Vice-President, and it was another two hours before McGovern was finally given the floor. By then, the Harrimans had given up and driven back up to Hobe Sound. For Averell, it was worse than the 1968 Chicago debacle. Then, he had at least been enthusiastic about Humphrey as a candidate.

Ironically, Harriman's retirement gave him more opportunity to delve into U.S.-Soviet affairs than he had ever had in his years working for Kennedy and Johnson. After visiting Moscow with Muskie in 1971, he went back five more times, the last when he was past ninety but unable to stay away because the Kremlin was heading into a time of unpredictable transition.

Each time he returned, he appeared to be saying his farewell. In 1974, he went to introduce Pamela, the year after that to lead an American delegation observing the thirtieth anniversary of the end of World War II. He went back again in 1976 intent upon establishing communications between Soviet officials and the new leadership in Washington. Two years later, he astonished the Kremlin by publicly reminding Communist leaders of their Stalinist past; and finally, he returned to urge Yuri Andropov to negotiate arms controls in spite of tensions with the Reagan administration.

After his three private visits to Moscow and regular meetings with Ambassador Anatoly Dobrynin during the Nixon-Ford years, he was eager to make himself at least an informal conduit between Jimmy Carter and Leonid Brezhnev. He had hardly been more enthusiastic about the former Georgia governor than he had been about George McGovern. But to make sure that he was not left on the shelf in Georgetown by newcomers operating a presidential campaign out of Atlanta, he did the same thing he had in 1960 when he was about to be overlooked by the Kennedys. Recovered from a broken hip he had suffered in a fall on the sidewalk in front of his house, he planned his own diplomatic mission and offered the candidate his services.

Richard Holbrooke, a State Department protégé during the last years of the Johnson administration, had moved onto the Carter campaign staff in Atlanta. Through him, Harriman arranged a meeting with the nominee in Washington. In earlier times, the candidate might have called at N Street; but since Carter was not hotly pursuing him, Averell hastened to the Capitol Hill townhouse of Carter aide Peter Bourne and waited his turn among a new generation of party functionaries lined up for a moment with the candidate. When he was called, he took the stairs to the second floor study two at a time, with a copy of his notes from his last conversation with Brezhnev.

Instead of fishing for an assignment, he informed Carter that he would shortly be traveling to the Soviet Union again, and since he would certainly see Brezhnev in the course of his visit, he would be pleased to deliver any message Carter cared to send. The candidate was happy to have the opportunity, but rather than jot anything down, he casually suggested that Harriman just tell Brezhnev that if Carter became President, he would be prepared to deal with the Soviet government directly and seriously. The administration's first priority would be nuclear-arms reduction and cooperation in inhibiting nuclear proliferation. As President, he would be anxious to engage Moscow on both Soviet immigration policy and Moscow's involvement in the affairs of other governments. He would be ready for a face-to-face meeting with Brezhnev.[13]

On September 20, Averell arrived at the Kremlin for his third meeting with the Soviet Communist party's general secretary. It was the first time he had talked with a Soviet leader in the middle of a presidential race and as the representative of a candidate. His chief reason for coming, he told Brezhnev, was to have him understand that the 1976 campaign rhetoric had become especially exaggerated because of Ronald Reagan's challenge to President Ford for the Republican party nomination. Threatened by a member of his own party, Ford had been forced to the right; and, to avoid being isolated, the Democratic nominee had taken more hawkish positions as well.

Carter, he assured Brezhenev, was interested in serious U.S.-Soviet diplomacy. In the Georgia governor's view, it was essential for Moscow and Washington to avoid surprising each other on crucial matters such as arms control. Carter supported the interim strategic weapons ceilings set by Ford and Brezhnev at their 1974 Vladivostok summit but considered them too high and wished to achieve substantial nuclear-arms reductions. Although he had no intention of interfering in the Soviets' internal affairs, he supported all of the provisions of the Helsinki accords on European security, including those pertaining to human rights. In America, the issue of Soviet Jewish emigration could not "be put under the rug."[14]

Anxious to brief Carter on the conversation, Harriman cut short a London visit with Pamela's son on the way home so he could get back to Washington while Carter was there for a few hours later in the week.

Although the polls still showed him substantially ahead, the Democratic nominee was campaigning at a frenetic pace. Harriman returned only to find there was not a moment in the campaign schedule for his report. However, Holbrooke arranged for him to catch up with Carter and his entourage in Bethesda, Maryland, where the candidate was making a stop at a 4-H Club function, and then ride with him to Dulles Airport in Virginia. The circumstances were hardly ideal for a serious diplomatic report. In keeping with his common man's image, Carter was being driven in mid-sized sedan rather than in a limousine. And since he was accompanied by a Secret Service bodyguard who required the front seat, Carter, Harriman, and Holbrooke were jammed into the back, with Averell in the middle. The party was, as usual, behind schedule. It was pouring rain; and with all of them packed into the vehicle in their damp raincoats, the windows fogged and they could scarcely see anything as they careened through traffic behind blaring sirens.

Carter had only a vague recollection of what he had told Harriman to pass along to Brezhnev; and under the circumstances, it was difficult for him to take in any of the reply, much less the nuances that Averell thought were fraught with significance.

The ambassador talked nonstop throughout the twenty-five-mile trip, reciting one by one all of the major points that each had made. Brezhnev had liked the idea of a postelection summit, and he had seemed favorably disposed to Harriman's suggestion that he say something positive about U.S.-Soviet relations after the election to give the winner an opportunity to respond in kind and get the new administration off to a positive start. It was of considerable interest, Harriman thought, that Brezhnev had not talked of "wars of liberation," as Khrushchev always did, but spoke of "liberation movements."

When they reached Carter's chartered plane at the airport, the candidate rushed for the ramp, and Harriman followed across the tarmac in the downpour. The engines were already whining, and Harriman shouted the last of his report as Carter turned and hurried up the stairs. Carter later mentioned to Holbrooke that it had been a remarkable and appreciated display of commitment and tenacity by a man eighty-five years old; but it was Brezhnev who took Harriman's mission as serious diplomacy.

A few days after the election, Dobrynin arrived at Hobe Sound with a personal message from the Soviet leader, requesting that Averell put it in the hands of the President-elect. Having heard Carter's views from Harriman, it said, Brezhnev was prepared to proceed in a "positive, constructive spirit" with efforts to end the arms race "in the center of these relations." It was the opening Averell had suggested.[15]

Delivering the message gave Harriman his chance to talk with Carter about administration appointments before the process of filling the ranks had gathered full steam. His foremost interests were to lobby for Cyrus Vance to become secretary of state and to discourage Carter from making James Schlesinger either secretary of defense or arms-control negotiator. He further wanted to put in strong reservations about Zbigniew Brzezinski as the White House national security adviser. He found the thought of Schlesinger in the Pentagon appalling because of his notions that nuclear weapons could have utility in fighting a war. He disliked Brzezinski personally and considered his views too rigidly anti-Soviet.

In spite of his age, some of Harriman's friends, including Holbrooke, were hoping he would volunteer for one more tour as ambassador-at-large; but for the first time since he became a Democrat, he wasn't actively interested in a presidential assignment, though he would have undoubtedly accepted an offer. The time had come, he told Carter, for a youth movement.

That was anything but a retirement announcement, however. The fact that he would not have government office space or civil servants working for him did not mean that he had no role. His house and offices adjacent to his residence became his own little embassy. Two apartments at the back became temporary bachelor quarters for Carter men moving into town ahead of their families, as well as for transient diplomats. Confirming his determination to remain involved, he suppressed his dislike for Brzezinski and invited the new national security adviser to make one of the apartments his home while he shopped for a house. Marshall Shulman, a onetime aide to Acheson, who returned to work for Vance at State, moved in for several weeks, followed by Holbrooke. Becoming concerned that he would overstay his welcome, Shulman more than once mentioned moving out; but Harriman was anxious not to lose a tenant who was in the thick of the action at Foggy Bottom, and Shulman found his quarters enlarged.

When he and the other guests came home in the afternoon, they were invited next door to watch the news, have a drink, and sometimes stay for dinner. Before they departed, they had always been fully debriefed on their day at State or at the White House and had the full benefit of Averell's reaction.

Later, during the furious congressional debate over ratification of the Panama Canal treaties and the Carter administration's long—and ultimately unsuccessful—effort to get Senate approval of the SALT II Treaty putting the first controls on offensive nuclear weapons, the house became headquarters of a lobbying effort reminiscent of Averell's Blue Eagle crusade during the New Deal. Since it was no longer possible for him to get out and work the country as he had for Johnson on Vietnam, people important to the effort were shuttled in to see him—reporters, editors, civic leaders, Democratic politicians during the day, crucial senators and administration strategists for cocktails and dinner.

"I live for SALT II," he told Holbrooke as his citizens committee went to work to fan grass roots support for the agreement in 1979. "I live for SALT II."[16]

But after seven years of negotiation and months of congressional debate, the arms treaty died with the Soviet invasion of Afghanistan, withdrawn from Senate consideration in the realization that the chance of getting the necessary two thirds approval was nil. It was justifiably Harriman's most crushing disappointment of the Carter administration. Had Carter—and Brzezinski—taken his visit with Brezhnev more seriously, the treaty might have been ratified before the war in Afghanistan made it politically unpalatable. At the outset of the Carter administration, Brezhnev had laid heavy emphasis on the interim agreement that he and Gerald Ford had made at their November 1974 meeting at Vladivostok, seeing it as a stepping stone to a SALT II treaty. But the new administration had, against the advice of Cyrus Vance, struck out on a new, more ambitious course in arms control rather than picking up the framework left behind by Ford and Henry Kissinger. Carter sent Vance to Moscow with a proposal for deep reductions in offensive nuclear armaments, and the Soviet Union had backed away, throwing deliberations into limbo. Disputes over human rights and other disagreements unrelated to the arms issue added to the delay, and it was June 1979 before Carter and Brzezinski had an agreement ready for consideration by the U.S. Senate.

With Vance, who regarded Harriman as his mentor, in charge at Foggy Bottom, Averell was more comfortable with the State Department than he had ever been when he was part of it. In the fall of 1977, he bought a place in the Virginia hunt country outside Middleburg, and he and Pamela often had Vance and his wife, Gay, as guests. Although there were recurrent suggestions from Holbrooke and others that Averell be brought into the administration for another tour as ambassador-at-large, nothing happened when the recommendation was sent on to the White House, because Brzezinski didn't approve of it. Especially where the

Kremlin was concerned, the national security adviser's views and Harriman's collided head-on. Brzezinski thought Averell overly eager to find agreements with Moscow, and Averell would often tell people that it was a fundamental mistake to have a Pole giving advice on Soviet policy. There were few occasions during the Carter administration when Harriman was moved to ask to see the President; and when he showed up to see him, he was always intercepted by Brzezinski, who would stroll into the Oval Office with him uninvited.

Without portfolio, he contented himself to work on his volunteer campaigns for the Panama Canal and SALT treaties, and to give occasional advice on ambassadorial appointments. When Carter did call on him, it seemed that more often than not the assignment was to represent the President at the funeral of old friends—Lord Mountbatten, wartime Australian prime minister Robert Menzies, Marshal Tito.

Nonetheless, Averell recharged his batteries with private trips. He went back to Hungary and Romania, and then, in the wake of U.S. recognition of Communist China, he planned a ten-day visit to Peking, Shanghai, and Hangchow. With the detailed schedule in place, however, his doctor called the mission off. There was too much danger of a bronchial infection. Only once during the Carter years did he get to return to Moscow—on a nongovernment mission to promote U.S.-Soviet trade, during which he had an hour-and-a-half talk with Brezhnev on the stalemated SALT negotiations.

But with the atmosphere between Washington and Moscow deteriorating, he decided speak his more important piece on Soviet-American relations in public rather than in private conversation with Brezhnev. Shortly before a luncheon where he was to be the speaker, he casually told Brezhnev he had decided to talk about Stalin.

No longer able to read from a text, he had rehearsed his remarks aloud with Peter Swiers. It was his valedictory. He recalled his first visit to the Soviet Union and his wartime diplomatic service. He reaffirmed his long-ago controversial assertion that the Soviet Union and the United States harbored irreconcilable differences. His point was that cooperation was still possible; to emphasize it, he dragged Josef Stalin—a man of "extraordinary brutality" and "extraordinarily able leadership"—out of the closet. In spite of the ideological differences, he said, even Stalin had acknowledged that World War II would have been lost without American Lend-Lease.[17]

Soviet officials squirmed in discomfort at public mention of the dictator's name. Astonished waiters stopped working and lined up against the wall to listen. When he finished, there was a moment of silence, wary glances between Russians, tentative applause from a few of them, and then a huge ovation.

He did not go back for another five years. By then, Ronald Reagan was in the White House; Brezhnev was dead; the never-ratified SALT II Treaty was a fading memory; and the deepest chill since the Cold War began had settled over relations between Washington and Moscow.

Unlike his father, who had settled his estate with his cryptic will leaving everything to his wife, Averell spent years systematically disposing of a fortune that grew to the neighborhood of $100 million while he pursued his government career. In part because of tax laws encouraging gifts, he and Roland donated land to the state of New York, and to the towns of Harriman, Woodbury, and Monroe, and to Columbia University.

By the time their estate plans were completed, E.H.'s empire in the Ramapos, once spreading over 40,000 acres, had been reduced to 3,500, three fourths of it divided equally among Averell's daughters and their families, and Roland's heirs, with the last fourth held by all of them in a single partnership. The 10,000 acres given for the Palisades Interstate Park in 1910 by their mother was followed many years later by 12,000 acres for Harriman State Park, and thousands more for the New York State Thruway. Averell's gift of Arden House and 1,000 acres to Columbia University would be followed thirty years later by the gift of Roland's Homestead and the 500 acres that went with it.

In Idaho, the 10,000-acre "railroad ranch" that Roland had loved as much as Arden itself was given to the state, becoming another Harriman State Park, where conditions of the gift prevented hunting and established a game preserve. By the time the brothers wound up their careers, most of their personal wealth was in stocks, bonds, and securities owned by their private corporations. Like his brother, Roland Harriman suffered from severe loss of hearing, but unlike Averell he did not have the stubbornness and defiance to fight through it. He had stepped aside as chairman of the Union Pacific in 1953, turning the job over to Bob Lovett, and thereafter devoted much of his energy to the American Red Cross. Appointed by President Truman to succeed General Marshall as national chairman, he was named to new terms by Eisenhower, Kennedy, Johnson, and Nixon. Typically without notice, he had in his own way served as many presidents as had Averell.

In February 1978, Roland died at the Homestead at the age of eighty-two; only Averell was left from E.H.'s brood. Their sister Carol had died in 1948, and Cornelia in 1966. And since neither he nor Roland had produced a son, he was the last to bear old William Harriman's name.

Feeling alone again and sick with a cold, he and Pamela set out for yet another funeral at Arden, accompanied by George Elsey, a onetime aide in the Truman White House who had for years worked closely with Roland at the Red Cross. On the Union Pacific corporate plane to New

York, Averell sat with a blanket around his shoulders, sipping hot bouillon and talking about the brother who had been so entirely different. Aside from family, they had shared few interests in their adult years. But going back to St. John's Church, where the family had gathered at its saddest and most joyful moments, Averell found their boyhood three quarters of a century earlier still vivid. He talked about their trips to Alaska and Japan, rowing on Forest Lake, hunting at their father's camp in Oregon, and looking out for one another at Groton. When his voice choked up, he coughed and sipped his bouillon and complained about his cold, but Elsey could tell that the old man was fighting back tears and struggling to keep his voice from breaking.

He was soon back into the swing in Washington, immersing himself in the SALT II debate, but he no longer received the satisfaction from politics that he had before, even in the Johnson administration. He had never overcome personal reservations about Jimmy Carter, but that had not diminished his loyalty. When Senator Edward Kennedy challenged the President in the 1980 Democratic primaries, he resisted pressure to endorse him against the President. The political mantle in fact had passed to Pamela, who would, at the Democrats' darkest moment following Carter's loss to Reagan, found her own political action committee with the audacious goal of recapturing the U.S. Senate from Republican control. Her prominence pleased him because it kept him engaged, but the shift of power in the family brought with it painful moments. His friendship with Daniel Patrick Moynihan, his aide from Albany days, suffered in part because Pamela supported Congresswoman Bella Abzug against him in his race for the Senate nomination. His warm relationship with Peter Duchin waned, first because Peter had been so close to Marie and later because he married Pamela's nemesis, Brooke Hayward.

As his wife turned the Georgetown house into the country's classiest salon, welcoming Democratic politicians and astounding party professionals with her ability to raise money, Averell spent most of his time at the Willow Oaks estate in Virginia, which, for tax reasons, became their official residence. There, realizing that his time was growing short, he took renewed interest in planning for the disposal of his estate. Though he could no longer see the words on the pages, he several times went over his will with William Rich, who handled his financial affairs, making sure that every tax issue was considered and that the estate was left in condition to support his branch of the Harriman family far into the next century.

In 1982, he gave $10 million to Columbia University's Russian Institute, along with $1.5 million from the Roland and Gladys Harriman Foundation. In appreciation, the university changed the name to the Harriman Institute for Advanced Study of the Soviet Union. With the SALT treaty dead and the Reagan White House yet to show any serious attention in arms control, the gift provided him an occasion for a broadside at administration Soviet policy. Misinformation about the Soviet Union was pervasive, he said, "beginning with those in highest authority in government," hence the grant that would create his memorial.[18]

Initially, the plan was for his personal papers covering his association with the Soviet Union to go to the new institute. But when the university sought an additional grant to process and preserve them, they were put in storage, the entire collection eventually being left to the Library of Congress, with copies of the Soviet material being provided to the institute.

All of his beloved art collection, including his famous van Gogh, *White Roses*, had been given to Pamela in January 1982. Experts later estimated that it would sell at auction for $60 million in the inflated art market of the 1980s. His five grandsons and one granddaughter, whose ages ranged from twenty-nine to forty-four, were to receive $100,000 each upon his death. A $6 million trust was established to begin providing proceeds to them and their offspring after twenty-five years. The rest of the fortune was left to Pamela. "I have intentionally refrained from making substantial provision for my beloved daughters, Kathleen Lanier Harriman Mortimer and Mary Averell Harriman Fisk, in this my will," he wrote, "not from any lack of love and affection for them but because I know them to be otherwise well provided for."[19]

In Barbados, on Christmas Eve, 1983, Harriman and Pamela walked down the driveway from their winter house to the sea. It was a little windy, but a good day for their regular stroll along the beach in the warm tropical surf. They had only started out, when both were knocked sprawling by a late-breaking wave. Although she scrambled quickly to her feet, he had a shooting pain in his right leg just above the ankle. After crawling onto the sand, he was able to get back to his feet; but he was unable to walk, and an X ray showed a fracture.

Unlike the time he had fallen on the sidewalk and cracked his hip, he did not bounce back. The best-kept secret in Washington was that in addition to his increasing deafness and blindness, he had been been suffering from bone cancer for several years. After he had decided against radiation or chemotherapy, he and Pamela had mentioned it to no one; and if he was in pain, he never admitted it.

But after the fracture from the fall in the surf healed, he never walked normally again; he grew increasingly stooped and required a walker to get about. Unable to make it up and down the stairs, he quit holding office hours. There were times when it seemed that he might die, but month in and month out he kept death at bay. When he returned from his last trip to the Soviet Union, he went back to ophthalmologists at Johns Hopkins University, but they had concluded that nothing more could be done about his blindness. He took the news with greater anger than sorrow. When NBC correspondent John Chancellor asked him one afternoon how Andropov had looked, he replied with the old crocodile snap, "How the hell should I know? I can't even see you."[20]

In spite of his severely impaired hearing, he could still manage one-on-one conversations, with the help of advancing technology. As his hearing declined, he got a new aid nearly every year. When he discovered that he could take a tax deduction if he gave the old ones to charity, he sent his secretary to find all the cast offs and turn them in. If batteries were left from a model taken out of service, they were sent back to the drugstore for a refund. The last model came with a microphone that could be placed near a visitor and transmit to a pocket receiver connected to his earpiece. One evening at Willow Oaks, his guests forgot about the transmitter and, while he had gone off to the bathroom, candidly talked about his condition. When he returned and began challenging most of what they'd said, they realized with horror that he had heard everything.

He still demanded that the newspapers be read to him every day, answered his mail, and stubbornly swam his laps wherever he was in residence, even when a nurse was required to help him in and out of the pool. When Pamela was away, friends joined him for lunch and dinner. In the summer of 1985, Anatoly Dobrynin came to a luncheon arranged for about a dozen friends, made a little speech and presented him with the Soviet government's Medal of the Patriotic War, with a citation formally expressing appreciation for his work for peace. After a patter of applause, to the surprise of the ambassador and all the rest, he got to his feet. Leaning heavily on his walker, he touched on all of his favorite themes on U.S.-Soviet relations. He still twinkled. He had found it necessary to decline the honor during the war, he said, and now it came to him as the first thing he had received from the Soviets since Stalin had presented him with two horses. All things considered, he added, he still preferred the horses. By the time he sat down, the eyes of several around the table had flooded with tears.

But except when allies from long past adventures called, he remained more interested in talking politics or about the news in the morning paper than in reminiscing. No matter how he tried to stay in touch, though, Washington had slipped away from him. It was impossible for him to be at dinners and parties surrounded by Democrats from several generations, journalists, and the old pros of the foreign service; and once there was a hint of autumn chill in the air, he longed for the sun and the ocean breeze at Barbados.

During the Christmas and New Year's holidays of 1985 and 1986, Peter and Karen Swiers flew in from Copenhagen, where they had been posted for two years. He was as frail as they had expected, but there had been a remarkable psychological rebound. He enjoyed his guests, his swims, his Christmas gifts, and asked to be taken on drives. On several days, they traveled the Upper Road around the coast to the north side of the island, where the Caribbean merges into the Atlantic. There, he liked to stop, because he still had enough peripheral vision to appreciate the view, and he could faintly hear the crashing surf.

He went back to Virginia to catch the best days of spring at Willow Oaks, high on a bluff overlooking Goose Creek in the foothills of the Blue Ridge Mountains. Then, as the dog days of summer arrived, he was driven to Dulles Airport and flown to the Westchester County Airport for the short trip to Birch Grove. The heat was blistering, and he arrived exhausted. But he recovered enough to board his golf cart every day and ride out to the pool for his regular swim.

Several days later, he developed pneumonia and no longer wanted to leave his room. He quit eating and lapsed into semiconsciousness, and Pamela realized that he had decided to die. She called Kathleen and Mary, who were on vacation in Alaska, Peter Swiers in Copenhagen, and her son, Winston, in London.

He recognized them all when they arrived; and during the times he was awake, Kathleen sat by his bed reading to him from the chapters of a new biography of General Ira Eaker, recounting the Fifteenth Air Force leader's arrival at Poltava after the first shuttle bombing of Hitler's eastern strongholds in June 1944.

At last, his kidneys quit. Three days later, sometime not long after midnight on the morning of July 26, 1986, the nurse summoned the family. Moments later, with Pamela, Kathleen, Mary, Peter, and Winston at his side, he died.

"He just decided that enough was enough," Pamela said.[21]

EPILOGUE

The funeral, with one eulogy and several scriptural readings, was at St. Thomas's Episcopal Church in Manhattan, where his mother had attended services every Sunday when she was in the city. When it was over, nine hundred mourners—a few stooped survivors from the Roosevelt years, more from the Fair Deal, plus a host from the Kennedy-Johnson period and from his old team at Albany—stood and sang "The Battle Hymn of the Republic" as his five grandsons, young Winston Churchill, and Peter Duchin carried the coffin down the aisle; Julia Ward Howe's Civil War anthem had likewise concluded the funeral of two of the people he best loved and most admired—Churchill and Robert Kennedy. Afterward, a motorcycle contingent of New York City's finest escorted the cortege across the George Washington Bridge. On the New Jersey shore, a contingent of New York State troopers met the party and led it up the Palisades Parkway through Harriman State Park and back to Arden.

The afternoon sun filtered through the hemlocks onto the solid rock ledge where his parents, his brother Harry, Mary Rumsey, her son Bronson, and Marie had been buried in a row. Beside Marie, workmen on the estate had opened a grave for Averell.

Down the hill, beneath small, almost unnoticeable native stones lay Roland, Gladys, and their daughter, Elizabeth Bliss, who had died in 1968, the family hierarchy preserved, at Roland's instructions, even in death.

After the words at the graveside, Episcopalian bishop Paul Moore, Jr., sprinkled sand on the coffin, and the family and the several dozen close friends who had driven up from the city drifted away, walking down the narrow road past St. John's Church.

It was more than two months later, however, before he was finally laid to rest. After the last of the mourners had gone, the body was taken to the funeral home that had arranged the service.

In the end, the family had decided to bury him beside Forest Lake, where he had rowed and fished and camped eighty years earlier and where he and Pamela had returned to picnic during the summers they had spent across the Hudson at Yorktown Heights. His grandson, David Mortimer, had chosen the spot, but there hadn't been time to get the permits necessary for a new cemetery. Instead of later transferring the body, Pamela had opted to go ahead with the graveside rites in the old family plot but to postpone the burial until the lake site was ready. Set off by the deep blue of the lake, his monument was visible from his boathouse and the dock.

The words beneath his name on the native stone read, "PATRIOT, PUBLIC SERVANT, STATESMAN."

NOTES

Chapter I

1. George Kennan, *E. H. Harriman, A Biography*, Vol. I (Boston: Houghton Mifflin, 1922), p. 13
2. Emma Lazarus, "The New Colossus: Inscription for the Statue of Liberty."
3. Recollections of Rosamond Holmes, Harriman papers
4. ibid.
5. ibid.
6. St. John's vestry letter to E. H. Harriman, May 14, 1859, Harriman papers
7. C. M. Keys, *World's Work*, February 1905
8. Kennan, *E. H. Harriman, A Biography*, Vol. I, p. 12
9. ibid., p. 17
10. ibid., p. 16
11. Letter to Mary Williamson Averell from Mrs. Orlando Harriman, Jan. 15, 1879, Harriman papers
12. Carlton J. Corliss, *Main Line of Mid-America, The Story of the Illinois Central*, (New York: Creative Age Press, 1950), p. 32
13. "Colossus of Roads," *Review of Reviews*, January 1907
14. Kennan, *E. H. Harriman*, Vol. I, p. 73
15. ibid., p. 80

16. Corliss, *Main Line of Mid-America*, p. 324
17. Kennan, *E. H. Harriman*, Vol. I, p. 94
18. E. H. Harriman letter to Mary A. Harriman, June 21, 1897, Harriman papers
19. ibid.
20. Kennan, *E. H. Harriman*, Vol. I, p. 72
21. Jonathan Hughes, *The Vital Few, America's Economic Progress and Its Protagonists* (Boston: Houghton Mifflin, 1966), p. 371
22. Kennan, *E. H. Harriman*, Vol. I, p. 90

Chapter II

1. Kennan, *E. H. Harriman*, Vol. I, p. 342
2. ibid., p. 124
3. ibid., p. 126
4. ibid., p. 132
5. ibid., p. 141
6. ibid., p. 148
7. ibid., p. 157–163
8. Letter from W. L. Park to Mary A. Harriman, Sept. 3, 1912
9. Author interview with WAH
10. Kennan, *E. H. Harriman*, Vol. I, p. 166
11. W. Almon Wolff, *Elks Magazine*, Sept. 1927
12. Maury Klein, *Union Pacific: The Rebirth, 1894–1969*, Vol. II (New York: Doubleday, 1990), p. 89
13. Memorandum by General Grenville Dodge, undated, Harriman papers
14. C. M. Keys, *World's Work*, April 1905.
15. Kennan, *E. H. Harriman*, Vol. I, p. 296
16. John Moody, *Masters of Capital* (New Haven, Ct.: Yale University Press, 1919), p. 101
17. W. Almon Wolff, *Elks Magazine*, Oct. 1927
18. ibid.
19. ibid.
20. Kennan, *E. H. Harriman*, Vol. I, p. 313
21. ibid.
22. Bernard Baruch, *Baruch, My Own Story* (New York: Henry Holt, 1957), p. 41
23. Kennan, *E. H. Harriman*, Vol. I, p. 314
24. ibid., p. 393
25. ibid., p. 395
26. ibid., p. 399

Chapter III

1. Craigie School report, May 28, 1904, Harriman papers
2. WAH letter to Christine S. Danzige, March 12, 1980, Harriman papers
3. William H. Goetzman and Kay Sloan, *Looking Far North: The Harriman Expedition to Alaska, 1899* (New York: Viking, 1982), p. xi
4. E. H. Harriman letter to Mary A. Harriman, undated, Harriman papers
5. Author interview with WAH "Uncle Willie" was William M. Harriman, the youngest of E.H.'s three brothers, and briefly E.H.'s partner on Wall Street. He died while Averell was still a student at Groton
6. Cornelia Harriman letter to WAH, undated, Harriman papers
7. E. H. Harriman letter to WAH, Oct. 7, 1906, Harriman papers
8. E. H. Harriman letter to WAH, Oct. 13, 1906, Harriman papers
9. E. H. Harriman letter to WAH, April 28, 1907
10. WAH letter to E. H. Harriman, Nov. 16, 1907
11. George Kennan, *E. H. Harriman's Far East Plans* (New York: Country Life Press, 1917), p. 3
12. ibid.
13. Lloyd C. Griscom, *Diplomatically Speaking* (New York: Literary Guild, 1940), p. 263
14. Kennan, *E. H. Harriman*, Vol. II, p. 6
15. George Biddle, "As I Remember Groton School," *Harpers Magazine*, August 1939
16. E. Roland Harriman, *I Reminisce* (Garden City, N.Y.: Doubleday, 1975), p. 14
17. E. H. Harriman letter to Mary A. Harriman, Aug. 19, 1907, Harriman papers
18. E. Roland Harriman, *I Reminisce*, p. 18
19. Kennan, *The Salton Sea: An Account of Harriman's Fight with the Colorado River* (New York: Macmillan 1917), p. 78
20. ibid., p. 80
21. *New York Times*, April 3, 1907
22. Kennan, *E. H. Harriman*, Vol. II, p. 201. William D. Haywood, the militant labor activist and organizer of International Workers of the World, and Charles Moyer, president of the Western Federation of Minters, were arrested in early 1906 and charged with the murder of Idaho governor Frank Steunenberg. Eugene V. Debs, a former railroad union organizer, was then making his name a household word as leader of the American Socialist party.
23. ibid., p. 205
24. *Savannah Morning News*, Jan. 26, 1909

25. E. H. Harriman letter to Mary A. Harriman, February 1909, Harriman papers
26. E. H. Harriman letter to WAH, Feb. 2, 1909, Harriman papers
27. E. H. Harriman letter to WAH, Feb. 16, 1909, Harriman papers
28. WAH letter to E. H. Harriman, March 7, 1909, Harriman papers
29. Richard Danielson letter to E. H. Harriman, April 1909, Harriman papers
30. Stanley Jackson, *J. P. Morgan: A Biography* (New York: Stein and Day, 1983), p. 282

Chapter IV

1. WAH letter to E. H. Harriman, July 1909, Harriman papers
2. *New York Evening Post*, Nov. 8, 1932
3. *New York World*, Feb. 23, 1910
4. *New York World*, Feb. 25, 1910
5. *New York Herald*, Oct. 30, 1910
6. *Junior League Review*, Fall, 1983
7. Mary A. Harriman letter to WAH, Feb. 12, 1912, Harriman papers
8. Author interview with WAH
9. WAH notes on 1912 visit to Oxford and Cambridge universities, Harriman papers
10. ibid.
11. W. Averell Harriman and Eli Abel, *Special Envoy to Churchill and Stalin, 1941–1946* (New York: Random House, 1975), p. 36
12. WAH letter to G. S. MacLagen, undated, Harriman papers
13. *New York Times*, March 30, 1913
14. *Yale Alumni Weekly*, November 1913
15. Author interview with WAH
16. Harriman and Abel, *Special Envoy*, p. 36
17. WAH letter to Mary A. Harriman, undated, Harriman papers
18. Mark L. Chadwin interview with Robert A. Lovett, Harriman papers
19. WAH letter to Mary A. Harriman, Sept. 25, 1914, Harriman papers
20. Harriman and Abel, *Special Envoy*, p. 46
21. Author interview with WAH

Chapter V

1. Robert Lansing, *War Memoirs of Robert Lansing* (New York: Bobbs-Merrill, 1935), p. 210
2. Hans Peter Hanssen, *Diary of a Dying Empire*, trans. Oscar Osburn,

ed. Philip Lutz, Mary Schofield, O. O. Winter (Bloomington, Ind.: Indiana University Press, 1955), p. 165

3. Author interview with WAH
4. Frederick G. Fassett, Jr., ed., *The Shipbuilding Business in the United States of America*, Vol. I (New York: Society of Naval Architects and Engineers, 1948), p. 51
5. Larry Irvin Bland, *W. Averell Harriman: Businessman and Diplomat, 1891–1945*, Ph.D. dissertation, University of Wisconsin, 1972
6. ibid.
7. R.H.M. Robinson, *International Marine Engineering*, Dec. 1917
8. W. C. Mattox, *Building the Emergency Fleet* (Cleveland: Penton Publishing, 1920)
9. E. Roland Harriman, *I Reminisce*, p. 54
10. Fassett, ed., *The Shipbuilding Business*, p. 52
11. Burnet Landreth diaries, Bristol Public Library, Bristol, Pa.
12. R.H.M. Robinson letter to E. N. Hurley, National Archives, RG 32 U.S. Shipping Board General Files, 582-176, Merchant Shipbuilding Corp.
13. WAH letter to Mary A. Harriman, Sept. 1918, Harriman papers
14. Robert A. Kilmarx, ed., *America's Maritime Legacy: A History of the U.S. Merchant Marine and Shipbuilding Industry Since Colonial Times* (Boulder, Colo.: Georgetown University Center for Strategic and International Studies, Westview Press, 1979), p. 126
15. *Marine Review*, April 1921
16. WAH letter to Mary A. Harriman, Feb. 14, 1919
17. *New York Times*, Jan. 24, 1920
18. WAH letter to Adm. William S. Benson, National Archives, RG 32, U.S. Shipping Board general files, 580–914, W. A. Harriman & Co., Inc.
19. Adm. William S. Benson letter to Averell Harriman, National Archives, RG 32 32, U.S. Shipping Board general files, W. A. Harriman & Co., 582-176
20. Author interview with Robert A. Lovett
21. *The Nation*, Oct. 20, 1920
22. *Marine Review*, Nov. 1919
23. London *Times*, Sept. 8, 1920
24. *New York Times*, Oct. 6, 1920
25. *Marine Review*, April 1921
26. *Forbes Magazine*, Oct. 1920
27. *Marine Review*, March 1921
28. Kilmarx, ed., *America's Maritime Legacy*, p. 140
29. Merchants Shipbuilding Co., annual report for 1920, Harriman papers

30. John Higham, *Strangers in the Land, Patterns of American Nativism,*
    1860–1925 (New Brunswick, N.J.: Rutgers University Press, 1955)
31. *Marine Review*, April 1921
32. National Archives, Records Group 32, U.S. Shipping Board general
    file, 582-115
33. ibid.
34. Author interview with Allen Grover
35. Kilmarx, ed., *America's Maritime Legacy*, p. 140
36. *New York Times*, Jan. 21, 1921
37. *New York Times*, Feb. 6, 1921
38. Adm. William S. Benson letter to WAH, Feb. 9, 1921, Harriman
    papers
39. National Archives, Records Group 32, U.S. Shipping Board general
    file, 582-176
40. ibid.
41. Alfred Clegg letter to Kermit Roosevelt, Dec. 29, 1921, Kermit Roo-
    sevelt papers, Library of Congress
42. National Archives, Records Group 32, U.S. Shipping Board general
    file, 582-176
43. WAH letter to Admiral William S. Benson, April 24, 1922, Harriman
    papers
44. Kermit Roosevelt letter to H. F. Kerr, Kermit Roosevelt papers,
    Library of Congress
45. Author interview with Allen Grover
46. Author interview with Luther Gulick
47. WAH letter to United American Lines, Feb. 26, 1926, Harriman
    papers
48. WAH letter to Mary A. Harriman, Mar. 4, 1926

Chapter VI

1. V. I. Lenin, "Capitalist Discords and the Concession Policy; Report
   to the Eighth Congress of Soviets on Dec. 21, 1920," *The Lenin*
   Anthology, ed. Robert C. Tucker (New York: W. W. Norton, 1975).
2. John Speed Elliott letter to WAH, undated, Harriman papers
3. National Archives, Record Group 59, State Department decimal file
   861.637/1
4. *New York Times*, Nov. 11, 1925
5. A. A. Djakelli letter to WAH, Aug. 30, 1926, Harriman papers
6. WAH letter to Mary A. Harriman, March 25, 1925, Harriman papers
7. National Archives, Record Group 59, State Department decimal file
   861.51/2013

8. National Archives, Record Group 59, State Department decimal file 861.51/2051
9. William Hamilton letter to WAH, May 19, 1926, Harriman papers
10. ibid.
11. National Archives, Record Group 59, State Department decimal file 861.637/25
12. WAH letter to Mary A. Harriman, Dec. 8, 1926, Harriman papers
13. National Archives, Record Group 59, State Department decimal file 861.637/30
14. National Archives, Record Group 59, State Department decimal file 861.637/33
15. Maxim Litvinov, *Notes for a Journal* (New York: William Morrow, 1955), p. 23
16. *Geneva* (N.Y.) *Times*, Nov. 11, 1957, report on Hobart College lecture by Boris Stanfield
17. Johan Wulfsberg, *Diary of Johan Wulfsberg*, Harriman papers
18. WAH letter to Richard H. M. Robinson, Jan. 13, 1927, Harriman papers
19. ibid.
20. WAH memo, Oct. 1953, Harriman papers
21. Author interview with WAH
22. WAH press release issued Feb. 9, 1927, Harriman papers
23. National Archives, Record Group 59, State Department decimal file 862.51/2168
24. *New York Times*, Aug. 18, 1928
25. National Archives, Record Group 59, State Department decimal file 860c.6463/Harriman & Co./21
26. National Archives, Record Group 59, State Department decimal file 860c.63/16
27. National Archives, Record Group 59, State Department decimal file 860c.6463/Harriman & Co./23
28. National Archives, Record Group 59, State Department decimal file 861.637/36
29. December 1927 monthly report to WAH from Jules LaBarthe, Harriman papers
30. National Archives, Record Group 59, State Department decimal file 861.637
31. *London Daily Mail* May 6, 1928
32. *New York Times*, June 17, 1928
33. WAH letter to Richard H. M. Robinson, June 6, 1928, Harriman papers
34. WAH cable to Georg Solmssen, July 27, 1928, Harriman papers
35. Georg Solmssen letter to WAH, Aug. 14, 1928, Harriman papers

36. Anthony C. Sutton, *Western Technology and Soviet Economic Develop-ment, 1917 to 1930* (Stanford, Calif.: Hoover Institution on War, Revolution, and Peace, Stanford University, 1968), p. 91
37. National Archives, Record Group 59, State Department decimal file 861.637/23
38. National Archives, Record Group 59, State Department decimal file 861.637/27

Chapter VII

1. Author interview with Robert A. Lovett
2. Nelson W. Aldrich, Jr., *Tommy Hitchcock: An American Hero* (Gaithers-burg, Md.: Fleet Street Corp., 1984), p. 165. Copyright Margaret Mellon Hitchcock.
3. George Gordon Moore letter to WAH, Aug. 12, 1963, Harriman papers
4. *The Blood Horse*, April 30, 1979
5. ibid.
6. *New York Daily News*, Mar. 26, 1925
7. ibid.
8. Author interview with Kathleen Harriman Mortimer
9. WAH cable to Kitty Lanier Harriman, Jan. 3, 1925, Harriman papers
10. E. Roland Harriman letter to WAH, April 17, 1925, Harriman papers
11. Ronald L. Davis, ed., *The Social and Cultural Life of the 1920's* (New York: Holt, Rinehart and Winston, 1972), p. 12
12. Author interview with Luther Gulick
13. Author interview with Frances Norton Lord
14. ibid.
15. Author interview with Ellen Barry
16. Author interview with Peggy Hitchcock
17. *New York Times*, Sept. 13, 1928
18. Aldrich, *Tommy Hitchcock*, p. 208
19. ibid.
20. New York *Herald Tribune*, Sept. 30, 1928
21. *New York Times*, Sept. 30, 1928

Chapter VIII

1. *New York Times*, June 15, 1929
2. LaMotte Cohu interview, Sherman Fairchild papers, Library of Con-gress

3. Roland Palmedo and Sherman Fairchild interview, Fairchild papers, Library of Congress
4. Author interview with Charles Collis
5. Robert S. McElvaine, *The Great Depression* (New York: Times Books, 1984), p. 34
6. Harriman and Abel, *Special Envoy*, p. 47
7. John A. Kouwenhoven, *Partners in Banking: An Historical Portrait of a Great Private Bank, Brown Brothers Harriman & Co., 1818–1968* (Garden City, N.Y.: Doubleday, 1981), p. 13
8. E. Roland Harriman letter to WAH, Sept. 9, 1925, Harriman papers
9. ibid.
10. Kouwenhoven, *Partners in Banking*, p. 16.
11. ibid., p. 71
12. E. Roland Harriman, *I Reminisce*, p. 77
13. Brown Brothers Harriman & Co. historical files, New York Historical Society
14. *Wall Street Journal*, Dec. 18, 1931
15. E. Roland Harriman, *I Reminisce*, p. 74
16. ibid., p. 77
17. WAH letter to David Bruce, Aug. 4, 1932, Harriman papers
18. Sherman Fairchild letter to WAH, Aug. 4, 1932, Harriman papers
19. Sherman Fairchild interview, Fairchild papers, Library of Congress
20. Lyndol Young interview, Sherman Fairchild papers, Library of Congress
21. LaMotte Cohu interview, Fairchild papers, Library of Congress
22. New York *Herald Tribune*, Nov. 17, 1932
23. New York *Herald Tribune*, Nov. 15, 1932
24. Richard Hoyt letter to WAH, March 1, 1933, Harriman papers
25. WAH resignation notice, March 15, 1933, Harriman papers
26. Klein, *Union Pacific: The Rebirth, 1894–1969*, p. 235
27. Memorandum by S. B. Brown, Brown Brothers Harriman & Co. historical file, New York Historical Society
28. Affidavit by George A. Ellis, Oct. 11, 1933, Harriman papers, New York
29. James Brown letter to WAH, April 15, 1933, Harriman papers, New York

Chapter IX

1. John Stover, *The Death and Decline of the American Railroad* (Oxford, England: Oxford University Press, 1970), p. 17
2. Edwin G. Nourse and associates, *Railroad Transportation and Public Policy* (Washington, D. C.: Brookings Institution, 1934), p. 123

3. Corliss, *Main Line of Mid-America*, p. 427
4. ibid., p. 428
5. WAH letter to David Bruce, Aug. 4, 1932, Harriman papers
6. WAH personal notes Jan. 15–Jan. 25, 1932, Harriman papers
7. Carl Gray letter to WAH, Jan. 8, 1929, Harriman papers
8. *Industrial News Review*, Dec. 1936
9. Union Pacific Railroad press release, May 24, 1933, Harriman papers
10. Robert A. Lovett letter to WAH, Feb. 1934, Harriman papers
11. ibid.
12. *Washington Star*, Feb. 16, 1934
13. *Business Week*, Feb. 17, 1934
14. Carl Gray telegram to Harriman, Feb. 29, 1934, Harriman papers
15. *New York Times*, May 7, 1934
16. *Newsweek*, Nov. 3 1934
17. New York *Herald Tribune*, Oct. 26, 1934
18. *Forbes Magazine*, December 15, 1936
19. *Time*, May 11, 1936
20. Felix Schaffgotsch letter to WAH, Dec. 23, 1935, Harriman papers
21. Doug Oppenheimer and Jim Poore, *Sun Valley: A Biography* (Boise, Ida.: Beatty Books, 1976), p. 29
22. Author interview with WAH
23. Dorice Taylor, *Sun Valley* (Sun Valley, Ida.: Ex Libris, 1980), p. 27
24. Steve Hannagan letter to WAH, April 15, 1936, Harriman papers
25. *Skiing News Magazine*, anniversary edition, 1961.
26. Author interview with WAH
27. David Niven, *The Moon's a Balloon* (New York: Putnam, 1972), p. 189
28. William Jeffers cable to WAH, Feb. 8, 1937, Harriman papers
29. Union Pacific Railroad annual report for the year ending Dec. 31, 1938, Harriman papers
30. Author interview with Robert S. McNamara
31. Klein, *Union Pacific: The Rebirth*, p. 378

Chapter X

1. Author interviews with Joseph Lash and Franklin Roosevelt, Jr.
2. Author interview with WAH
3. *New York Times*, March 5, 1933
4. *The Public Papers and Addresses of Franklin D. Roosevelt*, Vol. II, 1933, (New York: Random House, 1933)
5. James Warburg interview, p. 350, Columbia University Oral History
6. ibid.

7. Raymond Moley, *After Seven Years* (New York: Harper and Brothers, 1939), p. 178
8. ibid., pp. 178–179
9. James Warburg interview, p. 476, Columbia Oral History
10. Arthur M. Schlesinger, Jr., *The Coming of the New Deal* (Boston: Houghton Mifflin, 1958), p. 444
11. Harriman and Abel, *Special Envoy*, p. 54
12. Prescott Bush interview, Columbia Oral History
13. Mary Harriman Rumsey letter to Franklin D. Roosevelt, May 27, 1933, Harriman papers
14. WAH memo to Hugh Johnson, Dec. 1933, Harriman papers
15. The Unofficial Observer, *The New Dealers* (New York: Simon and Schuster, 1934), p. 325
16. Schlesinger, *The Coming of the New Deal*, p. 231
17. Moley, *After Seven Years*, p. 280
18. Arthur Brisbane letter to WAH, Dec. 14, 1933, Harriman papers
19. Robert A. Lovett letter to WAH, April 25, 1934 Harriman papers
20. Raymond Moley memo to *Newsweek* staff, Harriman papers
21. Broadus Mitchell, *Depression Decade: From New Era through New Deal, 1921–1941* (New York: Rinehart, 1955), p. 239
22. McElvaine, *The Great Depression*, p. 160
23. Kenneth S. Davis, *FDR: The New Deal Years, 1933–1937* (New York: Random House, 1979), p. 268
24. Author interview with Dexter Keezer
25. Dexter Keezer, unpublished manuscript, Harriman papers
26. ibid.
27. Author interview with Dexter Keezer
28. Mary Harriman (Rumsey) undated letter to WAH, Harriman papers
29. Mary Harriman Rumsey undated letter to staff, Harriman papers
30. Dr. D. W. Atchley letter to Dr. James F. Mitchell, Feb. 6, 1935, Harriman papers
31. Mitchell, *Depression Decade*, p. 258
32. Donald R. Richberg, *My Hero: The Indiscreet Memoirs of an Eventful but Unheroic Life* (New York: G. P. Putnam's Sons, 1954), p. 104
33. E. Roland Harriman, *I Reminisce*, p. 97
34. Klein, *Union Pacific*, p. 436
35. E. J. Kahn, Jr., *The World of Swope: A Biography* (New York: Simon and Schuster, 1965), p. 326

Chapter XI

1. Edward R. Stettinius papers, Box 120, University of Virginia Library
2. Author interview with John J. McCloy

3. WAH speech to Greater Omaha Association, June 1, 1940, Harriman papers
4. WAH memo to E. R. Stettinius, Box 79, Stettinius papers, University of Virginia Library
5. Eliot Janeway, *The Struggle for Survival* (New York: Weybright and Talley, 1951), p. 183
6. Author interview with WAH
7. Harriman and Abel, *Special Envoy*, p. 9
8. Robert Sherwood, *Roosevelt and Hopkins: An Intimate History* (New York: Harper Brothers, 1948), p.7
9. Author interview with Franklin D. Roosevelt, Jr.
10. Author interview with Robert Meiklejohn
11. Author interview with WAH
12. *New Yorker*, Aug. 14, 1943
13. Author interview with WAH
14. Harriman recorded reminiscences, 1953, Harriman papers
15. Henry H. Adams, *Harry Hopkins* (New York: G. P. Putnam's Sons, 1977), p. 149
16. Prepared testimony for Harry Hopkins confirmation hearing before Senate Commerce Committee, Jan. 11, 1939, Harriman papers
17. Sherwood, *Roosevelt and Hopkins*, p. 111
18. Prepared remarks for Winston-Salem, N. C., speech, Jan. 15, 1940, Harriman papers
19. WAH letter to Harry Hopkins, June 6, 1940, Harriman papers
20. *The Public Papers and Addresses of Franklin D. Roosevelt*, 1940 Vol. I: *War—and Aid to Democracies* (New York: Macmillan 1941)
21. Harriman and Abel, *Special Envoy* p. 10
22. Sherwood, *Roosevelt and Hopkins*, p. 243
23. John Colville, *Fringes of Power: 10 Downing Street Diaries, 1939–1955* (New York: W. W. Norton, 1985), p. 347
24. Harriman and Abel, *Special Envoy*, p. 5
25. WAH memorandum, March 11, 1941, Harriman papers
26. ibid.
27. ibid.
28. Harriman and Abel, *Special Envoy*, p. 22
29. ibid., p. 23
30. Harry Hopkins letter to WAH, June 4, 1941, Harriman papers
31. WAH letter to FDR, April 10, 1941, President's personal files, 6207, Franklin D. Roosevelt Library
32. Colville, *The Fringes of Power*, p. 375
33. WAH letter to FDR, President's personal files, 6207, Franklin D. Roosevelt Library
34. Harry Hopkins letter to WAH, May 6, 1941, Harriman papers
35. WAH letter to William Jeffers, May 30, 1941, Harriman papers

36. Sherwood, *Roosevelt and Hopkins*, p. 276
37. Colville, *The Fringes of Power*, p. 391
38. Harriman and Abel, *Special Envoy*, p. 63
39. WAH report to Churchill, July 1, 1941, Harriman papers
40. WAH memorandum of conversation, Aug. 6, 1941, Harriman papers
41. ibid.
42. Winston Churchill, *The Second World War*, Vol. III: *The Grand Alliance* (Boston: Houghton Mifflin, 1950)
43. Robert Meiklejohn, *Diary*, p. 144 Harriman papers
44. Harriman and Abel, *Special Envoy*, p. 92
45. ibid., p. 93
46. ibid.
47. Text, Harriman BBC and CBS broadcast, Oct. 13, 1941, Harriman papers
48. E. R. Stettinius memo to Harry Hopkins, Nov. 11, 1941, Harriman papers
49. Stettinius memorandum, Box 135, Hopkins file, Stettinius papers, University of Virginia Library
50. Harriman and Abel, *Special Envoy*, p. 111
51. John Gilbert Winant, *Letter from Grosvenor Square: An Account of a Stewardship* (Boston: Houghton Mifflin, 1947), p. 277
52. Churchill, *The Grand Alliance*, p. 605
53. ibid.
54. WAH-Churchill cable to Hopkins, Dec. 7, 1941, Harriman papers

Chapter XII

1. Beatrice Kaufman and Joseph Hennessey, eds., *Letters of Alexander Woollcott* (New York: Viking, 1944), p. 283
2. Memorandum of conversations, May 5–9, 1943, Harriman papers
3. Churchill, *The Grand Alliance*, p. 50
4. Author interview with Mary Soames
5. Mary Churchill letter to WAH, May 13, 1941, Harriman papers
6. WAH memorandum dictated Oct. 6, 1962, Harriman papers
7. John Colville, *Winston Churchill and His Inner Circle* (New York: Wyndham Books, 1981), p. 121
8. Mary Soames, *Clementine Churchill: The Biography of a Marriage* (Boston: Houghton Mifflin, 1979), p. 465
9. Author interview with John Colville
10. Author interview with Harrison Salisbury
11. Raymond E. Lee, *The London Journal of General Raymond E. Lee*, ed. James Leutze (Boston: Little, Brown, 1971), p. 359

12. Hastings Ismay memorandum to Edward Bridges, U.K. Public Records Office, Cabinet Papers/127/326
13. WAH letter to FDR, Franklin D. Roosevelt Presidential Library, President's Personal Files, Box 6207
14. Lee, *London Journal*, p. 353
15. Author interview with Pamela C. Harriman
16. Joseph P. Lash, *Eleanor and Franklin* (New York: W. W. Norton, 1971), p. 659
17. Lee, *London Journal*, p. 382
18. Kathleen Harriman letter to Marie Harriman, May 17, 1941, Harriman papers
19. Kathleen Harriman letter to Mary Harriman Fisk, May 30, 1941, Harriman papers
20. Mark Amory, ed., *The Letters of Evelyn Waugh* (New York: Ticknor and Fields, 1980), p. 514
21. Kathleen Harriman letter to Mary Harriman Fisk, Dec. 16, 1941
22. Anita Leslie, *Cousin Randolph: The Life of Randolph Churchill* (London: Hutchinson, 1985), p. 47
23. Author interview with Pamela C. Harriman
24. ibid.
25. ibid.
26. *Washington Post*, June 12, 1983
27. Kathleen Harriman letter to Mary Harriman Fisk, June 1941
28. Kathleen Harriman letter to Mary Harriman Fisk, June 21, 1942
29. Amory, ed., *Letters of Evelyn Waugh*, p. 154
30. Martin Gilbert, *Winston S. Churchill: Finest Hour, 1939–41* (Boston: Houghton Mifflin, 1983), p. 1050
31. Pamela Churchill cable to WAH, Jan. 7, 1942, Harriman papers
32. WAH cable to Randolph Churchill, Jan. 7, 1942, Harriman papers
33. Author interview with John Colville
34. ibid.
35. ibid.
36. Author interview with Pamela C. Harriman
37. Martin Gilbert, *Winston S. Churchill, 1945–65: Never Despair* (Boston: Houghton Mifflin, 1988), p. 179

Chapter XIII

1. Churchill, *The Grand Alliance*, p. 641
2. Harriman and Abel, *Special Envoy*, p. 114
3. Churchill, *The Grand Alliance*, p. 664
4. Harriman and Abel, *Special Envoy*, p. 115
5. Richard M. Leighton and Robert W. Cookley, *Global Logistics and*

Strategy (Washington D.C.: Office of the Chief of Military History, Department of the Army, 1955), p. 197

6. Harriman and Abel, *Special Envoy*, p. 120
7. Leighton and Cookley, *Global Logistics*, p. 198
8. Harriman and Abel, *Special Envoy*, p. 121
9. Sherwood, *Roosevelt and Hopkins*, p. 464
10. WAH letter to Stalin, Jan. 28, 1942, Harriman papers
11. Harriman and Abel, *Special Envoy*, p. 101
12. Winston Churchill, *The Second World War*, Vol. IV: *The Hinge of Fate* (Boston: Houghton Mifflin, 1950), p. 314
13. ibid., p. 320
14. WAH, Harvard oral history interview, Harriman papers
15. Harriman and Abel, *Special Envoy*, p. 133
16. G. R. Urban, ed., *Stalinism: Its Impact on Russia and the World* (New York: St. Martin's Press, Inc.)
17. Hastings Ismay, *The Memoirs of Lord General Ismay*, (New York: Viking, 1960), p. 250, 1960.
18. Sherwood, *Roosevelt and Hopkins*, p. 577
19. Churchill, *The Hinge of Fate*, p. 342
20. Harriman and Abel, *Special Envoy*, p. 138
21. Churchill, *The Hinge of Fate*, p. 381
22. FDR memo to WAH, June 20, 1942, Harriman papers
23. Churchill, *The Hinge of Fate*, p. 383
24. Sherwood, *Roosevelt and Hopkins*, p. 604
25. Forrest C. Pogue, *George C. Marshall: Ordeal and Hope, 1939–1942*, (New York: Viking, 1966), p. 346
26. Harriman and Abel, *Special Envoy*
27. ibid.
28. ibid., p. 147
29. Meiklejohn, *Diary*, p. 233, Harriman papers
30. Ivan Maisky, *Memoirs of a Soviet Ambassador: The War 1939–1943*, (New York: Charles Scribner & Sons, 1968), p. 297
31. Harriman and Abel, *Special Envoy*, p. 147
32. Churchill, *The Hinge of Fate*, p. 259
33. Sherwood, *Roosevelt and Hopkins*, p. 575
34. ibid., p. 526
35. Martin Gilbert, *Winston S. Churchill: Road to Victory, 1941–1945* (Boston: Houghton Mifflin, 1986), p. 713
36. Churchill, *The Hinge of Fate*, p. 473
37. Churchill, *The Hinge of Fate*.
38. Harriman and Abel, *Special Envoy*.
39. ibid., p. 154
40. ibid., pp. 154–156
41. ibid.

42. Gilbert, *Winston S. Churchill: Road to Victory*, p. 185
43. Harriman and Abel., *Special Envoy*, p. 157
44. UK Public Records Office, Premier Papers, 3/76A/11, folder 16
45. ibid.
46. Churchill, *The Hinge of Fate*, p. 502
47. Harriman and Abel, *Special Envoy*, p. 164
48. ibid. p. 165
49. T. H. Vail Motter, *The Persian Corridor and Aid to Russia (US Army in World War II, Middle East Theater)* (Washington, D.C.: Department of the Army), p. 190

Chapter XIV

1. William H. Standley and Arthur A. Ageton, *Admiral Ambassador to Russia* (Chicago: Henry Regnery Co., 1955), p. 341
2. ibid., p. 195
3. ibid., p. 209
4. ibid., p. 213
5. ibid., p. 308
6. ibid., p. 358
7. Adams, *Harry Hopkins*, p. 318
8. *Foreign Relations of the United States 1943*, Vol. I, p. 531
9. Harriman and Abel, *Special Envoy*, p. 214
10. Archibald Clark Kerr letter to Sir Stafford Cripps, June 3, 1943, Harriman papers
11. Harriman and Abel, Special Envoy, p. 219
12. Standley and Ageton, *Admiral Ambassador*, p. 490
13. Forrest C. Pogue, *George C. Marshall: Organizer of Victory, 1943–1945* (New York: Viking Press, 1973), p. 288
14. WAH memorandum, Oct. 23, 1953, Harriman papers
15. Maj. Gen. John R. Deane, *Strange Alliance* (Bloomington, Ind.: Indiana University Press, 1973), p. 11
16. Meiklejohn, *Diary*, p. 423, Harriman papers
17. WAH letter to Marie Harriman, Feb. 3, 1944, Harriman papers
18. Meiklejohn, *Diary*, p. 477, Harriman papers
19. WAH memorandum, Nov. 7, 1943, Harriman papers
20. Meiklejohn, *Diary*, p. 424, Harriman papers
21. Deane, *Strange Alliance*, p. 36
22. WAH letter to Marie Harriman, Dec. 19, 1943, Harriman papers
23. Harriman and Abel, *Special Envoy*, p. 294
24. WAH memo of conversation with Marshall, May 11, 1944, Harriman papers

25. Kathleen Harriman letter to Mary Harriman Fisk, June 26, 1944, Harriman papers
26. Kathleen Harriman, Feb. 23, 1944, report on Jan. 23 trip to Smolensk, Harriman papers
27. Harrison Salisbury, *A Journey for Our Times* (New York: Harper & Row, 1983), p. 215
28. WAH cable to FDR, Jan. 24, 1944, Harriman papers
29. *Hearings before the Select Committee to Conduct an Investigation of the Facts, Evidence, and Circumstances of the Katyn Forest Massacre*, Part 7 (82nd Congress, 2nd session), p. 2125
30. Harriman and Abel, *Special Envoy*, p. 314
31. ibid.
32. George F. Kennan, *Memoirs, 1925–1950* (Boston: Atlantic Monthly and Little, Brown, 1967), p. 233
33. Alexander Cadogan, *The Diaries of Sir Alexander Cadogan, 1938–1945*, ed. David Dilks (New York: G. P. Putnam's Sons, 1972)
34. Keith Eubank, *Summit at Teheran: The Untold Story* (New York: William Morrow, 1985), p. 176–77
35. Harriman and Abel, *Special Envoy*, p. 264
36. ibid., p. 265
37. Meiklejohn, *Diary*, p. 447, Harriman papers
38. Sherwood, *Roosevelt and Hopkins*, p. 847
39. WAH memorandum, Oct. 15, 1944, Harriman papers
40. Harriman and Abel, *Special Envoy*, p. 370
41. Charles E. Bohlen with Robert H. Phelps, *Witness to History, 1929–1969* (New York: W. W. Norton, 1973), p. 197
42. Harriman and Abel, *Special Envoy*, p. 399
43. ibid., p. 400

Chapter XV

1. *Foreign Relations of the United States, 1943*, Vol. III, p. 736.
2. Meiklejohn, *Diary*, Harriman papers
3. Kathleen Harriman letter to Mary Harriman Fisk, Jan. 13, 1942, Harriman papers
4. WAH cable to Churchill, Nov. 3, 1943, Harriman papers
5. Sherwood, *Roosevelt and Hopkins*, p. 814
6. Harriman and Abel, *Special Envoy*, p. 339
7. ibid.
8. WAH letter to Ira Eaker, Ira Eaker papers, Library of Congress
9. George F. Kennan, *Memoirs, 1925–1950*, p. 211
10. WAH draft cable to FDR, Aug. 25, 1944, Harriman papers

11. WAH cable to Hopkins, Sept. 10, 1944, *Foreign Relations of the United States 1944*, Vol. IV, p. 988
12. Kathleen Harriman letter to Mary Harriman Fisk, Aug. 20, 1944, Harriman papers
13. WAH cable to Hopkins, *Foreign Relations of the United States, 1944*, Vol. IV, p. 1130
14. Harriman and Abel, *Special Envoy*, p. 355
15. Stanislaw Mikolajczyk, *The Rape of Poland: Pattern of Soviet Aggression* (New York: McGraw Hill 1948), p. 95
16. Herbert Feis, *Churchill, Roosevelt, and Stalin: The War They Waged and The Peace They Sought* (Princeton, N.J.: Princeton University Press, 1957), p. 457
17. WAH memo of conversations with FDR, Oct. 21–Nov. 19, 1944, Harriman papers
18. Harriman and Abel, *Special Envoy*, p. 370
19. Deane, *The Strange Alliance*, p. 259
20. ibid., p. 84
21. *Report of the Crimea Conference*, Department of State Bulletin, Feb. 18, 1945, p. 215
22. Sherwood, *Roosevelt and Hopkins*, p. 870
23. WAH, Harvard oral history interview, p. 341, Harriman papers
24. George F. Kennan, *Memoirs, 1925–1950*, p. 212
25. WAH cable to FDR, *Foreign Relations of the United States 1945*, Vol. V, p. 1075
26. FDR cable to Stalin, *Foreign Relations of the United States 1945*, Vol. V, p. 1082
27. WAH cable to State Department, March 13, 1945, Harriman papers
28. WAH cable to General Marshall, March 17, 1945, Harriman papers
29. WAH cable to State Department, March 17, 1945, Harriman papers
30. FDR cable to Stalin, *Foreign Relations of the United States 1945*, Vol. III, p. 742
31. WAH cable to FDR, April 12, 1945, Harriman papers
32. FDR cable to WAH, April 12, 1945, Harriman papers
33. Harry S Truman, *Truman Memoirs*, Vol. I, *Year of Decisions* (Garden City, N.Y.: Doubleday, 1955), p. 71
34. Harriman and Abel, *Special Envoy*, p. 453
35. WAH oral history interview, postpresidential files, Harry S Truman Library, Independence, Mo.
36. Harriman and Abel, *Special Envoy*, p. 474
37. ibid., p. 482
38. Henry L. Stimson and McGeorge Bundy, *On Active Service in Peace and War*, Vol. II (New York: Harper and Brothers, 1948), p. 641
39. Harriman and Abel, *Special Envoy*

40. Ronald H. Spector, *Eagle Against the Sun: The American War with Japan* (New York: Random House, 1985), p. 505
41. Harriman and Abel, *Special Envoy*, p. 496
42. Meiklejohn, *Diary*, Harriman papers
43. ibid.
44. Harriman and Abel, *Special Envoy*, p. 510
45. ibid., p. 530
46. WAH cable to Louise Hopkins, Harriman papers

Chapter XVI

1. Henry A. Wallace, *The Price of Vision: The Diary of Henry A. Wallace, 1942–1946*, ed. John Morton Blum (Boston: Houghton Mifflin, 1974), p. 560
2. *New York Times*, March 20, 1946
3. Allen Nevins interview, p. 224, Columbia oral history
4. Author interview with Pamela C. Harriman
5. Harriman and Abel, *Special Envoy*, p. 553
6. Author interview with Waldemar Nielsen
7. *New York Times*, September 24, 1946
8. *Journal of Commerce*, Sept. 25, 1946
9. Theodore H. White, *Fire in the Ashes: Europe in Mid Century* (New York: William Sloane Associates, 1953), p. 34
10. Author interview with Waldemar Nielsen
11. Michael J. Hogan, *The Marshall Plan: America, Britain, and the Reconstruction of Western Europe, 1947–1952* (New York: Cambridge University Press, 1987), p. 34
12. Truman address to Congress, presidential papers, March 12, 1947
13. *New York Times*, May 20, 1947
14. *Foreign Relations of the United States*, Vol. III, pp. 237–239
15. Author interview with Richard Bissell
16. Paul Hoffman interview with Mark Chadwin, Harriman papers
17. Harry S Truman, *Truman Memoirs*, Vol. II: *Years of Trial and Hope* (Garden City, N.Y.: Doubleday, 1956), p. 121
18. Author interview with Richard Bissell
19. *Department of State Bulletin*, Nov. 16, 1947, p. 937
20. WAH oral history interview, postpresidential papers, Harry S Truman Library, Independence, Mo.
21. Arthur Vandenberg letter to WAH, Nov. 9, 1947, Harriman papers
22. Arthur H. Vandenberg, Jr., ed., *The Private Papers of Senator Vandenberg* (Boston: Houghton Mifflin, 1952), p. 379
23. Author interview with Waldemar Nielsen

24. ibid.
25. Alfred Friendly letter to WAH, June 1949, Harriman papers
26. Author interview with Waldemar Nielsen
27. Adrian Fisher interview with Mark Chadwin, Harriman papers
28. Vernon A. Walters, *Silent Missions* (Garden City, N.Y.: Doubleday, 1978), p. 161
29. ibid.
30. Paul G. Hoffman, *Peace Can Be Won* (Garden City, N.Y.: Doubleday, 1951), p. 36
31. Paul Hoffman interview with Mark Chadwin, Harriman papers
32. Harry B. Price, *The Marshall Plan and Its Meaning* (Ithaca, N.Y.: Cornell University Press, 1955), p. 32
33. *Foreign Relations of the United States, 1948*, Vol. III, p. 426
34. Author interview with Richard Bissell
35. Theodore H. White, *In Search of History: A Personal Adventure* (New York: Harper and Row, 1978), p. 283
36. Theodore H. White, *Fire in the Ashes*, p. 52–53
37. UK Public Records Office, Foreign Office papers, 371/71864/UR 1663
38. WAH oral history interview, John F. Kennedy School of Government
39. Transcript, CIA Foreign Broadcast Information Branch, Nov. 25, 1947, Harriman papers
40. WAH letter to Paul Hoffman, Nov. 6, 1948, Harriman papers
41. Edmund Hall-Patch letter to Foreign Office, UK Public Records Office, Foreign Office papers, T232/201/EEC7/8/07119954
42. Oliver Franks letter to Foreign Office, UK Public Records Office, Foreign Office papers, 371/77985/UR 2182
43. WAH oral history interview, postpresidential papers, Harry S Truman Library, Independence, Mo.
44. Paul Hoffman interview with Mark Chadwin, Harriman papers
45. Vernon A. Walters, *Silent Missions*, p. 176
46. Herbert Swope letter to WAH, Nov. 4, 1948, Harriman papers
47. William J. Donovan letter to WAH, Dec. 17, 1948, Harriman papers
48. Author interview with Alfred Friendly
49. WAH cable to Dean Acheson, Jan. 7, 1949, Harriman papers
50. Hugh Gaitskell, *Diary of Hugh Gaitskell, 1945–1956*, ed. Philip M. Williams (London: Jonathan Cape, 1983), p. 112
51. Alan Bullock, *Ernest Bevin, Foreign Secretary* (New York: W. W. Norton, 1983), p. 732
52. Paul Hoffman interview with Mark Chadwin, Harriman papers
53. *New York Times*, April 21, 1950

54. WAH letter to Truman, President's Secretary's files, Harry S Truman Library, Independence, Mo.
55. Milton Katz interview with Mark Chadwin

Chapter XVII

 1. Author interview with Alfred Friendly
 2. WAH testimony before Senate Foreign Relations Committee, April 29, 1949, Harriman papers
 3. WAH letter to Truman, President's Secretary's files, Harry S Truman Library
 4. Robert J. Donovan, *Tumultuous Years: The Presidency of Harry S Truman, 1949–1953* (New York: W. W. Norton, 1982), p. 131
 5. White House press release, June 16, 1950, Official file, Harry S Truman Library
 6. Adrian Fisher interview with Mark Chadwin, Harriman papers
 7. Author interview with Marshall Shulman
 8. Dean Acheson, *Present at the Creation: My Years at the State Department* (New York: W. W. Norton, 1969), p. 410
 9. Truman, *Years of Trial and Hope*, p. 339
10. Acheson, *Present at the Creation*, p. 410
11. WAH oral history interview, p. 227, John F. Kennedy Library
12. Truman, *Years of Trial and Hope*, p. 340
13. ibid., p. 60
14. Harriman oral history interview, p. 227, John F. Kennedy Library
15. New York *Herald Tribune*, June 20, 1950
16. Transcript of WAH remarks to Associate Press Managing Editors' Association, Nov. 16, 1950, Harriman papers
17. Author interview with Theodore Tannenwald
18. Author interview with Hildy Shishkin
19. Author interview with Clark Clifford
20. Clifford remarks to WAH 90th birthday party, Harriman papers
21. Memorandum to the President, signed by Harriman, Norstad, and Ridgway, Aug. 8, 1950, Harriman papers
22. Harriman undated memorandum of conversation, Harriman papers
23. Walters, *Silent Missions*, p. 197
24. Harriman undated memorandum of conversation, Harriman papers
25. Douglas MacArthur, *Reminiscences* (New York: McGraw-Hill, 1964), p. 340
26. *U.S. News and World Report*, Sept. 1, 1950

27. Truman, *Years of Trial and Hope*, p. 356
28. Omar N. Bradley and Clay Blair, *A General's Life* (New York: Simon and Schuster, 1983), p. 355
29. Theodore Tannenwald memorandum, Aug. 17, 1950, Harriman papers
30. Author interview with Theodore Tannenwald
31. Bradley and Blair, *A General's Life*, p. 579
32. Acheson, *Present at the Creation*, p. 521
33. Bradley and Blair, *A General's Life*, p. 631
34. WAH letter to Eisenhower, prepresidential papers, Dwight D. Eisenhower Library
35. Truman note to George Elsey, July 13, 1951, Harriman papers
36. Bradley and Blair, *A General's Life*, p. 609
37. Morton Kaplan, *The Rationale for NATO* (American Enterprise Institute, Hoover Policy Studies, 1973)
38. *New York Times*, May 21, 1951
39. WAH letter to Eisenhower, May 22, 1951, prepresidential papers, Dwight D. Eisenhower Library
40. Eisenhower letter to WAH, June 30, 1951, prepresidential papers, Dwight D. Eisenhower Library
41. WAH memo to Truman, July 5, 1951, Harriman papers
42. Acheson, *Present at the Creation*, p. 559
43. ibid., p. 560
44. WAH letter to Eisenhower, Sept. 19, 1951, Harriman papers
45. Author interview with Eric Roll
46. Edwin Plowden to WAH, Nov. 14, 1951, Harriman papers
47. Col. G. A. Lincoln interview with Mark Chadwin, Harriman papers
48. Acheson, *Present at the Creation*, p. 623
49. Author interview with Edwin Plowden

Chapter XVIII

1. *New York Times*, March 8, 1951
2. *Foreign Relations of the United States, 1952–1954*, Vol. X, Iran, pp. 80–81
3. Bullock, *Ernest Bevin*, p. 35
4. *Foreign Relations of the United States, 1952–1954*, Vol. X, Iran, p. 83
5. ibid., pp. 84–85
6. Acheson, *Present at the Creation*, p. 508
7. *Foreign Relations of the United States, 1952–1954*, Vol. X, Iran, pp. 88–89
8. ibid., p. 94
9. Walters, *Silent Missions*, p. 250

10. *New York Times*, July 18, 1951
11. WAH memorandum, July 25, 1951, Harriman papers
12. Walters, *Silent Missions*, p. 255
13. WAH cable to Truman, President's Secretary's files, Harry S Truman Library
14. *Foreign Relations of the United States 1952–1954*, Vol. X, Iran, p. 109
15. ibid., p. 112
16. ibid., p. 123
17. Author interview with Walter Levy
18. *Business Week*, Aug. 4, 1951
19. *Newsweek*, Aug. 13, 1951
20. WAH cable to Truman, Aug. 8, 1951, Harriman papers
21. Author interview with William Roundtree
22. Walters, *Silent Missions* p. 257
23. *Foreign Relations of the United States 1952–1954*, Vol. X, Iran, p. 145
24. *Newsweek*, Sept. 3, 1951
25. WAH Columbia University oral history interview with Edward Barrett, p. 306
26. WAH memorandum, Aug. 24, 1951, Harriman papers
27. ibid.
28. WAH Columbia University oral history interview with Edward Barrett, p. 309
29. Walters, *Silent Missions*, p. 267
30. *Foreign Relations of the United States 1952–1954*, Vol. X, Iran, pp. 150–152
31. UK Public Records Office, Prem 8/1432
32. Acheson, *Present at the Creation*, p. 510

Chapter XIX

1. *Public Papers of the Presidents: Harry S Truman 1952–53* (Washington, D.C.: U.S. Government Printing Office, 1953), p. 222
2. ibid., p. 224
3. John Bartlow Martin, *Adlai Stevenson of Illinois: The Life of Adlai Stevenson* (Garden City, N.Y.: Doubleday, 1976), p. 547
4. Herbert Swope letter to Harriman, June 19, 1950, Harriman papers
5. Author interview with George Elsey
6. Text, September 1950 speech, Harriman papers
7. *Washington Star*, Sept. 20, 1950
8. Author interview with James Lanigan
9. *New York Times*, April 17, 1952
10. *Time*, April 28, 1952
11. ibid.

12. New York *Herald Tribune*, April 21, 1952
13. Martin, *Adlai Stevenson of Illinois*, p. 566
14. James Loeb, unpublished memoir, Harriman papers
15. New York *Herald Tribune*, May 29, 1952
16. Author interview with Arthur Schlesinger, Jr.
17. *New York Times*, May 14, 1952
18. Charles Murphy memorandum, May 5, 1952, papers of Charles S. Murphy, Harry S Truman Library
19. James Loeb, unpublished memoir, Harriman papers
20. Author interview with Julius Edelstein
21. Author interview with Joe Rauh
22. Author interview with Joseph Laitin
23. Author interview with Frank Kelly
24. *Rocky Mountain News*, June 28, 1952
25. Arthur Schlesinger, Jr., memo to WAH, July 9, 1952, Harriman papers
26. ibid.
27. Paul T. David, Malcolm Moos, and Ralph M. Goldman, *Presidential Nominating Politics in 1952* (Baltimore: Johns Hopkins University Press, 1954), p. 107
28. ibid., p. 109
29. New York *Herald Tribune*, July 23, 1952
30. Author interview with Arthur Schlesinger, Jr.
31. *New York Post*, July 23, 1952
32. New York *Herald Tribune*, July 26, 1952
33. Author interview with Theodore Tannenwald
34. Martin, *Adlai Stevenson of Illinois*, p. 597
35. Text of WAH withdrawal statement, July 26, 1952, Harriman papers
36. Author interview with James Lanigan
37. Text, Oct. 18, 1952, Madison Square Garden speech, Harriman papers
38. Author interview with Frances Lord
39. Author interview with Milton Stewart
40. ibid.
41. *New York Times*, July 25, 1954
42. *New York Times*, Sept. 9, 1954
43. Author interview with Franklin D. Roosevelt, Jr.
44. Author interview with Bernard Ruggieri
45. *New York Times*, Oct. 20, 1954
46. ibid.
47. *New York Times*, Oct. 22, 1954
48. *New York Times*, Oct. 29, 1954

Chapter XX

1. *New York Times*, Jan. 1, 1955
2. Richard Norton Smith, *Thomas E. Dewey and His Times*, (New York: Simon and Schuster, 1982), p. 576
3. *Time*, Nov. 14, 1955
4. Undated memorandum by Julius Edelstein, Thomas Finletter, and George Backer, Harriman papers, Arents Research Library, Syracuse University
5. George Backer interview with Frank Munger, Harriman papers, Arents Research Library, Syracuse University
6. *New York Times*, Jan. 6, 1955
7. *New York Times*, Jan. 8, 1955
8. Author interview with Jack Germond
9. *Colliers Magazine*, Oct. 28, 1955
10. Robert Sherwood letter to Marie Harriman, Sept. 13, 1955, Harriman papers
11. Author interview with Michael Forrestal
12. *Public Papers of Governor Averell Harriman*, Vol. I (Albany, N.Y.: State of New York, 1959), p. 500
13. Author interview with Daniel Gutman
14. *Saturday Evening Post*, March 3, 1958
15. WAH interview with Frank Munger, Harriman papers, Arents Research Library, Syracuse University
16. Author interview with Daniel Gutman
17. George Backer interview with Mark Chadwin, Harriman papers
18. John Bartlow Martin, *Adlai Stevenson and the World: The Life of Adlai Stevenson* (Garden City, N.Y.: Doubleday, 1977), p. 202
19. *Colliers Magazine*, Oct. 28, 1955
20. Author interview with James Sundquist
21. ibid.
22. Author interview with Theodore Tannenwald
23. James Sundquist interview with Frank Munger, Harriman papers, Arents Library
24. James Sundquist interview with Kathleen Kenney, Harriman papers, Arents Library
25. George Backer interview with Mark Chadwin, Harriman papers
26. Author interview with Jack Germond
27. Author interview with James Sundquist
28. *New York Times*, June 10, 1955
29. *New York Times*, May 13, 1956
30. *New York Times*, Aug. 10, 1956
31. *New York Times*, June 17, 1956

32. *Public Papers of Gov. Averell Harriman*, Vol. II, p. 1342
33. Author interview with Theodore Tannenwald
34. Author interview with James Sundquist
35. New York *Herald Tribune*, Aug. 11, 1956
36. *New York Times*, Aug. 12, 1956
37. Daniel Gutman interview with Mark Chadwin, Harriman papers
38. Author interview with Jonathan Bingham
39. Author interview with Mrs. Daniel Patrick Moynihan
40. New York *Herald Tribune*, Aug. 16, 1956
41. New York *Herald Tribune*, Aug. 17, 1956

Chapter XXI

1. Peter Collier and David Horowitz, *The Rockefellers: An American Dynasty* (New York: Holt, Rinehart and Winston, 1976), p. 267
2. Milton Stewart interview with Mark Chadwin, Harriman papers
3. Joseph E. Persico, *The Imperial Rockefeller: A Biography of Nelson A. Rockefeller* (New York: Simon and Schuster, 1982), p. 38
4. Milton Stewart interview with Mark Chadwin, Harriman papers
5. Author interview with Jonathan Bingham
6. *New York Times*, April 16, 1958
7. *New York Times*, June 6, 1958
8. *New York Times*, May 23, 1958
9. WAH interview with Frank Munger, Harriman papers, Arents Library, Syracuse University
10. *Adirondack* (N.Y.) *Daily Enterprise*, Aug. 21, 1957
11. Truman letter to Roger Tubby, Sept. 19, 1957, President's personal file, Harry S Truman Library
12. Jeffrey Potter, *Men, Money, and Magic: The Story of Dorothy Schiff* (New York: Coward, McCann & Geoghegan, 1976), p. 258
13. Author interview with Robert Wagner
14. ibid.
15. *New York Times*, Aug. 7, 1958
16. *New York Times*, Aug. 11, 1958
17. *New York Times*, Aug. 15, 1958
18. Eleanor Roosevelt letter to WAH, Aug. 19, 1958, Harriman papers.
19. Author interview with Charles Van Devander
20. Author interview with Robert Wagner
21. WAH interview with Frank Munger, Harriman papers, Arents Library
22. ibid.
23. Warren Moscow, *The Last of the Big Time Bosses: The Life and Times of*

Carmine De Sapio and The Decline and Fall of Tammany Hall (New York: Stein and Day, 1971), p. 146
24. Daniel Gutman interview with Mark Chadwin, Harriman papers
25. Author interview with Philip Kaiser
26. Author interview with Daniel Gutman
27. *New York Times*, Sept. 2, 1958
28. Arthur Schlesinger, Jr., letter to WAH, Oct. 20, 1958, Harriman papers
29. Milton Stewart interview with Mark Chadwin, Harriman papers
30. Author interview with Penn Kimball
31. *New York Times*, Sept. 20, 1958
32. *New York Times*, Oct. 15, 1958
33. *New York Times*, Oct. 26, 1958
34. Potter, *Men, Money, and Magic: The Story of Dorothy Schiff*, p. 257
35. *New York Post*, Nov. 3, 1958
36. *New York Times*, Nov. 5, 1958
37. Author interview with Mrs. Jonathan Bingham

Chapter XXII

1. Author interview with Michael Forrestal
2. Author interview with Bernice McCray
3. Author interview with William Attwood
4. Reprints of articles for North American Newspaper Alliance, February and March 1959, Harriman papers
5. WAH memorandum, June 23, 1959, Harriman papers
6. Llewellyn Thompson cable to State Department, June 24, 1959, Harriman papers
7. *Harpers Magazine*, February 1971
8. ibid.
9. *New York Times*, Sept. 18, 1959
10. Author interview with William Walton
11. WAH letter to John F. Kennedy, Sept. 14, 1960, Harriman papers
12. WAH memorandum to Theodore Sorensen and Archibald Cox, Sept. 30, 1960, Harriman papers
13. Author interview with William Walton
14. ibid.
15. WAH letter to John F. Kennedy, Nov. 15, 1960, Harriman papers
16. WAH letter to John F. Kennedy, Nov. 12, 1960, Harriman papers
17. Arthur M. Schlesinger, Jr., *Robert Kennedy and His Times* (Boston: Houghton Mifflin, 1978), p. 223
18. WAH Harvard oral history interview, Harriman papers

19. Arthur M. Schlesinger, Jr., *A Thousand Days: John F. Kennedy in the White House* (Boston: Houghton Mifflin, 1965), p. 149

20. Author interview with John Kenneth Galbraith

21. ibid.

22. *New York Times*, Dec. 31, 1960

23. *Public Papers of the Presidents of the United States: John F. Kennedy, 1963* (Washington, D.C.: U.S. Government Printing Office, 1963), p. 650

24. U. Alexis Johnson with Jef Olivarius McAllister, *The Right Hand of Power: The Memoirs of an American Diplomat* (Englewood Cliffs, N.J.: Prentice-Hall, 1984), p. 233

25. WAH interview, p. 223 Columbia University oral history

26. Dean Rusk cable to WAH, June 23, 1961, Harriman papers

27. Author interview with Chester Cooper

28. WAH cable to secretary of state, July 18, 1961, Harriman papers

29. Schlesinger, *A Thousand Days: John F. Kennedy in the White House*, p. 514

30. WAH to secretary of state, Sept. 26, 1961, Harriman papers

31. Bernard B. Fall, *Anatomy of a Crisis: The Laotian Crisis of 1960–61* (Garden City, N.Y.: Doubleday, 1969), p. 228

32. John F. Kennedy Library, National Security File, regional security, Box 231a

33. C. L. Sulzberger, *Seven Continents and Forty Years: A Concentration of Memoirs* (New York: New York Times Book Co., 1977), p. 321

34. Author interview with Michael Forrestal

35. WAH letter to Winthrop Brown, March 1, 1962, Harriman papers

36. WAH oral history, John F. Kennedy Library

37. Author interview with Michael Forrestal

38. WAH letter to Ambassador Alan G. Kirk, Oct. 12, 1962, Harriman papers

39. Box 36, Charles E. Bohlen papers, Library of Congress

40. George W. Ball, *The Past Has Another Pattern: Memoirs* (New York: W. W. Norton, 1982), p. 297

41. WAH to Robert F. Kennedy, Oct. 22, 1962, Harriman papers

42. Schlesinger, *A Thousand Days: John F. Kennedy in the White House*, p. 822

43. WAH memorandum of conversation with Khrushchev, April 26, 1963

44. Glenn T. Seaborg with Benjamin S. Loeb, *Kennedy, Khrushchev and the Test Ban*, Glenn T. (Berkeley, Calif.: University of California Press, 1981), p. 178

45. William Sullivan oral history interview, John F. Kennedy Library

46. Benjamin Read oral history, John F. Kennedy Library

47. WAH Harvard oral history interview, Harriman papers

48. W. Averell Harriman, *America and Russia in a Changing World* (Garden City, N.Y.: Doubleday, 1971), p. 93
49. WAH Harvard oral history, Harriman papers
50. Seaborg, *Kennedy, Khrushchev and the Test Ban*, p. 241
51. ibid., p. 242
52. Ben Read oral history interview, John F. Kennedy Library

Chapter XXIII

1. John F. Kennedy Library, President's Office File, Box 65
2. Johnson, *The Right Hand of Power*, p. 340
3. Author interview with Michael Forrestal
4. ibid.
5. *Los Angeles Times*, Jan. 19, 1969
6. Author interview with Richard Holbrooke
7. WAH memorandum, July 22, 1961, Harriman papers
8. WAH letter to John Kenneth Galbraith, Oct. 31, 1961, Harriman papers
9. John F. Kennedy Library, President's Office File, Countries: Vietnam, Box 128a
10. John F. Kennedy Library, National Security File, Countries: Vietnam, Box 195
11. John Kenneth Galbraith letter to JFK, April 15, 1962
12. John Kenneth Galbraith, *Ambassador's Journal* (Boston: Houghton Mifflin, 1969), p. 297
13. John F. Kennedy Library, National Security File, Box 320
14. Author interview with Frederick Nolting
15. Frederick Nolting oral history interview, Lyndon B. Johnson Library
16. Edwin O. Guthman and Jeffrey Shulman, eds., *Robert F. Kennedy in His Own Words: The Unpublished Recollections of the Kennedy Years* (New York: Bantam Books, 1988), p. 279
17. Author interview with Michael Forrestal
18. Author interview with Fred Dutton
19. *New York Times*, July 11, 1963
20. Author interview with Carl Kaysen
21. Guthman and Shulman, eds., *Robert F. Kennedy in His Own Words*, p. 7
22. Roger Hilsman, *To Move a Nation: The Politics of Foreign Policy in the Administration of John F. Kennedy* (New York: Doubleday, 1967), p. 461
23. John F. Kennedy Library, National Security Files, Countries: Vietnam, Box 197

24. Author interview with Frederick Nolting
25. ibid.
26. Hilsman and Harriman cable to Henry Cabot Lodge, John F. Kennedy Library, National Security Files, Countries: Vietnam, Box 198
27. Michael Forrestal cable to JFK, John F. Kennedy Library, National Security Files, Countries: Vietnam, Box 198
28. State Department to Henry Cabot Lodge, John F. Kennedy Library, National Security Files, Countries: Vietnam, Box 198
29. ibid.
30. George Ball oral history interview, Lyndon B. Johnson Library
31. Maxwell D. Taylor, *Swords and Plowshares* (New York: W. W. Norton, 1972), p. 292
32. Ball, *The Past Has Another Pattern*, p. 370
33. Lodge cable to State Department, John F. Kennedy Library, National Security Files, Countries: Vietnam, Box 198
34. Author interview with Michael Forrestal
35. Maxwell Taylor cable to Paul Harkins, John F. Kennedy Library, National Security Files, Countries: Vietnam, Box 198
36. David Halberstam, *The Best and the Brightest* (New York: Random House, 1972), p. 332
37. Guthman and Shulman, eds., *Robert F. Kennedy In His Own Words*, p. 397
38. *Public Papers of the Presidents of the United States: John F. Kennedy, 1961*, p. 224
39. John F. Kennedy Library, National Security Files, Countries: Vietnam, Box 3, Roger Hilsman papers
40. William Sullivan oral history interview, John F. Kennedy Library
41. Guthman and Shulman, eds., *Robert F. Kennedy in His Own Words*, p. 10
42. Author interview with Roger Hilsman
43. Robert F. Kennedy oral history interview, John F. Kennedy Library
44. WAH memorandum, Harriman papers

Chapter XXIV

1. WAH letter to LBJ, Dec. 17, 1964, Harriman papers
2. WAH memo to LBJ, Nov. 9, 1964, Harriman papers
3. Lyndon B. Johnson Library, Famous Names File: Harriman
4. WAH oral history interview, Lyndon B. Johnson Library
5. Cyrus L. Sulzberger, *The Last of the Giants* (New York: Macmillan, 1970), p. 728
6. Douglass Cater memorandum to LBJ, Lyndon B. Johnson Library, Famous Names File: Harriman

7. WAH memorandum to LBJ, Oct. 3, 1964, Harriman papers
8. WAH letter to LBJ, March 16, 1965, Harriman papers
9. Author interview with Michael Forrestal
10. Author interview with Chester Cooper
11. Author interview with Milton Katz
12. WAH Harvard oral history interview, Harriman papers
13. Lyndon B. Johnson Library, Trip File: Harriman
14. WAH memorandum to McGeorge Bundy, July 11, 1964, Harriman papers
15. WAH memo of conversation with Cyrus Vance, Oct. 29, 1964, Harriman papers
16. Earle Wheeler letter to Harriman Sept. 3, 1970, Harriman papers
17. Author interview with Jack Valenti
18. WAH memorandum of conversation with Arthur Schlesinger, March 20, 1965, Harriman papers
19. WAH memorandum to LBJ, Jan. 19, 1965
20. WAH memorandum of conversation with Arthur Schlesinger, March 20, 1965
21. *New York Journal American*, April 17, 1965
22. WAH memorandum to LBJ, May 15, 1965, Harriman papers
23. WAH memorandum of conversation with Aleksey Kosygin, July 21, 1965, Harriman papers
24. WAH Harvard oral history interview, Harriman papers
25. WAH memorandum of conversation with LBJ, Dec. 28, 1965, Harriman papers
26. Ball, *The Past Has Another Pattern*, p. 408
27. WAH cable to State Department, Dec. 30, 1965, Harriman papers
28. WAH memorandum to Dean Rusk, Jan. 26, 1966, Harriman papers
29. Author interview with James Thomson
30. WAH memorandum to LBJ, March 11, 1966
31. Author interview with Chester Cooper
32. David Kraslow and Stuart Loory, *The Secret Search for Peace in Vietnam* (New York: Random House, 1968), p. 25
33. WAH undated memorandum of conversation with LBJ, Harriman papers
34. WAH memorandum to LBJ and secretary of state, Nov. 28, 1966, Harriman papers
35. WAH memorandum of conversation with Robert McNamara, Nov. 26, 1966, Harriman papers
36. WAH memorandum to Dean Rusk, Jan. 16, 1967, Harriman papers
37. WAH memorandum to LBJ and secretary of state, Feb. 2, 1967, Harriman papers
38. Author interview with Chester Cooper
39. WAH memorandum to LBJ, June 17, 1967, Harriman papers

40. Author interview with Chester Cooper
41. Author interview with Joseph Sisco
42. Author interview with James Stockdale
43. Author interview with Chester Cooper

Chapter XXV

1. Central Intelligence Agency summary, Feb. 12, 1968, Harriman papers
2. WAH memorandum of conversation with LBJ, Feb. 20, 1968, Harriman papers
3. WAH memorandum of conversation with Anatoly Dobrynin, March 10, 1968, Harriman papers
4. WAH memorandum of conversation with Robert Kennedy, March 20, 1968
5. Clark Clifford and Richard Holbrooke, *Counsel to the President*, (New York: Random House, 1991), p. 455
6. Stanley Karnow, *Vietnam: A History* (New York: Viking, 1983), p. 562
7. Averell Harriman memo to Dean Rusk, March 29, 1968, Harriman papers
8. *Public Papers of the Presidents of the United States: Lyndon Johnson, 1968–69*, Vol. I (Washington, D.C.: U.S. Government Printing Office, 1970), p. 470
9. WAH memorandum of telephone conversation with LBJ, April 11, 1968
10. WAH memorandum, April 9, 1968, Harriman papers
11. Lyndon B. Johnson, *The Vantage Point: Perspectives of the Presidency, 1963–1969* (New York: Holt, Rinehart and Winston, 1971), p. 505
12. Harriman-Vance cable to State Department, May 31, 1968, Harriman papers
13. Text of WAH June 12, 1968 speech, Harriman papers
14. WAH memorandum, Dec. 14, 1968, Harriman papers
15. Author interview with Cyrus Vance
16. WAH memorandum, Dec. 14, 1968, Harriman papers
17. Carl Solberg, *Hubert Humphrey: A Biography* (New York: W. W. Norton, 1984), p. 361
18. Author interview with Nicholas Katzenbach
19. WAH memorandum, Dec. 14, 1968, Harriman papers
20. Clifford and Holbrooke, *Counsel to the President*, p. 570
21. ibid.
22. Harriman-Vance cable to State Department, Sept. 21, 1968, Harriman papers

23. WAH memorandum of conversation with George Ball, Sept. 18, 1968, Harriman papers
24. Carl Solberg, *Hubert Humphrey*, p. 384
25. Harriman-Vance cable to State Department, Oct. 18, 1968, Harriman papers
26. WAH memorandum, Dec. 14, 1968, Harriman papers
27. WAH letter to William P. Rogers, Dec. 15, 1968, Harriman papers
28. *Time*, Dec. 13, 1968
29. *New York Times*, Jan. 20, 1969

Chapter XXVI

1. Author interview with Mrs. Jonathan Bingham
2. Undated Ethel Kennedy letter to WAH, Harriman papers
3. Author interview with Donald Klopfer
4. Matthew Josephson, *The Robber Barons* (New York: Harcourt Brace Jovanovich, 1962)
5. Author interview with Peter Duchin
6. John Muir, *Edward Henry Harriman*, a monograph, Harriman papers
7. *The Diary of James C. Hagerty: Eisenhower in Mid Course, 1954–1955*, ed. Robert H. Ferrell Indiana (Bloomington, Ind.: Indiana University Press, 1983), p. 240
8. Pamela Churchill letter to Averell Harriman, June 21, 1944, Pamela Harriman private collection
9. Brooke Hayward, *Haywire* (New York: Alfred A. Knopf, 1977)
10. Author interview with Pamela Harriman
11. ibid.
12. Author interview with Michael Forrestal
13. WAH memorandum of conversation with Jimmy Carter, Aug. 31, 1976, Harriman papers
14. WAH memorandum of conversation with Leonid Brezhnev, Sept. 20, 1976
15. Undated message, Leonid Brezhnev to Jimmy Carter, Harriman papers
16. Author interview with Richard Holbrooke
17. Peter Swiers's notes of Harriman remarks, Dec. 6, 1978, Harriman papers
18. *New York Times*, Oct. 22, 1982.
19. W. Averell Harriman last will and testament on file, Loudoun County, Va., recorder's office, Leesburg, Va.
20. Author interview with Richard Holbrooke
21. Author interview with Pamela Harriman

INTERVIEWS

Elie Abel
Mrs. Dean Acheson
Joseph Alsop
Mrs. Stewart Alsop
Mrs. Tilly Arnold
William Attwood
The Countess of Avon
George W. Ball
Mrs. Ellen Barry
Lucius Battle
Jacob Beam
Allen Betts
Jonathan Bingham
Mrs. June Bingham
Richard Bissell
Thomas Blaisdell
Benjamin Bradlee
Lionel Bond
Mrs. Fanny Meyers Brennan
Kingman Brewster
Nicolette Brierly
J. Carter Brown
Art Buchwald

McGeorge Bundy
William P. Bundy
Ellsworth Bunker
Ben Buttenweiser
Mark L. Chadwin
Mrs. Margaret Chapman
Marcus Childs
Virginia Childs
Winston Churchill II
Blair Clark
Clark Clifford
Charles Collingwood
Charles Collis
John Colville
Chester Cooper
Alan Crawford
Mrs. Polly Kraft Cutler
Margaret Truman Daniel
Dan Davidson
John Payton Davies
Mrs. Lucinda Dietz
Douglas Dillon
Richard Dougherty

Peter Duchin
Ernest Dunbar
Elbridge Durbrow
Fred Dutton
Julius Edelstein
George Elsey
Herbert Evans
James H. Evans
Mary Fisk
Robert Fisk
Mrs. Beulah Foster
William C. Foster
Allistair Forbes
Phyllis Forbes
Michael Forrestal
Alfred Friendly
Mrs. Alfred Friendly, Sr.
Mrs. Alfred Friendly, Jr.
J. William Fulbright
Clayton Fritchey
John Kenneth Galbraith
Jack Germond
Elbridge Gerry
Mrs. Ann Sardi Giná
Bernard Gladieux
Gen. Andrew Goodpaster
Lincoln Gordon
Gen. Paul Gorman
Allen Grover
Tom Guinzburg
Luther Gulick
Daniel Gutman
Philip Habib
Lord Hailsham
Katherine Halle
Armand Hammer
Averell Harriman
Pamela Harriman
Louis Harris
Helen Hayes
Ulrich Haynes
Richard Helms
Roger Hilsman
Richard Holbrooke

Ruth Hunsberger
Philip Iglehart
Stewart Iglehart
Roy Jenkins
U. Alexis Johnson
William Jorden
Philip Kaiser
Paul Kattenburg
Milton Katz
Carl Kaysen
Dexter Keezer
Frank Kelly
Leon Keyserling
Mary Keyserling
Penn Kimball
Mrs. James Kitchen
Donald Klopfer
Foy Kohler
Robert Komer
Joseph Kraft
James Lanigan
Gen. Lyman Lemnitzer
Walter Levy
Mrs. Frances Lord
Mrs. Katy Louchheim
Mrs. Nancy Lutz
Bernice McCray
John McCloy
George McGhee
Robert S. McNamara
Charles Maechling
Frank Mankiewicz
Robert Manning
John Marcum
Murray Marder
Earl Mazo
John Melby
Thomas C. Mendenhall
Josephine Merget
Robert Meiklejohn
Drew Middleton
Helen Kirkpatrick Millbank
Alice Leone Moats
Kathleen H. Mortimer

Daniel Patrick Moynihan
Elizabeth Moynihan
Edmund S. Muskie
John Negroponte
Waldemar Nielsen
Frederick Nolting
Leo Norodny
Gen. Lauris Norstad
George Paffenbarger
Mrs. Drew Pearson
Otis Pike
Edwin Plowden
Joe Rauh
Benjamin Read
Permelia Reed
Helen Reeves
William Rich II
Marie Ridder
Eric Roll
Franklin D. Roosevelt, Jr.
James Roosevelt
Walt W. Rostow
William Roundtree
James Rowe
Bernard Rugierri
Charles C. Rumsey, Jr.
Dean Rusk
Mary Russell
Harriman Salisbury
Stewart Scheftel
Dorothy Schiff
Arthur Schlesinger, Jr.
Lt. Gen. George Seignious
John Seigenthaler
Henry Shapiro

Hildy Shishkin
Marshall Shulman
Frank Sievarts
Julius Silver
Joseph Sisco
Cecil Smith
Mary Soames
Theodore Sorensen
Clara Spiegel
Monteagle Stearns
Milton Stewart
Adm. James Stockdale
Sybil Stockdale
Annette Stohlworthy
William Sullivan
James Sundquist
Peter Swiers
Herbert Swope, Jr.
Theodore Tannenwald
Dorice Taylor
Gen. Maxwell Taylor
Mrs. Llewellyn Thompson
James Thomson
Kemp Tolley
Betty Tomlinson
Roger Tubby
Janet Travell
Cyrus Vance
Charles Van De vander
Vernon A. Walters
William Walton
Warren Weaver
Thomas Whitney
Solly Zuckerman

SELECTED
BIBLIOGRAPHY

Acheson, Dean. *Present at the Creation: My Years in the State Department.*
New York: W. W. Norton, 1969.

Adams, Henry H. *Harry Hopkins.* New York: G. P. Putnam's Sons, 1977.

Adler, Cyrus. *Jacob H. Schiff, His Life and Letters* (3 volumes). New York:
Doubleday, 1928.

Aldrich, Nelson W., Jr. *Tommy Hitchcock: An American Hero.* Fleet Street
Corp., 1984.

Allen, Frederick. *Since Yesterday: The 1930's in America.* New York: Harper
and Row, 1939.

———. *The Lords of Creation.* Harper and Row, 1935.

Ball, George W. *The Past Has Another Pattern: Memoirs.* New York: W. W.
Norton, 1982.

Baltzell, E. Digby. *The Protestant Establishment Aristocracy and Caste in
America.* New York: Random House, 1964.

Beard, Charles A. and Mary R. *America in Midpassage.* New York: Macmillan, 1945.

Beschloss, Michael R. *Kennedy and Roosevelt: The Uneasy Alliance.* New
York: W. W. Norton, 1980.

Birmingham, Stephen. *The Right People.* New York: Little, Brown, 1958.

Blum, John Morton, ed. *The Price of Vision: The Diary of Henry A. Wallace,
1942–1946.* Boston: Houghton Mifflin, 1974.

———. *V Was for Victory: Politics and American Culture During World War
II.* New York: Harcourt Brace Jovanovich, 1976.

Bohlen, Charles E. *Witness to History*. New York: W. W. Norton, 1973.
———. *The Transformation of American Foreign Policy*. New York: W. W. Norton, 1969.
Bradley, Omar N., and Clay Blair. *A General's Life*. New York: Simon and Schuster, 1983.
Byrnes, James F. *Speaking Frankly*. New York: Harper and Brothers, 1974.
Campbell, Persia. *Mary Williamson Harriman*. New York: Columbia University Press, 1960.
Churchill, Winston S. *The Second World War*. Vol. III, *The Grand Alliance*. Boston: Houghton Mifflin, 1950.
———. Vol. V, *Closing the Ring*, 1951.
———. Vol. VI, *Triumph and Tragedy*, 1953.
Clemens, Diane Shaver. *Yalta*. New York: Oxford University Press, 1970.
Colville, John. *The Fringes of Power: 10 Downing Street Diaries, 1939–1955*. New York: W. W. Norton, 1989.
Commager, Henry Steele, and Alan Nevins. *The Heritage of America*. New York: Little, Brown, 1939.
Cooper, Chester L. *The Lost Crusade*. New York: Dodd, Mead, 1970.
Corliss, Carlton J. *Main Line of Mid America: The Story of the Illinois Central*. New York: Creative Age Press, 1950.
David, Paul T., Malcolm Moos, and Ralph M. Goldman. *Presidential Nominating Politics in 1952*. Baltimore: Johns Hopkins Press, 1954.
Davies, R.E.G. *Airlines of the United States Since 1914*. Washington: Smithsonian Institution Press, 1972.
Davis, Kenneth S. *FDR: The New Deal Years, 1933–1937*. New York: Random House, 1979.
Davis, Ronald L., ed. *The Social and Cultural Life of the 1920's*. New York: Holt, Rinehart and Winston, 1972.
Deane, Maj. Gen. John R. *Strange Alliance*. New York: Viking, 1946.
Dilks, David, ed. *The Diaries of Sir Alexander Cadogan*. New York: G. P. Putnam's Sons, 1972.
Dommen, Arthur J. *Conflict in Laos*. New York: Praeger Publishers, 1964.
Donovan, Robert J. *Conflict and Crisis: The Presidency of Harry S Truman, 1945–1948*. New York: W. W. Norton, 1977.
———. *Tumultuous Years, 1949–1953*. New York: W. W. Norton, 1982.
Eckenrode, H. J., and Pocahontas Wright Edmunds. *E. H. Harriman: The Little Giant of Wall Street*. New York: Greenberg, 1933.
Eden, Anthony. *The Reckoning*. Boston: Houghton Mifflin, 1965.
Eisenhower, Dwight D. *Crusade in Europe*. New York: Doubleday, 1948.
Eubank, Keith. *Summit at Teheran: The Untold Story*. New York: William Morrow, 1985.
Fall, Bernard B. *Anatomy of a Crisis: The Laotian Crisis of 1960–61*. New York: Doubleday, 1969.

Fassett, Frederick, Jr., ed. *The Shipbuilding Business in the United States of America*. Vol. I. New York: Society of Naval Architects and Marine Engineers, 1948.

Feis, Herbert. *Churchill, Roosevelt, and Stalin: The War They Waged and the Peace They Sought*. Princeton: Princeton University Press, 1957.

————. *From Trust to Terror: The Onset of the Cold War, 1945–50*. New York: W. W. Norton, 1970.

Filene, Peter G. *Americans and the Soviet Experiment, 1917–1933*. Cambridge: Harvard University Press, 1967.

Finder, Joseph. *The Red Carpet*. New York: The New Republic/Holt, Rinehart and Winston, 1983.

Fontenay, Charles L. *Estes Kefauver: A Biography*. Knoxville: University of Tennessee Press, 1980.

Freidel, Alfred. *America in the Twentieth Century*. New York: Alfred A. Knopf, 1970.

Galbraith, John Kenneth. *A Life in Our Times*. Boston: Houghton Mifflin, 1981.

————. *The Great Crash*. Boston: Houghton Mifflin, 1972.

Gilbert, Martin. Vol. VI. *Winston S. Churchill, Finest Hour, 1939–1941*. Boston: Houghton Mifflin, 1984.

————. Vol. VII. *Road to Victory, 1941–1945*. Boston: Houghton Mifflin, 1986.

————. Vol. VIII. *Never Despair, 1945–65*. Boston: Houghton Mifflin, 1988.

Goetzmann, William H., and Kay Sloan. *Looking Far North: The Harriman Expedition to Alaska, 1899*. New York: Viking, 1982.

Goulden, Joseph C. *Korea: The Untold Story of the War*. New York: McGraw-Hill, 1982.

Griscom, Lloyd C. *Diplomatically Speaking*. New York: Literary Guild, 1940.

Guthman, Edwin O., and Jeffrey Shulman, eds. *Robert F. Kennedy in His Own Words: The Unpublished Recollections of the Kennedy Years*. New York: Bantam Books, 1988.

Halberstam, David. *The Best and the Brightest*. New York: Random House, 1972.

Halley, Kay, ed. *The Grand Original: Portraits of Randolph Churchill by His Friends*. Boston: Houghton Mifflin, 1971.

Hammer, Armand. *The Quest of the Romanoff Treasure*. New York: The Paisley Press, 1936.

Hammer, Ellen J. *A Death in November: America in Vietnam 1963*. New York: E. P. Dutton, 1987.

Harriman, E. Roland. *I Reminisce*. New York: Doubleday, 1975.

Harriman, W. Averell, and Elie Abel. *Special Envoy to Churchill and Stalin, 1941–1946*. New York: Random House, 1975.

Hartman, Susan. *The Marshall Plan.* Columbus: Charles E. Merrill, 1968.

Herz, Martin F. *Beginnings of the Cold War.* Bloomington: Indiana University Press, 1966.

Higham, John. *Strangers in the Land: Patterns of American Nativism, 1860–1925.* New Brunswick: Rutgers University Press, 1955.

Hilsman, Roger. *To Move a Nation: The Politics of Foreign Policy in the Administration of John F. Kennedy.* New York: Doubleday, 1967.

Hoffman, Paul G. *Peace Can Be Won.* New York: Doubleday, 1951.

Hogan, Michael J. *The Marshall Plan: America, Britain, and the Reconstruction of Western Europe.* Cambridge: Cambridge University Press, 1955.

Hoopes, Townsend. *The Limits of Intervention.* New York: David McKay, 1969.

Hughes, Jonathan. *The Vital Few: American Economic Progress and Its Protagonists.* Boston: Houghton Mifflin, 1966.

Infield, Glenn B. *The Poltava Affair.* New York: Macmillan, 1973.

Isaacson, Walter, and Evan Thomas. *The Wise Men.* New York: Simon and Schuster, 1986.

Jackson, Stanley. *J. P. Morgan: A Biography.* New York: Stein and Day, 1983.

Johnson, Lyndon Baines. *The Vantage Point: Perspectives on the Presidency 1963–1969.* New York: Holt, Rinehart and Winston, 1976.

Johnson, U. Alexis, and Jef Olivarius McAllister. *The Right Hand of Power.* Englewood Cliffs: Prentice-Hall, Inc., 1984.

Jones, Jesse H., with Edward Angly. *Fifty Billion Dollars.* New York: Macmillan, 1951.

Josephson, Matthew. *The Robber Barons: The Great American Capitalists, 1861–1901.* New York: Harcourt Brace Jovanovich, 1962.

Kahn, E. J., Jr. *The World of Swope: A Biography of Herbert Bayard Swope.* New York: Simon and Schuster, 1965.

Karnow, Stanley. *Vietnam: A History.* New York: Viking, 1983.

Kattenburg, Paul M. *The Vietnam Trauma in American Foreign Policy.* New Brunswick: Transaction Books, 1980.

Kennan, George. *E. H. Harriman: A Biography* (two volumes). Boston: Houghton Mifflin, 1922.

———. *E. H. Harriman's Far East Plans.* New York: Country Life Press, 1917.

———. *The Salton Sea: An Account of Harriman's Fight with the Colorado River.* New York: Macmillan, 1917.

Kennan, George F. *Russia and the West Under Lenin and Stalin.* Boston: Little, Brown, 1960.

———. *Memoirs, 1925–1950.* Boston: Atlantic/Little, Brown, 1967.

Kilmarx, Robert A., ed. *America's Maritime Legacy: A History of the U.S.*

Merchant Marine and Shipbuilding Industry Since Colonial Times. Boulder: Westview Press, 1979.

Klein, Maury. *Union Pacific*. Vol. II, *The Rebirth*. New York: Doubleday, 1990.

Kouwenhoven, John A. *Partners in Banking: An Historical Portrait of a Great Private Bank, Brothers Harriman & Co. 1818–1968*. New York: Doubleday, 1968.

Kraslow, David, and Loory Stewart. *The Secret Search for Peace in Vietnam*. New York: Random House, 1968.

Lansing, Robert. *War Memoirs of Robert Lansing*. New York: Bobbs-Merrill, 1935.

Lash, Joseph P. *Roosevelt and Churchill, 1939–41*. New York: W. W. Norton, 1976.

———. *Eleanor and Franklin*. New York: W. W. Norton, 1971.

Leahy, Admiral William D. *I Was There*. New York: Curtis Publishing Co., 1950.

Leighton, Richard M., and Robert W. Coakley. *Global Logistics and Strategy*. Washington: Department of the Army, 1955.

Leslie, Anita. *Cousin Randolph: The Life of Randolph Churchill*. London: Hutchinson and Co., 1985.

Leutze, James, ed. *The London Journal of Gen. Raymond E. Lee, 1940–41*. Boston: Little, Brown, 1971.

Lewis, Alfred Allan. *Man of the World: Herbert Bayard Swope: A Charmed Life of Pulitzer Prizes, Poker, and Politics*. New York: Bobbs-Merrill, 1978.

Lewis, Oscar. *Sea Routes to the Gold Fields: The Migration by Water to California in 1849–52*. New York: Alfred A. Knopf, 1949.

MacArthur, General Douglas. *Reminiscences*. New York: McGraw-Hill, 1964.

McGhee, George. *Envoy to the Middle World*. New York: Harper and Row, 1969.

Mahoney, Richard D. *JFK: Ordeal in Africa*. New York: Oxford University Press, 1983.

Maisky, Ivan. *Memoirs of a Soviet Ambassador: The War 1939–1943*. New York: Charles Scribner and Sons, 1968.

Manchester, William. *American Caesar: Douglas MacArthur, 1880–1964*. Boston: Little, Brown, 1978.

Marcuse, Maxwell F. *This Was New York!* New York: Carlton Press, 1965.

Martin, Albro. *Enterprise Denied*. New York: Columbia University Press, 1971.

———. *James J. Hill and the Opening of the Northwest*. New York: Oxford University Press, 1976.

Martin, George. *Madam Secretary: Frances Perkins: A Biography of America's First Woman Cabinet Member.* Boston: Houghton Mifflin, 1976.

Martin, John Bartlow. *Adlai Stevenson of Illinois: The Life of Adlai Stevenson.* New York: Doubleday, 1976.

————. *Adlai Stevenson and the World.* New York: Doubleday, 1977.

Mattox, W. C. *Building the Emergency Fleet.* Cleveland: Penton Publishing Co., 1920.

May, Ernest R. *The World War and American Isolation, 1914–1917.* Cambridge: Harvard University Press, 1959.

Mecklin, John. *Mission in Torment: An Intimate Account of the U.S. Role in Vietnam.* New York: Doubleday, 1965.

Mee, Charles L., Jr. *Meeting at Potsdam.* New York: Evans and Co., 1975.

Millis, Walter, ed. *The Forrestal Dairies.* New York: Viking, 1951.

Mitchell, Broadus. *Depression Decade: From New Era Through New Deal, 1921–41.* New York: Rinehart and Co., 1955.

Moley, Raymond. *After Seven Years.* New York: Harper and Brothers, 1939.

————. *Masters of Politics.* New York: Funk and Wagnalls, 1949.

Moody, John. *The Railroad Builders: A Chronicle of the Welding of the United States.* New Haven: Yale University Press, 1919.

Moscow, Warren. *The Last of the Big Time Bosses: The Life and Times of Carmine De Sapio and the Rise and Fall of Tammany Hall.* New York: Stein and Day, 1971.

Motter, T. H. Vail. *The Persian Corridor and Aid to Russia.* Washington: Department of the Army, 1952.

Murray, Robert K. *The Harding Era.* Minneapolis: University of Minnesota Press, 1969.

Nelson, James C. *Railroad Transportation and Public Policy.* Washington: The Brookings Institution, 1959.

Newman, Robert P. *The Cold War Romance of Lillian Hellman and John Melby.* Chapel Hill: University of North Carolina Press, 1989.

Nolting, Frederick. *From Trust to Tragedy.* New York: Praeger Publishers, 1988.

Oppenheimer, Doug, and Jim Poore. *Sun Valley: A Biography.* Boise: Beatty Books, 1976.

Paley, William. *As It Happened.* New York: Doubleday, 1979.

Persico, Joseph E. *The Imperial Rockefeller: A Biography of Nelson A. Rockefeller.* New York: Simon and Schuster, 1982.

Pogue, Forrest. *George C. Marshall: Ordeal and Hope, 1939–42.* New York: Viking, 1966.

————. *George C. Marshall: Organizer of Victory, 1943–45.* New York: Viking, 1973.

Price, Harry. *The Marshall Plan and Its Meaning.* Ithaca: Cornell University Press, 1955.

Roosevelt, Kermit. *Countercoup: The Struggle for the Control of Iran.* New York: McGraw-Hill, 1979.

Rusk, Dean, with Richard Rusk. *As I Saw It.* New York: W. W. Norton. 1990.

Rust, William J. *Kennedy in Vietnam: American Vietnam Policy, 1960–63.* New York: Charles Scribner's Sons, 1985.

Schandler, Herbert. *The Unmaking of a President: Lyndon Johnson and Vietnam.* Princeton: Princeton University Press, 1977.

Schlesinger, Arthur, Jr. *The Coming of the New Deal.* Boston: Houghton Mifflin, 1958.

———. *A Thousand Days: John F. Kennedy in the White House.* Boston: Houghton Mifflin, 1965.

———. *Robert Kennedy and His Times.* Boston: Houghton Mifflin, 1978.

Schmidt, Margaret Fox. *Passion's Child: The Extraordinary Life of Jane Digby.* New York: Harper and Row, 1976.

Schoenbaum, Thomas J. *Waging Peace and War: Dean Rusk in the Truman, Kennedy and Johnson Years.* New York: Simon and Schuster, 1988.

Seaborg, Glenn T., with Benjamin Loeb. *Kennedy, Khrushchev, and the Test Ban.* Berkeley: University of California Press, 1981.

Sherwood, Robert. *Roosevelt and Hopkins: An Intimate History.* New York: Harper and Brothers, 1948.

Smith, Gene. *The Shattered Dream: Herbert Hoover and the Great Depression.* New York: McGraw-Hill, 1970.

Smith, Richard Norton. *Thomas E. Dewey and His Times.* New York: Simon and Schuster, 1982.

Soames, Mary. *Clementine Churchill: The Biography of a Marriage.* Boston: Houghton Mifflin, 1979.

Solberg, Carl. *Hubert Humphrey: a Biography.* New York: W. W. Norton, 1984.

Sorensen, Theodore. *Kennedy.* New York: Harper and Row, 1965.

Spaak, Paul-Henri. *The Continuing Battle: Memoirs of a European, 1936–66.* London: Weidenfeld and Nicholson, Ltd., 1971.

Spector, Ronald H. *Eagle Against the Sun.* New York: Macmillan, 1985.

Stettinius, Edward R., Jr. *Roosevelt and the Russians.* Westport: Greenwood Press, 1949.

———. *Lend Lease: Weapon for Victory.* New York: Macmillan, 1944.

Stikker, Dirk U. *Men of Responsibility.* New York: Harper and Row, 1965.

Sulzberger, Cyrus L. *An Age of Mediocrity.* New York: Macmillan, 1973.

———. *Seven Continents and Forty Years.* New York: Quadrangle Books, 1977.

Sutton, Anthony C. *Wall Street and the Bolshevik Revolution.* New York: Arlington House, 1974.

———. *Western Technology and Soviet Economic Development, 1917 to 1930.*

Stanford: Hoover Institution on War, Revolution, and Peace, Stanford University, 1968.

Talbot, Strobe, ed. and trans. *Khrushchev Remembers: The Last Testament.* New York: Little, Brown, 1974.

Taylor, Dorice. *Sun Valley.* Sun Valley, Ida.: Ex Libris, 1980.

Taylor, General Maxwell. *Swords and Plowshares.* New York: W. W. Norton, 1972.

Thomas, Gordon, and Morgat Witts. *The San Francisco Earthquake.* New York: Stein and Day, 1971.

Toland, John. *The Last 100 Days.* New York: Random House, 1965.

Tolley, Kemp. *Caviar and Commissars: The Experience of a U.S. Naval Officer in Stalin's Russia.* Annapolis: U.S. Naval Institute, 1983.

Truman, Harry S. *Memoirs.* Vol. I: *Year of Decisions.* New York: Doubleday, 1956.

———. Vol. II: *Years of Trial and Hope,* 1956.

Tugwell, Rexford G. *The Democratic Roosevelt: A Biography of Franklin D. Roosevelt.* New York: Doubleday, 1957.

Vandenberg, Arthur H., Jr., ed. *The Private Papers of Senator Vandenberg.* Boston: Houghton Mifflin, 1952.

Van der Beugel, Ernst H. *From Marshall Aid to Atlantic Partnership.* Amsterdam: Elsevier Publishing Co., 1986.

Walters, Vernon A. *Silent Missions.* New York: Doubleday, 1978.

Walton, Richard J. *Henry Wallace, Harry Truman, and the Cold War.* New York: Viking, 1976.

Warburg, James P. *The Long Road Home.* New York: Doubleday, 1964.

Werstein, Irving. *The Shattered Decade, 1919–1929.* New York: Charles Scribner's Sons, 1970.

White, Theodore H. *Fire in the Ashes: Europe in Mid-Century.* New York: William Sloane Associates, 1953.

———. *In Search of History,* New York: Harper and Row, 1978.

Whitney, Thomas P. *Russia in My Life.* New York: Reynal and Co., 1962.

Williams, Philip M., ed. *The Diary of Hugh Gaitskell, 1945–1956.* London: Jonathan Cape, Ltd., 1983.

Wilson, Neill C., and Frank J. Taylor. *Southern Pacific: The Story of a Fighting Railroad.* New York: McGraw-Hill, 1952.

Wilson, Theodore. *The First Summit: Roosevelt and Churchill at Placentia Bay.* Boston: Houghton Mifflin, 1941.

Yergin, Daniel H. *Shattered Peace: The Origins of the Cold War and the National Security State.* Boston: Houghton Mifflin, 1977.

PHOTOGRAPH
CREDITS

Averell and Roland Harriman.   RAPPAPORT STUDIOS, HARRIMAN FAMILY COLLECTION
Harriman Brothers at Arden.   HARRIMAN FAMILY COLLECTION
Groton School's Varsity Crew.   CURTISS STUDIO, HARRIMAN FAMILY COLLECTION
E.H. and Mary Harriman.   HARRIMAN FAMILY COLLECTION
Freshman at New Haven.   CURTISS STUDIO, HARRIMAN FAMILY COLLECTION
Launching.   HARRIMAN FAMILY COLLECTION
Harriman II, Steamship King.   HARRIMAN COLLECTION, LIBRARY OF CONGRESS
Homestretch at Belmont.   UNION PACIFIC MUSEUM COLLECTION
An Eight and Three Tens.   HARRIMAN COLLECTION, LIBRARY OF CONGRESS
The Former Mrs. Whitney.   HARRIMAN COLLECTION, LIBRARY OF CONGRESS
In E.H.'s Shoes.   UNION PACIFIC MUSEUM COLLECTION
Union Station, Washington, D.C.   UNION PACIFIC MUSEUM COLLECTION
Little Mary.   HARRIMAN FAMILY COLLECTION
Sun Valley, Idaho.   UNION PACIFIC MUSEUM COLLECTION
On Dollar Mountain.   UNION PACIFIC MUSEUM COLLECTION
The Young Churchills.   ASSOCIATED PRESS
Mission Accomplished.   PRESS ASSOCIATION, INC
Levity in the Kremlin.   HARRIMAN COLLECTION, LIBRARY OF CONGRESS
Bound for the Crimea.   HARRIMAN COLLECTION, LIBRARY OF CONGRESS
Summit in the Crimea.   HARRIMAN COLLECTION, LIBRARY OF CONGRESS
Atop Lenin's Tomb.   HARRIMAN COLLECTION, LIBRARY OF CONGRESS
The Brothers.   HARRIMAN COLLECTION, LIBRARY OF CONGRESS
Fueling the Recovery of Europe.   HARRY S. TRUMAN LIBRARY

Troubleshooter.   HARRY S. TRUMAN LIBRARY

Oil Crisis.   ASSOCIATED PRESS

The Peoples' Choice.   NEW YORK *DAILY NEWS*

The Governor. Sedge LeBlang, Metropolitan Opera.   HARRIMAN COLLECTION,
     LIBRARY OF CONGRESS

A Run for the White House.   HARRIMAN COLLECTION, LIBRARY OF CONGRESS

On the Hustings.   UNITED PRESS

The Last Campaign.   UNITED PRESS

Allies.   NEW YORK *DAILY NEWS*

In the Better Days of the Shah.   HARRIMAN COLLECTION, LIBRARY OF CONGRESS

To Moscow for Kennedy.   ASSOCIATED PRESS

Loyalty Put to the Test.   LYNDON B. JOHNSON LIBRARY

Preparing for Paris.   LYNDON B. JOHNSON LIBRARY

The Peace Team.   LYNDON B. JOHNSON LIBRARY

Reunion.   ASSOCIATED PRESS

Elder Statesman.   JIMMY CARTER LIBRARY

Changing Guard at the Kremlin.   TASS

INDEX

X